TRUTH IN MEMORY

Truth in Memory

Edited by

Steven Jay Lynn
Kevin M. McConkey

THE GUILFORD PRESS
New York   London

©1998 The Guilford Press
A Division of Guilford Publications, Inc.
72 Spring Street, New York, NY 10012
http://www.guilford.com

Printed in the United States of America

This book is printed on acid-free paper.

Last digit is print number: 9   8   7   6   5   4   3   2

Library of Congress Cataloging-in-Publication Data

Truth in memory / edited by Steven Jay Lynn, Kevin M.
   McConkey.
      p.   cm.
   Includes bibliographical references and index.
   ISBN 1-57230-345-X
   1. False memory syndrome.   2. Recovered memory.
3. Autobiographical memory.   I. Lynn, Steven J.
II. McConkey,
   Kevin M.
RC455.2.F35T78   1998
616.85′822390651—dc21   98-6870
                                                                CIP

CONTRIBUTORS

Jean Maria Arrigo, MA, School of Behavioral and Organizational Science, Claremont Graduate University, Claremont, CA

Amanda J. Barnier, PhD, School of Psychology, University of New South Wales, Sydney, New South Wales, Australia

Roy F. Baumeister, PhD, Department of Psychology, Case Western Reserve University, Cleveland, OH

Jason M. Blackwell, PhD, Department of Psychology, State University of New York at Binghamton, Binghamton, NY

George A. Bonanno, PhD, Department of Psychology, Catholic University of America, Washington, DC

Bette L. Bottoms, PhD, Department of Psychology, University of Illinois at Chicago, Chicago, IL

Suzanne L. Davis, MA, Department of Psychology, University of Illinois at Chicago, Chicago, IL

Duncan Day, PhD, Concordia University, Montreal, Quebec, Canada

Susan C. DuBreuil, PhD, University of Washington, Seattle, WA; Carleton University, Ottawa, Ontario, Canada

Mitchell L. Eisen, PhD, Department of Psychology, California State University, Los Angeles, Los Angeles, CA

Maryanne Garry, PhD, Department of Psychology, Victoria University, Wellington, New Zealand

Louise Gaston, PhD, McGill University, Montreal, Quebec, Canada

R. Edward Geiselman, PhD, Department of Psychology, University of California, Los Angeles, Los Angeles, CA

Gail S. Goodman, PhD, Department of Psychology, University of California, Davis, Davis, CA

Michael M. Gruneberg, PhD, Department of Psychology, University of Wales, Swansea, Singleton Park, Swansea, Wales, UK

Jeanne Albronda Heaton, PhD, Counseling and Psychological Services, Ohio University, Athens, OH

Douglas J. Herrmann, Department of Psychology, Indiana State University, Terre Haute, IN

Edward R. Hirt, PhD, Department of Psychology, Indiana University, Bloomington, IN

David J. Keuler, PhD, Department of Psychology, Catholic University of America, Washington, DC

John F. Kihlstrom, PhD, Department of Psychology, University of California, Berkeley, Berkeley, CA

Richard P. Kluft, MD, Department of Psychiatry, Temple University School of Medicine, Philadelphia, PA

Jean-Roch Laurence, PhD, Department of Psychology, Concordia University, Montreal, Quebec, Canada

D. Stephen Lindsay, PhD, Department of Psychology, University of Victoria, Victoria, British Columbia, Canada

Elizabeth F. Loftus, PhD, Department of Psychology, University of Washington, Seattle, WA

Steven Jay Lynn, PhD, Department of Psychology, State University of New York at Binghamton, Binghamton, NY

Peter Malinoski, MS, Department of Psychology, Ohio University, Athens, OH

Keith D. Markman, PhD, Psychology Department, Marywood University, Scranton, PA

Kevin M. McConkey, PhD, School of Psychology, University of New South Wales, Sydney, New South Wales, Australia

Hugh E. McDonald, PhD, Department of Psychology, San Diego State University, San Diego, CA

Michael R. Nash, PhD, Department of Psychology, University of Tennessee, Knoxville, TN

Leonard S. Newman, PhD, Department of Psychology, University of Illinois-Chicago, Chicago, IL

David G. Payne, PhD, Department of Psychology, State University of New York at Binghamton, Binghamton, NY

Kathy Pezdek, PhD, School of Behavioral and Organizational Science, Claremont Graduate University, Claremont, CA

Jianjian Qin, MA, Department of Psychology, University of California, Davis, Davis, CA

Karen J. Saywitz, PhD, Department of Psychiatry, School of Medicine, University of California, Los Angeles, Los Angeles, CA; Harbor–UCLA Medical Center, Torrance, CA

Phillip R. Shaver, PhD, Department of Psychology, University of California, Davis, Davis, CA

Peter W. Sheehan, PhD, Vice-Chancellery, Australian Catholic University, Sydney, New South Wales, Australia

Harry Sivec, PhD, WCA Hospital, Jamestown, NY

Ralph Underwager, PhD, MDiv, Private Practice at the Institute for Psychological Therapies, Northfield, MN

Hollida Wakefield, MA, Private Practice at the Institute for Psychological Therapies, Northfield, MN

Nona Leigh Wilson, PhD, Counseling and Human Resource Development Department, South Dakota State University, Brookings, SD

PREFACE

The title of this book, *Truth in Memory*, might seem like an oxymoron, at least to those who are well versed in the literature on human memory. To say that there is "truth in memory" perhaps implies that memory is a complete, static, and accurate record of the past. But this description falls short of conveying the "truth" about memory. In fact, a virtual consensus now exists among memory researchers that memory is a dynamic medium of experience shaped by expectancies, needs, and beliefs, imbued with emotion, and enriched by the inherently human capacity for narrative creation (cf. Lynn & Payne, 1997). Memories are, as a rule, a construction or, perhaps more accurately, a reconstruction of past events in the present, whether the remembrances are of mundane daily activities or of anomalous, life-altering events.

To contend that memory is reconstructive is not to disparage the human memory system. Rather, it is to recognize that reconstruction is the natural process for the creation of true memories as well as for false memories. And this process serves most of us well, most of the time. Indeed, the reconstructive nature of memory has evolved over the course of human history to help us understand who we are and what we do. However, the fact that memory is reconstructive underscores the fact that memory is, at times, sensitive to changes across the life span, to changes in our feelings and life situations, and to our interactions in different social settings. Hence, memory can be inaccurate in part or in whole, even when it has the semblance of truth.

The fact that memory is reconstructive raises a host of questions. To what extent and under what circumstances are memories accurate? Are certain memories, like very early memories, more accurate than others? Are there important differences in the quantity, quality, and accuracy of memories across the life span? Can certain memories, including traumatic ones, be forgotten or repressed for long periods only to resurface, with force and feeling, many years later in psychotherapy and other situations? Are certain procedures, in and apart from the context of psychotherapy, more useful than others in obtaining accurate memories?

These and other questions are at the core of the debate about the recovery of memory associated with childhood abuse, which has sharply divided scientific opinion, professional practice, and legal judgments. The issues involved in this debate have touched the lives of people on a daily basis. These lives have included a father accused of molesting his daughter who suddenly recovered graphic and detailed memories of sexual abuse, a sexual assault survivor whose memories of that assault are doubted and questioned by family and friends, and the therapist grappling with the best way, in both a clinical and a legal sense, to interview a possible victim of incest.

These scientific, clinical, and inherently personal issues and questions are the focal points of this book. Because the questions and issues are complex and multidimensional, the book contains contributions from individuals who hold a variety of viewpoints and who do not necessarily agree with one another on general or specific issues. However, all the contributors are active and articulate researchers and clinicians who present their views with candor and conviction. We anticipate that some readers will feel a stronger connection with some contributors and contributions than with others. Nevertheless, we hope that the book is useful for anyone who wants to learn more about memory. It can serve both as an introduction to a variety of issues in the literature and as a more advanced guide to conceptual approaches and empirical findings. Whereas some of the chapters convey well-established scientific findings and proven clinical procedures, other chapters contain material that will challenge entrenched views and clinical practices.

The book presents detailed theoretical analyses and novel empirical findings on selected issues in a way that will allow readers not only to understand the perspectives of the contributors but also to formulate defensible and coherent views of their own. The book incorporates information that will allow readers to understand the place of memory in the lives of individuals as well as to understand how broad social institutions shape and influence how we think about the memory of others and ourselves. Importantly, the book raises questions that cannot be answered fully or clearly at this stage and underscores the importance of knowing what those questions are and of seeking to answer them openly and honestly rather than denying that they exist or trying to pretend that all the answers are in hand.

Finally, even while recognizing the imperfect state of some of the answers, the book recognizes that individuals and professionals must not be paralyzed by uncertainty but, rather, must move forward. There is a way forward, and that is presented in the book. That way forward needs to be taken with care and with recognition of the need to incorporate new findings and new techniques in the future.

The book contains six sections and 19 chapters. Section I sets out various conceptual issues and empirical findings that are critical to formulating a firm foundation of understanding of memory. In Chapter 1, Kihlstrom traces the history of the interest in the recovery of memory from the work of Breuer and Freud to the present day. He launches a defense of the term "false memory syndrome" against those who argue that "no such entity is recognized by duly constituted medical authorities." He also disparages the idea that narrative truth can be a substitute for historical truth and notes that it does not help patients to persuade them to believe something that is not true. To do so would be to divert patients from confronting issues that are important to their current problems in living.

In Chapter 2, Payne and Blackwell argue that the subjectively compelling nature of false memories can best be understood and appreciated when memory errors are viewed as analogues of perceptual illusions. Their perception/reperception model views memory errors as normal processes by which we interpret the world around us, rather than bothersome anomalies, and it highlights the fact that the way in which events are experienced may lead to changes in behavior. The model leads researchers to examine the manner in which illusions of memory differ from "the real thing."

In Chapter 3, Hirt, McDonald, and Markman focus on how expectation for stability or change of an attribute or performance over time lead to expectancy-congruent recall of the past. These authors describe how motivations and desires may exert an effect on memory, and they illustrate how strongly held expectations may make it difficult for individuals to distinguish actual from expected events.

In Chapter 4, Nash provides a conceptual framework for understanding memory errors associated with reports of early sexual trauma during psychotherapy. He argues, for example, that a psychotherapy patient may believe she was not traumatized as a child when in fact she was (a false negative), or she may believe she was traumatized when in fact she was not (a false positive). Nash contends that it is exceedingly important to realize that the problem of false positives and the problem of false negatives are distinct. If patients sometimes report a traumatic event when it did not happen, this does not require us to reject the possibility that patients may fail to remember such an event when it did occur. Nash reviews three related research traditions that support the contention that false positives are an important part of human cognition: memory research, developmental psychopathology, and contemporary psychoanalytic theory.

Section II considers early autobiographical memories. In Chapter 5, Malinoski, Lynn, and Sivec review the assessment, reliability, and determinants of early memory reports. In their review of the literature on early memory reports, these authors provide a methodological critique of much of the available evidence and address the degree to which early memory reports represent constructed experiences that are malleable and shaped by personal, interpersonal, and situational influences.

In Chapter 6, DuBreuil, Garry, and Loftus present research that indicates that some adults are able to generate fantasies about early infancy that fit with their expectations and beliefs concerning infantile experiences. They incorporate suggested details transmitted to them by an experimenter. Not only are subjects willing to generate fantasies about childhood experiences but some of these adults later insist that their fantasized construction is a real memory.

Section III examines suggestion and suggestibility in children. In Chapter 7, Eisen, Goodman, Qin, and Davis focus on memory and suggestibility in maltreated children and review relevant studies on memory and suggestibility in children, including the developmental literature on the effects of stress and trauma on memory. They examine the possible role of individual differences in children's memory performance and the importance of ecological validity in studying children's eyewitness memory. Also, these authors summarize a recent study they conducted concerning the effects of age, dissociation, and stress arousal on memory and suggestibility in abused and neglected children.

In Chapter 8, Saywitz and Geiselman consider how to maximize completeness and minimize error when interviewing the child witness. They delineate factors affecting the incompleteness and inconsistency of children's memory reports and describe two innovative approaches, narrative elaboration and cognitive interviewing, to elicit more complete and consistent memory reports from children. Both approaches strive to assist children in narrating a past event more fully with less need for leading questions, thus reducing the risk of contamination.

Section IV presents research findings and clinical considerations that are directly relevant to understanding memory in the context of psychotherapy. In Chapter 9, McConkey, Barnier, and Sheehan examine the findings on the topic of hypnosis and pseudomemory and set out the implications. Contemporary interest in hypnosis is high theoretically, experimentally, clinically, and forensically, and there is special interest in the effect of hypnosis on memory, particularly on hypnotically suggested false memory, or hypnotic pseudomemory. The aim of their chapter is to delineate the nature and characteristics of hypnotically suggested memory by focusing on historical and clinical applications of hypnotically suggested false memory and experimental investigations of hypnotic pseudomemory.

In Chapter 10, Qin, Goodman, Bottoms, and Shaver discuss the results of two nationwide surveys they conducted that probed claims of repressed memory of satanic ritual abuse and religion-related abuse. They found that the evidence that clinicians provided for satanic ritual abuse was weak, and that a large proportion of the evidence came from only a few clinicians. Also, clinicians' acceptance of ritual and religious elements of cases was not related to the evidence provided but to the bizarreness and extremity of the allegations. The authors hypothesize that there is a subset of clinicians who accept, and even help to create, "false memories" of satanic ritual abuse.

In Chapter 11, Newman and Baumeister argue that UFO accounts can be understood as fantasies that, like masochistic ones, derive from a motivation to escape the self. They argue that UFO abduction memories may be constructed by a combination of suggestive cues, protracted retrieval efforts, and the elaboration of memories and knowledge with uncertain sources during free association or hypnosis. The authors consider that fantasies of sexual masochism bear a close resemblance in many respects to the UFO abduction experience.

In Chapter 12, Kluft reports a study in which he indicates that he was able to confirm recollections of abuse in 56% of the dissociative identity disorder patients he studied. For 38% of the patients, documentation was found for events that they had not recalled prior to their work in therapy; hypnosis was used in the recovery of confirmed memories with 32% of the individuals in the total sample. Of the confirmed memories reported in therapy, Kluft was able to directly confirm 50% of these memories; only 9% of the patients were demonstrated to have reported pseudomemories. Kluft believes that the confirmation of such memories justifies the careful use of hypnosis in exploring the experience of the dissociative identity disorder patient.

In Chapter 13, Laurence, Day, and Gaston take therapists to task for, perhaps unconsciously, yet actively, collaborating with their patients to create false memories. Whereas the authors hold that reconstructive effects of human memory are the norm and not generally the result of pathological processes, they also maintain that there are situations in which these basic processes become extremely damaging if left unchecked. Specifically, any situation that demands that individuals' memories be accurate, truthful records of the past exerts pressure on their ability to recall and illustrates the risk of false memories.

Section V considers false memories in the domains of law, textbooks, and the media. In Chapter 14, Heaton and Wilson focus on memory as it is portrayed in the media and underscore the factors that lead to the creation of confusion. They argue that a complete understanding of the false memory debate requires a careful examination of the media's role in calling the public's attention to the issue of repressed memory and framing the debate about recovered memory. Heaton and Wilson trace how movies and television talk shows foster misunderstanding about repressed memories and dissociation. The authors identify theatrical devices and media tactics that have influenced the debate about false memories, and they make a forceful case for increased awareness and continued examination of the media's role in the evolution of the memory recovery debate.

In Chapter 15, Arrigo and Pezdek review textbook models of multiple personality and argue the case for particular biases and social consequences. They evaluate the way four distinct models of multiple personality disorder (MPD; now dissociative identity disorder) have been presented in introductory psychology textbooks. These models include what the authors term "Trait MPD" (i.e., poor coping skills, predisposition to self-hypnosis, and/or the good–evil split in the psyche), "Fake MPD" (i.e., MPD as an iatrogenic creation), "Trauma MPD" (i.e., MPD as a response to severe trauma), and "Measurable MPD" (i.e., psychometric or physiological differences between MPDs and non-MPDs). The authors performed content and citation analyses to characterize textbook writers' selection and use of sources that supported the models. Various analyses converged on a differential/biased pattern of reporting MPD models that could not be explained by textbook "demographics" (e.g., edition and recency of references). The authors believe their data should serve as a call to action to textbook writers and their editors to rely on scientific data and to be true to their sources.

In Chapter 16, Underwager and Wakefield consider the recovered memory cases that have appeared in the court systems and argue that mental health professionals can provide information to help the finder of fact sort out the truth and falsity of an allegation. The authors present their views on the implications of the influential *Daubert* ruling regarding information that will be admissible as scientific evidence in judicial proceedings. In doing so, the authors examine the scientific status of repression, dissociation, and trauma memories and discuss these concepts in light of civil litigation and the problems and issues involved in evaluating the claims of recovered memories.

Section VI presents a way forward. In Chapter 17, Bonnano and Keuler consider psychotherapy without repressed memory and provide an alternative model to the concept of repressed memory based on contemporary concepts derived from experimental cognitive psychology. Psychotherapy is effective when patients are able to substitute a faulty construction of reality with a more suitable or effective construction, one created by the patient with the therapist and one containing elements of narrative truth as well as historical truth. This process of narrative revision represents the integration of memory fragments and constructions of the past with a more efficacious and functional story.

In Chapter 18, Gruneberg and Herrmann provide a tutorial about practical truths in memory and the implications of those truths. They examine the strengths and weaknesses of basic and applied research into memory and trace the history of interest in the practical memory movement. They discuss the ways in which the focus on practical memory has contributed to applied memory research and survey technologies relevant to improving memory in children, the elderly, and cognitively impaired populations. They conclude that it is necessary not only to establish practical truths in memory but also to use them in ways that serve society.

Finally, in Chapter 19, Lindsay presents a personal perspective on the need to depolarize the views that exist about recovered memory experiences. He strives to present a way forward by citing a number of factors that led to polarization of opinion about both therapies oriented to the recovery of childhood memories and the related controversy about the validity of so-called recovered memories. Lindsay highlights the aspects of the recovered memory controversy that contribute to contentiousness and specifies the conclusions permitted by existing scientific evidence on recovered memories.

This book is not the first and will not be the last word on truth in memory. We hope though that the words it contains are ones that will help professionals, both scientists and practitioners, become familiar with current findings and current views and to formulate views of their own. Scientists and practitioners interested in memory should not come from the red and the blue corners of a boxing ring to sometimes slug it out in the center and then return to those opposing corners. Rather, scientists and practitioners should come from the neutral corners to slug it out against ignorance and suffering, which are lurking in the red and blue corners. We believe that there is much in this book that will help shift the focus of the fight.

We are grateful to a number of people. This book was initially conceived some years ago by Steven Lynn and Nicholas Spanos. Nick died in 1994 when the plane he was piloting crashed. There is much in this book that Nick would disagree with, and there is much that he would agree with; however, we hope that this book is one he would respect.

Steven Lynn is grateful to his wife, Jennifer, and his daughter, Jessica, for their love, support, and understanding, and to his students Bonnie Hawk, Elisa Krackow, Tim Lock, Peter Malinoski, Lisa Marmelstein, Jeffrey Neuschatz, and Jane Stafford for their assistance during the preparation of this book. Kevin McConkey is grateful to the Australian Research Council and the University of New South Wales for grant support and is grateful to Amanda Barnier for assistance during the preparation of the book.

STEVEN JAY LYNN
KEVIN M. MCCONKEY

REFERENCE

Lynn, S. J., & Payne, D. G. (1997). Memory as the theater of the past: The psychology of false memories. *Current Directions, 6,* 55.

CONTENTS

III. SUGGESTION AND SUGGESTIBILITY IN CHILDREN

IV. MEMORY AND PSYCHOTHERAPY: RESEARCH FINDINGS AND CLINICAL CONSIDERATIONS

V. FALSE MEMORIES IN THE DOMAINS OF THE LAW, TEXTBOOKS, AND THE MEDIA

VI. A WAY FORWARD

SECTION I

FOUNDATION

CHAPTER 1

EXHUMED MEMORY

John F. Kihlstrom

Psychoanalysis is not an ordinary psychological analysis which is trying to discover any kind of phenomena and the laws which regulate the occurrence of these phenomena; it is a criminal investigation which aims at the discovery of a culprit, at the unearthing of a past happening which is responsible for extant troubles, an event which must be recognized and tracked through all its disguises. (pp. 610–611)

If an investigator has made up his mind to discover in every neuropathic patient the memory of some incident which left a powerful impress on the emotions and was able to stagger consciousness; if he holds a priori that this memory may be partially or wholly repressed and may be masked by symbols or metaphors, and if he believes that the patient will be so reticient [*sic*] about the matter that only through effort can it be brought back into the light of day, this investigator will almost inevitably be led to probe the mind for the discovery of sexual secrets. (p. 621)

The psychoanalysts invariably set to work in order to discover a traumatic memory, with the a priori conviction that it is there to be discovered. . . . Owing to the nature of their methods, they can invariably find what they seek. (p. 653)

—PIERRE JANET(1925, Vol. 1)

The recovery of memory has been a topic of considerable interest to both clinicians and experimenters for well over 100 years. In 1993, in fact, we celebrated the centenary of the work that brought this problem to the attention of clinicians, researchers, and the public at large—Breuer and Freud's (1893–1895/1955) "Studies on Hysteria"—or, at least, that of their "Preliminary Communication," published in the January 1 and January 15, 1893, issues of the *Neurologisches Centralblatt*. Reporting on their treatment of Anna O., Emmy von M., and other patients suffering from a variety of neurotic disorders collectively labeled "hysteria," these pioneers of psychotherapy claimed that their patients' symptoms were relieved when they remembered (usually while hypnotized) the traumatic incident that precipitated their illness—provided that the accompanying affect was also aroused, as an abreaction leading to a catharsis.

From these observations, Breuer and Freud concluded that "hysterics suffer from reminiscences" (1893–1895/1955, p. 7). Their famous passage is worth extended quotation:

> We may reverse the dictum "*cessante causa cessat effectus*" [when the cause ceases the effect ceases] and conclude from these observations that the determining process continues to operate in some way or other for years—not indirectly, through a chain of intermediate causal links, but as a *directly* releasing cause— just as a psychical pain that is remembered in waking consciousness still provokes a lachrymal secretion long after the event. *Hysterics suffer mainly from reminiscences.* (p. 7)

> Our observations have shown . . . that the memories which have become the determinants of hysterical phenomena persist for a long time with astonishing freshness and with the whole of their affective colouring. We must, however, mention another remarkable fact . . . that these memories, unlike other memories of their past lives, are not at the patients' disposal. On the contrary, *these experiences are completely absent from the patients' memory when they are in a normal psychical state, or are only present in highly summary form.* Not until they have been questioned under hypnosis do these memories emerge with the undiminished vividness of a recent event. (p. 9)

THE ROLE OF MEMORY IN PSYCHOTHERAPY

In the interests of historical accuracy, it is worth noting that the notion that memory and psychopathology are linked was not original with Breuer and Freud. They themselves cite both Delboeuf and Janet as precedents (Macmillan, 1979, 1986, 1996). In particular, Pierre Janet (1889, 1925), Charcot's protégé at the Salpêtrière and Freud's great rival (Perry & Laurence, 1984), also traced the problems of hysterical patients to their past experiences, though he treated these memories quite differently. Consider the case of Marie (Janet, 1889, 1925; see also Ellenberger, 1970), who experienced attacks of hysterical delirium, hallucinations, and automatisms following the onset of her menstrual periods. While hypnotized, Marie reported that she had been surprised and ashamed by her menarche, at age 13, and in an attempt to stop the flow of blood had plunged herself in a bath of ice water. This had the effect of stopping the menses, but it also produced an episode of delirium. In response, Janet used hypnotic suggestion to alter Marie's memory of the formative incident to something less traumatic; when he did so, the hysterical symptoms disappeared, never to return. Janet did not rely on abreaction and catharsis, as Breuer and Freud did, but his technique shows clearly that he felt that memory plays an important role in the development and maintenance of symptoms.

After Freud's triumph over Janet, psychoanalysis and similar psychody-namic theories dominated psychotherapy from the 1920s onward, but toward the end of the 1950s a new point of view arose, namely, behavior therapy. Behavior therapists taught that the symptom is the disease, and that it may be treated as a bad habit, independent of its origins (although, arguably, knowledge of the formative experience might be of use in the construction of a desensitization hierarchy). Similarly, beginning in the late 1960s and early 1970s, cognitive therapists claimed that mental illness derived from a set of maladaptive beliefs and expectations held by the patient, and that these could be corrected by quasi-educational interventions without inquiry into where and how they were acquired. Still and all, the implication of conditioning theory, and of cognitive–social learning theory as well, was that there must have been a learning experience sometime in the past, and even if therapists could remain disinterested in origins, theorists could not. Thus, there was considerable puzzlement when, for example, relatively few phobic patients were able to remember the circumstances under which they acquired their pathological fears.

More recently, psychodynamic forms of psychotherapy have been re-vived, thankfully without much reference to such surplus conceptual baggage as infantile sexuality and the Oedipus complex, in the treatment of posttrau-matic stress disorder. Thus, for example, it has been claimed that a whole host of problems, including anxiety, depression, and eating disorders, have their origins in childhood experiences of incest and other sexual trauma, abuse, neglect, and deprivation—memories of which were repressed by the patient (e.g., Bass & Davis, 1988, 1994; Blume, 1990; Frederickson, 1992; Herman, 1992; Terr, 1994). Therefore, many therapists seek to recover these memories, and bring them into conscious awareness so that the patient can deal with them more adaptively. It should be understood that, in essence, this *trauma-memory argument* (Kihlstrom, 1994d) is essentially the same as Breuer and Freud's (1893–1895/1955), and the method of treatment is essentially Breuer and Freud's technique of catharsis and abreaction: The patient exhumes forgotten material and reexperiences the associated emotion, a sequence that purifies the mind and frees it from conflict.

Of course, the fundamental idea that memory lies at the root of neurosis underwent modification as psychoanalysis developed. One change concerned the nature of the traumatic memories in question. Although the "Studies on Hysteria" (and other early works of Freud) contained hints of a sexual origin of neurosis, the memories detailed there are not always (or even often) particularly sexual in nature. But by 1896, in his essay "The Aetiology of Hysteria" (Freud, 1896/1962c), Freud firmly conceived the idea that the most important etiological factor was sexual abuse inflicted by an adult (almost always the father) when the patient was a young child—a memory that was lost to consciousness but to which the patients' symptoms were attributed. But then Freud almost immediately rejected his own notion and substituted the theory of seduction fantasy—formally announced in the "Three Essays on Infantile Sexuality" (Freud, 1905/1953b).

We all know the reasons that Freud himself gave for these revisions: that the recovery and abreaction of seduction memories did not result in cure, that cases of infantile seduction were rare, that the unconscious mind had difficulty distinguishing reality from imagination, and that no evidence of infantile seduction was found in the recollections of psychotic patients, whose thought processes were (in theory) not subject to repression. Whatever the reasons, it is a good thing that Freud abandoned the seduction theory because in fact he never had any positive evidence for it. In the three 1896 papers announcing the seduction theory, Freud describes a total of 18 new cases (1896/1962a, 1896/1962b, 1896/1962c). But, in fact, as Schimek (1987) and Macmillan (1996) note, the majority of the seductions reported by Freud were at the hands of other children, or of adults who were unrelated to the patient. For example, in the only case reported in any detail, Frau P., who suffered from chronic paranoia, remembered that she and her brother exposed themselves to each other as children. From this, Freud developed the "conjecture that we had to do with an affair between children" (Freud, 1896/1962b, p. 179).

Moreover, and the case of Frau P. illustrates this point, Schimek (1987) showed convincingly that most of these patients did not report any seductions at all (for a detailed analysis, see Macmillan, 1996). Instead, what Freud recorded were his *interpretations* of their memories, not the memories as reproduced by the patients themselves. Rarely was a seduction spontaneously remembered by his patients. Rather, the recollection of the past, and the interpretation made of those recollections, was clearly guided by Freud. The following passage from "The Aetiology of Neuroses" is particularly revealing: "If the memory which we have uncovered does not answer our expectations, it may be that we ought to pursue the same path a little further" (1896/1962c, p. 195). And just so the reader will not miss the point: "If the first-discovered scene is unsatisfactory, we tell our patient that this experience explains nothing, but behind it there must be hidden a more significant, earlier experience" (1896/1962c, pp. 195–196). It should be clearly understood that by this time Freud already had a well-developed theory that there was a sexual etiology for all the neuroses, and that he pressured his patients to produce memories that conformed to his expectations. This process was not subtle, and it continued after the theory of infantile seduction was thrown over for the theory of infantile sexuality. It remains a problem for psychoanalytical therapy even today (Brenneis, 1994a).

Anyone who does not believe this should reread the Dora case, published as "Fragment of an Analysis of a Case of Hysteria" (Freud, 1905/1953a; for an extended treatment, see Lakoff & Coyne, 1993). Here was a young woman, whose real name was Ida Bauer, brought to Freud by her father for treatment of a number of dramatic hysterical symptoms. Dora was quite clear about the source of her problems in living: She was being pressed to have an affair with a family friend, Herr K., but her father would not protect her from Herr K.'s advances. Herr K.'s wife, in turn, was serving as Dora's father's nurse while he suffered from complications of syphilis. It is quite clear that Dora's father and Frau K. were having an affair, and that Dora was effectively traded to Herr K. in return for his wife. Today we would call this a dysfunctional family. But reality was not enough for Freud, who considered Dora's rejection of Herr K., and her symptoms in general, as evidence of her "infantile affection for her father" (1905/1953a, p. 58), as well as a latent bisexual attraction to Frau K. The fact that Dora repeatedly and vehemently denied his interpretation only confirmed to Freud that he was correct. Freud even informed Dora that "no" might well mean "yes." Freud made it clear to Dora that the analysis must continue until she accepted his interpretation or she had no hope of getting well. Much to her credit, Dora summoned the strength to terminate treatment on New Year's Eve, 1900

The old joke about Freud is that he made two mistakes: first he believed his patients, and then he did not believe them. It is a good joke, but it is not right. It should be clear that Freud always assumed that his patients' memories were accurate. What changed was what Freud considered to be a memory. In "Studies on Hysteria" (Breuer & Freud, 1893–1895/1955), and in "The Aetiology of Neuroses" (Freud, 1896/1962a), the memories in question are Freud's interpretations of events that occurred in the real world outside the person. In the "Three Essays on Infantile Sexuality" (Freud, 1905/1953b), the memories in question are his interpretations of thoughts, images, and impulses that passed through the mind of the child. But the memories are always considered to be accurate—*provided that they conform to Freud's expectations.* The fact of the matter, then, is that Freud only made one mistake: He believed his own theory.

This is a mistake that is being repeated by many in clinical practice today.

HYPNOANALYSIS AND NARCOSYNTHESIS

The contemporary revival of Breuer and Freud's technique was foreshadowed in the efforts of psychiatrists and psychologists, themselves mostly psychoanalytically inclined, to treat cases of war neurosis (Grinker & Spiegel, 1943/1945b, 1945a; Hadfield, 1920; Kardiner, 1941; Watkins, 1949) in the two world wars. One of the legacies of the World War I was a large number of cases of traumatic war neurosis, now known as posttraumatic stress disorder (for the earliest discussions, see Brown, 1918, 1919, 1920a, 1920b; MacDougall, 1920; Myers, 1920). Such cases were observed in the past but not in such large numbers; in any case, the lack of an adequate psychological theory in the 18th and 19th centuries led them to be attributed to cowardice rather than diagnosed as instances of psychopathology.

The new psychological theory, itself heavily influenced by psychoanalysis, was that the victims of war neurosis had a personal or family history of neurosis that acted as a kind of diathesis, or predisposition, to mental breakdown. In civilian life these individuals made a more or less adequate adjustment, but they decompensated under wartime conditions of extreme and prolonged stress. This breakdown of established defense mechanisms led to the war neurosis itself. The theory of treatment was analogous to Breuer and Freud's (1893–1895/1955) original: For the short term, the goal of treatment was to get the patient to recover memories of trauma and promote abreaction and catharsis. This would put the patient back the way he was before the war. The long-term goal of treating the underlying neurotic disposition was left for others, later, after the patient was discharged from the military. The same approach was taken to cases encountered in the civilian sector.

Especially in the military hospitals, abreaction and catharsis had to be accomplished quickly, so that the patient could be returned to duty or discharged to civilian life. For this reason, clinicians returned to the very technique that Breuer and Freud pioneered: hypnosis. Of course, the clinicians knew that Freud had rejected hypnosis, but they also felt that hypnosis could facilitate treatment in at least some cases and therefore ought to be returned to the clinician's armamentarium. This decision was itself influenced by the development of a psychoanalytical theory of hypnosis, that hypnosis was a regression *in the service of the ego*, involving a transference-like relationship between subject and hypnotist. The combination of regression, permitting access to the unconscious, and transference, fomenting obedience and dependence, was irresistible for those who wanted to hasten the process of psychoanalysis.

Thus was born the technique of *hypnoanalysis*, so named by Hadfield (1920) and used by him in the apparently successful treatment of anxiety and conversion hysteria. Hadfield's technique consisted of two phases: *abreaction*, in which the patient was hypnotized and instructed to recall and relive the experiences leading to his or her breakdown, and to retain access to this memory in the normal waking state; and *adjustment*, in which the patient worked through the experience, accompanied by hypnotic suggestions for ego strengthening. The technique was successful in some cases, but clinicians were immediately reminded of why Freud abandoned hypnosis in the first place. When patients are not hypnotizable, or resist hypnosis, hypnosis does not help. Thus, in a classic study of psychogenic fugue, Abeles and Schilder (1935) reported that hypnosis was completely successful in only 8 of the 25 cases in which it was attempted and partially successful in only another 6.

What was needed was a technique that would work for everyone, and a possible solution quickly presented itself in the old aphorism, *in vino veritas*. In the early 1930s, two simultaneous lines of work led to the development of a pharmacological technique that came to be known as narcosynthesis. In one, Eric Lindemann (1932), the American psychiatrist and psychologist, then working at the University of Iowa, reported the first experiments on the psychological effects of a new class of cortical depressants, the *barbiturates*. Blackwenn (1930a, 1930b), a psychiatrist, had already reported that when these drugs were administered to catatonic schizophrenics, the patients became lucid and able to discuss their illnesses. Working with both patients and normals, Lindemann observed an increased tendency toward self-disclosure; the fact that his subjects were unable to refuse to answer his questions was apparently the origin of the label *truth serum* for these drugs.

At around the same time, J. S. Horsley (1936a, 1936b, 1937, 1943), a British physician and psychoanalyst, observed that pregnant women who were sedated with Nembutal were amnesic for the events of childbirth, but that this amnesia could be reversed by a subsequent administration of the same drug—apparently an early observation of what we now know as *state-dependent memory*. In later experiments, Horseley also observed that by virtue of barbiturates he could extract confessions from persons who were guilty of a crime but not those who were innocent. Based on the analogy to hypnosis and posthypnotic amnesia, Horsley initially called his technique *narcohypnosis*. When he turned from obstetrics to psychiatry, he developed the technique of *narcoanalysis*, in which barbiturates were used to facilitate transference and recover memories of both repressed traumatic events and forgotten experiences of childhood that might relate to the patient's current troubles (see also Kubie & Margolin, 1945).

The technique quickly caught on. Herman (1938) reported on six cases of psychogenic amnesia, in which only sodium amytal succeeded in restoring the patient's memory, including recovery of the event that precipitated the amnesia. And, of course, both Sargant and Slater (1940) and Grinker and Spiegel (1943/1945b, 1944, 1945a; Grinker, 1944), among others, used the technique widely in the treatment of war neuroses encountered in World War II. Grinker and Spiegel's (1945a) technique was as follows: After a low dose of barbiturate was slowly infused intravenously, the clinician would suggest to the patient that he was back at the scene of the trauma; he himself might even play a role in the scene. Grinker and Spiegel (1945a) observed that under these conditions, the patient typically recovered and abreacted a traumatic memory, at which time the neurotic symptoms would spontaneously disappear. But Grinker and Spiegel (1945a) argued that it was not enough to recover the memory: Steps must be taken to make the memory accessible in the undrugged state, work through the memory, and reintegrate the patient's personality. Because in their view the recovered memory had to be synthesized with the patient's conscious personality to be therapeutically effective, Grinker and Spiegel (1945a) renamed their technique *narcosynthesis* (see Tilken, 1949).

World War II also revived the use of hypnosis in the treatment of war neurosis: There was lots of war neurosis, and relatively few psychiatrists, and so clinical psychologists used the psychological techniques that were available to them. This work is well represented by Watkins's classic *Hypnotherapy of War Neuroses* (1949). The success of hypnosis in the war led to its revival in civilian psychotherapy as well. The signal event was the publication of Lindner's (1944) *Rebel without a Cause* (the source of the classic 1955 Nicholas Ray film starring James Dean, Natalie Wood, and Sal Mineo), in which a "neurotic psychopath" was regressed to the first year of his life, where he recovered a memory of witnessing his parents having sexual intercourse—the kind of primal scene that, according to psychoanalysis, lies at the heart of neurosis. Within the psychoanalytic community, hypnosis was revived by Margaret Brennman and Merton Gill, first in their *Hypnotherapy: A Survey of the Literature* (Brennman & Gill, 1947) and later in *Hypnosis and Related States: Psychoanalytic Studies in Regression* (Gill & Brennman, 1959). This tradition was continued by Erika Fromm (1992) and Doris Gruenewald (1982) at the University of Chicago and their many students (e.g., Brown & Fromm, 1986), among others.

As far as the barbiturates are concerned, their use also continued after the war. One aspect of this history was chronicled by Marks (1978), an investigative journalist who documented the quite unsuccessful quest by the U.S. Central Intelligence Agency (CIA) for a "truth drug" (and other techniques of behavioral control) to be used in the cold war (see also Thomas, 1988). Under the umbrella of the Human Ecology Fund, a large number of psychiatrists and social scientists, mostly in the United States and Canada, were involved in a CIA-sponsored program of behavioral research—originally named Project BLUEBIRD, then ARTICHOKE, then MKULTRA—intended to develop new methods of interrogation and the means of resisting them. But we digress. Let us instead turn to the primary question about these techniques: Are the memories recovered by hypnosis and barbiturates valid? That is, do the memories bear any positive relationship to what actually happened?

There is, unfortunately, a virtual lack of controlled clinical studies on the accuracy of hypnotically refreshed memories. Only two controlled experiments were carried out in field settings (forensic, rather than psychotherapeutic), and neither showed any advantage for hypnosis (Sloane, 1981; Timm, 1981). Of course, a wealth of controlled laboratory research exists on the issue of hypnotically refreshed memory (for reviews, see Erdelyi, 1988; Kihlstrom & Barnhardt, 1993; Kihlstrom & Eich, 1994; Lynn & Nash, 1994; Nash, 1987; Smith, 1983). The general thrust of this literature may be summarized as follows.

1. Hypnotic suggestions for hypermnesia are no more effective than nonhypnotic procedures in enhancing recall.
2. Any increases in valid memory produced by means of hypnosis are accompanied by increased production of inaccurate recollections.
3. There is no evidence that hypnotic age regression improves access to memories of past events.
4. Because hypnosis entails responsiveness to suggestion, the use of hypnosis to enhance memory may increase the subject's vulnerability to leading questions and interrogative biases.

5. For the same reason, hypnosis may diminish his or her ability to discriminate between memory and fantasy.

6. Explicit suggestions that certain events occurred, or might have occurred, may be especially perilous in this regard. For these reasons, both the medical establishment (Council on Scientific Affairs, 1985) and the courts (Laurence & Perry, 1988; Orne, Whitehouse, Dinges, & Orne, 1988; Scheflin & Shapiro, 1989) expressed doubts about forensic hypnosis and urged extreme caution in its use. The same considerations apply to clinical settings in which memories are exhumed.

With respect to drug effects on memory, there is again a dearth of relevant evidence. Despite the attention accorded to the amytal interview over the past half-century, there is apparently no controlled research in either the clinic or the laboratory that attempts to verify new memories ostensibly recovered by barbiturate drugs (for a comprehensive review, see Piper, 1994; see also Perry & Jacobs, 1982; Ruedrich, Chu, & Wadle, 1985). Lambert and Rees (1944) reported that barbiturate was superior to hypnosis and unaided psychological methods in producing relief from conversion and dissociative symptoms (see also Morris, 1945); however, their study suffers from a number of methodological problems, beginning with nonrandom assignment of patients to conditions and ending with a general failure to validate the patients' memories. A later series of placebo-controlled studies did indicate that patients became more responsive and voluble when sedated, but this is not the same as producing valid new recollections (Buckman, Hain, Smith, & Stevenson, 1973; Hain, Smith, & Stevenson, 1966; Smith, Hain, & Stevenson, 1970; Stevenson, Buckman, Smith, & Hain, 1974).

In routine clinical practice, it appears that the memories produced by both hypnosis and barbiturates are considered valid because they are vividly detailed and recalled with emotion. Thus, in his 1943 monograph on narcoanalysis, Horsley wrote: "In spite of the difficulty of establishing the validity of narco-hypnotic hypermnesia, there is abundant clinical evidence of its occurrence. This power of recalling seemingly forgotten incidents, especially those of childhood, is one of the most valuable results of this use of narcotics" (p. 19).

Similarly, Grinker and Spiegel wrote in their report on war neurosis:

The minuteness and wealth of detail which flood the memory, even of events which took place many months and even years before, is always impressive. The events which are depicted with the realistic impact of an expert dramatic production are probably always true counterparts of what actually took place, rather than fantasies such as are produced in dreams or hypnotic states. The emotional reactions, however, do not necessarily represent the actual behavior . . . during the original episode, but rather what he repressed and controlled in order to carry on his job. (1945a, p. 173)

Of at least equal importance, it appears that the memories were believed because the symptoms disappeared when the memory was recovered—a variant on the doctrine cited by Breuer and Freud: *cessante causa cessat effectus*. Finally, it should be understood that the memories were considered valid because they made sense—that is, the memories were believed *because they confirmed the clinicians' expectations of what they would find*. This, of course, is what Grünbaum (1984), in his discussion of the scientific status of psychoanalysis, called the "tally argument": The memories are believed because they tally with our theory of the case. It should go without saying that none of this—the vividness of the recollection, the fact that symptoms disappear, or that the memory conforms to our a priori beliefs—substitutes for objective evidence, independently obtained, that the memory is an accurate representation of some event that actually occurred in the past.

EXHUMED MEMORIES AND FALSE MEMORY SYNDROME

This history is crucially relevant to a highly visible problem in contemporary clinical practice: the exhumation of ostensibly repressed (or, perhaps, dissociated) memories of early childhood incest, sexual assault, and other forms of trauma, abuse, neglect, and deprivation (for other views of this problem, see Baker, 1992; Herman, 1992; Loftus, 1993, 1994; Loftus & Ketcham, 1994; Loftus, Polonsky, & Fullilove, 1994; Terr, 1994; Yapko, 1994). In recent years, the claim is frequently made that such memories, long denied entry into consciousness, lie at the heart of many cases of depression, anxiety disorder, eating disorder, and substance abuse—that, in many cases, these syndromes represent a form of posttraumatic stress disorder similar to that observed in the sufferers of war neurosis. Accordingly, it is claimed, the proper treatment of these problems involves the exhumation of these memories, accompanied by abreaction, and followed by catharsis. Furthermore, these therapeutic processes are no longer confined to the consulting room: Catharsis often involves confronting the parent or other figure who allegedly perpetrated the abuse, even to the point of bringing criminal or civil charges in a court of law. Sometimes the accused admits guilt, and sometimes independent evidence is found to corroborate the patient's memory and impeach the denial of the accused. But sometimes the accused denies the charge, and no corroboration is available. In this case, the question is: Who is to be believed?

In many ways, public attention to this problem began with the 1990 murder trial of George Franklin, in San Mateo County, California (for an account of this case, see MacLean, 1993). Franklin was accused by his daughter, Eileen, of killing Susan Nason, her childhood friend, in September 1969, when the two children were 8 years old. According to Eileen Franklin's account, she was reminded of the incident when an expression on the face of her own 5-year-old daughter, Jessica, reminded her of Susan's facial expression at the time she was killed—some 20 years previously. Gradually a fully detailed memory of the incident emerged. There being no statute of limitations on murder, Franklin was tried and subsequently convicted—even though there was no physical evidence to corroborate Eileen Franklin's memory, and her account of the episode changed from time to time, and even though some of the details in her memory had been published in local newspapers at the time of Susan's death.

Over the last several years we have witnessed a virtual pandemic of such reports, accompanied by a host of television dramas based on the theme of exhumed memory for incest and other sexual abuse. And we are beginning to see other forms of exhumed memories as well: of satanic (or sadistic) ritual abuse (Pazder & Smith, 1980; Sakheim & Devine, 1992; Tate, 1991; for a critical overview, see Richardson, Best, & Bromley, 1991), of abduction by aliens in unidentified flying objects (Jacobs, 1992; Mack, 1994), and of trauma in past lives (Fiore, 1977, 1987; Goldberg, 1982; Hubbard, 1968; Sparrow, 1988; Woolger, 1987; see also Stevenson, 1974, 1987). Some of these exhumed memories of child abuse have found their way into the courts—not necessarily as criminal charges, where the statute of limitations applies and the standard of evidence is "beyond a reasonable doubt," but often in civil suits where claims can be brought at any time, and the standard of evidence is the looser "reasonable certainty." In some jurisdictions, like Washington State, exhumed memories are allowed into evidence under the doctrine of "delayed discovery," by which cases may be brought if new evidence is uncovered after the statute of limitations would ordinarily have expired.

In trying to respond to this phenomenon as psychologists, we need to do several things immediately. The first is to agree that child abuse, neglect, and deprivation, including incest and other forms of sexual trauma, are much more common than we might like to think, and constitute a serious social problem. Revised data from the 1988 Study of National Incidence and Prevalence of Child Abuse and Neglect provide an estimated incidence of 14.8 to 22.6 abused children per thousand, including 1.9 to 2.1 children per thousand who are victims of sexual abuse; and there are reasons to think that these numbers may be increasing (National Center on Child Abuse and Neglect, 1988; Sedlak, 1990).

The second is to agree that legitimate claims of incest and other forms of child abuse, when corroborated by independent objective evidence, are fair game for pursuit in the courts as well as in the consulting room.

The third is to recognize that even in the absence of actual incest or sexual abuse, girls and women live in a sexually oppressive society.

The fourth is to recognize that individuals who make claim to be victims of sexual abuse are deeply troubled by *something* in our lives, even if they were not actually abused, and deserve our sympathy and support. But in the case of uncorroborated memories we are presented with a further and more difficult problem of resolving the conflict between the accuser and the accused—one that boils down to a conflict between one person's memories and those of another.

It should be understood that although the notion of repression is intuitively plausible (Singer, 1990), the evidence for the delayed recovery of valid repressed memories of incest and other forms of abuse is rather thin. Certainly there is considerable evidence that therapy patients report histories of incest and sexual abuse with considerable frequency. So, for example, in a study by Herman, Perry, and van der Kolk (1989), fully 81% of a sample of 21 patients with borderline personality disorder reported physical abuse, sexual abuse, witnessing domestic violence, or other traumata before age 18, and in most cases before age 6; 73% of 11 patients with borderline traits, but not borderline personality, gave similar reports; for 23 patients with antisocial or schizotypal personality disorders, the figure was 57%. These figures are comparable to those obtained by others. Unfortunately, it is not clear that these patients are representative of their diagnostic categories. And, in any event, there was no independent validation of these retrospective self-reports.

With respect to the validity issue, perhaps the most commonly cited study is that of Herman and Schatzow (1987). In this study there were 53 participants in a therapy group for incest survivors. Of these, 14 patients had a severe amnesia for the incidents in question. Some patients "strongly suspected" that they were abused but "could not remember clearly" (pp. 3–4). As part of the therapeutic process, the patients were offered the opportunity to gather evidence that would corroborate their memories, or suspicions, of abuse. Such efforts were successful for 74% of the cases, 39 of 53. However, 74% (39 of 53) of the group members had little or no amnesia to begin with. If these were the individuals who were able to validate their memories, this is not evidence of verification of exhumed memory. What is at issue is not confirmation of reported abuse but, rather, confirmation of abuse in cases of amnesia or exhumed memory.

Herman and Schatzow (1987) further reported that their amnesic patients gave an average age of onset for the abuse of 4.9 years of age, whereas the nonamnesic patients reported onsets at about 8 to 11 years of age. We may ask how the amnesic patients arrived at the age at which they were abused. From this evidence, Herman and Schatzow concluded that "massive repression appeared to be the main defensive resource available to patients who were abused early in childhood" (p. 11). Unfortunately, Herman and Schatzow failed to consider other possibilities. For example, what was the impact of infantile and childhood amnesia arising from normal physiological, cognitive, and environmental changes occurring normally over the course of early development? An attributional account of these dates also suggests itself. These patients, believing that they were incest survivors but lacking actual memories for abuse, and knowing something of the concept of repressed memory but little or nothing of normal infantile and childhood amnesia, may have *assumed* that their abuse occurred during that period, early in childhood, when their memories were poorest. Thus, the dating of their abuse may be based on attributional processes, not fact retrieval.

A similar criticism applies to a study by Briere and Conte (1993), also often cited in support of exhumed memory. In this research, a total of 468 psychotherapy patients (mostly women) with self-reported histories of sexual abuse completed a questionnaire in response to a solicitation by their therapists. Almost 69% of the respondents reported that they had not remembered their abuse at some point in time after it occurred (although they now remembered it). Briere and Conte (1993) then determined which attributes discriminated between those patients who were amnesic for their abuse (or who had been amnesic at one time) and those who always remembered the abuse. Out of 40 variables examined with a discriminant function analysis, 10 proved significant. Of these predictors, the age of the patient at the time the abuse began was by far the strongest: Patients who had been amnesic for their abuse were molested earlier than those who had not experienced amnesia at any time.

Again, it is important to understand just how ambiguous this finding is. First, the molestations were self-reported but not independently corroborated. Second, Briere and Conte (1993) made no distinction between repression and ordinary forgetting due to infantile and childhood amnesia and other benign factors. As in the case of the Herman and Schatzow (1987) study, it is entirely possible that many of the ostensibly amnesic patients inferred that they were molested as children and then attributed their molestation to a period in their lives covered by normal infantile and childhood amnesia.

In this respect, Williams (1992, 1994a, 1994b) made something of an advance. She followed up a group of women who were treated for sexual abuse as children some 17 years earlier (for a precedent, see Robins, 1966). Under the cover of an ostensibly routine interview about the medical care they received as children, these subjects were asked questions about childhood sexual victimization. A total of 38% of the informants failed to disclose their previous abuse to the interviewer. Williams (1992) reports that "qualitative analysis of these reports and non-reports suggests that the vast majority of the 38% were women who did not remember the abuse" (p. 20). Although the single anecdote supporting this conclusion is fairly compelling, no quantitative evidence is given to support the assertion that these women were actually amnesic for their abuse. Moreover, even accepting the conclusion that they had in fact forgotten the episode, there is no reason to conclude that the forgetting was due to repression as opposed to benign processes. The Williams (1992, 1994) study is an important advance because it allows for the independent confirmation of self-reports of childhood trauma but by itself it is not nearly enough to permit the conclusion that "a large proportion of women do not recall childhood sexual victimization experiences" (1992, p. 21). Better methodology is required to distinguish between those who do not recall actual abuse and those who merely do not report it (Della Femina, Yeager, & Lewis, 1990). Among the the former, furthermore, it is important to distinguish between memory failures that reflect repression and other pathological processes and those that are benign.

The difficulties with exhumed memories are further exacerbated by the patient's strategies of coping with them. A childhood history of incest or other forms of abuse certainly seems to provide a compelling explanation for the patient's current problems in living. Once they draw the conclusion that they were abused, patients (sometimes acting on professional advice) may withdraw from their families, which effectively prevents false recollections of abuse from being challenged by those implicated in them. They may also go so far as to reconstruct their lives and personalities around the memories of abuse and their new identities as survivors of trauma.

This is all right if the memory is accurate—although Kaminer (1992) writes compellingly of the dark side of the survivor and recovery movements. But when the memory is distorted, or confabulated, the result can be what is called *false memory syndrome*—a condition in which a person's identity and interpersonal relationships are centered around a memory of traumatic experience which is objectively false but in which the person strongly believes. Note that the syndrome is not characterized by false memories as such. We all have memories that are inaccurate. Rather, the syndrome may be diagnosed when the memory is so deeply engrained that it orients the individual's entire personality and lifestyle, in turn disrupting all sorts of other adaptive behaviors. The analogy to personality disorder is intentional. False memory syndrome is especially destructive because the person assiduously avoids confrontation with any evidence that might challenge the memory. Thus it takes on a life of its own, encapsulated and resistant to correction. The person may become so focused on the memory that he or she may be effectively distracted from coping with the real problems in his or her life. It should be noted as well that even when the memory is valid, or of unknown (and unknowable) validity, the person can take on an identity as a survivor that is not necessarily in the best interests of getting on with life. As Kaminer (1992) notes, such identifications are not uncommon in the recovery movement, of which the trauma-survivor movement is only one example (see also Tavris, 1993).

Some colleagues object to the term "false memory syndrome" on the ground that no such entity is recognized by duly constituted medical authorities, or that it represents an inappropriate medicalization of a social phenomenon (e.g., Carstensen et al., 1993; Pope, 1996). Although the word "syndrome" may be commonly associated with the medical model of psychopathology, it is important to understand that the medical community has no exclusive rights to its use. Language is for everyone. Put concisely, a syndrome is a collection of symptoms, or attributes, that tend to co-occur. *Webster's Ninth New Collegiate Dictionary* (1984) offers two formal definitions of the word: (1) "a group of signs and symptoms that occur together and characterize a particular abnormality"; and (2) "a set of concurrent things that usually form an identifiable pattern." Although the first definition is arguably medical, the second is certainly not. So, the word "syndrome" can be used, properly, without necessarily implying any medical diagnosis. Usually, we think of a *disease* as a syndrome whose cause is known. However, *Webster's* says otherwise: (1) "trouble," or (2) "a condition . . . that impairs the performance of a vital function," or (3) "a harmful development (as in a social institution." Even *disease* can be used without medical connotations.

As a test of this view, a scan of all books in the main library (*not* the medical library) of the University of Arizona that contained the word "syndrome" in their titles produced the following list of syndromes:

accident syndrome, acquired immune deficiency syndrome, Afghan syndrome, alcoholic Korsakoff's syndrome, Asperger syndrome, attention deficit disorder syndrome, battered woman syndrome, battered child syndrome, Bhopal syndrome, binge-purge syndrome, blue light syndrome, buckram syndrome, cabbage syndrome, California syndrome, carpal tunnel syndrome, Chinese restaurant syndrome, chronic fatigue syndrome, conflict resolution syndrome, crowding syndrome, Cushing's syndrome, De Lange syndrome, disuse syndrome, doomsday syndrome, Down's syndrome, editorial syndrome, Einstein syndrome, energy syndrome, fear of Jews syndrome, female stress syndrome, fetal alcohol syndrome, gemini syndrome, general adaptation syndrome, Gilles de la Tourette syndrome, good girl syndrome, good soldier syndrome, Hamlet syndrome, Japan syndrome, left-hander syndrome, low back pain syndrome, Maginot Line syndrome, male stress syndrome, maltreatment syndrome, maternal depletion syndrome, minimal brain dysfunction syndrome, mother syndrome, Munchausen by proxy syndrome, Munich syndrome, obesity as a culture-bound syndrome, Peter Pan syndrome, post-Tridentine syndrome, power syndrome, premenstrual syndrome, Prometheus syndrome, romantic syndrome, Shek Kip Mei syndrome, sissy boy syndrome, Sizewell syndrome, Spender syndrome, Stockholm syndrome, sudden infant death syndrome, suicide syndrome, Sunday syndrome, superwoman syndrome, thanatos syndrome, theta syndrome, Tory syndrome, toxic shock syndrome, traumatic cervical syndrome, UFO syndrome, vanishing lung syndrome, vibration syndrome, Vichy syndrome, Wacousta syndrome, and Weiner's syndrome.

Apparently, the earliest nonmedical usage of the term "syndrome" was by Simone de Beauvoir (1959), in her feminist classic *Brigitte Bardot and the Lolita Syndrome*. More recently, a film entitled *The China Syndrome*, directed by James Bridges and starring Jane Fonda, Jack Lemmon, and Michael Douglas, was very popular. There have been many references to both *Vietnam syndrome* and *post-Vietnam syndrome* in the popular media.

As with the psychoanalytically derived term "complex," the nonmedical usage of *syndrome* is very common nowadays, with new variants added frequently. Nobody who accepts a term such as "survivor syndrome" (a term apparently introduced to characterize Danish prisoners in Nazi concentration camps; see Eitinger & Krell, 1985; Helwig-Larsen, Hoffmeyer, Kieler, Thaysen, Thygesen, & Wulff, 1952)—or for that matter, "repressed memory syndrome"

(Frederickson, 1992, p. 40) to describe a pattern of behavior and a social problem can have any principled objection to false memory syndrome.

ON VALIDATING MEMORIES

What are research psychologists and science-oriented clinicians to make of all this? Scientific psychologists are supposed to be experts on such things as memory, and in fact we know a great deal about how memory is encoded, stored, and retrieved. In describing how memory works, psychologists often resort to the metaphor of a library: Memory traces are like books that must be purchased and catalogued; the prospective user must look up the book in the catalog to know where to find it. For the search to succeed, the book must not have been eaten by worms or displaced by a careless user. The library metaphor will take us a long way, but the notion of memory retrieval obscures the fact that memories can be distorted, biased, and otherwise changed by changes in perspective and other events that occur after the time of encoding (Kihlstrom, 1994b). In the final analysis, memory is not analogous to reading a book; it is more like *writing* a book from fragmentary notes. The principle of memory reconstruction (Kihlstrom, 1994a; Kihlstrom & Barnhardt, 1993) is of utmost importance in the present context because it means that any particular memory is only partly derived from trace information encoded at the time of the event. Recall that most if not all of the verifiable information recalled by Eileen Franklin about Susan Nason's murder was available for 20 years in various newspaper accounts, and also that Eileen Franklin's memory changed over time, in conformance with known facts of the case (MacLean, 1993). This does not mean that Eileen Franklin's memories are the product of confabulation, but it does mean that the possibility of confabulation cannot be ruled out.

Do we have any way of telling which memories are valid and which are the products of imagination? The short answer is no (for a detailed review of the available evidence, see Kihlstrom, 1994a). Johnson and her colleagues proposed a number of attributes that tend to distinguish between the two types of memories (Johnson, Foley, Suengas, & Ray, 1988), but none of these attributes, and no package of attributes, is diagnostic in this respect. In another line of research, Raskin, Steller, and their colleagues developed a *criteria-based statement analysis* (Raskin & Steller, 1989; Steller & Koehnken, 1989), but in the final analysis the criteria they propose are only those that tend to make statements *appear* credible and do not actually distinguish between accurate and inaccurate memories. In the final analysis, then, in the absence of independent corroboration, no criteria appear to distinguish reliably between accurate recollections and fabrications and confabulations.

The point is that the techniques used by many counselors and therapists to promote the recovery of memory *might* succeed as they are intended to.

But they may also promote confabulation, and in such a manner that neither the counselor nor the patient will be able to determine, with accuracy, whether the recollection is accurate. Because by their very nature these memories are often not subject to independent corroboration, therapists and their patients, and counselors and their clients, are treading on very thin ice. As far as the therapy is concerned, the patient may be distracted from grappling with issues that are centrally involved with his or her presenting complaint, the patient's family relations may be inappropriately disrupted, and if the recollection is brought into the legal system, people may be unjustly accused and lives unjustifiably ruined.

Consider, first, the cultural atmosphere that surrounds the recovery of these memories. It is perhaps only a slight exaggeration to say that we are living and working in a time that a history of childhood incest or sexual abuse is the default option. That is, it is widely believed that a large majority, or at least a substantial minority, of individuals have been victims of incest or sexual abuse. If a majority, or even a substantial minority, of people are believed to have been abused as children, it becomes easier for individuals to believe, or to be convinced, that they themselves were abused.

Then there is the claim that specific symptoms are the effects of child-hood sexual abuse. A number of authors offer symptom checklists for self-diagnosis (Bass & Davis, 1988, 1994; Blume, 1990; Frederickson, 1992). Typically, the authors provide no information about the manner in which their list was derived, and in fact there is no good evidence that any psychological symptom is pathognomonic of sexual abuse. The list proposed by Bass and Davis (1988) consists of 74 different characteristics ostensibly associated with sexual abuse. The list includes such attributes as feeling different from other people; having trouble expressing one's feelings; diffi-culty in accepting one's own body; having relationships that do not work out; using sex to meet needs that are not sexual; having difficulty in setting boundaries with one's children; and feeling dissatisfied with family relation-ships. Taken together, these attributes constitute a kind of "Barnum descrip-tion" (Meehl, 1956; Ulrich, Stachnik, & Stainton, 1963) in that they are so general they apply to some extent to everyone.

It may be true that abuse victims show these signs and symptoms, but it does not follow that everyone who displays these attributes is an abuse victim. In any event, it should be clear that such checklists have no scientific standing: Their authors provide no standardized procedures for administration and scoring, no norms by which individual responses can be evaluated, no indices of reliability or validity. It remains to be seen which of these items, if any, bear any specific relation to childhood incest and sexual abuse (Beitchman, Zucker, Hood, daCosta, & Akman, 1991; Beitchman, Zucker, Hood, daCosta, Akman, & Cassavia, 1992; Kendall-Tackett, Williams, & Finkelhor, 1993; for a further discussion of this problem, see Kihlstrom, 1997).

The problem occurs when well-intentioned counselors conclude, from their patients' symptoms, that they are victims of abuse—*in the absence of any independent evidence for the abuse.* Patients come to therapists because they are puzzled and concerned about what is happening to them and about what they are experiencing. They are looking for answers. If the therapist responds to the patient's complaint with an authoritative diagnosis of child abuse, it should surprise nobody that reports of abuse ensue. Therapists are supposed to know about these things. But whether these reports reflect the patient's actual experience or simply unfold by virtue of the self-fulfilling prophecy remains undetermined—and, frankly, they remain indeterminate.

The situation is compounded by the media attention given to childhood incest and sexual abuse and the adult recovery of ostensibly repressed memories of these experiences. In much the same way that the anticommunist films of the 1950s (e.g., *My Son John,* released in 1952) created a society in which there seemed to be a subversive under every bed, these media portrayals provide a distorted representation of repressed memories—typically complete with so-called experts who testify about the high incidence of child abuse and the inerrancy of late-recovered repressed memories. Bass and Davis (1988), in *The Courage to Heal,* note that "As the media focus on sexual abuse has increased, more and more women have had their memories triggered" (p. 75). But the fact is that memories are not triggered at all. They are *reconstructed* (Bartlett, 1932; Kihlstrom & Barnhardt, 1993). Whether the reconstruction is historically accurate is an empirical question; in individual cases, including many cases of repressed memories of childhood abuse, it is also an unanswerable one.

Further difficulty is created by the fact that we remember very little of our early childhoods. The theory of repressed memories is that the abused child defends against his or her experience by erecting a repressive or dissociative barrier, which blocks the memories from conscious awareness. But infantile and childhood amnesia are universal phenomena: They occur even in laboratory rats (for overviews, see Fivush & Hudson, 1990; Howe & Courage, 1993; Moscovitch, 1984; Spear & Campbell, 1979). For most of us, our earliest recollection is dated between the third and fourth birthday, and the first signs of a continuous record of autobiographical memory do not appear until sometime between 5 and 6 years of age (Kihlstrom & Harackiewicz, 1982). Thus, the theory offers a ready explanation of why some patients, who manifest symptoms ostensibly characteristic of abuse, remember nothing of the kind: Memory for the incidents is repressed. Sometimes a hand is waved in the direction of infantile and childhood amnesia. Thus, Bass and Davis (1988) offer the following caution: "If you ask friends who weren't abused, you will find that most of them also don't remember a great number of details from their childhood" (p. 71). But just a few pages later, they assert:

> If you don't remember your abuse, you are not alone. Many women don't have memories, and some never get any memories. This doesn't mean they weren't abused. (p. 81)

If you don't have any memory of it, it can be hard to believe the abuse really happened. You may feel insecure about trusting your intuition and want "proof" of your abuse. This is a very natural desire, but it is not always one that can be met. . . . (p. 82)

And elsewhere they write:

If you are unable to remember any specific instances . . . but still have a feeling that something abusive happened to you, it probably did. (p. 21)

Often the knowledge that you were abused starts with a tiny feeling, an intuition. It's important to trust that inner voice and work from there. Assume your feelings are valid. So far, no one we've talked to thought she might have been abused, and then later discovered she hadn't been. The progression always goes the other way, from suspicion to confirmation. If you think you were abused, and your life shows the symptoms, then you were. (p. 22)

And in another place:

Many survivors suppress all memories of what happened to them as children. . . . Survivors often doubt their own perceptions. Coming to believe that the abuse really happened, and that it really hurt you, is a vital part of the healing process. (p. 58)

Thus, in a peculiarly perverse logic, the very fact that someone cannot remember instances of abuse is turned into evidence that they were in fact abused. There are no warnings here about infantile and childhood amnesia or the strong possibility that one's inability to remember much from child-hood may reflect nothing more than universal facts about the maturation of brain structures, the growth of information-processing capacity, and the absence of environmental cues to space and time that are necessary for the encoding of memorable episodic memories.

Bartlett (1932), in his classic monograph on *Remembering*, concluded that recollection begins with an attitude around which the memory is recon-structed. In the present instance, the attitude is conveyed by a popular culture that embraces child abuse as a widespread fact of life and the therapist's suggestion—it is often much more than just a hypothesis—that the patient was in fact abused. Remembering continues with further reconstructive activity. Bass and Davis (1988) write:

If you don't remember what happened to you, write about what you *do* remember. Re-create the context in which the abuse happened even if you don't remember the specifics of the abuse yet. Describe where you lived as a child. What was going on in your family, in your neighborhood, in your life? Often when women think they don't remember, they actually remember quite a lot. But since the picture isn't in sequence and isn't totally filled in, they don't feel they have permission to call what they know "remembering." Start with what you have. When you utilize that fully, you usually get more. (p. 83)

The general idea here is a good one: According to the encoding specificity principle (Tulving & Thomson, 1973; Kihlstrom & Barnhardt, 1993), reinstating the context in which an event occurred can improve memory for the event. The problem is that in reinstating the context, the person's speculations about what *might* have happened may well be confused with the person's memory about what *did* happen—especially in the presence of an authoritative, supportive therapist who assumes that the speculations are true.

The process continues with dreams, images, sensations, feelings, and thoughts. As with Freud, these phenomena are supposed to represent the return of the repressed—the first glimmerings of repressed memories emerging into consciousness (Bass & Davis, 1988, 1994; Frederickson, 1992). Terr (1994) attempted to connect this clinical lore to the research literature on implicit memory (for an analysis, see Kihlstrom, 1994c). And, again, the idea is good: We know that memories can be expressed implicitly in thoughts, images, and dreams (Schacter, 1987; Schacter, Chiu, & Ochsner, 1993). But again, it does not follow that every thought, image, and dream about incest and abuse is an expression of a repressed memory of incest and abuse. These things may simply reflect what Freud called "day residues" of conscious experience, or, they may be entirely irrelevant to the person's actual experiences. It should surprise no one that an anxious and depressed person who is informed by his or her therapist that he or she is likely to be a victim of child abuse, and who is offered the theory of repressed memory to explain why he or she has no memory for such abuse, and who is the recipient of countless messages from the media that says that both abuse and repression are ubiquitous, should start thinking and dreaming about incest and child abuse. Victims of the San Francisco Earthquake suffered nightmares and other symptoms of posttraumatic stress syndrome for many months (Cardeña & Spiegel, 1993; Wood, Bootzin, Rosenhan, Nolen-Hoeksema, & Jourden, 1992); many teachers have "schoolmares" before the beginning of classes each fall; students dream about the exams they are to take the next day; we all ruminate over the insults that are inflicted on us or the social blunders we make. Why shouldn't someone who is concerned about incest and abuse do the same? The problem comes when these phenomena are attributed to actual past experiences, in the absence of any independent corroboration of these memories (Brenneis, 1994b).

Near the beginning of their chapter on "Remembering," Bass and Davis write: "There is no right or wrong when it comes to remembering" (1988, p. 71). Of course, this statement is not remotely true.[1] Memories are personal, and no one can say to someone else that he or she does not have a particular memory. And, for that matter, nobody can say to someone else that he or she *does* have a particular memory but just cannot remember it. But that does not mean that there is no right or wrong in memory. The crucible for memory is the truth about what happened, the fact of the matter. Incest and other forms of abuse and trauma occur all too frequently in our society, and the survivors of these experiences deserve our respect and support. But uncorroborated memories of these sorts of things have no special status. They should be taken seriously, and they should be investigated, but they should not be accepted uncritically by either the patient who remembers them or the therapist who receives the report. There is a fact of the matter, and the truth sometimes lies elsewhere.

Unfortunately, the vagaries of memory are such as to make it impossible to get at the truth by remembering alone. Many people, including many counselors, do not seem to understand this. In many cases, therapeutic work with patients is based on a view of memory processes that is simply, but wildly, incongruent with established principles. Many therapists and their patients are satisfied with a story that provides a plausible explanation of current difficulties. But, as Spence (1982, 1987, 1994) argues, narrative truth is no substitute for historical truth. It does not help a patient to persuade him or her to believe something that is not true. Not only will the belief have unpleasant consequences for innocent people, but the patient will be effectively diverted from confronting issues that *are* important to his or her current problems in living.

There seems to be increasing understanding of the difficulties posed by exhumed memory. For example, both the American Psychiatric Association (Board of Trustees, 1993) and the American Medical Association (AMA; Council on Scientific Affairs, 1994) have issued official statements of concern about the uses to which uncorroborated exhumed memories of sexual abuse should be put. The AMA statement, in particular, "considers recovered memories of childhood sexual abuse to be of uncertain authenticity, which should be subject to external verification. The use of recovered memories is fraught with problems of potential misapplication" (p. 4). And in the spring of 1994, a jury heard a groundbreaking suit in which Gary Ramona, who was accused by his daughter Holly of incest, sued the daughter's therapists and the medical center in which they worked for malpractice. On May 13, 1994, the jury returned a verdict for the father, agreeing that the therapists had inappropriately used aggressive therapeutic techniques, including barbiturate drugs, to help the daughter exhume memories of incest (Johnston, 1997).

Possibly, Breuer and Freud (1893–1895/1955) were right: The problems of many clinical patients can be traced to their life histories, including the experiences of early childhood. And perhaps memory remains important for psychotherapy, or at least some forms of it. The problem is in figuring out which memories are true, and which are not.

ACKNOWLEDGMENTS

An earlier version of this chapter ("The Recovery of Memory in the Laboratory and Clinic") was presented as an invited address to the 1993 joint convention of the Rocky Mountain Psychological Association and the Western Psychological Association,

Phoenix, Arizona, April 1993. The point of view represented in this chapter is based on research supported by Grant No. MH-35856 from the National Institute of Mental Health. I thank Terrence Barnhardt, Lawrence Couture, Jennifer Dorfman, Elizabeth Glisky, Travis Gee, Martha Glisky, Victor Shames, Michael Valdiserri, and Susan Valdiserri for their comments during the preparation of this chapter.

I owe special thanks to Malcolm Macmillan, on whose work, *Freud Evaluated: The Completed Arc* (1996), I relied greatly in my effort to understand the role of memory in psychoanalysis.

I also wish to acknowledge the contribution of Paul Buttenweiser (1993), who coined the phrase "exhumed memory." *Exhumed memory* seems better than either *repressed memory* or *dissociated memory* as a label for the phenomenon at issue in this chapter because the phrase so nicely captures the process by which ostensibly forgotten events are discovered in the course of therapy or self-help, and because it is neutral with respect to the mechanism (repression, dissociation, etc.) ostensibly responsible for the forgetting.

NOTE

1. This statement is repeated in the second (1992, p. 71) and third (1994, p. 78) editions of the book. The second edition is essentially the same as the first edition, from which the quotes in this essay were drawn; the major difference is an expanded resource guide. The third edition was more substantially revised. Of greatest relevance to this chapter, the statements in the chapter on memory were qualified somewhat. I retained the quotations from the first edition because of its status as the leading self-help book in the area of child sexual abuse—perhaps the leading self-help book in any category (Santrock, Minnett, & Campbell, 1994)—and the role it has played in disseminating the trauma-memory argument to the public at large. In the third edition, an entirely new chapter attempts to analyze what the authors call a "backlash against survivors and their supporters" (1994, p. 16). This chapter also attempts to confront the memory literature more directly and cites three papers as documentation for the authors' claims about traumatic amnesia and the exhumation of memory—Herman and Schatzow (1987), Briere and Conte (1993), and Williams (1992)—the same three papers that were analyzed and found inadequate earlier in this chapter.

REFERENCES

Abeles, M., & Schilder, P. (1935). Psychogenic loss of personal identity. *Archives of Neurology and Psychiatry, 34,* 587–604.

Baker, R. A. (1992). *Hidden memories: Voices and visions from within.* Buffalo, NY: Prometheus Press.

Bartlett, F. C. (1932). *Remembering: A study in experimental and social psychology.* Cambridge, UK: Cambridge University Press.

Bass, E., & Davis, L. (1988). *The courage to heal: A guide for women survivors of child sexual abuse.* New York: Harper & Row.

Bass, E., & Davis, L. (1992). *The courage to heal: A guide for women survivors of child sexual abuse* (2nd ed.). New York: Harper & Row.

Bass, E., & Davis, L. (1994). *The courage to heal: A guide for women survivors of child sexual abuse* (3rd ed.). New York: Harper & Row.

Beitchman, J. H., Zucker, K. J., Hood, J. E., daCosta, G. A., & Akman, D. (1991). A review of the short-term effects of child sexual abuse. *Child Abuse and Neglect, 15,* 537–556.

Beitchman, J. H., Zucker, K. J., Hood, J. E., daCosta, G. A., Akman, D., & Cassavia, E. (1992). A review of the long-term effects of child sexual abuse. *Child Abuse and Neglect, 16,* 101–118.

Blackwenn, W. J. (1930a). Narcosis as therapy in neuropsychiatric conditions. *Journal of the American Medical Association, 95,* 1168–1171.

Blackwenn, W. J. (1930b). Production of sleep and rest in psychotic cases. *Archives of Neurology and Psychiatry, 24,* 365–372.

Blume, E. S. (1990). *Secret survivors: Uncovering incest and its aftereffects on women.* New York: Wiley.

Board of Trustees. (1993, December 12). *Statement on memories of sexual abuse.* Unpublished report, American Psychiatric Association.

Brenman, M., & Gill, M. (1947). *Hypnotherapy: A survey of the literature* (Menninger Foundations Monograph Series, 5). New York: International Universities Press.

Brenneis, C. B. (1994a). Belief and suggestion in the recovery of memories of childhood sexual abuse. *Journal of the American Psychoanalytic Association, 42,* 1027–1053.

Brenneis, C. B. (1994b). Can early childhood trauma be reconstructed from dreams? On the relationship of dreams to trauma. *Psychoanalytic Psychology, 11,* 429–447.

Breuer, J., & Freud, S. (1955). Studies on hysteria. In J. Strachey (Ed. & Trans.), *The standard edition of the complete psychological works of Sigmund Freud* (Vol. 2). London: Hogarth Press. (Original work published 1893–1895)

Briere, J., & Conte, J. (1993). Self-reported amnesia for abuse in adults molested as children. *Journal of Traumatic Stress, 6,* 21–31.

Brown, D., & Fromm, E. (1986). *Hypnotherapy and hypnoanalysis.* Hillsdale, NJ: Erlbaum

Brown, W. (1918). Treatment of cases of shellshock in an advanced neurological centre. *Lancet, 2,* 197–200.

Brown, W. (1919). War neurosis. *Proceedings of the Royal Society of Medicine, 12,* 52–61.

Brown, W. (1920a). The revival of emotional memories and its therapeutic value: I. *British Journal of Psychology, 1,* 16–19.

Brown, W. (1920b). The revival of emotional memories and its therapeutic value: IV. *British Journal of Psychology, 1,* 30–33.

Buckman, J., Hain, J. D., Smith, B. M., & Stevenson, I. (1973). Controlled interviews using drugs: II. Comparisons between restricted and freer conditions. *Archives of General Psychiatry, 29,* 623–627.

Buttenweiser, P. (1993, August 1). The exhumed memory [book review of *Once upon a time: A true story of memory, murder, and the law* by H. N. MacLean]. *New York Times Book Review,* pp. 9–10.

Cardeña, E., & Spiegel, D. (1993). Dissociative reactions to the San Francisco Bay area earthquake of 1989. *American Journal of Psychiatry, 150,* 474–478.

Carstensen, L., Gabrieli, J., Shepard, R., Levenson, R., Mason, M., Goodman, G., Bootzin, R., Ceci, S., Bronfenbrenner, U., Edelstein, B., Schober, M., Bruck, M.,

Keane, T., Zimering, R., Oltmanns, T., Gotlib, I., & Ekman, P. (1993, March). Repressed objectivity. *APS Observer*, p. 23.

Council on Scientific Affairs. (1985). Scientific status of refreshing recollection by the use of hypnosis. *Journal of the American Medical Association, 253*, 1918–1923.

Council of Scientific Affairs. (1994). *Memories of childhood abuse.* Unpublished report, American Medical Association.

de Beauvoir, S. (1959). *Brigitte Bardot and the Lolita syndrome.* New York: Reynal.

Della Femina, D., Yeager, C. A., & Lewis, D. O. (1990). Child abuse: Adolescent records vs. adult recall. *Child Abuse and Neglect, 14*, 227–231.

Eitinger, L., & Krell, R. (1985). *The psychological and medical effects of concentration camps and related persecutions on survivors of the Holocaust.* Vancouver, BC: University of British Columbia Press.

Ellenberger, H. L. (1970). *The discovery of the unconscious: The history and evolution of dynamic psychiatry.* New York: Basic Books.

Erdelyi, M. H. (1988). Hypermnesia: The effect of hypnosis, fantasy, and concentration. In H. M. Pettinati (Ed.), *Hypnosis and memory* (pp. 64–94). New York: Guilford Press.

Fiore, E. (1977). *You have been here before.* New York: Coward-McCann.

Fiore, E. (1987). *The unquiet dead.* New York: Doubleday.

Fivush, R., & Hudson, J. A. (Eds.). (1990). *Knowing and remembering in young children.* New York: Cambridge University Press.

Fredrickson, R. (1992). *Repressed memories: A journey to recovery from sexual abuse.* New York: Simon & Schuster.

Freud, S. (1953a). Fragment of an analysis of a case of hysteria. In J. Strachey (Ed. & Trans.), *The standard edition of the complete psychological works of Sigmund Freud* (Vol. 7, pp. 7–122). London: Hogarth Press. (Original work published 1905)

Freud, S. (1953b). Three essays on the theory of sexuality. In J. Strachey (Ed. & Trans.), *The standard edition of the complete psychological works of Sigmund Freud* (Vol. 7, pp. 130–243). London: Hogarth Press. (Original work published 1905)

Freud, S. (1962a). Heredity and the aetiology of the neuroses. In J. Strachey (Ed. & Trans.), *The standard edition of the complete psychological works of Sigmund Freud* (Vol. 3, pp. 143–156). London: Hogarth Press. (Original work published 1896)

Freud, S. (1962b). Further remarks on the neuro-psychoses of defence. In J. Strachey (Ed. & Trans.), *The standard edition of the complete psychological works of Sigmund Freud* (Vol. 3, pp. 159–185). London: Hogarth Press. (Original work published 1896)

Freud, S. (1962c). The aetiology of hysteria. In J. Strachey (Ed. & Trans.), *The standard edition of the complete psychological works of Sigmund Freud* (Vol. 3, pp. 191–221). London: Hogarth Press. (Original work published 1896)

Freud, S. (1963). Repression. In J. Strachey (Ed. & Trans.), *The standard edition of the complete psychological works of Sigmund Freud* (Vol. 14, pp. 7–66). London: Hogarth Press. (Original work published 1915)

Fromm, E. (1992). An ego-psychological theory of hypnosis. In E. Fromm & M. R. Nash (Eds.), *Contemporary hypnosis research* (pp. 131–148). New York: Guilford Press.

Gill, M. M., & Brenman, M. (1959). *Hypnosis and related states: Psychoanalytic studies in regression* (Austin Riggs Center Monograph 2). New York: International Universities Press.

Goldberg, B. (1982). *Past lives, future lives.* New York: Newcastle.

Grinker, R. (1944). Treatment of war neuroses. *Journal of the American Medical Association, 126*, 142–145.

Grinker, R., & Spiegel, J. P. (1944). Brief psychotherapy in war neuroses. *Journal of Psychosomatic Medicine, 6*, 123–131.

Grinker, R., & Spiegel, J. P. (1945a). *Men under stress*. Philadelphia: Blackiston.

Grinker, R., & Spiegel, J. P. (1945b). *War neuroses*. Philadelphia: Blackiston. (Originally published 1943)

Gruenewald, D. (1982). A psychoanalytic view of hypnosis. *American Journal of Clinical Hypnosis, 24*, 185–190.

Grünbaum, A. (1984). *The foundations of psychoanalysis: A philosophical critique.* Berkeley: University of California Press.

Hadfield, J. A. (1920). Treatment by suggestion and persuasion. In H. Crichton-Miller (Ed.), *Functional nerve disease: An epitome of war experience for the practitioner* (pp. 61–87). London: Frowde; Hodder & Stoughton.

Hain, J. D., Smith, B. M., & Stevenson, I. (1966). Effectiveness and processes of interviewing with drugs. *Journal of Psychiatric Research, 4*, 95–106.

Helweg-Larsen, P., Hoffmeyer, H., Kieler, J., Thaysen, J. H., & Wulff, M. H. (1952). Famine disease in German concentration camps: Complications and sequelae. *Acta Psychiatrica et Neurologica Scandinavica* (Suppl. 83).

Herman, J. L. (1992). *Trauma and recovery*. New York: Basic Books.

Herman, J. L., Perry, J. C., & van der Kolk, B. A. (1989). Childhood trauma in borderline personality disorder. *American Journal of Psychiatry, 146*, 140–145.

Herman, J. L., & Schatzow, E. (1987). Recovery and verification of memories of childhood sexual trauma. *Psychoanalytic Psychology, 4*, 1–14.

Herman, M. (1938). The use of intravenous sodium amytal in psychogenic amnesic states. *Psychiatric Quarterly, 12*, 738–742.

Horsley, J. S. (1936a). Narco-analysis. *Lancet, 130*, 55–56.

Horsley, J. S. (1936b). Narco-analysis. *Journal of Mental Science, 82*, 416–422.

Horsley, J. S. (1937). Therapeutic narcosis with soneryl. *Journal of Mental Science, 83*, 25–39.

Horsley, J. S. (1943). *Narco-analysis, a new technique in short-cut psychotherapy: A comparison with other methods and notes on the barbiturates.* London: Oxford University Press.

Howe, M. L., & Courage, M. L. (1993). On resolving the enigma of infantile amnesia. *Psychological Bulletin, 113*, 305–326.

Hubbard, L. R. (1968). *Have you lived before this life? A scientific Survey: A study of past lives through Dianetic engrams.* Los Angeles: Church of Scientology of California.

Jacobs, D. M. (1992). *Secret life: Firsthand accounts of UFO abductions*. New York: Simon & Schuster.

Janet, P. (1889). *L'Automatisme psychologique*. Paris: Alcan.

Janet, P. (1925). *Psychological healing: A historical and clinical study* (2 vols.). New York: Macmillan.

Johnston, M. (1997). *Spectral evidence: The Ramona case: Incest, memory and truth on trial in Napa Valley.* Boston: Houghton Mifflin.

Johnson, M., Foley, M. A., Suengas, A. G., & Raye, C. L. (1988). Phenomenal characteristics for perceived and imagined autobiographical events. *Journal of Experimental Psychology: General, 117*, 371–376.

Kaminer, W. (1992). *I'm dysfunctional, you're dysfunctional: The recovery movement and other self-help fashions.* Reading, MA: Addison-Wesley.

Kardiner, A. (1941). *The traumatic neuroses of war.* New York: Hoeber.

Kendall-Tackett, K. A., Williams, L. M., & Finkelhor, D. (1993). Impact of sexual abuse on children: A review and synthesis of recent empirical studies. *Psychological Bulletin, 113,* 164–180.

Kihlstrom, J. F. (1994a). Delayed recall and the principles of memory. *International Journal of Clinical and Experimental Hypnosis, 42,* 357–345.

Kihlstrom, J. F. (1994b, July). *The social construction of memory.* Paper presented at the annual meeting of the American Psychological Society, Washington, DC.

Kihlstrom, J. F. (1996). The trauma-memory argument and recovered-memory therapy. In K. Pezdek & W. P. Banks (Eds.), *The recovered memory/false memory debate* (pp. 297–311). San Diego: Academic Press.

Kihlstrom, J. F. (1997). Suffering from reminiscences: Exhumed memory, implicit memory, and the return of the repressed. In M. A. Conway (Ed.), *Recovered memories and false memories* (pp. 100–117). Oxford, UK: Oxford University Press.

Kihlstrom, J. F., & Barnhardt, T. M. (1993). The self-regulation of memory, for better and for worse, with and without hypnosis. In D. M. Wegner & J. W. Pennebaker (Eds.), *Handbook of mental control* (pp. 88–125). Englewood Cliffs, NJ: Prentice-Hall.

Kihlstrom, J. F., & Eich, E. (1994). Altering states of consciousness. In D. Druckman & R. A. Bjork (Eds.), *Learning, remembering, and believing: Enhancing performance* (pp. 207–248). Washington, DC: National Academy Press.

Kihlstrom, J. F., & Harackiewicz, J. M. (1982). The earliest recollection: A new survey. *Journal of Personality, 50,* 134–148.

Kubie, L. S., & Margolin, S. (1945). The therapeutic role of drugs in the process of repression, dissociation, and synthesis. *Psychosomatic Medicine, 7,* 147–151.

Lakoff, R. T., & Coyne, J. C. (1993). *Father knows best: The use and abuse of power in Freud's case of "Dora."* New York: Teachers College Press.

Lambert, C., & Rees, W. L. (1944). Intravenous barbiturates in the treatment of hysteria. *British Medical Journal, 2,* 70–73.

Laurence, J.-R., & Perry, C. (1988). *Hypnosis, will, and memory: A psycho-legal history.* New York: Guilford Press.

Lindemann, E. (1932). Psychological changes in normal and abnormal individuals under the influence of sodium amytal. *American Journal of Psychiatry, 11,* 1083–1091.

Lindner, R. M. (1944). *Rebel without a cause: The hypnoanalysis of a criminal psychopath.* New York: Grune & Stratton.

Loftus, E. (1993). The reality of repressed memories. *American Psychologist, 48,* 518–537.

Loftus, E. F. (1994). The repressed memory controversy. *American Psychologist, 49,* 443–445.

Loftus, E., & Ketcham, K. (1994). *The myth of repressed memory: False memories and accusations of sexual abuse.* New York: St. Martin's Press.

Loftus, E. F., Polonsky, S., & Fullilove, M. T. (1994). Memories of childhood sexual abuse: Remembering and repressing. *Psychology of Women Quarterly, 18,* 67–84.

Lynn, S. J., & Nash, M. R. (1994). Truth in memory: Ramifications for psychotherapy and hypnotherapy. *American Journal of Clinical Hypnosis, 36,* 194–208.

MacDougall, W. (1920). The revival of emotional memories and its therapeutic value: III. *British Journal of Psychology, 1,* 23–29.

Mack, J. E. (1994). *Abduction: Human encounters with aliens.* New York: Scribner's.

MacLean, H. N. (1993). *Once upon a time: A true story of memory, murder, and the law.* New York: HarperCollins.

Macmillan, M. B. (1979). Delboeuf and Janet as influences in Freud's treatment of Emmy von N. *Journal of the History of the Behavioral Sciences, 15,* 299–309.

Macmillan, M. B. (1986). Souvenir de la Salpêtrière: M. le Dr Freud à Paris, 1885. *Australian Psychologist, 21,* 3–29.

Macmillan, M. B. (1996). *Freud evaluated: The completed arc* (rev. ed.). Cambridge, MA: MIT Press.

Marks, J. (1978). *The search for the Manchurian candidate.* New York: Times Books.

Meehl, P. (1956). Wanted–a good cookbook. *American Psychologist, 11,* 263–272.

Morris, D. P. (1945). Intravenous barbiturates: An aid in the diagnosis and treatment of conversion hysteria and malingering. *Military Surgeon, 96,* 509–513.

Moscovitch, M. (1984). *Advances in the study of communication and affect: Vol. 9. Infant memory: Its relation to normal and pathological memory in humans and other animals.* New York: Plenum.

Myers, C. S. (1920). The revival of emotional memories and its therapeutic value: II. *British Journal of Psychology, 1,* 20–22.

Nash, M. R. (1987). What, if anything, is age regressed about hypnotic age regression? A review of the empirical literature. *Psychological Bulletin, 102,* 42–52.

National Center on Child Abuse and Neglect. (1988). Executive summary: Study of national incidence and prevalence of child abuse and neglect: 1988. Washington, DC: Author.

Orne, M. T., Whitehouse, W. G., Dinges, D. F., & Orne, E. C. (1988). Reconstructing memory through hypnosis: Forensic and clinical implications. In H. M. Pettinati (Ed.), *Hypnosis and memory* (pp. 21–63). New York: Guilford Press.

Pazder, L., & Smith, M. (1980). *Michelle remembers.* New York: St. Martin's Press.

Perry, C., & Laurence, J.-R. (1984). Mental processing outside of awareness: The contributions of Freud and Janet. In K. S. Bowers & D. Meichenbaum (Eds.), *The unconscious reconsidered* (pp. 9–48). New York: Wiley-Interscience.

Perry, J. C., & Jacobs, D. (1982). Clinical applications of the amytal interview in psychiatric emergency settings. *American Journal of Psychiatry, 139,* 552–559.

Piper, A. (1993). "Truth serum" and "recovered memories" of sexual abuse: A review of the evidence. *Journal of Psychiatry and the Law, 21,* 447–471.

Pope, K. S. (1996). Memory, abuse, and science: Questioning claims about the false memory syndrome epidemic. *American Psychologist, 51,* 957–974.

Raskin, D. C., & Steller, M. (1989). Assessing credibility of allegations of child sexual abuse: Polygraph examinations and statement analysis. In H. Wegener, F. Losel, & J. Haisch (Eds.), *Criminal behavior and the justice system: Psychological perspectives* (pp. 290–302). New York: Springer-Verlag.

Richardson, J. T., Best, J., & Bromley, D. G. (1991). *The satanism scare.* New York: de Gruyter.

Ruedrich, S. L., Chu, C.-C., & Wadle, C. V. (1985). The amytal interview in the treatment of psychogenic amnesia. *Hospital and Community Psychiatry, 36,* 1045–1046.

Sakheim, D. K., & Devine, S. E. (Eds.). (1992). *Out of darkness: Exploring satanism and ritual abuse.* New York: Lexington Books.

Santrock, J. W., Minnett, A. M., & Campbell, B. D. (1994). *The authoritative guide to self-help books.* New York: Guilford Press.

Sargant, W., & Slater, E. (1940). Acute war neuroses. *Lancet, 2,* 1–2.

Schacter, D. L. (1987). Implicit memory: History and current status. *Journal of Experimental Psychology: Learning, Memory, and Cognition, 13*, 501–518.

Schacter, D. L., Chiu, C.-Y. P., & Ochsner, K. N. (1993). Implicit memory: A selective review. *Annual Review of Neuroscience, 16*, 159–182.

Scheflin, A. W., & Shapiro, J. L. (1989). *Trance on trial.* New York: Guilford Press.

Schimek, J. G. (1987). Fact and fantasy in the seduction theory: A historical review. *Journal of the American Psychoanalytic Association, 35*, 937–965.

Sedlak, A. J. (1990). Technical amendment to the study findings—National incidence and prevalence of child abuse and neglect: 1988. Rockville, MD: Westat.

Singer, J. L. (Ed.). (1990). *Repression and dissociation: Implications for personality theory, psychopathology, and health.* Chicago: University of Chicago Press.

Sloane, M. C. (1981). A comparison of hypnosis vs. waking state and visual vs. non-visual recall instructions for witness/victim memory retrieval in actual major crimes (Doctoral dissertation, Florida State University). *University Microfilms International,* #8125873.

Smith, B. M., Hain, J. D., & Stevenson, I. (1970). Controlled interviews using drugs. *Archives of General Psychiatry, 22*, 2–10.

Smith, M. C. (1983). Hypnotic memory enhancement of witnesses: Does it work? *Psychological Bulletin, 94*, 387–407.

Sparrow, L. E. (1988). *Reincarnation: Claiming your past, creating your future. Edgar Cayce's wisdom for the new age.* San Francisco: Harper & Row.

Spear, N. E., & Campbell, B. A. (Eds.). (1979). *Ontogeny of learning and memory.* Hillsdale, NJ: Erlbaum.

Spence, D. P. (1982). *Narrative truth and historical truth: Meaning and interpretation in psychoanalysis.* New York: Norton.

Spence, D. P. (1987). *The Freudian metaphor: Toward paradigm change in psychoanalysis.* New York: Norton.

Spence, D. P. (1994). *The rhetorical voice of psychoanalysis: Displacement of evidence by theory.* Cambridge, MA: Harvard University Press.

Steller, M., & Koehnken, G. (1989). Criteria-based statement analysis. In D. C. Raskin (Ed.), *Psychological methods in criminal investigation and evidence* (pp. 217–245). New York: Springer.

Stevenson, I. (1974). *Twenty cases suggestive of reincarnation* (2nd ed.). Charlottesville, VA: University of Virginia Press.

Stevenson, I. (1987). *Children who remember previous lives: A question of reincarnation.* Charlottesville, VA: University of Virginia Press.

Stevenson, I., Buckman, J., Smith, B. M., & Hain, J. D. (1974). The use of drugs in psychiatric interviews: Some interpretations based on controlled experiments. *American Journal of Psychiatry, 131*, 707–710.

Tate, T. (1991). *Children for the devil: Ritual abuse and satanic crime.* London: Methuen.

Tavris, C. (1993, January 3). Beware the incest-survivor machine. *New York Times Book Review,* pp. 1, 16–17.

Terr, L. (1994). *Unchained memories: True stories of traumatic memories, lost and found.* New York: Basic Books.

Thomas, G. (1988). *Journey into madness: Medical torture and the mind controllers.* London: Bantam.

Tilken, L. (1949). The present status of narcosynthesis using sodium pentothal and sodium amytal. *Diseases of the Nervous System, 10*, 215–218.

Timm, H. W. (1981). The effect of forensic hypnosis techniques on eyewitness recall and recognition. *Journal of Police Science and Administration, 9*, 188–194.

Tulving, E., & Thomson, D. M. (1973). Encoding specificity and retrieval processes in episodic memory. *Psychological Review, 80*, 352–373.

Ulrich, R. E., Stachnik, T. J., & Stainton, S. R. (1963). Student acceptance of generalized personality interpretations. *Psychological Reports, 13*, 831–834.

Watkins, J. (1949). *Hypnotherapy of war neuroses*. New York: Ronald.

Williams, L. M. (1992, Summer). Adult memories of childhood abuse: Preliminary findings from a longitudinal study. *APSAC Advisor*, 19–21.

Williams, L. M. (1994a). Recall of childhood trauma: A prospective study of women's memories of child sexual abuse. *Journal of Consulting and Clinical Psychology, 62*, 1167–1176.

Williams, L. M. (1994b). What does it mean to forget child abuse? A reply to Loftus, Garry, & Feldman (1994). *Journal of Consulting and Clinical Psychology, 62*, 1182–1186.

Wood, J. M., Bootzin, R. R., Rosenhan, D., Nolen-Hoeksema, S., & Jourden, F. (1992). Effects of the 1989 San Francico earthquake on frequency and content of nightmares. *Journal of Abnormal Psychology, 101*, 219–224.

Woolger, R. *Other lives, other selves*. New York: Doubleday.

Yapko, M. D. (1994). *Suggestions of abuse: True and false memories of childhood sexual trauma*. New York: Simon & Schuster.

CHAPTER 2

TRUTH IN MEMORY
Caveat Emptor

David G. Payne
Jason M. Blackwell

> There are no whole truths; all truths are half truths. It is trying to treat
> them as whole truths that plays the devil.
>
> —ALFRED NORTH WHITEHEAD (1954)

In many situations we rely on our memories to establish the truth. Establishing
the truth about past events requires memory systems that are able to (1) create
some record(s) of the events, (2) retain this information over time, and (3) use
this information to answer questions concerning these events. Humans have
evolved biological memory systems that generally allow us to easily remember
important events. More recently, people have developed technologies that
allow us to retain physical records (e.g., written descriptions and visual and
auditory recordings) of the past. Although these technologies are relevant to
the general issue of "truth in memory," we focus on a more specific issue,
namely, to what extent does human memory allow us to accurately recollect
the past? If we wish to establish the historical truth about events that were not
recorded with some technological device (e.g., a videocassette recorder), then
we must consider whether human memory is likely to provide an accurate
record. Spence (1984) and others (e.g., Ganaway, 1989; Howard, 1991)
discussed the distinction between narrative truth and historical truth, which
is important for our discussion. *Historical truth* refers to events that actually
occurred in the rememberer's past whereas *narrative truth* refers to events that
either may or may not have actually happened in the (historical) past but are
believed to be true (in the psychological sense) by the rememberer. Narrative
truth in some sense refers to our life story as we remember it; the historical

accuracy of this narrative truth is often indeterminate. Throughout this chapter when we refer to "truth" we are referring to historical truth.

As the quote from Alfred North Whitehead suggests, problems arise when we overlook the fact that some of what we believe to be true is, in reality, only partially true or false. In this chapter we consider whether human memory provides information sufficient for establishing whole truths or only partial truths. In the first section of the chapter we briefly review studies examining people's beliefs regarding human memory. We also consider studies that assess how people use their memories. These latter studies provide windows other than self-reports for looking at people's beliefs about the normal functioning of memory. In the second section we discuss metaphors that people use to explain memory, and we argue that these metaphors are intimately related to the beliefs we have about memory. In the third section we review evidence that shows that there are many ways in which normal human memory does not yield a veridical account of past events. Some of the memory errors that are now well established include misremembering details of events, recollecting events that never occurred, and recalling information correctly but attributing the information to an incorrect source (e.g., remembering that a joke was told at a party but attributing the joke to Mary when in fact Dean told the joke). In the final section we propose a conceptualization of human memory that focuses on both the quantity and accuracy of human memory. Our approach has many advantages over extant conceptualizations of human memory, and ideally it can alter our beliefs concerning what we might reasonably expect from our memories and the types of questions researchers should ask about memory functioning.

BELIEFS ABOUT HUMAN MEMORY

Autobiographical Memories

Many aspects of our lives hinge on what we believe about the functioning of our memory, and these beliefs can have major effects on the decisions we make as individuals and as a society. As individuals, our memories of the interactions we have with friends, family members, coworkers, and so forth affect how we view ourselves and how we think others perceive us. At the societal level, the fact that approximately half the states in the United States recently changed their statute of limitations for filing charges based on "recovered" memories—memories for which the rememberer was not able to recollect the event(s) earlier in his or her life but is now able to do so, often as a result of psychotherapeutic treatment—speaks volumes to the major impact beliefs about memory have on society.

Basing our individual behaviors and societal decisions on beliefs about memories would be fine—if these beliefs about memory were always accurate. Unfortunately, we are convinced—and we hope to convince the reader—that these beliefs are often not accurate, and people have serious misperceptions about how memory operates. Everyone knows that we forget things, but what people do not appear to appreciate is that we also misremember. We think we are remembering accurately, but our memories do not mirror reality. For example, do you remember where you were, whom you were with, what type of emotional reaction you had, when you heard about the space shuttle *Challenger* accident on February 3, 1986?

Many people, including us (D. G. P. and J. M. B.), report that they have a very vivid memory of where they were, who they were with, and how they learned about the *Challenger* disaster. Depending on your age you might have a similar vivid memory for what you were doing and how you felt on receiving the news of President Kennedy's assassination in 1963, the attempt on President Reagan's life in 1981, or the assassination of Itzhak Rabin in 1995.

Brown and Kulik (1977) coined the term "flashbulb memory" to refer to those recollections of autobiographical events which carry with them strong emotional reactions. Although researchers continue to question the specific details of flashbulb memories, as well as whether these memories are different from normal memories (e.g., McCloskey, Wible, & Cohen, 1988; Neisser & Harsch, 1992), most people report that they have recollections for certain unique events that are particularly clear and often involve a strong affective component. As such, flashbulb memories are particularly relevant to the topic of truth in memory, as these memories appear to provide the rememberer with a clear, accurate, and vivid memory of personally experienced, unusual, and unexpected events. Because they appear to be accurate and are relatively permanent, people often point to these sorts of memories as evidence of veridical and detailed memory.

There is, however, growing evidence that even flashbulb memories may be inaccurate. For example, memory researcher Ulric Neisser (1982) reported that for many years he had a vivid memory of how he heard of the Japanese attack on Pearl Harbor on December 6, 1941. He was listening to a baseball game on the radio when the game was interrupted with an announcement of the attack. Years later he realized that the "memory" was absurd—no one was playing baseball in December! In another often-cited case, developmental psychologist Jean Piaget (1945/1962) described a memory he had for an episode in which, as a young child, his caretaker protected him from an attacker; his memory included details of the attack as well as the injuries suffered by the caretaker. Years later the caretaker confessed that she had fabricated the entire event—but Piaget nonetheless had a clear and vivid memory of the episode that never occurred. This memory was presumably a consequence of hearing family stories about the attack.

These two anecdotal reports are but the tip of an iceberg of growing evidence which indicates that human memory often differs in systematic and major ways from the actual events of interest; we review additional evidence concerning the accuracy of flashbulb memories later in the chapter. Furthermore, these inaccurate memories are often very compelling to the rememberer—in many ways these false memories appear to the person as being indistinguishable from real, or veridical, memories of actual events. People apparently have great faith in the accuracy of their memories of unique and personally relevant events. We return to the issue of the accuracy of human memory later in the chapter; the next question we consider is, What do people believe about how long memories persist?

The Permanence of Stored Information

Loftus and Loftus (1980) conducted a survey to examine people's beliefs about how memory functions. Their sample included 75 individuals with graduate training in psychology and 94 nonpsychologists from a variety of backgrounds. All subjects were given the following question:

> Which of these statements best reflects your view on how human memory works?
>
> 1. Everything we learn is permanently stored in the mind, although sometimes particular details are not accessible. With hypnosis, or other special techniques, these inaccessible details could eventually be recovered.
>
> 2. Some details that we learn may be permanently lost from memory. Such details would never be able to be recovered by hypnosis, or any other special technique, because these details are simply no longer there.

Results showed that 84% of the psychologists and 69% of the nonpsychologists selected option 1. One of us (D.G.P.) replicated this informal study several times (in undergraduate and graduate classes, memory improvement seminars taught in the community, etc.), and the results were always consistent with those of Loftus and Loftus.

Yapko (1994) surveyed more than 850 psychotherapists in clinical practice regarding their beliefs on memory and other issues. A significant portion of these individuals expressed the belief that all events are permanently recorded in memory; they also reported a belief that these memories are recoverable through the use of clinical techniques (e.g., hypnosis). Garry, Loftus, Brown, and DuBreuil (1997) recently surveyed 116 graduate students from a variety of disciplines about their memory beliefs. Nearly two-thirds of these subjects agreed with the notion that once an event is experienced it is permanently stored in the brain. Furthermore, two-thirds of the respondents also agreed with the view that forgetting is caused by an inability to locate stored information.

There is also evidence that people believe in a variety of memory-enhancement techniques. For example, Whitehouse, Orne, Orne, and Dinges (1991) reported that 93% of their college-age subjects believed that hypnosis enhances memory retrieval; this belief stands in firm contrast to studies showing that hypnosis can affect how much a person will report but not the accuracy of their memory (e.g., Smith, 1983). Whitehouse et al.'s finding is consistent with the survey data reported by Yapko (1994) and converges on the conclusion that, by and large, most people believe that human memory works by storing a permanent record of events and that forgetting involves a failure to locate, or retrieve, these records from memory.

One question that arises from these studies in memory beliefs is, Why do people have such a strong belief in the permanence of memories? Subjects in the Loftus and Loftus (1980) study cited a variety of forms of evidence to support their belief that memories are permanently stored and potentially accessible, including Wilder Penfield's (1969) studies on electrical stimulation of the human brain in the 1950s, hypnosis, and laboratory studies showing that changes in retrieval cues can lead to the recall of previously unrecalled information (e.g., Tulving & Thomson, 1973). People also mentioned personal episodes of spontaneous recovery or reminiscence (i.e., the recovery of a sought after memory after previously failing to recall the event). There are indeed data from the basic research literature that, at one level, might be construed as support for the belief in permanent memories. For example, in a series of large-scale naturalistic memory studies Bahrick and his colleagues (e.g., Bahrick, 1984; Bahrick, Bahrick, & Wittlinger, 1975; Bahrick & Hall, 1991; Bahrick, Hall, Goggin, Bahrick, & Berger, 1994) have demonstrated that, over retention intervals of up to 50 years, there is little forgetting of foreign-language vocabulary and grammar, memory for faces and names, or foreign-language comprehension. Bahrick (1984) proposed that there is a "permastore" which maintains well-learned information for very long periods. In addition to these data showing good retention of information over very long intervals, Usher and Neisser (1993) recently reported data that lead them to argue that people can report reliable autobiographical event memories before age 3. Note that the data from the Usher and Neisser (1993) study do not refute the well-documented phenomena of infantile amnesia (Spear, 1979). Rather, they raise questions concerning the offset of this amnesia as well as methodological concerns about how to measure infantile amnesia.

Studies of the permastore construct introduced by Bahrick (1984) and the establishment of reliable early memories attest to the fact that some information may be well retained and there may be some reliable memories from early in life. However, data from these studies do not indicate that all memories are permanently recorded. Loftus and Loftus (1980) reviewed the scientific evidence relevant to the two options regarding how memory works given to subjects in their survey. They concluded that "contrary to popular belief, the evidence in no way confirms the view that all memories are permanent and thus potentially recoverable" (p. 420). Our reading of the scientific literature during the 18 years since the Loftus and Loftus study appeared leads us to the same conclusion that Loftus and Loftus drew in 1980.

It thus appears that people's beliefs about the permanence of memories are at odds with the available evidence. Furthermore, evidence concerning the mnemonic strategies people employ indicates that people do not understand how normal adult memory operates. For example, one of the most robust and reliable findings in the memory literature is the spacing effect (e.g., Greene, 1989; Woodworth, 1938). This refers to the fact that if people study information more than one time, their memory for these materials is better if the repetitions of the study episodes are spaced out in time than if they ocur back to back or in a massed format.

Despite the overwhelming evidence to support the validity and reliability of the spacing effect, there is very little application of this finding in the general population (Dempster, 1988). That is, it appears that individuals are unaware of the benefits of spacing. For example, Zechmeister and Shaughnessy (1980) presented subjects with lists of words to study, some of which appeared more than once in the list. The repeated words were presented in either a spaced or a massed format. After the repeated items were presented a second time, subjects were asked to estimate the likelihood that they would be able to recall these items on a later test. Although subjects rated the massed presentation items as more likely to be recalled than the spaced items, the recall data showed that there was a significant spacing effect with the spaced items better recalled than the massed items (for a review of related studies, see Payne and Wenger, 1996, pp. 126–130).

MEMORY METAPHORS

The results reviewed here suggest that people's implicit theories of memory do not agree with what we know about the normal functioning of human memory. Because many people subscribe to views of memory that are not supported by scientific facts, it is useful to consider in more detail the types of conceptualizations people employ as their implicit theory of human memory.

When people are confronted with phenomena that they do not understand or that are extremely complex, they often try to explain the phenomena by comparing or relating them to things with which they are more familiar. Metaphors and analogies are used in many domains including education and science, and they are often quite useful in making complex ideas seem more understandable. For example, Kosslyn and Koenig (1995) describe how concepts such as "parallel distributed processing" and "neural network" systems are used in cognitive neuroscience to account for a variety of phenomena. These systems can be rather complex and students often have difficulty appreciating how these systems function, with their abstract concepts such as input units, hidden units, feedforward, and connection strengths. To illustrate how these systems operate, Kosslyn and Koenig likened them to a fictional zoological system in which there were three layers of octopi in a shallow tidal pool. When octopi at the lower level felt anything with their tentacles, they squeezed the tentacles of octopi in the middle level who in turn squeezed the tentacles of those in the top row. The octopi in the top row would then wave their tentacles out of the water. Seagulls had supposedly learned to observe the octopi in the top row as an indication of fish available in the tidal pool. Kosslyn and Koenig's metaphor is an effective one because the student is able to visualize the three layers of octopi and compare these with the various output layers of a "neural network." Kosslyn and Koenig further developed this metaphor to explain several features of neural networks.

Lakoff and Johnson (1980) argued strongly that in our attempts to understand we routinely employ metaphors that structure the way we think, perceive, and act. We agree with Lakoff and Johnson's general claim regarding the prevalence of metaphorical thinking, and we believe that the metaphors people use to understand/explain memory affect both what people come to expect from memory and aspects of remembering/misremembering that are ignored or minimized in our theoretical accounts of memory. Lakoff and Johnson (1980) refer to these two functions of metaphors as *highlighting* and *hiding*, respectively (pp. 10–12).

What sorts of metaphors do laypersons and scholars employ to explain memory? Roediger (1980) reviewed the memory metaphors used in cognitive psychology and noted that the vast majority of these metaphors are spatial in nature. Table 2.1 lists a subset of the spatial analogies with search metaphors described by Roediger (1980).

Generally speaking, within the spatial analogy with search models, the mind is likened to a physical space. When we learn, we place objects (memories) into this space and when we remember we locate these objects via a search process. By utilizing a spatial metaphor for the mind we can attempt to understand something that is not known (e.g., mind, memory, and recollec-

---

TABLE 2.1. Spatial Analogies Used to Explain Human Memory

Spatial analogies with search

Wax tablet (Plato, Aristotle)
Gramophone (Pear, 1922)
Aviary (Plato)
House (James, 1890)
Rooms in a house (Freud, 1924/1952)
Switchboard (see John, 1972)
Purse (G.A. Miller, 1956)
Leaky bucket or sieve (Miller, 1956)
Stores (Atkinson & Shiffrin, 1968)
Mystic writing pad (Freud, 1940/1950)
Workbench (Klatzky, 1975)
Cow's stomach (Hintzman, 1974)
Library (Broadbent, 1971)
Dictionary (Loftus, 1977)
Tape recorder (see Posner & Warren, 1972)
Garbage can (Landauer, 1975)

Note. Adapted from Roediger (1980, Table 1). Copyright 1980 by the Psychonomic Society. Adapted by permission.

tion) by analogy to something that is familiar, such as objects within a three-dimensional space. Thus we might compare memory to a library, with memories for specific events being similar to books stored on the library shelf. Remembering the event then involves searching the library for the appropriate book; forgetting involves a failure to locate the sought-after book. Note that this storehouse metaphor accords well with the common view of memory documented in Loftus and Loftus's (1980) informal survey: When we forget something it is because we cannot "locate" that memory. Presumably if we used a better search strategy, took more time, and so forth, we would be able to remember the event of interest.

To use Lakoff and Johnson's (1980) terms, the various spatial and search metaphors that have been developed to explain memory (e.g., library, rooms in a house, and computer storage) function to highlight forgetting and to deemphasize memory errors. These metaphors are used by laypersons and scientists alike, and the use of these metaphors affects the beliefs and behaviors of these individuals.

What are the effects of metaphors on memory researchers? If memories are likened to a physical object that is deposited into a storehouse, the following types of questions are likely to be addressed by memory researchers: What factors affect the ease of locating an item in memory? What makes a retrieval cue effective in helping us recover a memory? How does our ability to retrieve information change across the retention interval? As these questions indicate, an important consequence of adopting a spatial metaphor is that it focuses attention on (or highlights) the *quantity* of information remembered and downplays, or hides, variations in the *accuracy* or *quality* of memories. If memory is likened to a library with books stored in it, there is little reason to question whether a retrieved memory is accurate—just as there is little reason to doubt that the text one finds on the library shelf is in fact the sought-after text. Nonetheless, there are situations in which our memories are inaccurate. In the next section we review studies of memory errors. Before discussing these, however, we comment briefly on the relation between technology and the metaphors people use to explain memory.

As Table 2.1 indicates, the analogies that people use to explain memory (as well as other perceptual and cognitive processes) tend to mirror the levels of technology available at the time. Over time, we have seen analogies move from wax tablets to rooms in a house, switchboards, workbenches, computers, tape recorders, and videocassette recorders in more recent yeras. As our technologies for recording information (or storing artifacts, records, etc.) advance, we see parallel developments in the relative sophistication/elaboration of our memory metaphors. If the metaphors we use to explain memory parallel the available technology, this suggests that nowadays people are likening memory to physical devices that rapidly developed in terms of the amount and ease of accessing stored information.

We suggest that we have passed the point when it is helpful or appropriate to draw analogies between human memory and the technology available to record events in the world around us. Our point here is not simply that the mind is not like a computer, for the mind is also not like a wax tablet, or workbench, for example. Rather, our point is that there are many negative consequences of continuing to draw analogies between human memory and modern technologies. These analogies and metaphors imply that human memory possesses many of the characteristics of these technological devices, and these comparisons are extremely misleading and can have unfortunate and unintended side effects. To give but one example, one psychotherapist recommends that patients who are attempting to recall a "repressed memory" should "pick up a videocassette from the side of the chair. Our mind is very much like a giant video library. Take the tape that we need to review today. . . . Put the cassette into the VCR, and as the picture starts to appear on the screen [signal] yes" (cited in Ofshe & Watters, 1994, p. 152).

Certainly not everyone draws such a literal comparison between existing technology and human memory. However, the pervasive acceptance of these high-tech metaphors in modern society suggests that the common implicit theories people have about human memory involve comparisons with modern technologies that far outstrip human memory capabilities. Furthermore, the impact of the spatial metaphor of memory is not limited to peoples' implicit theories of memory. Koriat and Goldsmith (1994, 1996) argue that most laboratory research on memory following Ebbinghaus's (1885/1964) pioneering studies embraced a spatial, or "storehouse," metaphor, with its attendant focus on the quantity of information retained. Koriat and Goldsmith outlined an alternative, the correspondence metaphor, which draws attention to the issue of how faithfully memory reports correspond to actual events/episodes. The correspondence metaphor highlights the extent to which what a person reports corresponds to what actually happened.

Koriat and Goldsmith (1994, 1996) acknowledge that there is no single metaphor (such as a storehouse) that captures all of the essential features of their correspondence metaphor. In describing this metaphor, they note that it has three attributes. First, memory is viewed as *being about* some past event and thus consists of a representation (or description) of the event. Second, the metaphor focuses on the extent to which the memory is *reliable*, or *accurate*. Thus, rather than ask questions about the loss or forgetting of information over time, the correspondence metaphor suggests that we consider the loss of correspondence between memory reports and actual events. Finally, the metaphor highlights *what* is remembered rather than the focus on the quantity of information retained fostered by the storehouse metaphor.

The model we present in the final section fo the chapter is consistent with this focus on the correspondence between experienced events and our recollections of these events. To summarize, then, in Lakoff and Johnson's (1980) terms, the metaphors used by laypersons and scientists highlight accurate and permanent retention as features of human memory, and there is ample evidence that these are not characteristics of normal human memory. Human memory is fallible, and not simply in terms of retrieval failures. We regularly misremember the details of events and in some cases we "remember" events that in fact never occurred. We now turn our attention to some of the growing empirical evidence which supports these conclusions.

NONTRUTH IN MEMORY: THE FOIBLES OF HUMAN MEMORY

Our goal in this section is to convince the reader of three things. First, there are many situations in which subjects come to sincerely believe that erroneous details of certain events are in fact veridical. Second, these memory errors can be observed in both laboratory and real-world situations with a wide range of stimuli and manipulations. Finally, a storehouse view of memory is largely incompatible with these findings.

One of the oldest and more thoroughly examined issues in the realm of memory errors concerns the effects of prior knowledge and beliefs on memory performance. Bartlett (1932) provided a classic demonstration of memory distortions in free recall by having Cambridge University students read a Native American folktale, "The War of the Ghosts." After reading the story subjects attempted to recall the story following various retention intervals varying from 15 minutes to 10 years. Bartlett found that subjects not only forgot details but also added or altered details, and these altered details often seemed to match the subjects' personal experiences. Bartlett suggested that this may occur because his subjects were not simply retrieving an exact representation of the story but rather attempting to recreate or "reconstruct" the story based on frameworks of knowledge Bartlett called *schemas*. For example, one of the "facts" Bartlett's subjects frequently reported was that the characters in the "War of the Ghosts" were fishing when, in fact, they were going to hunt seals. Subjects may have remembered that the characters in the story were in a boat and were seeking sustinence and assumed that they must have been fishing (fishing is presumably a more common activity for the British than seal hunting).

Perhaps due to rather lax experimental control (Kintsch, 1995) and a general failure to replicate his findings, Bartlett's (1932) work was largely ignored by experimental psychologists for several decades. In the 1970s, however, a number of important studies examined "reconstructive" memory (e.g., Bransford, 1979; Bransford & McCarrel, 1974; Spiro, 1977). For example, Snyder and Uranowitz (1978) had subjects read a short passage that described the life of a fictional character, "Betty K." The passage included details concerning Betty's social life, such as the fact that she dated some in high school. After reading the narrative, half the subjects were told that Betty had had an encounter with another woman and was now a lesbian; the remaining subjects were told that Betty was heterosexual.

One week later, subjects were given a multiple-choice test concerning the details of Betty's life. Snyder and Uranowitz (1978) found that subjects receiving the lesbian label tended to make errors that were consistent with the lesbian stereotype. For example, many of these subjects indicated that Betty had never dated men—a fact that was inconsistent with the narrative. Similar effects were obtained by a number of researchers, including Dooling and Christiaansen (1977), who examined how subjects' memory differed when a man's name was "Gerald Martin" versus "Adolph Hitler."

Read and Rosson (1982) provided further evidence of memory errors reflecting preexisting beliefs. They assessed subjects' attitudes toward nuclear power and then later had them read a narrative describing a fire at a nuclear power plant. After a 1- or 2-week delay, subjects then completed a recognition test for their memory of the narrative which included both veridical facts and pronuclear and antinuclear distortions. Subjects rated not only whether they thought the fact was consistent with the details of the narrative but also how confident they were in this judgment.

Read and Rosson found that subjects were often very confident that the distorted facts they "recognized" were consistent with the narrative. This was most notable for the subjects possessing antinuclear beliefs in the 2-week delay condition, where their confidence for these distortions was close to their confidence in true items.

Bransford and Franks (1971) and their colleagues (e.g., Bransford, Barclay, & Franks, 1972; Johnson, Bransford, & Solomon, 1973) demonstrated other potent forms of memory errors which involve inferences affecting memory for events. For example, Bransford et al. (1972) had subjects study simple sentences, such as "Three turtles rested on a floating log, and a fish swam beneath them." Later, subjects performed an old/new recognition test for their memory of the target sentences. The recognition test included old sentences as well as new sentences that were implied but not actually stated in the study phase. For example, "Three turtles rested on a floating log and a fish swam beneath it" was implied (i.e., the turtles were on a log, the fish swam beneath the turtles, therefore the fish swam beneath the log), but it was never stated verbatim in the study phase and thus subjects should have responded "new." Bransford et al. found that subjects frequently responded "old" to these implied sentences, suggesting they were not responding based on a verbatim representation of the sentences.

Other researchers (e.g., Harris, 1974) also provided evidence that implied information is often remembered as if it actually occurred. For example, Brewer (1977) presented subjects with sentences such as "The safe-cracker put the match to the fuse." These sentences implied, but did not explicitly state, a slightly different message (e.g., "The safe-cracker lit the fuse"). Brewer found that in a cued recall test, 19% of the items were recalled correctly, whereas 26% of the incorrect responses were consistent with the pragmatic implications of the sentence but were not explicitly stated. Taken together, the results reviewed here suggest that when subjects are given sentences to study, they do not simply store representations of the verbatim sentences but also conclusions and/or inferences that may be drawn from these sentences. Thus memory for sentences is often based on both the details provided in the sentence and inferences that can be drawn from these sentences.

Bransford and Franks (1971) demonstrated that subjects also combine separate but related pieces of information into a single, larger "idea unit" that was not actually presented. Bransford and Franks created their stimuli from several complex sentences (e.g., "The old car pulling the trailer climbed the steep hill"; "The ants in the kitchen ate the sweet jelly which was on the table") that were divided into sentences containing one (e.g., "The ants ate the jelly," "The jelly was sweet"), two, or three of the component ideas. Subjects were presented with target sentences containing between one to three ideas and answered a short question about each sentence. Later subjects performed an unexpected, old/new recognition test that included old sentences (i.e., sentences from the question answering phase), new sentences that were constructed from related sentences that were presented in the question-and-answering phase (e.g., "The ants ate the sweet jelly"), and noncase sentences that were created by taking ideas from different complex sentences (e.g., "The ants climbed the hill"). Subjects were also asked to rate how confident they were in the accuracy of these old/new decisions.

Based on a storehouse metaphor, one would expect that when subjects read the original sentences, they stored a separate representation for each sentence. These stored representations would be consulted on the recognition test, and subjects should respond "old" for old sentences (i.e., the ones they have representations for) at a high rate while new and noncase sentences, having no representation stored for them would be called "old" rather infrequently. Bransford and Franks indeed found a high rate of "old" responses for old items and a low rate for noncase items. However, the rate of "old" responses for new items was also often very high, especially when the new sentence contained all four component ideas that had been presented for study. That is, although none of the sentences presented during the study phase contained all four idea units, when the new sentences presented during the testing phase contained all four idea units that were presented, subjects were very likely to call this sentence old. This suggests that subjects had somehow taken the ideas from a number of sources (i.e., separate sentences) and used them to compile a coherent complex sentence that contained all four idea units. This general finding was replicated several times (e.g., Bransford & Franks, 1972; Cofer, 1973; Flagg, 1976; Singer, 1973).

Another interesting aspect of Bransford and Franks's (1971) data involved the relation between subjects' confidence in the accuracy of their responses and the number of idea units contained in the sentences. Not surprisingly, for the sentences that were presented during the study phase, the more idea units a sentence contained, the more confident the subjects were that the sentence was an old sentence. Interestingly, the same increase in confidence with increasing numbers of idea units was observed with the new sentences as well. Thus, subjects appeared to store the overall, abstracted meaning of the four idea units in each set. The more idea units contained in the test item, the more closely it matched this abstracted meaning and the more confident subjects were of their responses, regardless of whether or not the item had appeared in the study phase.

Further support for the idea that we often combine different sources of information to form unique wholes when we attempt to recollect an event comes from the eyewitness memory literature. Loftus and her colleagues (e.g., Loftus, Miller, & Burns, 1978; Loftus & Palmer, 1974) created a standard eyewitness memory paradigm that has been followed by countless studies. Basically, this preparation consists of presenting subjects first with some sort of event, such as a slide sequence depicting a car driving past a stop sign. Subjects then read a narrative that contains misleading information on certain facts of the event (e.g., referring to the stop sign as a yield sign), while no misleading information is given for other facts. In the early research in this area subjects' memories were typically tested using a forced-choice recognition test, known as a standard test (McCloskey & Zaragoza, 1985). In a standard test, subjects are asked to choose between the item that appeared in the slides versus the item mentioned in the postevent narrative (e.g., stop sign vs. yield sign).

Results from many studies showed that subjects were less accurate in identifying the original event/detail in the misleading condition than in the neutral condition (cf. Lindsay & Johnson, 1989; Loftus, 1979b; Loftus & Palmer, 1974), a finding referred to as the misinformation effect (see Loftus, 1979a, for a review of this literature). Loftus argued that the misinformation effect obtained with the standard test indicates that the misleading postevent information somehow overwrites the memory for the original event.

However, not all theorists agree with Loftus's overwriting hypothesis (e.g., Bekerian & Bowers, 1983; McCloskey & Zaragoza, 1985), and a number of alternative explanations have been offered. For example, subjects might remember both the original item and the item refered to in the postevent narrrative but select the postevent item because they believe the experimenter who wrote the narrative must have known what was depicted in the film. The debate over the "fate" of the memory for the original event (e.g., is it overwritten or does it coexist with the memory for the postevent information) has not been adequately resolved and research continues in this domain (see Lindsay, 1990, for a review).

Regardless of the final resolution to this debate over the fate of the memory of the original event, eyewitness memory research over the past two decades provides clear evidence that what people *report* about an event is affected by what they are exposed to during the retention interval. Recently there was a shift in emphasis in this area with researchers now examining whether the subjects believe that the misleading items occurred in the original episode. For example, Weingardt, Toland, and Loftus (1994) found that subjects were often willing to wager large sums of money that their inaccurate memory for an event was veridical. Zaragoza, who originally argued that misleading information has no effect on subjects memory for the original event (McCloskey & Zaragoza, 1985), now comes to a somewhat different conclusion: "Recent evidence has clearly established that adults do, under some conditions, come to believe they actually remember seeing suggested items" (Ackil & Zaragoza, 1995, p. 60).

Overall, then, it seems that it is possible for an external source to suggest misleading information that individuals ultimately accept as accurate. However, given that much of the evidence we focused on thus far comes from laboratory studies, one might question how commonly these various memory errors occur on a day-to-day basis. Fortunately, the eyewitness memory literature provides some indication of the commonality of these effects. For example, several researchers applied the eyewitness paradigm to real-world settings (e.g., Baker-Ward, Gordon, Ornstein, Larus, & Clubb, 1994; Ornstein, Gordon, & Larus, 1992; Saywitz, Goodman, Nicholas, & Moan, 1991). Oates and Shrimpton (1991), for example, asked children about an actual medical exam and found that some children fall prey to suggestions, such as reporting that the doctor looked in their ear when the doctor actually did not. More unsettling, Rudy and Goodman (1991) found that some children are influenced by even less plausible suggestions, such as "How many times did the doctor kiss you?"

Furthermore, the "misinformation" needs to be neither particularly strong nor particularly direct for eyewitness memory performance to be unreliable. For example, Ross, Ceci, Dunning, and Toglia (1994) suggest that peripheral details surrounding an event often become inappropriately combined with central ones. Ross et al. (1994) showed that subjects often mistakenly believe that innocent bystanders and people they have only seen in police pictures or lineups were actually the perpetrators of the crime. The authors suggest that this may occur because these individuals seem familiar; after all, the witness saw the bystander at the scene of the crime or in photographs. This "feeling of familiarity" may ultimately lead subjects to believe these individuals are, in fact, the perpetrators. Note that this explanation is similar to the one offered for the "false frame" effect found by Jacoby, Woloshyn, and Kelly (1989). Jacoby et al. (1989) showed that under some conditions, subjects come to mistakenly believe that nonfamous names (e.g., "Sebastian Weisdorf") presented to them earlier in the experiment are actually famous names.

Surprisingly, it seems that some "suggestions" do not even need to be external. In fact, a sizable body of literature suggests that we can also be mislead by our own, internally generated misinformation. Johnson, Taylor, and Raye (1977), for example, found that subjects often confuse events that actually occurred with those they were only asked to imagine. This general finding has been replicated many times (e.g., Anderson, 1984; Foley, Durso, Wilder, & Friedman, 1991; Foley & Johnson, 1985; Johnson, Foley, Suengas, & Raye, 1989). Relatedly, Johnson, Foley, and Leach (1988) found that subjects had notable difficulty discriminating words spoken by the experimenter versus those that subjects imagined the experimenter saying. This failure to monitor the sources of information is not limited to verbal materials, either.

Lindsay, Johnson, and Kwon (1991) had children and adults either perform a simple action (e.g., cross their arms, touch their nose) or simply imagine doing it. Results showed that imagined actions were mistakenly identified as having actually been performed; this confusion was most pronounced for children imagining themselves performing the action. Perhaps even more startling are the findings of Intraub and Hoffman (1992) who tested subjects under high memory-load conditions (60 pictures and 50 paragraphs to remember over a 1-week retention interval). They found that subjects would frequently claim to remember photographs that were never actually presented if these photographs were similar to scenes described in the paragraphs. Taken together, these studies demonstrate that memories for events and images that are only imagined can often be confused with memories of real, external events.

In a similar vein, Schooler and Engstler-Schooler (1990) presented subjects with faces to remember and in some conditions had subjects verbally describe a face after it was presented or had subjects perform an unrelated task. Amazingly, Schooler and Engstler-Schooler (1990) found that verbally describing the face actually inhibited later facial recognition, with subjects being more accurate when they performed the unrelated task. It seems that the act of verbalization led to faulty inferences that were incorporated in later recall attempts.

Several researchers also examined memory errors in naturalistic settings using naturally occurring stimuli. Along with the large body of anecdotal examples such as the Piaget abduction described earlier (see also Lindsay & Read, 1994), a handful of researchers attempted a more systematic study of the memory for personal, real-world events (i.e., "autobiographical memory").

Linton (1982) reported an interesting study that demonstrates impressive personal dedication. Using herself as the sole subject, she wrote short daily descriptions of life events over 6 years (more than 5,500 items) on which she tested herself monthly (with each test lasting 6–12 hours). As expected, Linton found more and more forgetting with increasing retention intervals. More important, her data also suggested that the manner in which we remember and interpret life events is anything but stable. "Just as historians must interpret and rewrite history as time passes, so we all rewrite our own personal histories" (Linton, 1982, p. 88). In a similar fashion, Conway, Collins, Gathercole, and Anderson (1996) found that two diarists often falsely recognized plausible but inaccurate events as having occurred.

Nickerson and Adams (1979) reported a study that demonstrates that even after literally hundreds of thousands of exposures, memory can be quite inaccurate. To appreciate this study, try to recall what is on the side of a penny that has a head on it. If you are having trouble doing this, perhaps a recognition test would be easier. Look at Figure 2.1 and find the picture that matches what a true penny looks like. If you are having some difficulty finding the correct one, you are not alone as Nickerson and Adams found that the

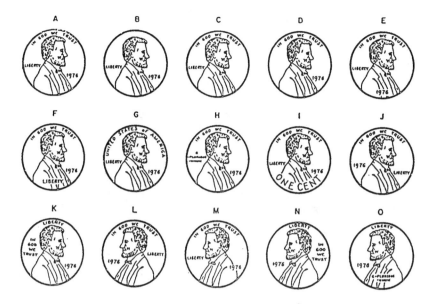

FIGURE 2.1. Possible pennies. Which picture is the true likeness of the front of a penny? From Nickerson & Adams (1979). Copyright 1979 by Academic Press. Reprinted by permission.

majority of their subjects could not identify the correct one, either (the upper left is correct). This finding, which has been replicated several times (e.g., Rubin & Kontis, 1983), is rather impressive: Despite countless exposures, the simplicity of the image, and our usually very accurate recognition memory for pictorial stimuli (e.g., Shepard, 1967; Standing, 1973), many people's memory for the front of a penny seems to be inaccurate.

Perhaps the largest body of literature on autobiographical memories is studies similar to the ones we used to introduce this chapter: studies of so-called flashbulb memories (Brown & Kulik, 1977). As noted previously, the concept behind flashbulb memories is simple and intuitive: Certain events are so emotionally charged (e.g., John F. Kennedy's assassination and a white Ford Bronco with a celebrity fleeing the authorities) that the moment becomes "burned" into memory in a seemingly complete and permanent fashion. However, research calls into question the veracity of such a claim. Neisser and Harsch (1992) asked subjects about the circumstances surrounding their learning of the *Challenger* disaster both 1 day following the event and 3 years later. Neisser and Harsch found that not only was there often little agreement between the two accounts subjects gave at these times but subjects were as confident in their inaccurate memories as their accurate ones, again suggesting there is very little difference from the rememberer's perspective between a "true" memory and a "false" one. Likewise, researchers found that flashbulb memories are susceptible to some of the memory distortions already mentioned, such as the effects of prior knowledge (Christianson, 1989). Wright (1993) found that subject's recollections concerning a disaster at a sporting event in the United Kingdom, the Hillsborough football disaster, were rather strongly influenced by the subjects' biases concerning the event itself and other events of which Hillsborough reminded them. Wright (1993a) concluded that "flashbulb memories . . . are susceptible to the same type of systematic biases as everyday memories" (p. 129).

Loftus and Pickrell (1995) provide an interesting demonstration of people recalling memories for events that did not occur. Loftus and Pickrell had older siblings reminisce with younger brothers and sisters about "events" that occurred in the younger sibling's childhood, including a false event concerning getting lost in a shopping mall. They found that through repeated questioning, some of the younger siblings came to "remember" the false event. Subjects did not appear to merely acquiesce to the older sibling's assertions, but rather they seemed to actively "remember" the incident such that they could provide what they felt was an accurate (and surprisingly detailed) account of the false event that, based on parents reports, never occurred. Not only were they seemingly sincere, but furthermore they sometimes elaborated on the story, providing details beyond what was suggested (a more detailed description of a man who found them in the mall, what they felt, etc.).

Following Loftus and Pickrell (1995), several other researchers further examined "implanted" memories (e.g., Ceci, Loftus, Leichtman, & Bruck, 1994). Despite severe limitations due to ethical concerns and methodological complexity, these researchers provided a number of impressive demonstrations. Hyman, Husband, and Billings (1995) asked the parents of college students to provide details of their children's early lives and used this information to cue the college students' memories for these events. In addition to the veridical facts provided by the parents, in a series of two interviews the subjects were also asked to remember a fictitious event, such as a clown at their fifth birthday party. Hyman et al. (1995) found that in their second interview, a number of subjects reported the event that was only suggested as if it actually occurred, even when they denied the event in the first interview. Note that Hyman et al. (1995) simply asked about the fictitious event, which seems to be a fairly mild sort of misinformation. In a similar fashion, Ceci, Huffman, and Smith (1994) asked children about real and fictitious events across a series of 7 to 10 interviews. Impressively, they found that by the final interview these children were assenting to over 30% of the false events.

These demonstrations of implanted memories may lack some of the scientific control that most empiricists would prefer. However, using a design first introduced by Deese (1959), Roediger and McDermott (1995) recently reported impressive levels of false memories in a laboratory setting. They presented subjects with lists of items such as *bed, rest, awake, tired, dream, wake, night, blanket, doze, slumber, snore, pillow, peace, yawn,* and *drowsy,* all of which are associates of the critical nonpresented item, *sleep.* They found that subjects recalled the critical non-presented items at rates approximately equal to those for the studied items. Subjects also frequently falsely recognized the critical nonpresented items, and the false alarm rate for these items was comparable to the hit rate for studied items.

Roediger and McDermott (1995) also examined subjects' phenomenological experience with the critical nonpresented and studied items that were called old on the recognition test. Toward this goal, they included a *remember/know* judgment (Tulving, 1985) on the recognition test. Basically, this consisted of asking subjects to make a judgment concerning the quality of their memory for items they believed were presented. If the subject could mentally relive the presentation of the item (perhaps by what they were doing when they heard the word or the words that were presented with it) they were to respond *remember*. If they were confident an item was presented but could not actually mentally relive its presentation, they were to respond *know*.

Because the critical nonpresented items were never given, there would be no way for subjects to mentally relive such a presentation and hence one would expect that these items would be labeled *know* items. Previous studies using the remember/know task show that new items that are mistakenly labeled old are generally perceived as *know* items (e.g., Rajaram, 1993). Roediger and McDermott's (1995) results, however, showed exactly the opposite pattern. Critical nonpresented items that were (falsely) recognized on the recognition test were more likely to be called remember items than know items. Furthermore, the proportion of remember responses for the critical nonpresented items was comparable to that for the studied items.

Payne, Elie, Blackwell, and Neuschatz (1996) replicated and extended Roediger and McDermott's (1995) results. Payne et al. (1996) found that, as one would expect, the hit rate for studied items decreased across a 24-hour retention interval. In contrast, the proportion of critical nonpresented items that were falsely recognized did not change across this retention interval. Furthermore, when subjects were asked to try to recall the list items on several successive recall tests, the false-recall rate increased across tests.

A final result from the Payne et al. (1996) study speaks to the issue of failures in source monitoring for false memories. Payne et al. wondered if, when falsely recalling a critical nonpresented item, subjects came to believe that they "remembered" the source that presented these items. To address this question they videotaped a male and a female experimenter reading a long list of words that were related to several critical nonpresented items (e.g., sleep, needle, king). After the list was presented, subjects were asked to recall the list on three successive tests. At the end of the third test subjects were instructed to look over the words they recalled and attempt to indicate which of the two experimenters read each word by writing the person's initial beside the word. The instructions stressed that this source monitoring task was a difficult one and that the subjects should leave blank any word for which they could not recollect which experimenter read the word.

Results showed that subjects identified a source (i.e., one of the two speakers in the videotape) for the falsely recalled items 87% of the time. This failure of source monitoring was not only large numerically but was compelling to the subjects. During debriefing, many subjects claimed that they were certain the critical nonpresented words were presented, and when the videotape was replayed the subjects refused to believe that the same tape was being shown.

A PERCEPTION–REPERCEPTION MODEL OF MEMORY

We demonstrated that the predominant type of metaphor used to explain memory is a storehouse metaphor which assumes that records of events are placed within some multidimensional space. Remembering is then viewed as the act of locating these records within the storehouse and examining the record. Metaphors of this type tend to focus on the quantity of information returned rather than the accuracy of the information (Koriat & Goldsmith, 1994, 1996).

We also showed that, perhaps as a consequence of these metaphors, people typically do not appreciate the many ways in which memory fails, other than forgetting. In the previous section we reviewed evidence indicating that there are many ways in which memory produces systematic errors, including misremembering details, remembering events that did not occur, "blending" information from multiple sources to produce a single recollection, and various types of source monitoring errors. These types of memory errors are difficult to explain within a simple storehouse model of memory, although with little effort one can devise a more complex model that posits retrieval processes as the culprit responsible for these errors. For example, much of the debate over the misinformation effect in eyewitness memory in essence involves questions over whether the memory for the original event is changed or the memory is intact but we somehow fail to retrieve that memory and instead base our responses on our memory of the postevent information.

In this final section we propose a perception–reperception model of memory that begins to flesh out the manner in which memory can function other than by locating records stored in some multidimensional space. Memory researchers typically use the term "memory errors" to refer to behaviors such as reporting an item on a recall test that was not on the study list or confusing the source of some piece of information. Indeed, we used this term repeatedly in the previous section. We believe that this terminology is linked to the use of storehouse metaphors.

There are, however, other ways to conceptualize situations in which what a person recollects is at odds with what actually happened. Bartlett's (1932) arguments concerning reconstructive processes of memory are one example of such an alternative view. The conceptualization we offer here is somewhat different in orientation from Bartlett's in that we posit a very close link between the perceptual processes that organize sensory information into a meaningful representation of the world and recollective processes that yield meaningful representations of past events. Other theorists also pointed to the close relation between perception and memory (e.g., Craik & Lockhart, 1972; Kolers & Roediger, 1984), but for present purposes there is one major difference between our model and these other proposals: We are offering here a metaphor for memory rather than an explicit scientific theory. We are currently in the process of developing this model into a more formal, albeit verbal, scientific model. This formal model is akin to the levels-of-processing (Craik & Lockhart, 1972) framework and the procedures-of-mind (Kolers & Roediger, 1984) conceptualizations.

Our model grew in part out of arguments made by Roediger (1996) concerning false memories. Roediger suggested that many memory errors can be viewed as memory illusions. He also suggests that just as researchers learned a great deal about the functioning of the sensory and perceptual systems by studying perceptual illusions, so can memory researchers profit by studying memory illusions. Memory illusions here refer to situations in which memory reports are discrepant from the actual events of interest. One of the primary advantages of calling memory errors memory illusions is that it changes how these behaviors are viewed. In the storehouse metaphor, errors are generally viewed as a nuisance to be avoided, with the primary interest centered on the amount of information accurately reported. Refering to errors as memory illusions makes these same behaviors (e.g., misremembering the details of an event and recalling an event that never occurred) legitimate topics of study. We thus endorse Roediger's main argument concerning the utlity of viewing memory errors as memory illusions.

The perception–reperception model we are proposing suggests that what is normally called "encoding" in the memory literature can be replaced by perception—that is, the processes involved with interpreting sensory signals (Craik & Lockhart, 1972, made a similar suggestion). The perception–reperception model likens "retrieval" to reperceiving the stimulus event, with the two main differences between perception of the original event and reperception of the remembered event being (1) a temporal distinction and (2) the "source" of the information that is being interpreted.

To appreciate these latter two points, consider the two tables illustrated in Figure 2.2. Do the tabletops in these drawings appear to be identical in size and shape? Most people are certain that the answer is no. As you may have guessed, the two tabletops are in fact identical—trace them onto a sheet of paper if you do not believe us. This visual illusion was created by Shepard (1990) and it demonstrates convincingly that our perception of the world can be quite at odds with objective reality. In perceptual illusions such as this, the physical stimuli are literally "right in front of us" and yet our interpretation of these stimuli is wrong. If what we remember of an event depends on how we perceive the event, then errors in perception can lead to errors in memory. It seems likely that if you showed someone Figure 2.2 and then later asked that person to describe what he or she remembered of that event, the person

FIGURE 2.2. Table illusion. The two tabletops appear to be very different but in fact are identical. From Shepard (1990), p. 48. Copyright 1990 by Roger N. Shepard. Used with permission of W. H. Freeman & Co.

might describe one long, thin table and another wider, shorter table, especially if the individual used these labels to describe the tables initially (Carmichael, Hogan, & Walter, 1932). In this case it seems likely that this "memory error" is really a perceptual error because the person might have described these two tables in the same way even if the figure were in clear view.

Consider next the geometric display presented in Figure 2.3. Take a look at that figure, then turn to page 54 and read the caption for Figure 2.4. If, like many people, you cannot identify the correct parallelogram in Figure 2.4, does this indicate that it is a perceptual illusion or a memory illusion? What is the primary difference between the visual illusion presented in Figure 2.2 and the "memory illusion" presented in Figures 2.3 and 2.4? For one thing,

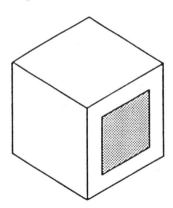

FIGURE 2.3. A simple box . . . Take a moment to carefully examine this picture, then turn to Figure 2.4 (p. 54). From Deregowski (1984). Copyright 1984 by Routledge & Kegan Paul. Reprinted by permission.

to select the correct parallelogram from Figure 2.4, an individual needs to remember what the display in Figure 2.3 looked like, whereas in Figure 2.2 the individual can scan back and forth between the two tables. However, what if we changed these figures slightly so that two tables in Figure 2.2 were presented on two separate pages of the chapter and the individual had to turn pages to compare the two tables. Is the visual illusion now a memory illusion?

Our point here is that there is no clear distinction between visual illusions and memory illusions, except perhaps a temporal distinction. Figure 2.5 contains a highly schematized depiction of the processes involved in performing a perceptual task (like comparing the two tabletops in Figure 2.2) versus a memory task (like remembering words in a list or performing the recognition task using Figures 2.3 and 2.4). In both cases, the person is exposed to some real-world event, he or she processes that information and responds based on the information provided by the event along with his or her general knowledge, decision-making processes, and so on. As Figure 2.5 illustrates, there are many similarities between perceptual tasks and memory tasks, including the establishment of an internal representation of the external world and responding based, in part, on this representation. Perceptual and memory tasks also can involve the retention of these representations over time. For example, a subject in a perception experiment might be asked to decide if two successive stimuli are the same or different; subjects in a memory experiment might study a list of items and then complete a recognition test in which they are asked to identify items in a test list that are the same as items from the study list.

We propose that rather than viewing memory as the storage and retrieval of accurate records of external events, responding based on prior events involves the active interpretation of internal representations that arise from sensory and perceptual processes. Furthermore, these "internal representations" are not separate and distinct from the sensory and perceptual processes that give rise to them. Rather, the same underlying representations that are used to perform tasks that, for ease of expostion, we refer to as sensory or perceptual tasks (e.g., detecting the presence of a faint stimulus and identifying an object in a complex visual array) are also used when we remember. Metaphorically speaking, we are suggesting here that the act of remembering involves the reperception of internal representations that are created from our experiences with the world around us. Whatever long-lasting changes in the nervous system result from our interactions with the world can be interpreted later in time and the interpretive processes that are utilized to "remember" what happened are quite similar to those perceptual processes that are used to interpret events as they unfold.

A number of advantages come from the perception–reperception model. First, memory errors are not bothersome anomalies to be explained away or minimized, but rather they reflect the normal processes by which we interpret the world around us. As such, studying these discrepancies between what "really happened" and what people recollect about those events is a legitimate,

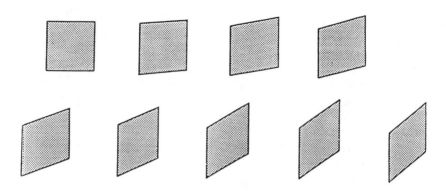

FIGURE 2.4. A diamond in the rough. Which one of these diamonds most closely matches the shaded are in the previous figure? The answer may surprise you. From Deregowski (1984). Copyright 1984 by Routledge & Kegan Paul. Reprinted by permission.

and indeed very useful research strategy. Second, because most people are familiar with visual illusions the fact that our behaviors based on memory show similar types of illusions should not be viewed as an unusual occurrence. Note that whereas the storehouse metaphor highlights accurate responding, the perception–reperception metaphor highlights the possibility of illusions.

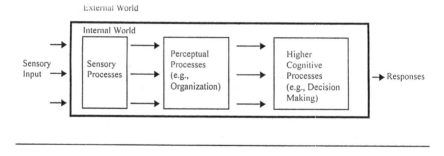

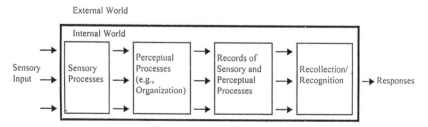

FIGURE 2.5. Conceptual flow charts of perception (upper panel) and memory (lower panel). Note the similarities in the involved processes.

We would argue that, in terms of possible impact on our implicit memory metaphors, this is a marked advantage over the storehouse metaphors.

A third strength of the perception–reperception model is that it highlights the close relation between the manner in which we experience an event and any subsequent changes in our behavior that occur as a function of that experience. The recent explosion of research on implicit memory documents that there are many situations in which prior events affect subsequent behavior even when the person cannot recollect the prior event (see Roediger & McDermott, 1993, for a review). Furthermore, many implicit memory studies show that the similarities of the processes invoked at study and test determine the overall performance levels obtained, with better performance in situations in which the processes "match" than when they are dissimilar.

A fourth advantage of the perception–reperception model is that it changes the types of questions one might ask about memory. For example, as noted earlier, one of the main issues debated in the eyewitness memory literature is whether misleading postevent information somehow overwrites the memory for the original event or whether there are two memories, one for the original event and a second for the misinformation. Although some progress was made in this debate, there is no final resolution to the question, and it appears that researchers have now turned their attention to such questions as, "Does the person really believe that the details specified in the misinformation really occured in the original event?" (e.g., Ackil & Zaragoza, 1995). According to the perception–reperception model, the misinformation effect arises because, at the time the memory test is administered, the individual can reperceive the internal representation ocorresponding to either event.

Critics might argue that the foregoing account does not really "explain" the misinformation effect but simply describes what happens. This misses the important point that the perception–reperception model forces one to ask different types of questions than one would ask if using a storehouse metaphor. For example, within the perception–reperception model it is reasonable to ask what factors increase the likelihood of people responding on the basis of one episode rather than another? To take another example, the false memory effect described in the last section represents a situation in which people's behaviors indicate that they believe that the critical nonpresented items actually occurred in the study list. It is difficult to account for this within the storehouse metaphor, but the same behaviors raise a host of interesting questions when viewed within the perception–reperception model. Just as one can ask what are the factors responsible for producing the visual illusion in Figure 2.2, one can (and should) ask what factors modulate the false memory effects that are so convincing to subjects in these experiments.

Finally, in our view, the perception–reperception model of memory represents both an advance and a retreat in terms of our theoretical accounts of memory. It represents an advance in that it causes us to think about (or rethink) questions such as the following: What functions does memory serve?

Under what conditions might we expect memory illusions to occur? and How might our beliefs about memory be altered by this conceptualization? The model is a "retreat" in the sense that it is a functional model rather than an explicitly stated model that postulates storage systems, retrieval processes, diverse sorts of memory traces, and so on. In some sense we are suggesting that we study memory in a manner similar to how we have studied the sensory and perceptual systems, namely, by seeking to specify the transfer functions that relate behavior to real-world events. Specifying these transfer functions requires that we continue to increase how closely the functions we propose approximate real behavior. In this sense we are heeding Alfred North Whitehead's (1954) sage advice concerning whole truths and half truths that we presented in the quote at the start of the chapter. Whereas the storehouse metaphor implicitly held that memories reflected whole truths, the perception–reperception model acknowledges that what we extract from the world around us is an approximation to the truth, and any time we need to respond on the basis of our understanding of what occurred, we are subject to interpretive errors. For those of us interested in establishing truth in memory, the perception–reperception model also reminds us that we would be well served to heed the subtitle of this chapter: When it comes to truth in memory, let the buyer beware.

REFERENCES

Ackil, J. K., & Zaragoza, M. S. (1995). Developmental differences in eyewitness suggestability and memory for source. *Journal of Experimental Child Psychology, 60*, 57–83.

Anderson, R. E. (1984). Did I do it or did I only imagine doing it? *Journal of Experimental Psychology: General, 113*, 594–613.

Atkinson, R. C., & Shiffrin, R. M. (1968). Human memory: A proposed system and its control processes. In K. W. Spence & J. T. Spence (Eds.), *The psychology of learning and motivation* (Vol. 2, pp. 89–195). New York: Academic Press.

Bahrick, H. P. (1984). Semantic memory content in permastore: Fifty years of memory for Spanish learned in school. *Journal of Experimental Psychology: General, 113*, 1–29.

Bahrick, H. P., Bahrick, P. O., & Wittlinger, R. P. (1975). Fifty years of memory for names and faces: A cross-sectional approach. *Journal of Experimental Psychology: General, 104*, 54–75.

Bahrick, H. P., & Hall, L. K. (1991). Lifetime maintenance of high school mathematics content. *Journal of Experimental Psychology: General, 120*, 20–33.

Bahrick, H. P., Hall, L. K., Goggin, J. P., Bahrick, L. E., & Berger, S. A. (1994). Fifty years of language maintenance and language dominance in bilingual Hispanic immigrants. *Journal of Experimental Psychology: General, 123*, 264–283.

Baker-Ward, L., Gordon, B. N., Ornstein, P. A., Larus, D. M., & Clubb, P. A. (1993). Young children's long-term retention of a pediatric examination. *Child Development, 64*, 1519–1533.

Bartlett, F. C. (1932). *Remembering: A study in experimental and social psychology.* Cambridge, UK: Cambridge University Press.

Bekerian, D. A., & Bowers, N. J. (1983). Eyewitness testimony: Were we misled? *Journal of Experimental Psychology: Learning, Memory, and Cognition, 1,* 139–145.

Bransford, J. D. (1979). *Human cognition: Learning, understanding and remembering.* Belmont, CA: Wadsworth.

Bransford, J. D., Barclay, J. R., & Franks, J. J. (1972). Sentence memory: A constructive versus interpretive approach. *Cognitive Psychology, 3,* 193–209.

Bransford, J. D., & Franks, J. J. (1971). The abstraction of linguistic ideas. *Cognitive Psychology, 2,* 331–350.

Bransford, J. D., & Franks, J. J. (1972). The abstraction of linguistic ideas: A review. *Cognition: International Journal of Cognitive Psychology, 1,* 211–249.

Bransford, J. D., & McCarrell, N. S. (1974). A sketch of a cognitive approach to comprehension. In W. Weimer & D. S. Palermo (Eds.), *Cognition and the symbolic processes* (pp. 189–229). Hillsdale, NJ: Erlbaum.

Brewer, W. F. (1977). Memory for the pragmatic implications of sentences. *Memory and Cognition, 5,* 673–678.

Broadbent, D. E. (1971). *Decision and stress.* New York: Academic Press.

Brown, R., & Kulik, J. (1977). Flashbulb memories. *Cognition, 5,* 73–99.

Carmichael, L., Hogan, H. P., & Walter, A. A. (1932). An experimental study of the effect of language on the reproduction of perceived forms. *Journal of Experimental Psychology, 15,* 73–86.

Ceci, S. J., Huffman, M. L. C., & Smith, E. (1994). Repeatedly thinking about a non-event: Source misattributions among preschoolers. *Consciousness and Cognition, 3,* 388–407.

Ceci, S. J., Loftus, E. F., Leichtman, M. D., & Bruck, M. (1994). The possible role of source misattributions in the crreation of false beliefs among preschoolers. *International Journal of Clinical and Experimental Hypnosis, 42,* 304–320.

Christianson, S. A. (1989). Flashbulb memories: Special, but not so special. *Memory and Cognition, 17,* 435–443.

Cofer, C. N. (1973). Constructive processes in memory. *American Scientist, 61,* 537–543.

Conway, M. A., Collins, A. F., Gathercole, S. E., & Anderson, S. J. (1996). Recollections of true and false autobiographical memories. *Journal of Experimental Psychology: General, 125,* 69–95.

Craik, F. I. M., & Lockhart, R. S. (1972). Levels of processing: A framework for memory research. *Journal of Verbal Learning and Verbal Behavior, 11,* 671–684.

Deese, J. (1959). On the prediction of occurrence of particular verbal intrusions in immediate recall. *Journal of Experimental Psychology, 58,* 17–22.

Dempster, E. N. (1988). The spacing effect: A case study in the failure to apply the results of psychological research. *American Psychologist, 43,* 627–634.

Deregowski, J. B. (1984). *Distortion in art: The eye and the mind.* London: Routledge and Kegan Paul.

Dooling, D. J., & Christiaansen, R. E. (1977). Episodic and semantic aspects of memory for prose. *Journal of Experimental Psychology: Human Learning and Memory, 3,* 428–436.

Ebbinghaus, H. (1964). *Memory: A contribution to experimental psychology.* New York: Dover. (Original work published 1885)

Flagg, P. W. (1976). Semantic integration in sentence memory. *Journal of Verbal Learning and Verbal Behavior, 15,* 491–504.

Foley, M. A., Durso, F. T., Wilder, A., & Friedman, R. (1991). Developmental comparisons of explicit versus implicit imagery and reality monitoring. *Journal of Experimental Child Psychology, 51,* 1–13.

Foley, M. A., & Johnson, M. K. (1985). Confusions between memories for performed and imagined actions. *Child Development, 56,* 1145–1155.

Freud, S. (1952). *A general introduction to psychoanalysis.* New York: Washington Square Press. (Original work published 1924)

Freud, S. (1950). A note upon the "mystic writing pad." In J. Strachey (Ed.), *Collected papers of Sigmund Freud.* London: Hogarth Press. (Original work published 1940)

Ganaway, G. K. (1989). Historical versus narrative truth: Clarifying the role of exogenous trauma in the etiology of MPD and its variants. *Dissociation, 2,* 201–205.

Garry, M., Loftus, E. F., Brown, S. W., & DuBreuil, S. C. (1997). Womb with a view: Memory beliefs and memory-work experiences. In D. G. Payne & F. G. Conrad (Eds.), *Intersections in basic and applied memory research* (pp. 233–255). Hillsdale, NJ: Erlbaum.

Greene, R. L. (1989). Spacing effects in memory: Evidence for a two-process account. *Journal of Experimental Psychology: Learning, Memory, and Cognition, 15,* 371–377.

Harris, R. J. (1974). Memory and comprehension of implications and inferences of complex sentences. *Journal of Verbal Learning and Verbal Behavior, 13,* 626–637.

Hintzman, D. L. (1974). Psychology and the cow's belly. *Worm Runner's Digest, 16,* 84–85.

Howard, G. S. (1991). Culture tales: A narrative approach to thinking, cross-cultural psychology, and psychotherapy. *American Psychologist, 46,* 187–197.

Hyman, I. E., Jr., Husband, T. H., & Billings, F. J. (1995). False memories of childhood experiences. *Applied Cognitive Psychology, 9,* 181–197.

Intraub, H., & Hoffman, J. E. (1992). Reading and visual memory: Remembering scenes that were never seen. *American Journal of Psychology, 105,* 101–114.

Jacoby, L. L., Woloshyn, V., & Kelley, C. (1989). Becoming famous without being recognized: Unconscious influences of memory produced by dividing attention. *Journal of Experimental Psychology: General, 118,* 115–125.

James, W. (1890). *Principles of psychology.* New York: Holt.

John, E. R. (1972). Switchboard versus statistical theories of learning and memory. *Science, 177,* 849–864.

Johnson, M. K., Bransford, J. D., & Solomon, S. K. (1973). Memory for tacit implications of sentences. *Journal of Experimental Psychology, 98,* 203–205.

Johnson, M. K., Foley, M. A., & Leach, K. (1988). The consequences for memory of imagining in another person's voice. *Memory and Cognition, 16,* 337–342.

Johnson, M. K., Foley, M. A., Suengas, A. G., & Raye, C. L. (1989). Phenomenal characteristics of memories for perceived and imagined autobiographical events. *Journal of Experimental Psychology: General, 117,* 371–376.

Johnson, M. K., Taylor, T., & Raye, C. L. (1977). Fact and fantasy: The effects of internally generated events on the apparent frequency of externally generated events. *Memory and Cognition, 5,* 116–122.

Kintsch, N. (1995). Introduction. In F.C. Bartlett, *Remembering: A study in experimental and social psychology.* Cambridge, UK: Cambridge University Press.

Klatzky, R. L. (1975). *Human memory: Structure and processes.* San Francisco: Freeman.

Kolers, P. A., & Roediger, H. L. (1984). Procedures of mind. *Journal of Verbal Learning and Verbal Behavior, 23*, 425–449.

Koriat, A., & Goldsmith, M. (1994). Memory in naturalistic and laboratory contexts: Distinguishing the accuracy-oriented and quantity-oriented approaches to memory assessment. *Journal of Experimental Psychology: General, 123*, 297–315.

Koriat, A., & Goldsmith, M. (1996). Memory metaphors and the laboratory/real life controversy: Correspondence versus storehouse views of memory. *Brain and Behavior, 19*, 167–228.

Kosslyn, S. M., & Koenig, O. (Eds.). (1995). *Wet mind.* New York: Free Press.

Lakoff, G., & Jonson, M. (1980). The metaphorical structure of the human conceptual system. *Cognitive Science, 4*, 195–208.

Landauer, T. K. (1975). Memory without organization: Properties of a model with random storage and undirected retrieval. *Cognitive Psychology, 7*, 495–531.

Lindsay, D. S. (1990). "Misleading suggestions can impair eyewitnesses' ability to remember event details." *Journal of Experimental Psychology: Learning, Memory, and Cognition, 16*, 1077–1083.

Lindsay, D. S., & Johnson, M. K. (1989). The eyewitness suggestibility effect and memory for source. *Memory and Cognition, 17*, 349–358.

Lindsay, D. S., Johnson, M. K., & Kwon, P. (1991). Developmental changes in memory source monitoring. *Journal of Experimental Child Psychology, 52*, 297–318.

Lindsay, D. S., & Read, J. D. (1994). Psychotherapy and memories of childhood sexual abuse: A cognitive perspective. *Applied Cognitive Psychology, 8*, 281–338.

Linton, M. (1982). Transformations of memory in everyday life. In U. Neisser (Ed.), *Memory observed: Remembering in natural contexts* (pp. 77–91). San Francisco: Freeman.

Loftus, E. F. (1979a). Eyewitness testimony. Cambridge, MA: Harvard University Press.

Loftus, E. F. (1979b). The malleability of human memory. *American Scientist, 67*, 312–320.

Loftus, E. F., & Loftus, G. R. (1980). On the permanence of stored information in the human brain. *American Psychologist, 35*, 409–420.

Loftus, E. F., Miller, D. G., & Burns, H. J. (1978). Semantic integration of verbal information into a visual memory. *Journal of Experimental Psychology: Human Learning and Memory, 4*, 19–31.

Loftus, E. F., & Palmer, J. C. (1974). Reconstruction of automobile destruction: An example of the interaction between language and memory. *Journal of Verbal Learning and Verbal Behavior, 13*, 585–589.

Loftus, E. F., & Pickrell, J. E. (1995). The formation of false memories. *Psychiatric Annals, 25*, 720–725.

McCloskey, M., Wible, C. G., & Cohen, N. J. (1988). Is there a special flashbulb-memory mechanism? *Journal of Experimental Psychology: General, 117*, 171–181.

McCloskey, M., & Zaragoza, M. (1985). Misleading postevent information and memory for events: Arguments and evidence against memory impairment hypotheses. *Journal of Experimental Psychology: General, 114*, 1–16.

Miller, G. A. (1956). Human memory and the storage of information. *IRE Transactions on Information Theory, IT-2*, 129–137.

Neisser, U. (1967). *Cognitive psychology.* New York: Appleton-Century-Crofts.

Neisser, U. (1982). John Dean's memory: A case study. In U. Neisser (Ed.), *Memory observed: Remembering in natural contexts* (pp. 139–159). San Francisco: Freeman.

Neisser, U., & Harsch, N. (1992). Phantom flashbulbs: False recollections of hearing the news about Challenger. In E. Winograd & U. Neisser (Eds.), *Affect and accuracy in recall: Studies of "flashbulb memories"* (pp. 9–31). Cambridge, UK: Cambridge University Press.

Nickerson, R. S., & Adams, M. J. (1979). Long-term memory for a common object. *Cognitive Psychology, 11,* 287–307.

Oates, K., & Shrimpton, S. (1991). Children's memories for stressful and nonstressful events. *Medicine, Science, and the Law, 31,* 3–10.

Ofshe, R., & Watters, E. (1994). *Making monsters: False memories, psychotherapy, and sexual hysteria.* New York: Charles Scribner's Sons.

Ornstein, P. A., Gordon, B. N., & Larus, D. M. (1992). Children's memory for a personally experienced event: Implications for testimony. *Applied Cognitive Psychology, 6,* 49–60.

Payne, D. G., Elie, C. J., Blackwell, J. M., & Neuschatz, J. S. (1996). Memory illusions: Recalling, recognizing and recollecting events that never occurred. *Journal of Memory and Language, 31,* 261–285.

Payne, D. G., & Wenger, M. J. (1996). Practice effects in memory. In D. J. Herrmann, C. McEvoy, C. Hertzog, P. Hertel, & M. K. Johnson (Eds.), *Basic and applied memory research: Practical applications* (Vol. 12, pp. 45–68). Mahwah, NJ: Erlbaum.

Pear, T. H. (1922). *Remembering and forgetting.* London: Metheun.

Penfield, W. (1969). Consciousness, memory, and man's conditioned reflexes. In K. Pribram (Ed.), *On the biology of learning.* New York: Harcourt, Brace & World.

Piaget, J. (1962). *Play, dreams, and imitation in childhood* (C. Cattegno & F. M. Hodgsen, Trans.). New York: Norton. (Original work published 1945)

Posner, M. I., & Warren, R. E. (1972). Traces, concepts, and conscious constructions. In A. W. Melton & E. Martin (Eds.), *Coding processes in human memory.* Washington, DC: Winston.

Rajaram, S. (1993). Remembering and knowing: Two means of access to the personal past. *Memory and Cognition, 21,* 89–102.

Read, S. J., & Rosson, M. B. (1982). Rewriting history: The biasing effects of attitudes on memory. *Social Cognition, 1,* 240–255.

Roediger, H. L. (1980). Memory metaphors. *Memory and Cognition, 8,* 231–246.

Roediger, H. L. (1996). Memory Illusions. *Journal of Memory and Language, 35,* 76–100.

Roediger, H. L., & McDermott, K. B. (1993). Implicit memory in normal human subjects. In H. Spinnler & F. Boller (Eds.), *Handbook of neuropsychology.* Amsterdam: Elsevier.

Roediger, H. L., & McDermott, K. B. (1995). Creating false memories: Remembering words not presented in lists. *Journal of Experimental Psychology: Learning, Memory, and Cognition, 21,* 803–814.

Ross, D. R., Ceci, S. J., Dunning, D., & Toglia, M. P. (1994). Unconscious transference and mistaken identity: When a witness misidentifies a familiar with an innocent person. *Journal of Applied Psychology, 79,* 918–930.

Rubin, D. C., & Kontis, T. C. (1983). A schema for common cents. *Memory and Cognition, 11,* 335–341.

Rudy, L., & Goodman, G. S. (1991). Effects of participation on children's reports: Implications for children's testimony. *Developmental Psychology, 27,* 527–538.

Saywitz, K. J., Goodman, G. S., Nicholas, E., & Moan, S. F. (1991). Children's memories of a physical examination involving genital touch: Implications for reports of child sexual abuse. *Journal of Consulting and Clinical Psychology, 59,* 682–691.

Schooler, J. W., & Engstler-Schooler, T. Y. (1990). Verbal overshadowing of visual memories: Some things are better left unsaid. *Cognitive Psychology, 22,* 36–71.

Shepard, R. N. (1967). Recognition memory for words, sentences, and pictures. *Journal of Verbal Learning and Verbal Behavior, 6,* 156–163.

Shepard, R. N. (1990). *Mind sights: Original visual illusions, ambiguities, and other anomalies, with a commentary on the play of mind in perception and art.* New York: Freeman.

Singer, M. (1973). A replication of Bransford and Franks' (1971). The abstraction of linguistic ideas. *Bulletin of the Psychonomic Society, 1,* 416–418.

Smith, M. (1983). Hypnotic memory enhancement of witnesses: Does it work? *Psychological Bulletin, 94,* 387–407.

Snyder, M., & Uranowitz, S. W. (1978). Reconstructing the past: Some consequences of person perception. *Journal of Personality and Social Psychology, 36,* 941–950.

Spear, N. E. (1979). Experimental analysis of infantile amnesia. In J. F. Kihlstrom & F. J. Evans (Eds.), *Functional disorders of memory* (pp. 75–102). Hillsdale, NJ: Erlbaum.

Spence, D. P. (1984). *Narrative truth and historical truth.* New York: Norton.

Spiro, R. J. (1977). Remembering information from text: The "state of schema" approach. In R. C. Anderson, R. J. Spiro, & W. E. Montague (Eds.), *Schooling and the acquisition of knowledge* (pp. 137–165). Hillsdale, NJ: Erlbaum.

Standing, L. (1973). Learning 10,000 pictures. *Quarterly Journal of Experimental Psychology, 25,* 207–222.

Tulving, E. (1985). Memory and consciousness. *Canadian Psychologist, 26,* 1–12.

Tulving, E., & Thomson, D. M. (1973). Encoding specificity and retrieval processes in episodic memory. *Psychological Review, 80,* 353–373.

Usher, J. A., & Neisser, U. (1993). Childhood amnesia and the beginnings of memory for four early life events. *Journal of Experimental Psychology: General, 122,* 155–165.

Weingardt, K. R., Toland, H. K., & Loftus, E. F. (1994). Reports of suggested memories: Do people truly believe them? In D. F. Ross, J. D. Read, & M. P. (Eds.), *Toglia Adult eyewitness testimony: Current trends and developments* (pp. 3–26). New York: Cambridge University Press.

Whitehead, A. N. (1954). *Dialogues of Alfred North Whitehead* (L. Price, ed.). Boston: Little, Brown.

Whitehouse, W. G., Orne, E. C., Orne, M. T., & Dinges, D. F. (1991). Distinguishing the source of memories reported during prior waking and hypnotic recall attempts. *Applied Cognitive Psychology, 5,* 51–59.

Woodworth, R. S. (1938). *Experimental psychology.* New York: Henry Holt.

Wright, D. B. (1993). Recall of the Hillsborough Disaster over time: Systematic biases of 'flashbulb' memories. *Applied Cognitive Psychology, 7,* 129–138.

Yapko, M. D. (1994). Suggestibility and repressed memories of abuse: A survey of psychotherapists' beliefs. *American Journal of Clinical Hypnosis, 36,* 163–171.

Zechmeister, E. B., & Shaughnessy, J. J. (1980). When you know that you know and when you think that you know but you don't. *Bulletin of the Psychonomic Society, 15,* 41–44.

CHAPTER 3

EXPECTANCY EFFECTS IN RECONSTRUCTIVE MEMORY
When the Past Is Just What We Expected

Edward R. Hirt
Hugh E. McDonald
Keith D. Markman

Memories of the past play an essential role in our everyday lives. We recollect past events and experiences shared with our families and friends. We assess our students' learning by examining their retention and memory for past information covered in our courses. We evaluate social change by comparing the present to our memory for what things were like in the past. Given the importance we place on memory, a critical issue is the potential accuracy of these memories.

Although people would like to believe that their memories are veridical, the dominant view emerging from the psychological literature emphasizes the constructive nature of memory. This view, dating back to the seminal work of Sir Frederick Bartlett (1932), illustrates the role that prior knowledge structures or schemas play in recalling past information. Bartlett gave his subjects an unusual and unfamiliar text, a Native American folk tale titled "The War of the Ghosts," and asked them to recall the story as accurately as possible. He found that subjects often distorted the story to fit with their expectations. His work emphasized the theory-driven nature of memory and the biasing effect that schemas and expectancies have on what information is retrieved. This work on reconstructive memory paints a bleak picture of the potential accuracy of past memories.

SOURCES OF SCHEMATIC EFFECTS ON MEMORY

As we begin, it would be helpful to first discuss what we mean by the term "schema". Schemas are organized knowledge structures stored in memory that are developed through experience. Basically, schemas represent summaries and abstractions derived from prior experience. For example, most of us (based on similar experiences) have a schema for an event such as a wedding. Weddings have a bride and groom, a wedding party, a ceremony that typically includes certain features (e.g., a procession, an exchange of vows, exchange of wedding rings, and a celebrant/justice of the peace), a receiving line, a reception, wedding toasts, a wedding cake, and so on. People have schemas for events and activities (e.g., chess, football games, and whodunnit mystery novels), individuals or groups of people (e.g., stereotypes), and social roles (e.g., occupations). Schemas are very useful in that they provide us with a frame of reference from which to perceive new experiences. Do any of you remember attending your first football game? For novices, it seems like a bunch of people running chaotically around a field: They have little idea where to focus their attention, and they can attach little meaning to the events going on around them. However, with more and more experience, they develop an understanding of the game, are able to notice and identify entire plays (larger units of analysis), and can compare the present to past performances by the same players and teams. Schemas have implications for all phases of information processing—from attention and perception, to encoding (interpreting and attaching meaning to perceived events), to memory (storage and retrieval of information). In this chapter, we focus on the implications that schemas have for memory (and the accuracy of memory).

How do schemas exert such a powerful influence on memory? In general, schema theories propose two different processes by which schemas affect memory. First, schemas drive encoding. Based on prior knowledge, schemas generate expectancies that direct and guide our attention to schema-consistent information. As a result, schema-consistent rather than schema-inconsistent or schema-irrelevant information is preferentially encoded and thus is "available" (Tulving & Pearlstone, 1966) for later recall. A number of studies illustrate how schematic expectations lead to the preferential encoding of schema-consistent information (Rothbart, Evans, & Fulero, 1979; Zadny & Gerard, 1974), resulting in better recall of schema-consistent information. For example, Cohen (1981) had participants watch a videotape of a woman and were told that she was employed as either a waitress or a librarian. Although all participants saw the same videotape, Cohen found that participants in the waitress condition noticed and remembered more details consistent with their stereotype of a waitress (e.g., she owned a bowling ball and she drank beer), whereas those in the librarian condition noticed and remembered more details consistent with their stereotype of a librarian (e.g., she had many bookshelves and she wore glasses).

Furthermore, people tend to interpret ambiguous information in a manner consistent with their expectations (Darley & Gross, 1983), leading to the perception of greater support for one's expectations than is objectively warranted. Chapman and Chapman's (1967) work on the "illusory correla- tion" phenomenon illustrated how clinicians holding expectations about the relationship between specific symptoms and clinical diagnoses found evi- dence supporting their beliefs even in a set of data in which no such relationship actually existed. Thus, according to this view, schemas act as filters that selectively encode schema-consistent information and render it available for later recall.

However, other research has qualified the effects of schemas on encod- ing. Although it is true that schema-relevant information consistently shares a memory advantage over schema-irrelevant information (Anderson & Pichert, 1978; Brewer & Treyens, 1981), whether schema-consistent or schema- inconsistent information is better recalled is a topic of some debate. Whereas some studies found better recall of consistent information, several studies (Hastie & Kumar, 1979; Srull, 1981; Wyer & Gordon, 1982) indicated that inconsistent information is better recalled than consistent information.

Indeed, on the surface, these results appear to directly contradict the implications of schema theories; yet a careful examination of these studies reveals that this is not the case. In these studies, participants were often given the goal of integrating all the available information to form an overall impression (often called an impression set). Schema-consistent information fits in well with prior expectancies and thus can be processed quickly and easily. Inconsistent information is particularly salient and requires greater attention and effort to integrate it with the other available information. As a result, a greater number of associative links are formed between schema- inconsistent and other items than between schema-consistent and other items, resulting in better subsequent recall of inconsistent information (cf. Srull, Lichtenstein, & Rothbart, 1985). However, this memory advantage for schema- inconsistent information occurs only when individuals are both motivated (cf. Fiske & Neuberg, 1990) and have sufficient opportunity and cognitive re- sources (cf. Bargh & Thein, 1985) to engage in these inconsistency-resolution processes (for reviews of this literature, see Stangor & McMillan, 1992; von Hippel, Sekaquaptewa, & Vargas, 1996). Thus, these data further attest to the directive influence of schemas on the encoding of available information.

A second process by which schemas are hypothesized to influence memory occurs at retrieval. Schemas serve as effective retrieval cues for schema-consistent information. For instance, Anderson and Pichert (1978) asked participants to read a description of a home using either the perspective of a burglar or the perspective of a prospective home buyer. After a week's delay, participants were asked to recall the description. In this recall task, information consistent with the participants' given perspective was preferen- tially recalled. Following this initial recall task, participants were then pro- vided with the alternative perspective and asked to recall the description again. Their results indicated the successful retrieval of previously unrecallable information following the receipt of the second perspective.

Furthermore, the organized structure of schemas allows one to make inferences about information not recalled (and perhaps not presented), leading to schema-consistent intrusions in memory. Numerous studies (Cantor & Mischel, 1977; Dooling & Christiaansen, 1977; Snyder & Uranowitz, 1978; Spiro, 1980) demonstrate that people misremember not presented but schema-consistent information in memory. Dooling and Christiaansen (1977), for instance, had participants read a passage about a fictitious ruthless dictator named Gerald Martin. Some participants were later told that the character described in the passage (Gerald Martin) was actually Adolf Hitler. In a subsequent recognition test, participants were presented with some questions which were consistent with their schema about Hitler but were not contained in the passage (e.g., he persecuted Jews); participants made a number of such schema-consistent intrusions, incorrectly believing that this information was in the passage. This research suggests that schemas can also operate postencoding, influencing memory for information that was encoded prior to the activation of the schema. Thus, schemas can influence memory at the time of recall, resulting in the selective retrieval of schema-consistent information and the potential importation of schema-based intrusions in memory.

However, these schematic postencoding effects have proven to be far more controversial than schematic effects at encoding. A number of studies attempted to assess whether schematic effects on memory occur at encoding or at retrieval by presenting schematic information either before or after encoding (Rothbart et al., 1979; Wyer, Srull, Gordon, & Hartwick, 1982; Zadny & Gerard, 1974). The logic of these studies is as follows: If schemas exert their effects only at encoding, memory should be biased by one's schemas in before but not in after conditions because schemas must be present at encoding to affect memory. Alternatively, if schemas operate at both encoding and retrieval, schema-consistent biases in memory should be observed in both before and after conditions. These studies typically show that the effects of schematic information presented before encoding are much stronger than the effects of schematic information presented after information is encoded.

Several of these studies (Rothbart et al., 1979; Wyer et al., 1982) found no effects in the after (i.e., postencoding) conditions. Furthermore, the few studies that successfully demonstrated postencoding effects have been questioned on both empirical and methodological grounds. For example, Bartlett's (1932) original work has failed to replicate (Gauld & Stephenson, 1967; Zangwill, 1972) and was criticized as being unrepresentative of normal prose (Mandler & Johnson, 1977). Other studies were criticized for simply demonstrating that later information interferes with memory for earlier information, a phenomenon known as retroactive inhibition effects in recall (Tulving & Psotka, 1971).

Finally, a number of these studies relied exclusively on recognition data.

Unlike recall, recognition tests used a forced-choice procedure in which participants must choose an answer even when they do not know it. When they are uncertain, participants who cannot remember the information may be likely to guess based on their schema, resulting in schema-consistent response biases. This process is best illustrated in a study by Snyder and Uranowitz (1978), who had participants read a passage about a woman named Betty K. and were later told that she was currently living either a heterosexual or lesbian lifestyle. Participants were then given a recognition test over the material contained in the passage. They found that participants distorted their memory of the original information to be in line with their current schema (Betty K.'s current lifestyle). But did these recognition responses really indicate that participants' memory were altered or could they merely reflect schema-consistent guessing or response biases under uncertainty? By employing signal detection analyses of their recognition data (procedures designed to separate true memory from guessing), both Bellezza and Bower (1981) and Clark and Woll (1981) found that the reconstructive memory effects observed by Snyder and Uranowitz (1978) were solely the result of schema-consistent guessing or response biases under uncertainty. Indeed, several reviews of this literature (Alba & Hasher, 1983; Higgins & Bargh, 1987) not only question the inevitability of schematic reconstruction of the past but claim there is insufficient evidence to support the notion that reconstructive or schematic postencoding effects reliably occur.

The goal of this chapter is to provide definitive evidence that postencoding effects can reliably influence reconstructive memory for past information. In particular, we demonstrate how expectancies concerning the stability or change of an attribute or performance over time lead to expectancy-congruent recall of the past. Take, for example, a situation in which a woman is retrospectively asked to report her symptoms during her last period (McFarland, Ross, & DeCourville, 1989). McFarland et al. (1989) conducted a diary study in which women were asked to complete daily questionnaires assessing their symptomology for 4 to 6 weeks. Later, participants were asked to recall their symptoms on a day when they were menstruating or not menstruating (at the time of recall, all participants were in the intermenstrual phase). They found that women's recall of their physical and affective symptoms were biased by their theories of menstrual distress. Women who believed that they suffered from PMS exaggerated the negativity of their symptoms in their recall.

At the same time, we acknowledge that schematic reconstruction is not an inevitable process. Indeed, there are many situations in which individuals demonstrate remarkably accurate recall of the past, even over prolonged periods of time (e.g., Bates, Masling, & Kintsch, 1978; Hasher, Attig, & Alba, 1981; Keenan, MacWhinney, & Mayhew, 1977; McCloskey & Zaragoza, 1985). Thus, it is important to elucidate the conditions under which schematic reconstruction of the past is likely or unlikely to occur. In this chapter, we present a model of the reconstructive memory process that attempts to delineate the conditions that result in accurate and inaccurate memory for the past.

THE ROSS AND CONWAY MODEL

Work by Michael Ross and his colleagues (Conway & Ross, 1984; McFarland et al., 1989; McFarland, Ross, & Giltrow, 1992; Ross, McFarland, & Fletcher, 1981) demonstrated that subjects' recall of the past is often a function of their idiosyncratic expectancies of change. In one experiment, participants were exposed to a persuasive counterattitudinal message that successfully changed their attitudes toward the benefits of toothbrushing (Ross et al., 1981). However, when participants were asked to recall their past attitude toward toothbrushing (i.e., their attitude before they were exposed to the persuasive message), they reported their past attitude to be the same as their current attitude. Participants misrecalled their past attitude despite knowing that the experimenter could check their recall for accuracy (participants had completed an attitude measure before the experimental session). Ross et al. (1981) argue that this result was obtained because participants held an expectancy that attitudes are stable over time and allowed this expectancy to guide their recall of the past. Indeed, Ross (1989) reports that people commonly hold stability expectancies for traits and attitudes (see also Hamilton & Sherman, 1996).

In other circumstances, we hold theories or expectancies of change. For instance, people who participate in self-help or self-improvement courses usually expect that they will improve. Despite the fact that many of these courses result in no objective change or improvement, people report that they are much better off than they were before. Conway and Ross (1984) found that participants in a study-skills improvement course recalled their previous skill level as worse than it really was (even though the course had no measurable effect), presumably because of their reliance on their expectancy of improvement at the time of retrieval. Conversely, individuals holding a expectancy of decline over time should recall the past as better than it actually was, consistent with a theory of decline over time. McFarland et al. (1992) found that elderly individuals believed that some characteristics (e.g., physical strength/agility, energy level, or ability to remember details) decline with age, whereas others (e.g., wisdom or maturity) improve with age. Thus, an elderly individual might recall him- or herself in the past to have been much stronger, with more energy and a better memory, but a fool.

Based on this work, Ross and Conway (1986) proposed a model of personal recall (see Figure 3.1). Imagine you are asked to report your attitude toward abortion 10 years ago. Ross and Conway suggest that individuals answer such questions by means of a two-step process: First, the individual consults his or her present status or standing on the attribute in question. The present, which is more salient and available to us, serves as a benchmark or

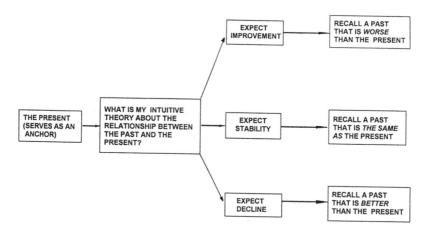

FIGURE 3.1. Schematic of the Ross and Conway (1986) model.

anchor from which the past is inferred. Thus, in the above example, the individual would consider his or her current attitude toward abortion. Second, the individual invokes his or her theory or expectancy of stability or change. The expectancy guides the reconstructive process such that the individual infers an expectancy-congruent past. If, for example, a person believes her attitude toward abortion has not changed much over the past decade, she would recall her past attitude as roughly the same as the present. If she expects that her attitude has changed (e.g., "I've become more liberal in my beliefs"), she might recall her past attitude as different (e.g., more conservative) than the present.

Ross and Conway's (1986) model has considerable intuitive appeal and is supported by a number of studies. However, in these studies, participants' expectancies were never actually manipulated. Thus, Hirt (1990) attempted to provide a more critical test of the model by directly manipulating both participants' expectancies and the "present" (outcome information). In these studies, participants were given information about a hypothetical college student and his past grades in his courses. After a delay, participants were given information inducing expectancies of future academic improvement (the student was now being tutored), decline (the student was losing his tutor), or stability (the student was continuing to be tutored). Finally, participants were given the target's current grades (the outcome information) and were then asked to recall his past grades. Hirt's results strongly supported the Ross and Conway (1986) model: participants' recall of the past scores (which were the same for all) was significantly affected by the outcome information. Participants who received a final grade of 84 recalled a higher past score than participants who received final grades of 78 or 72, indicating that participants were indeed using the outcome information as a benchmark from which they adjusted their recall of the past. Furthermore, participants were also significantly influenced by the expectancy manipulation. Regardless of the specific final score given, participants expecting improvement recalled lower past scores than those expecting stability or decline. Thus, these results illustrate that both outcome and expectancy powerfully influence recall.

HIRT'S MODEL OF RECONSTRUCTIVE MEMORY

In addition to providing empirical support for the Ross and Conway model, Hirt's (1990) research extended the model beyond the domain of personal recall to memory for others, suggesting it may have broad applicability. Nonetheless, one might ask what role accuracy plays in this model. According to Ross and Conway, accurate recall of the past occurs as a result of the serendipitous match of expectancy and outcome: If the relationship between past and present happens to be consistent with one's expectancy, then recall of the past using the expectancy should be fairly accurate. However, when the relationship between the past and present is not consistent with an expectancy, the model predicts expectancy-consistent distortion of the past.

Indeed, several observations in Hirt's (1990) data indicated that participants were doing more than simply engaging in an expectancy-based inference (guessing) process. Hirt (1990, Study 2) manipulated the past scores that participants received (and that were to be recalled later) to examine whether participants' recall was sensitive to variations in the original information. Participants were given a past score of either 70, 74, or 78 in the critical target course (Chemistry). All participants were given the same outcome or anchor (a final grade of 80) and one of two expectancies (improvement or no expectancy/control). His findings indicated that participants' recall, given the same outcome and expectancy, was significantly influenced by the manipulation of the prior scores. Participants given an original score of 70 recalled a lower score than participants given an original score of 74 or 78, illustrating that participants were not solely using the outcome and expectancy as a basis for recall. Nonetheless, the recall of participants given the same original scores continued to be affected by their expectancies of change. Expect-improvement participants recalled significantly lower scores than did no-expectancy (control) participants, emphasizing the biasing influence of one's expectancies on memory.[1] Thus, these results suggest that participants were consulting their memory trace of the original information as well as the implications of the expectancy and the outcome at the time of retrieval.

These observations led Hirt to propose his own model of reconstructive memory in which individuals are conceptualized as integrating information from three sources at retrieval: (1) the present (outcome), which serves as an anchor; (2) the expectancy regarding the relationship between the past and the present; and (3) the episodic memory trace of the original information. A critical implication of this model is that accurate recall can occur in two ways. First, recall should be accurate to the degree that the outcome matches one's expectancy. Indeed, in a study similar to Hirt's (1990) research, Hirt, Erickson, and McDonald (1993) provided participants with mixed feedback, half of which was consistent with their induced expectancy and half of which was inconsistent with their expectancy. Their results demonstrated that subjects are relatively accurate in their recall of information consistent with their expectancy but show expectancy-congruent distortion for information inconsistent with their expectancy. Second, recall can be more accurate to the degree that subjects give greater relative weight to the memory trace of the original information and/or reduced weight to the expectancy at retrieval. Thus, the relative weighting that individuals give to the memory trace as opposed to the expectancy also determines the accuracy of recall.

MODERATORS OF THE RELATIVE WEIGHTING OF EXPECTANCY VERSUS MEMORY TRACE

Accessibility

What factors determine the relative weighting given to the expectancy as opposed to the memory trace? Certainly, one important factor is the salience or accessibility of these two sources of information. We would argue that in nearly all cases, the memory trace of the original information is going to be weaker and less accessible than the trace of information presented more recently (the "present"). Under these conditions, the presence of a salient expectancy about the relationship between the past and present provides a ready "heuristic" with which to infer the past. Clearly, this was the case in our previous research (Hirt, 1990). In our paradigm, participants studied the original information and then worked on a set of distractor problems for 20 minutes. After this retention interval, participants received the expectancy manipulation, followed by the outcome information. Participants were then asked to recall the original information. Given that participants received the expectancy and outcome information immediately prior to the recall task, it is no surprise that they gave greater relative weight to the expectancy than to the memory trace at retrieval. However, we reasoned that to the extent that we reduced the differential salience of the expectancy over the memory trace at retrieval, we should see less weight given to the expectancy and correspondingly increased weight given to the memory trace, and thus greater memory accuracy.

Hirt et al. (1993) manipulated the relative salience of the expectancy versus the memory trace by varying the timing at which participants received the expectancy information (see Figure 3.2). In the first condition (T1), participants received the expectancy information immediately after the original scores, prior to the retention interval. In a second condition (T2), participants received the expectancy information halfway through the reten-

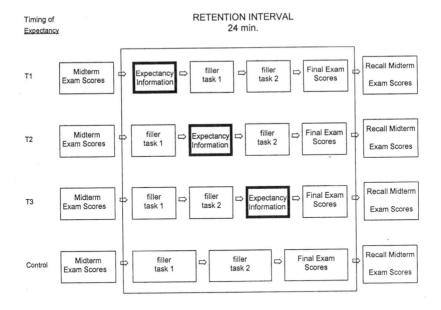

FIGURE 3.2. Schematic of the manipulation of the timing condition (T) of the expectancy information.

tion interval. Finally, in a third condition (T3), participants received the expectancy information following the retention interval and immediately prior to the outcome information and recall task, paralleling our past work. Our predictions were that by varying the timing of the expectancy information, we could reduce its relative salience at retrieval and thereby reduce the relative weight given to the expectancy and increase memory accuracy.

Methodology

In these studies, all participants received outcome information in which half the scores improved and half declined (for a net change of 0). Thus, for each expectancy condition, half the scores were consistent and half inconsistent with their expectations. By this procedure, we could obtain an index of participants' reliance on their expectancy at retrieval by comparing the relative accuracy of their recall of the consistent and inconsistent scores. Specifically, we measured recall accuracy in terms of the absolute difference between a participants' recalled score and the actual score. Greater weight given to the expectancy would result in relatively accurate recall of the consistent scores but expectancy-congruent distortion of the inconsistent scores. Thus, participants expecting improvement should recall the improving scores accurately but distort the declining scores to be lower than they actually were (consistent with their expectancy of net improvement in performance).

Conversely, participants expecting decline should recall the declining scores accurately but distort the improving scores to be higher than they actually were (consistent with their expectancy of net decline in performance). Greater weight given to the memory trace should result in accuracy for both expectancy-consistent *and expectancy-inconsistent* information. Thus, the critical measure is the amount of distortion displayed in the recall of the inconsistent scores.

In addition, we included a recognition task following the recall task. Participants were given a two-alternative forced-choice task for each of the original midterm scores. Following the procedure outlined by Bellezza and Bower (1981), we varied the incorrect alternative (or foil) presented with the correct original score: In half the cases, it was expectancy congruent (e.g., a lower score than the correct score in the expect improvement condition) and in half the cases it was expectancy incongruent (e.g., a higher score than the correct original score in the expect improvement condition). In this way, signal detection analyses could be performed to discriminate true memory from expectancy-congruent guessing or response bias; if participants are simply guessing based on their expectancy, they should display high accuracy when the correct score is paired with an expectancy-incongruent foil but poor accuracy when the correct score is paired with an expectancy-congruent foil. On the other hand, if participants display equally high accuracy when an expectancy-congruent or an expectancy-incongruent foil is paired with the correct score, it indicates true memory for the original score. Thus, via both of these indices, we can assess the relative weight given the expectancy as opposed to the memory trace at retrieval.

The results supported our predictions: Participants in both the T2 and T3 conditions (i.e., conditions in which receipt of the expectancy was delayed) displayed expectancy-congruent distortion of inconsistent scores and relatively accurate recall of the consistent scores, indicating that they gave greater weight to the expectancy at retrieval. Analyses of the recognition data also revealed that T2 and T3 participants showed enhanced expectancy-congruent response bias (i.e., consistently guessing the most expectancy-congruent of the two alternatives) relative to no-expectancy (control) participants, further illustrating their reliance on their expectancy. Interestingly, the performance of T2 and T3 participants did not differ on any of these measures. In contrast, T1 participants (i.e., those who received the expectancy immediately after the original information) showed significantly less expectancy-congruent distortion in their recall of the inconsistent scores and little or no response bias on the recognition items, suggesting that they gave less weight to the expectancy at retrieval. Thus, it appears that the salience of the expectancy at retrieval indeed affects the relative weight given to the expectancy in their recall and recognition performance.

However, comparisons between the performance of T1 and no expectancy (control) participants revealed a surprising set of results. T1 participants showed greater overall recall and recognition accuracy than did the control (no-expectancy) participants. Signal detection analyses revealed that T1 participants showed better true memory for the original scores than did the controls, suggesting that they were not only giving less weight to the expectancy but also giving significantly greater weight to the memory trace at retrieval. What might be the source of this enhanced memory? Recall that T1 participants received the expectancy immediately after the original information (and prior to the retention interval). This expectancy information alerted participants to the relevance of the target's academic performance and to the possibility that a change would occur. Thus, it is likely that upon receipt of this expectancy information, participants would be motivated to go back and mentally review or "reprocess" the original scores in light of this expectation (asking themselves, "What were those scores again?"). Because of the temporal proximity of the expectancy to the original scores in the T1 condition, participants were able to successfully reprocess the original information, resulting in a stronger memory trace for later recall. However, participants in the T2 and T3 conditions would be less able to reprocess the original scores because the original information was no longer as salient and accessible by the time they received the expectancy.

This explanation provides a reasonable account for the Hirt et al. (1993) data. Moreover, research by Wyer et al. (1982) corroborates this reprocessing notion. Wyer et al. used the same perspective manipulation (home buyer vs. burglar) as Anderson and Pichert (1978) used. In their study, Wyer et al. (1982) found that supplying participants with a new perspective after the information was initially received led them to reconsider and reprocess the information, resulting in better overall memory for that information. This research suggests that discrediting testimony or other cues presented shortly after information is processed might similarly motivate reconsideration and reprocessing of the original information, the end result being not only disregard for the discredited information but also better overall memory.

Indeed, in a follow-up experiment (Hirt, McDonald, Erickson, & Gruberth, 1997), we tested the strength of the memory trace in our three timing conditions (T1, T2, T3). The experiment followed the same procedure used by Hirt et al. (1993). However, to test the strength of the memory trace more directly, participants did not receive the outcome information. Instead, borrowing from a methodology used by Fazio, Lenn, and Effrein (1983), we gave participants a reaction time task in which they were presented with questions about the original information as well as some filler trials (to provide a baseline index of each individual's response time). The questions were true–false statements and participants were asked to respond as quickly as possible without sacrificing accuracy. Three questions about each original score were presented, one with the correct score (e.g., midterm Chemistry score—75%?) and two foils, one higher (e.g., 79) and one lower (e.g., 71). The results indicated that T1 participants were not only more accurate in their memory for the original scores but also quicker in their responses. These results thus support the notion that these T1 participants have a stronger memory trace for the original scores, resulting in better overall accuracy at retrieval.

Nature of the Memory Trace

The effects observed in the T1 condition highlight the role that the nature of the memory trace plays in the relative weighting process. Certainly, we would predict that strong memory traces will receive greater weight at retrieval than weaker traces. Imagine a case in which an individual has verbatim memory for the past ("I know for a fact he got an 87 in American History"). In such circumstances, the memory trace receives exclusive weighting and the expectancy and outcome information are weighted zero. However, in most circumstances, memory traces are weak or incomplete or have decayed with time to the point that accuracy (or confidence in accuracy) is substantially reduced.

What factors contribute to the development of strong memory traces? The most obvious answer to this question involves the way the original information is initially encoded. Indeed, a great deal of research manipulated the goals with which individuals encode information. Although a comprehensive review of this work on encoding goals is beyond the scope of this chapter, we focus our discussion on the three most frequently used encoding set manipulations: recall set, impression set, and comprehension set. Our choice in focusing on these encoding sets is based on both theoretical and empirical grounds. A recall set is important because it offers an index of participants' performance when their goal is explicitly to remember the information for later recall. Another useful condition is a comprehension set condition, in which participants are told to merely comprehend the information and to focus on the coherence and grammaticality of the statements (Lichtenstein & Srull, 1987); this condition establishes a baseline of incidental learning when participants' goal is not to focus on the content of the presented information. An impression set (in which participants are told to form an impression of the target) is important given that it is arguably the dominant encoding set operative during social interaction, and based on the vast empirical literature on the memory effects associated with this goal.

The most straightforward prediction that one could make is that individuals under a recall set would give the greatest weight to the memory trace and show the most accurate recall and least amount of expectancy-congruent distortion. Recall sets promote individuals to rehearse and learn the information verbatim (i.e., memorize), resulting in a stronger and more detailed memory trace. Conversely, comprehension set individuals should have a very weak memory trace and be forced to rely heavily on their expectancies to reconstruct the past. Predictions regarding the impression set condition are more difficult. On the one hand, numerous studies in the person memory literature demonstrate superior memory in impression set over recall set conditions (e.g., Hamilton, Katz, & Leirer, 1980; Srull et al., 1985). Specifically,

given sets of behaviors performed by a target person, impression set participants were able to recall a greater number of these behaviors in a later recall
test than were recall set participants. Additional studies (Lichtenstein & Srull,
1987) comparing performance across recall, impression, and comprehension
set conditions again found better recall by impression set subjects, though
recall in both impression set and recall set conditions was superior to that in
comprehension set conditions. Presumably, these effects occur because the
memory traces formed under impression set instructions are well organized
and coherent, characterized by numerous interconnections among items in
memory. Thus, on the basis of this evidence, one might expect the performance of impression set individuals to equal or exceed that of recall set
individuals.

On the other hand, individuals given an impression set tend to form
global or summary evaluations of the original information. There is literature to suggest that these summary structures are stored independently
from the original information on which they were based (Carlston, 1980;
Lingle & Ostrom, 1979; Schul & Burnstein, 1985a; Wyer, Srull, & Gordon,
1984). Indeed, these studies show that impression set individuals tend to
base later judgments on these summary evaluations rather than accessing
the details of the original information. For instance, Carlston (1980) had
participants read behavioral descriptions that could be interpreted in
multiple ways under an impression set. One such behavior would be a
person Paul who helps a friend complete a take-home exam. This behavior
could be interpreted as "helpful" or "dishonest." Participants in Carlston's
(1980) experiments were asked to make a judgment about either Paul's
helpfulness or his dishonesty immediately after reading the behavioral
description. After a delay, participants were asked to judge Paul on the other
trait dimension. If participants used their impression as a basis for the later
trait judgment (rather than the original information), those who judged
Paul as helpful should rate Paul more positively (more honest) than participants who earlier rated Paul as dishonest. If participants instead rated Paul
on the basis of the original information, they should not be affected by the
earlier judgment. Carlston found that impression set participants used their
prior impressions as opposed to the actual original information as a basis
for subsequent trait judgments.

Moreover, Higgins's work on "changes of standard" (Higgins & Lurie,
1983; Higgins & Stangor, 1988) finds that the recall of subjects given an
impression set is strongly affected by changes in the contextual information
provided. In Higgins's work, participants typically read about a judge (Judge
Jones) and his sentencing decisions for different crimes and are asked to make
a judgment about the severity versus the leniency of this particular judge.
Participants are also given the sentencing decisions of other judges as a context
for making this judgment; however, in these experiments, the sentencing
decisions of the other judges are manipulated so that Judge Jones either looks
harsh relative to the others or lenient relative to the others. Participants are

later asked to recall the specific sentencing decisions of Judge Jones. Higgins et al. find that participants' recall is strongly biased by their impressions of Judge Jones such that those who judged him as lenient (but given the identical original information) recall shorter sentences than those who judged him as harsh. Thus, the context biased their impressions of Judge Jones, leading participants later to distort their memory of the original information to be consistent with their current impressions. Similarly, in our reconstructive memory paradigm, the expectancy information provides a ready context within which to assimilate one's recall of the past. Thus, based on this literature, we predicted that the performance of impression set individuals should be worse than that of recall set individuals (though still better than that of comprehension set individuals).

Hirt, McDonald, and Erickson (1995) tested these predictions. Participants encoded the original information about the target person under either recall, impression, or comprehension set instructions and then completed a task designed to solidify those encoding instructions. Recall set participants were asked to recall all the information they could from the original information sheet. Impression set participants were asked to give their general impression of the target person. Comprehension set participants rated the original information passage in terms of its grammar and comprehensibility. From that point on, the study followed the standard T3 procedure in which all participants completed a series of filler tasks during the retention interval, received the expectancy and outcome information, and then completed the recall and recognition tasks. The results indicated that recall set participants were quite accurate in both their recall and recognition performance and gave little weight to the expectancy during retrieval. Impression set and comprehension set participants both showed significant expectancy-congruent distortion in their responses, indicating that they were giving considerable weight to the expectancy during retrieval.

The second study (Hirt et al., 1995, Study 2) included a delay condition in which participants came back 2 days later to complete the recall and recognition measures. Importantly, for these delay condition participants, the expectancy and outcome information was also provided after the 2-day interval to equate the salience of these sources of information at retrieval. The results of this study illustrated that the differences between the encoding set conditions were enhanced with delay. Recall set participants continued to show no expectancy-congruent distortion even over the delay, whereas the magnitude of the distortion was significantly greater over the delay for both impression set and comprehension set participants. In fact, the responses of comprehension set participants in the delay condition revealed a pattern of expectancy-based guessing (cf. Ross & Conway, 1986), indicating no contribution of any memory trace to their recall and recognition responses.

These results emphasize the role of the nature of the original memory trace in reconstructive memory. Individuals under recall set instructions formed memory traces that resulted in more accurate memory for the past and reduced the weight given to the expectancy at retrieval. The memory traces of participants under impression and comprehension set instructions were weaker, leading participants to weight the expectancy more heavily and thus show greater expectancy-congruent distortion. Based on these results, it is tempting to conclude that recall sets are likely to consistently result in more accurate reconstructive memory. However, we believe it is important to acknowledge that in this research, we were assessing memory for details (i.e., specific grades). Because recall sets lead to more precise, verbatim encoding of the original information, participants are likely to display better memory for details (see also Cohen & Ebbesen, 1979). However, although there are many situations in which accurate recall of specific details is very important (e.g., eyewitness testimony and academic test taking), in other situations memory for the "gist" of the information is sufficient. In such circumstances, the use of abstracted, trait-based representations of the original information formed under an impression set would facilitate greater organization and interconnections between items in memory, resulting in the successful retrieval of more of the original information (Hamilton et al., 1980).

Thus, the implications of this work for the accuracy of reconstructive memory depends on which definition of "accuracy" one uses. When accuracy is defined in terms of memory for specific details, then a recall set will result in more accurate memory. However, when accuracy is defined in terms of the recall of a greater amount of the available information (or of summary evaluations of that information), then an impression set will result in more accurate memory.

Motivation

To this point, we have focused exclusively on more structural factors that affect the relative weighting of the expectancy versus the memory trace. However, we have neglected the role that motivational factors play in determining which source of information receives greater weighting at retrieval. A number of different motivations may be operative when one attempts to reconstruct the past. Kunda (1990) distinguishes between two major classes of motivational goals: (1) accuracy goals, in which one desires to arrive at an accurate conclusion; and (2) directional goals, in which one desires to arrive at a particular (desired) conclusion. We discuss each of these goals separately, emphasizing their implications for the accuracy of reconstructed memories.

Accuracy Motives

In most tasks we perform, accuracy is not our primary goal. Indeed, the view that individuals are "cognitive misers" (Fiske & Taylor, 1991), limited in their capacity to process information and primarily interested in conserving mental resources, once dominated the field of social psychology. However, more recently, this view has been replaced with one emphasizing that people are "motivated tacticians" who have multiple cognitive strategies available to them and choose among them based on their motives and goals (Fiske & Taylor, 1991). According to this view, people who are motivated to do so can use more complex, effortful, and effective strategies when processing information, resulting in greater accuracy; however, unmotivated individuals use shortcuts and simplifying tools or heuristics to get a task done more quickly. In our reconstructive memory paradigm, reliance on the expectancy at retrieval can be construed as such a shortcut: A great deal of mental effort is necessary to access the memory trace of the original information, so that it is tempting to simply infer the past based on the outcome and expectancy. However, to the extent that individuals are motivated to be accurate in their recall of the past, they should expend greater mental effort and thus give greater weight to the memory trace at retrieval.

Hirt (1990, Study 3) tested this hypothesis by providing some participants with accuracy motivation immediately prior to the recall task. Accuracy motivation was induced by one of two different means. One group of participants was told that they would receive a monetary incentive for accurate performance (namely, accurate recall of all of the past scores would qualify them for a lottery with a $100 cash prize). Another group of participants was given context reinstatement instructions (cf. Bekerian & Bowers, 1983; Hasher & Griffin, 1978; Tulving & Thomson, 1973). Specifically, these participants were told to try to "picture the original information sheet in their minds" in a manner similar to how an eyewitness might try to mentally "recreate the scene of the crime." The results indicated that both of these accuracy motivation manipulations were successful at reducing the amount of expectancy-congruent distortion in recall. Participants given accuracy motivation gave greater weight to the memory trace at retrieval, resulting in more accurate recall of the past.

On the surface, these findings are not particularly surprising—people are more accurate when they are motivated to be accurate (cf. Aderman & Brehm, 1976; Brockway, Chmielewski, & Cofer, 1974; Gauld & Stephenson, 1967). However, a number of memory studies (Fischhoff, 1975; Loftus, Miller, & Burns, 1978) found that accuracy incentives fail to increase memory accuracy. Indeed, for accuracy goals to work, individuals must be able to gain access to the original trace and must decide to expend the necessary effort to do so. In the present context, participants know that the original information is "in there," so the motivation simply encourages them to work harder to access this information. Conversely, in many of the studies that fail to find effects of accuracy incentives, it is unclear whether participants either had access to the original information and/or believed that their current memory was in fact inaccurate (and that they needed to modify their recall of the event). Nonetheless, this is an area of reconstructive memory that clearly merits further investigation.

Directional Motives

Another set of motives can often exert a directive influence on information processing. In many cases, people are motivated to see particular outcomes. For example, when I (E. R. H.) go to my physician for a series of tests done, I am motivated to have the test results come out negative, indicating that I am healthy and have nothing to worry about. Research illustrates how the motivation to see desired outcomes leads to biased information processing strategies. People motivated to maintain certain beliefs were shown to selectively focus on supportive rather than opposing beliefs (Kunda, 1987; Pyszczynski & Greenberg, 1987), to evaluate data inconsistent with a desired conclusion more critically than information consistent with it (Ditto & Lopez, 1992; Fazio & Williams, 1986; Lord, Ross, & Lepper, 1979), and to choose inferential rules (Ginossar & Trope, 1987) and test strategies (Quattrone & Tversky, 1984) that increase the likelihood that evidence in favor of the desired conclusion will be obtained. Importantly, Kunda (1990) points out that people are not simply free to engage in "wishful thinking" and believe whatever they want to believe, independent of any evidence. Instead, she argues, that people "attempt to be rational and construct a justification of their desired conclusion that would persuade the dispassionate observer" (p. 482). Thus, people are compelled to construct an evidentiary base to justify their motivated beliefs.

Reconstruction of the past is one means by which people might justify their desired conclusion. If a student wants to convince him- or herself that studying hard is a waste of time, he or she might selectively recall situations in the past in which he or she did not study and still did quite well. Kunda and her colleagues demonstrated such effects in a clever set of studies (Kunda & Sanitioso, 1989; Sanitioso, Kunda, & Fong, 1990). Participants in their studies were led to believe that either introversion or extraversion was associated with future academic success and then later given an autobiographical memory task. Participants who were led to believe that introversion was desirable were more likely to report memories of past introverted behavior first and reported more introversion-related memories overall than did participants who were led to believe that extraversion was desirable (Sanitioso et al., 1990). By selectively recruiting memories, participants were able to conclude that they in fact had the more desirable trait.

On the surface, one might question whether these results reflect memory or merely strategic self-presentation. That is, are participants really remembering different events when they are motivated to do so or are they simply reporting or confabulating events that portray themselves in the most positive light? This is clearly a difficult issue to answer, particularly in studies of autobiographical memories—after all, one cannot assess the veracity of these memories without independent verification. However, several findings in this literature render a self-presentational explanation of these results unlikely. First, a number of studies show that individuals' memory for the past is not particularly self-aggrandizing. For instance, Conway and Ross (1994) found that participants in a study skills improvement course recalled their past level of study skills as worse than they actually were, in the service of their expectancy of improvement. Similarly, McFarland et al. (1992) found that older participants who believed that certain attributes declined over time recalled the past as better, making the present look even more bleak. Second, a number of studies (Bem & McConnell, 1970; Conway & Ross, 1984; Goethals & Reckman, 1973) illustrated that these motivated distortions in memory appear even when participants are fully aware that the accuracy of their recall can be checked. Thus, there is solid evidence that these results reflect biased memory search over and above self-presentational concerns.

These studies illustrate the powerful biasing effects of directional motives on memory search processes. However, McDonald and Hirt (1997) hypothesized that expectancy use at retrieval might likewise be a function of motivational goals: namely, people would give greater weight to their expectancy in their reconstruction of the past to the extent that they desired to see their expectancy confirmed. Certainly, in many cases, we are motivated to see our expectancies confirmed. After all, many of the expectancies we hold derive from our wishes and desires (cf. Pyszczynski & Greenberg, 1987; Trope & Liberman, 1996). In these circumstances, when expectancies match our desires, we should be strongly compelled to use our expectancies as a basis of reconstructing the past, resulting in significant expectancy-congruent distortion of the past. However, when expectancies and desires mismatch (e.g., "My team is lousy and is expected to fail but I really want them to win"), we would expect people to give little weight to their expectancies ("We're going to do it!").

McDonald and Hirt (1997) tested their hypotheses using the standard Hirt et al. paradigm. Participants were given either improvement or decline expectancies about the target person's academic performance. In the improvement scenario, participants were told that the target (J. W., a male college student) had recently begun to date another student who was serious about academics. His new girlfriend was having a very positive influence on him, such that he was now putting greater effort into his schoolwork and was gaining greater confidence in his abilities, suggesting continued improvement. In the decline scenario, participants were again told that the target had a new relationship, but in this case his girlfriend was not at all serious about school. She was clearly having a negative influence on him, encouraging him to put less effort into his schoolwork so he could stay out late and party (implying continued decline).

In these studies, however, we also manipulated participants' motivations to see either a positive (improvement) or negative (decline) outcome for the target via a likability manipulation. Participants watched a videotaped interview in which the target person (J. W.) interviewed a fellow student. Ostensibly, participants believed that they were watching the interview to evaluate the interviewer's skills and performance. Three different versions of the interview were created to manipulate participants' liking for the target. In the likable condition, the interviewer was very polite and friendly, clearly making an effort to put the interviewee at ease. In the dislikable condition, the interviewer was rude, abrupt, and unfriendly, making for a painfully uncomfortable interaction. In the neutral condition, the interviewer was businesslike and expressed no affect either way. All participants received the same set of original (midterm) scores and the identical set of outcome (final) scores and then completed recall and recognition measures assessing memory for the original information.

We expected that participants would want to see the positive expectancy (improvement) confirmed for a liked target but would want to see the negative expectancy (decline) confirmed for a disliked target. Thus, under conditions in which their expectancy and liking "matched" (expect improvement for a liked target, expect decline for a disliked target), we predicted that participants would be motivated to see their expectancy confirmed and thus give significant weight to their expectancies during retrieval and show expectancy-congruent distortion of the past. Conversely, under conditions in which expectancy and liking "mismatched" (expect improvement for a disliked target, expect decline for a liked target), we predicted that participants would be motivated to discount their expectancy (e.g., "It isn't going to happen—he's too nice a guy to let her ruin his life"), giving little or no weight to the expectancy at retrieval.

Although these predictions appear straightforward, we want to highlight the counterintuitive nature of these predictions. In the "match" conditions, participants are hypothesized to give greater weight to their expectancies, resulting in a pattern of expectancy-congruent distortion. Thus, we predicted that participants would recall *lower* past grades for a liked target (consistent with an expectancy of improvement) and *higher* past grades for a disliked target (consistent with an expectancy of decline). Conventional wisdom would suggest that we would like to see a liked target do well and a disliked target do poorly, all other things being equal. Indeed, when we ran a separate set of subjects who were given the liking manipulation and no outcome information, individuals who liked the target did in fact recall his original scores (which were the same for all participants) as higher overall than individuals who disliked the target. But in our paradigm, participants received outcome information (his final scores) so that their recall of the past is constrained by the present. In this case, the focus is on performance *change* rather than absolute level of performance. Thus, participants who liked the target would be motivated to recall lower past performance, indicative of a positive change; likewise, participants who disliked the target would be motivated to recall higher past performance, indicative of a negative change.

The results of McDonald and Hirt's (1997) experiments found support for their hypotheses. Participants in match conditions showed significant expectancy-congruent distortion in both their recall and recognition responses. Participants in the mismatch conditions, however, displayed little expectancy-congruent distortion in their responses. Mismatch condition participants appeared to be discounting the expectancy at retrieval and instead revealed a tendency to either (1) distort their recall in a manner consistent with their liking for the target (rather than the expectancy) or (2) engage in more effortful, data-driven retrieval of the original information, resulting in more accurate overall performance.

These results provide strong evidence in support of the notion that people weight their expectancies based on their motivational goals. When the expectancy leads one to recall a desired past, one will be motivated to give it greater weight at retrieval. If the expectancy works against one's motivational desires (and points to an undesired past), one will be motivated to give it little or no weight at retrieval. Moreover, by reconstructing the past in this way, people create justifications that allow them to maintain desired beliefs. Sanitioso et al. (1990) illustrated how biased recruitment of memories can justify desired beliefs about one's level of introversion–extraversion. Similarly, here we see that participants are able to justify their "just world" beliefs (Lerner, 1980) that good things happen to good people and bad things happen to bad people. Moreover, these perceptions of change have important implications for our predictions about the future (cf. Silka, 1989). Participants recalled the likable target as showing improvement over time, a desired outcome that has positive implications for the future; conversely, participants recalled the dislikable target as declining, a desired outcome that has negative implications for the future (e.g., "He is getting what he deserves").

To test these notions, McDonald and Hirt (1997) included measures that asked participants to predict the future of the target's relationship with his girlfriend as well as his academic performance the following school year. Participants in the match conditions predicted J. W.'s relationship was more likely to be maintained and predicted that his academic performance would continue in the expectancy-congruent direction (i.e., improving for the liked target, declining for the disliked target). Moreover, regression analyses indicated that participants' biased recollections of the past partially mediated their predictions of J. W.'s future performance. In other words, the more participants distorted their recall of the past in an expectancy-congruent manner, the more strongly they made expectancy-congruent predictions of the target's future performance. Thus, these data provide empirical support not only for the idea that motivational goals can bias memory reconstruction as well as memory search processes but also for the notion that motivated distortion of the past can serve as justification for desired beliefs.

CONCLUSION

We believe that the research that we have presented in this chapter provides strong evidence that expectancies presented after information is encoded can have strong biasing effects on memory. Although expectancy effects on encoding have been robustly demonstrated, many researchers (Alba &

Hasher, 1983; Higgins & Bargh, 1987) have questioned whether there is sufficient evidence that expectancies introduced after the encoding of the original information can bias memory. Many of the extant studies have been criticized as demonstrating nothing more than retroactive inhibition effects or response biases at retrieval. The present research controlled for these factors and reliably demonstrates that expectancies induced at retrieval can lead to systematic distortion of the past. Moreover, these studies emphasize that expectancy manipulations not only result in the selective retrieval of expectancy-congruent items in memory (cf. Sanitioso et al., 1990) but can also lead to expectancy-congruent distortion of memory of the same information (cf. Vorauer & Ross, 1993). Thus, not only do people expecting a particular outcome selectively recall *different* information, but they may also recall the same information differently—in other words, they may distort it in a manner that confirms their expectancies.

Despite these powerful biasing effects of expectancies, however, we know that people can also be quite accurate in their recall of the past. Moreover, their responses indicate that they are not entirely "theory driven" and oblivious to the actual data. Indeed, the Hirt (1990) model emphasizes the role of the memory trace at retrieval and the fact that the relative weighting given to the memory trace as opposed to the expectancy determines the accuracy of reconstructed memories. This model thus incorporates the potential for either theory-driven or more data-driven processing at retrieval. A number of moderator variables have already been identified that predict when individuals tend to give greater weight to the memory trace as opposed to their expectancy (e.g., the temporal relationship between encoding and the receipt of the expectancy, the perceiver's goals during encoding, incentive for accuracy, and mismatches between motivation and expectancy). We are also exploring other moderator variables that might affect the relative weights given to these factors.

One factor that we have not explored sufficiently is the nature of the expectancy (cf. Olson, Roese, & Zanna, 1996). Expectancies, like memory traces, can vary in strength. In our experiments, we have given participants powerful expectancies that virtually guaranteed that the expected outcome would occur. However, most expectancies that we hold are more probabilistic in nature—stereotypic expectancies about others, expectancies about potential health outcomes or health risks, expectancies about the effectiveness of an intervention or a social program. It remains to be seen whether individuals are sensitive to the probabilistic nature of expectancies or whether they treat them in an "all or nothing" fashion. Evidence from work in hypothesis testing suggests that individuals test even tentative hypotheses using strategies that increase the likelihood of hypothesis confirmation (Devine, Hirt, & Gehrke, 1990; Skov & Sherman, 1986). Thus, it would be important to examine memory effects using a broader range of expectancies that vary in strength and/or likelihood of occurrence.

Finally, an important but unanswered question with this research is the permanence of these reconstructive memories. Once individuals reconstruct an expectancy-congruent past, does this become their "memory" for the past or is there the potential for individuals to go back and reaccess their memory trace? A number of studies using discrediting manipulations (e.g., Schul & Bernstein, 1985b) found mixed results regarding participants' abilities to ignore discredited or inadmissable evidence. These questions raise the larger issue of the extent to which the reconstructive process occurs on-line as participants receive the information or whether it must be prompted (e.g., by a memory test).

Our earlier research clearly emphasized the extent to which individuals could control the relative weight given to their expectancy as opposed to the memory trace at retrieval. However, our more recent work examining the influence of directional motives on memory (McDonald & Hirt, 1997) suggests to us that motivations and desires may exert a less conscious and more automatic effects on memory. As Kunda (1990) argues, individuals may be strongly biased by their motives, and yet convinced themselves that they are being completely rational and objective in retrieving information from memory. This argument suggests a more insidious kind of influence far more difficult to detect and control.

Indeed, we see our work on reconstructive memory as having important implications for work on false memories. For us, one of the most intriguing aspects of the Roediger and McDermott (1995) work on false memories is the fact that these memories are generated spontaneously and yet are held with such great confidence: Participants are more convinced that these strongly associated (but not presented) words were included on the list—and say that they specifically remember actually seeing or hearing them—than many of the items that were actually included on the list. Prior work on reality monitoring (cf. Johnson & Raye, 1981) also illustrated how people have great difficulty distinguishing real from imagined events. We believe that strongly held expectations may similarly make it difficult for individuals to distinguish actual from simply expected events. The extent to which such "wishful thinking" can result in systematic reconstruction and distortion in memory remains to be determined but is an interesting avenue for future research. Indeed, it is these aspects of reconstructive memory that have engaged researchers and laypersons alike since the time of Bartlett, because the study of memory touches something deep and fundamental about ourselves and our lives. We are continuing our own exploration of these reconstructive memory processes and *expect* the compelling nature of these questions to inspire future research for years to come.

NOTE

1. Interestingly, in the present research, we observed a tendency for participants not given an expectancy to self-generate an expectancy of stability. Moreover, the

recall and recognition responses indicated that no-expectancy participants weighted their self-generated expectancies to a similar degree as did participants whose expectancies were explicitly manipulated. These results emphasize the ubiquitous role that expectations play in guiding memorial reconstruction.

REFERENCES

Aderman, D., & Brehm, S. (1976). On the recall of initial attitudes following counterattitudinal advocacy: An experimental reexamination. *Personality and Social Psychology Bulletin, 2,* 59–62.

Alba, J. W., & Hasher, L. (1983). Is memory schematic? *Psychological Bulletin, 93,* 203–231.

Anderson, R. C., & Pichert, J. W. (1978). Recall of previously unrecallable information following a shift in perspective. *Journal of Verbal Learning and Verbal Behavior, 17,* 1–12.

Bargh, J. A., & Thein, R. D. (1985). Individual construct accessibility, person memory, and the recall–judgment link: The case of information overload. *Journal of Personality and Social Psychology, 49,* 1129–1146.

Bartlett, F. C. (1932). *Remembering: A study in experimental and social psychology.* Cambridge, UK: Cambridge University Press.

Bates, E., Masling, M., & Kintsch, W. (1978). Recognition memory for aspects of dialogue. *Journal of Experimental Psychology: Human Learning and Memory, 4,* 187–197.

Bekerian, D. A., & Bowers, J. M. (1983). Eyewitness testimony: Were we misled? *Journal of Experimental Psychology: Learning, Memory, and Cognition, 9,* 139–145.

Bellezza, F. S., & Bower, G. H. (1981). Person stereotypes and memory for people. *Journal of Personality and Social Psychology, 41,* 856–865.

Bem, D. J., & McConnell, H. K. (1970). Testing the self-perception explanation of dissonance phenomena: On the salience of premanipulation attitudes. *Journal of Personality and Social Psychology, 14,* 23–31.

Brewer, W. F., & Treyens, J. C. (1981). Role of schemata in memory for places. *Cognitive Psychology, 13,* 207–230.

Brockway, J. F., Chmielewski, D., & Cofer, C. N. (1974). Remembering prose: Productivity and accuracy constraints in recognition memory. *Journal of Verbal Learning and Verbal Behavior, 13,* 194–208.

Cantor, N., & Mischel, W. (1977). Traits as prototypes: Effects on recognition memory. *Journal of Personality and Social Psychology, 35,* 38–48.

Carlston, D. E. (1980). The recall and use of traits and events in social inference processes. *Journal of Experimental Social Psychology, 16,* 303–328.

Chapman, L. J., & Chapman, J. P. (1967). Genesis of popular but erroneous diagnostic observations. *Journal of Abnormal Psychology, 72,* 193–204.

Clark, L. F., & Woll, S. B. (1981). Stereotype biases: A reconstructive analysis of their role in reconstructive memory. *Journal of Personality and Social Psychology, 41,* 1064–1072.

Cohen, C. E. (1981). Person categories and social perception: Testing some boundaries of the processing effects of prior knowledge. *Journal of Personality and Social Psychology, 40,* 441–452.

Cohen, C. E., & Ebbesen, E. B. (1979). Observational goals and schema activation: A theoretical framework for behavior perception. *Journal of Experimental Social Psychology, 15*, 305–329.

Conway, M., & Ross, M. (1984). Getting what you want by revising what you had. *Journal of Personality and Social Psychology, 47*, 738–748.

Darley, J. M., & Gross, P. G. (1983). A hypothesis-confirming bias in labeling effects. *Journal of Personality and Social Psychology, 44*, 20–33.

Devine, P. G., Hirt, E. R., & Gehrke, E. M. (1990). Diagnostic and confirmation strategies in trait hypothesis testing. *Journal of Personality and Social Psychology, 58*, 952–963.

Ditto, P. H., & Lopez, D. F. (1992). Motivated skepticism: Use of differential decision criteria for preferred and nonpreferred conclusions. *Journal of Personality and Social Psychology, 63*, 568–584.

Dooling, D. J., & Christiaansen, R. E. (1977). Episodic and semantic aspects of memory for prose. *Journal of Experimental Psychology: Human Learning and Memory, 3*, 428–436.

Fazio, R. H., Lenn, T. M., & Effrein, E. A. (1983). Spontaneous attitude formation. *Social Cognition, 2*, 217–234.

Fazio, R. H., & Williams, C. J. (1986). Attitude accessibility as a moderator of the attitude–perception and attitude–behavior relations: An investigation of the 1984 Presidential election. *Journal of Personality and Social Psychology, 51*, 505–514.

Fischhoff, B. (1975). Hindsight ≠ foresight: The effects of outcome knowledge on judgment under uncertainty. *Journal of Experimental Psychology: Human Perception and Performance, 1*, 288–299.

Fiske, S. T., & Neuberg, S. L. (1990). A continuum of information processing from category-based to individuating processes: Influences of information and motivation on attention and interpretation. In M. P. Zanna (Ed.), *Advances in experimental social psychology* (Vol. 23, pp. 1–74). New York: Academic Press.

Fiske, S. T., & Taylor, S. E. (1991). *Social cognition* (2nd ed.). New York: McGraw-Hill.

Gauld, A., & Stephenson, G. M. (1967). Some experiments relating to Bartlett's theory of remembering. *British Journal of Psychology, 58*, 39–49.

Ginossar, Z., & Trope, Y. (1987). Problem solving in judgment under uncertainty. *Journal of Personality and Social Psychology, 52*, 464–474.

Goethals, G. R., & Reckman, R. F. (1973). The perception of consistency in attitudes. *Journal of Experimental Social Psychology, 9*, 491–501.

Hamilton, D. L., Katz, L. B., & Leirer, V. O. (1980). Cognitive representation of personality impressions: Organizational processes in first impression formation. *Journal of Personality and Social Psychology, 39*, 1050–1063.

Hamilton, D. L., & Sherman, S. J. (1996). Perceiving persons and groups. *Psychological Review, 103*, 336–355.

Hasher, L., Attig, M. S., & Alba, J. W. (1981). I knew it all along: Or did I? *Journal of Verbal Learning and Verbal Behavior, 20*, 86–96.

Hasher, L., & Griffin, M. (1978). Reconstructive and reproductive processes in memory. *Journal of Experimental Psychology: Human Learning and Memory, 4*, 318–330.

Hastie, R., & Kumar, P. (1979). Person memory: Personality traits as organizing principles in memory for behaviors. *Journal of Personality and Social Psychology, 37*, 25–38.

Higgins, E. T., & Bargh, J. A. (1987). Social cognition and social perception. *Annual Review of Psychology, 38*, 369–425.

Higgins, E. T., & Lurie, L. (1983). Context, categorization, and memory: The "change of standard" effect. *Cognitive Psychology, 15*, 525–547.

Higgins, E. T., & Stangor, C. (1988). A "change-of-standard" perspective on the relations among context, judgment, and memory. *Journal of Personality and Social Psychology, 54*, 181–192.

Hirt, E. R. (1990). Do I see only what I expect?: Evidence for an expectancy-guided retrieval model. *Journal of Personality and Social Psychology, 58*, 937–951.

Hirt, E. R., Erickson, G. A., & McDonald, H. E. (1993). The role of expectancy timing and outcome–consistency in expectancy-guided retrieval. *Journal of Personality and Social Psychology, 65*, 640–656.

Hirt, E. R., McDonald, H. E., & Erickson, G. A. (1995). How do I remember thee? The role of encoding set and delay in reconstructive memory processes. *Journal of Experimental Social Psychology, 31*, 379–409.

Hirt, E. R., McDonald, H. E., Erickson, G. A., & Gruberth, G. (1997). *Spontaneous reprocessing and future projection: Clarifying the role of expectancy timing in reconstructive memory.* Unpublished manuscript, Indiana University–Bloomington.

Johnson, M. K., & Raye, C. L. (1981). Reality monitoring. *Psychological Review, 88*, 67–85.

Keenan, J. M., MacWhinney, B., & Mayhew, D. (1977). Pragmatics in memory: A study in natural conversation. *Journal of Verbal Learning and Verbal Behavior, 16*, 549–560.

Kunda, Z. (1987). Motivated inference: Self-serving generation and evaluation of causal theories. *Journal of Personality and Social Psychology, 53*, 636–647.

Kunda, Z. (1990). The case for motivated reasoning. *Psychological Bulletin, 108*, 480–498.

Kunda, Z., & Sanitioso, R. (1989). Motivated changes in the self-concept. *Journal of Experimental Social Psychology, 25*, 272–285.

Lichtenstein, M., & Srull, T. K. (1987). Processing objectives as a determinant of the relationship between recall and judgment. *Journal of Experimental Social Psychology, 23*, 93–118.

Lingle, J. H., & Ostrom, T. M. (1979). Retrieval selectivity in memory-based impression judgments. *Journal of Personality and Social Psychology, 37*, 180–194.

Loftus, E. F., Miller, D. G., & Burns, H. J. (1978). Semantic integration of verbal information into visual memory. *Journal of Experimental Psychology: Human Learning and Memory, 4*, 19–31.

Lord, C. G., Ross, L., & Lepper, M. (1979). Biased assimilation and attitude polarization: The effects of prior theories on subsequently considered evidence. *Journal of Personality and Social Psychology, 37*, 2098–2109.

Mandler, J. M., & Johnson, N. S. (1977). Rememberance of things parsed: Story structure and recall. *Cognitive Psychology, 9*, 111–151.

McCloskey, M., & Zaragoza, M. (1985). Misleading postevent information and memory for events: Arguments and evidence against memory impairment hypotheses. *Journal of Experimental Psychology: General, 114*, 1–16.

McDonald, H. E., & Hirt, E. R. (1997). When expectancy meets desire: Motivational effects in reconstructive memory. *Journal of Personality and Social Psychology, 72*, 5–23.

McFarland, C., Ross, M., & DeCourville, W. (1989). Women's theories of menstruation and biases in recall of menstrual symptoms. *Journal of Personality and Social Psychology, 57*, 522–531.

McFarland, C., Ross, M., & Giltrow, M. (1992). Biased recollections in older adults: The role of implicit theories of aging. *Journal of Personality and Social Psychology, 62*, 837–850.

Olson, J. M., Roese, N. J., & Zanna, M. P. (1996). Expectancies. In E. T. Higgins & A. W. Kruglanski (Eds.), *Social psychology: Handbook of basic principles* (pp. 211–238). New York: Guilford Press.

Pyszczynski, T., & Greenberg, J. (1987). Toward an integration of cognitive and motivational perspectives on social inference: A biased hypothesis-testing model. In L. Berkowitz (Ed.), *Advances in experimental social psychology* (Vol. 20, pp. 297–340). New York: Academic Press.

Quattrone, G. A., & Tversky, A. (1984). Causal versus diagnostic contingencies: On self-deception and on the voter's illusion. *Journal of Personality and Social Psychology, 46*, 237–248.

Roediger, H. L., & McDermott, K. B. (1995). Creating false memories: Remembering words not presented in lists. *Journal of Experimental Psychology: Learning, Memory, and Cognition, 21*, 803–814.

Ross, M. (1989). Relation of implicit theories to the construction of personal histories. *Psychological Review, 96*, 341–357.

Ross, M., & Conway, M. (1986). Remembering one's own past: The construction of personal histories. In R. M. Sorrentino & E. T. Higgins (Eds.), *Handbook of motivation and cognition: Foundations of social behavior* (Vol. 1, pp. 122–144). New York: Guilford Press.

Ross, M., McFarland, C., & Fletcher, G. J. O. (1981). The effect of attitude on recall of personal histories. *Journal of Personality and Social Psychology, 10*, 627–634.

Rothbart, M., Evans, M., & Fulero, S. (1979). Recall for confirming events: Memory processes and the maintenance of social stereotyping. *Journal of Experimental Social Psychology, 15*, 343–355.

Sanitioso, R., Kunda, Z., & Fong, G. T. (1990). Motivated recruitment of autobiographical memory. *Journal of Personality and Social Psychology, 59*, 229–241.

Schul, Y., & Burnstein, E. (1985a). The informational basis of social judgments: Using past impression rather than the trait description in forming a new impression. *Journal of Experimental Social Psychology, 21*, 421–439.

Schul, Y., & Burnstein, E. (1985b). When discounting fails: Conditions under which individuals use discredited information in making a judgment. *Journal of Personality and Social Psychology, 49*, 894–903.

Silka, L. (1989). *Intuitive judgments of change.* New York: Springer-Verlag.

Skov, R. B., & Sherman, S. J. (1986). Information gathering processes: Diagnosticity, hypothesis-confirming strategies, and perceived hypothesis confirmation. *Journal of Experimental Social Psychology, 22*, 93–121.

Snyder, M., & Uranowitz, S. W. (1978). Reconstructing the past: Some cognitive consequences of person perception. *Journal of Personality and Social Psychology, 36*, 941–950.

Spiro, R. J. (1980). Accommodative reconstruction in prose recall. *Journal of Verbal Learning and Verbal Behavior, 19*, 84–95.

Srull, T. K. (1981). Person memory: Some tests of associative storage and retrieval models. *Journal of Experimental Psychology: Human Learning and Memory, 7*, 440–462.

Srull, T. K., Lichtenstein, M., & Rothbart, M. (1985). Associative storage and retrieval processes in person memory. *Journal of Experimental Psychology: Learning, Memory, and Cognition, 11,* 316–345.

Stangor, C., & McMillan, D. (1992). Memory for expectancy-congruent and expectancy-incongruent information: A review of the social and social developmental literatures. *Psychological Bulletin, 111,* 42–61.

Trope, Y., & Liberman, A. (1996). Social hypothesis testing: Cognitive and motivational mechanisms. In E. T. Higgins & A. W. Kruglanski (Eds.), *Social psychology: Handbook of basic principles* (pp. 239–270). New York: Guilford Press.

Tulving, E., & Pearlstone, Z. (1966). Availability versus accessibility of information in memory for words. *Journal of Verbal Learning and Verbal Behavior, 5,* 381–391.

Tulving, E., & Psotka, J. (1971). Retroactive inhibition in free recall: Inaccessibility of information available in the memory store. *Journal of Experimental Psychology, 87,* 1–8.

Tulving, E., & Thomson, D. M. (1973). Encoding specificity and retrieval processes in episodic memory. *Psychological Review, 80,* 352–373.

von Hippel, W., Sekaquaptewa, D., & Vargas, P. (1996). On the role of encoding processes in stereotype formation. In M. P. Zanna (Ed.), *Advances in experimental social psychology* (Vol. 27, pp. 177–254). New York: Academic Press.

Vorauer, J. D., & Ross, M. (1993). Exploring the nature and implications of functional independence: Do mental representations of the self become independent of their bases? In T. K. Srull & R. S. Wyer (Eds.), *Advances in social cognition* (Vol. 5, pp. 157–169). Hillsdale, NJ: Erlbaum.

Wyer, R. S., & Gordon, S. E. (1982). The recall of information about persons and groups. *Journal of Experimental Social Psychology, 18,* 128–164.

Wyer, R. S., Srull, T. K., & Gordon, S. E. (1984). The effects of predicting a person's behavior on subsequent trait judgments. *Journal of Experimental Social Psychology, 20,* 29–46.

Wyer, R. S., Srull, T. K., Gordon, S. E., & Hartwick, J. (1982). Effects of processing objectives on the recall of prose material. *Journal of Personality and Social Psychology, 43,* 674–688.

Zadny, J., & Gerard, H. B. (1974). Attributed intentions and informational selectivity. *Journal of Experimental Social Psychology, 10,* 34–52.

Zangwill, O. L. (1972). Remembering revisited. *Quarterly Journal of Experimental Psychology, 24,* 123–138.

CHAPTER 4

PSYCHOTHERAPY AND REPORTS OF EARLY SEXUAL TRAUMA
A Conceptual Framework for Understanding Memory Errors

Michael R. Nash

Although psychoanalytical theorists such as Roy Schafer (1983) have been beating the hermeneutic drum for many years now, and researchers like Elizabeth Loftus (1993), Donald Spence (1982), and Martin Orne (Orne, Whitehouse, Dinges, & Orne, 1988) have issued many an empirical caution about the reconstructive nature of memory, practitioners retained a deeply entrenched conviction that when our patients report a "memory" of a childhood trauma it must in some essential way be true. But there is now a growing sensitivity to the possibility that at least some reports of early trauma may not in fact be true (Tavris, 1993). It is not that all adults who suddenly report a memory of early trauma are somehow indulging in a believed-in fantasy but that in some cases the trauma happened and in some cases it did not.

It may be argued with some justification that the historical veridicality of such reports are irrelevant to the process of psychotherapy. In short, it may not really matter whether the event actually happened or not—here the premise is that if the meaning of the report is properly managed therapeutically, the patient will get better. Of course, for forensic purposes it *does* matter whether or not the event happened. And certainly, if we are to ever construct a scientifically viable theory of human psychological development we must know what actually happened in the child's environment and we must not be satisfied with retrospective reports. Moreover, if we are to ever understand the relationship between trauma, dissociation, and hypnotizability, we must know what really happened.

Logically, two broad types of mnemonic errors are possible when adult psychotherapy patients reflect on whether or not they were traumatized as children (see Figure 4.1.). They may believe they were not traumatized when in fact they were (false negative), or they may believe they were traumatized when in fact they were not (false positive). It behooves science to consider the incidence, importance, and clinical implications of these two types of errors so that we may adjust the epistemological status we give reports of abuse/non-abuse. I contend that it is exceedingly important to realize that the problem of false positives and the problem of false negatives are distinct. The existence of one type of error does not necessarily eliminate the possibility of the other type of error. For instance, proponents of pseudomemory sometimes employ a curious twist of logic such that if false positives are demonstrated to occur, the validity of false negatives (e.g., repression and dissociation) is necessarily negated. Logically this does not follow at all. If patients sometimes report a traumatic event when it did not happen (a false positive), we are not required to reject the possibility that patients may fail to remember such an event when it *did* occur (a false negative). After all, if cultural and psychological factors can create the need to believe that certain events occurred when they did not (false positives), why then can these same factors not operate in such a way as to engender *not* remembering certain events when they did in actuality occur? The conceptual sword cuts both ways. A more productive approach to both false positive and false negative mnemonic errors is to treat them separately and to develop a healthy appreciation for the malleability of human memory and the fallibility of self-report. Champions of pseudomemory and champions of repression/dissociation would do well to empirically (and separately) test whether, and how, false positives and false negatives present clinically and cease trying to argue that the existence of one precludes the existence of the other.

| | EVENT ACTUALLY OCCURRED | |
	YES	NO
EVENT REMEMBERED AS HAPPENING — YES	ACCURATE	ERROR (FALSE POSITIVE)
EVENT REMEMBERED AS HAPPENING — NO	ERROR (FALSE POSITIVE)	ACCURATE

FIGURE 4.1. The relationship of a mnemonic experience to the historical event.

As a small step toward that end I first very briefly review the theoretical and empirical foundations that argue respectively for the existence of false positives ("pseudomemory")and false negatives ("repression"). Second, I delineate the reasons why we cannot rely on clinical efficacy as a way of ruling out either type of error. Third, I present summaries of two successful therapies, one illustrating an example of an almost certain instance of a false-positive error and the other a fairly certain instance of a false-negative error.

THEORETICAL AND EMPIRICAL GROUNDING FOR THE OCCURRENCE OF FALSE POSITIVES

At least three related research traditions support the contention that false positives are indeed an important part of human cognition: memory research, developmental psychopathology, and contemporary psychoanalytical theory. It is abundantly clear now that human memory is not immutably stored in pristine form somewhere in the brain as Freud and his contemporaries supposed. Indeed organization, encoding, and recall are highly dependent on meaning structures at the time of the event and subsequent beliefs about feeling and reality (Bradburn, Rips, & Shevell, 1987; Goodman & Hahn, 1987; Loftus, Korf, & Schooler, 1989). Loftus sums up the memory research on this topic quite eloquently:

> Thus our representation of the past takes on a living, shifting reality; it is not fixed and immutable, not a place way back there that is preserved in stone, but a living thing that changes shape. expands, shrinks, and expands again, an amoebalike creature with powers to make us laugh, and cry, and clench our fists. Enormous powers—powers even to make us believe in something that never happened. (Loftus & Ketcham, 1991, p. 20)

In addition, many contemporary psychoanalytical theorists and developmental theorists argue that the psychic structure of a child is unalterably changed during the course of development. As a consequence, old stages, or infantile modes of functioning, are simply not "there" to be retrieved (Bruner, 1968; Erdelyi, 1985; Gill, cited in Tuttman, 1982; Peterfreund, 1978; Piaget, 1973; Rubinfine, 1981; Spitz, 1965; Westin, 1989). These theorists offer persuasive evidence that humans do not passively record the events around them, thereby creating exact copies in the mind. Instead, memories and cognitive schemas appear to be transformed into the structure of successive stages and thereby changed forever (Eagle, 1984; Piaget, 1973; Piaget & Inhelder, 1969). Indeed, contrary to earlier notions of psychopathology as a return to infantile phases of development, a growing research literature fails to support the notion that adult psychopathology is similar to, or even properly analogous to, normal phases in child development (Donaldson &

Westerman, 1986; Flavell, 1985; Harter, 1977, 1983, 1986; Harter & Buddin, 1987; Westin, 1989).

Though perhaps not the most compelling, certainly the most controversial evidence for false positives emerges from the dramatic increase in reports of bizarre satanic ritual abuse, especially among dissociative patients. Ganaway (1991) found that up to 50% of dissociative disordered patients report satanic ritualistic abuse involving heinous, even cannibalistic crimes carried out by an organized network of secret covens. These fantastic accounts, though compellingly rendered, have rarely, if ever, been confirmed by law enforcement authorities. Finally, several studies appear to document that false memories can, and do, occur under laboratory and field conditions (Abelson, Loftus, & Greenwald, 1992; Haugaard, Reppucci, Laurd, & Nauful, 1991; Laurence & Perry, 1983; Neisser & Harsch, 1992; Piaget, 1962; Pynoos & Nader, 1989; Weeks, Lynn, Green, & Brentar, 1992).

Taken together, there appears to be a sufficient theoretical and empirical basis to support the contention that at least under some circumstances, individuals report memory for events that did not in fact occur. The caveat here is that no laboratory researcher has yet produced false memories of the emotional intensity and gravity of early sexual trauma. While clinicians and researchers will undoubtedly continue to debate the ecological validity of these theories and their associated studies, no responsible investigator can simply ignore the possibility of this form of memory error.

As to the evidence about whether hypnosis contributes to the problem of false-positive memories, the findings from the lab and the field are about as clear as they can get. False positives happen, hypnosis may have something to do with it, and the responsible elements of the hypnosis community acknowledge this fact.

But it is important to note that hypnosis has gotten a bit of a raw deal on this issue. Of the hundreds of expressive therapeutic techniques now extant, hypnosis is the only one for which there is substantial data on memory and its accuracy. For various historical reasons, no other therapy technique was so scrupulously examined as to its effect on memory. Because for decades the hypnosis research community stood alone as concerned about this issue, they are the only ones with the data. As a result, hypnosis became a kind of whipping boy for the sins of expressive psychotherapy in general. The media and the courts focus on the memory-distorting effects of hypnosis precisely because it is the hypnosis literature that so rigorously documented how plastic memory is in treatment. Hypnosis researchers painfully and tediously documented the role of expectation, suggestion, imagination, and fantasy as codeterminants of what patients report remembering *in* treatment and outside of it. It is not that these factors are absent in other expressive therapies; it is just that if researchers attempt to find out what science has to say about how memories can be distorted in therapy, they are going to encounter hypnosis and not much of anything else.

I believe a more realistic assessment of the situation is that–hypnosis research has delivered an important and disturbing message to society at large: Passionately believed-in recollections about the past are not always what they appear to be. This message is so profoundly upsetting to cherished conventional notions of memory that courts, and some elements of the mental health community, yearn to kill the messenger.

The 1992 debate on recovered memories provides an excellant example of this type of thinking. During the well-publicized and attended convention debate between Elizabeth Loftus and John Briere, Briere somewhat piously cautioned that, although he believes in the accuracy of recovered memories, he does not recommend hypnosis be used in the treatment of abuse cases because of problems with suggestion. Apparently John Briere believes that therapists can avoid the operation of expectation, suggestion, fantasy, transference, and imagination merely by not doing hypnosis. This kind of logic betrays a recklessly naive model of human cognition.

It is indeed chilling to contemplate the possibility that there simply is no structural difference between believed-in fantasy and memory of historical fact, and that patients might get better regardless of whether or not new "insights" are true. But it is the special responsibility of clinicians to be mindful that getting better in therapy does not bestow on the patient a mantle of infallibility. Indeed what we call insight may be more a process of creation than a process of discovery.

THEORETICAL AND EMPIRICAL GROUNDING FOR THE OCCURRENCE OF FALSE NEGATIVES

The research literature on repression is complex and exceedingly controversial. Two influential reviews of the research literature presented diametrically opposite conclusions, with Holmes (1974, 1990) asserting that repression does not exist and Erdelyi and Goldberg (1979) that it does. But as R. Hansen and C. Hansen (1988) observe: "a consensus for the existence of repression may be emerging" (p. 811). Freud (1915/1957) asserted that "the motive and purpose of repression was nothing else than the avoidance of unpleasure" (p. 153), and current research definitions generally operationalize repression along these lines (Davis & Schwartz, 1987). Three research traditions contributed to recent developments in our understanding of repression since the Holmes (1974) and Erdelyi and Goldberg (1979) reviews. I briefly review these areas next.

Research on the "Repressor Personality"

One recent approach to investigating the viability of the construct of repression is to view it not as a state phenomenon but as a trait. Weinberger and Schwartz (1979) developed a valid typology based on pattern of scores from self-report measures of defensiveness and anxiety, with "repressors" obtaining a pattern of low anxiety with high defensiveness. Subsequent research suggests that the patterns of emotion-laden memories for repressors are fundamentally different from those of nonrepressors with that of repressors being less elaborated and more constricted. Further, repression appears to involve a relative inaccessibility to unpleasant emotional memories, especially linked with fear or threat (Bonanno, Davis, Singer, & Schwartz, 1991; Davis & Schwartz, 1987; R. Hansen & C. Hansen, 1988; C. Hansen, R. Hansen, & Shantz, 1992).

Implicit Memory Research

A premise of those who stress the importance of repressive and dissociative mechanisms operative in the generation of false negatives is that patients' behavior and experience are in part determined by the early trauma even though memory of the event is outside awareness. Information processing studies appear to confirm that events can occur outside awareness that nonetheless dramatically affect mental functioning (Eich, 1984; Jacoby, 1988; Kihlsrom, 1987; Schacter & Graf, 1986; Zajonc, 1980, 1984). Schacter (1983) posits an explicit and implicit memory. The former involves conscious memory of an event, whereas the latter involves change in behavior and experience caused by the event but without conscious memory of the event. Though these theorists are in no way equating implicit memory with the symptoms of psychiatric patients, the cognitive science literature does provide ample evidence for the proposition that preferences, attitudes, and behaviors can be shaped by events that are not consciously perceived or remembered.

Hypnosis Research on Memory

Advances in research in nonconscious processing of information have established hypnosis as "perhaps the pre-eminent method for investigating different levels of consciousness" (Holroyd, 1992, p. 220). Here the nonconscious processing of information can take on the form of frank amnesia for what would otherwise be salient events in the laboratory or clinic (Bertrand, Spanos, & Parkinson, 1983; Howard & Coe, 1980; Kihlstrom, 1978, 1982, 1983; Kihlstrom, Evans, Orne, & Orne, 1980). Further, because phenomena such as posthypnotic amnesia are easily reversible upon administration of a prearranged cue, the amnesia is clearly not attributable to changes during the encoding stage of information acquisition (Holroyd, 1992; Kihlstrom, 1987). As Holroyd (1992) notes, theorists have hypothesized a number of mechanisms other than repression to account for the sometimes dramatic alterations in memory function following an amnesia suggestion: These include dissociation (Hilgard, 1977), disrupted search (Evans & Kihlstrom, 1973), strategic enactment (Spanos, 1986), and output inhibition (Huesmann, Gruder, & Dorst, 1987). Nevertheless, disruptions in the memory retrieval process of a kind at least analogous to those presented by patients can be reliably demonstrated with highly hypnotizable subjects. These distortions were demonstrated to involve shifts in retrieval process, memory organization, and manifestations of implicit memory.

As with false-positive errors, there appears to be sufficient research and theoretical support for the contention that false negative errors can occur. Under certain circumstances events that might otherwise be accurately represented in memory nonetheless fail to reach awareness. The repressor personality research further supports the view that this disengagement between memory and awareness can be engendered by strong feelings of threat or fear which may in turn alter the encoding process. The caveat here is that the kinds of longitudinal studies necessary to document the gross false negatives reported in the clinical literature are simply not extant. As with false positives, we can document the plausibility of these phenomena, but we cannot precisely replicate them in the laboratory.

In sum, there is sufficient evidence in the memory research to support a working hypothesis that both false-positive and false-negative errors may occur in the consultation room and in the work-a-day world. Although it is clearly premature to claim that either is definitively demonstrated to be operative in reports of early sexual trauma, neither is it possible to simply dismiss one or the other as unimportant or inoperative in such cases.

CLINICAL EFFICACY AND HISTORICAL VERIDICALITY

There is ample research evidence that expressive psychotherapies are beneficial. The process–outcome psychotherapy research demonstrates quite clearly that it is helpful for patients to reflect on their present feelings and their past in a disciplined and compassionate therapeutic context (Blanchard, Andrasik, Ahler, Teders, & O'Keefe, 1980; Lambert, Shapiro, & Bergin, 1986; Meltzoff & Kornreich, 1970; Miller & Berman, 1983; Nicholson & Berman, 1983; Rachman & Wilson, 1980; Smith, Glass, & Miller, 1980). Psychotherapeutic techniques (including hypnosis) can be quite efficacious and should continue to be used. What I contend is that this clinical utility may have little or nothing to do with uncovering the truth about the patient's past and we should stop claiming that it does in courtrooms and in our own clinical theories. In short, what patients think they have found out about their past may be helpful, but that does not necessarily mean it is accurate.

Examples abound in the historical reviews of healing (Spanos & Gottlieb, 1979). Three hundred years ago a young woman suffering from what we would call glove anesthesia might have sought help from the village priest. The causative agent may have been construed by the priest as demonic possession. The priest might invite the young woman to search her memory for relevant evidence concerning the specific nature of the demon; memories emerge of strange occurrences involving a hellish imp; an exorcism is performed; the woman is cured. Clearly the effectiveness of the therapy in no way supports the accuracy of the woman's memory concerning the existence of imps per se.

Let us consider why clinical utility and historical veridicality are so confounded in psychoanalytical and other insight-oriented therapies. The problem may reside in the very language used by clinical theorists to describe expressive, insight-oriented, or uncovering therapies. We assume that our patients are indeed *expressing* something that was there all along but somehow hidden; that they are *seeing* something that was there all along but somehow enshrouded; that we are *uncovering* something that was there all along but somehow obscured. And we assume this "thing" is the truth. I believe that patients who report newly remembered traumas, at least the neurotic-level patients, do eventually get better to the extent that they experience themselves as recognizing the past traumatic event and to the extent that they connect this event to their contemporary experience and behavior, especially in the arena of the relationship with the therapist. But does this mean that the report is really true. The language and basic tenet of dynamic therapies may seduce us into believing that we have indeed uncovered the truth, that we have discovered the pathogenic event and it has liberated our patient.

Why does it seem so natural for us to confound clinical utility and historical event? It must be remembered that Freud was as passionate and relentless a natural scientist as ever existed. It should not be surprising then that some of his theories were almost naive models of psychic cause and effect. I believe that at the root of this "truth–clinical utility" problem is one of Freud's earliest most appealing ideas about the lawfulness of psychopathology: his concept of temporal regression as enumerated in his 1917 supplement to *Interpretation of Dreams* (1917/1957). Freud based his concept of temporal regression on the assumption of an orderly pattern of human development from simpler, less organized states to more complex, advanced states. He (1915/1957) also maintained that these structures in human development are imperishable and under special circumstances may "again become the mode of expression of the forces in the mind" (p. 285), and that "the essence of mental disease lies in a return to earlier states of affective life and of functioning" (p. 286). Many contemporary psychoanalytical theorists and cognitive developmental psychologists embrace the idea that old developmental stages remain imperishable and that psychopathology is most essentially a regression to, or eruption of, one or more of these previously abandoned modes of relating to self and others (Balint, 1968; Bion, 1977; Kohut, 1971; Langer, 1970; Stolorow & Lachman, 1980; Werner, 1948).

The notion that temporal regression is possible and that psychopathology is a lawful undoing of development is exceedingly appealing to clinicians and theorists who struggle to make sense of the seemingly random disorganization arising from pathology. A formulation based on temporal regression defines a linear continuity between presumed etiological factors in childhood (like a trauma) and the adult symptoms themselves. It charts a course for treatment involving a therapeutic regression to the developmental stage in question, reemergence of long repressed memories and feeling states, and a gradual resumption of development from that point. I believe that it is Freud's mistaken concept of the imperishability of psychic structures (memories, modes of relating, psychosexual stages) and his related claim that patients have access to these stages through regression that underlie our propensity to infer that patient reports of trauma are quite literally reproductions of an historical event.

In sum, we cannot with certainty rely on clinical efficacy to validate the mnemonic experience of our patients in therapy—for some of our successful therapy patients, narrative truth and historical truth may be almost identical; for others there may be little or no correspondence (Spence, 1982). Thus the problem of false-positive and false-negative errors persists. For the purpose of clinical illustration, I present two cases which I believe demonstrate an occurrence of a false-positive memory error and a false-negative error respectively in the context of successful psychotherapy.

A UFO ABDUCTION: AN EXAMPLE OF A PROBABLE FALSE-POSITIVE MEMORY ERROR

A 31-year-old single, white male patient consulted me, reporting recent multiple flashbacks of a previously unremembered traumatic incident that occurred when he was 17 years old. He was acutely anxious, preoccupied with the incident, experiencing nightmares, interpersonally withdrawn, physiologically hyperreactive, and in short quite indistinguishable from posttraumatic stress disorder patients. Interviewing and testing revealed him to have a somewhat ruminative cognitive style, and he was clearly not psychotic. This was a quite successful professional young man whose sexual, family, interpersonal, and work adjustment had been reasonably satisfactory.

He related to me that he had always known that something odd had happened to him when he was 17. What he had *always* remembered was that on a hot summer day he and a male friend had taken a trip to a particularly scenic and isolated part of the Rocky mountains, only a few miles from his home. He and his friend both remember walking along a path together about twilight, near a stand of red woods trees. Then they came upon something very odd. It was a kind of brightly glowing grub (insect larva) on the path. They both moved up to the grub for a closer look. Suddenly there was a bright flash of light which startled them both. Then there was another flash of light. They had no idea what these things were. In some distress, they walked briskly back to the car. The odd thing was that when they returned home they discovered that it was 11:30 at night. They had lost approximately 2 hours of time. The patient reported that this occurrence was the basis for a scary story he and his friend would relate at appropriate times to friends around a campfire. Though it had always puzzled him, it was in a fanciful and not distressing way. Three months before he consulted me, however, he picked up one of the popular books about UFO abductions . . . and this caused quite a bit of distress. He read 60 pages and was so terrified that he had to put the book down. He contacted the author of the book who happened to be conducting a workshop in a neighboring state. In short, the patient and his friend visited the author; they were both hypnotized by the author twice during the weekend. My patient's friend reported no memories of being abducted, but my patient had two extraordinary hypnotic experiences filled with vivid details of the aliens, their spacecraft, and a peculiar machine that they attached to his penis to obtain samples of sperm (this instrument is a commonly reported among abductees). Further, other memories of previous abductions were revealed during the hypnosis. The author's conclusion was that although the patient's friend had not really been abducted, the patient had. As is seen so often in these cases the patient began to wonder whether there had been many more incidents of abduction throughout his life. As I mentioned earlier he was acutely anxious, sleep disordered, prone to night-mares, and physiologically hyperreactive. Thus, he came to me in a great deal of turmoil, acutely anxious, hoping that I might help him clarify what had and had not happened.

I believe I successfully treated this highly hypnotizable man over a period of 3 months using standard uncovering techniques and employing hypnosis on two occasions. My stance with him was that the abduction material as elaborated by the original hypnosis must be immensely important, but I told him that my operating hypothesis was that it was not literally true. Hypnosis and free association did enable him to elaborate more detail of the abduction with some attending dramatic abreaction. My persistent attention to symbolic manifestations of conflictual material contained in the abduction material, while decidedly unappreciated by him initially, did yield some insight around tolerating his own passive–dependent longings. About 2 months into this therapy his symptoms abated: He was sleeping normally again, his rumina-tions and flashbacks had resolved themselves, he returned to his usual level of interpersonal engagement, and his productivity at work improved. What we did, worked. Nevertheless, let me underscore this: He walked out of my office as utterly convinced that he had been abducted as when he walked in. As a matter of fact he thanked me for helping him "fill in the gaps of my memory."

Here we have a stark example of a tenaciously held conviction about the past, which is almost certainly not true in all its detail but which nonetheless has all the signs of a previously repressed traumatic event. I could discern no difference between this patient's clinical presentation regarding the trauma and that of my sexually abused patients. Nevertheless, the patient seemed to get better as he was able to elaborate on the report of trauma and integrate it into his own view of the world.

AN EARLY SEXUAL SEDUCTION: AN EXAMPLE
OF A PROBABLE FALSE-NEGATIVE MEMORY ERROR

A 46-year-old man presented with complaints of depression, social withdrawal, excessive sleeping, violent outbursts, sexual problems over the previous 2 months, and some mild suicidal ideation. The patient was a well-educated individual from the southwestern region of the United States with a sputtering career in electronic engineering. He was married, and at the time was taking courses at a community college to help redirect his career. He reported inconstant parenting in a rural community, with a father who had died when he was quite young and a mother who seemed prone to overly dramatic hysterical outbursts. From early adolescence through his mid-twenties the patient reported experimenting with drugs. But it was alcohol that became a serious problem. Throughout this period he seems to have been a vocational underachiever. Though he completed his bachelor's degree he was exceedingly dissatisfied with himself and was prone to emotional outbursts. Through Alcoholics Anonymous he had abstained from alcohol use entirely for the 10 years prior to treatment with me. But he remained an underachiever vocationally.

My initial formulation was of an introjective depression such that the patient experienced himself as unworthy of pleasure: sexually, at work, and in relationships with authority figures. There was a figural componant of self-punitiveness that moved the patient to undo and spoil anything phallic, from an erection to a work product, to school. I anticipated sessions of therapy that would address issues of inhibited aggression, and would be saturated with themes of competition, power, and guilt.

What brought the patient into treatment was the 2-month exacerbation of symptoms above noted. Interestingly this was coincident with the emergence of two very troubling and intrusive unbidden images. One image was of himself at the age of 9, being surrounded by a group of older threatening children in an unfamiliar house. This image was vague but nonetheless highly charged with fear. He wondered if something sexual had happened at that time. The second was an image of himself curled up on his bed at home, sucking his thumb. By the time therapy began the patient was becoming increasingly preoccupied with what these images could mean. As is my custom, I acknowledged his curiosity about the intrusive images and assured him that they must be important and that we should try to understand them. But I also shared with him the fundamentals of my clinical formulation and recommended that we focus our work on addressing his dramatically self-destructive flight from his own feelings and needs. He was amenable to this approach.

A period of five sessions followed, during which I introduced the patient to hypnosis, finding him to be highly hypnotizable. Initial work on the intrusive images was quite productive of intense emotion (mostly fear) but bereft of specific new content. Eventually, however, the patient began to elaborate on the first image as being of a familiar (not unfamiliar) house. It seemed to be a house in his rural Texas home, the house of an older child whom he knew only tangentially. Though details were still missing, he could identify a distant cousin who remained in the background during whatever attack there was, if any. He remembered lying face down with his buttocks exposed. He also remembered boys with erections, apparently masturbating. At his point (about 12 sessions into the therapy) the focus of our work returned to the initial formulation and symptom cluster involving introjective depression. Outside of hypnosis we explored and worked through his conflicts over "standing out" in any way, almost always utilizing the images of the trauma as an anchor. It was during this work that some of his more florid symptoms began to be resolved: sex with his wife became reasonably satisfying, his perfectionism at work was eased, his procrastination and self-sabotage at school ceased, his insomnia decreased. At this point I was satisfied but he was not. He wanted to know more precisely what had, and had not, happened to him at age 9. In this case there was a fairly definitive means of finding out, one which he hesitated to pursue: He could contact his cousin to ask him.

After much equivocation on this issue he finally decided to ask his cousin about the incident and to invite him to one of our last therapy sessions. His cousin was a 45-year-old oil contractor who lived out of town. Though reluctant initially, with acute embarrassment the patient's cousin declared that he remembered the incident quite clearly. Apparently there were four or five boys (variously related to one another) who during that time would became involved in mutual masturbation and sex play among themselves. During the incident in question the patient had stumbled upon their activities and was unwillingly incorporated into them. There was no sodomy, but the patient was masturbated upon by "several" of the boys. The cousin claimed to have been appalled by the incident but was unwilling to stop it. He was surprised to find that after the incident the patient acted as though it never happened.

It seems reasonable to infer from the third-party verification in this case that an emotionally charged sexual event had indeed occurred to the patient when he was 9 years old. We cannot know all the details of the incident with certainty, but we do know that the patient reported a period of not remembering the incident, had affect-laden imagery emerged relative to the incident later in his life, and that fuller (though not complete) elaboration of the incident was associated with hypnosis and psychotherapy.

OVERVIEW OF BOTH CASES

For the purpose of clinical efficacy all we need to know is that the patients were helped to resolve a cluster of debilitating symptoms in part by enabling them to elaborate more fully their mnemonic experience and by helping them to integrate these experiences into their own self-narratives. The issue of historical truth is another matter. In the UFO abduction case at least, getting better had nothing to do with real insight, recovery of real memories, or uncovering of the truth in any historical sense. Whether the mnemonic experience derives from highly symbolic imaginal material, screen memory, or actual memory traces, it is possible that constructing a compelling self-narrative provides some symptom relief. This is where the purposes of clinical utility and explication of developmental psychopathology may diverge. Clinically, the therapy was reasonably successful; but we cannot use this success alone to validate my UFO patient's stories of how his symptoms arose and what they mean historically.

CONCLUSION

Summarizing then, when we are faced with patients who experience themselves as suddenly and agonizingly remembering a previously forgotten trauma, either in the course of therapy or in spontaneous flashback states, we should above all else recognize the enormous clinical importance of this material. And we should indeed consider that these reports might represent memory traces of a historical event (in this sense an undoing of a false-negative error). But we owe it to ourselves, the patients, the patients' families, and society at large, to be mindful that a literal reliving of a historical event is not humanly possible. Memories do not literally *return* in pristine form, unsullied by contemporary factors like suggestion, transference, values, social context, and fantasies elaborated at the time of (and subsequent to) the event. In short, false positives can and do occur. The field must acknowledge the reality of both types of inferential errors concerning self-report of early trauma: false positives and false negatives.

ACKNOWLEDGMENT

This chapter was first published in the *International Journal of Clinical and Experimental Hypnosis* (Nash, 1994). It is adapted here by permission of the journal's editor.

NOTE

1.   It should be noted that Freud's ideas about the imperishability of psychic structures were embedded in the then prevailing *Zeitgeist* of neurophysiology which construed the central nervous system as layer, with archaic memory structures "underneath" more recent ones (Jackson, 1888/1931–1932). Even into the 1950s Penfield and Rasmussen (1950) contended that material emerging under electrode stimulation of discrete sites exposed during surgery was akin to a tape recording of the brain.

REFERENCES

Abelson, R. P., Loftus, E. F., & Greenwald, A. G. (1992). Attempts to improve the accuracy of self-reports of voting. In J. M. Tanur (Ed.), *Questions about survey questions: Meaning, memory, expression, and social interactions in surveys* (pp. 138–153). New York: Russell Sage.

Balint, M. (1968). *The basic fault: Therapeutic aspects of regression.* London: Tavistock.

Bertrand, L. D., Spanos, N. P., & Parkinson, B. (1983). Test of the dissipation hypothesis of hypnotic amnesia. *Psychological Reports, 52,* 667–671.

Bion, W. R. (1977). *Seven servants.* New York: Aronson.

Blanchard, E. B., Andrasik, F., Ahler, T. A., Teders, S. J., & O'Keefe, D. O. (1980). Migraine and tension headache: A meta-analytic review. *Behavior Therapy, 11,* 613–631.

Bonanno, G. A., Davis, P. J., Singer, J. L., & Schwartz, G. E. (1991). The repressor personality and avoidant information processing: A dichotic listening study. *Journal of Research in Personality, 25,* 386–401.

Bradburn, N. M., Rips, L. J., & Shevell, S. K. (1987). Answering autobiographical questions: The impact of memory and inference on surveys. *Science, 236*(10), 157–161.

Bruner, J. S. (1968). *Processes of cognitive growth: Infancy.* Worcester, MA: Clark University Press.

Davis, P. J., & Schwartz, G. E. (1987). Repression and the inaccessibility of affective memories. *Journal of Personality and Social Psychology, 52,* 155–162.

Donaldson, S. K., & Westerman, M. A. (1986). Development of children's understanding of ambivalence and causal theories of emotion. *Developmental Psychology, 22,* 655–662.

Eagle, M. N. (1984). *Recent developments in psychoanalysis: A critical evaluation.* New York: McGraw-Hill.

Eich, E. (1984). Memory for unattended events: Remembering with and without awareness. *Memory and Cognition, 12,* 105–111.

Erdelyi, M. H. (1985). *Psychoanalysis: Freud's cognitive psychology.* New York: Freeman.

Erdelyi, M. H., & Goldberg, B. (1979). Let's not sweep repression under the rug: Toward a cognitive psychology of repression. In J. F. Kihlstrom & F. J. Evans (Eds.), *Functional disorders of memory* (pp. 355–402). Hillsdale, NJ: Erlbaum.

Evans, F. J., & Kihlstrom, J. F. (1973). Posthypnotic amnesia as disrupted retrieval. *Journal of Abnormal Psychology, 82,* 317–323.

Flavell, J. (1985). *Cognitive development* (2nd ed.). Englewood Cliffs, NJ: Prentice-Hall.

Freud, S. (1957). Thoughts for the times on war and death. In J. Strachey (Ed. & Trans.), *The standard edition of the complete works of Sigmund Freud* (Vol. 14, pp. 275–300). London: Hogarth Press. (Original work published 1915)

Freud, S. (1957). A metapsychological supplement to the theory of dreams. In J. Strachey (Ed. & Trans.), *The standard edition of the complete psychological works of Sigmund Freud* (Vol. 14, pp. 222–235). London: Hogarth Press. (Original work published 1917)

Ganaway, G. (1991, August). *Alternative hypotheses regarding satanic ritual abuse memories.* Paper presented at the 99th annual meeting of the American Psychological Association, San Francisco.

Goodman, G. S., & Hahn, A. (1987). Evaluating eyewitness testimony. In I. B. Weiner & A. K. Hess (Eds.), *Handbook of forensic psychology* (pp. 258–292). New York: Wiley.

Hansen, R. D., & Hansen, C. H. (1988). Repression of emotionally tagged memories: The architecture of less complex emotions. *Journal of Personality and Social Psychology, 55,* 811–818.

Hansen, R. D., Hansen, C. H., & Shantz, D. W. (1992). Repression encoding: Discrete appraisals of emotional stimuli. *Journal of Personality and Social Psychology, 63,* 1026–1035.

Harter, S. (1977). A cognitive-developmental approach to children's expression of conflicting feelings and a technique to facilitate such expression in play therapy. *Journal of Consulting and Clinical Psychology, 45,* 417–432.

Harter, S. (1983). Children's understanding of multiple emotions: A cognitive-developmental approach. In W. F. Overton (Ed.), *The relationship between social and cognition development.* Hillsdale, NJ: Erlbaum.

Harter, S. (1986). Cognitive-developmental process in the integration of concepts about emotions and the self. *Social Cognition, 4,* 119–151.

Harter, S., & Buddin, B. J. (1987). Children's understanding of the simultaneity of two emotions: A five-stage developmental acquisition sequence. *Developmental Psychology, 23,* 388–399.

Haugaard, J. J., Reppucci, N. D., Laurd, J., & Nauful, T. (1991). Children definitions of the truth and their competency as witnesses in legal proceedings. *Law and Human Behavior, 15,* 253–272.

Hilgard, E. R. (1977). The problem of divided consciousness: A neodissociation interpretation. *Annals of the New York Academy of Sciences, 296,* 48–59.

Holmes, D. S. (1974). Investigations of repression: Differential recall of material experimentally or naturally associated with ego threat. *Psychological Bulletin, 81,* 632–53.

Holmes, D. S. (1990). The evidence for repression: An examination of sixty years of research. In J. Singer (Ed.). *Repression and dissociation: Implications for personality, theory, psychopathology, and health* (pp. 85–102). Chicago: University of Chicago Press.

Holroyd, J. (1992). Hypnosis as a methodology in psychological research. In E. Fromm & M. R. Nash (Eds.), *Contemporary hypnosis research* (pp. 201–226). New York: Guilford Press.

Howard, M. L., & Coe, W. C. (1980). The effects of context and subjects' perceived control in breaching posthypnotic amnesia. *Journal of Personality, 48,* 342–359.

Huesman, L. R., Gruder, C. L., & Dorst, G. (1987). A process model of posthypnotic amnesia. *Cognitive Psychology, 19,* 33–62.

Jackson, J. H. (1931–1932). *Selected writings of John Hughlings Jackson* (J. Taylor, Ed.). London: Hodder & Stoughton. (Original work published 1888)

Jacoby, L. L. (1988). Memory observed and memory unobserved. In U. Neisser & E. Winograd (Eds.), *Remembering reconsidered: Ecological and traditional approaches to the study of memory* (pp. 145–177). Cambridge, UK: Cambridge University Press.

Kihlstrom, J. F. (1978). Context and cognition in posthypnotic amnesia. *Journal of Clinical and Experimental Hypnosis, 26,* 246–267.

Kihlstrom, J. F. (1982). Hypnosis and the dissociation of memory, with special reference to posthypnotic amnesia. *Research Communications in Psychology, Psychiatry, and Behavior, 7,* 181–197.

Kihlstrom, J. F. (1983). Instructed forgetting: Hypnotic and nonhypnotic. *Journal of Experimental Psychology, 112,* 73–79.

Kihlstrom, J. F. (1987). The cognitive unconscious. *Science, 237,* 1445–1452.

Kihlstrom, J. F., Evans, F. J., Orne, E. C., & Orne, M. T. (1980). Attempting to breach posthypnotic amnesia. *Journal of Abnormal Psychology, 89,* 603–616.

Kohut, H. (1971). *The analysis of the self: A systematic approach to the psychoanalytic treatment of narcissistic personality disorders.* New York: International Universities Press.

Lambert, M. J., Shapiro, D. A., & Bergin, A. E. (1986). The effectiveness of psychotherapy. In S. L. Garfield & A. E. Bergin (Eds.), *Handbook of psychotherapy and behavior change* (3rd ed., pp. 157–211). New York: Wiley.

Langer, J., (1970). Werner's comparative organismic theory. In P. H. Mussen (Ed.), *Carmichael's manual of child psychology* (3rd ed., Vol. 1, pp. 733–771). New York: Wiley.

Laurence, J.-R., & Perry, C. (1983). Hypnotically created memory among highly hypnotizable subjects. *Science, 222,* 523–524.

Loftus, E. F. (1993). The reality of repressed memories. *American Psychologist, 48,* 518–537.

Loftus, E. F., & Ketcham, K. (1991). *Witness for the defense.* New York: St. Martin's Press.

Loftus, E. F., Korf, N. L., & Schooler, J. W. (1989). Misguided memories: Sincere distortions of reality. In J. C. Yuille (Ed.), *Credibility assessment* (pp. 155–174). Dordrecht, The Netherlands: Kluwer Academic.

Martindale, C., Covello, E., West, A. (1986). Primary process in cognition and hemispheric asymmetry. *Journal of Genetic Psychology, 147,* 79–87.

Meltzoff, J., & Kornreich, M. (1970). *Research in psychotherapy.* New York: Atherton Press.

Miller, R. C., & Berman, J. S. (1983). The efficacy of cognitive behavior therapies: A quantitative review of the research evidence. *Psychological Bulletin, 94,* 39–53.

Nash, M. R. (1994). Memory distortion and sexual trauma: The problem of false negatives and false positives. *International Journal of Clinical and Experimental Hypnosis, 42,* 346–362.

Neisser, U., & Harsch, N. (1992). Phantom flashbulbs: False recollections of hearing the news about Challenger. In E. Winograd & U. Neisser (Eds.), *Affect and accuracy in recall: Studies of "flashbulb" memories* (pp. 9–31). New York: Cambridge University Press.

Nicholson, R. A., & Berman, J. S. (1983). Is follow-up necessary in evaluating psychotherapy? *Psychological Bulletin, 93,* 261–278.

Orne, M. T., Whitehouse, W. G., Dinges, D. F., & Orne, E. C. (1988). Reconstructing memory through hypnosis: Forensic and clinical implications. In H. M. Pettinati (Ed.), *Hypnosis and memory* (pp. 21–63). New York: Guilford Press.

Penfield, W., & Rasmussen, T. (1950). *The cerbral cortex of man: A critical study of localization.* Boston: Little, Brown.

Peterfreund, E. (1978). Some critical comments on psychoanalytic conceptualizations of infancy. *International Journal of Psychoanalysis, 59,* 427–441.

Piaget, J. (1962). *Plays, dreams, and imitation in childhood.* New York: Norton.

Piaget, J. (1973). *The child and reality: Problems of genetic psychology* (A. Rosin, Trans.). New York: Grossman.

Piaget, J., & Inhelder, B. (1969). *The psychology of the child.* New York: Basic Books.

Pynoos, R. S., & Nader, K. (1989). Children's memory and proximity to violence. *Journal of the American Academy of Child and Adolescent Psychiatry, 28,* 236–241.

Rachman, S. J., & Wilson, G. T. (1980). *The effects of psychological therapy* (2nd ed.). New York: Pergamon Press.

Rubinfine, D. L. (1981). Reconstruction revisited: The question of the reconstruction of mental functioning during the earliest months of life. In S. Tuttman, C. Kaye, & M. Zimmerman (Eds.), *Object and self: A developmental approach: Essays in honor of Edith Jacobson* (pp. 383–395). New York: International Universities Press.

Schacter, D. L. (1987). Implicit memory: History and current status. *Journal of Experimental Psychology: Learning, Memory, and Cognition, 13*, 501–518.

Schacter, D. L., & Graf, P. (1986). Effects of elaborative processing on implicit and explicit memory for new associations. *Journal of Experimental Psychology: Learning, Memory, and Cognition, 12*, 432–444

Schafer, R. (1983). *The analytic attitude.* New York: Basic Books.

Smith, M. L., Glass, G. V., & Miller, T. I. (1980). *The benefits of psychotherapy.* Baltimore: Johns Hopkins University Press.

Spanos, N. P. (1986). Hypnotic behavior: A social psychological interpretation of amnesia, analgesia, and "trance logic." *Behavioral and Brain Sciences, 9*, 449–467.

Spanos, N. P., & Gottlieb, J. (1979). Demonic possession, mesmerism, and hysteria: A social psychological perspective on their historical interrelations. *Journal of Abnormal Psychology, 88*, 527–546.

Spence, D. P. (1982). *Narrative truth and historical truth.* New York: Norton.

Spitz, R. A. (1965). *The first year of life: A psychoanalytic study of normal and deviant development of object relations.* New York: International Universities Press.

Stolorow, R. D., & Lachmann, F. M. (1980). *Psychoanalysis of developmental arrests: Theory and treatment.* New York: International Universities Press.

Tavris, C. (1993, January). Beware the incest-survivor machine. *New York Times Book Review.*

Tuttman, S. (1982). Regression: Curative factor or impediment in dynamic psychotherapy. In S. Slip (Ed.), *Curative factors in dynamic psychotherapy* (pp. 177–198). New York: McGraw-Hill.

Weeks, J. R., Lynn, S. J., Green, J. P., & Brentar, J. T. (1992). Pseudo-memory in hypnotized and task motivated subjects. *Journal of Abnormal Psychology, 101*, 356–360.

Weinberger, D. A., & Schwartz, G. E. (1979). Low-anxious, high-anxious and repressive coping styles: Psychometric patterns and behavioural and physiological responses to threat. *Journal of Abnormal Psychology, 88*, 369–380.

Werner, H. (1948). *Comparative psychology of mental development.* Chicago: Follett.

Westin, D. (1989). Are "primitive" object relations really preoedipal. *American Journal of Orthopsychiatry, 59*, 331–345.

Zajonc, R. B. (1980). Feeling and thinking: Preferences need no inferences. *American Psychologist, 35*, 151–175.

Zajonc, R. B. (1984). On the primacy of affect. *American Psychologist, 37*, 117–123.

EARLY AUTOBIOGRAPHICAL MEMORIES

. . . .

CHAPTER 5

. . . .

THE ASSESSMENT, VALIDITY, AND DETERMINANTS OF EARLY MEMORY REPORTS
A Critical Review

Peter Malinoski
Steven Jay Lynn
Harry Sivec

Autobiographical memory is at the core of human experience and identity. Autobiographical memories can be defined as memories that are "specific, personal, long-lasting, and (usually) of significance to the self-system" (Nelson, 1993, p. 8). Not only do such memories constitute our unique personal makeup and thus define who we are (Singer & Salovey, 1993), but they also serve as the basis of the experiences we share with others and play an essential role in forming and structuring relationships.

It is no wonder, then, that clinicians have long regarded the exploration of memories—particularly early memories—as crucial to the enterprise of psychotherapy (Bindler & Smokler, 1980; Papanek, 1979). Adlerian clinicians (e.g., Adler, 1927; Wieland & Steisel, 1958) were the first to assert that the earliest memory has particular significance and provides a window to current mental status and functioning. Consider the following statement by Adler (1931): "The first memory will show the individual's fundamental view of life; his first satisfactory crystallization of his attitude. It offers us an opportunity to see at one glance what he has taken as the starting point of his development. I would never investigate a personality without asking for the first memory" (p.75). Relatedly, Saul, Snyder, and Sheppard (1956) asserted that early memories "reveal probably more clearly than any other single psychological datum, the central core of each person's psychodynamics, his chief motivations" (p. 229). And more recently, Olson (1979) articulated a belief shared by many therapists (Papanek, 1979) that "[early memories] when correctly interpreted often reveal very quickly the basic core of one's personality, or life-style, and suggest important, bedrock themes with which the therapist must currently deal in treating the client" (p. xvii).

Interest in the potential clinical value of early recollections led to a swell of research on early memories (Fakouri & Hafner, 1994; Watkins, 1992) over the past 20 years or so. Neisser (1982) echoes the sentiments of many researchers in his observation that the systematic investigation of earliest memories can provide important information about the human memory system.

In this chapter we review the literature on the topic of early memory reports. In so doing, we provide a methodological critique of much of the available evidence and address the degree to which early memory reports represent constructed experiences that are malleable and shaped by personal, interpersonal, and situational influences. To place the study of early memories in context, it is first necessary to discuss the phenomenon of infantile amnesia.

INFANTILE AMNESIA

Definitions of Infantile Amnesia

The research reviewed in this chapter is premised on a number of definitions of infantile amnesia. Infantile amnesia can be defined as the age before which an individual does not recall any events. This definition is not particularly useful because it does not take into account the accuracy of the memories reported. Indeed, some individuals report early memories of questionable accuracy such as from in the womb and shortly after birth (see DuBreuil, Garry, & Loftus, Chapter 6, this volume).

Another perhaps more useful way of defining infantile amnesia is the age before which an individual cannot *accurately* recall any event. Drawing from his clinical experience with neurotic patients and a survey conducted by Henri and Henri (1898), Freud (1901/1960) concluded that memories for childhood events occurring prior to the sixth or eighth year of life are hidden or disguised from conscious awareness. Moreover, Freud (1899/1973) considered memory fragments from prior to the age of 6 to be disconnected and infused with fantasy. He speculated that "it is only from the sixth or seventh year onwards that our lives can be reproduced in memory as a connected chain" (p. 47). Clearly, determining the accuracy of events from long ago is difficult and often impossible, and some memories of events are simply not verifiable. Nevertheless, this has not dissuaded investigators (Howes, Siegel, & Brown, 1993) from investigating the accuracy of early memory reports.

Infantile amnesia can be also be defined as the age before which there is an accelerated rate of nonreporting of life events in excess of the rate of normal memory decay. Because accelerated forgetting over the childhood years implies infantile amnesia (Wetzler & Sweeney, 1986), infantile amnesia represents *deficient* recall, rather than absolute amnesia, of personal childhood memories. Wetzler and Sweeney (1986) demonstrated that an accelerated rate of nonreporting of life events does occur, implying that infantile amnesia, as they defined it, does exist and has its offset at about age 5.

Finally, Usher and Neisser (1993) defined the offset of childhood amnesia as the age at which at least half the participants recall something about an event. These authors used specific, datable benchmark events, such as the birth of a sibling or the death of a family member in their research on early recall.

Age of Earliest Memories

We were unable to find any quantitative review of the ages of earliest reported memories. Table 5.1 lists the remarkably few research studies we identified that have required that participants respond to open-ended questions about their earliest memory and to specify the age at which the event occurred. In many studies (i.e., Allers, White, & Hornbuckle, 1992; Barrett, 1980) this information was solicited, but the investigators did not report descriptive statistics. Alternatively, some studies elicited specific earliest memories, such as the earliest memory with a strong emotional content (i.e., Cowan & Davidson, 1984); these studies are not included in Table 5.1 as they do not include all memories. Dudycha and Dudycha (1933a, 1933b) eliminated participants whose earliest memories dated from more than 5 years of age from their analyses, so their descriptive statistics on age of earliest memory are underestimates of the age of the participants' earliest memory. Gordon (1928) required participants to be very certain of their earliest memory reported, which may have resulted in an overestimate of the age of earliest memory because earlier memories recalled with less confidence were omitted.

In nearly all studies (Henri & Henri, 1898, and Waldfogel, 1948, were notable exceptions) the precise unit of measurement of the age of earliest memory (i.e., nearest month, nearest 6 months) was not specified; thus the precision with which the dating was measured is unknown. Moreover, in most studies, it is not clear if the age reported is the nearest age unit to the recalled time of the event or the lower bound of the interval. That is, in studies in which participants were not directed to the nearest precision level in dating their memories (i.e., Rabbitt & McInnis, 1988), a participant may have reported her age was 4 years when reporting an event that she knows occurred when she were 4 years 11 months old. If participants use the lower bound, either by direction or convention, the reported mean ages will be underestimates of the true age of earliest memory.

During the last century, the predominant means of securing data on the earliest memory was to administer questionnaires to groups of university

TABLE 5.1. Mean Age of Earliest Memory

Source	Subjects	Mean age of earliest memory (SD)	
Acklin, Sauer, Alexander, & Dugoni (1989)	160 nondepressed undergraduates (53 males and 107 females)	4.78	(2.74)
		5.03	(2.58)
	31 mildly depressed undergraduates (10 males and 21 females)	6.15	(3.23)
	21 depressed undergraduates (5 males and 16 females)		
Caruso & Spirrison (1994)	134 undergraduates, 86 females, 48 males	4.96	(3.12)
Hankoff (1987)	32 adult males with a history of serious crime and deliquency	4.37	(1.86)
	50 adult males with no legal history	3.75	(1.31)
Henri & Henri (1898)	Adults aged 16-65 from several nations 88 males, 35 females responding to mail survey	3.27	(2.33)
Howes, Siegel, & Brown (1993)	Approximately 200 undergraduate females	3.07	
	Approximately 100 undergraduate males	3.40	
Kihlstrom & Harackiewicz (1982)	150 high school students	3.91	(1.26)
	164 college/graduate students	3.24	(0.99)
Lynn, Malinoski, & Aronoff (1997)	71 male undergraduates	3.73	(1.54)
	160 female undergraduates	3.33	(1.39)
Malinoski & Lynn (1997a) (first questioning)	42 male undergraduates	4.10	(2.11)
	91 female undergraduates	3.51	(1.27)
Lynn & Malinoski (1997b) (first questioning)	38 male undergraduates	4.15	(1.44)
	45 female undergraduates	3.94	(1.54)
Miles (1893)	71 college student females and 29 female college faculty (89 usable responses)	3.04	
Potwin (1901)	75 female undergraduate	3.01	
	25 male undergraduates	4.4	
Rabbitt & McInnis (1988) (interview)	70 elderly people with low IQ test scores	4.79	(2.19)
	228 elderly people with average IQ scores	3.88	(1.76)
	79 elderly people with high IQ test scores	3.14	(1.06)
Rule (1983)	27 firstborn undergraduates	3.77	(1.63)
	37 laterborn undergraduates	3.70	(1.54)
Rule & Jarrel (1983)	66 undergraduates	3.70	(1.58)
Saunders & Norcross (1988)	184 undergraduates (108 males and 76 females)	3.8	(1.6)

TABLE 5.1. (*cont.*)

Source	Subjects	Mean age of earliest memory (*SD*)	
Sivec, Lynn, & Malinoski (1997a) (Non-hypnotic, non-age regression group)	20 undergraduates	4.05	(1.24)
Waldfogel (1948)	76 female undergraduates	3.23	
	48 male undergraduates	3.64	
Williams & Bonvillian (1989)	20 deaf college students with deaf parents	3.65	(1.23)
	33 deaf college students with hearing parents	3.83	(1.23)
	29 hearing college students	3.03	(1.16)

students. As Table 5.1 reveals, Dudycha and Dudycha's (1941) conclusion that the age of earliest memory for most people is between 3 and 4 years old was verified by research throughout the latter half of this century. The mean ages of earliest memory ranges from 3.01 years (Potwin's [1901] sample of female undergraduates) to 6.15 years for depressed undergraduates (Acklin, Sauer, Alexander, & Dugoni, 1989).

Most studies provide a mean age with a standard deviation, but the proportion of participants reporting memories from before the offset of infantile amnesia cannot be adequately estimated from these statistics alone because it is likely that age distributions are positively skewed. Few studies present frequency distributions that report the proportion of participants' earliest memories in well-defined age ranges (0–6 months, 6–12 months, etc.). Table 5.2 lists these studies with proportions of earliest memory reports from 0 to 24 months in 6-month increments.

Many participants appear to have difficulty estimating calendar time when attempting to recall very early events (Westman, 1995). Lynn and Malinoski (1997) asked subjects to report their earliest memories and estimate their age (to the nearest month) at the time of the recalled events in two separate interview contexts. Approximately 46% of the participants demonstrated at least a 6 month discrepancy in reported age for the same earliest memory over the two occasions. These unstable age estimates suggest that a significant proportion of participants had difficulty placing the event in calendar time.

A second way to study early memories is to inquire about specific, datable events that occur during childhood. Using this approach, Sheingold and Tenney (1982) found that only 3 of 22 college women with siblings born before the age of 36 months remembered anything at all about the sibling birth, and

TABLE 5.2. Proportions of Subjects Reporting Very Early Memories

Study	Sample size	0–6 months	6–12 months	12–18 months	18–24 months	Total 24 months
Dudycha & Dudycha (1933a)[b]	233	0 (00)	0 (00)[a]	0 (00)	10 (04)[a]	10 (04)
Dudycha & Dudycha (1933b)[b]	200	0 (00)	0 (00)[a]	0 (00)	1 (01)[a]	1 (01)
Gordon (1928)[c]	460	0 (00)	3 (01)	7 (02)	22 (05)	32 (07)
Henri & Henri (1898)	121	0 (00)	3 (02)	4 (03)	9 (07)	16 (13)
Sivec, Lynn, & Malinoski (1997a)	40 (non-hypnosis group)	1 (03)	0 (00)	0 (00)[a]	0 (00)	1 (03)
Malinoski & Lynn (1997)	133 (first questioning)	1 (01)	3 (02)	2 (02)	9 (07)	15 (11)
Lynn & Malinoski (1997)	83 (first questioning)	0 (00)	0 (00)	0 (00)	6 (07)	6 (07)

Note. For all age intervals, the lower bound is exclusive and upper bound inclusive; percentages are in parentheses.
[a]These studies measured age in 1-year, not 6-month, increments; thus the preceding column is collapsed into this one.
[b]These studies did not include any memory reports from greater than 5 years of age, so these percentages may be inflated.
[c]Subjects in this study were instructed to report early memories of which they were "very sure."

two of these participants were between 32 and 36 months of age at the time of the birth. Some of the questions the researchers asked may not have tapped personal memory but rather deductive processes or later retelling of the story of the birth (Pillemer & White, 1989). Sheingold and Tenney (1982) concluded that the period between 36 and 48 months of age was critical for recalling a sibling birth.

Similarly, Winograd and Killinger (1983) found that only about 15% of participants younger than 24 months at the time of the assassination of John F. Kennedy gave evidence of any significant recall of the shooting. According to Winograd and Killinger (1983, Fig. 2), only about 15% of individuals were able to report any memory at all for the JFK assassination when they were 24 to 36 months old. With more stringent reporting criteria (reporting of autobiographical information pertinent to the event in four of five recall categories), recall dropped to about 3% of 2-year-olds. Only 6% of participants who were 12–24 months old at the time of the assassination claimed to recall anything at all about it, and none of these participants met the stringent recall criteria. The "any memory at all" condition could be met by simply stating what city one was in at the time of the shooting, which is not dependent on personal memory for the event but, rather, memory of an autobiographical fact.

Terr (1988) interviewed 20 children who experienced documented trauma between 6 months and 5 years of age. The preadolescents she studied generally could provide verbal recall of the trauma if it occurred after 30 to 36 months of age. The earliest memory report of trauma was from a child who was 28 months of age at the time of the traumatic event.

Usher and Neisser (1993) stated that the offset of childhood amnesia depended on the to-be-recalled event. More than half the participants who experienced a sibling birth or hospitalization from 2.00 to 2.99 years could respond to three questions about the event, and their answers could be verified by their mothers. However, for death of a family member and family move to a new home, the offset of childhood amnesia climbed to 3.00 to 3.99 years. Significantly, Usher and Neisser's research indicated that regardless of the event, little or nothing was recalled when the event occurred before 24 months of age.

Loftus (1993) suggested that Usher and Neisser's participants' memory reports at age 2 did not necessarily reflect historically accurate memories. She noted that age 2 can indicate any point between 2.00 and 2.99 years. Moreover, Loftus argued that memories that Usher and Neisser rated as "accurate" may result from educated guesses, knowledge of what must have happened, or secondary information acquired after the event.

A third way of examining the age of earliest memory is to have individuals record all their childhood memories. Wetzler and Sweeney (1986) analyzed such data from Waldfogel (1948) and Rubin (1982, cited in Wetzler & Sweeney, 1986). The authors found that memories before the age of 36 months were rarely reported and that accelerated forgetting occurs as increasingly earlier childhood memories are reported.

Not all researchers agree that 36 to 48 months is the age for the offset of childhood amnesia. Howe and Courage (1993) maintained that the development of a sense of self is critical to the offset of infantile amnesia and the establishment of autobiographical memory. These authors conclude that a sense of self emerges between 18 to 24 months that is capable of acting as a referent essential to the arrangement of personal experiences in memory. From their review of the early autobiographical memory literature, Howe and Courage concluded that there "does appear to be solid evidence from most studies that memories are available for many individuals from the age of 2 years" (p. 315). However, they cited only two empirical studies on personal memory reports from adults to support this controversial conclusion: Winograd and Killinger (1983) and Usher and Neisser (1993), both described earlier. Neither study supports Howe and Courage's (1993) conclusion.

In summary, the age of earliest memory elicited in questionnaire research seems to fall between 36 and 48 months for most people. Few adults report early memories before the age of 30 months, and it is rare for adults to report memories before the age of 24 months. Though people vary in terms of the age of earliest memory reported, and females tend to have slightly younger ages of reported memories than males (Howes et al., 1993; Kihlstrom & Harackiewicz, 1982; Nelson, 1990), the available research implies that reports of memories reported by adults for events that occurred at or before 24 months of age can be considered unusual.

Individual Differences in Early Memories and Identified Populations

So far, we have reviewed research on the temporal boundaries of early recollections. In this section we review studies of individual differences in recall of the early memories and early memory reports in identified populations of participants. Although our review is not exhaustive, we highlight certain important areas of individual differences.

Depression

The available evidence implies that early memory reports may have some role in discriminating depressed and nondepressed individuals. Acklin et al. (1989) conducted a discriminant function analysis and determined that unpleasant affect, frustrated needs, and perceptions of the environment as unsafe or unpredictable in earliest memory reports correctly classified nondepressed, mildly depressed, and severely depressed individuals significantly better than chance. Another study (Fakouri, Hartung, & Hafner, 1985) revealed that neurotic depressives reported more fear-inducing and anxiety provoking incidents than controls in their earliest memories, and that depressives' early memories were more likely to involve disturbed relationships with family members. In their preliminary study of an elderly population, Allers, White, and Hornbuckle (1990) obtained a significant correlation between Beck Depression Inventory (BDI) scores and passivity, external locus of control, and negative affect in early memory reports. And in a later study (Allers et al., 1992), the authors found that BDI scores were significantly correlated with negative affect and passivity in the early memories of college students.

　　Brewin, Andrews, and Gotlib's (1993) review concluded that anxious and depressed adults, compared with matched controls, generally perceived their parents during childhood as more rejecting, less caring, and more overprotective. In an important and illustrative study, Lewinsohn and Rosenbaum (1987) found that acutely depressed participants recalled their parents in more negative terms than nondepressed controls. However, these negative memories were not a stable trait or personality characteristic of individuals who experience recurrent depression: Individuals who were in depression remission did not differ from nondepressed controls in parental recall. Thus, these authors demonstrated mood-dependent retrieval of early childhood experiences in clinically depressed individuals from a random sample of the general population. Lewinsohn and Rosenbaum's research implies that present mood state may infiltrate and/or distort recall of past events, raising serious questions about the stability and validity of certain early memory reports.

Offenders and Juvenile Delinquents

Hankoff (1987) asserted that the relative ease of eliciting early memories may facilitate the assessment of delinquent or criminal populations. This contention is suported by research indicating that early memories of incarcerated criminals and criminally dangerous psychiatric patients are more unpleasant and dramatic and marked by more disturbing or aggressive interactions with others than the early memories of control subjects (Hankoff, 1987; Tobey & Bruhn, 1992). Relatedly, the early memories of felony offenders include more themes of uncomfortable and unpleasant relationships with family members compared with the relatively bland memories of noncriminal control subjects (Elliot, Fakouri, & Hafner, 1993).

Attempts to classify criminally dangerous and delinquent persons with statistical procedures have, in the main, proven successful. For instance, Tobey and Bruhn (1992) used logistical regression analysis of early memory reports to correctly identify 50% of the criminally dangerous and 97% of the nondangerous patients studied. Bruhn and Davidow (1983) were able to use early memory reports to correctly identify 80% of 15 delinquent boys and 100% of 18 nondelinquents. Davidow and Bruhn (1990) used thematic data from early memories to correctly classify 81.7% of the 71 delinquents and 95.8% of the 71 nondelinquent boys. The delinquents scored higher on indices of harm to self, others, or animals; rulebreaking; and firesetting. Last and Bruhn (1983) showed that the content of early memory reports correctly classified well-adjusted, mildly maladjusted, and severely maladjusted boys in 44% of cases, well above chance levels. Finally, Last and Bruhn (1985) found that the thematic content of two early memories solicited from groups of delinquent, hyperactive, somatic, and schizoid boys correctly classified 41% of the participants.

Taken together, these findings warrant the tentative conclusion that early memory reports can provide useful information in the classification and assessment of criminal and delinquent populatons. Whether such reports contribute anything to classifying criminal and delinquent populations above and beyond other more traditional measures remains to be established by future research.

Borderline, Psychotic, and Inpatient Samples

Persons diagnosed with borderline personality experience high levels of negative affect which can be markedly labile. Not surprisingly, patients diagnosed with borderline personality disorder report both a greater preponderance of negative early memories and fewer positive memories than paranoid schizophrenic and neurotic patient groups. Nigg, Lohr, Westen, Gold, and Silk (1992) compared the earliest memories of patients with borderline personality with the earliest memories of patients with major depressive disorder and persons recruited from the general population with no psychiatric diagnosis. Compared with participants in the other groups, the borderline patients' earliest memories were more frequently characterized by deliberate injury and "malevolent representations" (p. 61). In a related study, Nigg et al. (1991) reported that such early memories appeared to be at least partially related to a history of childhood sexual abuse. Like borderline patients, paranoid schizophrenic patients, in turn, report fewer early positive memories than neurotic patients (Arnow & Harrison, 1991). Early memory reports also distinguish psychotic depressives and paranoid schizophrenic patients (Friedman & Schiffman, 1962).

Alcoholics

In addition to persons with serious psychological disorders, alcoholic and nonalcoholic persons' early memories differ on salient dimensions. In one study (Hafner, Fakouri, & Labrentz, 1982), alcoholics, compared with nonalcoholics, reported a greater degree of negative interactions with others and more anxiety-producing or threatening situations, as well as more memories from outside the home. Relatedly, Chaplin and Orlofsky (1991) found that the content of alcoholic veterans' early memories reflected more passivity, negative affect, negative self-perception, external locus of control, and less psychosocial maturity compared with the memory reports of nonalcoholic veterans.

The literature on persons with serious psychological disorders and alcohol-related problems implies that negative content of early memories is associated with a variety of psychological disorders and dysfunctions. The challenge of future research will be to determine whether disorder-specific early memories can be identified that facilitate the discriminative power of early memory reports.

Intelligence

Rule and Jarrell (1983) reported low negative correlations ($r = -.29$ and $-.35$) between the age of the earliest memory and two measures of intelligence, implying that greater intelligence is associated with earlier recall; however, no correlation was discerned between age of earliest memory and a third IQ measure. Whereas Rabbit and McInnis (1988) found that older adults with high IQ scores reported earlier memories than those with lower IQ scores, the content of early memories was unrelated to both age and intelligence. Due to the mixed nature of the findings, few generalizations can be made about the link between early memory reports and intelligence.

Negative Findings

Many of the findings reviewed so far imply that early memories are associated with a variety of personality characteristics and populations of interest. However, a subset of findings argue against attributing special significance to the earliest memory or very early memories. For example, Tylenda and

Dollinger (1987) noted that the earliest memory was no more emotionally significant than a recent memory reported by college students. In fact, the affective qualities of the earliest memory and the recent significant memory were so highly correlated as to be psychometrically equivalent. Salovey and Singer (1989) found that mood-congruent recall was more likely to occur with recent memories than with earliest memories, casting doubt on the special ability of current mood to predict early memory reports. Caruso and Spirrison (1994) evaluated the relationship of the "Big Five" personality domains (neuroticism, extroversion, openness, agreeableness and conscientiousness) assessed by the NEO and as rated in the earliest memory report of college students: only agreeableness demonstrated a significant correlation, and the obtained association was small in magnitude. Finally, Robbins and Tanck (1994) found no correlation between BDI scores and pleasantness ratings of early memories. In conclusion, these findings call into question the special significance of early memories as reflections or correlates of current personality characteristics.

Our review indicates that an abundance of research has been conducted on early memories, and that such memories have been accorded a special status among certain clinicians and researchers. Because strong claims require a close examination of the evidential base, it is essential to further explore whether early memories reflect a fundamental core of personality organization as well as current behavioral and affective functioning. In the next section, we discuss methodological issues and the determinants of early memory reports, and we conclude that it is premature to arrive at closure on the question of the special status of early memories.

METHODOLOGICAL ISSUES

Classification of Earliest Memories

Literally dozens of early memory classification schemes have been proposed in the last 36 years (e.g., Bruhn 1984, 1992a, 1992b; Clark, 1994; Dreikurs, 1973; Eckstein, 1976; Fowler, Hilsenroth, & Handler, 1995; Friedman & Schiffman, 1962; Last, 1983; Last & Bruhn, 1985; Levy, 1965; Linton, 1986, 1992; Manaster & Perryman, 1974; Mayman, 1968; Powers & Griffith, 1987; Quinn, 1973; Shulman & Mosak, 1988; Warren, 1990). Unfortunately, no single classification scheme has been widely used or accepted (Bruhn, 1984; Caruso & Spirrison, 1994). Instead, many researchers have modified existing memory protocols and scoring schemes to suit particular needs, essentially creating new protocols from extant ones (e.g., Saunders & Norcross, 1988). Although content classification procedures may be similar in certain respects (i.e. evaluating the "pleasantness" of expressed affect) across protocols, such procedures have demonstrated low interprocedure categorization consistency, reflecting authors' idiosyncratic beliefs about the relative importance of different characteristics of early memory reports (Bishop, 1993; Clark, 1994).

Of course, the failure to standardize memory and scoring protocols across studies renders comparisons across studies and paradigms hazardous. Moreover, whereas classification schemes may be clinically informative, researchers have failed to elaborate the psychometric properties of different approaches to eliciting early memories (Bishop, 1993). Lacking proper instruments with established psychometric properties, clinicians may depend too much on their intuition or on face-valid yet unsound instruments in evaluating the significance of early memory reports, thus leading to a decrease in the validity of data interpretation (Bishop, 1993).

Different memory elicitation protocols also pull for widely varying numbers of early memories. Most protocols inquire about the very earliest memory. However, some protocols also inquire about the next earliest memory (i.e., Bruhn, 1992a; Rabbit & McInnis, 1988), and other protocols inquire about several early childhood memories (i.e., Fowler et al., 1995). Whereas many protocols elicit memories for specific earliest memories, such as the earliest memory of mother, father, siblings, or school experience (e.g., Fowler et al., 1995), other protocols specifically inquire about the earliest positive and/or negative memory (e.g., Colker & Slaymaker, 1984). Comparison across these different earliest memory tasks is difficult at best, making generalization challenging and rendering meta-analytical techniques difficult, if not impossible to utilize.

The extent to which written versus interview methods have a differential impact on memory reports has not been explored. Although Fowler et al.'s (1995) research indicates that interview methods are superior to written methods, the question of whether laboratory-based interview-elicited memory reports are generalizable to clinical contexts has not been determined.

Atheoretical/Inadequate Research Paradigms

Watkins (1992) criticized some early memory researchers who used the Manaster–Perryman Manifest Content Scoring Manual by stating that they "seemingly have been guided by the following logic: 'Let's find two or more groups that differ, get some EMs [early memories] from them, rate their memories by means of the Manaster–Perryman, and see what results we get.' Too often, these studies seem lacking in a solid rationale or reason for being" (p. 261). In our opinion, this criticism can be leveled at early memory research in general, which often fails to articulate the theoretical underpinnings of the research.

Clinical versus Statistical Significance

The clinical significance of early memory reports is often approached by way of case examples. Case reports, however, are no substitute for controlled research demonstrating the clinical utility of early memory reports. Unfortunately, the vast majority of early memory studies we reviewed were designed to demonstrate statistically significant between-group differences, rather than addressing the clinical usefulness or significance of the findings. For example, the assessment of early memories has not been demonstrated to be superior to traditional means of detecting personality traits and current psychological functioning. We could find no empirical study that provided evidence that the assessment of early memory reports was superior to other means of assessing current anxiety, depression, psychopathology, or offender status, and although there are some indications that early memory reports predict physiological reactivity better than face-valid self-report measures (Shedler, Mayman, & Mannis, 1994), the incremental predictive validity of early memory measures has not, in general, been demonstrated.

Finally, most research on early and earliest memory focuses on white, middle-class participants who are usually college students (Watkins, 1992). In many cases, sample sizes were too small for analyses to have adequate power to detect differences among groups when they exist. In several studies (e.g., Grunberg, 1989) no comparison groups were used, limiting the inferences that can be drawn from the data.

The Lack of Normative Data

To evaluate the potential significance of an individual's memory reports, it is important to understand *normative* reporting of early memories. As Tylenda and Dollinger (1987) noted, "few descriptive generalizations can be made about childhood memories. Most of the extant literature provides only qualitative or clinical information about the early memories of particular individuals or groups of psychiatric patients" (pp. 361–362). The fragmentary nature of knowledge in the field and the implementation of many different and incompatible memory elicitation and scoring systems precludes the creation of a database of norms. Clinicians must resort to drawing inferences regarding the significance of clients' early memory reports from the available literature which is, perhaps, not much more informative than relying on "mere intuition."

Determinants of Early Memory Reports

These methodological difficulties notwithstanding, researchers have been able to examine a number of determinants of very early memory reports and the malleability of early memories. Not surprisingly, early memories, like memories of more recent events, often appear to be reconstructions rather than literal representations of actual events. In this section we review research conducted in our laboratory that examines a number of determinants of early memories as well as the extent to which early memories are malleable and responsive to social influence.

Since Adler's early writings on early memories, many clinicians have been aware that early memories are retrospective reconstructions that have a certain subjective or psychological truth that does not necessarily correspond with the historical record. In fact, early memories are viewed as largely projective measures that reflect important current concerns and dynamics. Bruhn (1992a, 1992b), for example, is a strong advocate of the use of early personal memories as projective techniques in assessment, and he stated that "personality and developmental variables—not the laws of memory—help us to understand what is retained and what is dropped from autobiographical memory" (p. 6). Binder and Smokler (1980) proposed that collecting a set of early memories can be an invaluable aid in selecting a defined area of conflict or problems to address in brief psychodynamic psychotherapy. And Savill and Eckstein (1987) argued that because early memories change as a function of mental status, they can provide an index of mental status, be used in the assessment of therapeutic outcome, aid in monitoring therapeutic progress, provide focal themes for therapy, and be used as a quick and easily administered and scored therapeutic tool.

Many of the studies we reviewed in our discussion of early memories in clinical populations indicate that past memories of individuals are consistent with current characteristics. Whereas early memories may be accurate representations of past events that determine, to some extent, current functioning, it could also be the case that current functioning affects the recall of past events. For example, it could be argued that individuals are depressed because they have very negative early life experiences as children, and they accurately remember these negative events as adults. However, recall that Lewinsohn and Rosenbaum's (1987) research indicated that when depressed persons are in remission, their childhood memories are no more negative than nondepressed persons' memories. In short, memories of the past appear to be strongly dependent on current mood state and may not mirror a childhood that is truly more negative or "depressogenic."

In keeping with this line of reasoning, one important determinant of early memories may be current functioning. Adcock and Ross (1983) found that the earliest memory "tenderness" and "neuroticism" thematic categories were significantly related to neuroticism as measured by the Eysenck Personality Questionnaire. Barrett (1980) secured a moderate correlation between thematic ratings of the earliest memory reports of college students and measures of current anxiety, locus of control, and social desirability, whereas Nichols and Feist (1994) noted that participants with optimistic explanatory styles reported earliest memories involving other persons, higher levels of activity, greater interpersonal contact and mastery, and more pleasant overall affect than participants who demonstrated pessimistic explanatory styles. Finally, Saunders and Norcross (1988) reported that college students with self-rated dysfunctional family relationships reported more unpleasant earliest memories; negative earliest memories were also significantly correlated with greater hostility, paranoia, and somatization. In summary, studies with nonclinical samples support the idea that early memories and indices of current functioning, affect, and personality are related.

One aspect of current functioning that we have examined in our laboratory is fantasy proneness. Wilson and Barber (1981, 1983) described a group of individuals they categorized alternatively as "fantasizers," "fantasy-prone personalities," and "fantasy addicts." The primary characteristic of these individuals was a deep, long-standing, and extensive immersion in fantasy and imagination. According to Wilson and Barber (1981), they comprise about 4% of the population and represented the extreme end of the continuum of the trait of fantasy proneness. Little has been reported about the relationship between fantasy proneness and early memory reports. Wilson and Barber (1983) found that 24 of 26 highly fantasy-prone women reported early memories of events prior to their third birthday. Of these 24 women, 8 reported clear memories of events that occurred on or before their first birthday, well before the offset of infantile amnesia.

Lynn, Malinoski, and Aronoff (1997a) investigated this relationship directly and found that fantasy proneness correlated significantly yet weakly ($r = -.18$) with the age of earliest reported memory, such that more fantasy-prone individuals reported earlier memories. Of 222 individuals who reported the age of their earliest memory, the 12 individuals who recalled memories from before 24 months of age were significantly more fantasy prone than individuals reporting earliest memories at later ages. Furthermore, the individuals who recalled memories before 24 months also reported more perceived detail and vividness in their early memories and rated their memories as more accurate than did individuals with later memories.

Our research implies that caution is warranted with respect to very early memory reports: The fact that persons who report very early memories during the period covered by infantile amnesia confidently report that these memories are relatively vivid and accurate implies that therapists may be tempted to give these memories greater credence than is probably warranted. The fact that these participants who report early memories are also more fantasy prone than participants who report later memories suggests that they may be particularly vulnerable not only to confusing fantasy and reality but also to the biasing effects of leading questions.

Hypnotizability

In a second study, Lynn et al. (1997b) hypnotized 150 participants and found that measures of number of suggestions passed and suggestion-related involvement and involuntariness correlated ($r = .22$ to $.35$) with early memory reports. That is, the more hypnotizable and involved in suggestions participants were, the more likely they were to confidently report early memories and to rate them as vivid and detailed. Interestingly, the results were not materially affected by whether the hypnotizability and memory measures were administered in the same test context or whether the hypnotizability and memory measures were administered in entirely different situations so that participants were unaware of the connection between any of the measures.

Hypnosis

Sivec, Lynn, and Malinoski (1997a) recently examined the influence of the hypnotic context on very early memory reports by interviewing 40 hypnotized and 40 nonhypnotized participants about their earliest memories. The first time they were asked to report their earliest memory, only 3% of the nonhypnotized participants recalled a memory earlier than 2 years of age. However, 23% of the hypnotized participants reported a memory earlier than age 24 months, 20% reported a memory earlier than 18 months, 18% reported a memory earlier than 1 year, and 8% reported a memory of earlier than 6 months. The second time they were asked for an early memory, only 8% of the nonhypnotized participants reported a memory earlier than 2 years, and only 3% reported memories of 6 months or earlier. In contrast, 35% of hypnotized participants reported memories earlier than 18 months, 30% of participants reported memories earlier than 1 year, and 13% of participants reported a memory before 6 months.

Although accurate recall of events at this very early age is implausible, the researchers did not corroborate participants' memories. Corroboration of early memories was attempted by Nash, Drake, Wiley, Khalsa, and Lynn (1986) who compared the early memories of hypnotized and nonhypnotized participants who participated in a prior age-regression experiment. This experiment involved age regressing hypnotized and nonhypnotized role-playing (i.e., simulating) participants to age 3 years to a scene in which they were in the soothing presence of their mothers. During the experiment, participants reported the identity of their transitional objects (e.g., blankets and teddy bears). Third-party verification (parent report) of the accuracy of recall was obtained for 14 hypnotized participants and 10 simulation control participants. Despite the similarity to children in their way of relating to transitional objects, hypnotic participants were less able than control participants to correctly identify the specific transitional objects actually used. Hypnotic subjects' hypnotic recollections, for example, matched their parent's report only 21% of the time, whereas simulators' reports after hypnosis were corroborated by their parents 70% of the time. All recollections obtained during hypnosis were incorporated into posthypnotic recollections, regardless of accuracy.

In another study, Sivec, Lynn, and Malinoski (1997b) age-regressed participants to the age of 5 and suggested that they played with a Cabbage Patch Doll if they were a girl or a He-Man toy if they were a boy. An important aspect of this study was that these toys were not released until 2 or 3 years after the target time of the age-regression suggestion. Half the participants received hypnotic age-regression instructions and half the participants received suggestions to age regress that were not administered in a hypnotic context. Interestingly, none of the nonhypnotized persons were influenced by the suggestion. In contrast, 20% of the hypnotized participants rated the memory of the experience as real and were confident that the event occurred at the age to which they were regressed.

In summary, studies that compare memory reports elicited in hypnotic and nonhypnotic conditions show that hypnosis results in more implausible memories, a higher percentage of memories that are impossible to corroborate, and a higher percentage of reports of events that could not have occurred at the target age. The studies reviewed reveal that certain early memory reports are imaginative constructions that are subjectively compelling yet inaccurate.

Interpersonal Influence

Although hypnosis is a social influence situation, implausible memory reports are by no means limited to hypnosis and may arise in response to interpersonal influences in a variety of situational contexts. To illustrate, we summarize Malinoski and Lynn's research (Lynn & Malinoski, 1997; Malinoski & Lynn, 1997) which implies that implausible memory reports (of very early events < 24 months, covered by infantile amnesia) can be quite readily established. In a one-on-one interview situation that was analogous to a clinical interview, 83 participants were repeatedly (four times) asked to tell about their earliest memories under different conditions (Lynn & Malinoski, 1997). In one condition (low interpersonal influence/demand), the questions were phrased in a very permissive manner, with statements such as, "If you don't remember, it's all right." In a second condition (high interpersonal influence/demand), the questions were worded to subtly suggest that participants should be able to recall earlier memories on each trial (i.e., "Tell me when you get an earlier memory"). This small change in wording resulted in a difference of average recall of nearly 1 year across groups (low demand earliest memory $M = 3.45$ years vs. high demand $M = 2.48$ years).

In the initial reported memory, only 7 of 83 or 8.4% of the participants across both groups reported a memory from age 24 months or younger. Three of these were from the high-demand and four from the low-demand group. By the end of the interview, 20% of the low-demand group reported at least one memory from 24 months of age or younger, whereas 43% of the high-demand group reported at least one such memory.

After the interview ended, participants were given accurate information about memory and fully debriefed. All the participants who completed the first session were recruited by phone to participate in another supposedly unrelated experiment. No mention was made of the previous session. The final sample consisted of 64 participants who completed the entire protocol (80% return rate).

The second interview occurred an average of 2 weeks after the first session. A second set of experimenters was used who were blind to the experimental hypotheses and the content of the first session, including participants' original high- or low-demand assignment. Participants were informed that they were participating in a self-disclosure interview experiment related to deep versus superficial cognitive processing. After a series of decoy questions designed to camouflage the session, the interviewer asked the participant to report his or her "very earliest memory; the very first thing you can recall."

After this task, participants were informed that this session was, in fact, connected to the previous session and the experimenter handed the participant a sealed photocopy of his or her earliest memory report from the previous session. At no point did the experimenter see this copy. The participant read the memory report and the experimenter asked if the memory reported in the current session was the same as the very earliest memory reported in response to the memory probes from the previous session. The majority of participants (58%) in the high-demand condition did *not* report the same earliest memories in the first and second sessions; 45% of participants in the low-demand condition also reported different earliest memories in the two sessions.

When the memory reports differed, the interviewer asked why the reports were discrepant. As noted previously, the most frequent reason for memory report inconsistency between the sessions, was a problem in determining the chronology of memories, a finding consistent with the observation that children have difficulty evaluating calendar time (Westman, 1995). These findings imply that not all implausible memories are inaccurate but may reflect events that occurred at later ages, past the offset of infantile amnesia. Hence, the content of the memory may be accurate in substance yet inaccurate in terms of the stated age of the event reported. Other reasons that participants gave for discrepancies across testing situations included questionable accuracy of memories, clarity of memories, and pressure to report increasingly early memories.

In a second study (Malinoski & Lynn, 1997), interviewers asked 133 participants to report their earliest memory. Interviewers probed for increasingly early memories until participants denied any earlier memories for two consecutive probes. After two such denials, participants received a strong suggestion to promote earlier memory reports using nonhypnotic "memory recovery techniques" similar to those promoted by some therapists (e.g., Farmer, 1989; Meiselman, 1990). Interviewers asked participants to close their eyes, see themselves "in their mind's eye" as a toddler or infant, and "get in touch" with memories of long ago. Interviewers also informed participants that most young adults can retrieve memories of very early events—including their second birthday—if they "let themselves go" and try hard to visualize, focus, and concentrate. Interviewers then asked for subjects' memories of their second birthday. Participants were complimented and reinforced for reporting increasingly early memories.

The mean age of the initial reported memory was 3.7 years, with only 11% of participants reporting initial earliest memories at or before age 24 months, and 3% of the sample reported an initial memory from age 12 months or younger. Fantasy proneness was weakly negatively correlated with the age of the initial reported memory. However, after receiving the visualization instructions, 59% of the participants reported a memory of their second birthday. The participants who reported birthday memories scored significantly higher on measures of compliance and hypnotizability than those who did not report such memories.

After the birthday memory was solicited, interviewers pressed participants for even earlier memories. The mean age of the earliest memory reported was 1.6 years, fully 2 years less than their initial memory report. Low but significant correlations were secured between the age of the earliest memory reported and compliance, interrogative suggestibility, and hypnotizability.

One of the most interesting findings was that 78.2% of the sample reported at least one memory that occurred at 24 months of age or earlier. Furthermore, more than half (56%) of the participants reported a memory between birth and 18 months of life, a third of the participants (33%) reported a memory that occurred at age 12 months or younger, and 18% reported at least one memory of an event that occurred at 6 months or younger, well outside the boundary of infantile amnesia. Finally, 4% of the sample reported memories from the first week of life. Participants who reported at least one memory from 24 months of age or earlier scored higher on compliance scores and interrogative suggestibility than participants who reported memories after 2 years of age.

It is worth underscoring the point that neither of these studies used particularly invasive methods for eliciting implausible memories; however, it is clear that with increasing pressure, participants report increasingly implausible memories. Other studies reviewed elsewhere in this book indicate that suggestive procedures can result in rich and detailed false memories of early life events (Hyman, Husband, & Billings, 1995; Loftus & Pickrell, 1995) in a minority of participants tested.

Accuracy of Earliest Memories

People are often very confident in the accuracy of their childhood memories (Lindsay & Read, 1994; Malinoski & Lynn, 1997), but very few studies address the accuracy of early childhood memories. Howes et al. (1993) attempted to verify the accuracy of early memory reports. These researchers asked 260 undergraduate students to report their three earliest memories. Participants then were asked to contact individuals who could potentially confirm the accuracy of their memories and to inquire about the nature of the remembered event in a neutral, nonleading manner.

A total of 21% of the memories reported were not confirmable (i.e., no one else was present at the time of the remembered event). However, 80% of the memories for which confirmation could be provided were rated as "all verified" or "partially verified," following comparison with the report of the verifier. Thirteen percent of the memories that could be confirmed were classified as "distorted," where the participant significantly altered the nature of the event and significant inaccuracies were evident. Less than 1% of the confirmable memories were rated as "disconfirmed" (i.e., pseudomemories). Approximately 2.5% of the memories were classified as containing "differences." That is, the verifier recalled a significantly different account of the memory but was not sure of the accuracy of his or her own memory. The researcher noted that no confirmation was reported for any memory of an event before the age of 12 months. However, they maintained that with respect to events dating from the second year of life to more recent events, there was no significant correlation between age of recalled event and frequency of confirmation.

Howes et al. (1993) concluded from these results that the majority of earliest childhood memories were historically accurate. The authors assumed that their procedure minimized the risk of mutual contamination of memory reports because participants reported their earliest memories before receiving instructions to contact verifiers and verifiers, purportedly, did not learn of the participants' accounts of events until after they reported their own memories of the events in question. However, the authors did not discuss the evident methodological shortcomings inherent in relying on the participants to report both sets of memories. That is, it is possible that participants subtly or overtly influenced the reports of the verifiers to align with their own memory reports, in conformance with the demands of the experiment. In the absence of independent corroboration of earliest memories, Howes et al.'s conclusions are questionable and must remain tentative at best.

Perceived Accuracy and Confidence of Memories

The participants in Malinoski and Lynn's (1997) research reported moderate-to-high levels of confidence in the accuracy of their early memory reports. For the initial memory reported, the mean confidence rating was 4.57 on a 5 point scale (1 = not at all confident, 3 = somewhat confident, and 5 = very confident). The mean confidence rating for memories of the second birthday was 3.27, and the mean confidence rating for the very earliest memory reported was 3.59. Moreover, there was a moderate to high correlation (r = .58) between the clarity of the earliest memory report and the confidence in the accuracy of the report. A poststudy questionnaire item indicated that participants believed their memories were, overall, quite accurate. Indeed, 94% of the participants stated that they believed their memory reports to be accurate at least to a moderate degree. In short, certain participants were confident in the accuracy of highly implausible memories.

In Malinoski and Lynn's (1997) research that compared participants in high-versus low-interpersonal-demand conditions, participants also rated their confidence in the accuracy of each of their memory reports on a 5-point scale. The high- and low-demand groups did not differ in their confidence ratings for either the initial memory reported (4.64 vs. 4.44, respectively) or the final memory reported (3.67 vs. 4.07). It is notable that the confidence ratings were well above the midpoint of the scale for both groups in both conditions. Hence, even when participants were pressured to recall increasingly early memories, they were reasonably confident in the accuracy of the memories elicited.

The researchers also found that confidence and clarity ratings were moderately and significantly correlated ($r = .41$) for the initial memory reported across all participants. Confidence and clarity ratings also correlated highly for the final earliest memory in both the high-demand ($r = .54$) and low-demand ($r = .69$) conditions.

If the eyewitness literature is any indication, there is only a weak relationship between between accuracy of recall of early memories and confidence in early recollections. Bothwell, Deffenbacher, and Brigham (1987) performed a meta-analysis on 35 staged-event eyewitness studies and found a correlation between confidence in recall and recall accuracy of only .25. Similarly, Wells and Murray (1984) showed that confidence accounts for less than 10% of the variance in eyewitness identification accuracy. This research strongly implies that confidence in memory accuracy is no guarantee of accurate recall. Indeed, many participants in our research vehemently asserted that memories that purportedly occurred before the offset of infantile amnesia occurred in reality.

FUTURE DIRECTIONS AND CONCLUSION

Clinicians have long recognized autobiographical memory as a foundation of human identity and experience. Some evidence suggests that characteristics of early memory reports may correlate with depression, delinquency, alcoholism, intelligence, and the presence of psychological disorders to a small or moderate degree. Much of this research, however, suffers from fundamental shortcomings, limiting the inferences that can be drawn from it.

To move our knowledge forward, it will be necessary for investigators to develop early memory interviews that can be administered reliably and that can assess early memories on a variety of dimensions including age of earliest memory, density of early memories across the first 10 years of life, expressed affect, confidence in the accuracy of early memory reports, and vividness of imagery associated with early memories. The development of well-standardized protocols with established psychometric properties will not only facilitate comparisons across studies but also provide normative data that will facilitate comparisons of findings across the life span and across different psychological disorders and dysfunctions.

Of course, the development of valid, standardized instruments should not deter investigators from customizing or tailoring early memory instruments to fit the unique research questions and requirements of the experimental design. Indeed, one of the problems we noted in previous investigations of early memory reports is the failure to elaborate the theoretical underpinnings of research conducted and to examine group differences in early memories between patient populations, for example, as a function of expected differences as predicted by a particular theoretical approach. For instance, according to psychoanalytical theory, psychotic and depressed patients may differ not so much in terms of the positive or negative content of their early memory reports as in terms of the primitivity or regressive quality of the memories or the way in which significant figures such as parents or caretakers are represented in the early memory reports.

In evaluating the "special properties" of early memories, workers in the field need to better articulate in what sense such reports are "special." That is, early memory reports could be examined in terms of their ability to predict not only personality characteristics or qualities but also the complexity of self-representations, the nature and quality of the therapeutic alliance, and treatment outcome. Regardless of the dimensions examined, before it can be asserted that early memories are somehow special, it will be necessary to specify "compared to what?" Relatedly, it would be useful to examine early memories vis-à-vis other well-established measures of personality, therapeutic alliance, and therapeutic outcome to determine the convergent, discriminant, and incremental validity of early memories reports across salient dimensions of personal and interpersonal functioning. This research is crucial insofar as the available evidence has not yet demonstrated that early memory reports are superior to traditional means of psychological assessment or that the addition of such reports to a battery of other assessment tools enhances the prediction of psychological functioning.

To draw meaningful conclusions from research on early memories, it is necessary to remedy some specific deficiencies of previous research. These deficiencies include the failure to examine early memories in ethnically and culturally diverse populations, the failure to include appropriate numbers of subjects to adequately test hypotheses, and the failure to include appropriate control groups. The research in this area has matured to the point that more rigorous experimental designs are required to provide convincing demonstrations of the role of early memories in understanding individual differences, self-perceptions, and current psychological functioning.

These methodological issues notwithstanding, progress has been made in explicating the determinants of early memory reports. For instance, the evidence reviewed indicates that the clarity, perceived accuracy, and age of early memory reports are related to the personality traits of fantasy proneness and hypnotizability. Consequently, therapists should be aware that the memory reports of highly fantasy-prone and highly hypnotizable individuals may differ from their other clients and be particularly sensitive to interpersonal influence.

Contextual variables such as hypnosis and moderate degrees of interpersonal influence also influenced earliest memory reports to a substantial extent, increasing the proportion of implausible memories without concomitant reductions in confidence levels in the accuracy of those memories. These contextual variables were also associated with earlier ages of recall of earliest memories. Although recent research has begun to shed light on potentially important modifiers of early memory reports, much needs to be learned about the factors associated with the plasticity of early memory reports. Nevertheless, it is already clear that early autobiographical memories, like more recent memories, are not necessarily accurate representations of historical events. Clinicians must therefore be wary of giving early memory reports special credence and examine potential suggestive, interpersonal, and cultural influences on reports of early life experience.

REFERENCES

Acklin, M. W., Bibb, J. L., Boyer, P., & Jain, V. (1991). Early memories as expressions of relationship paradigms: A preliminary investigation. *Journal of Personality Assessment, 57,* 177–192.

Acklin, M. W., Sauer, A., Alexander, G., & Dugoni, B. (1989). Predicting depression using earliest childhood memories. *Journal of Personality Assessment, 53,* 51–59.

Adcock, N. V., & Ross, M. W. (1983). Early memories, early experiences, and personality. *Social Behavior and Personality, 11,* 95–100.

Adler, A. (1927). *Understanding human nature.* New York: Greenberg.

Adler, A. (1931). *What life should mean to you.* Boston: Little, Brown.

Allers, C. T., White, J., & Hornbuckle, D. (1990). Early recollections: Detecting depression in the elderly. *Individual Psychology, 46,* 61–66.

Allers, C. T., White, J., & Hornbuckle, D. (1992). Early recollections: detecting depression in college students. *Individual Psychology, 48,* 324–329.

Arnow, D., & Harrison, R. H. (1991). Affect in early memories of borderline patients. *Journal of Personality Assessment, 56,* 75–83.

Barrett, D. (1980). The first memory as a predictor of personality traits. *Journal of Individual Psychology, 36,* 136–149.

Binder, J. L., & Smokler, I. (1980). Early memories: A technical aid to focusing in time-limited dynamic psychotherapy. *Psychotherapy: Theory, Research and Practice, 17,* 52–62.

Bishop, D. R. (1993). Applying psychometric priniciples to the clinical use of early recollections. *Individual Psychology, 49,* 153–165.

Bothwell, R. K., Deffenbacher, K. A., & Brigham, J. C. (1987). Correlation of eyewitness accuracy and confidence: Optimality hypothesis revisited. *Journal of Applied Psychology, 72,* 691–695.

Brewin, C. R., Andrews, B., & Gotlib, I. H. (1993). Psychopathology and early experience: A reappraisal of retrospective reports. *Psychological Bulletin, 113,* 82–98.

Bruhn, A. R. (1984). The use of earliest memories as a projective technique. In P.

McReynolds & C. J. Chelume (Eds.), *Advances in psychological assessment* (Vol. 6, pp. 109–150). San Francisco: Jossey-Bass.

Bruhn, A. R. (1992a). The early memories procedure: A projective test of autobiographical memory, part 1. *Journal of Personality Assessment, 58,* 1–15.

Bruhn, A. R. (1992b). The early memories procedure: A projective test of autobiographical memory, part 2. *Journal of Personality Assessment, 58,* 326–346.

Bruhn, A. R., & Davidow, S. (1983). Earliest memories and the dynamics of delinquency. *Journal of Personality Assessement, 47,* 476–482.

Caruso, J. C., & Spirrison, C. L. (1994). Early memories, normal personality variation, and coping. *Journal of Personality Assessment, 63,* 517–533.

Chaplin, M. P., & Orlofsky, J. L. (1991). Personality characteristics of male alcoholics as revealed through their early recollections. *Individual Psychology, 47,* 356–371.

Clark, A. J. (1994, December). Early recollections: A personality assessment tool for elementary school counselors. *Elementary School Guidance and Counseling, 29,* 92–101.

Colker, J. O., & Slaymaker, F. L. (1984). Reliability of idiographic interpretation of early recollections and their nomothetic validation with drug abusers. *Individual Psychology, 40,* 36–44.

Cowan, N., & Davidson, G. (1984). Salient childhood memories. *Journal of Genetic Psychology, 145,* 101–107.

Davidow, S., & Bruhn, A. R. (1990). Earliest memories and the dynamics of delinquency: A replication study. *Journal of Personality Assessment, 54,* 601–616.

Dreikurs, R. (1973). *Psychodynamics, psychotherapy, and counseling* (rev. ed.). Chicago: Alfred Adler Institute.

Dudycha, G. J., & Dudycha, M. M. (1933a). Adolescents' memories of preschool experiences. *Journal of Genetic Psychology, 42,* 468–480.

Dudycha, G. J., & Dudycha, M. M. (1933b). Some factors and characteristics of childhood memories. *Child Development, 4,* 265–278.

Dudycha, G. J., & Dudycha, M. M. (1941). Childhood memories: A review of the literature. *Psychological Bulletin, 38,* 668–682.

Eckstein, D. (1976). Early recollection changes after counseling: A case study. *Journal of Individual Psychology, 32,* 212–223.

Elliott, W. N., Fakouri, M. E., & Hafner, J. L. (1993). Early recollections of criminal offenders. *Individual Psychology, 49,* 68–75.

Fakouri, M. E., & Hafner, J. L. (1994). Adlerian-oriented early recollection studies: What do we ask? *Individual Psychology, 50,* 170–172.

Fakouri, M. E., Hartung, J. R., & Hafner, J. L. (1985). Early recollections of neurotic depressive patients. *Psychological Reports, 57,* 783–786.

Farmer, S. (1989). *Adult children of abusive parents: A healing program for those who have been physically, sexually, or emotionally abused.* Los Angeles: Lowell House.

Fowler, C., Hilsenroth, M. J., & Handler, L. (1995). Early memories: An exploration of theoretically derived queries and their clinical utility. *Bulletin of the Menninger Clinic, 59,* 79–98.

Freud, S. (1973). Screen memories. In J. Strachley (Ed. & Trans.), *Standard edition of the complete psychological works of Sigmund Freud* (Vol. 3). London: Hogarth Press. (Original work published 1899).

Freud, S. (1960). Childhood memories and screen memories. In J. Strachey (Ed. & Trans.), *Standard edition of the complete psychological works of Sigmund Freud.* (Vol. 6). London: Hogarth Press. (Original work published 1901)

Friedman, J., & Schiffman, J. (1962). Early recollections of schizophrenic and depressed patients. *Journal of Individual Psychology, 18,* 57–61.

Gordon, K. (1928). A study of early memories. *Journal of Delinquency, 12,* 129-132.

Grunberg, J. (1989). Early recollections and criminal behavior in mentally ill homeless men. *Individual Psychology, 45,* 289–299.

Hafner, J. L., Fakouri, M. E., & Labrentz, H. L. (1982). First memories of "normal" and alcoholic individuals. *Journal of Individual Psychology, 38,* 238–244

Hankoff, L. D. (1987). The earliest memories of criminals. *International Journal of Offender Therapy and Comparative Criminology, 31,* 195–201.

Henri, V., & Henri, C. (1898). Earliest recollections. *Popular Science Monthly, 53,* 108–115.

Howe, M. L., & Courage, M. L. (1993). On resolving the enigma of infantile amnesia. *Psychological Bulletin, 113,* 305–326.

Howes, M., Siegel, M., & Brown, F. (1993). Early childhood memories: Accuracy and affect. *Cognition, 47,* 95–119.

Hyman, I. E., Husband, T. H., & Billings, F. J. (1995). False memories of childhood experiences. *Applied Cognitive Psychology, 9,* 181–197.

Kihlstrom, J. F., & Harackiewicz, J. M. (1982). The earliest recollection: A new survey. *Journal of Personality, 50,* 134–148.

Last, J. M. (1983). *The Comprehensive Early Memories Scoring System Manual.* Unpublished manuscript. [Available from J. M. Last at 17117 West Nine Mile Rd., #423, Southfield, MI]

Last, J. M., & Bruhn, A. R. (1983). The psychodiagnostic value of children's earliest memories. *Journal of Personality Assessment, 47,* 597–603.

Last, J. M., & Bruhn, A. R. (1985). Distinguishing child diagnostic types with early memories. *Journal of Personality Assessment, 49,* 187–192.

Levy, J. (1965). Early memories: Theoretical aspects and applications. *Journal of Personality Assessment, 29,* 281–291.

Lewinsohn, P. M., & Rosenbaum, M. (1987). Recall of parental behavior by acute depressives, remitted depressives, and nondepressives. *Journal of Personality and Social Psychology, 52,* 611–619.

Lindsay, D. S., & Read, J. D. (1994). Psychotherapy and memories of childhood sexual abuse: A cognitive perspective. *Applied Cognitive Psychology, 8,* 281–338.

Linton, M. (1986). Ways of searching the contents of memory. In D. C. Rubin (Ed.), *Autobiographical memory* (pp. 50–67). Cambridge, UK: Cambridge University Press.

Loftus, E. F. (1993). Desperately seeking memories of the first few years of childhood: The reality of early memories. *Journal of Experimental Psychology: General, 122,* 274–277.

Loftus, E. F., & Pickerell, J. E. (1995). The formation of false memories. *Psychiatric Annals, 25,* 720–725.

Lynn, S. J., & Malinoski, P. T. (1997). *Early memory reports as a function of high versus low situational influence.* Unpublished manuscript, Ohio University, Athens, OH.

Lynn, S. J., Malinoski, P. T., & Aronoff, J. (1997a). *Dissociation, fantasy-proneness, and early memories.* Unpublished manuscript, Binghamton University, Binghamton, NY.

Lynn, S. J., Malinoski, P. T., & Aronoff, J. (1997b). *Hypnosis, early memories and context effects.* Unpublished manuscript, Binghamton University, Binghamton, NY.

Malinoski, P. T., & Lynn, S. J. (1997). *The pliability of early memory reports.* Unpublished manuscript, Ohio University, Athens, OH.

Manaster, G. J., & Perryman, T. B. (1974). Early recollections and occupational choice. *Journal of Individual Psychology, 30,* 232–237.

Mayman, M. (1968). Early memories and character structure. *Journal of Projective Techniques and Personality Assessment, 32,* 303–316.

Meiselman, K. (1990). *Resolving the trauma of incest: Reintegration therapy with survivors.* San Francisco: Jossey-Bass.

Miles, C. (1893). A study of individual psychology. *American Journal of Psychology, 6,* 534–558

Nash, M. R., Drake, S. D., Wiley, S., Khalsa, S., & Lynn, S. J. (1986). The accuracy of recall by hypnotically age regressed subjects. *Journal of Abnormal Psychology, 95,* 298–300.

Neisser, U. (1982). *Memory observed: Remembering in natural contexts.* San Francisco: Freeman.

Nelson, K. (1990). Remembering, forgetting, and childhood amnesia. In R. Fivush & J. A. Hudson (Eds.) *Knowing and remembering in young children* (pp. 301–316). New York: Cambridge University Press.

Nelson, K. (1993). The psychological and social origins of autobiographical memory. *Psychological Science, 4,* 7–14.

Nichols, C. C., & Feist, J. (1994). Explanatory style as a predictor of earliest recollections. *Individual Psychology, 50,* 31–39.

Nigg, J. T., Lohr, N. E., Westen, D., Gold, L. J., & Silk, K. R. (1992). Malevolent object representations in borderline personality disorder and major depression. *Journal of Abnormal Psychology, 101,* 61–76.

Nigg, J. T., Silk, K. R., Westen, D., Lohr, N. E., Gold, L. J., Goodrich, S., & Ogata, S. (1991). Object representations in the early memories of sexually abused borderline patients. *American Journal of Psychiatry, 148,* 864–869.

Olson, H. A. (1979). The hypnotic retrieval of early recollections. In H. A. Olson (Ed.), *Early recollections: Their use in diagnosis and psychotherapy* (pp. 223–229). Springfield, IL: Charles C. Thomas.

Papanek, H. (1979). The use of early recollections in psychotherapy. In H. A. Olson (Ed.), *Early recollections: Their use in diagnosis and psychotherapy* (pp. 163–171). Springfield, IL: Charles C. Thomas.

Pillemer, D. B., & White, S. H. (1989). Childhood events recalled by children and adults. In H. W. Reese (Ed.), *Advances in child development and behavior* (Vol. 21, pp. 297–340). New York: Academic Press

Potwin, E. B. (1901). Study of early memories. *Psychological Review, 8,* 596–601.

Powers, R. L., & Griffith, J. (1987). *Understanding life–style: The psychoclarity process.* Chicago: Americas Institute of Adlerian Studies.

Quinn, J. (1973). *Predicting recidivism and type of crime from early recollections of prison inmates.* Unpublished doctoral dissertation, University of South Carolina.

Rabbitt, P., & McInnis, L. (1988). Do clever old people have earlier and richer first memories? *Psychology and Aging, 3,* 338–341.

Robbins, P. R., & Tanck, R. H. (1994). Depressed mood and early memories: Some negative findings. *Psychological Reports, 75,* 465–466.

Rubin, D. C. (1982). On the retention function for autobiographical memory. *Journal of Verbal Learning and Verbal Behavior, 21,* 21–38.

Rule, W. R., & Jarrell, G. R. (1983). Intelligence and earliest memory. *Perceptual and Motor Skills, 56,* 795–798.

Salovey, P., & Singer, J. A. (1989). Mood congruency effects in recall of childhood versus recent memories. *Journal of Social Behavior and Personality, 4,* 99–120.

Saul, L. J., Snyder, R. R., & Sheppard, E. (1956). On early memories. *Psychoanalytic Quarterly, 25,* 228–237.

Saunders, L. M. I., & Norcross, J. C. (1988). Earliest childhood memories: Relationship to ordinal position, family functioning, and psychiatric symptomatology. *Individual Psychology, 44,* 95–105.

Savill, G. E., & Eckstein, D. G. (1987). Changes in early recollections as a function of mental status. *Individual Psychology, 43,* 3–17.

Schulman, B. H., & Mosak, H. H. (1988). *Manual for lifestyle assessment.* Muncie, IN: Accelerated Development.

Shedler, J., Mayman, M., & Manis, M. (1993). The illusion of mental health. *American Psychologist, 48,* 1117–1131.

Sheingold, K., & Tenney, Y. J. (1982). Memory for a salient childhood event. In U. Neisser (Ed.), *Memory observed* (pp. 201–212). New York: Freeman.

Singer, J. A., & Salovey, P. (1993). *The remembered self: Emotion and memory in personality.* New York: Free Press.

Sivec, H. J., Lynn, S. J., & Malinoski, P. T. (1997a). *Early memory reports as a function of hypnotic and nonhypnotic age regression.* Unpublished manuscript, Ohio University, Athens, OH.

Sivec, H. J., Lynn, S. J., & Malinoski, P. T. (1997b). *Hypnosis in the cabbage patch: Age regression with verifiable events.* Unpublished manuscript, Ohio University, Athens, OH.

Terr, L. (1988). What happens to early memories of trauma? A study of twenty children under age five at the time of documented traumatic events. *Journal of the American Academy of Child and Adolescent Psychiatry, 27,* 96–104.

Tobey, J. H., & Bruhn, A. R. (1992). Early memories and the criminally dangerous. *Journal of Personality Assessment, 59,* 137–152.

Tylenda, B., & Dollinger, S. J. (1987). Is the earliest childhood memory special? An examination of the affective characteristics of autobiographical memories. *Journal of Social Behavior and Personality, 2,* 361–368.

Usher, J. A., & Neisser, U. (1993). Childhood amnesia and the beginnings of memory for four early life events. *Journal of Experimental Psychology: General, 122,* 155–165.

Waldfogel, S. (1948). The frequency and affective character of childhood memories. *Psychological Monographs, 62*(4, Whole No. 291).

Warren, C. (1990). Use of hypnogogic reverie in collection of earliest recollections. *Indvidual Psychology, 46,* 317–322.

Watkins, C. E., Jr. (1992). Adlerian-oriented early memory research: What does it tell us? *Journal of Personality Assessment, 59,* 248–263.

Weiland, I. H., & Steisel, I. M. (1958). An analysis of the manifest content of the earliest memories of children. *Journal of Genetic Psychology, 92,* 41–52.

Wells, G. L., & Murray, D. M. (1984). Eyewitness confidence. In G. L. Wells & E. F. Loftus (Eds.), *Eyewitness testimony: Psychological perspectives* (pp. 155–170). New York: Cambridge University Press.

Westman, A. S. (1995). First memories seem quite complete, but when the event happened is recalled less frequently. *Psychological Reports, 77,* 543–546.

Wetzler, S. E., & Sweeney, J. A. (1986). Childhood amnesia: An empirical demonstration. In D. C. Rubin (Ed.), *Autobiographical memory* (pp. 191–201). Cambridge, UK: Cambridge University Press.

Williams, R. L., & Bonvillian, J. D. (1989). Early childhood memories in deaf and hearing college students. *Merrill Palmer Quarterly, 35,* 483–497.

Wilson, S. C., & Barber, T. X. (1981). Vivid fantasy and hallucinatory abilities is the life histories of excellent hypnotic subjects ("somnambules"): Preliminary report with female subjects. In E. Klinger (Ed.), *Imagery: Vol. 2. Concepts, results, and application* (pp. 133–149). New York: Plenum.

Wilson, S. C., & Barber, T. X. (1983). The fantasy-prone personality: Implications for understanding imagery, hypnosis, and parapsychological phenomena. In A. A. Sheikh (Ed.), *Imagery: Current theory, research and application* (pp. 340–390). New York: Wiley.

Winograd, E., & Killinger, W. A., Jr., (1983). Relating age at encoding in early childhood to adult recall: Development of flashbulb memories. *Journal of Experimental Psychology, 112,* 413–422.

CHAPTER 6

TALES FROM THE CRIB
Age Regression and the Creation of Unlikely Memories

Susan C. DuBreuil
Maryanne Garry
Elizabeth F. Loftus

It is now well established that recollections of the past may be distorted by postevent information given in the form of suggestion and leading and misleading questions. This can occur both with and without hypnosis (Barnier & McConkey, 1992; Loftus, 1979; Loftus & Palmer, 1974; Loftus & Zanni, 1975; Lynn, Milano, & Weekes, 1991; Spanos, Gwynn, Comer, Baltruweit, & deGroh, 1989; Spanos, Quigley, Gwynn, Glatt, & Perlini, 1992). The magnitude of suggestibility effects depends on factors such as the plausibility of the suggested event, delay between the actual event and the misleading postevent information, the context of the testing session, and the type of recall test administered (Barnier & McConkey, 1992; McCann & Sheehan, 1987; McConkey, Labelle, Bibb, & Bryant, 1990; Sheehan, Statham, & Jamieson, 1991).

Considerably more controversy surrounds whether entire autobiographical events can be created or fabricated using similar procedures. Interest in this question arose in response to increased litigation against alleged perpetrators of childhood sexual abuse that was largely based on plaintiffs' recovery of repressed memories. One line of research explores whether people can genuinely believe in memories of traumatic events that are highly unlikely to have occurred in real life. For example, Mulhern (1994) provides a sociohistorical analysis of claims of satanic ritual abuse, concluding that there is virtually no evidence to suggest that memories of ritualistic torture and abuse are veridical. Spanos, Burgess, and Burgess (1994) draw similar conclusions concerning the veracity of alien abduction and past-life reports.

A second line of research examines the cognitive and social psychological factors that can lead to the creation of false memories from childhood. Loftus and colleagues (Loftus, 1993; Loftus & Ketcham, 1994; Loftus & Pickrell, 1995) demonstrated that people can be *led* to integrate into their personal histories an entirely fabricated event. Over the course of several interviews that involved using a subject's family member as a confederate, subjects were led to believe that they had been lost in a shopping mall when they were young children. Several other studies demonstrated similar childhood memory creations with both children and adults (Ceci, Huffman, Smith, & Loftus, 1994; Ceci, Loftus, Leichtman, & Bruck, 1994; Hyman, Husband, & Billings, 1995).

These studies of false childhood memories have been criticized on several grounds. Often questioned is the extent to which their findings generalize to the implantation of traumatic events in real life and the extent to which the suggested memories are actually false rather than delayed remembrances of actual events. The centerpiece of this chapter is a study designed to address the second criticism. It demonstrates that some adults are able to generate fantasies about early infancy that fit with their expectations and beliefs concerning infantile experiences and incorporate suggested details transmitted to them by an experimenter. Not only are subjects willing to generate fantasies about childhood experiences, but some of these adults later insist that their fantasized constructions are real memories.

To reiterate, past research shows that subjects can be led, via suggestion, to remember false details as being part of actually experienced events. Moreover, they can even be led to believe and to remember that they experienced entirely false childhood memories after a false suggestion from a close relative that such an experience occurred. The particular suggestive procedures are still somewhat removed from the types of activities that go on in some clinical settings. In certain clinical settings, patients present with a set of symptoms, receive a suggestion that these symptoms point to buried memories, and participate in "memory work" designed to extract those buried memories. The claim by therapists who engage in these procedures is that authentic buried memories will be excavated and the patient will thus be cured. Critics argue that, on the contrary, these memory work procedures may unwittingly be eliciting fabricated recollections.

Could these procedures actually elicit fabricated recollections? To explore this issue, our research uses a false-feedback procedure. In the false-feedback paradigm, subjects are given misleading information about themselves as part of a manipulation designed to induce them to construct entirely false memories of the past. Our procedure, adapted from one first used at Carleton University by Spanos and Burgess (Burgess, 1994; Spanos, 1996), is designed to simulate certain features that are included in some questionable therapeutic settings. In the Carleton research, subjects were told that they have "symptoms" that strongly indicate they most probably saw a mobile over their cribs on the day after they were born. They were also supplied with misinformation indicating that a regression procedure would probably lead to retrieval of memories of the mobile. Hypnotic and nonhypnotic subjects were then age-regressed back to birth and asked to describe any experiences they could remember, including those involving a mobile. The surprising finding: Many hypnotic and nonhypnotic age-regressed subjects reported remembering the mobile.

In our adaptation of the false-feedback procedure, we also used symptom interpretation and imagery-based age regression to induce subjects to recall events from the first day of life. Other subjects were regressed back to kindergarten and induced to remember spiral disks hanging from the walls of their classrooms. We found many subjects who willingly accepted these suggestions and later claimed that the suggested experiences were real memories, not fantasies. We were also interested in the individual differences that predict who will be susceptible to such false memory creations, and, conversely, who would be resistant. For example, are people who have especially vivid imagery more susceptible? Are people who believe in the permanence of memory more susceptible? Before discussing the specific research paradigm, we provide more information about the conceptual evolution of the false feedback paradigm.

CLINICAL TECHNIQUES

The term "memory work" is used to refer to therapy that focuses on retrieving "repressed" memories of childhood sexual abuse (Loftus, 1994). Many therapeutic techniques fall under this umbrella category and include procedures such as hypnosis, imagery, age regression, and symptom interpretation. These techniques are used with two kinds of clients: those who remember abuse but wish to fill in more details and also those who suspect early childhood abuse but have no concrete memories.

Some researchers have begun to question the validity of using these techniques to uncover memories of past sexual abuse (e.g., Lindsay & Read, 1994; Loftus, 1994; Loftus & Ketcham, 1994). Some of these techniques are touted by others (e.g., Bass & Davis, 1992; Frederickson, 1992) as reliable tools for uncovering memories of childhood abuse. In fact, Poole, Lindsay, Memon, and Bull (1995) found that more three-quarters of the U.S. PhD-level psychotherapists sampled in their study reported using at least one questionable memory recovery technique to help clients remember childhood sexual abuse. Three of these techniques, imagery, age regression, and symptom interpretation, are particularly relevant to the false-feedback procedure we used in our research.

Imagery Techniques

Imagery procedures are used in therapeutic settings for a variety of purposes ranging from the elimination of psychosomatic symptomology such as warts (for a review see Johnson, 1989; Spanos, Stenstrom, & Johnston, 1988) to the retardation of anxiety-related disorders such as herpes (Longo, Clum, & Yaeger, 1988). These lines of research are promising and suggest a beneficial application of imagery procedures.

Other uses of imagery are highly controversial and even downright disconcerting (e.g., the use of imagery procedures in therapeutic settings to elicit recall of allegedly repressed or dissociated memories of childhood sexual abuse). Imagery techniques have surprisingly wide acceptance. Roland (1993), for example, proposes using a visualization technique for jogging "blocked" memories of sexual abuse and a "reconstruction" technique for recovering repressed memories of abuse. Siegel and Romig (1990) claim that hypnosis is especially reliable for recovering these memories. Moreover, Poole et al. (1995) found that a substantial number of practitioners use imagery procedures in their own practices to help clients retrieve memories of abuse. They found that 32% of the U.S. practitioners in their study reported using "imagery related to the abuse," and an astounding 22% reported using liberal imagery strategies in which clients are given "free reign" to their imaginings.

What are imagery-based procedures? Are they effective in enhancing accurate recall? Imagery procedures usually include some form of relaxation instructions followed by instructions to vividly re-create experiences. They may be used in isolation or they may be used with other techniques such as hypnosis and age regression. Much of the empirical data examining the purported memory-enhancing effect of imagery procedures is buried within the hypnosis and psycholegal literature. By and large, this literature suggests that imagery procedures are no more effective than hypnotic or control procedures in enhancing recall or recognition accuracy (Spanos et al., 1989; Yuille & McEwan, 1985; Sloane, 1981).

One problem with generalizing from the psycholegal literature is that there is a substantial difference in the delay interval between witnessing or experiencing a crime and recalling it and between witnessing or experiencing a childhood event and attempting to recall it in adulthood. It goes without saying that the delay intervals are typically far greater in the childhood case. Moreover, both laboratory and field studies establish that longer delays between experiencing an event and attempted recall are detrimental to the accuracy of memories. The relatively huge delays between childhood and adulthood would be expected to result in serious degradation of memory for those childhood experiences. Would imagery help? A number of researchers and clinicians worry that imagery-based techniques may lead to increased confabulation when used for attempted recall of childhood events (Lindsay & Read, 1994; Loftus & Ketcham, 1994).

Age Regression

Age regression involves regressing a person back through time to an earlier life period. Subjects are typically given relaxation instructions and then asked to mentally re-create events that occurred at a successively earlier period in the person's life. Poole et al. (1995) found that 17% of their U.S. practitioner sample reported using age-regression procedures with the explicit intent of retrieving memories of childhood abuse. Self-help resources also recommend regression procedures. For example, Bass and Davis (1992) indicate that one way to retrieve memories of childhood incest is by "going back" to earlier times using self- or therapist-guided regression. Bass and Davis (1992) provide the following example of an individual recounting a regressive episode:

> Most of the regressions I experienced felt almost like going on a ride. They'd last maybe three or four hours at a time. One of the most vivid regressions I went through was late one evening, when Barbara and I were talking about her going to visit a friend. I felt like I was being sucked down a drain. And then I felt like a real baby. I started crying and clinging and saying, "You can't go! You have to stay with me!" And I began to talk in a five-year-old's voice, using words and concepts that a five-year-old might use. All of a sudden I thought I was just going to throw up. I ran to the bathroom, and then I really started to sob. I saw lots of scenes from my childhood. Times I felt rejected flashed by me, almost in slides. (pp. 73–74)

At face value the passage reveals a woman who experienced childhood memories from a child's point of view. She took on the cognitions, behaviors, and emotions of the age to which she was regressed. She *felt* as if she were a child, she *behaved* as she believed a child would behave, and she *recalled* childhood experiences. Anecdotes such as this one are used to support the notion that the regressed person has actually gone back in time to an earlier life period. Some regression aficionados further believe that because the individual actually regressed to an earlier age, the regression experience accurately reflects what was genuinely experienced at that age. Proponents of this view point to cases like the one described previously and argue that the level of detail, the vividness of the recall, and the apparent accuracy of regression experiences indicate that age regression is an effective memory-retrieval technique. Of course, their argument deteriorates in the face of regression-prompted reports of prenatal, past-life, and alien-abduction memories. But suppose we put aside these bizarre reports and turn our attention to empirical issues. What does the research indicate about age regression?

The empirical literature suggests that the experiences of age-regressed individuals are contextually dependent, expectancy driven, social constructions (Spanos, Burgess, & Burgess, 1994). According to this view, age-regressed subjects behave according to cues they derive from the social situation and according to their knowledge and beliefs about age-relevant children. After reviewing the relevant literature, Nash (1987) concluded that the behavior of age-regressed adults was substantially different from the behavior of children at the age to which adults are regressed. This was elegantly demonstrated in one study in which adults were regressed back to age 3 (O'Connell, Shor, & Orne, 1970) and their regressed behavior was compared to age-relevant controls. Both groups of subjects were engaged in creating mud pies when they were interrupted with an enticing offer of a lollipop from the experimenter. The experimenter held the lollipop at an angle that required the subjects to awkwardly maneuver around the experimenter's hand to reach the stick. The children completed this task without difficulty. The age-regressed adults, on the other hand, failed to adopt such advanced cognitions. Instead, they grabbed the lollipop by the head and stuck the mud coated candy into their mouths—a behavior that clearly demonstrated the adults' mistaken beliefs about the probable behavior of young children. Put another way, the age-regressed adult subjects behaved as they believed 3-year-olds would behave rather than as 3-year-olds actually behave. Other researchers show that age-regressed subjects are also susceptible to pre- and postregression suggestions about the veracity of their experiences (Baker, 1982; Spanos, Menary, Gabora, DuBreuil, & Dewhirst, 1991).

Symptom Interpretation

McElroy and Keck (1995) describe the cases of three women who were diagnosed as survivors of childhood sexual abuse. All three women displayed symptoms meeting criteria according to the revised third edition of the *Diagnostic and Statistical Manual of Mental Disorders* (DSM-III-R; American Psychiatric Association, 1987) for obsessive–compulsive and/or eating disorders. None of the three women had memories of being sexually abused as a child before her prior therapy. Nonetheless, all three women were told by previous therapists that their physical and psychological complaints were symptoms of sexual or physical trauma that they suffered during childhood. Therapists told the women that remembering abuse was critical to their recovery. One of the three women was diagnosed during her first interview at an eating disorder clinic. Her proposed treatment program involved individual and group therapy directed toward recovering memories of the apparent abuse. This woman did not return to follow up her treatment plan at the clinic, she did not search for these apparent memories of abuse, and she did not confront her family.

The two other women were diagnosed as survivors in individual therapy sessions. Both women continued therapy, attempted to recover memories of abuse, and also confronted their families in the absence of such memories. Of course, we can never be entirely sure what those women believed during the course of their therapy, nor how their beliefs changed over the course of their therapy. Nevertheless, these reports are consistent with the idea that the interpretation of physical and psychological complaints by an authoritative and professionally educated source can have detrimental psychological and familial consequences. These clients were willing to believe and to behave in ways that were apparently inconsistent with what they knew about themselves.

Examples of symptom interpretation also exist in popular psychology readings and self-help sources (e.g., Bass & Davis, 1992; Blume, 1990; Fredrickson, 1992). Some popular self-help books on the topic of incest include lists of symptoms that are presented as possible/probable correlates of childhood incest. Blume's *Incest Survivors' Aftereffects Checklist* consists of 34 such correlates. The scale instructions read: *Do you find many characteristics of yourself on this list? If so, you could be a survivor of incest.* Blume also indicates that "clusters" of these items are significant predictors of childhood sexual abuse and that the predictive utility is additive; that is, the more items endorsed by an individual the more likely that there is a history of incest.

But sweeping indicators of sexual abuse are not supported by the empirical literature. Researchers agree that there may be numerous correlates of sexual abuse, but some agree that no clear-cut pattern of symptoms are shown to be causally associated with sexual abuse (Ceci & Loftus, 1994). In short, some genuine victims of childhood incest may experience many symptoms, others only some, and still others none. Moreover, nonvictims also experience many of the same symptoms often associated with sexual abuse (Tavris, 1993). However, Poole et al. (1995) found that therapists often view symptom interpretation as an important component of therapy aimed at recovering memories of suspected childhood sexual abuse. In fact, Poole et al. (1995) found that more than one-third of the U.S. practitioners sampled reported that they used this technique.

Imagery, age regression, and symptom interpretation are all questionable techniques when used as a regimen to recall or to diagnose repressed memories of childhood sexual abuse. A number of mental health professionals have now joined in their criticism of those who continue using the techniques (e.g., Merskey, 1996).

ATTRIBUTE AND SITUATION-SPECIFIC VARIABLES

Beliefs about Memory

It is likely that several beliefs are associated with the extent to which an individual is willing to try recalling memories of early childhood and the extent to which they define their memories as reality (Spanos, Cross, Dickson, & DuBreuil, 1993). At the very least, subjects must believe that (1) the memories are kept intact and stored safely away waiting to be retrieved, and (2) there are techniques that will enable them to retrieve these stored memories.

General Population

Laypeople often hold various misconceptions about the way human memory works. Survey studies show, for example, that some people believe in the permanence of human memory (Garry, Loftus, & Brown, 1994; Garry, Loftus, Brown, & DuBreuil, 1997; Loftus & Loftus, 1980; Yarmey & Tressellian-Jones, 1983). Surveys also indicate a belief in the effectiveness of various techniques (e.g., hypnosis) to aid in the retrieval of both recently experienced events (Labelle, Lamarche, & Laurence, 1990; McConkey & Jupp, 1985) and events from as far back as childhood (Garry et al., 1997). Some people hold even more extreme opinions concerning memory and memory-retrieval strategies. For example, a substantial proportion of subjects in Garry et al. (1994) and Garry et al. (1997) believed in the veridicality of memories retrieved from the womb and also believed in the existence of past lives (see also Yapko, 1994).

Practitioners

Some research shows that despite their training and education, practitioners' beliefs about memory are not very different from those of laypeople. For example, Yapko (1994) found that 47% of the professionals (the majority of whom were practitioners) had greater faith in hypnotic than in nonhypnotic memories, and 31% believed that events recalled under hypnosis were likely to be accurate. Furthermore, 54% of his sample believed to some degree in the effectiveness of hypnosis for recovering memories as far back as birth, and 28% believed in its effectiveness for recovering memories from past lives. Fortunately, the majority of his sample (79%) also recognized that false memories could emerge using hypnosis. Nonetheless, a noteworthy percentage of his subjects endorsed aspects of hypnosis that are inconsistent with the empirical literature on hypnosis (e.g., hypnotized people cannot lie and hypnotized people can access memories as far back as birth).

Beliefs and Bizarre Memories

Anecdotal and empirical evidence reveals that people who hold preexisting beliefs about the existence of a particular phenomenon may interpret ambiguous events in line with their preexisting beliefs. For example, Siegal (1992) found that anecdotal accounts of hallucination experiences were often interpreted in line with beliefs about the phenomenon even when there were more parsimonious physiological or external explanations for them. Siegal's subjects held various interpretations of their hallucinatory experiences. Interpretations included communication with a deceased, contact with alien beings, and telepathic communication with a Nazi sympathizer. Siegal's scientific beliefs led him to search for and to find relatively mundane explanations for the experiences reported by his subjects. The subjects' beliefs, on the other hand, led them to search for more elaborate explanations that were consistent with their preexisting beliefs concerning particular phenomenon (e.g., alien life, spiritual mediumship, and telepathy). This can occur even with instances that many might consider outright bizarre, namely, accounts of past lives and accounts of prenatal experiences. Those who a priori believe in these types of experiences are more likely to think that delayed recall of the experiences are veridical, although it is not clear which way the causal links run.

Belief in reincarnation is a particularly appropriate example of the effects of preexisting beliefs on behavior because it involves the apparent recall of long-term delayed memories. There are hundreds of anecdotal accounts of people who claim to recall past-life experiences (e.g., Wambach, 1978). To some laypersons, past-life accounts may be very convincing if they contain detailed information about the historical context of the remembrance. Nonetheless, when past-life reports are examined for historical accuracy in empirical studies, the reports typically come up short (Spanos et al., 1991). Beliefs seem to play an important role in these memories. Spanos et al. (1991) found that past-life reporters held significantly stronger beliefs in reincarnation than did non-past-life reporters. Moreover, they found that the strength of belief in reincarnation correlated with the reality subjects assigned to their experiences. Also important, these studies revealed the rather large number of subjects who were willing to generate the called-for images in response to a hypnotic age-regression instructions. Of course, a subset of these individuals, when asked about the veracity of their reports, were willing to acknowledge that their images were fantasy creations, but another subset insisted that the constructions were real.

A recently aired documentary (Frontline, 1995) showed a group therapy session in which a woman was age-regressed back through childhood, to the womb, to being trapped in her mother's Fallopian tube. The woman gave a convincing demonstration of the emotional and physical discomfort that one would experience if one were indeed stuck in such an uncomfortable position. Although the woman may have held a genuine belief in the veracity of her experience, the empirical literature indicates that the products of her regression experiences were not memory based. Unfortunately, her case is not an isolated example of the kind of experience we might call questionable. The mental health and counseling literature contains case studies of prenatal remembering that are nearly if not equally unlikely (Lawson, 1984; van Husen, 1988).

THE EFFECTS ON MEMORY OF IMAGERY, AGE REGRESSION, AND SYMPTOM INTERPRETATION

To say that a suggestive technique led to the creation of a false memory, one must be able to know for a fact that the "memory" produced is in fact false. Much of the research examining the impact of suggestive techniques on memory creation relied on pretest scores or else relied on the improbability of the suggested event to support the claim that the event never happened and the currently reported "memory" must be false. However, critics of the research claim that the reported memory is not improbable and that the suggestive technique in fact produced a real, genuine memory.

Spanos and colleagues (Burgess, 1994; Spanos, 1996) developed a paradigm to circumvent this criticism by capitalizing on *infantile amnesia*. Infantile amnesia is the inability of adolescents and adults to recall experiences from early childhood. The age before which adults cannot recall concrete episodic experiences is sometimes termed the "amnesic barrier." Most cognitive researchers agree that infantile amnesia exists; however, there is some controversy over the age below which people are unable to retrieve reliable memories. Usher and Neisser (1993) argued that the barrier hovers around 2 to 3 years of age, but others believe that it is closer to 3 or 4 years (e.g., Pillemer & White, 1989; Winograd & Killinger, 1983). Spanos and Burgess used the amnesic barrier to their advantage. They asserted that even if events from before the barrier actually occurred, the source of the reports would not be memory but some other factor.

Spanos and Burgess developed a multifaceted methodology for implanting into autobiographical memory a false event that allegedly occurred in early infancy (Burgess, 1994; Spanos, 1996). They chose as their target one day after birth, a time that falls within the boundaries of even the most optimistic views of infantile amnesia. There were four main components of the paradigm. First, subjects were told that they exhibited a unique personality profile. Second, they were given a reason to link their personality profile with early childhood experiences. Third, they were given misinformation promoting the permanence of human memory. Finally, they were given efficacy-enhancing instructions about a memory-retrieval strategy. These four components of the paradigm can be roughly equated to the therapeutic setting in which a diagnosis about childhood sexual abuse is made on the basis of a client symptomology and memory-retrieval therapy is used to elicit memories of abuse.

Like the Carleton University investigators, we attempted to simulate an atmosphere that reflected the social environment present in some client–therapist relationships. However, we used *only* nonhypnotic age-regression procedures and we regressed some subjects to the day after birth and others to the first day of kindergarten. We also explored the impact on false memory creation of prior beliefs about the efficacy of memory-retrieval strategies and the nature of human memory.

Thirty-six subjects were randomly selected from more than 400 who completed a modified version of Garry et al.'s (1997) memory beliefs survey and several nonrelated surveys during a mass testing session. Subjects from this pool were contacted by phone and invited to participate in a study about childhood experiences. No link was drawn between the memory beliefs survey and our regression study. All subjects were tested individually and were prescreened on several critical questions (e.g., Were you born in a hospital?

Did you attend kindergarten?). Subjects were then exposed to a complex set of instructions modeled after the basic components developed at Carleton.

Subjects completed what was ostensibly a prescreening battery of tests for participation in the study. The battery was described as an established personality profile and subjects were told that their responses on the questionnaire would dictate their eligibility to participate in the study. After subjects completed the battery, the experimenter collected the Scantron answer sheet and left the room under the guise of needing to wait while the computer analyzed their responses. Following the ruse, subjects were given false feedback concerning their responses. All subjects were given the same personality profile and the same feedback. The feedback included verbal information about their personality type, a brief written profile, and a computer-generated distribution that plotted the subject's bogus personality scores relative to the general population. All the feedback was designed to inculcate in subjects the belief that they showed a personality profile we called High Perceptual Cognitive Monitor.

The second component of the procedure was to inculcate the belief that subjects who showed this particular personality profile were probably exposed to visually stimulating environments at a given age (for half the subjects, the day after birth; for the other half, kindergarten). Specifically, subjects were told that they were probably participants in psychology programs in the late 1960s and early 1970s (in North American hospitals for the infancy subjects, and in kindergarten classrooms for the others). These programs were designed to enhance the cognitive capacities of infants (or young children). The dates varied with subject age and the range always included the year in which the subjects was born.

Here is a portion of the "cover story" that informed the subject about the "program" in hospitals:

> In the early l960s a great deal of work was done by psychologists on the effects of early experience, and more specifically on the importance of visual stimulation and exposure to varied visual environments in the development of personality and cognitive abilities. About 25 to 30 years ago . . . some hospitals . . . began hanging mobiles above the cribs of newborn infants. The mobiles moved, and were colored red and green in order to attract and hold the infant's visual attention, and to help the infant to coordinate their eye-movements and their eye–hand coordination.

The corresponding message for the kindergarten subjects was "some schools . . . began hanging spiral disks on the walls of kindergarten classes. The spirals moved, and were colored red and green in order to attract and hold the child's visual attention. . . ."

A third component of the misinformation procedure was to give subjects information supporting the idea that people can retrieve early childhood memories. To this end, all subjects were told the notorious videotape analogy of human memory. They were told that memory works like a videotape recorder and that retrieving memories is like hitting the playback button. Finally, subjects were presented with a technique that the experimenter indicated would enable them to retrieve these early childhood memories. They were given expectancy-enhancing instructions about the efficacy of the memory-retrieval strategy for enhancing recall. It is important to emphasize that the techniques used in this study are not infrequently used by practitioners and that the misinformation presented was not all that far-fetched. As discussed earlier, surveys indicated that some people hold controversial ideas about the nature of human memory, some practitioners believe that regression procedures are effective in enhancing human memory, and some practitioners use such techniques to elicit early childhood memories.

Twenty subjects were age-regressed to the day after birth and 16 subjects were age-regressed to kindergarten. To get a feel for what subjects did during the age-regression procedure, here is a portion of the specific instructions that were read to the "infancy" subjects:

> During the cognitive restructuring procedure I will ask you to imagine yourself at several younger ages. I will ask you to mentally place yourself back to each age and try your best to recreate the thoughts, feelings, emotions, and other experiences that you felt at each age. Recreating these experiences will trigger old memories, and those memories will trigger still other old memories. Finally, I will ask you to take yourself back to the day after your day of birth, and reexperience yourself as an infant in a hospital crib. During this process I will ask you to try to reexperience the sensations and feeling that you had as an infant. Once you are primed in this way to reactivate your infant memories, I will ask you to visualize a mental TV screen, and you will see yourself as an infant on your mental TV screen. Your memories will come to life and you will see yourself in your mind's eye in your crib a day after your birth.

All subjects were given at least two opportunities to practice describing their experiences before they reached the target date. In the infancy condition, they reported their experiences at ages 15, 10, and 5 years before recounting the experiences at birth. In the kindergarten condition, they reported their experiences at ages 15 and 10 years before recounting the kindergarten experience. After being probed for their memories about the critical period, all subjects were age-progressed to their current age and further questioned about their experiences.

OVERALL REGRESSION EXPERIENCES

Report Frequency

All 16 subjects regressed to kindergarten reported experiences that were consistent with being a child in a kindergarten class, and all but 2 of the 20 (i.e., 90%) of the subjects regressed to infancy reported experiences that were consistent with being in a hospital nursery. Presented next are verbatim reports from two subjects. Case 1 is a report from a subject regressed to infancy and Case 2 is a report from a subject regressed to kindergarten.

> *Case 1.* "Um, the thing that keeps going through my mind is where my sister is and there's crying alot and there's a window—like in the second row—it seems as if I were to look straight ahead there's a big glass window but only my Dad is standing there and um, there are little paper baby bottles hanging from the ceiling and there's a yellow bow tied to somebody's, um, crib but I don't know why and the crib that I'm in is like, um, a clear plastic thing and there's like a red . . . along the side. And actually I remember there's a mobile. If I'm lying like this, this is my head, and I'm lying on my back, it's hanging from the left corner. But it seems to be pastel colors. It's nothing bright. [Subject asked by experimenter to focus on the object]. It's dangling from this white plastic thing with has a knob on it you can turn. I think to start music but you can't—there's no music playing and it stands about like—kind of—like 6 or 8 inches above me and has an arm and this little part that's a cream color and hanging from it are like 5 . . . objects and they're like, um, let's see, a truck looking thing and just a circle and there's objects that really aren't anything in particular."

> *Case 2.* "Well, I sort of like, I don't know like, but there were a lot of neat things that I wanted to play with in there. There was a kitchen where you could play house and like there was . . . and stuff that you could take out of the wall for cooks and stuff. There was just like tables—there wasn't separate desks. [Subject asked by the experimenter to focus on the object]. There's just like letters and stuff on the wall. Like the alphabet and—I think there's pictures of animals—that they like—what—they say underneath them, like cow or like chicken. I see like a chicken. It's like brown feathers and like an orange beak. And like—it's not too detailed but it's like—I mean it's got some detail. It's not just like a cartoon figure. It's got a little bit of detail and it's like—standing on it's own."

Taken together, these two cases nicely illustrate the integration into reports of childhood of experimenter-suggested details and details generated by the subjects based on their own beliefs concerning their experiences. With regard to the latter, Case 1 illustrates that the subject included in her report details consistent with the fact that she is a twin and details consistent with a script or schema for the typical hospital nursery: specifically, that infants are surrounded by other infants, that there is a viewing window, and that the father is likely to be at the viewing window while the mother recuperates from the birth. Similarly, Case 2 reveals a woman who included in her report information consistent with what we all know about kindergarten classrooms: specifically, that kindergarten classrooms contain toys for children to play with and are decorated colorfully with things such as drawings and the alphabet.

Believed-In Authenticity

Subjects rated the degree to which they believed that their regression reports were fantasy creations versus actual memories. Ratings were made, after subjects were progressed to their current age, on a 5-point scale that ranged from 1 (definitely real memories) through 3 (unsure) to 5 (definitely fantasies). Recall that 18 of the 20 regressed to infancy generated infancy-consistent reports. One-third of these infancy subjects believed that their reported experiences were probably or definitely real memories, 50% were unsure about the reality of their reports, and the remaining subjects believed that their reports were probably fantasy creations. All the subjects regressed to kindergarten reported kindergarten-consistent reports and, in striking contrast to the infancy subjects, all the kindergarten subjects believed in the reality of their memories. Three-quarters of the kindergarten subjects believed that their reports were definitely real memories, and the remaining one-quarter believed that their reports were probably real memories.

TARGET EVENT

Frequency of Reports

Case 1 further illustrates the influence of experimenter suggestion on childhood reports. The subject spontaneously reported that she "saw" a mobile hanging above her crib, briefly described the mobile, and when prompted for more details, provided them. Case 2 reported on her kindergarten experience but without discussing the critical object, the spiral disk. We initially predicted that the kindergarten subjects would be more likely than the infancy subjects to report the critical object, reasoning that subject's metacognitive beliefs about the ability to recover very early memories might cause some subjects to reject the infancy suggestion. However, this is not what we found. Eleven of the 18 subjects (61%) who reported infancy experience included in their reports objects that they self-defined as a mobile or that were consistent with the general characteristics of a mobile (e.g., described objects hanging from strings above their cribs). In contrast, only 4 of the 16 subjects (25%) who reported kindergarten experiences included in their reports descriptions of objects that were consistent with the suggested spiral disk.

Believed-In Authenticity

Recall that subjects had to tell us later whether they thought their experiences constituted reality or fantasy. Recall that only four of the subjects in the kindergarten group reported the complementary spiral disk. Two of these subjects rated their reports as definitely real memories, and the other two rated their reports as probably real memories. These kindergarten subjects rated their memories as closer to reality when compared to the group of infancy subjects who had conjured up a memory of a mobile.

IMAGERY VIVIDNESS

Subjects rated the vividness of their experiences using a 5-point scale that ranged from 1 (extremely vivid) to 5 (not at all vivid). Ratings were collected after subjects were progressed from their regressed age to their current age. On average, subjects defined their experiences as moderately vivid, with a mean near 3 and vividness ratings did not differ between those regressed to infancy and kindergarten or between those who saw the target detail and those who did not.

Vividness ratings did, however, correlate with subjects' self-perceived authenticity of their experiences. Infancy subjects who reported more vivid images also tended to believe in the reality of their experiences, and, conversely, subjects who had less vivid experiences tended to define their experiences as fantasies. The corresponding analysis for subjects in the kindergarten condition was not computed because all these subjects reported that their reported images reflected actual memories.

BELIEFS ABOUT MEMORY

Recall that all subjects were pretested on their beliefs about memory. Seven items from Garry et al.'s (1997) Memory Beliefs scale were used as an index of beliefs about the permanence of human memory. All seven items were concerned with the extent to which subjects believe that experiences are permanently stored in human memory (e.g., precise records of all our experiences are permanently stored in the brain). Possible scores on this scale ranged from 7 to 35, and high scores indicated a belief in memory permanence. Fortunately, as expected, subjects regressed to infancy and those regressed to kindergarten did not differ significantly on these pretested beliefs. Surprisingly, beliefs about memory permanence did not differentiate those subjects who reported the target events and those who did not.

Two additional items from Garry et al. (1997) were used as an index of the extent to which subjects believed that techniques such as hypnosis are effective for retrieving nonconfabulated recollections from memory. These items were summed to yield one score. High scores indicate a belief in the effectiveness of hypnosis-like retrieval strategies and low scores indicate disbelief (scores range from 2 to 10). Fortunately, as expected, subjects regressed to infancy and kindergarten did not differ on this pretested belief dimension. However, beliefs in the memory-related efficacy of such techniques did differentiate subjects who reported the target events and those who did not.

DISCUSSION

Nearly all empirical researchers would agree that adults are exceedingly unlikely to reliably recall events that occurred before 2 years of age. Given this restriction on memory we can be fairly certain that memories about infancy are not based on genuine experiences but are due to some other factor. Subjects in this study were regressed to infancy to determine whether a multifaceted regimen involving imagery, age regression, and symptom interpretation would lead subjects to generate obviously false reports from the day after birth. Ninety percent of the subjects did so.

Of the 18 subjects who generated reports from the day after birth, one-third believed that their memories were probably or definitely actual memories. That subjects are willing to generate detailed and vivid fantasies about events for which they cannot possibly have memories is perhaps not so surprising. But that one-third of these subjects then go on to insist that their fantasy creations are real memories is perhaps more surprising. What do subjects rely on to make judgments concerning memory authenticity? The vividness of their images appears to be one variable. Subjects who rated their regression experiences as vivid were also more likely to report that their experiences were authentic memories. This finding is in line with other research showing a correlation between image vividness and subjective authenticity.

Subjects were given instructions designed to enhance the likelihood that they would recall that they were exposed to cognitively stimulating stimuli either as infants or as young children in kindergarten. Infancy subjects were told that their personality profile, High Perceptual Cognitive Monitor, indicated that they were probably exposed to a mobile hanging over their cribs in the hospital nursery and kindergarten subjects were told that they were probably exposed to rotating spiral disks in their kindergarten class. From the prior finding at Carleton University, we suspected that a large number of infancy subjects might incorporate the suggested visual stimuli into their accounts. However, we were curious as to whether subjects regressed to an older age would also succumb to the suggestion, and perhaps to a greater degree.

Subjects regressed to infancy described details that are routinely associated with a hospital room nursery (e.g., bright lights, viewing window, and parents watching them) and many of them also indicated that they saw the suggested mobile hanging over their hospital crib. Similarly, subjects regressed to kindergarten described details that were consistent with the experimenter's suggestion about the spiral disk. However, fewer subjects in the kindergarten condition succumbed to the target suggestion (i.e., rotating spiral disk) than subjects in the infancy condition. Whereas over 60% of subjects who reported infancy experiences included the critical suggested item in their reports, only 25% of those regressed to kindergarten included the suggested spiral disk.

At least three potentially interrelated hypotheses may explain these findings. Two can be answered easily with the findings from ongoing research in our lab, and the third and fourth involve the notions of reporting criterion and demand-related pressures. Could subjects be using their experiences with others as the source of their descriptions? If so, it seems that such an account could explain the discrepancy in target-stimuli report rates between the kindergarten and infancy conditions. It may be that subjects, in general, have a better conception of what a mobile looks like than a spiral disk and that it required less effort for them to generate an image of a mobile than a spiral disk. The image may have been taken from experiences with younger siblings, younger relatives, or friends. Given that it was relatively easy to visualize, they may have reported it. This account suggests that they may have blended the experiences of others with their own historical accounts. On the other hand, kindergarten subjects may have been less able to generate an image of a spiral disk because they are less likely to have been exposed to such devices directly or indirectly, and as such were less likely to generate and report the details in their regression accounts. Of course, there is always the possibility that kindergarten subjects believe less in the probability, in general, of the widespread implementation of kindergarten programs compared to the hospital programs and that their disbelief precluded them from entertaining the idea that they may have been participants in such programs. We were careful to equate the two conditions to the best of our ability by keeping the rationales in the two conditions identical. We did, however, deem it necessary to use a different visual stimulus because it is likely that mobiles are not uncommon decorations in kindergarten classrooms. Nonetheless, kindergarten subjects may have deemed the kindergarten ruse as less believable than the corresponding infancy ruse. Preliminary data, where subjects rate the believability of both programs, support this hypothesis.

The third explanation involves the concept of reporting criterion and demand. It may be that subjects in the kindergarten condition were less likely to report details that they were unsure about because they did not feel the pressure to do so as they already reported information about which they were relatively confident. Subjects in the infancy condition, however, may have been more likely to report details they were less confident in because their scripts for infancy were truncated by lack of actual or believed-in actual memories and they filled in the gaps in their presentation with details suggested to them by the experimenter. According to this hypothesis, subjects in the infancy condition may have felt stronger pressures to report detail of questionable veracity and thus lowered their reporting criterion. In so doing, infancy subjects may have been more likely to include the target stimuli in their reports than kindergarten subjects. It is important to note that these hypotheses do not assume a greater accuracy of report on behalf of the kindergarten subjects. In general, people are probably more likely to have reviewed or tried to dredge up memories from kindergarten rather than infancy. Regardless of whether these "memories" are accurate, partially accurate, or pure confabulation, subjects would probably have more confidence in these "rehearsed memories."

Within both the infancy and the kindergarten conditions, some subjects endorsed the suggested target detail and some did not. Are there any clues as to what influences whether subjects respond to the suggestion? Subjects who included the suggested detail in the reports and those who did not were equivalent in terms of their self-reported vividness of their images. Those who "remembered" the suggested detail and those who did not were also similar in the extent to which they generally believe that experiences are permanently stored in human memory. The "remembering" and the "nonremembering" subjects did, however, differ in their beliefs about the effectiveness of memory-retrieval strategies to dig out accurate memories. Subjects who reported the target detail believed to a greater extent in the efficacy of memory-retrieval techniques than those who did not report the target detail.

Infancy subjects who resisted the suggestion to see a mobile believed to a greater extent than those who did not that their regression experiences reflected actual memories. In thinking about why this might be so, at least one hypothesis comes to mind: Perhaps the overt suggestion and experimenter prompting leads to increased reporting of the detail, but, at the same time, these activities may also lead some subjects to question the veracity of their experiences. According to this notion, nonsuggestive regression procedures may foster genuine belief in fantastic tales of improbable events whereas more suggestive techniques may deflate these beliefs.

COMPARISONS BETWEEN THE CANADIAN AND AMERICAN SAMPLES

Our findings and those of Burgess (1994) demonstrate that most subjects were willing to generate reports about infancy (see Table 6.1 for a comparison). We found that 90% of our subjects who were regressed to infancy described age-consistent experiences and Burgess (1994) found that "almost all" of her 60 hypnotic and nonhypnotic subjects described similar experiences. Moreover, 55% (11 of 20) of our subjects and 50% of Burgess's generated infancy accounts that included the suggested mobile. These findings are clear in showing that many subjects are quite willing to generate obviously false memories from infancy. These false memories contain details derived from their own conceptions of the target situation and may also contain suggestion-induced information derived from the experimental setting.

The authenticity reports are also revealing. Across the two studies, just over 40% of the subjects conceded that their infancy accounts were probably or definitely fantasy creations. That is, they held at least a somewhat accurate perception of their experiences. However, nearly one-third of subjects were unsure about the validity of their memories or defined them as probable or definite memories. Given that we can be virtually certain about the implausibility of these infancy reports, we have evidence here for

TABLE 6.1. Comparisons Drawn betweeen the Canadian and American Samples

	Canadian		American	
	Hypnotic	Nonhypnotic	Infancy	Kindergarten
Reported experience (%)	"Almost all"		90	100
Authenticity (%)				
Real	47	47	33.3	100
Unsure	43	30	50	0
Fantasy	10	23	16.7	0
Reported target (%)	43	57	55	25
Authenticity				
Real	46	41	30	100
Unsure	46	35	50	0
Fantasy	8	24	20	0

Note. There were 30 subjects in each of the Canadian hypnotica and nonhypnotic conditions. The respective *n*'s in the American infancy and kindergarten condition were 20 and 16, respectively.

reports of memories that are false and a concomitant belief that these false memories are genuine.

Although the American and Canadian findings have some similarities there were some differences. The authenticity that subjects held in their reports differed somewhat between the two studies. Burgess found that nearly 47% of her sample believed that their experiences were based on probable or definite memories of infancy. We found that a substantially lower percentage of subjects believed that their reports were actual memories. Only 33% of the infancy subjects believed that their reports reflected probable or definite memories. Nonetheless, half of our subjects were unsure about the reality of their memories, thus demonstrating no intuitive awareness of the concept of childhood amnesia.

Why might the Canadian sample be more willing to embrace the suggested information? One hypothesis is that the "cover story" seems more plausible to those who grew up in a Canadian culture. Canada has a smaller population than does the United States and a provincially standardized health care system. In contrast, the United States has a greater diversity of health care resources ranging from private, to state, to federal institutions. Given this diversity, American subjects may have been less likely to believe that the psychological program described to them at the beginning of the study could have been implemented at a national level in the United States, and they may have been unable to make the link between their bogus personality profile and the purported earlier cognitive stimulation. This negative mind-set in the American subjects may then have influenced their receptivity to the regression experiences.

Of course, it is always possible that the Canadian experimenter was simply more skilled at conducting the regression procedures. This skill may have led to an increased belief on the part of subjects that their experiences were indeed veridical. It is also possible that the timing of the two studies might have made a difference. The Canadian study was run years earlier than the American one, and the level of publicity concerning memory issues was different at those times. Other variables such as the rapport developed between subject and experimenter may have also influenced the extent to which subjects defined their experiences as real rather than fantasy.

ALTERNATIVE ACCOUNTS OF FINDINGS

Source Confusion

Some may argue that age-regressed experiences are accurate reflections of the past, but the time at which the events occurred is distorted. According to this view, memories recalled from well before the infantile amnesic barrier are memories of actual events that occurred later on in life. However, in the present paradigm, half the subjects were regressed to the day after birth. The events to which a person is exposed in the first few days of life are experienced only once and it is difficult to conceive of situations that even closely resemble the hospital nursery environment. Given that the experience is a unique one, it is unlikely that subjects are recalling accurate memories of their own experiences while distorting their source.

Demand

Perhaps these results are due to nothing more than demand, as in Orne's (1973) concept of demand-related responding. In traditional laboratory research, compliance to experimental demand is considered a nuisance variable best treated with statistical or experimental control. The same concern could be applied to clinical settings, with the best situation arising when clients' responses are genuinely their own. However, client–therapist relationships are not demand-free. They are complex social relationships in which both the therapist and client are susceptible to the subtle and not-so-subtle pressures to respond according to situational demands and role assignments. Not only do the therapists place demands on clients to progress in therapy, but clients may themselves be similarly motivated. Such demands may play an important role in the initial development of memories to the extent that subjects are willing to go through with and to consider a therapist's interpretations of their complaints and suggestions for improvement. Anecdotes of women who accuse but then recant their allegations (Gavigan, 1992) and those who at their therapist's persuasion confront their alleged abusers in the absence of memories (e.g., McElroy & Keck, 1995) suggest that these demands are very real ones. Rather than dismissing these demands as nuisance variables, it is critical that we examine their possible influence in clinical settings.

Consequences of False Recall

In the studies just discussed, recalling the suggested stimuli resulted in relatively few consequences, good or bad. Pezdek (1994) argues that people are unlikely to recall false instances of childhood incest because the consequences of such recall are real life and traumatic. We argue that remembering false childhood sexual abuse does not necessarily have negative consequences for the client: There may be positive consequences for those who harbor false beliefs that they were sexually abused. Recovery of false memories of abuse may explain years of psychological and/or physical discomfort and be the impetus that allows them to move beyond their present-day pain—whatever its cause. Beyond the possible positive consequences derived from discovering an explanatory construct, however, clients may derive positive gain for recalling events that are in line with their therapist's expectations and beliefs.

CONCLUSION

A principal aim of this chapter is to report new research findings that might enhance understanding of potential precursors to and the conditions under which false memories may be generated. Imagery-based age-regression techniques allow subjects to generate fantastic stories of necessarily false experiences. Although some of our subjects did indeed recognize the fantastic nature of their regression reports, others claimed to believe in the authenticity of these reports. We urge caution in using these techniques to verify preexisting beliefs about the cause of a client's symptomology. Many questions in this chapter cry out for future empirical attention. In contrast, we can offer only one answer about the imagery-based techniques used in our study: If you use them, (pseudo)memories may come.

ACKNOWLEDGMENTS

Susan C. DuBreuil was supported by a postdoctoral fellowship award from the Social Sciences and Humanities Council of Canada. Maryanne Garry was supported by an NIH UW Cooperative Research Center STD New Investigator Award.

REFERENCES

American Psychiatric Association. (1987). *Diagnostic and statistical manual of mental disorders* (3rd ed., rev.). Washington, DC: Author.

Baker, R. A. (1982). The effect of suggestion on past-lives regression. *American Journal of Clinical Hypnosis, 25,* 71–76.

Barnier, A. J., & McConkey, K. M. (1992). Reports of real and false memories: The relevance of hypnosis, hypnotizability, and context of memory test. *Journal of Abnormal Psychology, 101*, 521–527.

Bass, E., & Davis, L. (1992). *The courage to heal: A guide for women survivors of child sexual abuse.* New York: HarperCollins.

Blume, E. S. (1990). *Secret survivors.* New York: Ballantine.

Burgess, M. F. (1994). *False memory reports in hypnotic and nonhypnotic subjects.* Unpublished master's thesis, Carleton University, Ottawa, Canada.

Ceci, S. J., Huffman, M. L. C., Smith, E., & Loftus, E. F. (1994). Repeatedly thinking about a non-event: Source misattributions among preschoolers. Special Issue: The recovered memory/false memory debate. *Consciousness and Cognition: An International Journal, 3*, 388–407.

Ceci, S. J., & Loftus, E. F. (1994). "Memory work": A royal road to false memories? *Applied Cognitive Psychology, 8*, 351–364.

Ceci, S. J., Loftus, E. F., Leichtman, M. D., & Bruck, M. (1994). The possible role of source misattributions in the creation of false beliefs among preschoolers. *International Journal of Clinical and Experimental Hypnosis, 42*, 304–320.

Ewin, D. M. (1994). Many memories retrived with hypnosis are accurate. *American Journal of Clinical Hypnosis, 36*, 174–176.

Frederickson, R. (1992). *Repressed memories.* New York: Fireside.

Frontline. (1995). *Divided memories.*

Garry, M., Loftus, E. F., & Brown, S. W. (1994). Memory: A river runs through it. Special Issue: The recovered memory/false memory debate. *Consciousness and Cognition: An International Journal, 3*, 438–451.

Garry, M., Loftus, E. F., Brown, S., & DuBreuil, S. C. (1997) Womb with a view: Memory beliefs and memory-work experiences. In D. G.Payne & F. G. Conrad (Eds.), *Intersections in basic and applied memory research* (pp. 233–256). Mahwah, NJ: Erlbaum.

Gavigan, M. (1992). False memories of child sexual abuse: A personal account. *Issues in Child Abuse Accusations, 4*, 246–247.

Hyman, I. E., Husband, T. H., & Billings, F. J. (1995). False memories of childhood experiences. *Applied Cognitive Psychology, 9*, 181–197.

Johnson, R. F. Q. (1989). Hypnosis, suggestion, and dermatological changes. In N. P. Spanos & J. F. Chaves (Eds.), *Hypnosis: The cognitive-behavioral perspective* (pp. 297–312). New York: Prometheus Books.

Labelle, L., Lamarche, M. C., & Laurence, J.-R. (1990). Potential jurors' opinions on the effects of hypnosis on eyewitness identification: A brief communication. *International Journal of Clinical and Experimental Hypnosis, 38*, 315–319.

Lawson, A. H. (1984). Perinatal imagery in UFO abduction reports. *Journal of Psychohistory, 12*, 211–239.

Lindsay, D. S., & Read, J. D. (1994). Psychotherapy and memories of childhood sexual abuse: A cognitive perspective. *Applied Cognitive Psychology, 8*, 281–338.

Loftus, E. F. (1979). The malleability of human memory. *American Scientist, 67*, 312–320.

Loftus, E. F. (1993). The reality of repressed memories. *American Psychologist, 48*, 518–537.

Loftus, E. F. (1994). The repressed memory controversy. *American Psychologist, 49*, 443–445.

Loftus, E. F., & Ketcham, K. (1994). *The myth of repressed memory.* New York: St. Martin's Press.

Loftus, E. F., & Loftus, G. R. (1980). On the permanence of stored information in the human brain. *American Psychologist, 35,* 409–420.

Loftus, E. F., & Palmer, J. (1974). Reconstruction of automobile destruction: An example of the interactin between language and memory. *Journal of Verbal Learning and Verbal Behavior, 13,* 585–589.

Loftus, E. F., & Pickrell, J. (1995). The formation of false memories. *Psychiatric Annals, 25,* 720–724.

Loftus, E. F., & Zanni, G. (1975). Eyewitness testimony: The influence of the wording of a question. *Bulletin of the Psychonomic Society, 5,* 86–88.

Longo, D. J., Clum, G. A., & Yaeger, N. J. (1988). Psychosocial treatment for recurrent genital herpes. *Journal of Consulting and Clinical Psychology, 56,* 61–66.

Lynn, S. J., Milano, M., & Weekes, J. R. (1991). Hypnosis and pseudomemories: The effects of prehypnotic expectancies. *Journal of Personality and Social Psychology, 60,* 318–326.

McCann, T. E., & Sheehan, P. W. (1987). The breaching of pseudomemory under hypnotic instruction: Implications for original memory retrieval. *British Journal of Experimental and Clinical Hypnosis, 4,* 101–108.

McConkey, K. M., & Jupp, J. J. (1985). Opinions about the forensic use of hypnosis. *Australian Psychologist, 20,* 283–291.

McConkey, K. M., Labelle, L., Bibb, B. C., & Bryant, R. A. (1990). Hypnosis and suggested pseudomemory: The relevance of test context. *Australian Journal of Psychology, 42,* 197–205.

McElroy, S. L., & Keck, P. E. (1995). Misattribution of eating and obsessive–compulsive disorder symptoms to repressed memories of childhood sexual or physical abuse. *Biological Psychiatry, 37,* 48–51.

Merskey, H. (1996). Recovered memories. *British Journal of Psychiatry, 169,* 665–673.

Mulhern, S. (1994). Satanism, ritual abuse, and multiple personality disorder: A sociohistorical perspective. *International Journal of Clinical and Experimental Hypnosis, 42,* 265–288.

Nash, M. R. (1987). What, if anything, is age regressed about hypnotic age regression? A review of the empirical literature. *Psychological Bulletin, 102,* 42–52.

O'Connell, D. N., Shor, R. E., & Orne, M. T. (1970). Hypnotic age regression: An empirical and methodological analysis. *Journal of Abnormal Psychology Monographs, 76*(3, Pt. 2).

Orne, M. T. (1973). Communication by the total experimental situation: Why it is important, how it is evaluated, and its significance for the ecological validity of findings. In P. Pliner, L. Krames, & T. Alloway (Eds.), *Communication and affect: Language and thought.* New York: Academic Press.

Pezdek, K. (1994). The illusion of illusory memory. *Applied Cognitive Psychology, 8,* 339–350.

Pillemer, D. B., & White, S. H. (1989). Childhood events recalled by children and adults. *Advances in Child Development and Behavior, 21,* 297–340.

Poole, D. A., Lindsay, S., Memon, A., & Bull, R. (1995). Psychotherapy and the recovery of memories of childhood sexual abuse: U.S. and British Practitioners' opinions, practices, and experiences. *Journal of Consulting and Clinical Psychology, 63,* 426–437.

Roland, C. B. (1993). Exploring childhood memories with adult survivors of sexual abuse: Concrete reconstruction and visualization techniques. *Journal of Mental Health Counseling, 15,* 363–372.

Sheehan, P. W., Statham, D., & Jamieson, G. A. (1991). Pseudomemory effects over time in the hypnotic setting. *Journal of Abnormal Psychology, 100*, 39–44.

Siegal, R. K. (1992). *Fire in the brain: Clinical tales of hallucination*. New York: Plume.

Siegel, D. R., & Romig, C. A. (1990). Memory retrieval in treating adult survivors of sexual abuse. *American Journal of Family Therapy, 18*, 246–256.

Sloane, M. C. (1981). A comparison of hypnosis vs. waking state and visual vs. nonvisual recall instructions for witness/victim memory retrieval in actual major crimes. *Dissertation Abstracts International, 42*, 2551.

Spanos, N. P. (1996). *Multiple identities and false memories: A sociocognitive perspective on multiple personality disorder, hypnosis, and spirit*. Washington, DC: American Psychological Association.

Spanos, N. P., Burgess, C. A., & Burgess, M. F. (1994). Past-life identities, UFO abductions, and satanic ritual abuse: The social construction of memories. *International Journal of Clinical and Experimental Hypnosis, 42*, 433–446.

Spanos, N. P., Cross, P. A., Dickson, K., & DuBreuil, S. C. (1993). Close encounters: An examination of UFO experiences. *Journal of Abnormal Psychology, 102*, 624–632.

Spanos, N. P., Gwynn, M. I., Comer, S. L., Baltruweit, W. J., & deGroh, M. (1989). Are hypnotically induced pseudomemories resistant to cross-examination? *Law and Human Behavior, 13*, 271–289.

Spanos, N. P., Menary, E., Gabora, N. J., DuBreuil, S. C., & Dewhirst, B. (1991). Secondary identity enactments during hypnotic past-life regression: A sociocognitive perspective. *Journal of Personality and Social Psychology, 61*, 308–320.

Spanos, N. P., Quigley, C. A., Gwynn, M. I., Glatt, R. L., & Perlini, A. H. (1992). Hypnotic interrogation, pretrial preparation and witness testimony during direct examination and cross-examination. *Law and Human Behavior, 15*, 639–653.

Spanos, N. P., Stenstrom, R. J., & Johnston, J. C. (1988). Hypnosis, placebo, and suggestion in the treatment of warts. *Psychosomatic Medicine, 50*, 245–260.

Tavris, C. (1993, January 3). Beware the incest survivor machine. *New York Times Book Review*, pp. 1, 16–17.

Usher, J. A., & Neisser, U. (1993). Childhood anmesia and the beginnings of memory for four early life events. *Journal of Experimental Psychology: General, 122*, 155–165.

van Husen, J. E. (1988). The development of fears, phobias, and restrictive patterns of adaptation following attempted abortions. *Pre- and Peri-Natal Psychology Journal, 2*, 179–185.

Wambach, H. (1978). *Reliving past lives: The evidence under hypnosis*. New York: Harper & Row.

Winograd, E., & Killinger, W. A. (1983). Relating age at encoding in early childhood to adult recall: Development of flashbulb memories. *Journal of Experimental Psychology: General, 112*, 413–422.

Yapko, M. D. (1994). Suggestibility and repressed memories of abuse: A survey of psychotherapist's beliefs. *American Journal of Clinical Hypnosis, 36*, 163–171.

Yarmey, A. D., & Tressellian-Jones, H. P. (1983). Is psychology of eyewitness testimony a matter of common sense? In S. M. A. Lloyd-Bostock & B. R. Clifford (Eds.), *Evaluating witness confidence*. New York: Wiley.

Yuille, J. C., & McEwan, N. H. (1985). Use of hypnosis as an aid to eyewitness memory. *Journal of Applied Psychology, 70*, 389–400.

SUGGESTION AND SUGGESTIBILITY IN CHILDREN

CHAPTER 7

MEMORY AND SUGGESTIBILITY IN MALTREATED CHILDREN
New Research Relevant to Evaluating Allegations of Abuse

Mitchell L. Eisen
Gail S. Goodman
Jianjian Qin
Suzanne L. Davis

In the late 1970s and early 1980s, a rash of sensational cases of mass molestation of children in day-care facilities was publicized in the popular media. At about the same time, investigators reported prevalence studies indicating that in the United States, approximately 25% of the adult female population and 9% of the adult male population suffered some form of sexual abuse as children or teenagers (Finkelhor, 1984; Russell, 1983). It was then unclear whether American society was coming to grips with an alarming rate of child abuse to which it had been turning a blind eye or whether society was overreacting to the imaginative creations of young children and the hysteria of front-line investigators faced with these new and alarming allegations. Deep divisions emerged within and across several professional fields, with advocates on one side claiming that children are incapable of lying and their reports of abuse should always be assumed valid, and advocates on the other side claiming that all memory reports that come without corroboration or physical evidence are suspect and likely corrupted through subtle means during undisciplined interviewing procedures or direct coaching. Although a vast literature of basic research on children's memory existed at that time, little scientific work was available on children's performance as eyewitnesses or on optimal interviewing techniques for children in abuse cases.

An increasing awareness of problematic questioning techniques employed in some high-profile investigations coupled with a dearth of corroborative evidence regarding the more bizarre allegations of rampant cult ritual abuse led to a backlash of cynicism. This cynicism, spawned by a concern with false reports, turned societal attention away from the earlier prevalence studies and mounting documentation of short- and long-term adverse mental health effects of child abuse (e.g., Kendall-Tackett, Williams, & Finkelhor, 1993; Kolko, 1992). A more balanced approach, we believe, is to acknowledge that society faces two serious problems: underreporting of abuse when it has indeed occurred and overreporting of abuse when it has not occurred. Although we view the former as the more prevalent problem, both problems are in need of remedy. Solutions to these problems rely in important ways on understanding children's memory and suggestibility about abusive acts. Specifically, society needs to know when we can or cannot rely on children's memories of abuse.

Debates about children's memory and suggestibility and how best to interview children about abuse are far from resolved. Fortunately, increased interest in these issues has spawned a flood of research. In this chapter, we review relevant studies on memory and suggestibility in children, including the developmental literature on effects of stress and trauma on memory. We also focus on the possible role of individual differences in children's memory performance. This review is followed by a discussion of the importance of ecological validity in studying children's eyewitness memory. Finally, we present an overview of a recent study we conducted concerning effects of age, dissociation, and stress arousal on memory and suggestibility in abused and neglected children (Eisen, Goodman, & Qin, 1995).

ACCURACY IN MEMORY

Although research on child witnesses is relatively new, it is grounded in an established literature on basic memory processes that provides a wealth of information on normal memory development. One of the most robust findings in this area indicates that remembering is, at least in part, a process of reconstruction for both children and adults (Bartlett, 1932; Loftus, 1979; Stein, Trabasso, & Liwag, 1993, 1997). This reconstruction is the result of an interpretative process based on original perceptions. Although the resulting recollection is never identical to the original perceptions, this does not demonstrate conclusively that memory is universally poor or highly suggestible. More accurately, it is generally believed that there are conditions in which memory is likely to be highly accurate and stable as well as conditions in which it may be inaccurate or modifiable (Pezdek & Roe, 1994; Stein, Wade, & Liwag, 1997). In addition, age differences exist in individuals' tendencies to distort perceived information at the points of encoding, retention, and retrieval, as discussed next.

It is generally believed that compared to adults, children have fewer cognitive resources and a more limited knowledge base available to help them encode and retrieve complex information. One consistent finding in the literature on children's memory is that the amount and accuracy of information reported in a memory interview typically increases with age (e.g., Goodman & Reed, 1986; Leippe, Romanczyk, & Manion, 1992) as does children's (especially preschoolers') resistance to misleading information (Ceci & Bruck, 1993; Goodman & Aman, 1991). It has been convincingly demonstrated that some memories are retained quite well by children over long durations (Fivush, 1993; Hudson & Fivush, 1987). However, data indicate that young children's memories are at times more fragile and fade relatively quickly compared to adults' memories of the same materials (Brainerd & Reyna, 1991; Flin, Boon, Knox, & Bull, 1992).

At the encoding level, young children may lack the ability to infer causal relations that link complex events (Stein & Trabasso, 1985), due in part to the lack of a well-developed knowledge base to give meaning to events (Chi, 1978). These difficulties in encoding are directly related to retention and retrieval. If information is not organized in a meaningful fashion initially, prolonged retention and accurate retrieval become increasingly difficult.

At the retrieval level, many young children lack the ability or motivation, especially in formal interview settings, to recall and report detailed episodic memories on their own, including memories of abuse (Keary & Fitzpatrick, 1994). Even when young children have accurately encoded and retained large amounts of information, considerable cuing and contextual support may be necessary for them to retrieve and report this information in a meaningful fashion (e.g., Fivush, 1993; Price & Goodman, 1990). With development, children exhibit greater conscious control of the memory process (Kail, 1990) and become better at accessing memories without cues from others (Price & Goodman, 1990). This gradual developmental process is accompanied by a steady increase in children's knowledge base, which fosters the ability to organize information in a meaningful fashion.

Despite clear age trends in the development of memory skills, it is also clear that even young children (i.e., preschoolers) can have accurate memories and are not necessarily highly suggestible (see Goodman & Bottoms, 1993; Spencer & Flin, 1993, for reviews). In a recent review of the literature, Stein, Wade, and Liwag (1997) note that certain memories are extremely accurate, robust, and resistant to updating (see Chinn & Brewer, 1993; Johnson & Siefert, 1994; Stein & Miller, 1993).

Existing evidence does not support either of the more extreme positions that (1) children are universally suggestible and unreliable as witnesses, or (2) children lack the ability to lie or deceive (in contrast, see Chandler, Fritz, & Hala, 1989; Ekman, 1989; Goodman & Bottoms, 1993; Orcutt, Goodman, Batterman-Faunce, Tobey, & Thomas, 1992). As data continue to be compiled, a clearer picture is emerging that some children are more suggestible than others and may be more likely to lie or deceive when interviewed. Moreover, there are several well-documented situational variables that can affect the accuracy of children's memory reports and resistance to suggestion. These issues are reviewed in the next section.

Factors That Influence Children's Eyewitness Memory

Eyewitness memory represents a complex, dynamic process that can be influenced by individual differences and interview factors. However, to date, relatively little attention has been given to individual differences in children's memory and suggestibility. One of the few individual differences addressed in the literature is age. Age was found to be an important predictor of children's resistance to pressure and response to persuasion (Ceci & Bruck, 1993). In all likelihood the roots of these age effects lie in differences in intellectual development, memory abilities, personality tendencies, language development, and emotional functioning. These individual-difference factors are likely to have important effects on children's memory performance. The study of such individual differences represents a vital domain for research on children's eyewitness memory.

Contrary to the dearth of studies in the literature examining the role of individual differences, a number of investigations have identified interview factors related to children's memory and resistance to misleading information that are especially relevant to assessing allegations of abuse. These factors include (1) the type of information recounted, (2) repeated versus single interviews, (3) the context surrounding an interview, (4) motivational factors and rapport, (5) the language used, and (6) the type of questions posed. We deal with each of these issues individually.

The type of information to be recounted is a key determinant of the accuracy of children's recollections and of children's resistance to misleading information. Information that is central or salient tends to be remembered with greater accuracy than peripheral or nonsalient information (Cassel & Bjorklund, 1995; Goodman & Reed, 1986; Loftus, 1979). As the strength of children's memory for an event increases, so often does their resistance to misleading information (but see Howe, 1991), although this trend can be overshadowed by social forces (e.g., intimidation) that also affect performance. Still, the centrality, salience, and memorability of information are important factors in understanding children's suggestibility. Thus, most laboratory studies that assess children's memory and suggestibility for nonmemorable events may be poor analogues for predicting children's reporting of significant events in their lives, such as experiences of abuse.

Repetition in questioning has long been regarded as a potential contaminant in information gathering. However, recent data on repeated interviewing of children do not necessarily support this contention. There has been a flourish of studies exploring the effects of repeated interviewing (see Poole & White, 1995, for a review). Repetition studies generally entail two types of designs. Some repetition studies involve questioning children about an event that actually occurred (Bruck, Ceci, Francoeur, & Barr, 1995; Dent & Stephenson, 1979; Fivush & Schwarzmueller, 1995; Goodman, Bottoms, Schwartz-Kenney, & Rudy, 1991; Leichtman & Ceci, 1995a, 1995b; Poole & Lindsay, 1994), whereas other repetition studies involve asking children about "nonevents" that never actually happened (e.g., Ceci, Loftus, Leichtman, & Bruck, 1995). Among studies in the former group, children may watch a filmed event, observe a staged event, or actively participate in an event. The children are then asked repeatedly about the event over a period of days, weeks, or months in a nonsuggestive fashion or with the repeated presentation of misleading information. Despite the pervasive belief that repeated interviewing has a corrupting influence on children's memory, findings from a number of studies generally indicate that repeatedly interviewing children in a nonmisleading fashion has no detrimental effect on memory and may actually improve recall through rehearsal and/or reminiscence (Brainerd & Ornstein 1991; Dent, 1991; Howe, 1991) or the process of memory reinstatement (Howe, Courage, & Bryant-Brown, 1993; Rovee-Collier & Shyi, 1992). In their review of relevant literature, Fivush and Schwarzmueller (1995) note that repeated interviews provide an opportunity for children to rehearse an event, noting that if a memory is not rehearsed, the event may remain relatively unorganized and fragmentary, becoming increasingly difficult to retrieve over time. This may be especially relevant to cases of abuse when children choose not to think or talk about the event. However, Fivush and Schwarzmueller (1995) add that once a coherently organized memory is established, recall seems to be quite robust and stable over time.

Other studies found that repeated interviewing with the use of misleading suggestions can lead to significant distortions in memory reports for many young children (e.g., Bruck, Ceci, Francoeur, & Barr, 1995; but see Goodman et al., 1991). However, a close examination of the results of several of these studies reveals that the lion's share of the variance in errors produced by misleading suggestions came after the first round of questioning, while increments in inaccuracies from repeated questioning were actually not significant or present only for a subset of children (Cassel, Roebers, & Bjorklund, 1996; Ceci, Crotteau-Huffman, Smith, & Loftus, 1995; Poole, 1995). Moreover, in some of these studies, children were told that their parents said the child experienced the event, thus making the studies uncharacteristic of a typical child abuse investigation.

Repeated questions within a single interview were also found to lead to errors in children's reporting (see Fivush & Schwarzmueller, 1995; Poole & White, 1995, for reviews). Such errors appear to be related to the social context demands of being asked the same question twice. In such cases children may assume they gave the wrong answer the first time and change their response due to the social demands of the encounter (Siegal, Waters, & Dinwiddie, 1988), although sometimes the change is simply to "I don't know" (Moston, 1987). Saywitz and Moan-Hardie (1994) found that instructing children that they might be asked the same question repeatedly, and that this does not mean that their first response was wrong, seems to help children maintain their initial response over repeated questioning. This finding is especially relevant to legal interrogations of children in abuse cases where repeated questioning techniques are not uncommon.

In a single interview, one runs the risk of not gaining important information the child has to offer due to initial fearfulness and/or guardedness on the part of the child. In addition, there is good evidence that young children do not necessarily recall all the information they are capable of in a single interview. They may describe bits and pieces of the event at different times, with each piece representing a valid part of the puzzle. The fact that children may focus on different aspects of the event at different times may make them appear to be inconsistent and thus unreliable witnesses (Fivush, 1993). This inconsistency is not so much a function of inaccuracy as it is a function of the questions the child is asked in each interview, the child's interpretation of the questions, and the child's ability to retrieve relevant information at that point in time.

The forensic interview context can often influence how children respond to the questioning. The abuse investigation provides a unique context for questioning children. For many children this is a very stressful and confusing time. When children are involved in such investigations they are often removed from their homes, subjected to repeated interviews from a variety of sources, and asked questions about whether their parents, neighbors, and friends have hit them, hurt them, or touched them in a sexualized manner. Tobey and Goodman (1992) found that providing an accusatory context (e.g., suggesting that someone did something bad) may lead to increased inaccuracies for some preschool children, although it did not lead to an increase in false abuse reports, whereas Lepore and Sescoe (1994) created an even stronger accusatory context which resulted in error to abuse-related questions.

Motivational factors that promote honesty or deception are always important to consider in dealing with allegations of abuse and neglect. Many children interviewed about allegations of abuse are keenly aware of what reporting means to their family. Such revelations could ostracize them, isolate them from their loved ones, and lead to the dissolution of the family as a whole, resulting in a total loss of the only support system these children know. Sometimes children are coached to repeat scripts to the interviewer or outright lie. Often this coaching involves parents telling children how the investigators are evil and trying to tear their family apart. Other times children are threatened with violence if they reveal what has happened to them. It is important to understand what children believe the interview is about, how they interpret the information in question, and, most of all, how they understand the repercussions of disclosing information.

Rapport has also been found to influence children's resistance to misleading information. A supportive context can bolster young children's resistance to suggestive misinformation about abuse, whereas intimidation can contribute to young children's suggestibility about abuse-related events (Carter, Bottoms, & Levine, 1997; Goodman et al., 1991).

Children's level of language development dictates the types of questions children can understand. Recent studies suggest that when children are questioned about a past event, they may try to answer questions they do not fully comprehend by responding to the part of the question they understand (Saywitz & Snyder, 1991). When presented with a lengthy question they cannot follow, young children may respond to the beginning or the end of the inquiry. As cooperative interviewees, they hold up their end of the conversation by answering questions to the best of their abilities (Goodman & Saywitz, 1994). Studies indicate that when children are in settings in which tasks and stimuli are complex and unfamiliar, young children may be less likely to know when they misunderstand questions and fail to request clarification from the interviewer (Asher, 1976; Markman, 1977; Patterson, Masad, & Cosgrove, 1978). In addition, children under about 8 or 10 years of age have difficulty comprehending legal terms commonly used in court (Flin, Stevenson, & Davies, 1989; Saywitz, Jaenicke, & Camparo, 1990). Studies investigating children's ability to respond accurately when interviewed with questions involving legal terminology and phrasing show significant increases in error rates (e.g., Carter et al., 1997; Perry, McAuliff, Tam, Claycomb, Dostal, & Flanagan, 1995). Even when children have the ability to report information accurately, poor questioning techniques that do not take into account children's language skills could lead to significant increases in errors. Interviewers must be sensitive to these issues when constructing questions, and researchers should consider language development in designing protocols and interpreting their findings.

The types of questions posed are an important consideration in a forensic interview, especially when one appreciates that the types of questions needed to elicit information from children about abuse may be deemed leading in a legal context. One robust finding from the research literature is that open-ended questions (e.g., "Tell me everything you can about what happened") typically result in the most accurate memory reports (e.g., Dent & Stephenson, 1979). When children are asked broad, open-ended questions, their memory is most likely to come mainly from their own experience. However, children's responses to open-ended inquiries tend to be the most circumscribed. Young children may give very brief and nondescript responses to open-ended questions even though the same children can demonstrate more detailed memory when asked specific questions (Hutcheson, Baxter, Telfer, & Warden, 1995).

Because open-ended questions tend to provide the least inaccurate information, they are often recommended for initial queries during an interview. However, the avoidance of all specific (e.g., leading) questions and the sole use of open-ended questions do not guarantee accurate and unbiased reporting. Recent work indicates that under certain conditions, even open-ended questions can elicit inaccurate reports. For example, this can occur when children report a different event than the one of interest to the interviewer. Such reports could lead to a great deal of confusion if interviewers do not realize that the children are recalling a totally different event than the one about which the interviewer asked (Rudy & Goodman, 1991). In addition, a minority of children in recent studies provided fantasy reports when asked about an event in their past (e.g., Goodman & Aman 1991; Rudy & Goodman, 1991). Moreover, if a child has incorporated repeated misinformation into memory, such information may infiltrate free recall (Leichtman & Ceci, 1995a; but see Goodman & Reed, 1986).

Despite data revealing that some young children's free recall in response to open-ended questions can be inaccurate or fanciful, young children typically answer such questions by providing overly succinct but accurate information. Because this information is often of limited use, interviewers usually need to ask specific questions of children. The amount of information an interviewer elicits is typically increased when children are asked specifically about an event of interest. However, this increase in accuracy is often accompanied by an increase in inaccurate information, especially from young children (Dent & Stephenson, 1979; Goodman & Reed, 1986; Hutcheson et al., 1995). Given the data revealing children's limited response to open-ended questions, coupled with the possible increase in inaccurate information when using leading questions, it is recommended that interviewers conservatively consider the cost–benefit ratio in balancing these concerns when probing for information in their interviews.

STRESS, TRAUMA, AND ECOLOGICAL VALIDITY

Ironically, much of the past research on children's memory that led to doubts about the reliability of their recollections was conducted in laboratory studies investigating recall or recognition of stories, pictures, or films (see Kail, 1990, for a review). Recently, however, investigators have attempted to enhance the ecological validity of their research by involving children as active participants rather than passive spectators in events. This is most evident in the recent flourish of studies assessing children's memory for stressful events in which the children actually took part (e.g., Goodman, Hepps, & Reed, 1986; Goodman , Hirschman, Hepps, & Rudy, 1991; Goodman, Quas, Batterman-Faunce, Riddlesberger, & Kuhn, 1997; Howe, Courage, & Peterson, 1994; Ornstein, Baker-Ward, Gordon, & Merritt, 1993; Steward, 1993; Vandermass, Hess, & Baker-Ward, 1993). The designs of these studies vary considerably in their relevance to eyewitness testimony in regard to accounting for effects of stress, history of trauma, context of the events and interviews, and mode of questioning.

Stress and Memory

Studies examining the influence of stress on memory yielded mixed results. The observation that higher levels of stress are at times associated with decreased task performance goes back at least to the turn of the century (Yerkes & Dodson, 1908). Recent evidence that stress impairs children's memory and heightens their suggestibility is based in part on studies in which memory for information peripheral to the stressor was tested (Bugental, Blue, Cortez, Fleck, & Rodriquez, 1992; Peters, 1987; but see Merritt, Ornstein, & Spicker, 1994). However, other recent work indicates that although peripheral details may or may not be as strongly encoded or retained, the central details of stressful events are retained especially well in memory (Christianson, 1992). This trend is hypothetically due to a significant narrowing of attention and subsequent increased concentration on central information in times of elevated stress and perceived threat. Several authors have hypothesized that increased stress may actually enhance rather than impair memory either through physiological (Gold, 1987) or psychological means (Bohannon, 1988; Goodman et al., 1991; Pillemer, 1993). In their studies of flashbulb memories, Warren-Leubecker and Swartwood (1992) found that children who were more upset about the space shuttle Challenger disaster reported more information and retained the event more consistently in memory than children who were less upset. Steward and Steward (1989) also discovered that children who reported that they were more distressed during painful medical procedures had more complete and accurate memory reports 6 months after the event.

An important trend across several studies and clinical reports is that individual differences exist in children's memories of stressful events. For example, in the Steward and Steward (1989) study, despite the general trend toward increased accuracy in the distressed children, some highly stressed children showed particularly high error rates. In recent research on a stressful medical procedure involving urethral penetration, Goodman and Quas (1997) report that when personality and family factors were controlled, stress in and of itself did not impair or strengthen children's memory at 1- to 4-week delays. Mixed results like these demonstrate the likely importance of individual differences in influencing children's memory.

Trauma and Memory

Currently, substantial debate exists as to whether traumatic memories require special explanatory mechanisms (Brown, 1995). A number of experimentalists argue that there is no special process involved in dealing with memories of trauma (Hembrooke & Ceci, 1995; Howe et al., 1994). Other theorists believe that traumatic memories are processed in a substantially different manner than ordinary events (Alpert, 1995; Whitfield, 1995) and that traumatic stress is qualitatively different from ordinary stress, resulting in unique variants in the way information is stored and retrieved (van der Kolk & Fisler, 1995). van der Kolk and Fisler (1995) argue that trauma stems from an inescapable stressful event that overwhelms one's coping mechanisms, and that memories from these traumatic events are encoded differently than ordinary events, by virtue of alterations in attentional focus from extreme emotional arousal. Bremner, Krystal, Southwick, and Charney (1995) report that traumatic stress interferes with the processing of information through the creation of abnormalities in the functioning of brain regions and systems involved in memory.

van der Kolk's model of trauma and memory is based on Janet's (1919/1925) pioneering work on dissociation. Janet initially described dissociation as a process in which persons faced with overwhelming emotions are unable to create a narrative memory for the event. They therefore compartmentalize this unintegrated memory. The person's fear of facing this overwhelming emotional memory which has been split off keeps them from adequately processing the event in a narrative form. Current theories of dissociation propose that these compartmentalized memories consist largely of sensory perceptions and affective states (Nemiah, 1995; van der Kolk & van der Hart, 1989, 1991).

Dissociation is increasingly being identified as a key defense mechanism employed by abused children (Briere, 1992; Chu & Dill, 1990; Frischholz, 1985; Lynn & Rhue, 1994; Putnam, 1985, 1991; Quimby & Putnam, 1991; Rhue, Lynn, Henry, Buhk, & Boyd, 1990). Theoretically, when children are confronted with the overwhelming stress of abuse or other traumas, they are unable to process the information and employ the defense of dissociation. This mode of cognitive avoidance results in the compartmentalization of the traumatic memory which prohibits the event from being adequately processed. It is hypothesized that the use of this strategy becomes habitual at some point. Supporters of this position note that dissociation exists on a continuum from minor dissociations of everyday life (e.g., daydreaming and instances of automaticity in everyday functioning) to such major forms of psychopathology as dissociative disorders (Carlson & Putnam, 1986; Hilgard, 1977).

It is generally believed that children who come to rely on this defense to deal with traumatic events would also be likely to "dissociate" when confronted with more minor stressful circumstances in everyday life (Bremner et al., 1995; Lynn & Rhue, 1994; Speigel, 1986). Generally, investigators report that a history of exposure to extreme stress (such as childhood physical abuse) increases the risk for stress-related symptomology when reexposed to traumatic stress later in life (see Bremner, Southwick, & Charney, 1994, for a review). There is also evidence that when children are sexually abused at a young age, they are more vulnerable to the development of posttraumatic stress symptoms and depression (Wolfe, Gentile, & Wolfe, 1989; Wolfe, Sas, & Wekerle, 1994), which may also affect memory performance.

Additional research indicating associations between abuse and memory problems exists. Bremner et al. (1995) report finding decrements in explicit memory function in survivors of childhood abuse and note similar findings for a variety of other traumatized groups, including concentration camp survivors (Helweg-Larsen et al., 1952), prisoners of the Korean war (Stuker, Winstead, Galina, & Allain, 1991), and Vietnam veterans (Bremner, Southwick, Johnson, Yehuda, & Charney, 1993). Bremner et al. (1995) also cite recent work that revealed lower left hippocampal volume in survivors of child physical and sexual abuse and decreases in hippocampal metabolism in patients with posttraumatic stress disorder, findings that may provide some evidence for physiological correlates to explicit memory problems in traumatized individuals.

Conversely, there is reason to believe that some abused and otherwise traumatized children may show better recall for personally experienced events in laboratory research by virtue of their being hypervigilant to the details of stressful and otherwise threatening events. In their review of the literature on the impact of long-term effects of chronic childhood abuse, Carlson, Furby, Armstrong, and Shales (1995) note that increased levels of hyperarousal were found in various samples of adults with a history of physical and/or sexual abuse (Briere, 1988; Browne & Finkelhor, 1986; Coons, Bowman, Pellow, & Schneider, 1989; Wolfe et al., 1989). Carlson et al. (1995) note that hyperarousal symptoms could be seen as the result of a preparatory response to a generalized expectation of danger. For some individuals, it is plausible that this increased preparatory response leads to an enhanced attention to the details of threatening situations. In addition, the high level of distrust found in many abused children coupled with this hypervigilance to details in stressful and possibly threatening situations may lead to better memory and enhanced resistance to misleading information. There is logically a point of watershed at which some children may become overly stressed and no longer able to process threatening information in a meaningful manner while other children remain alert and hypervigilant. This point may vary dramatically from child to child due to differences in such factors as social support, coping skills, hardiness, and a history of extreme trauma. Cicchetti, Rogosch, Lynch, and Holt (1993) found some children to be more resilient than others and as a result to show less severe consequences when suffering maltreatment.

In summary, a clear understanding of the relation between stress and memory eludes researchers, perhaps in part because they fail to take individual-difference factors into account. Coping mechanisms associated with experiences of abuse and other forms of victimization may create individual differences in the processing of stressful or traumatic events, with implications for memory. For instance, maltreated children who developed the coping mechanism of dissociation may "tune out" during traumatic experiences, and their memory may thus be adversely affected. Alternatively, abused children may be hypervigilant to threatening events and remember such events with particular clarity. Interesting theoretical formulations have been offered about the interplay of abuse, trauma, and memory, but surprisingly little research exists on maltreated children's memory performance.

The Issue of Ecological Validity

In attempting to understand the effects of stress and trauma on children's memory, the ecological validity of research has gradually progressed in recent years from studying children's memory for trips to the doctor's office (Ornstein et al., 1993; Saywitz, Goodman, Nicholas, & Moan, 1991) to studying their memory for having blood drawn (Goodman, Hirschman, et al., 1991) to studying their memory for having quite stressful and invasive medical procedures (Goodman et al., 1997; Merritt et al., 1994). To increase the ecological validity in relation to abuse investigations, several of these studies focused on children's memory for genital contact.

For example, Saywitz et al. (1991) examined children's suggestibility about an anogenital examination performed during a checkup by a pediatrician, which required that the children undress and that their genitals be touched. The authors proposed that questioning children about memories regarding this experience was more ecologically valid in relation to abuse investigations than previous studies that did not involve memory for genital contact. Like sexual abuse, genital touch might be particularly memorable to the child because it is a personally meaningful, salient, and novel event (see also Goodman, Rudy, Bottoms, & Aman, 1990). The authors found that regardless of the use of leading and misleading questions, 5- to 7-year-olds were unlikely to confuse the touching in an anogenital exam with inappropriate fondling or sexual misconduct even when this was suggested through misleading questioning. In other studies by Goodman and her colleagues (Goodman & Aman, 1991; Goodman, Bottoms et al., 1991; Tobey & Goodman, 1992), the authors reported that children as young as 4 years of age showed relatively high resistance to misleading abuse suggestions (e.g., "The man took your clothes off, didn't he?"). These basic results were maintained over the course of two repetitions of misleading abuse questions (Goodman, Bottoms et al., 1991) and when an accusatory context was introduced (Tobey & Goodman, 1992). However, young children (e.g., 2- and 3-year-olds) can be expected to make more errors than do older children to abuse-related leading and misleading questions (Bruck, Ceci, Francoeur, & Renick, 1995; Goodman & Aman, 1991).

Although these studies represent an important step toward creating ecologically valid models for assessing children's eyewitness memory, important aspects of the ecological validity of this work is still in question. In the Saywitz et al. (1991) study, all participants were young girls visiting a female pediatrician while their mothers accompanied them into the examination room and remained with them throughout the examination. Furthermore, neither the experience (e.g., the medical exam) nor the questioning took place within the context of an actual abuse investigation. In such investigations, children face significant and unique psychological demands in which they may be bombarded with questions and innuendo about sexual misconduct, physically abusive events, and other atrocities over a period of days, weeks, or even months.

It should also be noted that participants in former studies of children's memory for stressful events were not known victims of physical and/or sexual abuse. Moreover, the nonabused children tested in these studies typically were not representative of children who tend to be interviewed in abuse investigations (but see Goodman, Hirschman et al., 1991). If children who suffered maltreatment are developmentally delayed in cognitive or language skills, have deficient memory abilities, or suffer from heightened suggestibility, results from former research might not generalize to children who tend to be interviewed in typical abuse cases. It is also possible that abused children are hypervigilant regarding abusive actions or abuse suggestions and, as a result, would be more resistant to such questioning than nonabused children.

Therefore, there was a clear need for more ecologically valid research examining abused and neglected children's memory and resistance to suggestion when interviewed in a clinical/forensic context and for research that accounted for important intervening variables identified in the literature. In the remainder of this chapter we briefly review the initial project conducted at the Under the Rainbow program at Mt. Sinai Hospital in Chicago, Illinois, designed to help fill the need for an ecologically valid investigation of memory abilities of maltreated children. To accomplish this task we built on methodology traditionally employed in child-witness research to include variables related to stress and trauma that may affect memory in maltreated children, such as individual differences in dissociation, general psychopathology, and intellectual ability.

THE INITIAL "UNDER THE RAINBOW" STUDY

The Under the Rainbow (UTR) program at Mt. Sinai Hospital is dedicated to the assessment and treatment of abused and neglected children. The program has three components: inpatient assessment, outpatient assessment, and outpatient treatment. The inpatient assessment program involves hospitalizing children for 5 days who are in the midst of an ongoing forensic investigation. This hospitalization provides unique opportunities for the collection of data and control for extraneous variables. In addition to the fact that the children are removed from their homes, they are also subjected to the rigors of an intensive investigation that may influence their memory performance through increased stress as well as the emergence of relevant concerns (e.g., whether they will be returned to their families). At the time of admission, many of these children were questioned about allegations of abuse by the police, Department of Child and Family Services (DCFS) workers, relatives, emergency room physicians, teachers, and the like, whereas others did not talk with anyone about their experiences.

The present study was designed to assess the parameters of the reliability of abused and neglected children's memory and resistance to misleading information. This was accomplished by examining the effects of individual differences in age, stress arousal, dissociation, and other forms of gross psychopathology on the memory and suggestibility of maltreated children. By attempting to replicate and extend past findings on children's memory for experienced events, in particular a medical examination involving anogenital touch (Saywitz et al., 1991), we hoped to evaluate abused and neglected children's memory reports and susceptibility to suggestion. By studying children who were in the midst of actual abuse investigations, we also hoped to study these issues in a particularly ecologically valid fashion.

Two of our main interests were in examining (1) how individual differences in age, intellectual ability, dissociative tendencies, and general psychopathology relate to memory and resistance to misleading information; and (2) how level of stress arousal affects maltreated children's memory. In this chapter we briefly discuss the results of a preliminary analysis of the data from our initial study conducted at the UTR program. A second, larger study is currently under way.

The collection of data for the present study was designed to be conducted almost completely within the existing framework of the assessment protocol of the UTR inpatient program. During this evaluation, each child in our study received a complete physical examination, a review of the child's health records, updated vaccinations and needed medical attention, an anogenital examination to detect physical signs of abuse, a forensic interview directed at assessing allegations of abuse and neglect, and a psychological consultation which consisted of an assessment of each child's mental status, emotional functioning, and psychological sequelae of abuse and/or neglect. In addition, all parents and caretakers who were available were interviewed, and the child's records of past involvement with the social service system were reviewed. All children 6 years of age and under were screened for developmental delays, and those children suspected of having auditory and/or language delays or neurological problems received a thorough assessment of these problems during their hospitalization. The 5-day hospitalization provided a unique opportunity to examine each child's level of functioning.

On the first day of each child's hospitalization, the child received a complete physical exam and otherwise had a chance to become acclimated to the inpatient unit. On the second day of the stay, the child was given an anogenital examination for overt signs of physical and/or sexual abuse. At some point during the procedure the doctor took a sample of secretions from the child's genitals and rectum. The doctor also checked the muscle tone in the rectum by digitally penetrating the child. For our study, this examination marked the first point of data collection. These medical examinations are all standard parts of the UTR assessment. However, during the anogenital examination, we added collection of information on the child's heart rate and the doctors' and nurses' judgments of the child's level of stress arousal and discomfort. On the fifth and final day of the inpatient assessment, each child was administered a structured interview composed of a series of specific, leading, and misleading questions to assess the child's memory and resistance to misleading information for the details of the anogenital exam given 3 days earlier. Each child was thoroughly debriefed immediately after this interview.

At some point during this 5-day stay (usually on the third day), the child took part in a psychological consultation, again as part of UTR's standard assessment. During the psychological consultation a clinician looked for signs and symptoms of trauma and assessed each child's mental status, emotional functioning, cognitive level, and affective response to the alleged abuse. During the consultation, each child over 5 years of age had his or her intellectual functioning assessed through the administration of Raven's Progressive Matrices Test (Raven, Court, & Ravens, 1986). Following the interviews, clinicians provided an assessment of the child's functioning, specifically, a rating of Global Adaptive Functioning (GAF), using a scale described in the third revised edition of the *Diagnostic and Statistical Manual of Mental Disorders* (DSM-III-R; American Psychiatric Association, 1987).

Between the second and fifth days of the hospitalization, children were administered the Memory for Sentences Subtest of the Standford–Binet Intelligence Scale (fourth edition). Two dissociation measures were administered to children: All children over the age of 5 were administered the Children's Perceptual Alteration Scale (CPAS; Evers-Szostak & Sanders, 1990), and all children over 11 years of age were administered the Dissociative Experiences Scale for Adolescents (A-DES; Armstrong, Putnam, Carlson, Libero, & Smith, 1997). In addition, the parents and caretakers of all children who were available were administered the Child Dissociative Checklist (CDC; Putnam, Helmers, & Trickett, 1993).

Participants

The participants were 214 children referred to the UTR program at Mt. Sinai Hospital for the assessment of abuse and neglect (the full sample). Referrals of children to UTR typically come from the court system, DCFS, private agencies, family physicians, school counselors, clinic and emergency room doctors, and, on occasion, parents themselves. Of the 214 subjects, 108 received the memory test for the anogenital examination (the memory-suggestibility sample).

The subjects were predominantly low socioeconomic status African American children from the urban areas of Chicago surrounding the hospital. The mean age of the children was 7 years, 4 months (range = 3–15 years; n = 92 males, 122 females). In terms of ethnic background, 76% of the children were African American, 12% were Hispanic, 9% were Caucasian, and the remaining 3% of the children were of unknown ethnicity. The memory-suggestibility sample closely resembled the full sample in these demographic characteristics.

The maltreated group included those cases that were determined to be "founded" by DCFS after an extensive investigation by local law enforcement and child welfare authorities. The control group was composed of those patients who were referred for assessment but who had made no outcry of maltreatment, and lacked any suspicion of abuse or neglect by UTR staff or DCFS workers. In these cases, abuse could be reasonably ruled out based on the evidence from the 5-day assessment and a prolonged investigation by DCFS. In such instances, UTR staff also met with and interviewed the family members and determined that the likelihood of abuse, neglect, parental addiction, and/or domestic violence was minimal.

The children were primarily divided into groups by type of abuse. The groups were (1) children who were physically and/or sexually abused, (2) children with indicated cases of neglect (including lack of supervision, exposure to domestic violence, etc.) but no indication of abuse, and (3) children with no history of abuse or neglect. Of the 214 participants, 53% were classified as being either physically and/or sexually abused (see Table 7.1). Fifteen percent of the children had indicated cases of neglect, and 8% had documentation of parental addiction without neglect or abuse, whereas 22% of the children in the study had no documented history of abuse or neglect and thus served as a control group. Some children in each of the groups also had a history of corporal punishment of unspecified duration and magnitude. (In this chapter, we do not report analyses comparing the maltreated and control groups' memory performance. Preliminary analyses suggest that relatively few differences exist, but more thorough analyses are under way.)

It is worth noting how difficult it is to be certain of the range of abusive, neglectful, or traumatic experiences to which each child was exposed. For instance, it is safe to assume that many of the sexually and/or physically abused children in our study were neglected and/or had addicted parents or caretakers about whom we are unaware. In addition, it is almost impossible to document precise differences in varying types of neglect (e.g., emotional, environmental, medical, and physical) or the frequency and intensity of the maltreatments. Finally, even if we were able to define cleanly differentiated groups in terms of abuse and neglect, many of the children (including those in the control group) came from "war zones" in the housing projects of Chicago and may be equally or more traumatized by the gun shots and violence in their neighborhoods than aversive experiences at home.

Age, Memory, and Suggestibility

As noted earlier, the literature indicates that memory skills progressively improve with age. Based on this previous work we stratified our sample into

TABLE 7.1. Classification of Maltreatment and Control Subjects

Abuse status	Full sample	Memory-suggestibility sample
Sexual abuse	60 (28.6%)	33 (30.6%)
Physical abuse	28 (13.1%)	11 (10.2%)
Sexual and physical abuse	24 (11.2%)	17 (15.6%)
Neglect	32 (15.0%)	11 (10.2%)
Parental addiction	17 (7.9%)	10 (9.3%)
Nonabuse comparison	46 (21.5%)	24 (22.1%)

three age groups: 3–5 years, 6–10 years, and 11 years and above. As predicted, the results indicated an age progression for children's memory for the anogenital examination when answers to all questions were considered as a whole, with younger children performing more poorly than older children. An age effect was also apparent when examining children's resistance to misleading questions. The 3- to 5-year-old group made significantly more errors on misleading questions than the 6- to 10-year-old group and the 11- to 15-year-old group. Consistent with former research (Goodman & Aman, 1991), the youngest children were significantly less accurate on the misleading abuse-related questions than the 6- to 10-year-olds and the 11- to 15-year-olds (see Table 7.2).

However, despite performing more poorly than their older counterparts, the 3- to 5-year-olds still demonstrated relatively good resistance to misleading information in answering the abuse-related questions. When presented with misleading questions related to abusive or inappropriate behavior by the doctor and/or nurse (e.g., "How many times did the doctor kiss you?"), 3- to 5-year-olds answered 79% of the questions without making commission errors. Interestingly, approximately 40% of the errors made by 3- to 5-year-olds in response to the misleading abuse-related questions were produced by only 6 of the 29 children in this group. Due to the small number of children in this error-prone subgroup, it is difficult to identify possible communalities among

TABLE 7.2. Proportion of Correct, Incorrect, and "Don't Know" Responses to the Memory Test for the Anogenital Examination

	Age group			
	3–5 years	6–10 years	11–15 years	M
All questions				
Correct[a]	.63	.81	.92	.77
Incorrect[a]	.35	.16	.08	.21
Don't know	.02	.03	.004	.02
Misleading questions				
Correct[b]	.63	.83	.91	.77
Incorrect[b]	.36	.14	.08	.21
Don't know	.02	.03	.01	.02
Misleading abuse-related questions				
Correct[b]	.60	.81	.91	.75
Incorrect[b]	.40	.16	.09	.24
Don't know[c]	.01	.03	.00	.02

[a]Fs (2, 105) 51.20, ps < .001; planned comparisons revealed that the differences between all three age groups were significant.
[b]Fs (2, 105) 17.31, ps < .001; planned comparisons revealed that the youngest age group differed significantly from the two older groups, but the difference between the two older groups was not significant.
[c]The 6- to 10-year-old age group mean was combined with the 11- to 15-year-old age group mean and then compared to the 3- to 5-year-old age group mean. Across question categories, there were no significant differences for "don't know" responses.

these children that might explain their responses. However, research assistants collecting the data reported that many of these errors were made by children who were indiscriminately responding to the questions as a result of what the research assistants perceived as boredom, lack of understanding, or lack of cooperativeness. Even so, we cannot rule out possible memory impairment effects. Thus, although the 3- to 5-year-olds' proportion of commission errors to misleading abuse-related questions was relatively low on average, there were some children who were more error-prone than others. If such children were interviewed in an abuse investigation, a false accusation could potentially result.

Asking misleading abused-related questions about the anogenital examination in the context of an ongoing abuse investigation is in many ways a particularly good analogue to an actual forensic interview. Despite the UTR staff's attempts to reduce the number of times children were interviewed about abuse, by the time the children were questioned about their memory for the anogenital examination, the children had been repeatedly interviewed over a period of days and sometimes weeks, or even after months, being asked whether their parents and loved ones, neighbors, friends, or strangers touched them inappropriately, hit them, or attempted to hurt them in anyway. Therefore, this mode of inquiry was essentially normalized for these children. Asking them about possible transgressions by the doctors and nurses was expected and not outside reasonable expectations. Therefore, it is conceivable that this type of questioning was interpreted by the children as yet one more set of questions regarding who may have hit them, kissed them, or fondled them. If their friends, neighbors, and loved ones are not beyond suspicion, why should the doctors and nurses be? In addition, the actual genital touch and digital penetration that occurs during the anogenital examination combined with the confusing and often highly stressful circumstances of being removed from their homes and placed at the UTR program creates an even more ecologically valid framework for such questioning.

Individual Differences in Adaptive Functioning and Intellectual Ability

In this study we also examined how individual differences in psychopathology, short-term memory, and intellectual ability relate to memory and resistance to misleading information. Preliminary analysis indicated that children's level of functioning as measured by GAF was a good predictor of performance in the memory interviews, with the higher-scoring children (i.e., those judged to have a higher level of functioning) generally performing better on the anogenital examination memory test. GAF was also found to be related to the child's intellectual ability. In addition, children's performance on the standardized measures of memory ability (e.g., Memory for Sentences) was related to their performance in the memory interview. However, some of these relations varied across age groups and the measures employed. A preliminary examination of these data indicates that these are clearly important variables to be studied in future research. We will be examining these data from the present sample more closely and will report the findings in future papers.

Dissociation

The dissociation measures performed somewhat inconsistently. The A-DES and the CPAS were positively interrelated, but the CDC shared very little variance with either the A-DES or CPAS (see Table 7.3). A preliminary examination of the data indicated that only the CDC was related to a history of abuse, general psychopathology, and, in some instances, memory. However, these effects were not so robust as to be consistent across all age groups or across all measures employed.

Stress and Memory

In our preliminary analyses, stress arousal as measured by heart rate and doctors' and nurses' judgments of children's stress were not related to memory or suggestibility for the anogenital examination in any systematic fashion after the effects of age and base-level heart rate were controlled statistically. In our ongoing, large-scale study, we significantly improved our methodology for assessing stress arousal so as to examine possible relations between stress and memory in greater detail.

CONCLUSION

Assessing children's memory and resistance to misleading questions is particularly important for many reasons, including the need to obtain accurate disclosures of abuse from children and the need to understand the effects of casual or "reckless" interviewing techniques sometimes employed by nonprofessionals and professionals alike in abuse evaluations. It is commonly believed that if interviewers suggest abuse with leading or misleading questions, the memory of children can be easily corrupted. However, our data, along with past data collected on nonabused children,

TABLE 7.3. Intercorrelations among the CDC, CPAS, and A-DES

	CDC	CPAS	A-DES
CDC	1.00		
	($n = 80$)		
CPAS	.00	1.00	
	($n = 52$)	($n = 145$)	
A-DES	.28	.66	1.00
	($n = 14$)	($n = 42$)	($n = 42$)

indicate that even many relatively young children can be resistant to such inquiries, at least in a one-time, nonpressuring interview. Perhaps surprisingly, the accusatory and stressful context of an ongoing abuse investigation did not substantially change these trends, for instance, when our findings are compared to those our former studies (e.g., Tobey & Goodman, 1992). However, a subset of young children in our study did make errors that could lead to legal concerns.

Most interviewers (and parents) know that some young children will say "yes" to most anything given the right conditions: because they are tired of answering questions, they are being oppositional, they do not understand what is being asked, they think that is what the interviewer wants to hear, they are lying purposely, or their memory is actually corrupted, whereas other children will not respond in this way even when pressured to do so. Moreover, there is sufficient data from other studies to indicate that some children, under some circumstances, are particularly susceptible to altering their reporting and perhaps even their memory. It seems important to stay in touch with the fact that there are individual differences at work, some of which were revealed by the present study. Global adaptive functioning and increasing age were associated with children's resistance to misleading information.

It is also vital to note the influence of situational variables. Some children are suggestible in certain situations and not others, whereas other children appear to be quite resistant to misleading suggestions in most situations. These same patterns are repeatedly found in adults (Gudjonsson, 1986). Unfortunately, it appears that politics has entered the child-witness debate, with some scientists implying that virtually all children are highly suggestible and can be subject to memory distortion about any aspect of any event, and others implying that children's memory can never be corrupted in any significant way and that children are incapable of lying. As the data mount, it is becoming increasingly clear that neither implication is true and that the answers to these crucial questions fall somewhere in between these two extremes.

ACKNOWLEDGMENTS

We thank the director (Dr. Bruce Peters) and the staff of the Under the Rainbow Program, Mt. Sinai Hospital and Medical Center, for their assistance. We are also grateful to the Illinois Department of Child and Family Services and Dana Corwin, the Guardian of the State of Illinois, for support and approval of our project. A number of research assistants provided valuable help. We would especially like to thank Denise Scheaffer, Gary Lee, Jason Brown, Ellisa Faye, Clair Henn-Haas, Jennett Pearson, RN, and Ernestine Watts, RN. Writing of this chapter was facilitated by a grant from the National Center on Child Abuse and Neglect.

REFERENCES

Alpert, J. L. (1995). Trauma, dissociation, and clinical study as a responsible beginning. *Consciousness and Cognition, 4,* 125–129.

American Psychiatric Association. (1987). *Diagnostic and statistical manual of mental disorders* (3rd ed., rev.). Washington, DC: Author.

Armstrong, J., Putnam, F. W., Carlson, E., Libero, D., & Smith, S. (1997). Development and validation of a measure of adolescent dissociation: The Adolescent Dissociative Experiences Scales. *Journal of Nervous and Mental Disease,185,* 1–7.

Asher, S. (1976). Children's ability to appraise their own and other person's communication performance. *Developmental Psychology, 12,* 24–32.

Bartlett, F. (1932). *Remembering: A study in experimental and social psychology.* Cambridge, UK: Cambridge University Press.

Bohannon, J. N. (1988). Flashbulb memories for the space shuttle disaster. *Cognition, 29,* 179–196.

Brainerd, C., & Ornstein, P. (1991). Children's memory for witnessed events: The developmental backdrop. In J. Doris (Ed.), *The suggestibility of children's recollections* (pp. 10–20). Washington, DC: American Psychological Association.

Brainerd, C., & Reyna, V. (1991). Gist is the grist: Fuzzy-trace theory and the new institutionalism. *Developmental Review, 10,* 3–47.

Bremner, J. D., Krystal, J. H., Southwick, S. M, & Charney, D. S., (1995). Functional neuroanatomical correlates of the effects of stress on memory. *Journal of Traumatic Stress, 8,* 527–553.

Bremner, J. D., Southwick, S. M., & Charney, D. S. (1994). Etiologic factors in the development of posttraumatic stress disorder. In C. M. Mazure (Ed.), *Stress and psychiatric disorders* (pp. 149–186). Washington, DC: American Psychiatric Press.

Bremner, J. D., Southwick, S. M. Johnson, D. R., Yehuda, R., & Charney, D. S. (1993). Childhood physical abuse in combat-related posttraumatic stress disorder. *American Journal of Psychiatry, 150,* 235–239.

Briere, J. (1988). The long-term clinical correlates of childhood sexual victimization. *Annals of the New York Academy of Sciences, 528,* 327–334.

Briere, J. (1992). *Child abuse and trauma: Theory and treatment of lasting effects.* Newbury Park, CA: Sage.

Brown, L. S. (1995). Comment. *Consciousness and Cognition, 4,* 130–132.

Browne, A., & Finkelhor, D. (1986). Impact of child sexual abuse: A review of the research. *Psychological Bulletin, 99,* 66–77.

Bruck, M., Ceci, S. J., Francoeur, E., & Barr, R. (1995). "I hardly cried when I got my shot!": Influencing children's reports about a visit to their pediatrician. *Child Development, 66*(1), 193–208.

Bruck, M., Ceci, S.J., Francoeur, E., & Renick, A. (1995). Anatomically detailed dolls do not facilitate preschoolers' reports of a pediatric examination involving genital touching. *Journal of Experimental Psychology: Applied, 1,* 95–109.

Bugental, D., Blue, J., Cortez, V., Fleck, K., & Rodriguez, A. (1992). Influences of witnessed affect on information processing in children. *Child Development, 63,* 774–786.

Carlson, E. B., Furby, L., Armstrong, J., & Shales, J. (1997). A conceptual framework for the long-term psychological effects of severe and chronic childhood abuse. *Child Maltreatment, 2*(3), 272–295.

Carlson, E., & Putnam, F. W. (1986). An update on the Dissociative Experiences Scale. *Dissociation: Progress in the Dissociative Disorders, 6,* 16–21.

Carter, C., Bottoms, B. L., & Levine, M. (1997). Linguistic and socio-emotional influences on the accuracy of children's reports. *Law and Human Behavior, 20*(3), 335–358.

Cassel, W., & Bjorklund, D. F. (1995). Developmental patterns of eyewitness memory and suggestibility: An ecologically based short-term longitudinal study. *Law and Human Behavior, 19*(5), 507–532.

Cassel, W., Roebers, C., & Bjorklund, D. F. (1996). Developmental patterns of eyewitness responses to repeated and increasingly suggestive questions. *Journal of Experimental Child Psychology, 61*(2), 116–133.

Ceci, S. J., & Bruck, M. (1993). The suggestibility of the child witness: A historical review and synthesis. *Psychological Bulletin, 113*(3), 403–439.

Ceci, S. J., Crotteau-Huffman, M., Smith, E., & Loftus, E. F. (1995). Repeatedly thinking about nonevents. *Consciousness and Cognition, 3,* 338–407.

Ceci, S. J., Loftus, E. F., Leichtman, M. D., & Bruck, M. (1995). The possible role of source misattributions in the creation of false beliefs among preschoolers. *International Journal of Clinical and Experimental Hypnosis, 42,* 304–320.

Chandler, M., Fritz, A. S., & Hala, S. (1989). Small-scale deceit: Deception as a marker of 2-, 3-, and 4-year-olds' early theories of mind. *Child Development, 60*(6), 1263–1277.

Chi, M. (1978). Knowledge structures and memory development. In R. Siegler (Ed.), *Children's thinking: What develops?* Hillsdale, NJ: Erlbaum.

Chinn, C., & Brewer, W. F. (1993). The role of anomalous data in knowledge acquisition: A theoretical framework and implications for science instruction. *Review of Educational Research, 68*(1), 1–49.

Christianson, S. A. (1992). Emotional stress and eyewitness memory: A critical review. *Psychological Bulletin, 112,* 284–309.

Chu, J. A., & Dill, D. L. (1990). Dissociative symptoms in relation to childhood physical and sexual abuse. *American Journal of Psychiatry, 147,* 887–892.

Cicchetti, D., Rogosch, F. A., Lynch, M., & Holt, K. D. (1993). Resilience in maltreated children: Processes leading to adaptive outcome. *Developmental Psychopathology, 5,* 629–647.

Coons, P. M., Bowman, E., Pellow, T. A., & Schneider, P. (1989). Post-traumatic aspects of the treatment of victims of sexual abuse and incest. *Psychiatric Clinics of North America, 12,* 325–335.

Dent, H. (1991). Experimental studies of interviewing child witnesses. In J. Doris (Ed.), *The suggestibility of children's recollections* (pp. 138–146). Washington, DC: American Psychological Association.

Dent, H., & Stephenson, G. (1979). An experimental study of the effectiveness of different techniques of questioning child witnesses. *British Journal of Social and Clinical Psychology, 18,* 41–51.

Eisen, M., Goodman, G. S., & Qin, J. (1995, July). *Eyewitness testimony in victims of child maltreatment: Stress, memory, and suggestibility.* Paper presented at the meeting of the Society for Applied Research on Memory and Cognition, Vancouver, Canada.

Ekman, P. (1989). *Why kids lie.* New York: Penguin Books.

Evers-Szostak, M., & Sanders, S. (1990, August). *The validity and reliability of the Children's Perceptual Alteration Scale (CPAS): A measure of children's dissociation.*

Paper presented at the annual convention of the American Psychological Association, San Francisco.

Finkelhor, D. (1984). *Child sexual abuse*. New York: Free Press.

Fivush, R. (1993). Developmental perspective on autobiographical recall. In G. S. Goodman & B. L. Bottoms (Eds.), *Child victims, child witnesses: Understanding and improving testimony* (pp. 1–24). New York: Guilford Press.

Fivush, R., & Schwarzmueller, A. (1995). Say it once again: Effects of repeated questions on children's event recall. *Journal of Traumatic Stress, 8*, 555–580.

Flin, R., Boon, J, Knox, A., & Bull, R. (1992). The effects of a five month delay on children's and adults' eyewitness memory. *British Journal of Psychology, 83*, 323–336.

Flin, R., Stevenson, Y., & Davies, G. (1989). Children's knowledge of court proceedings. *British Journal of Psychology, 80*, 285–297.

Frischholz, E. J. (1985). The relationship among dissociation, hypnosis, and child abuse in the development of multiple personality disorder. In R. P. Kluft (Ed.), *Childhood antecedents of multiple personality disorder* (pp. 99–126). Washington, DC: American Psychiatric Press.

Gold, P. E. (1987). Sweet memories. *American Scientist, 75*, 151–155.

Goodman, G. S., & Aman, C. J. (1991). Children's use of anatomically detailed dolls to recount an event. *Child Development, 61*, 1859–1871.

Goodman, G. S., & Bottoms, B. L. (1993). *Child victims, child witnesses: Understanding and improving testimony*. New York: Guilford Press.

Goodman, G. S., Bottoms, B. L., Schwartz-Kenney, B., & Rudy, L. (1991). Children's memory for a stressful event: Improving children's reports. *Journal of Narrative and Life History, 1*, 69–99.

Goodman, G. S., Hepps, D., & Reed, R. S. (1986). The child victim's testimony. In A. Haralambie (Ed.), *New issues for child advocates*. Phoenix: Arizona Council of Attorneys for Children.

Goodman, G. S., Hirschman, J. E., Hepps, D., & Rudy, L. (1991). Children's memory for stressful events. *Merrill Palmer Quarterly, 37*, 109–158.

Goodman, G. S., & Quas, J. (1997). Trauma and memory: Individual differences in children's recounting of a stressful experience. In N. L. Stein, P. A. Ornstein, B. Tversky, & C. Brainerd (Eds.), *Memory for everyday and emotional events*. Mahwah, NJ: Erlbaum.

Goodman, G. S., Quas, J. A., Batterman-Faunce, J. M., Riddlesberger, M. M., & Kuhn, J. (1997). Predictors of accurate and inaccurate memories of traumatic events experienced in childhood. *Consciousness and Cognition: An International Journal, 3*, 269–294.

Goodman, G. S., & Reed, R. (1986). Age differences in eyewitness testimony. *Law and Human Behavior, 10*, 317–332.

Goodman, G. S. Rudy, L., Bottoms, B. L., & Aman, C. (1990). Children's concerns and memory: Issues of ecological validity in children's testimony. In R. Fivush & J. Hudson (Eds.), *Knowing and remembering in young children* (pp. 249–284). New York: Cambridge University Press.

Goodman, G. S., & Saywitz, K. J. (1994). Memories of abuse. *Child and Adolescent Psychiatric Clinics of North American, 3*, 645–662.

Gudjonsson, G. H. (1986). The relationship between interrogative suggestibility and acquiescence: Empirical findings and theoretical implications. *Personality and Individual Differences, 7*, 195–199.

Helweg-Larsen, P., Hoffmeyer, H., Kieler, J., Thaysen, E. H., Thaysen J. H., Thygesen, P., & Wulff, M. H. (1952). Famine disease in German concentration camps: Complications and sequels. *Acta Medica Scandinavica, 274*, 235–460.

Hembrooke, H., & Ceci, S. J. (1995). Traumatic memories: Do we need to invoke special mechanisms? *Consciousness and Cognition, 4*, 75–82.

Hilgard, E. R. (1977). *Divided consciousness: Multiple controls in human thought and action.* New York: Wiley.

Howe, M. (1991). Misleading children's story recall: Forgetting and reminiscence of the facts. *Developmental Psychology, 27*, 746–762.

Howe, M. L., Courage, M. L., & Bryant-Brown, L. (1993). Reinstating preschoolers' memories. *Developmental Psychology, 29*, 854–869.

Howe, M., Courage, M. L., & Peterson, C. (1994). How can I remember when "I" wasn't there: Long-term retention of traumatic experiences of the cognitive self. *Consciousness and Cognition: An International Journal, 3*(3–4), 327–355.

Hudson, J., & Fivush, R. (1987). *As time goes by: Sixth graders remember a kindergarten experience* (Emory Cognition Project Report No. 13). Atlanta, GA: Emory University Press.

Hutcheson, G., Baxter, J., Telfer, K., & Warden, D. (1995). Child witness statement quality: Question type and errors of omission. *Law and Human Behavior, 19*, 631– 648.

Janet, P. (1925). *Psychological healing* (Vols. 1-2). New York: Macmillan. (Original work published as *Les médications psychologiques* [Vols. 1–3], in 1919)

Johnson, H. M., & Siefert, C. M. (1994). Sources of the continued influence effect: When misinformation in memory affects later inferences. *Journal of Experimental Psychology: Learning, Memory, and Cognition, 20*(6), 1420–1436.

Kail, R. (1990). *The development of memory in children* (3rd. ed.). New York: Freeman.

Keary, K., & Fitzpatrick, C. (1994). Children's disclosure of sexual abuse during formal investigation. *Child Abuse and Neglect, 18*, 543–548.

Kendall-Tackett, K. A., Williams, L. M., & Finkelhor, D. (1993). Impact of sexual abuse on children: A review and synthesis of recent empirical studies. *Psychological Bulletin, 113*, 164–180.

Kolko, D. (1992). Characteristics of child victims of physical violence. *Journal of Interpersonal Violence, 7*, 244–276.

Leichtman, M., & Ceci, S. J. (1995a). Effects of stereotypes and suggestions on preschoolers' reports. *Developmental Psychology, 31*, 568–578.

Leichtman, M., & Ceci, S. J. (1995b). "The effects of stereotypes and suggestions on preschoolers' reports": Correction. *Developmental Psychology, 31*, 758.

Leippe, M., Romanczyk, A., & Manion, A. (1992). Eyewitness memory for a touching experience: Accuracy differences between child and adult witnesses. *Journal of Applied Psychology, 76*, 367–379.

Lepore, S., & Sesco, B. (1994). Distorting children's reports and interpretations of events through suggestion. *Journal of Applied Psychology, 79*, 108–120.

Loftus, E. F. (1979). *Eyewitness testimony.* Cambridge, MA: Harvard University Press.

Lynn, S. J., & Rhue, J. W. (1994). *Dissociation: Clinical and theoretical perspectives.* New York: Guilford Press.

Markman, E. M. (1977). Realizing that you don't understand: A preliminary investigation. *Child Development, 48*, 986–992.

Merritt, K. A., Ornstein, P. A., & Spicker, B. (1994). Children's memory for a salient medical procedure: Implications for testimony. *Pediatrics, 94*, 17–23.

Moston, S. (1987). The suggestibility of children in interview studies. *First Language*, 7, 67–78.

Nemiah, J. C. (1995). Early concepts of trauma, dissociation, and the unconscious: Their history and current implications. In D. Bremner & C. Marmar, (Eds.), *Trauma, memory, and dissociation*. Washington, DC: American Psychiatric Press.

Orcutt, H., Goodman, G. S., Tobey, A., Batterman-Faunce, J., & Thomas, S. (1993, August). *Fact finders' abilities to detect deception: Effects of closed circuit television*. Paper presented at the annual convetion of the American Psychological Association, Toronto, Canada.

Ornstein, P., Baker-Ward, L., Gordon, B., & Merritt, K. (1993). Children's memory for medical procedures. In N. Stein (Chair), *Children's memory for emotional events*. Symposium presented at the meeting of the Society for Research in Child Development, New Orleans.

Patterson, C., Masad, C., & Cosgrove, J. (1978). Children's referential communication: Components of plans for effective listening. *Developmental Psychology, 14*, 401–406.

Perry, N., McAuliff, B., Tam, P., Claycomb, L., Dostal, C., & Flanagan, C. (1995). When lawyers question children: Is justice served? *Law and Human Behavior, 19*, 609–630.

Peters, D. P (1987). The impact of naturally occurring stress on children's memory. In S. J. Ceci, M. P. Toglia, & D. F. Ross (Eds.), *Children's eyewitness memory* (pp. 122–141). New York: Springer-Verlag.

Pezdek, K., & Roe, C. (1994). Children's eyewitness memory: How suggestible is it? *Consciousness and Cognition, 3*, 374–387.

Pillemer, D. B. (1993). Preschool children's memories of personal circumstances: The fire alarm study. In E. Winograd & U. Neisser (Eds.), *Affect and accuracy in recall: The problem of flashbulb memories*. New York: Cambridge University Press.

Poole, D. A. (1995, May). *Trends in eyewitness testimony*. Paper presented at the Midwestern Psychological Association, Chicago.

Poole, D. A., & Lindsay, D. S. (1994, March). *Interviewing preschoolers: Effects of nonsuggestive techniques, parental coaching, and leading questions on reports of nonexperienced events*. Paper presented at the meeting of the American Psychology and Law Society, Santa Fe, NM.

Poole, D. A., & White, L. T. (1995). Tell me again and again: The stability and change in the repeated testimony of children and adults. In M. S. Zaragoza, J. R. Graham, G. C. N. Hall, R. Hirschman, & Y. S. Ben-Porath (Eds.), *Memory and testimony in the child witness* (pp. 24–43). Thousand Oaks, CA: Sage.

Price, D. W. W., & Goodman, G. S. (1990). Visiting the wizard: Children's memory of a recurring event. *Child Development, 61*, 664–680.

Putnam, F. W. (1985). Dissociation as a response to extreme trauma. In R. P. Kluft (Ed.), *Childhood antecedents of multiple personality disorder* (pp. 65–97). Washington, DC: American Psychiatric Press.

Putnam, F. W. (1991). Recent research on multiple personality disorder. *Psychiatric Clinics of North America, 14*, 489–502.

Putnam, F. W., Helmers, K., & Trickett, P. K. (1993). Development, reliability, and validity of a child dissociation scale. *Child Abuse and Neglect, 17*, 731–741.

Quimby, L. G., & Putnam, F. W. (1991). Dissociative symptoms and aggression in a state mental hospital. *Dissociation: Progress in the Dissociative Disorders, 4*, 21–24.

Raven, J. C., & Court, J. H., & Raven, J. (1986). *Manual for Raven's Progressive Matrices and Vocabulary Scales*. London: Lewis.

Rhue, J. W., Lynn, S. J., Henry, S., Buhk, K., & Boyd, P. (1990). Child abuse, imagination and hypnotizability. *Imagination, Cognition and Personality, 10*, 53–63.

Rovee-Collier, C., & Shyi, C. W. G. (1992). A functional and cognitive analysis of infant long-term retention. In M. L. Howe, C. J. Brainerd, & V. F. Reyna (Eds.), *Development of long-term retention* (pp. 3–55). New York: Springer-Verlag.

Rudy, L., & Goodman, G. S. (1991). Effects of participation on children's reports: Implications for children's testimony. *Developmental Psychology, 27*, 1–26.

Russell, D. (1983). The incidence and prevalence of intrafamilial and extra familial sexual abuse of female children. *Child Abuse and Neglect, 7*, 133–146.

Saywitz, K. J., Goodman, G. S. Nicholas, E., & Moan, S. F. (1991). Children's memories of a physical examination involving genital touch: Implications of reports of child abuse. *Journal of Consulting and Clinical Psychology, 59(5)*, 682–691.

Saywitz, K. J., Jaenicke, C., & Camparo, L. (1990). Children's knowledge of legal terminology. *Law and Human Behavior, 14(6)*, 523–535.

Saywitz, K. J., & Moan-Hardie, S. (1994). Reducing the potential for distortion of childhood memories. *Consciousness and Cognition, 3(3/4)*, 408–425.

Saywitz, K. J., & Snyder, L. (1991, April). *Preparing child witnesses: The efficacy of comprehension monitoring training*. Paper presented at the meeting of the Society for Research in Child Development, Seattle, WA.

Siegal, M., Waters, L., & Dinwiddie, L. (1988). Misleading children: Causal attributions for inconsistency under repeated questioning. *Journal of Experimental Child Psychology, 45*, 438–456.

Speigel, D. (1986). Dissociating damage. *American Journal of Clinical Hypnosis, 29(2)*, 122–131.

Spencer, J., & Flin, R. (1993). *The evidence of children: The law and the psychology*. London: Blackstone Press.

Stein, N. L., & Miller, C. A. (1993). The development of memory and reasoning skill in argumentative contexts: Evaluating, explaining, and generating evidence. In R. Glaser (Ed.), *Advances in instructional psychology* (Vol. 4, pp. 285–335). Hillsdale, NJ: Erlbaum.

Stein, N. L., & Trabasso, T. (1985). The search after meaning: Comprehension and comprehension monitoring. In F. Morrison, C. Lord, & D. Keating (Eds.), *Advances in applied developmental psychology* (Vol. 2, pp. 33–57). New York: Academic Press.

Stein, N. L., Trabasso, T., & Liwag, M. D. (1993). The representation and organization of emotional experience: Unfolding the emotion episode. In M. Lewis & J. Haviland (Eds.), *Handbook of emotions* (pp. 279–300). New York: Guilford Press.

Stein, N. L., Trabasso, T., & Liwag, M. D. (1997). The Rashomon phenomenon: Personal frames and future oriented appraisals in memory for emotional events. In M. Haith, J. B. Benson, R. J. Roberts, Jr., & B. F. Pennington (Eds.), *The development of future oriented processes*. Chicago: University of Chicago Press.

Stein, N., Wade, E., & Liwag, M. D. (1997). A theoretical approach to understanding and remembering emotional events. In N. L. Stein, P. A. Ornstein, B. Tversky, & C. Brainerd (Eds.), *Memory for everyday and emotional events*. Mahwah, NJ: Erlbaum.

Steward, M. (1993). Understanding children's memories for medical procedures: "He didn't touch me and it didn't hurt!" In C. Nelson (Ed.), *Memory and affect in development* (pp. 171–226). Hillsdale, NJ: Erlbaum.

Steward, M., & Steward, J. (1989). *The development of a model interview for young child victims of sexual abuse: Comparing the effectiveness of anatomical dolls, drawings, and videographics.* Final report to the National Center on Child Abuse and Neglect, Washington, DC.

Stuker, P. B., Winstead, D. K., Galina, Z. H., & Allain, A. N. (1991). Cognitive deficits and psychopathology among former prisoners of war and combat veterans of the Korean conflict. *American Journal of Psychiatry, 148,* 67–72.

Tobey, A., & Goodman, G. S. (1992). Children's eyewitness memory: Effects of participation and forensic context. *Child Abuse and Neglect, 16,* 779–796.

van der Kolk, B. A., & Fisler, R. E. (1995). Dissociation and the fragmentary nature of traumatic memories: Overview and exploratory study. *Journal of Traumatic Stress, 8,* 505–525.

van der Kolk, B. A., & van der Hart, O. (1989). Pierre Janet and the breakdown of adaptation in psychological trauma. *American Journal of Psychiatry, 146,* 1530–1540.

van der Kolk, B. A., & van der Hart, O. (1991). The intrusive past: The flexibility of memory and the engraving of trauma. *American Imago, 48*(4), 425–454.

Vandermass, M. O., Hess, T. M., & Baker-Ward, L. (1993). Does anxiety affect children's reports of memory for a stressful event? *Journal of Applied Cognitive Psychology, 7,* 109–128.

Warren-Leubecker, A., & Swartwood, J. (1992). Developmental issues in flashbulb memory research: Children recall the Challenger event. In E. Winograd & U. Neisser (Eds.), *Affect and accuracy in recall* (pp. 95–120). Cambridge, UK: Cambridge University Press.

Whitfield, C. L. (1995). The forgotten difference: Ordinary memory versus traumatic memory. *Consciousness and Cognition, 4,* 88–94.

Wolfe, V. V., Gentile, C., & Wolfe, D. A. (1989). The impact of sexual abuse on children: A PTSD formulation. *Behavior Therapy, 20,* 215–228.

Wolfe, D. A., Sas, L., & Wekerele, C. (1994). Factors associated with the development of post-traumatic stress disorder among child victims of sexual abuse. *Child Abuse and Neglect, 18,* 37–50.

Yerkes, R. M., & Dodson, J. D. (1908). The relation of strength of stimulus to rapidity of habit formation. *Journal of Neurology and Psychology, 18,* 459–482.

CHAPTER 8

INTERVIEWING THE CHILD WITNESS
Maximizing Completeness and Minimizing Error

Karen J. Saywitz
R. Edward Geiselman

Despite a surge of research on children's eyewitness memory, studies have not produced a gold-standard protocol for questioning children that guarantees accuracy and completeness. Nor have researchers produced a reliable test that discriminates true from false statements about past events. However, studies have identified some of the external factors that can undermine or facilitate children's recall, such as the use of suggestive questions or a child-centered setting free of distractions. Also, studies have identified internal factors, developmental processes such as vocabulary growth or retrieval strategy usage, which interact with external factors to determine the quality of children's reports. This chapter focuses on those external and internal factors germane to understanding one of the most problematic aspects of children's recall.

A common finding in contemporary research illustrates the problem young children present. In experimental studies, young children's spontaneous descriptions of past events provide the most accurate information, in comparison to responses to specific and leading questions. Unfortunately, these descriptions can be woefully incomplete. Hence, children's spontaneous-event recall, despite its accuracy, is often insufficient for decision making in the legal or clinical domains (Myers, 1998). Adults' liberties, children's safety, and victims' recoveries cannot be determined without further information. More information is forthcoming in response to additional questions and cues that trigger retrieval. However, the methods used to elicit additional information can undermine the accuracy, relevance, or consistency of children's statements. For example, repeated use of suggestive questions with very young children can create the potential for distortion (Ceci & Bruck, 1993). Stressful interview settings and long delays can interfere with recall of details, limiting amounts of recall (Brainerd, Reyna, Howe, & Kingma, 1990; Peters, 1991; Saywitz & Nathanson, 1993; Saywitz, Nathanson, Snyder, & Lamphear, 1993, Experiment 7). Moreover, developmentally inappropriate questions containing complex syntax and abstract concepts can create avoidable inconsistencies as children stretch to answer questions they do not fully understand (Saywitz, Nathanson, & Snyder, 1993).

In this chapter, we delineate component skills thought to be contributing to children's incompleteness and discuss implications for eliciting more complete and consistent recounts from children. Although theories of memory continue to evolve as science progresses, our intent is to inform experienced interviewers of research findings relevant to their task. We describe two innovative approaches to questioning children that were developed in our respective laboratories: *narrative elaboration* and *cognitive interviewing*. Both strive to aid children in narrating a past event more fully with less need for leading questions, thereby reducing the risk of contamination. Both are procedures that expand children's initial retelling to allow follow-up questions to clarify information from the original narrative, not adult supposition. In this way, the goals of both accuracy and completeness are served.

FACTORS AFFECTING CHILDREN'S INCOMPLETENESS AND INCONSISTENCY

Encoding and Storage

One reason for children's incompleteness is the fact that not all the information perceived is encoded or stored for later retrieval (see Ornstein, Gordon, Baker-Ward, & Merritt, 1995, for discussion). The forensic interview requires deliberate retrieval of information acquired incidentally. At the time of the incident, witnesses are not aware that the information will become important later. The information that is selected for encoding is determined in part by the child's level of prior knowledge and experience, which influences how the situation is interpreted, what kinds of information are noticed, and what is considered relevant and necessary for storage. As knowledge increases with maturation and experience, children's abilities to attend to, understand, encode, and store the kind of forensically relevant information required of a witness improve. Hence, children may encode less and different kinds of information than interviewers are seeking.

Studies suggest that the salience of the information, that is, the significance and importance of the information to the witness, is one determinant of what is encoded. In one study, 2- to 4-year-olds recalled a highly interesting event (e.g., getting candy) better than an uninteresting one (Somerville, Wellman, & Cultice, 1983). Children and adults often differ in terms of what they consider salient because children do not merely absorb the adult view of reality. They construct their own world view from their limited experiences. In one study, children outperformed adults in recall of someone's shoe type, including the brand name, because this type of sneaker was a status symbol to the young children but quite forgettable to adult subjects (King & Yuille, 1987).

On the other hand, in some situations children can be expected to fail to notice information that might be of critical importance because it is not significant to them. For example, the time of occurrence can be a vital piece of information for verifying an alibi. Children younger than 7 years of age may not have mastered the skill of telling time, do not have the world knowledge necessary to judge forensic relevance, and may not understand the principle that time flows independent of their own subjective experience to accurately estimate duration (Friedman, 1982; Saywitz, 1989). Many children would be unable to tell what time an event took place and how long it lasted. They may be able to recall what television program they were watching because it *was* of interest to them. The interviewer would then need to estimate time from the television guide.

Not only children may encode different kinds of information from what interviewers are seeking, but what is encoded may vary in terms of the strength of its trace (Ornstein et al., 1995). Some of the children's memory traces could be weaker and require greater effort and cuing to retrieve. Resistance of the trace to forgetting is thought to be, in part, a function of the degree to which the information was processed (i.e., superficially or completely and meaning-fully) (Craik & Lockhart, 1972). Young children may possess a greater number of weak traces because they process the information less fully as it happens.

Traces can be stronger if an individual is exposed to a piece of informa-tion for a longer period rather than a shorter period, perhaps allowing greater opportunity for more complete processing. Similarly, if the individual is personally involved in an event that is meaningful and embedded in the context of his or her life, it may result in a stronger trace (more easily recalled) than if the individual is a bystander (Goodman & Reed, 1986; Saywitz, Geiselman, & Bornstein, 1992). Individuals tend to have stronger recall for central actions and familiar settings than for peripheral details (e.g., eye color or hair color) and unfamiliar settings (Fivush, & Shukat, 1995; Saywitz, Goodman, Nicholas, & Moan, 1991; Tucker, Mertin, & Luszcz, 1990). Also, memory fades with time. Thus, longer retention intervals, created by the liberal use of continuances in court cases, contribute to incompleteness. If events are repeated, such as molestation that continues for months, individu-als tend to recall what usually happens (i.e., the generalized script for the event). More external guidance is needed to recall details unique to the individual episodes (Fivush & Hammond, 1990; Hudson & Nelson, 1986).

These characteristics of the event and the retention interval potentially influence the completeness of spontaneous recall and the need for specific questions to flush out additional information.

As they mature, children develop the ability to process information with greater speed and efficiency. With greater personal experience, children expand the knowledge base utilized to understand events and develop a greater ability to organize and select incoming information for encoding. There is greater overlap between the child's memory and the information needed in the forensic context. It is possible that the internal representation of the event becomes more detailed, organized, and relevant to the interviewer's purpose, and that traces become more fully elaborated. After the fact, little can be done to address incompleteness that is due to developmental limitations on encoding and storage. However, a number of other factors also contribute to the incompleteness of children's accounts. Several of these can provide insights for improving children's recall performance during the interview.

Context Dependence

Another contributor to children's incompleteness can be the context in which the questioning occurs. Generally, young children's behaviors are more easily influenced by the context than older children's or adults' behaviors (Donaldson, 1979). Nowhere is this more evident than in the preschooler's tendency to be distracted by the "perceptual pull" of intriguing aspects of the physical surroundings. Yet context is not simply the place in which remembering occurs, it is a constituent of the memory process itself (Ceci, Brofenbrenner, & Baker, 1988). The physical and psychological setting in which remembering transpires influences ability to recall. It is highly likely that the completeness and consistency of children's reports will be influenced by the contexts created by interviewers.

Laboratory studies amply demonstrate young children's tendencies to perform differently in different physical surroundings. For example, researchers found that children's uses of prospective memory strategies were less efficient in an unfamiliar laboratory than in the child's home (Ceci et al., 1988). They speculated that the laboratory setting induced anxiety incompatible with the deployment of the memory strategy under study. Hence, when statements across interviews are inconsistent and information is reported in one setting but not another, context rather than dishonesty could be responsible. The effect of the forensic context was apparent in a study of 8- to 10-year-olds. Half were questioned in a courtroom stocked with spectators, mock jurors, and a confederate judge (Saywitz & Nathanson, 1992, 1993; Saywitz, Nathanson, Snyder, & Lamphear, 1993). The other half were questioned in an adjacent room by the same interviewer asking the same questions. Children questioned in court showed significantly less complete free recall and more erratic heart rate patterns than children questioned in the private room. It is unlikely differences were due to a general memory failure; when children were asked specific questions, providing retrieval cues, the effect of setting disappeared. It is more likely that children stored information, but the information was less accessible in the courtroom context for free-recall purposes than in the noncourt setting.

Anxiety, confusion, or distraction due to the formality or unfamiliarity of the setting may have interfered with the motivation or effort required for independent retrieval. A significantly greater number of children questioned in court could not recall the staged event at all in response to free-recall instructions, in comparison to the noncourt group. Anecdotally, children in the courtroom made such comments as "I can't think in here." Such statements were not made in the small room. Studies such as these suggest that characteristics of the context can contribute to variability in completeness across settings, explaining some of the inconsistency noted between pretrial statements and courtroom testimony. Continued investigation of the specific setting characteristics that influence recall may provide guidelines for the reform of settings in which child interviews occur. Perhaps the practice of equating consistency with reliability should be reexamined as well.

For the purpose of this overview, we define context as more than the physical setting of the interview. Our discussion includes characteristics of the psychosocial atmosphere (e.g., formality, familiarity, interviewer demeanor, and mood) and certain task demands (e.g., difficulty level, cue availability, and complexity). Characteristics of the interviewer can contribute to an atmosphere of intimidation, support, empathy, or contempt that potentially influence children's statements. In one study, the autobiographical memories of a group of 3-year-olds were better in a supportive social atmosphere than in a neutral one. In fact, 3-year-olds in the supportive environment performed as well as 5-year-olds in the neutral environment (Goodman, Bottoms, Schwartz-Kenney, & Rudy, 1991). However, by the time children were 5 years of age there were no differences. In contrast, a coercive or intimidating demeanor creates the potential for inhibiting children's output. In one interviewing study, qualitative analyses suggested that condescending comments reduced children's productivity (Geiselman, Saywitz, & Bornstein, 1993). Of course, characteristics of the context are also linked to suggestibility (i.e., accusatory context); however, for the purpose of this chapter, we focus our discussion on findings relevant to completeness.

The way in which the adult constructs the memory task also affects children's performance. Depending on the purpose of the interview or the skill of the interviewer, one interview may require comprehension of complex linguistic constructions and provide few cues to guide retrieval efforts or to focus attention. Other interviews may constitute a task of far less difficulty, providing ample cues and demanding less verbal skill. In a study of recall context on preschoolers' memories for recurring events, younger children's recall (2 and one-half to 4 years of age) was more complete when the recall context included a greater number of stimulus supports (e.g., returning to the scene of the event to be recalled) and when the recall task was less verbal (e.g., opportunities to demonstrate what occurred with a model) than in situations providing less stimulus support during retrieval and requiring a verbal response (e.g., free recall in a waiting room) (Price & Goodman, 1990). In fact, the 2-year-olds appeared to be almost "totally ignorant of all aspects of a repetitive episode" when asked for verbal free recall in the waiting room. However, when stimulus support was increased, younger children's performance was in some cases brought up to the level of children in the next oldest age group, when the older age group was tested under conditions of less stimulus support. In short, completeness of the young children's recall was highly dependent on cues in the setting and nonverbal props available to supplement verbal statements.

Further, younger children are more dependent on adult questions for direction than older children to search their memories in an efficient, systematic, and organized fashion. For young children, much detail is elicited in a piecemeal fashion by a series of questions that tend to drive the organization of the material (Fivush, 1993; Fivush & Shukat, 1995). For better or worse, the way children are questioned surely influences the amount of information they provide. As they grow, children learn to function more independently of the setting, the interviewer, or variations in task demands. In sum, one factor contributing to the completeness and consistency of children's performance in forensic interviews is the context created by the interviewer.

Communication and Language

In the forensic context, memories must be transformed into words and communicated verbally, according to unfamiliar sociolinguistic principles. Large discrepancies between children's comprehension abilities and adult wording can create inconsistencies and limit the amount of information reported. Inconsistencies appear from question to question, depending on the wording. For example, in one instance a preschooler denied seeing a *weapon* at the scene of the murder. Later, when asked specifically if he saw a gun, he answered "yes," the correct response. The abstract, hierarchical, and categorical term, "weapon," was either unfamiliar or insufficient to trigger recall of the specific, concrete, visualizable object, "gun," that was perceived, encoded, stored, and potentially accessible to retrieval, depending on the way the question was worded. Even small differences in interviewer word choice may limit completeness and create inconsistencies across interviews.

Several studies examined transcripts of child witness testimony, then tested school children (matched in age to the witnesses) for comprehension of comparable question forms and vocabulary (Brennan & Brennan, 1988; Perry, McAuliff, Tam, & Claycomb, 1995; Saywitz, Jaenicke, & Camparo, 1990; Saywitz & Snyder, 1993). Researchers tended to find that the linguistic complexity and vocabulary of the question were not well matched to the child's stage of language acquisition. Elsewhere, Saywitz and her colleagues suggested that such discrepancies create the potential for misunderstanding and communication breakdown, creating the opportunity for incomplete and/or apparently inconsistent statements that are misinterpreted by adult listeners (Saywitz, Nathanson, & Snyder, 1993). Guidelines for talking to children in language they can understand are not difficult to construct from the language acquisition literature (see Brennan & Brennan, 1988; Perry et al., 1995; Saywitz, 1995; Saywitz & Elliott, in press; Saywitz, Nathanson, & Snyder, 1993; Walker, 1994, for attempts to begin to do so).

In addition to the language of the interviewer, successful communication and complete reporting depend on the children's abilities to monitor how well or poorly they understood the question. Language acquisition studies amply demonstrate young children's difficulties monitoring whether or not they fully comprehend language in ongoing conversation (Dickson, 1981). A recent study extended these findings by testing children's comprehension monitoring of questions about a previously staged event (Saywitz, 1995; Saywitz, Nathanson, Snyder, & Lamphear, 1993). The results of a study of 186 first- and third-graders suggested that during a recall interview composed of questions that varied in comprehensibility, children often tried to answer questions they did not fully understand, rarely asking for a rephrase. Often their responses were an association to a part of the question they did understand and remember, typically the beginning or ending of the utterance. They were correct about as often as they were incorrect in responding to incomprehensible questions. However, when a second group was warned before the interview that "some of the questions might be easy to understand, but that some questions might be hard to understand," and they were given permission to ask for a rephrase (e.g., "Tell me when you don't understand, say, 'I don't get it, I don't know what you mean' "), the accuracy of their responses improved significantly. Further, when a third group was given practice identifying noncomprehension and asking for a rephrase with modeling and feedback prior to the interview, they responded with the fewest errors and the most correct responses to interview questions of all three groups. In sum, children's incompleteness can be a function of a mismatch between the child's comprehesion and the interviewer's language. Unlike incompleteness due to encoding and storage differences, contextual and communicative factors could be manipulated by interviewers to maximize children's performance. Laboratory studies and further applied research ought to provide some guidance.

Retrieval Strategy Usage

Incompleteness and inconsistency in young children's recall may also be a function of limited or inconsistent use of memory-jogging strategies to aid retrieval during the interview. Older children and adults use more complex and successful retrieval strategies than younger children to increase the amount of information they retrieve independently (e.g., Ornstein, Naus, & Liberty, 1975; Pressley & Levin, 1977). Preschoolers show only rudimentary use of retrieval strategies on very simple tasks when experimenters suggest the strategies to the children (Ritter, 1978; Ritter, Kaprove, Fitch, & Flavell, 1973). Hence, 3-year-olds require a good deal of prompting, 5-year-olds less so. From 4 to 12 years of age, children demonstrate increasing efficiency and flexibility in retrieval strategy usage. For example, in one study, 6- to 11-year-olds were presented with lists of categorizable items to learn for later recall (e.g., animals). At the time of recall, children were presented with pictures of category cues (e.g., zoo). The 6-year-olds did not use the category cues to aid recall; the 8- to 11-year-olds did (Kobasigawa, 1974, 1977).

Generally, studies suggest that by third grade (8 to 9 years of age) children generate and use a variety of retrieval strategies spontaneously. Still, complex heuristics resulting in exhaustive memory searches are rarely seen until the end of grade school and may not be mastered until adolescence (Salatas & Flavell, 1976). A list of the most thoroughly investigated retrieval strategies includes rehearsal, clustering, category cues (Kobasigawa, 1974, 1977; Perlmutter & Myers, 1979) and the use of external cues, such as pictures or props (Fivush, 1993; Hudson & Fivush, 1987; Pipe, Gee, & Wilson, 1993).

Studies also demonstrate that children can be taught to use retrieval strategies to improve recall, although they might not use such strategies spontaneously (Flavell, 1970; Paris, Newman, & McVey, 1982). First-graders who used a verbal-rehearsal strategy spontaneously when learning a list for later recall showed more complete recall than first-graders who did not use this strategy spontaneously. But when the latter group was taught to use the strategy, their performance improved (Keeney, Cannizzo, & Flavell, 1967). Similarly, children who failed to use a sorting–clustering strategy to recall categorizable pictures had inferior recall for the pictures than a group of peers who used this strategy. Again, when taught this strategy, the former group improved. In past laboratory studies, children often profited from instruction; however, their gains did not necessarily transfer to new situations and tasks. Young children use the strategies provided by adults but have difficulty independently generating strategies and planning for retrieval. Some researchers propose that children can also learn to use retrieval strategies suggested by interviewers in the forensic context to enhance completeness (Saywitz, 1995). In fact, the experimental techniques described later in this chapter attempt to do just that. Unfortunately, a review of past laboratory studies finds that researchers focused primarily on encoding strategies and deliberate memory, limiting their usefulness for child witnesses who must recall incidentally stored information and rely on strategies at the time of retrieval. Still, these training studies offer one springboard for development of techniques for teaching children to improve the completeness of their reports.

Maintenance and Generalization

Available laboratory studies suggest that a number of interventions can improve children's ability to maintain newly learned strategies and use them efficiently on such new tasks as forensic interviews or courtroom testimony. (e.g., Cavanaugh & Borkowski, 1979; Pressley, Forrest-Pressley, & Elliott-Faust, 1988; Ringel & Springer, 1980). For example, children benefit from practice if given explicit feedback on their progress. In one representative study, practice using a memory strategy increased children's knowledge of whether the strategy worked better than other strategies, but it did not facilitate the use of the strategy on new memory tasks. Yet, when practice was combined with explicit feedback on performance, recall was promoted. A similar improvement emerged when practice was combined with a prompt to use the strategy just before the memory test (Pressley, Ross, Levin, & Ghatala, 1984). Children possess information gained through practice with a particular strategy, but they may not necessarily utilize the information in the service of recall without hints, prompts, and feedback. Even older children can benefit. The keyword strategy has been used extensively to promote memory of foreign-language vocabulary. After being taught to use this strategy on one recall task, 18-year-olds transferred its use to a second task, but 12-year-olds did not (Pressley & Dennis-Rounds, 1980). However, when 12-year-olds were told to use a technique similar to the one practiced on the first task, they were able to use the keyword strategy on a second task.

Such training studies can be mined for promising approaches to facilitate children's completeness in the forensic setting. Strategy instruction, practice with feedback, and hints or reminders immediately prior to questioning may maximize completeness and minimize generalization problems (Pressley & Dennis-Rounds, 1980; Pressley et al., 1988). Both narrative elaboration and the enhanced cognitive interview make use of instruction, feedback, hints, and practice prior to the interview for these reasons.

Metacognitive Knowledge and Awareness

Metamemory

With age and experience, children learn more about how and when to apply retrieval strategies with maximal success (Flavell & Wellman, 1977). Such knowledge is thought to increase generalization of newly learned strategies to novel tasks, such as the forensic interview. As children grow, they learn which strategies are more effective for recalling details, how to evaluate if a strategy is effective, and how to generate alternatives if a strategy fails. They learn to discriminate easy from difficult recall tasks and predict the likelihood of success or failure in a given situation. They learn to select from among several strategies the most appropriate for a given situation. These metamemory skills may facilitate complete reporting.

Metamemory studies demonstrate that increased awareness of how memory works can result in improved strategy use and better recall. For example, increased awareness of the value of the strategy for improving performance is related to better recall (e.g., Lodico, Ghatala, Levin, Pressley, & Bell, 1983; Ringel & Springer, 1980) and to selecting more effective strategies (Pressley et al., 1984). Children credited their newfound successes to their strategic behavior in comparison to control groups that did not receive training (Ghatala, Levin, Pressley, & Lodico, 1985; Lodico et al., 1983). Further, there is evidence that knowledge concerning the value of the strategy helps to maintain strategy use after initial training and to generalize its application to new tasks (Borkowski, Milstead, & Hale, 1988; Lodico et al., 1983; Pressley et al., 1988). Limited metacognitive knowledge is associated with more difficulty transferring gains to new situations in laboratory studies (Cavanaugh & Borkowski, 1979); however, age-related differences are reduced by metamemory training (Ghatala et al., 1985; Kurtz & Borkowski, 1984, 1987). Hence, increasing children's awareness of how and when to employ newly learned strategies during the forensic interview through preparation could be a source of increased completeness.

Metacommunication

In addition to increased awareness of the workings of their memory (metamemory), children increase their ability to decipher the task demands and response consequences of verbal exchanges. Children increase their ability to estimate the listener's need to know, his or her prior knowledge on the topic, who is at fault for miscommunication, the consequences for miscommunication, and how to orient the listener to time, place, and perspective. Hence, with age and experience, children learn to take the listener's perspective, to anticipate the listener's needs, to provide missing context cues, and to elaborate on the unfamiliar spontaneously. One can observe the beginnings of these metalinguistic skills when preschoolers reformulate utterances that were misunderstood; however, these skills continue to develop throughout the school-age years. Limited metalinguistic awareness may contribute to incompleteness and inconsistency of children's reports. Consider the following paths as an illustration.

Young children, again relying on their limited personal experience, are likely to assume that the rules for everyday communication pertain to the forensic interview as well (Keenan, MacWhinney, & Mayhew, 1977). This is clearly not the case (Saywitz, Nathanson, & Snyder, 1993; Walker, 1993). Violations of numerous postulates of conversation occur with frequency in the forensic context. For example, at least one researcher noted a tendency for children to change their answer when questions are repeated, presumably assuming that the interviewer was dissatisfied with the first answer (Moston, 1987). Also, listeners typically assume speakers are sincere unless presented with information to the contrary (Grice, 1975). Children under 9 to 13 years of age tend to interpret remarks as sincere (Demorest, Meyer, Phelps, Gardner, & Winner, 1984). Unexpected violations of the sincerity postulate are not infrequent in the adversarial process. We speculated elsewhere that failure to understand a speaker's true intent could influence how much information children report and how readily they acquiesce to misleading questions (Saywitz & Moan-Hardie, 1994).

Consider another example. Typically, grammatical conventions are used to introduce, maintain, and change topics in conversation. Comments that link one topic of conversation with the next are frequent in conversations between adults and children. Young children rely heavily on adults to structure the conversation and to elaborate on their responses (Newhoff & Launer, 1984). These transitional comments (e.g., "Before we were talking about school. Now we are going to talk about your Uncle John.") are often omitted in the forensic context (Brennan & Brennan, 1988). It is suggested that without proper introduction, children are left disoriented with little understanding of how and why questions are being asked, unable to switch frames of reference without the necessary signals (Brennan & Brennan, 1988; Saywitz, Nathanson, & Snyder, 1993). In such situations, listeners cannot be certain they have the same antecedents in mind as the children, for example, when using pronouns (e.g., he and they) that refer to persons previously named. Consequently, there is fertile ground for misinterpretation of children's meaning as inconsistent or incomplete.

In sum, some portion of children's incompleteness may be due to their limited metacognitive awareness of memory and communication in the interview. One way to compensate for limited metacognitive awareness might be through the application of instructions. For example, instructions announcing that the interviewer was not present at the event in question and could not know what happened may address children's misperceptions about the interviewer's knowledge base and expectations. This instruction was included with others in a study designed to promote children's resistance to misleading questions (Saywitz & Moan-Hardie, 1994). However, the independent contributions of such instructions have rarely been tested.

Knowledge of the Legal System

Limited knowledge of the legal system may be another source of children's incompleteness. For example, unrealistic expectations regarding the purpose of the interview, the intentions and behaviors of the interviewer, or the limits on confidentiality could undermine effort and motivation applied to retrieval. Lack of familiarity could foster confusion or fear of the unknown which could distract children from the task at hand and lower productivity.

Studies generally find that children under 10 years of age have somewhat limited knowledge of the legal system (Flin, Stevenson, & Davies, 1989; Melton, Limber, Jacobs, & Oberlander, 1992; Sas, 1991; Saywitz, 1989). For example, many 4- and 5-year-olds did not know that the judge is in charge of the courtroom or that the judge has decision-making responsibilities. They described the judge's function in terms of appearances ("He wears a robe, bangs a gavel, and sits up high." "He listens."). They expressed the belief that the judge is omniscient (e.g., "He knows if you are telling the truth or not"). Young children expressed the belief that jurors were mere spectators. Many did not understand that they were impartial but believed these unfamiliar adults must be friends of the defendant. Some children believed they would go to jail if they made an inadvertent mistake on the stand. Many children did not understand the flow of information from the police officer to the attorney to the judge, expressing surprise or betrayal when they learned that strangers have knowledge that was disclosed in private. As children develop greater knowledge of the investigative and judicial process, they are in a better position to decipher the demands of the interview task, the purpose of the questioning, and the role of the interviewer.

Given such limited understanding of the roles of the professionals, the rules by which they interact, or the requirements of the system, it is easy to postulate that children could have trouble formulating an accurate appraisal of task demands and response consequences in the forensic context. For example, expectations that error leads to jail could raise the threshold for responding, resulting in more "I don't knows" and more incomplete recall. Or, it could increase motivation and effort because the cost of error is so high, thereby improving recall performance. Fear of the unknown could lead to avoidance, thus thwarting completeness.

Two studies demonstrated that children can be taught to understand relevant aspects of the investigative and judicial process (Sas, 1991; Saywitz, Nathanson, Snyder, & Lamphear, 1993, Experiment 7). In one study, alleged victims of child abuse demonstrated more legal knowledge after receiving individual preparation than those who received status quo services (Sas, 1991). In another study, children were taught about the legal process and then questioned in a mock testimony paradigm with a simulated trial environment (Saywitz, Nathanson, Snyder, & Lamphear, 1993, Experiment 7). Although children demonstrated increased legal knowledge as a result of preparation, knowledge of the legal system was not associated with memory benefit. This could be due to the fact that the experiment did not recreate the complexities of actual trials or the feelings of actual witnesses.

Two additional studies of children's recall for staged events in a courtroom context examined the relation between legal knowledge, memory, and anxiety. In one study, greater legal knowledge was associated with less anxiety about testifying in a simulated trial and more correct responses to direct questions (Goodman et al., in press). In another study, when compared to children questioned in a private adjacent room, children questioned in a courtroom demonstrated greater heart rate reactivity, indicative of a stress response, and expressed greater confusion over not knowing what to do in court. However, legal knowledge was unrelated to measures of anxiety in this paradigm. Greater legal knowledge was, however, related to more productivity in free recall, more correct responses to specific questions, and fewer "I don't know" responses, suggesting a relation independent of anxiety.

More research regarding the effects of preparation to enhance legal knowledge and thereby to reduce stress and/or improve memory performance is clearly warranted. Yet we are beginning to see some evidence that lack of familiarity with the legal system may exacerbate children's tendencies to provide incomplete reports, perhaps reducing effort or motivation required for successful retrieval. Limited knowledge of the legal system, especially its purposes and procedures, may contribute to children's incompleteness by hampering their abilities to infer the purpose and intentions of the interviewer or to judge the forensic relevance of the information potentially available for retrieval. Making sense of the unfamiliar processes and procedures could divert attentional resources necessary for complete retrieval.

Narrative Discourse

Children's descriptions could also be constrained by their limited ability to narrate past events. A narrative is a description of a past event that is minimally cued by external sources (i.e., questions). The organizational pattern of the narrative reflects the child's prior understanding of the events and other information-processing capabilities. A narrative is a unit of discourse with its own form (e.g., underlying organizational rules, that is, its own grammar) and content (e.g., expectations about event sequences built up from past experience about the temporal and causal relations among events). To the degree that children's organizational patterns for mentally representing events are undeveloped or rudimentary, their narrative descriptions could be circumscribed.

The ability to produce narrative recounts emerges during the preschool and early elementary school years (Fivush & Hammond, 1990). Children's early narratives are skeletal and can be loosely organized according to what is salient to the individual child based on his or her immature and often egocentric perspective of the world (Nelson, 1978; Nelson, Fivush, Hudson, & Lucariello, 1983). With maturation and experience, children's narratives become more fully elaborated and relevant to the context at hand. Older children provide longer, more elaborate narratives with more spontaneity and less need for direct questions (Fivush & Shukat, 1995). Younger children require direct questions to recall as much as older children. In one study, 3- to 6-year-olds were asked to recount a trip to Disney World 6 or 18 months prior (Hammond, 1987). To recount as much information as older children, the younger ones needed more questions and prompts from interviewers. In such studies, young children rarely provided more information than was asked for by the adult (Fivush & Shukat, 1995). When repeatedly interviewed about a past event, subsequent interviews elicited a good deal of accurate new information not reported in the original interview, creating the appearance of inconsistency (Fivush & Hammond, 1990).

Adults' questions guide children toward the categories of information relevant to the topic at hand. The didactic role of adults' questions in children's development of conversational forms and in the development of narrative recounts is well-known (Heath, 1983; Rice, Wilcox, & Hadley, 1992). Adult questioning can play a facilitative role on children's recall (Flavell, 1985) or become an interfering, or, worse, a contaminating factor, if highly suggestive questions are used (Ceci & Bruck, 1993). The dilemma for the interviewer is that children can remember autobiographical information for long periods, and with the assistance of questions they can recount it. Still, their recounts can be compromised by limited language and narrative production skills or by coercive techniques that distort their statements.

Children's narratives improve with age as they begin to internalize the process of cuing recall. In short, children learn what questions to ask themselves to search their memory more effectively and efficiently. They have learned that their narratives should include the who, what, when, where, and why. It is no longer the adult's responsibility to ask for each of these individually; they are often included in the initial narrative spontaneously. Children develop a greater understanding of the listener's needs and goals, of the kind of information and the level of detail expected in the interview setting (Eisenberg, 1985; Stein, 1988). Narratives improve with age as children learn to structure the flow of information to guarantee understanding by the listener. They use cohesion devices which are linguistic tools speakers use to link sentences and build coherence, that is, ties between ideas and pieces of information to create a coherent narrative. This is often accomplished with the use of conjunctions. In short, limited ability to narrate a past event can be a significant contributor to the incompleteness of children's accounts.

EXPERIMENTAL INTERVIEW TECHNIQUES

Contributors to children's incompleteness include their limited knowledge base, infrequent or rigid use of retrieval strategies, immature language and narrative production skills, nascent metacognitive knowledge, and dependence on the context. As we highlighted in our review of these factors, there is a rich quarry of laboratory findings to be mined in pursuit of techniques to enhance children's completeness in the forensic context. Two innovative techniques developed in our laboratories attempt to address this challenge. Next we describe these techniques, narrative elaboration and cognitive interviewing, and several studies that examine their efficacy. Then, in the final section of the chapter, we discuss guidelines for interviewing children extrapolated from the research reviewed.

Narrative Elaboration

Narrative elaboration is both a preparation procedure and an interview format developed by Saywitz and Snyder (1996) to facilitate more complete, detailed, and relevant descriptions of past events from school-age children in response to general, open-ended questions, such as "Tell me what happened." Narrative elaboration utilizes memory-retrieval mnemonics from the experimental literature on memory development. This technique requires interviewers to teach children what it means to be interviewed prior to questioning them about the event under investigation. Children learn some of the task demands of the forensic interview, that is, the kind of information and the level of detail the interviewer requires. Children learn a new strategy for improving the completeness of their reports and practice it with modeling and feedback on the recall of unrelated events. Feedback is designed to promote more fully elaborated narratives and shared expectations about the interviewer's purpose. Then children are prompted to use the new strategy in the future when they are asked about the event under investigation.

Narrative elaboration is based on six factors found to benefit children's recall in the experimental literature: memory strategy instruction, practice with feedback, rationales for strategy utility, organizational guidance according to category cues, external memory aids (i.e., pictorial cues), and reminders to use the new strategy prior to interviewing.

First, children are given a rationale for learning a new retrieval strategy (strategy utility). They learn that there are better and worse ways to remember, using examples that differ depending on the child's age. For example, older children discuss that they would remember more items from a grocery list if the items were written down than if they had to be recalled without a written list.

Then children are taught that event recall is comprised of four types of information: participants, settings, actions, and conversations. They are instructed that it is important to tell as much as they can remember about each of these parts, without guessing. Each category is represented pictorially on a card. Children are taught through an analogy to a street light ("Red tells you to stop, green tells you to go") that the reminder cards are also "signs that tell you what to do." For example, the *people* card "reminds you to tell as much as you can remember about who the people were and what each one looked like." Then, children practice using the cards to elaborate on each category while recalling a story, a video, or an unrelated autobiographical event (e.g., what they did this morning from the time they got up until the time they arrived at the interview). During practice, interviewers model additional details that could have been reported if available in memory from each category (hair color and style, clothing, age, race, etc.,). School-age children learn rather quickly that they can recall several additional pieces of relevant information in response to each card to expand their initial narrative.

Then, the interview regarding the incident under investigation begins. Open-ended questions are used to request the description of the event. After the child indicates that her uninterrupted narrative is complete, the interviewer presents each card individually asking, "Does this card remind you to tell something else?" Follow-up questions can focus on expanding or clarifying information elicited from the child in this relatively unbiased manner rather than resorting to questions based on adult supposition or other sources of information that create the potential for distortion.

Four studies were conducted to test the effectiveness of this technique (Dorado & Saywitz, 1997; Saywitz, Nathanson, Snyder, & Lamphear, 1993, Experiments 1–3; Saywitz & Snyder, 1996; Saywitz, Snyder, & Lamphear, 1996). In one study of 132 7- and 10-year-olds, the procedure increased completeness of children's recall of a classroom activity by 53%, in comparison to a control group (Saywitz & Snyder, 1996). Improvements were found in the amount of additional information reported about the participants, setting, and conversations. The 7- to 8-year-olds who received the intervention performed at the level of 10- to 11-year-olds in the control group. A second study was conducted to determine whether benefits would generalize to a new interviewer who was an unfamiliar authority figure in an interview subsequent to the training (Saywitz et al., 1996). The results were similar. Most of the benefit of the training is found in children's responses to the reminder cards in comparison to free recall or responses to specific follow-up questions. The cards allow children additional unbiased opportunities to expand their reports by adding the kind to detail that is relevant in a forensic investigation. Practice with the technique before the interview helps children develop an accurate understanding of the interviewers' expectations, needs, intentions, and memorial as well as communicative task demands of the interview. It also discourages children from pushing themselves too hard to report information about which they are unsure. In a recent study, a simplified version of narrative elaboration was also successful at improving the recall of middle- and low-income preschoolers, without the use of leading questions (Dorado & Saywitz, 1997).

Cognitive Interviewing

In response to the need for assisting witnesses and victims in their recollections of persons and events, Geiselman et al. (1984), and Geiselman, Fisher, MacKinnon, and Holland (1985, 1986) constructed an interview format that includes memory retrieval mnemonics from the literature in cognitive psychology. The resulting technique was labeled the cognitive interview (CI). It has been tested with favorable results in more than 36 experiments with both adults and children (Koehnken, Milne, Memon, & Bull, 1994).

The Original Cognitive Interview

The original CI consists of four general retrieval methods that can be used in most interview situations, plus additional, more specific techniques that are appropriate for retrieving specific kinds of information, such as names, numbers, or conversation. Of the four general methods, two attempt to increase the feature overlap between the memory record for the event and the memory-retrieval aid: (1) mentally reconstructing the environmental and personal (emotional) context that existed at the time of the events (Bower, Gilligan, & Monteiro, 1984), and (2) reporting everything, even partial information, regardless of the perceived importance of the information (Smith, 1983). The other two methods encourage using many retrieval paths: (3) recounting the events in a variety of orders (Geiselman & Callot, 1990), and (4) reporting the events from a variety of perspectives (Anderson & Pichert, 1978).

The original version of the CI also contains several specific suggestions to facilitate recall of physical appearance, speech characteristics, conversation, names, and numbers. For example, "Did the person (or voice) remind you of anyone (or any voice) you know. If so, why?" This technique was found to elicit additional details about the target person's mannerisms and appearance, and also to aid the witness in recalling what was said, "Think about your reactions to what was said and the reactions of others who were there. Maybe by thinking about your reactions, you will remember what was said to you." Further, if the witness is blocking on a name he or she is asked to go through the alphabet searching for the first letter of the name. In laboratory experiments, this "first letter" technique was found to be successful roughly two-thirds of the time that someone is blocking on a name (Gruneberg & Monks, 1976). A series of questions also was developed to help witnesses recollect numbers by recalling partial information (MacKinnon, O'Reilly, & Geiselman, 1990). Although this research addressed memory for license plates in particular, the questions apply to numbers in general. The technique includes queries about numerical magnitude, character shape, proximity, and cognitive impressions.

The Enhanced Cognitive Interview

The original version of the CI was elaborated to address, in addition to the original issue of memory enhancement, the rememberer's control over his or her emotional state, the social dynamics of the interview, and several procedures to promote effective communication. Crucial to the revised, or enhanced, CI procedure (ECI) is the sequencing of the primary sections of the interview. The general strategy is to guide the witness to those memory images that are richest in relevant information and to facilitate communication when these memories are activated. Each section of the procedure makes a unique contribution to ensuring the success of the interview.

To become completely conversant in the ECI, the interviewer must learn 13 basic skills: establishing rapport, listening actively, telling the rememberer to actively generate information and not wait passively for the interviewer to ask questions, asking open-ended questions, pausing after the rememberer's response before asking follow-up questions, not interrupting, explicitly requesting detailed descriptions, encouraging the rememberer to concentrate intensely, encouraging the rememberer to use imagery, recreating the original context, adopting the rememberer's perspective, asking eyewitness-compatible questions, and following the sequence of the CI. (For an in-depth description of the ECI, see Fisher, Geiselman, Raymond, Jurkevich, & Warhaftig, 1987a; Fisher, McCauley, & Geiselman, 1994; and the more comprehensive volume on investigative interviewing by Fisher & Geiselman, 1992.)

The Cognitive Interview for Use with Children

From the literature on child development, there is reason to believe that the memory-retrieval mnemonics from the CI would be useful with child witnesses. The techniques that comprise the CI provide explicit retrieval strategies, specific retrieval cues, and strategies for organizing information. Although young children show limited memory strategy usage, they are known to be able to use strategies provided by adults at the moment of retrieval that they cannot spontaneously generate and employ on their own.

With respect to reconstructing the circumstances, Pressley and Levin (1980) observed that imagery instructions enhance recall performance of children. Dent (1982) suggested such a technique with child witnesses. With respect to reporting everything, children's spontaneous reports often are found to be less complete than those of adults. In addition, children do not have a good idea of what has investigative value because they have limited knowledge of the legal system and they may have many misconceptions about the forensic context (Saywitz, 1989). Thus, children also may benefit from this instruction. On the other hand, the usefulness of varied recall orders and perspectives is likely to be a function of cognitive and social development. The ability to order recall chronologically was shown to develop gradually with age (Brown, 1975). With regard to varied perspectives, the ability to draw inferences about the perspectives of others also was shown to develop gradually (Shantz, 1975). Thus, developmental differences in children's ability to take advantage of these techniques to improve recall are in need of investigation.

Saywitz et al. (1992) tested a modified version of the original CI with children between the ages of 7 and 12, employing experienced detectives to conduct the interviews. Reconstruction of the circumstances surrounding the event was carried out with the child describing the environmental and personal context *aloud*, to ensure that the child expended the mental effort required. Before the children gave their narrative accounts of the stage event, the cognitive interviewers asked them to "picture that time when you were taken out of class to a room that had balloons in it, as if you were there right now. Think about what it was like. What did the room look like? Tell me out loud. Were there any smells in the room? Was it dark or light in the room? Picture any other people who were there. Who else was there? What things were there in the room? How were you feeling when you were in that room?" The cognitive interviewers also were instructed to avoid using such terms as "pretend" and "imagine" in an attempt to maintain the child in reality and minimize fantasy.

The second CI technique was rephrased into more developmentally appropriate language. The cognitive interviewers were instructed to tell the child, "Now I want you to start at the beginning and tell me what happened, from the beginning to the middle, to the end. Tell me everything you remember, even little parts that you don't think are very important. Sometimes people leave out little things because they think little things are not important. Tell me everything that happened."

Following the narrative report, the cognitive interviewers asked any specific questions necessary to clarify what was reported thus far (as would be the case with standard questioning). Then, the interviewers asked the children to recall the events in backward order, starting at the end, then the middle, then the beginning. To prevent the child from making grand leaps backward in time, as observed by Geiselman and Padilla (1988), the interviewer repeatedly prompted the children with the question, "Then what happened *right* before that?"

The cognitive interviewers also were instructed in the use of the specific memory-jogging techniques developed by Geiselman et al. (1986) where appropriate. These included techniques for recalling numbers, names, and further descriptions of people (e.g., "Did the man remind you of anyone you know, and if so, why?").

When the child appeared to have exhausted memory for the event, the cognitive interviewers asked the child to "Put yourself in the body of _____, and tell me what that person saw." This was done to evaluate any effects (positive or negative) of the change-perspectives technique at each of the two age levels.

In Experiment 1, a staged event was carried out that involved a private encounter between an unfamiliar man and two children. The results showed that the CI significantly increased the number of correct facts recalled by both 7- to 8-year-olds and 10- to 11-year-olds over that gained with standard police interview procedures. This positive effect was achieved without affecting the number of incorrect items generated. These results were replicated in Experiment 2 with a different staged event and with 8- to 9-year-olds and 11- to 12-year-olds. A prior practice CI concerning an unrelated event was found to enhance the success of the CI about the target event at both age levels. With practice, the children achieved a 45% increase over standard procedures.

In one sense, the recommendation in favor of a practice CI creates a dilemma. As noted previously, victims and witnesses of child abuse must undergo several interview sessions regarding the alleged criminal act, and this opens the door for numerous psychological and legal complications. MacFarlane (cited in Cody, 1989), for example, estimated that some victims of child abuse are asked to retell their story to as many as 15 different parties. The "practice" interview could be seen as just another interview session for the child, although it does not involve the potentially harmful component of retelling or reliving a traumatic event to a stranger.

On the other hand, with a more complete report from the child early on in the process (due to more effective interview techniques), less time should be required for interviewing the child overall. The practical implication is that children who are witness/victims could receive practice at being interviewed without necessitating the child to retell frightening or anxiety-producing experiences for the currently required (or accepted) number of times (Cody, 1989). Minimal additional time and personnel would be necessary to carry out a "practice interview" with children, and the apparent positive impact on the target interview seems well worth the expense.

In the field, the practice interview could concern some innocuous event staged in a waiting room, so that the interviewer would have knowledge of the approximate facts as they actually happened. Alternatively, the practice interview could concern some standard aspect of the day's activities, such as what transpired at school on an earlier day. The advantage for having prior knowledge of the event is that the questioner in the practice session could identify when a child reports information that clearly is in error. At that point, the interviewer could pursue the possible source of the error to clarify what is expected of the child during an interview. For example, the interviewer might need to further explain the meaning of saying, "I don't know," for certain children.

There was some evidence that the change-perspectives technique was confusing for the very youngest subjects, as also noted by Geiselman and Padilla (1988). If used with young children, this technique should be tried at the end of the interview to avoid confusing them midway through and influencing future responses. In addition, this technique could be upsetting for children if they were asked to report the event from the viewpoint of an alleged perpetrator. In such cases, the perspectives of other victims or even a stuffed animal may not carry similar emotional overtones.

The ECI also was evaluated for use with children by Fisher and McCauley (1995). Seven-year-old children interacted with an adult experimenter by going through a series of actions in a Simon-says game. Two weeks later, the children were interviewed about the activities. The ECI elicited almost twice as many correct actions as the standard interview without an increase in errors. For further discussion of recent research readers are referred to Milne (in press).

IMPLICATIONS FOR IMPROVING COMPLETENESS AND REDUCING ERROR

What conclusions can be drawn from the studies reviewed to guide future research and practice? To maximize completeness and minimize error, the literature suggests that interviewers strive to create an opportunity for children to provide the most spontaneous and complete description of a past event possible in their own words. This avenue promotes accuracy by reducing the need for leading questions that introduce information from other sources or adult supposition. The experimental literature highlights several avenues worth pursuing in research and in practice to achieve maximal completeness and minimal error. These include the following:

1. Physical surroundings that are not distracting, confusing, or fearful.
2. A psychosocial atmosphere that is not accusatory, intimidating, or condescending but is supportive of maximal motivation and effort.
3. Preparation to demystify the legal context, to allay unrealistic fears, to help children understand the interviewer's purpose and expectations, and to judge forensic relevance.
4. Instructions to help children decipher the task demands and response consequences, circumventing some of their metacognitive limitations.
5. Age-appropriate language of questions, well matched to children's comprehension level to promote successful communication.
6. Memory-enhancement techniques, including retrieval strategies, prompts, and cues suggesting strategies to aid retrieval and to organize narration of relevant detail.
7. Modified task demands that lower the difficulty level of the interview task such as external cues and props the reduce verbal demands.
8. A general approach to questioning that begins with the most nonleading approaches first to elicit a relatively spontaneous narrative, followed by questions that guide the memory search to relevant topics and details without generating error or distortion.

Creating the Context

With regard to the psychosocial atmosphere created, there is little research relating the development of rapport to more complete free recall. However, studies of the authority status differential between interviewer and child imply that an intimidating atmosphere could foreclose a child's productivity. For the very youngest children, a supportive atmosphere may be optimal. A supportive demeanor does not prevent the interviewer from maintaining an objective neutral stance with regard to the veracity of the child's allegations and exploring alternative explanations for a child's statements. An objective mind-set can be maintained alongside a respectful and even kind approach to the child. For example, one can recognize a child's effort without reinforcing any specific content ("Thank you for trying so hard to listen carefully and tell me what you have heard or seen"). In addition, some evidence suggests that comments perceived to be coercive ("You can go to the bathroom after you tell me the answer to my question") or condescending ("You probably won't remember what color his eyes were"), even when they are not intended as such, reduce children's productivity and thus should be avoided.

With regard to the physical surroundings, the limited research available suggests that children ought to be able to provide a more complete report when surroundings are child centered. By this we mean the removal of distracting and intriguing items from offices (e.g., computers and calculators) and provision of time, for children to acclimate to the new surrounding, so that they can attend to the questions. For preschoolers, child-size furniture is desirable. The table should be the right height for the chair and the size of the child. Similarly, answering phone calls and beepers during the interview gives the impression that other things are more important. It does not convey the level of attention and seriousness that the interview demands. When the interviewer demonstrates motivation and attention, the child is more likely to respond in kind. Creating a context that is most conducive to provision of a complete report will be a matter of creativity, ingenuity, and further research.

Preparing Children

Past studies suggest that there might be some benefit to developing techniques of preparation to increase children's awareness of the interview's purpose, task demands, and response consequences. Increased awareness may have the potential for expanding children's initial retelling of past events. For example, studies reviewed suggested that practice with comprehension monitoring and cognitive interviewing before questioning the child about the event under investigation resulted in more complete recall of the event at hand in comparison to control groups without preparation. Moreover, preparation to demystify the investigative and judicial process in general may free up attentional resources for retrieving details rather than wondering about unknowns, such as the limits on confidentiality or the intentions of the police officer. Some of the studies reviewed suggested there may be a relation between greater legal knowledge and better recall in a mock courtroom environment. Programs preparing child witnesses for court by educating them about the legal system are being developed in the United States, Canada, and the United Kingdom. Similarly, time spent preparing children for the forensic interview may also be time well spent. Studies of legal knowledge highlighted children's lack of relevant information. Studies of preparation efforts suggested that school-age children can learn a good deal about the investigative process (e.g., flow of information and role of police, attorney, or judge), the interviewer's role (e.g., a child welfare worker might explain that her job is to ensure that children and families stay safe and healthy), and the child's role (e.g., a witness is someone who tells what they have heard and seen and felt). Further, there was some evidence to suggest that this information may make the unfamiliar more familiar, reducing fears of the unknown, and liberating the attentional resources and effort necessary for retrieval.

Instructing Children

The studies reviewed suggest there may be merit in providing instructions to children who have little knowledge from which to infer the purpose of the interview, the expectations and intentions of the interviewer, or the consequences of disclosure. For example, instructions could increase awareness of parameters unique to the forensic interview task (e.g., "Tell the truth. Do not make anything up. Do not guess."). Instructions could address the listener's perspective (e.g., "I was not there and do not know what happened. Sometimes I repeat myself because I am confused. This doesn't mean you need to change your answer.") as well as the constraints of the legal process (e.g., "I will need to write down [or audiotape] what we are saying so that I can remember it accurately later because what you are telling me is important"). Instructions could also address the consequences of making detailed statements (e.g., limits on confidentiality). Instructions could help children make a better metacognitive appraisal of whether the consequences will be worth the effort required for detailed retrieval, and greater effort applied to the deployment of retrieval strategies could enhance recall of detail.

The appendix lists a number of instructions utilized in research studies of school-age children conducted by the authors. Most are included as part of an experimental package. Thus, the independent contributions of individual instructions have rarely been tested. Three of these were tested independently—two with positive effects, one with no measurable effects.

As previously mentioned, in a study of the effects of comprehension monitoring training, instructions warning school-age children that some questions would be easy to understand and others would be difficult for them to understand, in concert with permission to ask for a rephrase, were very successful (Saywitz, 1995; Saywitz, Nathanson, Snyder, & Lamphear, 1993, Experiment 4). In two other studies, motivating instructions ("Do your best, try your hardest") given to control groups appeared to be associated with more complete free recall of a past event for both preschoolers and school-age children, in comparison to control groups given no instructions in a third study (Dorado & Saywitz, 1997; Saywitz & Snyder, 1996; Saywitz et al., 1996).

Finally, in one study of the narrative elaboration technique (Saywitz & Snyder, 1996) a control group of school-age children received instructions to be accurate and complete ("Tell as much as you can about what really happened, even the little things, without guessing or making anything up"). These instructions alone were of no measurable benefit in comparison to a control group.

One last word of caution on the use of instructions and preparation is in order. In a study of children's resistance to suggestion, instructing children to admit lack of knowledge rather than go along with suggestive questions resulted in both expected benefits and unintended consequences. As expected, errors on misleading questions dropped significantly and "I don't know" responses increased. However, correct responses to some types of questions diminished in favor of the "I don't know" response as well, although errors did not increase (Saywitz & Moan-Hardie, 1994). Perhaps children became more cautious about guessing, even in situations in which they would have been correct. A follow-up study eliminated this adverse effect by including instructions to "Tell the answer when you know the answer," among a few other changes. We present these findings here to highlight the need for empirical investigation of various interview instructions before application.

Questioning Children

Past studies inform us that young children can benefit from questions that guide the memory search in an efficient and systematic manner. In developing guidelines for questioning children, several principles are clear.

Communication

Successful communication is critical to a complete accounting of what occurred. Questions should be phrased in grammar and vocabulary children can easily comprehend. Interviewers should use age-appropriate rules of discourse. Moreover, questions should be matched to children's level of cognitive development. Questions involving abstract concepts or skills children have not yet mastered should be avoided. If deployed, responses should be interpreted within a developmental framework. For example, answers to questions asking children how many times something happened or what time an event began will be suspect if children have not yet learned to count or tell time.

Retrieval Strategies

Interviewers can provide cues, retrieval strategies, and prompts to facilitate retrieval as long as these do not generate unintended errors. Further research is necessary to illuminate the best methods of accomplishing these goals. Narrative elaboration and cognitive interviewing are examples of two techniques designed to provide children with such memory-jogging opportunities.

Open-Ended Questions

Memory-development research prompts many authors to suggest that interviews begin with open-ended questions, such as "Why do you think you are here today? Is there anything you want to tell me?" (e.g., Bull, 1995). Again, we remind the reader that the likelihood of these questions being successful at eliciting genuine abuse experiences is, in part, related to how well children understand the role, purpose, and expectations of the interviewer as well as the overall functioning of the legal system. For example, asking an open-ended question, such as "Is there anything you want me to tell the judge?" will only be useful if children understand the role of the judge as a decision maker in their lives.

Our review of the literature suggests that an interviewer strives to elicit the most complete report possible with the least risk of distortion. In general, studies suggest that the least biasing method of questioning would be to proceed from relatively open-ended efforts to elicit an independent narrative along a continuum to progressively more focused and specific questions, some of which may be considered leading (see Lamb et al., 1996; Myers, Saywitz, & Goodman, 1997). Young children need help judging forensic relevance; organizing and elaborating a narrative description; and anticipating the listener's needs, expectations, and knowledge. Studies examining the effects of different question forms are clearly needed to facilitate practical guidelines. Generally, if open-ended questions are successful at producing a narrative, no matter how skeletal, then interviewers can prompt children to elaborate on their narratives by offering general prompts, such as repeating the end of the statement with rising intonation or asking, "What happened next?" or "Tell me more."

Although a number of researchers advocate that interviewers avoid specific questions completely, the exclusive use of general questions does not guarantee accuracy any more than specific questions guarantee contamination. Children can be highly resistant to leading questions under many conditions and sometimes general questions result in avoidable error. For example, in a study of children's recall for a physical examination, 5- and 7-year-olds were asked if the doctor put something in their mouths. Many incorrectly answered, "No." When asked specifically if the doctor took their temperature, these same children correctly answered, "Yes," spontaneously offering that a thermometer was put in their mouths. The more general question was perhaps less leading in the technical sense, but it also elicited the greater number of incorrect responses. Moreover, with very young children aged 18 to 36 months, general questions may be of limited value (Hewitt, in press).

Focused Questions

If open-ended questions fail, interviewers might consider focused questions, which merely focus a child's attention to the topic at hand ("Let's talk about preschool now") (Myers et al., 1997). Next, categorical or "Wh" questions that cue children to report certain types of information (what, who, where, when) might be useful, especially if responses are followed with queries to help children elaborate ("Tell me more"), justify ("What makes you say so?"), or clarify ("I'm confused") in their own words.

Studies of the development of organizational strategies, cuing, and story recall suggest that categorical prompts might focus children's attention on forensically relevant categories and increase memory performance. Particularly useful might be "Wh" questions regarding the participants (e.g., "What clothes were the people wearing?" "What did their hair look like?"), the setting (e.g., "What was the weather like that night?" "Was it inside or outside?"), and the conversations (e.g., "What did he say?"). These categories are typically found in mental representations of events (Stein & Glenn, 1978) but are not the categories that tend to be mentioned spontaneously in children's narrative reports (Fivush & Shukat, 1995, Saywitz, Nathanson, Snyder, & Lamphear, 1993, Experiments 2–3). Their narratives are typically composed of the actions that occurred. Hence, "Wh" questions could provide an opportunity for elaboration that involves little if any suggestion, especially if interviewers follow a protocol that calls for using similar questions to enhance elaboration in all cases (Dorado & Saywitz, 1997).

For the most part, the memory-jogging techniques derived from the experimental literature are useful only once interviewers establish with the child that there is a relevant event to be explored. Procedures are needed for raising sensitive topics in the first place (e.g., abuse) without the use of leading questions. Suggestions in the clinical literature include discussions of safety rules, problem-solving strategies, or body parts inventories (e.g., Morgan, 1995). However, the effects of these techniques have not been tested. Certainly, this is one area for future research worthy of pursuit.

Short-Answer Questions

Finally, the interviewer can consider short-answer questions (e.g., "What color was it?") to elicit further details about information provided in the initial narrative. In the real world, the use of specific short-answer questions is often guided by practical considerations of risk assessment. In cases with significant corroborative evidence that raises the concern over a child's immediate safety, there is greater justification of the use of specific questions in comparison to cases that lack such corroborative evidence or when children are already in a safe place. For example, some questions may be not be justified, or necessary, in interviews with 3- to 5-year-olds who are not in imminent danger and who comprise the age group most susceptible to distortion, especially if they have been repeatedly interviewed about events in the distant past with highly suggestive techniques. However, the same questions may not be problematic in an early interview with an 8-year-old, who is more resistant to suggestion by virtue of her age and the freshness of her memory, and/or in a case with corroborating physical evidence to suggest this child may be in imminent danger if returned home. Again, answers can be followed with requests for elaboration, clarification, and justification in the child's own words to minimize misinterpretation and maximize completeness.

Although it is clear that tag questions (e.g., ". . . , isn't that true?" or ". . . , didn't you?") should be avoided, the effects of yes–no and multiple-choice questions are poorly understood. One study, however, demonstrated the superiority of "Wh" question types over yes–no questions for preschoolers (Peterson & Biggs, 1997). It is probably useful to rephrase yes–no questions as "Wh" questions whenever possible. For example, "Did he hurt your pee pee?" can be rephrased as "What did he do with his hands?" (Morgan, 1995). Multiple-choice questions are a relative unknown in the forensic context. More research is needed on the effects of such questions to help guide interviewers' efforts.

CONCLUSION

Our discussion of interviewing principles that are designed to maximize the completeness of children's reports is based primarily on results of experimental studies of children's free recall and not on the realities of work conditions on the frontlines. Whether interview protocols should be based exclusively or even primarily on the results of laboratory studies is questionable. In reality, limits on the ecological validity of paradigms are bound to hamper generalization. In many ways, these studies raise more questions than they answer. And, there is no doubt that the application of research-based guidelines will be filtered through the financial, political, and logistical realities of the legal, mental health, and social services systems in a given community. Still, our goal was to educate the experienced interviewer with regard to some of the most relevant findings from child development laboratories. Ideally, interviewers can integrate the research findings with their own experiences and practical considerations to inform decision making in the field. Researchers can continue to develop innovative approaches to expand a child's initial retelling, without adversely impacting accuracy. With developmentally sensitive, empirically tested, and forensically sound procedures, children should be able to provide both reliable and meaningful information to decision makers in the field.

APPENDIX: Instructions That May Clarify Interview Task Demands for School-Age Children

1. Your job is to tell what you saw and what you heard, the best you can. Tell the truth. Just tell what you really remember. Do not guess. Do not make anything up.
2. Do your best. Try your hardest.
3. Tell me what happened from the beginning to the middle to the end. Tell as much as you can remember about each part.
4. You may not understand all the questions. Some may be easy and some may be hard to understand. I am used to talking to other adults, not children. When you don't understand a question, tell me that you don't understand. You can say, "I don't get" or "I don't know what you mean."
5. I may ask some questions more than once. Sometimes I forget that I already asked you that question. You don't have to change your answer, just tell me what you remember the best you can.
6. If you do not want to answer some of the questions, you can say, "I don't want to answer that question."
7. Sometimes you may not know the answer to a question. That's okay. Nobody can remember everything. If you don't know the answer to a question, then say, "I don't know," but do not guess or make anything

up. It is very important to tell me only what you really remember, only what really happened.

8. If you don't know the answer, you can say, "I don't know," but if you do know the answer, tell the answer.

9. Sometimes I may put my guess into a question. You should tell me if I am wrong. I was not there, and I could not know what happened.

10. I want to write down what we say because what you're telling me is important. Later, if I forget what we said, I can look it up.

11. Tell me as much as you can about what happened. Tell me everything, even the little things that you might not think are very important.

Note. This list is not intended to be read to children as a script in its totality. Individual instructions have been used in separate studies. See above text for discussion of their empirical investigation.

REFERENCES

Anderson, R. C., & Pichert, J. W. (1978). Recall of previously unrecallable information following a shift in perspective. *Journal of Verbal Learning and Verbal Behavior, 17,* 1–12.

Borkowski, J. G., Milstead, M., & Hale, C. (1988). Components of children's Metamemory: Implications for strategy generalization. In F. E. Weinert & M. Perlmutter (Eds.), *Memory development: Universal changes and individual differences* (pp. 73–100). Hillsdale, NJ: Erlbaum.

Bower, G. H., Gilligan, S. C., & Monteiro, K. P. (1984). Selectivity of learning caused by affective states. *Journal of Experimental Psychology: General, 110,* 451–472.

Brainerd, C. J., Reyna, V. F., Howe, M. L., Kingma, J. (1990). The development of forgetting and reminiscence. *Monographs of the Society for Research in Child Development, 55*(3–4, Serial No. 222).

Brennan, M., & Brennan, R. (1988). *Strange language: Child victims under cross examination.* Riverina, Australia: Charles Stuart University Press.

Brown, A. (1975). The development of memory: Knowing, knowing about knowing, and knowing how to know. In H. W. Reese (Ed.), *Advances in child development and behavior* (Vol. 10). New York: Academic Press.

Bull, R. (1995). Innovative techniques for the questioning of child witnesses, especially those who are young and those with learning disability. In M. S. Zaragoza, G. R. Graham, G. C. N. Hall, R. Hirschman, & Y. S. Ben-Porath (Eds.), *Memory and Testimony in the Child Witness* (pp. 179–194). Thousand Oaks, CA: Sage.

Cavanaugh, J. C., & Borkowski, J. G. (1979). The metamemory-memory "connection": Effects of strategy training and maintenance. *Journal of General Psychology, 101,* 161–174.

Ceci, S., Brofenbrenner, U., & Baker, J. (1988). Memory in context: The case of prospective remembering. In F. Weinert & M. Perlmutter (Eds.), *Universal changes and individual differences* (pp. 243–256). Hillsdale, NJ: Erlbaum.

Ceci, S. J., & Bruck, M. (1993). Suggestibility of the child witness: A historical review and synthesis. *Psychological Bulletin, 113,* 403–439.

Cody, K. (1989). The McMartin question: The "no-maybe-sometimes-yes" syndrome. *Easy Reader, 19,* 16–25.

Craik, F. I. M., & Lockhart, R. S. (1972). Levels of processing: A framework for memory research. *Journal of Verbal Learning and Verbal Behavior, 11,* 671–684.

Demorest, A., Meyer, C., Phelps, E., Gardner, H., & Winner, E. (1984). Words speak louder than actions: Understanding deliberately false remarks. *Child Development, 55,* 1527–1534.

Dent, H. R. (1982). The effects of interviewing strategies on the results of interviews with child witnesses. In A. Trankell (Ed.), *Reconstructing the past* (pp. 279–297). Stockholm, Sweden: Norstedt.

Dickson, P. (1981). *Children's oral communication skills.* New York: Academic Press.

Donaldson, M. C. (1979). *Children's minds.* New York: Norton.

Dorado, J., & Saywitz, K. (1997). Interviewing preschoolers: A test of an innovative technique. In B. Clark (Chair), *Assessment of child maltreatment.* Symposium conducted at the 105th annual convention of the American Psychological Association, Chicago.

Eisenberg, A. R. (1985). Learning to describe past experiences in conversation. *Discourse Processes, 8,* 177–204.

Fisher, R. P., & Geiselman, R. E. (1992). *Memory enhancing techniques for investigative interviewing.* Springfield, IL: Charles C. Thomas.

Fisher, R. P., Geiselman, R. E., Raymond, D. S., Jurkevich, L. M., & Warhaftig, M. L. (1987). Enhancing enhanced eyewitness memory: Refining the cognitive interview. *Journal of Police Science and Administration, 15,* 291–297.

Fisher, R. P., & McCauley, M. R. (1995). Facilitating children's recall with the revised cognitive interview. *Journal of Applied Psychology, 80,* 510–516.

Fisher, R. P., McCauley, M. R., & Geiselman, R. E. (1994). Improving eyewitness testimony with the cognitive interview. In D. Ross, J. D. Read, & M. Toglia (Eds.), *Adult eyewitness testimony and current trends and developments* (pp. 245–269). New York: Springer-Verlag.

Fivush, R. (1993). Developmental perspectives on autobiographical recall. In G. S. Goodman & B. L. Bottoms (Eds.), *Child victims, child witnesses: Understanding and improving testimony* (pp. 1–24). New York: Guilford Press.

Fivush, R., & Hammond, N. R. (1990). Autobiographical memory across the preschool years: Toward reconceptualizing childhood amnesia. In R. Fivush & J. A. Hudson (Eds.), *Knowing and remembering in young children* (pp. 223–248). New York: Cambridge University Press.

Fivush, R., & Shukat, R. (1995). Content, consistency, and coherence of early autobiographical recall. In M. S. Zaragoza, G. R. Graham, G. C. N. Hall, R. Hirschman, & Y. S. Ben-Porath (Eds.), *Memory and testimony in the child witness* (pp. 179–194). Thousand Oaks, CA: Sage.

Flavell, J. H. (1970). Developmental studies of mediated memory. In H. W. Reese & L. P. Lipsitt (Eds.), *Advances in child development and behavior* (pp. 181–211). New York: Academic Press.

Flavell, J. H., & Wellman, H. M. (1977). Metamemory. In R. V. Kail & J. W. Hagen (Eds.), *Perspectives on the development of memory and cognition* (pp. 3–33). Hillsdale, NJ: Erlbaum.

Flin, R. H., Stevenson, Y., & Davies, G. (1989). Children's knowledge of court proceedings. *British Journal of Psychology, 80,* 285–297.

Friedman, W. (1982). *The developmental psychology of time.* New York: Academic Press.

Geiselman, R. E., & Callot, R. (1990). Reverse versus forward recall of script-based texts. *Applied Cognitive Psychology, 3,* 141–144.

Geiselman, R. E., Fisher, R. P., Firstenberg, I., Hutton, L. A., Sullivan, S., Avetissian, I., & Prosk, A. (1984). Enhancement of eyewitness memory: An empirical evaluation of the cognitive interview. *Journal of Police Science and Administration, 12,* 74–80.

Geiselman, R. E., Fisher, R. P., MacKinnon, D. P., & Holland, H. L. (1985). Eyewitness memory enhancement in the police interview: Cognitive retrieval mnemonics versus hypnosis. *Journal of Applied Psychology, 70,* 401–412.

Geiselman, R. E., Fisher, R. P., MacKinnon, D. P., & Holland, H. L. (1986). Enhancement of eyewitness memory with the cognitive interview. *American Journal of Psychology, 99, 385–401.*

Geiselman, R. E., & Padilla, J. (1988). Interviewing child witnesses with the cognitive interview. *Journal of Police Science and Administration, 16,* 236–242.

Geiselman, R. E., Saywitz, K. J., & Bornstein, G. K. (1993). Effects of cognitive questioning techniques on children's recall performance. In G. S. Goodman & B. L. Bottoms (Eds.), *Child victims, child witnesses: Understanding and improving testimony* (pp. 71–93). New York: Guilford Press.

Ghatala, E. S., Levin, J. R., Pressley, M., & Lodico, M. G. (1985). Training cognitive strategy monitoring in children. *American Educational Research Journal, 22,* 199–216.

Goodman, G. S., Bottoms, B., Schwartz-Kenney, B., & Rudy, L. (1991). Children's testimony about a stressful event: Improving children's reports. *Journal of Narrative and Life History, 7,* 69–99.

Goodman, G. S., & Reed, R. (1986). Age differences in eyewitness testimony. *Law and Human Behavior, 10,* 317–332.

Goodman, G., Tobey, A., Batterman-Faunce, J., Orcutt, H., Thomas, S., & Shapiro, C. (in press). Face to face confrontation: Effects of closed circuit testimony and jurors' decisions. *Law and Human Behavior.*

Grice, H. (1975). Logic and conversation. In R. Cole & J. Morgan (Eds.), *Syntax and semantics: Speech acts.* New York: Academic Press.

Gruneberg, M. M., & Monks, J. (1976). The first letter search strategy. *IRCS Medical Science: Psychology and Psychiatry, 4,* 307.

Hammond, N. R. (1987). *Memories of Mickey Mouse: Young children recount their trip to Disney World.* Unpublished master's thesis, Emory University, Atlanta.

Heath, S. (1983). *Ways with words: language, life and work in communities and classrooms.* Cambridge, UK: Cambridge University Press.

Hewitt, S. (in press). Small voices. Thousand Oaks, CA: Sage.

Hudson, J. A., & Fivush, R. (1987). *As time goes by: Sixth graders remember a kindergarten experience* (Emory Cognition Project Report No. 13). Atlanta, GA: Emory University Press.

Hudson, J. A., & Nelson, K. (1986). Repeated encounters of a similar kind: Effects of familiarity on children's autobiographic recall. *Cognitive Development, 1,* 253–271.

Keenan, J., MacWhinney, B., & Mayhew, D. (1977). Pragmatics in memory: A study of natural conversation. *Journal of Verbal Learning and Verbal Behavior, 16,* 549–560.

Keeney, T. J., Cannizzo, S. R., & Flavell, J. H. (1967). Spontaneous and induced verbal rehearsal in a recall task. *Child Development, 38*, 953–966.

King, M. A., & Yuille, J. C. (1987). Suggestibility and the child witness. In S. J. Ceci, M. P. Toglia, & D. F. Ross (Eds.), *Children's eyewitness memory* (pp. 24–35). New York: Springer-Verlag.

Kobasigawa, A. (1974). Utilization of retrieval cues by children in recall. *Child Development, 45*, 127–134.

Kobasigawa, A. (1977). Retrieval strategies in the development of memory. In R. V. Kail & J. W. Hagen (Eds.), *Perspectives on the development of memory and cognition* (pp. 177–201). Hillsdale, NJ: Erlbaum.

Koehnken, G., Milne, R., Memon, A., & Bull, R. (1994). *A meta-analysis on the effects of the cognitive interview.* Paper presented at the biennial conference of the American Psychology and Law Society, Santa Fe, NM.

Kurtz, B., & Borkowski, J. (1984). Children's metacognition: Exploring relations among knowledge, process, and motivational variables. *Journal of Experimental Child Psychology, 43*, 129–148.

Kurtz, B., & Borkowski, J. (1987). Development of strategic skills in impulsive and reflective children: A developmental study of metacognition. *Journal of Experimental Child Psychology, 43*, 129–148.

Lamb, M. E., Hershkowitz, I., Sternberg, K. J., Esplin, P. W., Hovav, M., Manor, T., & Yudilevitch, L. (1996). Effects of investigative utterance types on Israeli children's responses. *International Journal of Behavioral Development, 19*(3), 627–637.

Lodico, M., Ghatala, E., Levin, J., Pressley, M., & Bell, J. (1983). The effects of strategy monitoring on children's selection of effective memory strategies. *Journal of Experimental Psychology, 35*, 263–277.

MacKinnon, D. P., O'Reilly, K., & Geiselman, R. E. (1990). Improving eyewitness recall for license plates. Applied *Cognitive Psychology, 4*, 129–140.

Melton, G., Limber, S., Jacobs, J., & Oberlander, L. (1992). *Preparing sexually abused children for testimony: Children's perceptions of the legal process* (Final report to the National Center on Child Abuse and Neglect, Grant No. 90-CA-1274). Lincoln: University of Nebraska–Lincoln.

Milne, R. (in press). The cognitive interview: Recent research. *Journal of Applied Cognitive Psychology* (Special Issue).

Morgan, M. (1995). *How to interview sexual abuse victims.* Thousand Oaks, CA: Sage.

Moston, S. (1987). The suggestibility of children in interview studies. *First Language, 7*, 67–78.

Myers, J. (1998). *Legal issues in child abuse and neglect* (2nd ed.). Newbury Park, CA: Sage.

Myers, J., Saywitz, K., & Goodman, G. (1997). Psychological research on children as witnesses: Practical implications for forensic interviews and courtroom testimony. *Pacific Law Journal, 28*, 3–91.

Nelson, K. (1978). How young children represent knowledge of their world in and out of language. In R. Siegler (Ed.), *Children's thinking: What develops?* (pp. 255–273). Hillsdale, NJ: Erlbaum.

Nelson, K., Fivush, R., Hudson, J., & Lucariello, J. (1983). Scripts and the development of memory. In M. T. H. Chi (Ed.), *Trends in memory development research* (pp. 52–70). Basel, Switzerland: Karger.

Newhoff, N., & Launer, P. (1984). Input as interaction: Shall we dance? In R.

Naremore (Ed.), *Language science: Recent advances* (pp. 37–65). San Diego, CA: College Hill.

Ornstein, P. A., Gordon, B. N., Baker-Ward, L. E., & Merritt, K. A. (1995). Children's memory for medical experiences: Implications for Testimony. In D. P. Peters (Ed.), *The child witness in context: Cognitive, social, and legal perspectives.* Dordrecht, The Netherlands: Kluwer Academic.

Ornstein, P. A., Naus, M. J., & Liberty, C. (1975). Rehearsal and organizational processes in children's memory. *Child Development, 46,* 818–830.

Paris, S. G., Newman, R. S., & McVey, K. A. (1982). Learning the functional significance of mnemonic actions: A microgenetic study of strategy acquisition. *Journal of Experimental Child Psychology, 34,* 490–509.

Perlmutter, M., & Myers, N. A. (1979). Development of recall in 2- to 4-year-old children. *Developmental Psychology,* 78–83.

Perry, N., McAuliff, B., Tam, P., & Claycomb, L. (1995). When lawyers question children: Is justice served? *Law and Human Behavior, 19*(6), 609–629.

Peters, D. P. (1991). The influence of stress and arousal on the child witness. In J. Doris (Ed.), *The suggestibility of children's recollections: Implications for eyewitness testimony* (pp. 60–76). Washington, DC: American Psychological Association.

Peterson, C., & Biggs, M. (1997). Interviewing children about trauma: Problems with "specific" questions. *Journal of Traumatic Stress, 10*(2), 279–290.

Pipe, M.-E., Gee, S., & Wilson, C. (1993). Cues, props, and context: Do they facilitate children's event reports? In G. S. Goodman & B. L. Bottoms (Eds.), *Child victims, child witnesses: Understanding and improving testimony* (pp. 25–45). New York: Guilford Press.

Pressley, M., & Dennis-Rounds, J. (1980). Transfer of mnemonic keyword strategy at two age levels. *Journal of Educational Psychology, 72,* 575–582.

Pressley, M., Forrest-Pressley, D. J., & Elliott-Faust, D. J. (1988). What is strategy instructional enrichment and how to study it: Illustrations from research on children's prose memory and comprehension. In F. E. Weinert & M. Perlmutter (Eds.), *Memory development: Universal changes and individual differences* (pp. 101–130). Hillsdale, NJ: Erlbaum.

Pressley, M., & Levin, J. R. (1977). Developmental differences in subjects' associative learning strategies and performance: Assessing a hypothesis. *Journal of Experimental Child Psychology, 24,* 431–439.

Pressley, M., & Levin, J. (1980). The development of mental imagery retrieval. *Child Development, 51,* 558–560.

Pressley, M., Ross, K., Levin, J., & Ghatala, E. (1984). The role of strategy utility knowledge in children's strategy decision making. *Journal of Experimental Child Psychology, 38,* 491–504.

Price, D., & Goodman, G. (1990). Visiting the wizard: Children's memory for a recurring event. *Child Development, 61,* 664–680.

Rice, M., Wilcox, K., & Hadley, P. (1992). The role of language and social interaction skills. In F. L. Parker (Ed.), *New directions in child and family research* (pp. 320–322). Washington, DC: Administration on Children, Youth and Families, Department of Health and Human Services.

Ringel B. A., & Springer, C. J. (1980). On knowing how well one is remembering: The persistence of strategy use during transfer. *Journal of Experimental Child Psychology, 29,* 322–333.

Ritter, K. (1978). The development of knowledge of an external retrieval cue strategy. *Child Development, 49,* 1227–1230.

Ritter, K., Kaprove, B. H., Fitch, J. P., & Flavell J. H. (1973). The development of retrieval strategies in young children. *Cognitive Psychology, 5,* 310–321.

Salatas, H., & Flavell, J. H. (1976). Retrieval of recently learned information: Development of strategies and control skills. *Child Development, 47,* 941–948.

Sas, L. (1991). *Reducing the system-induced trauma for child sexual abuse victims through court preparation, assessment and followup* (Final Report for Project No. 4555-1-125). London, Canada: Health and Welfare, Canada, National Welfare Grants Division.

Saywitz, K. J. (1989). Children's conception of the legal system: Court is a place to play basketball. In S. J. Ceci, D. F. Ross, & M. P. Toglia (Eds.), *Perspectives on children's testimony* (pp. 131–157). New York: Springer-Verlag.

Saywitz, K. J. (1995). Improving children's testimony: The question, the answer and the environment. In M. S. Zaragoza, G. R. Graham, G. C. N. Hall, R. Hirschman, & Y. S. Ben-Porath (Eds.), *Memory and testimony in the child witness* (pp. 113–140). Thousand Oaks, CA: Sage.

Saywitz, K., & Elliott, D. (in press). Interviewing children in the forensic context. Washington, DC: American Psychological Association Press.

Saywitz, K., Geiselman, R. E., & Bornstein, G. (1992). Effects of cognitive interviewing and practice on children's recall performance. *Journal of Applied Psychology, 77*(5), 744–756.

Saywitz, K., Goodman, G., Nicholas, E., & Moan, S. (1991). Children's memories of physical examinations that involve genital touch: Implications for reports of sexual abuse. *Journal of Consulting and Clinical Psychology, 59*(5), 682–691.

Saywitz, K., Jaenicke, C., & Camparo, L. (1990). Children's knowledge of legal terminology. *Law and Human Behavior, 14*(6), 523–535.

Saywitz, K., & Moan-Hardie, S. (1994). Reducing the potential for distortion of childhood memories. *Consciousness and Cognition, 3,* 257–293.

Saywitz, K., & Nathanson, R. (1992). Effects of environment on children's testimony and perceived stress. In B. Bottoms & M. Levine (Chairs), *Actual and perceived competency of child witnesses.* Symposium conducted at the annual convention of the American Psychological Association, Washington, DC.

Saywitz, K., & Nathanson, R. (1993). Children's testimony and their perceptions of stress in and out of the courtroom. *Child Abuse and Neglect, 17,* 613–622.

Saywitz, K., Nathanson, R., & Snyder, L. (1993). Credibility of child witnesses: The role of communicative competence. *Topics in Language Disorders, 13*(4), 59–78.

Saywitz, K., Nathanson, R., Snyder, L., & Lamphear, V. (1993). *Preparing children for the investigative and judicial process: Improving communication, memory and emotional resiliency* (Final Report to the National Center on Child Abuse and Neglect, Grant No. 90-CA-1179). Los Angeles: University of California.

Saywitz, K. J., & Snyder, L. (1993). Improving children's testimony with preparation. In G. S. Goodman & B. L. Bottoms (Eds.), *Child victims, child witnesses: Understanding and improving testimony* (pp. 117–146). New York: Guilford Press.

Saywitz, K., & Snyder, L. (1996). Narrative elaboration: Test of a new procedure for interviewing children. *Journal of Consulting and Clinical Psychology, 64,* 1347–1357.

Saywitz, K., Snyder, L., & Lamphear, V. (1996). Helping children tell what happened:

A follow-up study of the narrative elaboration procedure. *Child Maltreatment, 1*(3), 200–212.

Shantz, C. (1975). *The development of social cognition.* Chicago: University of Chicago Press.

Smith, M. (1983). Hypnotic memory enhancement of witnesses: Does it work? *Psychological Bulletin, 94,* 384–407.

Somerville, S. C., Wellman, H. M., & Cultice, J. C. (1983). Young children's deliberate reminding. *Journal of Genetic Psychology, 143,* 87–96.

Stein, N. L. (1988). The development of children's storytelling skill. In H. B. Franklin & S. S. Barsen (Eds.), *Child language: A reader* (pp. 282–297). New York: Oxford University Press.

Stein, N., & Glenn, C. (1978). *The role of temporal organization in story comprehension* (Tech. Rep. No. 71). Urbana: University of Illinois, Center for the Study of Reading.

Tucker, A., Mertin, P., & Luszcz, M. (1990). The effect of a repeated interview on young children's eyewitness memory. *Australian and New Zealand Journal of Criminology, 23,* 117–124.

Walker, A. G. (1993). Questioning young children in court. *Law and Human Behavior, 17*(1), 59–81.

Walker, A. G. (1994). *Handbook of questioning children.* Washington, DC: ABA Center on Children and the Law.

MEMORY AND PSYCHOTHERAPY: RESEARCH FINDINGS AND CLINICAL CONSIDERATIONS

CHAPTER 9

HYPNOSIS AND PSEUDOMEMORY
Understanding the Findings and Their Implications

Kevin M. McConkey
Amanda J. Barnier
Peter W. Sheehan

You see how, with the help of artificial or natural sleep, a false idea, an illusory memory, or a false testimony can slip into the brain.

—Hippolyte Bernheim (quoted in Laurence & Perry, 1988, p. 238)

Contemporary interest in hypnosis is high theoretically, experimentally, clinically, and forensically (e.g., Fromm & Nash, 1992; Lynn & Rhue, 1991; McConkey & Sheehan, 1995; Rhue, Lynn, & Kirsch, 1993), and there is special interest in the effect of hypnosis on memory (e.g., Laurence & Perry, 1988; McConkey, 1992, 1995; Orne, 1979; Orne, Soskis, Dinges, & Orne, 1984; Pettinati, 1988; Scheflin & Shapiro, 1989; Smith, 1983; Spiegel & Spiegel, 1987; Wagstaff, 1989). In this chapter, we focus on hypnotically suggested false memory, or hypnotic pseudomemory. We aim to delineate the nature and characteristics of hypnotically suggested memory. To do this, we focus on (1) the historical and clinical applications of hypnotically suggested false memory and (2) the experimental investigations of hypnotic pseudomemory. By drawing inferences from selected clinical work and from the different experimental approaches within hypnosis and by looking for patterns of convergence and divergence across the data, we seek to specify the issues that are independent of hypnosis (that relate to memory, for example) and the issues that are distinctive to hypnosis. In the final section we attempt to define the major issues for research and resolution. To achieve these various aims, this chapter considers the available evidence in some detail. The experimental work, for example, needs to be discussed in depth to gain an appreciation of the consistencies and inconsistencies in approach and findings.

The boundaries of hypnotic pseudomemory are variable, and we exclude a number of aspects from consideration. First, we do not consider hypnotic pseudomemories in clinical or forensic settings when they occur as a by-product of therapeutic or investigative procedures. We note, however, that there is substantial evidence that hypnotic and nonhypnotic pseudomemories can be created and maintained unintentionally in those settings, often with dire consequences for the individual and others (e.g., Coons, 1988; Garry & Loftus, 1994; Levitt, 1990; Lynn & Nash, 1994; McConkey, 1992, 1995; Nash, 1994; Ofshe, 1992; Orne, 1979; Orne, Whitehouse, Dinges, & Orne, 1988; Perry, Laurence, D'Eon, & Tallant, 1988; Yapko, 1994a, 1994b). Second, we do not consider the intentional creation of hypnotic pseudomemories for past (or future) lives, human and nonhuman, in the experimental or clinical setting. We note, however, that there is substantial evidence that hypnotic and nonhypnotic pseudomemories of these kinds can be created in the experimental or clinical setting, especially for hypnotized, hypnotizable subjects, and subjects will sometimes hold created beliefs of a personal past (or future) life with fervor, possibly gaining some apparent personal benefit from their formation (e.g., Baker, 1982; Kampman, 1976; Kline, 1951; Kline & Guze, 1951; Spanos, Burgess, & Burgess, 1994; Spanos, Menary, Gabora, DuBreuil, & Dewhirst, 1991; Stevenson, 1994; Zolik, 1958). Third, we do not consider the use of hypnotic pseudomemories or paramnesias as experimental tools for investigating psychopathology (e.g., Burns & Reyher, 1976; Matthews, Kirsch, & Allen, 1984; Reyher, 1961, 1962; Reyher & Smyth, 1971; Sheehan, 1969, 1971; Smyth, 1982; Sommerschield & Reyher, 1973). This use typically involves the hypnotic creation of false memories to arouse unacceptable thoughts and feelings on the part of an individual. Typically, the paramnesia is covered with hypnotically suggested amnesia, and a posthypnotic suggestion is given that the feelings associated with the paramnesia will occur when, for instance, cue words are presented after hypnosis. Although this technique's usefulness for elucidating psychopathology is limited, there is reasonable consistency in the finding that hypnotized, hypnotizable subjects will accept a hypnotically suggested paramnesia. Although we do not review these associated lines of inquiry and application, they do nevertheless all under-score the need to understand more fully the hypnotic construction of memories that are not factually accurate.

At the outset, we note that the experience of hypnosis depends largely on the hypnotizability of the individual but is shaped in major ways by the communications of the hypnotist. Moreover, we note that the individual in hypnosis is actively involved in responding to the overall mass of messages that he or she receives, with the suggestions of the hypnotist playing a central role in that process (e.g., McConkey, 1991; Sheehan, 1991, 1992; Sheehan & McConkey, 1982). Similarly, we note that memory involves constructive and reconstructive processes, and that a person's ultimate recollections of episodic and semantic material are shaped by both the internal (e.g., cognitive and emotional) and the external (e.g., interpersonal and consequential) conditions that prevail during the acquisition, retention, and retrieval of memory material. We consider also that memory and belief are bidirectional in their influence and may be additive in their impact (see also Alba & Hasher, 1983; Bartlett, 1932; Kihlstrom, 1994; Kihlstrom & Barnhardt, 1993; Ross, 1989).

For us, hypnotic pseudomemory can be defined as memory reported when a suggestion is given following a hypnotic induction that a person will remember specific information that the hypnotist knows (or believes) to be false. Operationally, the testing of hypnotic pseudomemory typically involves (1) a not-yet-hypnotized subject either reporting an event he or she has experienced or participating in an event presented by the hypnotist, (2) the hypnotist then inducing hypnosis and suggesting false information relevant to the target event, and (3) the hypnotist then deinducing hypnosis and subsequently testing the subject's memory of the target event with regard to the suggested false information.

HISTORICAL PERSPECTIVES
AND CLINICAL APPLICATIONS

First we consider hypnotically suggested false memory or hypnotic pseudomemory in the clinical setting. The intentional falsification of memory for therapeutic benefit has a long history (e.g., Bernheim, 1888/1973; Burnham, 1889; Forel, 1906; Freud, 1909/1955; Janet, 1889/1973), and that history has been well reviewed in a number of places (e.g., Crabtree, 1994; Ellenberger, 1970; Laurence & Perry, 1983a, 1988; Macmillan, 1991; Nemiah, 1984; Perry & Laurence, 1984). For example, Bernheim (1888/1973) created and used "retroactive hallucinations"; Burnham (1889) noted that clinical benefits, but also legal problems, could be associated with "pseudoreminiscences or illusions of memory"; Forel (1906) referred to "illusory retroactive memory"; and Freud (1909/1955) spoke about "constructions" of the past that lead to therapeutic benefit. Across these 19th-century investigators, there was a general consensus that whereas false memories could be created during hypnosis, they could also be created without hypnosis especially in highly hypnotizable people. Janet (1889/1973), in particular, saw memory not only in terms of its reconstructive nature but also in terms of its essential creativity, and he noted that these aspects of memory could be used therapeutically. For Janet (1889/1973; see also Ellenberger, 1970; Laurence & Perry, 1983a, 1988; Nemiah, 1984; Perry & Laurence, 1984), psychopathology was the result of a "fixed idea," and successful treatment was based on not only uncovering the traumatic event but also reconstructing or replacing the original memory with a false, and more acceptable, memory. Janet's famous cases of Marie and Achille exemplify his treatment approach, and we focus here on Marie (Janet,

1889/1973; see Ellenberger, 1970; see also Crabtree, 1994, for a related discussion of Achille).

Marie was a 19-year-old woman who suffered from a number of hysterical symptoms. Twenty hours after the onset of menstruation, for instance, the flow stopped and she experienced violent trembling, severe pain, and a hysterical crisis. In addition, Marie suffered from anesthesia of the left side of her face and blindness in her left eye, both of which were present for many years. To treat the convulsive attacks, Janet hypnotically regressed Marie to 13 years, where she recalled her first menstruation and how she plunged herself into a bucket of cold water to stop the flow; she recalled experiencing violent shivering and days of sickness and delirium. Her menstruation did not reappear for 5 years, but when it did the observed disturbances occurred. To treat the hysterical symptoms, Janet first tried to remove from her "somnambulistic consciousness" the fixed idea that menstruation could be stopped by a cold bath, but he was unsuccessful. Janet described his second, and this time successful, approach in the following way:

> It was necessary to bring her back, through [hypnotic] suggestion, to the age of thirteen, put her back into the initial circumstances of the delirium, convince her that the menstruation had lasted for three days and was not interrupted through any regrettable incident. Now, once this was done, the following menstruation came at the due point, and lasted for three days, without any pain, convulsion, or delirium. (Janet, quoted in Ellenberger, 1970, p. 364)

In the case of Marie's anesthesia on the left side of her face and blindness in her left eye, Janet determined through hypnotic age regression that as a 6-year-old, she had slept with a child of the same age who had impetigo on the left side of her face. After this, Marie had developed an almost identical impetigo and had also developed blindness. Again, Janet hypnotically age-regressed Marie to the time of the traumatic incident and reconstructed the memory:

> I put her back with the child who had so horrified her; I make her believe that the child is very nice and does not have impetigo (she is half-convinced. After two re-enactments of this scene I get the best of it); she caresses without fear the imaginary child. The sensitivity of the left eye reappears without difficulty, and when I wake her up, Marie sees clearly with the left eye. (Janet, quoted in Ellenberger, 1970, p. 364)

The treatment was successful, and 5 months later there continued to be no signs of hysterical symptoms.

Janet's (1889/1973) contemporary, Freud (1937/1964), similarly recognized that "new constructions" as opposed to "reconstructions" of original memories could be therapeutically helpful. He wrote:

The path that starts from the analyst's construction ought to end in the patient's recollection; but it does not always lead so far. Quite often we do not succeed in bringing the patient to recollect what has been repressed. Instead of that, if the analysis is carried out correctly, we produce in him an assured conviction of the truth of the construction, which achieves the same therapeutic result as a recaptured memory. (Freud, quoted in Frankel, 1988, p. 251)

Thus, even when hypnosis is not involved, intentional and therapeutically helpful pseudomemories can occur in the clinical setting. As Macmillan (1991) points out, the suggestive pressures placed on clients in psychoanalysis (and in the absence of hypnosis) may result "in new creations such as fabricated or pseudo-memories" (p. 217), and this is a point being echoed strongly in contemporary writings about therapy in general (e.g., Loftus & Ketcham, 1994; Ofshe & Watters, 1994; Spence, 1982; Yapko, 1994b).

Further, Macmillan (1991) highlights the relevance of the interpersonal relationship between therapist and client to the creation and therapeutic use of pseudomemories. Macmillan (1991) notes that psychoanalytical procedures to bring material into consciousness "involve the emotional and intellectual dependence of a subject upon a mentor and an interaction allowing the transmission of the beliefs and expectations of the investigator," and that for false memories to be "integrated with each other and with the subject's real memories," an essential precondition is that "the subject divine the investigator's expectations" (p. 218). In the course of therapy, both therapist and client make an agreement (either explicitly or implicitly) to share in the development of an account of the past that will allow an abatement of symptoms. The consequences of that agreed-on memory change depends, at least in part, on the nature of the interpersonal relationship. Such a view of the centrality of the therapist–client dynamic can be seen in Barber's (1991) "locksmith" model of hypnotic responsiveness. He argues that "the personal qualities of the hypnotist, and the real and transferential relationship that develops between the hypnotist and subject, are critical. . . . These and other elements present in the hypnotherapeutic setting can liberate or 'unlock' a capacity for hypnotic responsiveness that remains otherwise inaccessible and dormant" (pp. 258–260).

In addition to the work of the 19th-century investigators and of Milton Erickson (1935, 1944; Erickson & Rossi, 1980; Huston, Shakow, & Erickson, 1934) earlier this century, there are many contemporary examples of the clinical use of intentionally falsified memory in the treatment of phobias and anxiety (e.g., Baker & Boaz, 1983; Lamb, 1985; Miller, 1986). Although these later clinicians used different language to characterize their approaches, the aim of treatment and its formula was essentially identical. In general, treatment aimed to replace or reconstruct an original traumatic memory, which was believed to be the cause of the phobic or anxious symptoms, with an intentionally created false memory that involved safety or comfort (depending on the particular case). Treatment usually lasted only a few sessions and often included some assessment of hypnotizability and a discussion of appropriate new memories to replace the old. Treatment, however, always included an interview (sometimes hypnotic) to ascertain the source of the symptoms and a hypnosis session that incorporated a suggestion for age regression to when the client first experienced the initial traumatic event. Following this, hypnotic suggestions were given for the false memory that restructured, rewrote, or replaced the original memories with new, agreed-on desirable endings. Typically, the client reported the false memories with the same level of conviction and belief as the original memory, and successful treatment led to an abatement of the symptoms.

To give a flavor of the clinical utility of this technique, we sample from some clinical case reports (viz., Baker & Boaz, 1983; Lamb, 1985; Miller, 1986). Baker and Boaz (1983) reported treatment of a 30-year-old woman's severe dental phobia. She could not specify the reason for her anxiety, but she had not been to a dentist in 20 years and needed extensive dental treatment. During hypnosis, the client was age-regressed to when she first became frightened of the dentist. She reported being taken to the hospital for a tooth extraction at the age of 9, and becoming terror stricken during the procedure; she could not recall being comforted by anyone. The therapist then falsified her original memory by suggesting that as she thought about being taken into the operating room, she would remember the doctor holding her and stroking her forehead and telling her that she should not be afraid. The client reported that she could hear the doctor comforting her and subsequently reported that her fear was diminished as she reexperienced going into the operating room. The second session involved hypnotic age regression to the operation and repetition of the suggestion that the doctor was comforting her; the client continued to report reduction of her anxiety. This treatment enabled the woman to undergo extraction of two wisdom teeth without fear of the dentist or the treatment. During follow-up, the client recalled the implanted material as original memory, without awareness of either the construction of the suggested pseudomemory or the trauma associated with the original memory.

Lamb (1985) reported successful treatment of three phobic clients (fear of the dark, dental phobia, and fear of flying). Lamb replaced the traumatic experiences of the past with new, nonthreatening experiences that decreased or eliminated the anxiety. For example, the client who was afraid of the dark believed that her fear was based on the following incident from when she was 5 years old: The client's mother had shut the client and her two siblings in their bedroom, after some misbehavior on their part, closing the door behind her; the client had run to the door screaming for her mother to come back. Her father, hearing the screams, ran to the bedroom and pushed the door open; this action accidentally tore off the client's toenail and caused severe pain. During hypnosis, the client was age-regressed to the incident and the therapist gave suggestions to recall more "desirable endings" (e.g., the children would not misbehave, she would fall asleep, and her mother would leave and close the door). The client accepted and believed in the pseudomemory and within 6 months she was no longer frightened of the dark. Lamb (1985) concluded that, "although the new ending is in fact the result of reconstructed memory, the client can then react emotionally to it and, therefore, transform it into an important part of his or her psychic life" (p. 61).

Miller (1986) reported the use of "reconstructive hypnotherapy" for anxiety reactions with three clients (two cases of performance anxiety and one case of separation anxiety). For example, the client with separation anxiety presented with anxiety about pain from an impending surgical procedure and anxiety about separation from her parents; her problems appeared to be based on a separation from her parents at a parents' and children's overnight camp when she was 4 years old. To "transform the trauma into a coping state" (p. 140) during hypnosis the therapist suggested that rather than being separated from her parents and being refused permission to visit them by her camp counselor, she would remember the counselor being berated by her parents for keeping her from them. During the session her parents (who were present during therapy) acted out their anger at the counselor. Following this session, the client experienced being able to visit her parents and returned to her own tent feeling happy and safe. Consequently, the client's other experiences when there had been separation anxiety (e.g., going to camp at age 10) were remembered without anxiety, and her visit to the hospital for surgery was free of anxiety. Her "rewritten" memory helped her to "master and dispel the anxiety" (p. 139) and led to a reduction in anxiety.

An analysis of this work underscores for us that intentionally created false memories can be therapeutically beneficial. Clients can show commitment to and belief in intentionally falsified memories to the extent that they are indistinguishable from the original memory. Further, the interpersonal relationship between the therapist and client seems central to the shared development of accounts (false or otherwise) of the past and their successful integration into memory. However, despite the range of uses and apparent beneficial impact of hypnotic pseudomemories in therapy, experimental work has largely ignored clinically created hypnotic pseudomemories except when they are relevant forensically. We return to this issue briefly later in this chapter (see also McConkey & Sheehan, 1995) and note that the forensic implications of false memories are a major focus of discussion elsewhere (e.g., Loftus & Ketcham, 1994; Ofshe & Watters, 1994; Pendergrast, 1994; Yapko, 1994b).

CRITICAL REVIEW OF EXPERIMENTAL INVESTIGATIONS

We now consider briefly the forensic impetus behind the experimental investigation of hypnotic pseudomemory and then evaluate the experimental work in some detail. The experimental investigation of hypnotic pseudomemory is stimulated in large part by issues associated with the forensic use of hypnosis (e.g., Orne, 1979; Orne et al., 1984; Orne et al., 1988; Perry et al., 1988). Perhaps one of the most striking examples of the possible creation of a hypnotic pseudomemory in the forensic setting was presented in Orne's (1979) analysis of *State v. White* (1979; for other examples, see Kirby, 1984; Perry et al., 1988). In this case, the hypnotist gave the following suggestion to a woman who was a close friend of the murder victim ("Sweetie Pie") and who was living with a suspect ("Joe White"); the relationship between the woman and Joe White was known to be a violent one.

> "For the moment I want you to think about just you and me and Sweetie Pie, who got strangled, thrown out on the road, taken to the morgue, put in a box, and buried in the ground. Now somebody did that. I don't know who, but you know that Joe White is a suspect in this case, don't you? Do you think that there is any reason why Joe White should or should not be a suspect in this case?" (quoted in Orne, 1979, p. 330)

The hypnotist also gave the subject a posthypnotic suggestion that she would think about telling the truth, how good it would be to tell the truth, and that she would eventually tell the truth. The woman subsequently reported that Joe White had told her that he had killed Sweetie Pie. Although he was arrested and sent to trial, "the court recognized the danger of permitting hypnosis to be used in a context where it is more likely to create a memory than to refresh it" (Orne, 1979, p. 331).

This example of the apparent vulnerability of memory to suggestion sparked public debate about the serious ethical and legal questions regarding the usefulness of hypnotic techniques in the forensic arena. However, the finding that pseudomemories could be created relatively easily was not new, although little empirical attention had until then focused on it. Over 100 years ago, Bernheim (1888/1973, 1891) demonstrated this ease by suggesting to a female patient that she had awakened four times during a particular night to visit the toilet and had slipped and fallen on her nose on the fourth occasion. Following hypnosis, the patient said that she had had diarrhea on that night, which led to the four visits, and that she had fallen and hit her nose on the final visit. She was convinced that these events were veridical memories, even in the face of Bernheim's insistence that the events had been suggested. In a similar vein, Orne (1979) presents a simple demonstration along the following lines: (1) establish that the subject went to bed at (say) midnight and rose at (say) 8 a.m. on a particular night (e.g., last Wednesday); (2) during hypnosis, age-regress the subject to relive that night; (3) during this reliving, ask the subject whether he or she heard two loud noises—this is, in fact, a subtle suggestion; (4) ask the subject to describe the noises, and what he or she does in response to them; and (5) after hypnosis ask the subject about the night. According to Orne (1979), "The subject's altered memory concerning the night . . . will tend to persist (unless suggestions are given to the contrary) particularly because the subject was asleep at the time and there are no competing memories. The more frequently the subject reports the event, the more firmly established the pseudomemory will become" (p. 323). Based on demonstrations such as this, as well as on various forensic cases, Orne (1979) concluded that pseudomemories developed in hypnosis may be accepted by people as their actual memory of the original events, and that this false memory will be held with subjective certainty and reported with conviction. This conclusion and its forensic implications generated an enormous amount of empirical interest and activity.

Using the basic procedure of Orne (1979), Laurence and Perry (1983b; see also Laurence, Nadon, Nogrady, & Perry, 1986) hypnotically regressed 27 high hypnotizable subjects to a night of the previous week and asked them if they heard loud noises; subjects who reported having heard noises were asked to describe them in detail. Seventeen subjects accepted the suggestion and described the noises, and either 1 day or 1 week later, they were asked by another experimenter about that night. False memory reporting occurred in 13 subjects; 6 said the noises definitely had occurred on the night even after they were told that the hypnotist suggested them; the remaining 7 said they were confused about the source of the noises. In this first empirical demonstration of the procedure of Orne (1979), Laurence and Perry (1983b) concluded that false memories can be hypnotically created in high hypnotizable individuals. McCann and Sheehan (1988, Study 1) repeated the major procedures with high hypnotizable subjects, but tested for the occurrence of false memory immediately after hypnosis. During the deinduction procedure, however, experimental subjects were told they would remember the events of the night, whereas control subjects were told that they would remember the events of the hypnosis session. Experimental subjects, more than control subjects, showed false memory after hypnosis, by either saying they heard noises on the night or reporting confusion about hearing noises on the night. McCann and Sheehan (1988, Study 1) concluded from these findings that context is a significant determinant of false memory reporting, especially the degree to which context can blur together parts of the session that establish the suggestion and later procedures that test for the false memory.

The impact of context on pseudomemory reporting was highlighted also by Spanos and McLean (1986a; see also McConkey & Kinoshita, 1986; Spanos & McLean, 1986b; Zamansky, 1986), who hypnotically regressed high hypnotizable subjects to a night of the previous week and gave them a subtle suggestion of hearing noises. This suggestion was accepted by one-third of the subjects and, after hypnosis, most of them reported that the noises occurred on the night. However, when these subjects were rehypnotized and told that the hypnotist would talk with the "hidden part, that knows what is really going on," only two subjects said the noises occurred on the night. Then, when they were "informed that the hypnotist would recontact their 'hypnotized part'" all subjects reported that the noises occurred on the night. Finally, when the hypnotist said they should remember their "hidden part," approximately one-third of the subjects said the noises occurred on the night. Overall, the subjects' false memory reports followed the shifting messages, and their reports of whether the noises occurred on the night or were suggested during hypnosis changed in accordance with the cues carried by the testing context. Spanos and McLean (1986a, 1986b) concluded that hypnotically suggested false memory is essentially an artifactual phenomenon that reflects socially determined bias in memory reports rather than a reflection of actual changes in memory. These studies, however, were unable to conclude whether pseudomemory was specific to hypnosis (i.e., an effect not found outside of hypnosis).

To investigate this phenomenon, Weekes, Lynn, Green, and Brentar (1992) used the essential procedures of Laurence and Perry (1983b) and tested high hypnotizable subjects in either hypnosis or task-motivation conditions. That is, the subjects were age-regressed to a night of the previous week and given a suggestion of hearing noises, and their reporting of these noises was tested after hypnosis. The findings indicated that an equivalent number of hypnotized and task-motivated subjects reported the false memory after hypnosis. Thus, pseudomemories are not restricted to hypnosis and may occur in other motivational and situational contexts, at least for high hypnotizable subjects. Notably, the criterion for pseudomemory was strict, and those subjects who indicated confusion or uncertainty were not considered to be displaying pseudomemory. In an attempted replication of Spanos and McLean's (1986a) context manipulation, Weekes et al. (1992) attempted to reverse pseudomemory reporting by using a "deep concentration" procedure, in which the subjects were told they would be able "to think clearly, never confusing fantasy with reality or reality with fantasy" (p. 357). However, this procedure did not change the incidence of pseudomemory reporting; an equivalent number of hypnotized and task-motivated subjects reported the pseudomemory. Thus, unlike Spanos and McLean (1986a), different cues did not shift pseudomemory reporting. This may have been, of course, because the deep concentration and hidden observer instructions differed in important ways in the degree to which they legitimized shifts in reporting. This failure to shift pseudomemory suggests that it is not simply an hypnotic effect but, rather involves other processes that affect memory in a meaningful way. In support of this hypothesis, during an inquiry into the experiences of subjects, Weekes et al. (1992) found that hypnotized rather than task-motivated subjects were more likely to report novel sounds that were additional to the suggested noises. This finding is consistent with the argument of Barnier and McConkey (1992) that hypnotized subjects tend to experience unsuggested elaborations that work to integrate suggested information into existing memory.

In a subsequent study, Lynn, Rhue, Myers, and Weekes (1994) revised the deep concentration instructions of Weekes et al. (1992) to separate more clearly the contexts of testing and thus more obviously legitimize the reversal of pseudomemory reporting. Following the procedures of Weekes et al.

(1992), Lynn et al. (1994) tested hypnotizable subjects and unhypnotizable subjects simulating a hypnotized state in an application of the real–simulating model of hypnosis (Orne, 1959, 1971). The findings indicated that an equivalent number of reals and simulators displayed pseudomemory. As in Weekes et al. (1992), the deep concentration instructions did not shift the incidence of pseudomemory, and a similar number of reals and simulators reported hearing noises on a night of the previous week. Moreover, and unlike Weekes et al. (1992), both reals and simulators reported additional novel sounds during an inquiry into their experiences. Overall, the essential similarity between real and simulating subjects raised the possibility that the pseudomemory reports of hypnotized subjects may reflect the influence of demand characteristics, as indexed by the responses of simulating subjects (Orne, 1959, 1971). However, it was not clear whether real and simulating subjects behaved similarly, but for different reasons, reflecting either response bias or memory change.

In an attempt to answer this question, Murrey, Cross, and Whipple (1992) conducted a further replication of Spanos and McLean (1986a). They tested high hypnotizable subjects and randomly selected subjects by first showing them a videotape of a mock robbery in which the robber was not wearing a hat. In the week following when the subjects watched the videotape, they were placed in either hypnosis or waking conditions and played an audiotape to enhance their memory of the videotape; this audiotape included subtle suggestions for a false memory of the robber wearing a hat. One week after viewing the videotape, the subjects were administered a memory test for the videotape; also, some subjects were offered a monetary reward if they achieved the most correct answers on the test. More high hypnotizable subjects who were hypnotized, given the suggestion, and not offered the monetary reward reported the false memory than high hypnotizable subjects who were hypnotized, given the suggestion, and offered the monetary reward. The offer of a monetary reward appreciably reduced false memory reporting. Notably, pseudomemory reporting by high hypnotizable subjects who were hypnotized, given the suggestion, and offered the monetary reward did not differ from that of randomly selected subjects who were not hypnotized and either given the suggestion and offered the reward or not given the suggestion and not offered the reward. Murrey et al. (1992) concluded from this complex set of findings that response bias influences the reporting of hypnotically suggested false memory. They further argued that if response bias is controlled, "there may not be significant differences in manifestation of pseudomemories between highly hypnotizable subjects and subjects representative of the general population" (p. 77).

One of the ways in which Murrey et al. (1992) differed markedly from Laurence and Perry (1983b), Lynn et al. (1994), McCann and Sheehan (1988, Study 1), Spanos and McLean (1986a), and Weekes et al. (1992) was in their use of an actual event that subjects watched before the suggestion for false memory was given. In this respect, they followed the work of McCann and

Sheehan (1988, Studies 2 and 3) who argued that some fundamental weaknesses in the earlier work included not only the lack of objective verification of the events of the night to be remembered but also the ambiguity of the criteria for determining whether a false memory was actually occurring.

Accordingly, McCann and Sheehan (1988, Study 2) showed high hypnotizable subjects a videotape of a bank robbery and 1 week later hypnotized them and gave them strong suggestions for two false items (viz., the robber wearing a mask and the robber swearing). Also, in two different conditions, some subjects were given amnesia instructions and others were not during the deinduction. After hypnosis, all subjects were given recall and recognition tests of the videotape and were scored as showing pseudomemory if they mentioned the robber wore a mask and/or swore during free recall. Overall, less than one-third of the subjects reported a pseudomemory, and there were no appreciable differences across the memory items or the experimental conditions. Notably, of the subjects who showed pseudomemory during free recall, two-thirds identified the original videotape during recognition testing even when a nonoriginal videotape consistent with their false memory (i.e., a masked and swearing robber) served as a distractor. As McCann and Sheehan (1988) noted, this finding indicates both apparent acceptance and rejection of the false memory when it was tested in different ways. McCann and Sheehan (1988, Study 3; see also Kinoshita, 1989; Labelle, Dixon, & Laurence, 1989; McCann & Sheehan, 1989a, 1989b) used the same procedures with high hypnotizable subjects in an attempt to contrast the effects for long (1 week) and short (immediate) delay in the occurrence of hypnotically suggested false memory. Also in this study, a third false item was used (viz., the robber entering from the right, rather than from the left), and the subjects were shown the videotape in one of two different conditions. Specifically, half the subjects watched the videotape with the audio on and the other half watched it with the audio off. Findings indicated that there were no appreciable differences whether testing happened with a long or short delay, or whether subjects watched the videotape with the audio on or off. Overall, the majority of subjects reported a false memory of one sort or another. Given this finding, McCann and Sheehan (1988) argued that the incidence of pseudomemory lies along a continuum where the degree of stimulus salience or extent of compatibility of the suggested false information with the original stimulus is critical. Thus, the mask was a salient and compatible cue that reflected an existing cognitive schema (i.e., robbers and masks go together) which helped to facilitate the subjects' acceptance of the suggested false memory. McCann and Sheehan (1988, Study 3) noted that approximately three-quarters of the subjects who reported the mask during their free recall nevertheless correctly identified the original videotape in which the robber was not wearing a mask; this somewhat paradoxical finding was compatible with that of McCann and Sheehan (1988, Study 2). Both findings suggest that whereas hypnotically suggested false information can have an appreciable impact on memory, it does not necessarily destroy the capacity of subjects to recognize the original material. Further, in commenting on the finding that pseudomemory was no different on the immediate and the 1-week tests, McCann and Sheehan (1988) argued that if hypnotically created pseudomemory reflected the simple influence of hypnotic suggestion rather than implicating nonhypnotic processes as well, it should have weakened over time according to theoretical notions about the posthypnotic persistence of hypnotically suggested effects (e.g., Sheehan & Orne, 1968). Given this hypothesis, pseudomemory response cannot be viewed as a standard posthypnotic reaction (McCann & Sheehan, 1988). Pseudomemory clearly involves a memory effect that is influenced by both stimulus and testing characteristics.

The specific impact of particular memory testing was assessed further by McCann and Sheehan (1987a; see also, Gregg, 1987; McCann & Sheehan, 1987b). They allocated high hypnotizable subjects to conditions in which hypnotic pseudomemories were tested either first by recall and then by recognition or first by recognition and then by recall. Subjects were shown the videotape used by McCann and Sheehan (1988), then hypnotized and asked to reexperience watching the videotape. The hypnotist then suggested the three false items (viz., the robber wearing a mask, entering from the right, and swearing). After hypnosis, the subjects in the recall-first group recalled the videotape and were asked to select the original videotape from four they were shown; the four varied in whether the robber wore a mask and/or swore. Subjects in the recognition-first group were tested in the reverse order. During recall, more subjects in the recall-first than in the recognition-first group showed pseudomemory; during recognition, the majority of subjects identified the original videotape. The finding that memory testing order was associated with different rates of pseudomemory reporting highlighted again the impact of context of testing. Moreover, McCann and Sheehan (1987a, 1987b) concluded that hypnotically created pseudomemory can clearly be breached by exposure to the original material. They argued that this means that original memories are not lost irretrievably, and that pseudomemory elements are not irreversibly integrated with the original memories (McCann & Sheehan, 1987a, 1987b).

Across all this experimental work, although high hypnotizable subjects in hypnosis are more likely to accept and report pseudomemories, there is a clear finding that not all high hypnotizable subjects display pseudomemory. This finding raises the question of the particular characteristics (if any, perhaps cognitive) of subjects who do or do not display pseudomemory reporting. For this reason, McCann and Sheehan (1987a) also assessed the capacity of their subjects to display the hidden observer effect (Hilgard, 1977; Nogrady, McConkey, Laurence, & Perry, 1983; Zamansky & Bartis, 1985). Specifically, they asked subjects who were experiencing hypnotically suggested anosmia whether a hidden part could identify what they themselves could not identify during a suggestion for hypnotic anosmia. They found that five subjects in the recall-first group showed the hidden observer effect, and most of these showed pseudomemory; eight subjects in the recognition-first group showed the hidden observer effect, but none of these showed pseudomemory. Although limited by the small number of subjects, this research suggests an appreciable interaction of the association of hidden observer and pseudomemory reporting and order of memory testing (McCann & Sheehan, 1987a). Such an association of hidden observer and pseudomemory reporting was reported also by Laurence et al. (1986) in their extended analysis of the findings of Laurence and Perry (1983b). In that study, 13 high hypnotizable subjects showed pseudomemory in response to a hypnotic suggestion that they had heard noises on a night of the previous week. Using the procedures of Laurence and Perry (1981) and Nogrady et al. (1983), those subjects were rated in terms of whether they showed a duality report during hypnotic age regression and whether they showed a hidden observer effect during hypnotic analgesia; a significant relationship was found between these two types of responses (see also Laurence & Perry, 1981; Nogrady et al., 1983). Of the subjects who displayed pseudomemory, approximately three-quarters showed duality; moreover, of the subjects who showed a hidden observer effect, the majority displayed pseudomemory. These findings underscore the possibility that particular characteristics of high hypnotizable subjects, such as cognitive style, may be linked also to the acceptance and integration into memory of hypnotically suggested false information.

The relationship of pseudomemory reporting to subject characteristics was examined also by Labelle, Laurence, Nadon, and Perry (1990), who tested high, high-medium, and low hypnotizable subjects with the procedures of Laurence and Perry (1983b); that is, they suggested that noises occurred on a night of the previous week. During hypnosis, two-thirds of the high and high-medium subjects, but only one low hypnotizable subject, accepted the suggestion. After hypnosis, an equivalent number of high and high-medium subjects reported the noises as a pseudomemory; two-thirds said the noises occurred on the night, and one-third were confused about the source of the noises. Notably, no low hypnotizable subjects incorporated the suggested noises into memory after hypnosis. The presence of pseudomemory was associated with hypnotizability (Shor & Orne, 1962; Weitzenhoffer & Hilgard, 1962), absorption (Tellegen, 1981; Tellegen & Atkinson, 1974; see also Roche & McConkey, 1990), and preference for an imagic cognitive style (Isaacs, 1982; see also Nadon, Laurence, & Perry, 1987). Moreover, discriminant analysis indicated that a combination of hypnotizability and preference for an imagic cognitive style was the strongest predictor of pseudomemory occurrence. Labelle et al. (1990) concluded "that persons who possess both strong hypnotic abilities and high imagery preference are particularly vulnerable to suggested distortions of memory given the appropriate context" (p. 227). Although this is an appealing conclusion there is limited empirical support from other studies. McConkey, Labelle, Bibb, and Bryant (1990) and Barnier and McConkey (1992), for instance, both reported that neither absorption nor preference for an imagic cognitive style was associated with pseudomemory responding. It should be noted, however, that the type of pseudomemory responding being investigated across these two studies differed in a number of ways from that of Labelle et al. (1990). Similarly, McCann and Sheehan (1988, Study 3) reported that absorption was not associated with pseudomemory. Again, it should be noted that absorption was measured differently and the type of pseudomemory responding being investigated in this study varied from that in Labelle et al. (1990). The role of hypnotizability in hypnotic pseudomemory reporting is, however, central and consistent.

The central relevance of hypnotizability was investigated also by Sheehan, Statham, and Jamieson (1991a), who tested a large number of high, medium, and low hypnotizable subjects in either hypnosis or waking conditions. They followed the procedures of McCann and Sheehan (1988, Studies 2 and 3). Subjects were shown a videotape of a bank robbery, and during hypnosis it was suggested that the robber wore a mask and swore. (Notably, a number of subjects reported one or the other of these false items even before the suggestion was given, but these subjects were excluded from the analyses.) After hypnosis on free-recall testing, pseudomemory occurred more for subjects in the hypnosis than the waking condition on one or both of the items, and more for high than for medium or low hypnotizable subjects. On recognition testing, pseudomemory reporting was very low overall but highest for high hypnotizable subjects in the hypnosis condition. In addition to demonstrating the impact of testing context on pseudomemory, Sheehan et al. (1991a) showed once again that hypnotizability is especially relevant to the occurrence of pseudomemory; this is consistent with Labelle et al. (1990). Importantly, with the additional use of a waking condition Sheehan et al. (1991a) demonstrated an interaction between hypnotizability and the presence of hypnotic induction. Specifically, pseudomemory was greatest in high hypnotizable subjects who were given suggestions for false memory following an hypnotic induction. This interaction between hypnotizability and hypnotic induction focuses on the questions of what specific processes are associated with the assumed change in memory. Sheehan et al. (1991a) explored this question through use of the Experiential Analysis Technique (EAT; Sheehan & McConkey, 1982), which is a method designed to investigate the phenomenal experiences of subjects. That analysis showed that "in some subjects, pseudomemory suggestion created new experiences in ways that cannot be classified as simple compliance ... [and] that for many subjects, pseudomemory responses were accompanied by experiences that reflected substantial delusion or confusion" (Sheehan et al., 1991a, p. 136). Sheehan et al. (1991a) concluded that hypnotic pseudomemory is a phenomenon that requires both high hypnotizability and the presence of hypnotic induction, and these together lead to the experience of hypnosis and the reported alteration of old or the creation of new memories. Pseudomemory is not simply the result of response bias but, rather, is determined by multiple, interacting factors that include individual differences, situational variables, and memory processes.

Consistent with this notion, Sheehan, Statham, Jamieson, and Ferguson (1991) examined the impact on hypnotic pseudomemory of the ambiguity of the hypnotist's communications. In Study 1, they tested a large number of high, medium, and low hypnotizable subjects in hypnosis and waking conditions and followed the procedures of McCann and Sheehan (1988, Studies 2 and 3). They showed subjects a videotape of a bank robbery and subsequently gave hypnotic suggestions that the robber wore a mask, entered from the right, and swore. On free-recall testing after hypnosis, more high hypnotizable subjects in the hypnosis condition reported pseudomemories compared to all other subjects. Following Sheehan et al. (1991a), they used the EAT to analyze the experiences of subjects. That use indicated that high hypnotizable subjects in the hypnosis condition showed the greatest amount of reported memory change. Thus, Sheehan, Statham, Jamieson, and Ferguson (1991, Study 1) completed an effective replication of Sheehan et al. (1991a). In Study 2, they again tested a large number of high, medium, and low hypnotizable subjects in either hypnosis or waking conditions using the same procedures as Study 1 but attempted to shift pseudomemory by lessening ambiguity in the hypnotist's communication about whether it was appropriate to continue to report the suggested false items after hypnosis. The essential difference in this study was the deletion of any reference to false memories continuing after hypnosis. After hypnosis on free-recall testing, there was no difference in the incidence of pseudomemory associated with hypnotizability, but more subjects in the hypnosis than the waking condition still reported pseudomemories. Sheehan, Statham, Jamieson, and Ferguson (1991) argued that this finding indicated that the occurrence of pseudomemory was lessened considerably when ambiguity about the appropriateness of continued response away from the context of the hypnotic suggestion for false memory is reduced. Nevertheless, they acknowledged that the findings overall could be interpreted in terms of pseudomemory either being the outcome of multiple, interacting factors (viz., hypnotic induction, hypnotizability, prevailing conditions, and method of memory test) or a response that moves across different contextual settings if the appropriate signal or cue to respond consistent with the suggestion for false memory is present (see Sheehan & Orne, 1968; Weitzenhoffer, 1957).

Posthypnotic effects tend to dissipate over time (Edwards, 1963; Kellogg, 1929; Patten, 1930; Sheehan & Orne, 1968), and the role that time plays in the occurrence of pseudomemory is a relevant parameter. This finding was investigated by Sheehan, Statham, and Jamieson (1991b). They tested a large number of high, medium, and low hypnotizable subjects in hypnosis and waking conditions and followed the procedures of McCann and Sheehan (1988, Studies 2 and 3), with the exception that they tested pseudomemory 2 weeks after subjects watched the videotape of the bank robbery and were given hypnotic suggestions for the false items of the robber wearing a mask and swearing. Sheehan et al. (1991b) considered that there would be particular value in determining "whether false memory suggestions persist in their effect when a substantial period of time (2 weeks) has lapsed after implantation of the false memories . . . because temporary effects have then the opportunity to dissipate or extinguish" (p. 40). On free-recall testing 2 weeks after the suggestion was given, more high and medium hypnotizable subjects in the hypnosis condition reported pseudomemories compared to the other subjects. Notably, and consistent with McCann and Sheehan (1987a, 1988, Studies 2 and 3), pseudomemory virtually disappeared on recognition testing with most subjects identifying the original videotape even when distractor videotapes that included the robber wearing a mask and swearing were shown. Nevertheless, the performance of subjects on free recall indicated that suggested pseudomemory persisted over a reasonably long period, and that the effect was most obvious in high hypnotizable subjects in the hypnosis condition. As Sheehan et al. (1991b) pointed out, the persistence of the effect may be explained in part by subjects' tacit acceptance that hypnotically suggested false memories will last in their influence beyond hypnosis to some unspecified point in time, and the strength with which the ultimate testing context is linked in this way to the context of suggestion is predictive of the degree and durability of the pseudomemory.

The issue here, in part, is the extent to which the hypnotically suggested false memory is an effect of hypnotic process or an effect of nonhypnotic changes in memory. If it is an effect primarily of hypnosis, a transient memory report is created and should dissipate over time or cease when canceled directly or indirectly; the actual memory should not be altered irretrievably. If it is an effect of changed memory, either the actual memory is altered irretrievably or the actual and the suggested memory coexist and interactively influence performance on memory tests of one sort or another. The coexistence of multiple memories of the same event is possible, we would argue, with different versions being available and accessible under different prevailing conditions of the individual and the social setting in which subjects are recollecting. In this sense, it seems reasonable to argue that real and suggested memories may coexist and compete for verbal report, as it were, while the person works through confusion and uncertainty about the memories that are available and eventually comes to commit to a developed account of the event that meets and satisfies the internal and external requirements for appropriate memory reporting.

The clinical data we discussed earlier suggest that one of the prevailing conditions that may influence pseudomemory is the relationship with the hypnotist. To investigate this aspect, Sheehan, Green, and Truesdale (1992, Study 1) tested high and low hypnotizable subjects in hypnosis and waking conditions on the procedures of McCann and Sheehan (1988, Studies 2 and 3). They varied the degree to which rapport with the subjects was present at either normal or reduced levels, with rapport being reduced by the hypnotist and the second experimenter (who tested pseudomemory) acting in a cold and distant fashion and making critical comments to the subjects. After hypnosis, on free recall, the strongest pseudomemory effect occurred for high hypnotizable subjects in the hypnosis condition; there was no difference on free recall for the two rapport conditions. On a structured-recall test, however, the strongest pseudomemory effect occurred for high hypnotizable subjects in the hypnosis condition and in the rapport-present condition; in the rapport-reduced condition, the pseudomemory effect was substantially less. To explore this further, Sheehan et al. (1992, Study 2) tested high and low hypnotizable subjects in hypnosis and in either rapport-present or rapport-reduced conditions, with the rapport reduction involving only the second experimenter acting coldly and making critical comments. Sheehan et al. (1992, Study 3) tested high hypnotizable subjects in hypnosis and in either rapport-present or rapport-reduced conditions, with the rapport reduction involving only the hypnotist acting coldly and making critical comments. These studies showed that when either the second experimenter alone (Study 2) or the hypnotist alone (Study 3) was critical of subjects, there was no detrimental effect on pseudomemory reporting. Thus, Sheehan et al. (1992) concluded that in recall where directive questioning is involved, the inhibition of rapport lessens pseudomemory responding, but only when rapport is inhibited by both the hypnotist in the hypnotic setting and the person who tests for pseudomemory. According to Sheehan et al. (1992), "rapport with the hypnotist that is reinforced in the testing context . . . is the variable of consequence" (p. 699) in influencing hypnotically suggested false memory. This finding supports our notion that interpersonal interaction processes that occur during and after hypnosis critically shape the reports that subjects give as pseudomemory.

The relevance to pseudomemory of interaction processes in different interpersonal settings was investigated by McConkey et al. (1990), who tested high and low hypnotizable subjects in hypnosis and waking conditions. Subjects were shown a series of slides of a purse snatching, and following hypnotic induction (for those in the hypnosis condition) or a filler task (for those in the waking condition), the experimenter asked subjects to think about the slides and gave them the suggestion that the thief wore a scarf. Subjects were asked to focus on and describe that scarf. After hypnosis, pseudomemory was tested by a second experimenter via free recall. Then this experimenter told subjects (incorrectly) that the first experimenter had shown some subjects the thief with a scarf and others the thief without a scarf; she then asked them what their memory was now of the thief. These comments were intended to allow subjects legitimately to report or not to report a memory for a scarf. Unknown to either of the first two experimenters, a third experimenter contacted subjects by telephone between 4 and 24 hours after their session in the laboratory and asked them a number of questions about that session including their memory of the thief and the scarf. More high than low hypnotizable subjects showed pseudomemory on the first test after hypnosis, but there was no difference across the hypnosis and waking conditions. Pseudomemory did not change appreciably at the second test after hypnosis, but it did change dramatically on the test conducted away from the laboratory by the third experimenter. The major finding of McConkey et al. (1990) was the drop in pseudomemory from the laboratory to the nonlaboratory context, and this finding is consistent with the notion that pseudomemory decreases when the link between the contexts of suggestion and testing is weakened (see also McCann & Sheehan, 1987a, 1988). Thus, it again appears that hypnotically suggested false memory is likely to vary as a function of the strength of the link between the setting in which the material is suggested and that in which memory is tested. As argued by Spanos and McLean (1986a) and Sheehan et al. (1991a, 1991b), contextual shifts may significantly influence memory reports.

To explore this issue further, Barnier and McConkey (1992) followed the major procedures of McConkey et al. (1990) and tested high and low hypnotizable subjects in hypnosis or waking conditions. Subjects were shown a series of slides depicting a purse snatching and then asked in either hypnosis or waking conditions to reexperience seeing the slides; the experimenter suggested that the thief had a moustache (which he did), wore a scarf (which he did not), and helped pick up flowers dropped by his victim (which he did not). Pseudomemory was tested by a second experimenter during an inquiry session that used the EAT (Sheehan & McConkey, 1982). Toward the end of that inquiry session, pseudomemory was tested again when the experimenter gave the appearance of ending the session and thus gave subjects a reason for either maintaining or changing their previous memory reports by telling them (incorrectly) that there were versions of the slide series being shown to subjects that differed on whether the thief had a moustache, wore a scarf, and helped his victim pick up flowers. Barnier and McConkey (1992) found that subjects in the hypnosis and waking conditions responded similarly on pseudomemory reporting. Hypnotizability was relevant to the false items but not to the real item. Specifically, more high than low hypnotizable subjects reported pseudomemory for the scarf and the flowers but were similar in their reports of the moustache. A dramatic change occurred, however, when the second experimenter shifted the context of testing. When told (incorrectly) that the items may or may not have been present in the slides, high hypnotizable subjects moved from reporting to not reporting each of the items, and low hypnotizable subjects moved from reporting to not reporting the moustache (which was, in fact, present in the slides). The EAT inquiry into the experiences of subjects indicated that those who changed their reporting after the shift in context were those who, despite their initial pseudomemory reports to the experimenter, either experienced confusion in their original memory of the items or responded positively to the first experimenter because of the social demands of the setting. Barnier and McConkey (1992) concluded that hypnotizability rather than hypnosis was the major predictor of subjects' false memory reports and argued that high hypnotizable subjects tend to accept pseudomemory suggestions and cognitively elaborate them in a way that gives them personal meaningfulness; that is, high hypnotizable subjects have a tendency to "unsuggested elaboration of suggested pseudomemories"

(Barnier & McConkey, 1992, p. 526). The shift in context resulted in a substantial drop in subjects' pseudomemory reporting, and this was consistent with the importance of the link between the suggestion and the testing highlighted by McConkey et al. (1990), Sheehan et al. (1991a), and Sheehan, Statham, Jamieson, and Ferguson (1991). Notably, however, Barnier and McConkey (1992) saw the drop occur in subjects' reports of real as well as false memories. This suggests that subjects' memories of the real item were no more or less fixed in memory than were those associated with the false items. Clearly, reported memories of actual events are responsive to changes in the context of testing as well.

The change of context introduced by Barnier and McConkey (1992) strongly challenged subjects in their pseudomemory reports. The degree to which reported memories can be influenced by a strong challenge was also investigated by Spanos, Gwynn, Comer, Baltruweit, and de Groh (1989) who examined the effect of hypnosis and hypnotizability in response to pseudomemory suggestions and cross-examination of subjects. Spanos et al. (1989, Study 1) showed high and low hypnotizable subjects a videotape of a simulated robbery, and 1 week later showed them a videotape of a simulated newscast about the arrest of the (wrong) suspect. One week after that, they tested subjects in one of four conditions: hypnosis with pseudomemory suggestions that linked the arrested (wrong) suspect with the actual offender, imagery with pseudomemory suggestions, pseudomemory suggestions alone, or no pseudomemory suggestions. One week after that, they tested their subjects in a cross-examination context in which they "were asked to swear on a Bible that everything that they said in the session would be 'the truth, the whole truth, and nothing but the truth' " (Spanos et al., 1989, p. 276). The findings indicated that subjects in the hypnotic condition were as likely as those in both the imagery- and the suggestion-alone conditions to show misattributions about and misidentification of the offender. Moreover, hypnotic and nonhypnotic subjects were as likely to break down under cross-examination by disavowing their initial misattributions and their initial misidentifications. High rather than low hypnotizable subjects in each of the conditions made more misattributions and misidentifications; moreover, whereas both showed a drop in misattributions during the cross-examination, this drop was greater for high hypnotizable subjects. Spanos et al. (1989, Study 2) explored the effect of different cross-examination procedures on the degree to which high hypnotizable subjects changed their pseudomemory reports. Following the major procedures of the first study, in the second study high hypnotizable subjects were shown the videotape of the robbery and the videotape of the newscast and tested in the hypnosis-with-pseudomemory-suggestion condition. The subjects were then tested in one of three cross-examination conditions that differed in terms of the instructions given to subjects: the Bible (as in Study 1), hidden observer instructions ("there is another part of the mind that knows what is really going on, a hidden part that remains uninfluenced by suggestions. The hidden part can always distinguish between suggestions and reality," p. 285), or no instructions. The essential findings from the first study about pseudomemory-based misattributions and misidentifications were replicated, and subjects in the three cross-examination conditions disavowed many misattributions and misidentifications. The greatest breakdown occurred with the hidden observer instructions, the next with the control instructions, and the least with the Bible instructions. Subjects' comments indicated that those who were given the hidden observer instructions had a face-saving reason for changing their earlier accounts (viz., hypnosis confuses reality and fantasy; the hidden part allows them to be separated). Overall, Spanos et al. (1989) concluded that their experiments "contradict both the notion that hypnotic interrogations are more potent facilitators of pseudomemory reports than nonhypnotic interrogations and the notion that hypnotically engendered pseudomemories are particularly resistant to cross-examination. [Also,] variations in resistance to cross-examination are tied to subjects' perceptions about how their disavowals are likely to be evaluated by significant others" (p. 288).

In the final set of experimental studies relevant to our focus, Lynn, Weekes, and Milano (1989) tested hypnotizable subjects and unhypnotizable subjects simulating a hypnotized state in an application of the real–simulating model of hypnosis (Orne, 1959, 1971). In this study, the method of creating and testing a false memory was very different from that used in the previous studies we have considered. Specifically, following an hypnotic induction the subjects were either given or not given a suggestion that a telephone would ring and the experimenter would answer it; in reality, the telephone either did or did not ring. After the deinduction of hypnosis, the subjects completed questionnaires that contained a range of questions about the suggested and/or actual telephone ring and the conversation, and pseudomemory was assessed on the basis of subjects' responses to various questionnaire items. Only a handful of the real, hypnotizable subjects who were given the telephone suggestion reported that the telephone rang in their open-ended reports; none of the real, hypnotizable subjects reported the pseudomemory when asked in a structured way whether they had heard an actual telephone or whether the ring was suggested. The pattern of responses of real and simulating subjects was similar across the conditions in which a pseudomemory suggestion was given. This pattern underscores the possible role of demand characteristics in the occurrence of hypnotically suggested false memories, and the finding is consistent with Lynn et al. (1994). It should be noted, however, that the incidence of pseudomemory reporting in this study was very low, which may be because of the immediacy and verifiability of the suggested event. Labelle et al. (1990) considered that the relevance of this work to hypnotic pseudomemory was limited because it essentially assessed whether subjects could determine the source of a suggested auditory hallucination after hypnosis. They noted that there was nothing in the suggestion that the telephone ring would become integrated posthypnotically, and that the questionnaire assessment essentially communicated the suggested nature of the telephone ring. These concerns aside, however, Lynn et al. (1989) reasonably concluded from the data that "although hypnotic suggestions produce shifts in awareness and attention, subjects are not deluded by suggestions into confusing fantasy with reality. Instead, they remain attuned to their environment and successfully discriminate suggestions and external events" (p. 143). For us, however, this does not necessarily mean that the hypnotically suggested memory and the actual memory are essentially independent and will never become confused or fused.

Lynn, Milano, and Weekes (1991) extended their experimental approach in a way that overcame in part the concerns of Labelle et al. (1990). Specifically, they hypnotically regressed high hypnotizable subjects to a hypnosis session of the previous week in which a confederate of the experimenter entered the test room and spilled pencils. While asking subjects to reexperience this session, the hypnotist suggested that the telephone rang two times after the confederate spilled the pencils and left the room. Moreover, prior to hypnotic age regression in the second session, the subjects were given no particular expectancy, the expectancy that hypnosis is an altered state and enhances memory, or the expectancy that hypnosis is not an altered state and does not enhance memory. After hypnosis, pseudomemory was assessed via subjects' responses to various questionnaire items. The expectancies conveyed to subjects before hypnosis did not influence pseudomemory reporting; also, the incidence of pseudomemory reporting was low with no subjects reporting that the telephone definitely rang, and most indicating that the telephone definitely did not ring. The remaining subjects showed some uncertainty about whether the telephone rang in the first session. Notably, only one-quarter of the subjects recalled that the pencils spilled, and one-third said they did not spill. The remaining subjects showed uncertainty about whether the pencils spilled. It is noteworthy that regardless of whether the suggested event occurred (pencils dropped) or did not occur (telephone ringing), there was substantial uncertainty about whether it had happened. As Lynn et al. (1991) pointed out, because the base rate of uncertainty about remembered events is reasonably high, substantial care is needed in defining what constitutes a reasonable criterion for the occurrence of a hypnotic pseudomemory. This is especially the case because in this study the subjects were more likely to believe that events that really happened the week before did not in fact happen than they were to believe that the suggested events actually occurred (Lynn et al., 1991).

In a subsequent study, Lynn, Milano, and Weekes (1992) replicated the essential procedures of Lynn et al. (1991) but did not link the telephone ringing to the pencils dropping; rather, in the first session there was no confederate and no dropped pencils. Lynn et al. (1992) included a simulating condition to index the potential effect of demand characteristics and age-regressed real (hypnotizable) and simulating (unhypnotizable) subjects to the first session; in doing so, they gave the subjects the suggestion of the telephone ringing. Pseudomemory reporting was indexed again through various questionnaire items, and this assessment indicated that no subjects reported a pseudomemory of the telephone ringing. Lynn et al. (1992) argued that this very low rate of pseudomemory reporting was consistent with the impact of using a target stimulus that was publicly verifiable and occurring in the subjects' direct field of experience. As they acknowledged, however, it may have been that the pseudomemory suggestion was too artificial or unconvincing and therefore did not override the subjects' existing memory that a telephone did not ring during their previous session.

ISSUES FOR RESEARCH AND RESOLUTION

Five main issues about hypnotically suggested false memories need further attention: (1) the role of hypnotizability, (2) the relevance of hypnosis, (3) the impact of demand characteristics, (4) the role of context, and (5) the durability of hypnotically created memory. The empirical work that has been conducted allows each of these issues to be addressed.

Hypnotizability is a clearly critical variable in the occurrence of hypnotic pseudomemories. High hypnotizable subjects are more likely than low hypnotizable subjects to accept, incorporate, and maintain hypnotically suggested false memories in the experimental setting (e.g., Barnier & McConkey, 1992; Labelle et al., 1990; McConkey et al., 1990; Sheehan et al., 1991a, 1991b; Sheehan, Statham, Jamieson, & Ferguson, 1991). What is more, high hypnotizable subjects who accept suggestions for pseudomemories appear to be characterized, to some extent at least, by particular abilities (e.g., Labelle et al., 1990; Laurence et al., 1986; McCann & Sheehan, 1987a, 1987b). Low hypnotizable subjects are not immune entirely from the effects, but they are much less likely to show them. When they do, it is probably more of an effect of nonhypnotic changes to memory. The presence of hypnotic induction typically interacts with hypnotizability to produce the greatest effects of pseudomemory in high hypnotizable subjects, although this is not invariably the case. Subjects in nonhypnotic waking, task-motivated, and simulating conditions all show pseudomemory effects that are comparable to those shown by subjects in hypnotic conditions (e.g., Barnier & McConkey, 1992; Lynn et al., 1994; McConkey et al., 1990; Murrey et al., 1992; Sheehan et al., 1991a, 1991b; Sheehan, Statham, Jamieson, & Ferguson, 1991; Sheehan et al., 1992; Weekes et al., 1992).

Whereas it might be argued that pseudomemory is not strictly an hypnotic effect, it should be noted, of course, that these nonhypnotic and hypnotic pseudomemory effects may be similar in their incidence but different in terms of the processes that give rise to them. Clearly, pseudomemory effects that look similar may arise in hypnotic and nonhypnotic settings for quite different reasons. The important point to underscore is that when hypnotic induction has an appreciable impact, it appears to do so in combination with high hypnotizability. The impact of demand characteristics—demonstrating also the role of context—was shown most obviously by the similar reactions of hypnotic and simulating subjects when presented with a suggestion for hypnotic pseudomemory. A substantial amount of research now indicates that hypnotically created memory is present or absent depending on the social context of testing and the specific type of memory test used (e.g., Barnier & McConkey, 1992; Lynn et al., 1994; McCann & Sheehan, 1987a, 1987b; McConkey et al., 1990; Murrey et al., 1992; Spanos & McLean, 1986a). These findings raise major questions about the nature and durability of the hypnotically created memory, and those questions are ones that require further research.

Returning to our comments earlier in this chapter, future research needs to take into account lines of activity and inquiry that are highlighted by the historical and clinical material but ignored in large part by those investigating hypnotic pseudomemories. First, the historical and clinical material points to the importance of investigating false memories for nontrivial, personal events; of suggesting false memories for events that are emotionally toned; of suggesting false memories that will have positive consequences for the individual; and of testing and reinforcing different consequences of incorporating the false memory. Second, and relatedly, future research should incorporate notions of gist recall (Bartlett, 1932; Neisser, 1982). Much of the experimental work focused on nongist details that in a sense "don't matter" to the individual. They may matter forensically but have little importance to the individual. For example, whether the thief was wearing a mask may be totally obliterated by whether a victim survived. Within the clinical sphere of intentionally created false memory, the therapist typically focuses on gist recall; he or she changes the meaning of the memory material, and details are by and large often irrelevant. Third, research needs to recognize specifically the importance of the personal relationship between the hypnotist and the subject in determining whether hypnotically suggested false memory is accepted, incorporated, and maintained. The importance of these variables is highlighted consistently in the historical and clinical work. We would argue that if a hypnotist who has a strong and positive interpersonal relationship with a subject gives a suggestion about a personal event that shifts the emotional valence of that event from negative to positive, and if the acceptance of the false memory has positive consequences for the individual, with those consequences being reinforced by the hypnotist and others, then that false memory will be accepted and integrated into memory. With commitment on the part of the subject, any distinction between the real and the false memory will lose psychological meaning. And the subject will seek information that converges with the memory to which he or she has become committed. The point we wish to reinforce here is that there is a strong need for genuine experimental–clinical rapprochement in the area of hypnotically suggested false memory.

Experimental research raises further questions to explore. Investigators should consider, for example, the extent to which pseudomemory is similar to, or different from, other hypnotic effects. Sheehan, Statham, Jamieson, and Ferguson (1991) explored whether hypnotic pseudomemory could usefully be viewed as a posthypnotic suggestion effect. However, although intentionally created false memory seems to behave like a posthypnotic suggestion in some respects (e.g., dependence on test context), it is clearly unlike a posthypnotic suggestion in other respects (e.g., pseudomemory does not dissipate sufficiently over time). The main question for us is whether pseudomemory follows the same pattern as posthypnotic suggestion (or other hypnotic effects) or whether it is qualitatively different by virtue of its interaction with the dynamic processes of memory and their operation in a social context.

There is a strong need also for research to absorb the questions and designs of those investigating the creation of false memories and the factors that influence their nature and reporting outside the area of hypnosis (e.g., Garry & Loftus, 1994; Loftus, 1992; Loftus, Donders, Hoffman, & Schooler, 1989; Loftus & Hoffman, 1989; Schooler, Gerhard, & Loftus, 1986). Such research can ultimately inform us of what is the "memory" character of hypnotic pseudomemory rather than what makes it "hypnotic." Research outside the area of hypnosis typically shows that misleading information can cause people to believe that they saw things that never actually happened, or that they saw things differently from the way things actually occurred. Misinformation may lead to the creation of new memories, the alteration of old memories, and the reporting of blended memories of perceived and suggested information (Garry & Loftus, 1994). In work such as this, important theoretical and empirical issues are addressed. For example, issues associated with the misremembering of the source of information and with the familiarity of the material (e.g., Begg, Anas, & Farinacci, 1992), the miscombination of different features of the original memory event (e.g., Reinitz, Lammers, & Cochran, 1992), repetition of information about the original memory event (e.g., Begg & Armour, 1991), and perceptions occurring outside of consciousness (e.g., Jacoby & Whitehouse, 1989) can all lead to false memories when hypnosis is not involved. Even highly public and emotional flashbulb events such as the *Challenger* disaster can be associated with false memories about where people were when they heard the news, and false memories out of hypnosis can be held with acute emotional intensity (e.g., Neisser & Harsch, 1993).

Research outside the area of hypnosis points to a number of other relevant specific issues that influence memory. Although some hypnotic research has addressed matters such as the influence of the method of memory reinforcement or challenge and type of memory test, other aspects need to be additionally considered. These include the characteristics and expectancies of the individual; the type, extent, age, and meaning of the memory; the nature and purpose of the subject–inquirer interaction; the type, strength, credibility, and compatibility of the suggestion for false memory; the commitment of the subject to the memory required, and the consequences of that commitment to others; and the ongoing appropriateness and adequacy of the inserted false memory, until it takes on a life of its own. As a specific example, research might usefully address whether memories, false as opposed to real, can be discriminated by their characteristics on a probabilistic basis. Clinical work tells us that an individual's level of belief in his or her memory, or the degree of its clinical efficacy, is no real indication of "true memory"; that is, false memories can be therapeutic, but this does not make them true.

Finally, it is worth noting that hypnotic research can in turn inform research outside the area of hypnosis. The findings reviewed in this chapter, for instance, have important implications for nonhypnotic work on memory. First, the hypnotic work highlights in a distinctive way the special importance of the consequences of creating memories, and this may be linked to the nature of the interpersonal relationships. Clinical work underscores the fact that therapist and client generally agree in some way to develop an account of the past that will help to create a better future, and there are usually agreed-on consequences of memory change in the therapeutic setting. Yet outside the area of hypnosis, the interpersonal processes associated with memory change appear to be unrecognized to a large degree. Second, hypnosis research consistently and importantly highlights the importance of individual differences. These variables are relevant even when hypnosis is not involved (e.g., Barnier & McConkey, 1992); however, they are most relevant, as expected, when hypnosis is involved. Somewhat disappointingly, work outside the area of hypnosis typically ignores the relevance and potential importance of individual differences.

CONCLUSION

With these thoughts in mind, what is needed for a better understanding of hypnotically suggested false memory is a specific delineation of it as a phenomenon that can guide both research and application. In our view, hypnotic pseudomemory reflects the interaction of multiple social and psychological processes. It demonstrates not only the influence of the communications of one person on the experiences and responses of another but also on the plasticity and the persistence of recollections. There is persistence and plasticity in memory, but we are as yet unclear about the conditions of persistence and those of plasticity. The research reviewed here begins to delineate some of those conditions and to inform us that when people develop accounts of past events the strength of their commitment will depend on individual, interpersonal, and contextual factors. Hypnosis potentiates the plasticity of memory for some people under certain circumstances. In the same way, however, memory may be changed for these and other individuals out of hypnosis. In hypnosis, we are dealing with the occurrence of real events, but we are dealing also with the influence of factors that operate on memory when hypnosis is not involved.

ACKNOWLEDGMENTS

The preparation of this chapter was supported in part by a grant from the Australian Research Council to Kevin M. McConkey, an Australian Postgraduate Award to Amanda J. Barnier, and an independent grant from the Australian Research Council to Peter W. Sheehan.

REFERENCES

Alba, J. W., & Hasher, L. (1983). Is memory schematic? *Psychological Bulletin, 93*, 203–231.

Baker, R. A. (1982). The effect of suggestion on past-lives regression. *American Journal of Clinical Hypnosis, 25*, 71–76.

Baker, S. R., & Boaz, D. (1983). The partial reformulation of a traumatic memory of a dental phobia during trance: A case study. *International Journal of Clinical and Experimental Hypnosis, 31*, 14–18.

Barber, J. (1991). The locksmith model: Accessing hypnotic responsiveness. In S. J. Lynn & J. W. Rhue (Eds.), *Theories of hypnosis: Current models and perspectives* (pp. 241–274). New York: Guilford Press.

Barnier, A. J., & McConkey, K. M. (1992). Reports of real and false memories: The relevance of hypnosis, hypnotizability, and context of memory test. *Journal of Abnormal Psychology, 101*, 521–527.

Bartlett, F. C. (1932). *Remembering*. Cambridge, UK: Cambridge University Press.

Begg, I. M., Anas, A., & Farinacci, S. (1992). Dissociation of processes in belief: Source recollection, statement familiarity, and the illusion of truth. *Journal of Experimental Psychology: General, 121*, 446–458.

Begg, I. M., & Armour, V. (1991). Repetition and the ring of truth: Biasing comments. *Canadian Journal of Behavioral Science, 23*, 195–213.

Bernheim, H. (1891). *Hypnotisme, suggestion, psychothérapie; études nouvelles*. Paris: Octave Doin.

Bernheim, H. (1973). *Hypnosis and suggestion in psychotherapy*. New York: Aronson. (Original work published 1888)

Burnham, W. H. (1889). Memory, historically and experimentally considered. III: Paramnesia. *American Journal of Psychology, 2*, 430–464.

Burns, B., & Reyher, J. (1976). Activating posthypnotic conflict: Emergent uncovering psychopathology, repression, and psychopathology. *Journal of Personality Assessment, 40*, 492–501.

Coons, P. M. (1988). Misuse of forensic hypnosis: A hypnotically elicited false confession with the apparent creation of a multiple personality. *International Journal of Clinical and Experimental Hypnosis, 36*, 1–11.

Crabtree, A. (1994). *From Mesmer to Freud: Magnetic sleep and the roots of psychological healing*. New Haven, CT: Yale University Press.

Edwards, G. (1963). Duration of post-hypnotic effect. *British Journal of Psychiatry, 109*, 259–266.

Ellenberger, H. F. (1970). *The discovery of the unconscious: The history and evolution of dynamic psychiatry*. New York: Basic Books.

Erickson, M. H. (1935). A study of an experimental neurosis hypnotically induced in a case of ejaculatio praecox. *British Journal of Medical Psychology, 15*, 34–50.

Erickson, M. H. (1944). The method used to formulate a complex story for the induction of an experimental neurosis in a hypnotic subject. *Journal of General Psychology, 31*, 67–84.

Erickson, M. H., & Rossi, E. L. (1980). The February man: Facilitating new identity in hypnotherapy. In E. L. Rossi (Ed.), *The collected papers of Milton H. Erickson on hypnosis* (Vol. 4, pp. 525–542). New York: Irvington.

Forel, A. (1906). *Hypnotism or suggestion and psychotherapy: A study of the psychological, psychophysiological, and therapeutic aspects of hypnotism* (N.W. Armit, Trans.). New York: Rebman.

Frankel, F. H. (1988). The clinical use of hypnosis in aiding recall. In H. M. Pettinati (Ed.), *Hypnosis and memory* (pp. 247–264). New York: Guilford Press.

Freud, S. (1955). Analysis of a phobia in a five-year-old boy. In J. Strachey (Ed. & Trans.), *The standard edition of the complete psychological works of Sigmund Freud* (Vol. 10, pp. 5–149). London: Hogarth Press. (Original work published 1909)

Freud, S. (1964). Constructions in analysis. In J. Strachey (Ed. & Trans.), *The standard edition of the complete works of Sigmund Freud* (Vol. 23, pp. 255–269). London: Hogarth Press. (Original work published 1937)

Fromm, E., & Nash, M. R. (Eds.). (1992). *Contemporary hypnosis research.* New York: Guilford Press.

Garry, M., & Loftus, E. F. (1994). Pseudomemories without hypnosis. *International Journal of Clinical and Experimental Hypnosis, 42*, 363–378.

Gregg, V. H. (1987). Hypnotic pseudomemory: Continuing issues. *British Journal of Experimental and Clinical Hypnosis, 4*, 109–111.

Hilgard, E. R. (1977). *Divided consciousness: Multiple controls in human thought and action.* New York: Wiley-Interscience.

Huston, P. E., Shakow, D., & Erickson, M. H. (1934). A study of hypnotically induced complexes by means of the Luria technique. *Journal of General Psychology, 11*, 65–97.

Isaacs, P. (1982). *Hypnotic responsiveness and the dimensions of imagery and thinking style.* Unpublished doctoral dissertation, University of Waterloo, Waterloo, Ontario, Canada.

Jacoby, L. L., & Whitehouse, K. (1989). An illusion of memory: False recognition influenced by unconscious perception. *Journal of Experimental Psychology: General, 118*, 126–135.

Janet, P. (1973). *L'Automatisme psychologique.* [Psychological automatism.] Paris: Centre National de las Recherche Scientifique. (Original work published 1889)

Kampman, R. (1976). Hypnotically induced multiple personality: An experimental study. *International Journal of Clinical and Experimental Hypnosis, 24*, 215–227.

Kellogg, E. R. (1929). Duration of the effects of post-hypnotic suggestion. *Journal of Experimental Psychology, 12*, 502–514.

Kihlstrom, J. F. (1994). Hypnosis, delayed recall, and the principles of memory. *International Journal of Clinical and Experimental Hypnosis, 42*, 337–345.

Kihlstrom, J. F., & Barnhardt, T. M. (1993). The self-regulation of memory: For better and for worse, with and without hypnosis. In D. M. Wegner & J. W. Pennebaker (Eds.), *Handbook of mental control* (pp. 88–125). Englewood Cliffs, NJ: Prentice-Hall.

Kinoshita, S. (1989). Re-interpreting a re-analysis: A comment on McCann and Sheehan. *British Journal of Experimental and Clinical Hypnosis, 6*, 160–162.

Kirby, M. D. (1984). Hypnosis and the law. *Criminal Law Journal, 8*, 152–165.

Kline, M. V. (1951). A note on primate-like behavior induced through hypnosis. *Journal of Genetic Psychology, 81*, 125–131.

Kline, M. V., & Guze, H. (1951, Winter). The use of a drawing technique in the investigation of hypnotic age regression and progression. *British Journal of Medical Hypnotism*, 1–12.

Labelle, L., Dixon, M., & Laurence, J.-R. (1989). Pseudomemory creation and confidence ratings: A theory still in search of supportive data. *British Journal of Experimental and Clinical Hypnosis, 6*, 163–165.

Labelle, L., Laurence, J.-R., Nadon, R., & Perry, C. (1990). Hypnotizability, preference for an imagic cognitive style, and memory creation in hypnosis. *Journal of Abnormal Psychology, 99*, 222–228.

Lamb, C. S. (1985). Hypnotically-induced deconditioning: Reconstruction of memories in the treatment of phobias. *American Journal of Clinical Hypnosis, 28*, 56–62.

Laurence, J.-R., Nadon, R., Nogrady, H., & Perry, C. (1986). Duality, dissociation and memory creation in highly hypnotizable subjects. *International Journal of Clinical and Experimental Hypnosis, 34*, 295–310.

Laurence, J.-R., & Perry, C. (1981). The "hidden observer" phenomenon in hypnosis: Some additional findings. *Journal of Abnormal Psychology, 90*, 334–344.

Laurence, J.-R., & Perry, C. (1983a). Forensic hypnosis in the late nineteenth century. *International Journal of Clinical and Experimental Hypnosis, 31*, 266–283.

Laurence, J.-R., & Perry, C. (1983b). Hypnotically created memory among highly hypnotizable subjects. *Science, 222*, 523–524.

Laurence, J.-R., & Perry, C. (1988). *Hypnosis, will, and memory: A psycho-legal history.* New York: Guilford Press.

Levitt, E. E. (1990). A reversal of hypnotically "refreshed" testimony. *International Journal of Clinical and Experimental Hypnosis, 38*, 6–9.

Loftus, E. F. (1992). When a lie becomes memory's truth: Memory distortion after exposure to misinformation. *Current Directions in Psychological Science, 1*, 121–123

Loftus, E. F., Donders, K., Hoffman, H. G., & Schooler, J. W. (1989). Creating new memories that are quickly accessed and confidently held. *Memory and Cognition, 17*, 607–616.

Loftus, E. F., & Hoffman, H. G. (1989). Misinformation and memory: the creation of new memories. *Journal of Experimental Psychology: General, 118*, 100–104.

Loftus, E. F., Ketcham, K. (1994). *The myth of repressed memory: False memories and allegations of sexual abuse.* New York: St. Martin's Press.

Lynn, S. J., Milano, M., & Weekes, J. R. (1991). Hypnosis and pseudomemories: The effects of prehypnotic expectancies. *Journal of Personality and Social Psychology, 60*, 318–326.

Lynn, S. J., Milano, M., & Weekes, J. R. (1992). Pseudomemory and age regression: An exploratory study. *American Journal of Clinical Hypnosis, 35*, 129–137.

Lynn, S. J., & Nash, M. R. (1994). Truth in memory: Ramifications for psychotherapy and hypnotherapy. *American Journal of Clinical Hypnosis, 36*, 194–208.

Lynn, S. J., & Rhue, J. W. (Eds.). (1991). *Theories of hypnosis: Current models and perspectives.* New York: Guilford Press.

Lynn, S. J., Rhue, J. W., Myers, B. P., & Weekes, J. R. (1994). Pseudomemory in hypnotized and simulating subjects. *International Journal of Clinical and Experimental Hypnosis, 42*, 118–129.

Lynn, S. J., Weekes, J. R., Milano, M. J. (1989). Reality versus suggestion: Pseudomemory in hypnotizable and simulating subjects. *Journal of Abnormal Psychology, 98,* 137–144.

Macmillan, M. (1991). *Freud evaluated: The completed arc.* Amsterdam: North-Holland.

Matthews, W. J., Jr., Kirsch, I., & Allen, G. (1984). Posthypnotic conflict and psychopathology—controlling for the effects of posthypnotic suggestions: A brief communication. *International Journal of Clinical and Experimental Hypnosis, 32,* 363–365.

McCann, T. E., & Sheehan, P. W. (1987a). The breaching of pseudomemory under hypnotic instruction: Implications for original memory retrieval. *British Journal of Experimental and Clinical Hypnosis, 4,* 101–108.

McCann, T., & Sheehan, P. W. (1987b). Pseudomemory reports and their variable explanations. *British Journal of Experimental and Clinical Hypnosis, 4,* 112–114.

McCann, T., & Sheehan, P. W. (1988). Hypnotically induced pseudomemories—sampling their conditions among hypnotizable subjects. *Journal of Personality and Social Psychology, 54,* 339–346.

McCann, T., & Sheehan, P. W. (1989a). Pseudomemory creation and confidence in the experimental hypnosis context. *British Journal of Experimental and Clinical Hypnosis, 6,* 151–159.

McCann, T., & Sheehan, P. W. (1989b). Confident persistence in the face of disbelief: A response to commentaries. *British Journal of Experimental and Clinical Hypnosis, 6,* 166–170.

McConkey, K. M. (1991). The construction and resolution of experience and behavior in hypnosis. In S. J. Lynn & J. W. Rhue (Eds.), *Theories of hypnosis: Current models and perspectives* (pp. 542–563). New York: Guilford Press.

McConkey, K. M. (1992). The effects of hypnotic procedures on remembering: The experimental findings and their implications for forensic hypnosis. In E. Fromm & M. R. Nash (Eds.), *Contemporary hypnosis research* (pp. 405–426). New York: Guilford Press.

McConkey, K. M. (1995). Hypnosis, memory, and the ethics of uncertainty. *Australian Psychologist, 30,* 1–10.

McConkey, K. M., & Kinoshita, S. (1986). Creating memories and reports: Comment on Spanos and McLean. *British Journal of Experimental and Clinical Hypnosis, 3,* 162–166.

McConkey, K. M., Labelle, L., Bibb, B. C., & Bryant, R. A. (1990). Hypnosis and suggested pseudomemory: The relevance of test context. *Australian Journal of Psychology, 42,* 197–205.

McConkey, K. M., & Sheehan, P. W. (1995). *Hypnosis, memory, and behavior in criminal investigation.* New York: Guilford Press.

Miller, A. (1986). Brief reconstructive hypnotherapy for anxiety reactions. *American Journal of Clinical Hypnosis, 28,* 138–146.

Murrey, G. J., Cross, H. J., & Whipple, J. (1992). Hypnotically created pseudomemories: Further investigation into the "memory distortion or response bias" question. *Journal of Abnormal Psychology, 101,* 75–77.

Nadon, R., Laurence, J.-R., & Perry, C. (1987). Multiple predictors of hypnotic susceptibility. *Journal of Personality and Social Psychology, 53,* 948–960.

Nash, M. R. (1994). Memory distortion and sexual trauma: The problem of false negatives and false positives. *International Journal of Clinical and Experimental Hypnosis, 42,* 346–362.

Neisser, U. (1982). *Memory observed: Remembering in natural contexts*. San Francisco: Freeman.

Neisser, U., & Harsch, N. (1993). Phantom flashbulbs: False recollections of hearing the news about Challenger. In E. Winograd & U. Neisser (Eds.), *Affect and accuracy in recall: Studies of "flashbulb" memories* (pp. 9–31). New York: Cambridge University Press.

Nemiah, J. C. (1984). The unconscious and psychopathology. In K. S. Bowers & D. Meichenbaum (Eds.), *The unconscious reconsidered* (pp. 49–87). Toronto: Wiley.

Nogrady, H., McConkey, K. M., Laurence, J.-R., & Perry, C. (1983). Dissociation, duality, and demand characteristics in hypnosis. *Journal of Abnormal Psychology, 92*, 223–235.

Ofshe, R. J. (1992). Inadvertent hypnosis during interrogation: False confession due to dissociative state; mis-identified multiple personality and the satanic cult hypothesis. *International Journal of Clinical and Experimental Hypnosis, 40*, 125–156.

Ofshe, R. J., & Watters, E. (1994). *Making monsters: False memories, psychotherapy, and sexual hysteria*. New York: Charles Scribner's Sons.

Orne, M. T. (1959). The nature of hypnosis: Artifact and essence. *Journal of Abnormal and Social Psychology, 58*, 277–299.

Orne, M. T. (1971). The simulation of hypnosis: Why, how, and what it means. *International Journal of Clinical and Experimental Hypnosis, 19*, 183–210.

Orne, M. T. (1979). The use and misuse of hypnosis in court. *International Journal of Clinical and Experimental Hypnosis, 27*, 311–341.

Orne, M. T., Soskis, D. A., Dinges, D. F., & Orne, E. C. (1984). Hypnotically induced testimony. In. G. L. Wells & E. F. Loftus (Eds.), *Eyewitness testimony: Psychological perspectives* (pp. 171–213). New York: Cambridge University Press.

Orne, M. T., Whitehouse, W. G., Dinges, D. F., & Orne, E. C. (1988). Reconstructing memory through hypnosis: Forensic and clinical implications. In H. M. Pettinati (Ed.), *Hypnosis and memory* (pp. 21–63). New York: Guilford Press.

Patten, E. F. (1930). A note on the persistence of hypnotic suggestion. *Journal of Abnormal and Social Psychology, 25*, 319–334.

Pendergrast, M. H. (1994). *Victims of memory: Incest accusations and shattered lives*. Hinesburg, VT: Upper Access Press.

Perry, C., & Laurence, J.-R. (1984). Mental processing outside of awareness: The contributions of Freud and Janet. In K. S. Bowers & D. Meichenbaum (Eds.), *The unconscious reconsidered* (pp. 9–48). New York: Wiley.

Perry, C. W., Laurence, J.-R., D'Eon, J., & Tallant, B. (1988). Hypnotic age regression techniques in the elicitation of memories: Applied uses and abuses. In H. M. Pettinati (Ed.), *Hypnosis and memory* (pp. 128–154). New York: Guilford Press.

Pettinati, H. M. (Ed.). (1988). *Hypnosis and memory*. New York: Guilford Press.

Reinitz, M. T., Lammers, W. J., Cochran, B. P. (1992). Memory conjunction errors: Miscombination of stored stimulus features can produce illusions of memory. *Memory and Cognition, 20*, 1–11.

Reyher, J. (1961). Posthypnotic stimulation of hypnotically induced conflict in relation to psychosomatic reactions and psychopathology. *Psychosomatic Medicine, 23*, 384–391.

Reyher, J. (1962). A paradigm for determining the clinical relevance of hypnotically induced psychopathology. *Psychological Bulletin, 59*, 344–352.

Reyher, J., & Smyth, L. D. (1971). Suggestibility during the execution of a posthypnotic suggestion. *Journal of Abnormal Psychology, 78*, 258–265.

Rhue, J. W., Lynn, S. J., & Kirsch, I. (Eds.). (1993). *Handbook of clinical hypnosis.* Washington, DC: American Psychological Association.

Roche, S. M., & McConkey, K. M. (1990). Absorption: Nature, assessment, and correlates. *Journal of Personality and Social Psychology, 59,* 91–101.

Ross, M. (1989). Relation of implicit theories to the construction of personal histories. *Psychological Review, 96,* 341–357.

Scheflin, A. W., & Shapiro, J. L. (1989). *Trance on trial.* New York: Guilford Press.

Schooler, J. W., Gerhard, D., & Loftus, E. F. (1986). Qualities of the unreal. *Journal of Experimental Psychology: Learning, Memory, and Cognition, 12,* 171–181.

Sheehan, P. W. (1969). Artificial induction of posthypnotic conflict. *Journal of Abnormal Psychology, 74,* 16–25.

Sheehan, P. W. (1971). An explanation of the real-simulating model: A reply to Reyher's comment on "artificial induction of posthypnotic conflict." *International Journal of Clinical and Experimental Hypnosis, 19,* 46–51.

Sheehan, P. W. (1991). Hypnosis, context, and commitment. In S. J. Lynn & J. W. Rhue (Eds.), *Theories of hypnosis: Current models and perspectives* (pp. 520–541). New York: Guilford Press.

Sheehan, P. W. (1992). The phenomenology of hypnosis and the experiential analysis technique. In E. Fromm & M. R. Nash (Eds.), *Contemporary hypnosis research* (pp. 364–389). New York: Guilford Press.

Sheehan, P. W., Green, V., & Truesdale, P. (1992). Influence of rapport on hypnotically induced pseudomemory. *Journal of Abnormal Psychology, 101,* 690–700.

Sheehan, P. W., & McConkey, K. M. (1982). *Hypnosis and experience: The exploration of phenomena and process.* Hillsdale, NJ: Erlbaum.

Sheehan, P. W., & Orne, M. T. (1968). Some comments on the nature of posthypnotic behavior. *Journal of Nervous and Mental Disease, 146,* 209–220.

Sheehan, P. W., Statham, D., & Jamieson, G. A. (1991a). Pseudomemory effects and their relationship to level of susceptibility to hypnosis and state instruction. *Journal of Personality and Social Psychology, 60,* 130–137.

Sheehan, P. W., Statham, D., & Jamieson, G. A. (1991b). Pseudomemory effects over time in the hypnotic setting. *Journal of Abnormal Psychology, 100,* 39–44.

Sheehan, P. W., Statham, D., Jamieson, G. A., & Ferguson, S. R. (1991). Ambiguity in suggestion and the occurrence of pseudomemory in the hypnotic setting. *Australian Journal of Clinical and Experimental Hypnosis, 19,* 1–18.

Shor, R. E., & Orne, M. T. (1962). *Harvard Group Scale of Hypnotic Susceptibility, Form A.* Palo Alto, CA: Consulting Psychologists Press.

Smith, M. C. (1983). Hypnotic memory enhancement of witnesses: Does it work? *Psychological Bulletin, 94,* 387–407.

Smyth, L. D. (1982). Psychopathology as a function of neuroticism and a hypnotically implanted aggressive conflict. *Journal of Personality and Social Psychology, 43,* 555–564.

Sommerschield, M., & Reyher, J. (1973). Posthypnotic conflict, repression and psychopathology. *Journal of Abnormal Psychology, 82,* 278–290.

Spanos, N. P., Burgess, C. A., & Burgess, M. F. (1994). Past-life identities, UFO abductions, and satanic ritual abuse: The social construction of memories. *International Journal of Clinical and Experimental Hypnosis, 42,* 433–446.

Spanos, N. P., Gwynn, M. I., Comer, S. L., Baltruweit, W. J., & de Groh, M. (1989). Are hypnotically induced pseudomemories resistant to cross-examination? *Law and Human Behavior, 13,* 271–289.

Spanos, N. P., & McLean, J. (1986a). Hypnotically created pseudomemories: Memory distortions or reporting biases? *British Journal of Experimental and Clinical Hypnosis, 3,* 155–159.

Spanos, N. P., & McLean, J. (1986b). Hypnotically created false reports do not demonstrate pseudomemories. *British Journal of Experimental and Clinical Hypnosis, 3,* 167–171.

Spanos, N. P., Menary, E., Gabora, N. J., DuBreuil, S. C., & Dewhirst, B. (1991). Secondary identity enactments during past-life regression. *Journal of Personality and Social Psychology, 61,* 308–320.

Spence, D. P. (1982). *Narrative truth and historical truth.* New York: Norton.

Spiegel, D., & Spiegel, H. (1987). Forensic uses of hypnosis. In I. B. Wiener & A. K. Hess (Eds.), *Handbook of forensic psychology* (pp. 490–507). New York: Wiley.

State v. White, No. J-3665 (City Ct., Branch 10, Milwaukee County, Wis., March 27, 1979).

Stevenson, I. (1994). A case of the psychotherapist's fallacy: Hypnotic regression to "previous lives." *American Journal of Clinical Hypnosis, 36,* 188–193.

Tellegen, A. (1981). Practicing the two disciplines for relaxation and enlightenment: Comment on "Role of the feedback signal in electromyograph biofeedback: The relevance of attention" by Qualls and Sheehan. *Journal of Experimental Psychology: General, 110,* 217–226.

Tellegen, A., & Atkinson, G. (1974). Openness to absorbing and self-altering experiences (absorption), a trait related to hypnotic susceptibility. *Journal of Abnormal Psychology, 83,* 268–277.

Wagstaff, G. F. (1989). Forensic aspects of hypnosis. In N. P. Spanos & J. F. Chaves (Eds.), *Hypnosis: The cognitive–behavioral perspective* (pp. 340–357). Buffalo, NY: Prometheus Books.

Weitzenhoffer, A. M. (1957). Posthypnotic behavior and the recall of the hypnotic suggestion. *Journal of Clinical and Experimental Hypnosis, 5,* 41–58.

Weitzenhoffer, A. M., & Hilgard, E. R. (1962). *Stanford Hypnotic Susceptibility Scale, Form C.* Palo Alto, CA: Consulting Psychologists Press.

Weekes, J. R., Lynn, S. J., Green, J. P., & Brentar, J. T. (1992). Pseudomemory in hypnotized and task-motivated subjects. *Journal of Abnormal Psychology, 101,* 356–340.

Yapko, M. D. (1994a). Suggestibility and repressed memories of abuse: A survey of psychotherapists' beliefs. *American Journal of Clinical Hypnosis, 36,* 163–171.

Yapko, M. D. (1994b). *Suggestions of abuse: True and false memories of childhood sexual trauma.* New York: Simon & Schuster.

Zamansky, H. S. (1986). Hypnotically created pseudomemories: Memory distortions or reporting biases? *British Journal of Experimental and Clinical Hypnosis, 3,* 160–161.

Zamansky, H. S., & Bartis, S. P. (1985). The dissociation of an experience: The hidden observer observed. *Journal of Abnormal Psychology, 94,* 243–248.

Zolik, E. S. (1958). An experimental investigation of the psychodynamic implications of the hypnotic "previous existence" fantasy. *Journal of Clinical Psychology, 14,* 179–183.

CHAPTER 10

REPRESSED MEMORIES OF RITUALISTIC AND RELIGION-RELATED CHILD ABUSE

Jianjian Qin
Gail S. Goodman
Bette L. Bottoms
Phillip R. Shaver

The possibility that victims of child abuse can repress or otherwise lose memories of early traumatic experiences and then recover them years later is currently the subject of heated debate (Alpert et al., 1996). Concerns about false memories are particularly intense in cases involving repressed memory of alleged acts of satanic ritual abuse (Wright, 1994). Allegations of ritual abuse, which often arise in the context of psychotherapy (Bottoms, Shaver, & Goodman, 1996), typically include descriptions of bizarre, horrendous acts such as murder, torture, and sacrifice of humans and animals; cannibalism; and baby breeding to supply the sacrificial needs of satanic cults (e.g., Bottoms et al., 1996; Jonker & Jonker-Bakker, 1991; Ofshe, 1992, 1993; Victor, 1994). Such allegations were made in some of the most publicized trials of the past decade, such as the McMartin and Little Rascals prosecutions (Victor, 1994; Waterman, Kelly, Oliveri, & McCord, 1993). Claims of repressed memory of religion-related abuse (e.g., sexual abuse by Catholic priests) have also resulted in controversial legal cases. Both types of repressed memory claims have been the source of a backlash against child protection services and clinical psychology and psychiatry. Nevertheless, few studies directly examine the characteristics of ritual and religion-related repressed memory cases, the circumstances under which such memories are "recovered," the amount of evidence available to support claims of ritual and religion-related abuse, and the belief systems and training of clinicians who trust clients' repressed memory reports. In the present chapter, we address these issues by discussing the results of two nationwide surveys that probed claims of repressed memory of satanic ritual and religion-related abuse.

To provide a context for understanding allegations of ritualistic and religion-related abuse in repressed memory cases, we begin with a brief discussion of what we currently know about repressed memory and ritual abuse. We then address the topic of repressed memories of religion-related abuse. Next, we present the results of our initial survey, thereby providing a profile of cases involving allegations of repressed memories of ritual and religion-related abuse and detailing the nature of such cases. Finally, we describe the results of a second survey, one that concerned the belief systems and training of clinicians who deal with repressed memory cases. This chapter does not answer the ultimate question of the validity of repressed memory or abuse allegations. However, the findings from our surveys are relevant to understanding how such allegations emerge and the extent of evidence for them.

REPRESSED, RECOVERED, AND FALSE MEMORIES

We use the term "repressed memory" to describe a situation in which it is alleged, by a clinician and/or the clinician's client, that a traumatic childhood event was temporarily or permanently forgotten. We realize that the specific psychodynamic mechanism of repression might not be involved and that the allegation might be either true or false.

Repression is a key concept in psychoanalytic theory (Freud, 1915/1957). It refers to the avoidance of conscious representation of frightening ideas or memories and unwanted emotions (Singer, 1990). The existence of repression is not well established in laboratory experiments (Holmes, 1990); nevertheless, it is often evoked to account for the loss of memories of childhood abuse (e.g., Briere & Conte, 1993; Courtois, 1992; Herman, 1992; Herman & Schatzow, 1987). Consistent with the possibility of repression of traumatic experiences, available evidence indicates that sexual abuse experienced in childhood (including middle to late childhood) is not necessarily remembered or reported in adulthood (Briere & Conte, 1993; Herman & Schatzow, 1987; Loftus, Polonsky, & Fullilove, 1994; Widom & Morris, 1997; Williams, 1994). In addition, studies suggest that amnesia for early abuse experiences is related to early onset of abuse (Briere & Conte, 1993; Cameron, 1996; Herman & Schatzow, 1987; Williams, 1994), extreme, repeated, and violent abuse (Briere & Conte, 1993; Herman & Schatzow, 1987), abuse that is viewed as emotionally scarring (Elliot & Briere, 1995), and a close perpetrator–victim relationship (Williams, 1994). However, other studies indicate no relation between forgetting and early age of onset (Elliot & Briere, 1995), duration (Cameron, 1996; Elliot & Briere, 1995), emotional impact (Williams, 1995), or closeness to the perpetrator (Loftus et al., 1994). In any case, whether the available evidence indicates that "repression" rather than simple, motivated, or unmotivated forgetting occurred is still being debated (e.g., Alpert et al., 1996). Few studies address the important issue of whether memories of traumatic childhood experiences can be lost from consciousness for years and then gradually or suddenly reawakened.

Regardless of the possibility that memories of traumatic childhood events can be repressed and later recovered, there is also the interesting question whether false memories of such events can be induced or constructed. Loftus (1993) and Lindsay and Read (1994, 1995) argue that experimental research on suggestibility, memory impairment, and hypnosis in adults and children indicates that false memories can be created (also see Spanos, 1994). In several recent articles, researchers report implanting false memories of such events as being lost in a shopping mall or going to the hospital, although the criteria used to classify a report as false in these studies are sometimes open to question (Hyman, Husband, & Billing, 1995; Hyman & Pentland, 1996; Loftus & Pickrell, 1995; but see Pezdek, Finger, & Hodge, 1997). Anecdotal and case-study reports also indicate that under certain conditions, some people can be led to believe in vivid false memories of such acts as sexual abuse, murder, cannibalism, UFO abductions, and, in particular, satanic ritual abuse (Mack, 1994; Newman & Baumeister, 1996; Ofshe & Watters, 1994; Victor, 1994).

In summary, the existence of repression is not well established in laboratory experiments, but such experiments may not be relevant to memory for traumatic events. A substantial clinical literature supports the possibility of repression of traumatic experiences, but clinical studies rest largely on unvalidated self-reports or clinicians' inferences. However, consistent with the clinical literature, the most rigorous study to date (Williams, 1994) indicates that sexual abuse experienced in childhood (including middle to late childhood) is not necessarily remembered in adulthood. Whether this indicates "repression" rather than more normal forgetting is unclear. It is also unclear whether memories of traumatic childhood experiences can be reawakened in adulthood. There is, in addition, the important question whether false memories of traumatic childhood events can be induced. Based on current experimental literature and the reports of clinicians, the best answer to this question appears to be "yes."

RITUAL ABUSE

Repressed memory cases often include allegations of satanic ritual abuse. These allegations involve scenarios of abuse allegedly committed by Satan-worshipping cult members. Professionals who believe these allegations often take the severity of their clients' psychological symptoms, the clients' sincerity in recounting past abuse, and the similarity of reports by different patients as evidence of authenticity (Young, Sachs, Braun, & Watkins, 1991). Skeptics counter that these indicators are misleading and insufficient to compel belief and that corroborative physical evidence is lacking. An FBI expert on ritual abuse allegations, for example, asserts that despite the vivid and insistent nature of allegations of ritual abuse, "There is little or no evidence for the portion of the allegations that deals with large-scale baby breeding, human sacrifice, and organized satanic conspiracies" (Lanning, 1991, p. 173). This conclusion followed at least 8 years of investigation by American law enforcement agencies and has not been reversed in subsequent years.

Modern allegations of satanic ritual abuse seem to have appeared first in the 1980s and have grown steadily since that time, at least up to the early 1990s (Bottoms, Shaver, & Goodman, 1996). One of the first modern descriptions of a satanic ritual abuse survivor appears in *Michelle Remembers*, a supposedly nonfiction book written by a survivor in conjunction with her psychiatrist and eventual husband (Smith & Pazder, 1980). Among other extraordinary claims in the book, Michelle says she was saved by Mary and Jesus from a personal encounter with Satan during a satanic ritual and had horns and a tail surgically sewn on her flesh by members of a satanic cult.

Subsequent to the publication of *Michelle Remembers*, reports of ritual abuse increased. According to results of a survey conducted by the American Bar Association, about one-quarter of local prosecutors in the United States handled cases involving "ritualistic or satanic abuse" as of 1991 (Smith, Elstein, Trost, & Bulkley, 1993). Also during this time, researchers began to study the claims and symptoms of ritual abuse survivors. Young et al. (1991) examined 37 dissociative disorder patients who reported having been ritually abused in childhood by satanic cults. Memories of childhood ritual abuse emerged gradually in patients over the course of their therapy during hypnotic interviews or while patients were abreacting, dreaming, or experiencing flashbacks or dissociative states. Often, the memories at first lacked a clear sequencing of events but were elaborated and made more coherent as treatment progressed. Although Young et al. (1991) did not explicitly describe their patients' memories as repressed, it was clear that the patients initially did not have memories of ritual abuse but later did have them after various "memory recovery" techniques were applied.

Many adult survivors of alleged ritual child abuse have been diagnosed as suffering from posttraumatic stress disorder (PTSD) and other dissociative disorders, such as multiple personality disorder (MPD; now called dissociative identity disorder; Putnam, 1993; Rogers, 1992). For example, all 37 patients in the study reported by Young et al. (1991) had prominent PTSD symptoms with high levels of anxiety and panic, easy "triggering" of memories and thoughts by external stimuli, flashbacks, nightmares, and intrusive images. Some professionals believe that MPD can be caused by childhood sexual abuse (e.g., Kluft, 1985) and claim that dissociative disorders may underlie many repressed memory claims (e.g., Briere, 1993). However, according to Ganaway (1995), the hypothesized link between childhood abuse and the later discovery of MPD still lacks independent corroborative evidence. The supposed link is based almost completely on therapeutically constructed or reconstructed memories.

Is satanic ritual child abuse a growing risk to society or only an example of societal rumor, myth, and urban legend (Richardson, Best, & Bromley, 1991; Rogers, 1992) exacerbated by questionable therapeutic techniques used with suggestible clients? Skeptics point out that a few clinical psychologists account for a huge proportion of all ritual abuse case reports (Bottoms, Shaver, & Goodman, 1996). They criticize the lack of comparison groups in ritual child abuse studies, the nonspecificity of the satanic ritual abuse syndrome, and the lack of systematic analyses of the actual similarities among allegations. They also argue that social psychological and sociological research shows that rumors and urban legends can be spread throughout society rapidly and be shared by large numbers of people who have never met (Mulhern, 1991; Victor, 1993). If satanic ritual abuse of children does not occur, then repressed memories of it would obviously be false.

RELIGION-RELATED ABUSE

Claims of repressed memory do not appear only in satanic ritual abuse cases. Adults sometimes allege to have repressed their memories of other childhood traumas, such as religion-related child abuse. By religion-related abuse we mean abuse associated with religious beliefs or practices (e.g., religiously motivated medical neglect, severe beatings due to religious beliefs, abuse perpetrated by religious professionals, or abuse committed in religious settings). It is surprising that much less has been written about religion-related child abuse than about satanic ritual abuse because there is reason to believe that religion-related abuse is more common and verifiable than satanic ritual abuse (Bottoms, Shaver, & Goodman, 1996; Bottoms, Shaver, Goodman, & Qin, 1995).

Cases of repressed memory of religion-related abuse often involve allegations of sexual acts by religious professionals. Perhaps the most famous case concerned the late Cardinal Bernardin of Chicago (Sheler, 1993). In that case, a young man making allegations against the Cardinal eventually recanted, although he still maintained that he had been abused by other religious authorities. However, in another celebrated religion-related repressed memory case, Father Porter was convicted of abusing children who attended his Boston church. In this case, Father Porter's confession supported the claims of the adults who "recovered" memories that he had abused them as children (see also Horn, 1993). Thus, true memories of abuse may have been lost and then successfully recovered even though similar claims of recovered memories can sometimes be false.

THE CO-CREATION OF FALSE CLAIMS OF RITUAL AND RELIGION-RELATED ABUSE

Although the debate about the reality of recovered repressed memories is far from being settled, there is consensus that false memories sometimes occur. Bottoms and Davis (1997) describe how a confluence of social and psychological forces may have contributed to the creation of false memories of ritual and religion-related abuse in therapeutic settings (see also Loftus, 1993; Pendergast, 1995; Shaver, Bottoms, & Goodman, 1995; Spanos, 1996). Specifically, Bottoms and Davis proposed that sociocultural, client, and therapist factors interact in such a way that when a certain type of client enters therapy with a certain type of therapist, co-creation of false memories may result. Some of the important sociocultural influences on this process include family instability and fragmentation, publicity about the prevalence of child abuse, and reactions of religious groups to such publicity. Given this sociocultural milieu, client factors that may contribute include being an actual victim of child maltreatment (though not by satanic cults or religious professionals), depression or other forms of malaise, belief in Satan and satanic evil, and inherent suggestibility and hypnotizability. Finally, an essential ingredient for the formation in therapy of false memories of satanic or religion-related abuse is the entry of vulnerable clients into therapy with a clinician possessing the following characteristics: an emphasis on the powerful long-term effects of child sexual abuse, belief in repressed memories, use of highly suggestive memory-recovery techniques, and mixing of religion with therapy (see also Poole, Lindsay, Memon, & Bull, 1995). It should be noted that a number of these therapist characteristics and practices (e.g., a focus on the powerful long-term effects of child sexual abuse) are not necessarily problematic in and of themselves and may be quite justifiable in general or when dealing with child abuse victims. The point is that when a specific set of sociocultural, client, and therapist forces come together, the interaction may at times result in false memories of satanic or religion-related abuse.

Although the studies described in this chapter do not directly test this model, they do provide information relevant to it. For instance, our initial survey examined the presenting symptoms of clients who allege satanic ritual abuse, and our second survey investigated therapists' beliefs about ritual abuse.

A SURVEY CONCERNING RITUALISTIC AND RELIGION-RELATED CHILD ABUSE

Despite heated debates, there are only a few scientific studies of ritualistic and religion-related child abuse and even fewer studies of the subset of more questionable cases in which the allegations arise as recovered repressed memories. What is the specific nature of the abuse allegations? Are they supported by corroborative evidence? How credible do the claims seem to clinicians? To investigate these issues, we conducted a nationwide survey of clinical psychologists, psychiatrists, and clinical social workers. The data we obtained from this survey allowed us to compare ritual and religion-related abuse claims in repressed memory cases versus those in non-repressed memory cases. We turn now to a description of the methods and results of our study.

The Survey and the Sample

The survey was conducted in 1990–1991 and consisted of two phases: a preliminary postcard survey followed by a detailed questionnaire survey. During the postcard survey, each clinician received a cover letter explaining that we were interested in child abuse allegations involving ritualistic or religious practices (Table 10.1). Clinicians were asked to indicate on the postcard reply form the number of ritual and religion-related child abuse cases they had personally encountered since January 1, 1980. During the subsequent survey, a detailed questionnaire was sent to clinicians who had encountered at least one case. Each respondent was asked to provide specific information about typical or representative ritual and religion-related cases reported to them by either children or adult survivors. (By adult survivor we mean a person who was 18 years of age or older reporting abuse that allegedly occurred during childhood.) The issues covered by the detailed questionnaire included case characteristics such as type of abuse involved in the case and other case features; characteristics of the victims and perpetrators, such as number and gender, and victims' ages, presenting symptoms, and diagnoses; any evidence for the victims' claims; and the respondent's degree of belief in the claims. The list of case features we provided in the postcard survey was also included in the detailed questionnaire.

We surveyed nearly 20,000 professionals, about equally divided into clinical psychologists who were members of the American Psychological Association (APA), psychiatrists who were members of the American Psychiatric Association, and clinical social workers who were members of the National Association of Social Workers (NASW). To increase the likelihood of finding clinicians who had worked with victims of ritualistic abuse, we oversampled certain subcategories of the first two professions. Among clinical psychologists, we randomly selected a subgroup whose primary specialties were clinical, counseling, school, or child, although we also included a random selection of members of the APA representing other clinical specialties. Among psychiatrists, we randomly selected a subgroup of child psychiatrists, some of whom dealt with dissociative disorders and some of whom dealt with any of the other possible child psychiatry specialties. We sampled members of the NASW without regard for their area of specialization because NASW could not provide information regarding specialty categories.

After eliminating invalid respondents (e.g., those who were retired or

TABLE 10.1. List of Case Features

F1	Abuse by a member or members of any cult-like group in which members feel compelled to follow the orders of a leader or leaders
F2	Abuse related to any practice or behavior repeated in a prescribed manner (including prayers, chants, incantations, wearing of special costumes)
F3	Abuse related to symbols (e.g., 666, inverted pentagrams, inverted or broken crosses), invocations, costumes, beliefs, etc. associated with the devil
F4	Abuse related to belief in supernatural, paranormal, occult, or special powers (e.g., magical surgery, calling on spirits, magical flying)
F5	Abuse associated with threats or activities involving graveyards, crypts, bones, the dead, ghosts, etc.
F6	Abuse involving rituals using human or animal excrement or blood
F7	Abuse involving rituals that include special knives, candles, altars, etc.
F8	Abuse involving actual or staged sacrifice or killing of humans
F9	Abuse involving actual or staged torture of humans
F10	Abuse involving actual or staged cannibalism (eating human flesh)
F11	Abuse involving actual or staged sacrifice, killing, or torture of animals.
F12	Ritualistic abuse involving forced participation in or observation of sexual practices
F13	Ritualistic abuse involving child pornography
F14	Ritualistic abuse involving drugs
F15	Abuse involving the withholding of medical care for religious reasons, resulting in harm to a child
F16	Abuse related to attempts to rid a child of the devil or evil spirits
F17	Abuse by religious professional such as priests, rabbis, or ministers
F18	Abuse committed in a religious setting, a religious school, or a religious daycare center
F19	Abuse related to the "breeding" of infants for ritual sacrifice
F20	Ritualistic abuse resulting in amnesic periods or preoccupation with dates
F21	Abuse disclosed by an individual with a dissociative or multiple personality disorder traceable to earlier ritualistic or religious abuse

deceased) from the postcard survey, 6,939 (36%) valid respondents remained. Of these valid respondents, 2,136 (31%) reported that they had encountered at least one ritual or religion-related child or adult abuse case. A detailed survey was sent to each of these clinicians. There were 720 (34%) valid respondents to the detailed survey.

Case Definition

Respondents provided information about a total of 490 cases of ritual or religion-related child abuse reported by adult survivors. As explained next, these cases were classified along three dimensions: repressed memory cases versus non-repressed memory cases, ritual cases versus religion-related cases, and multiple-role cases versus single-role cases.

All the cases were classified as *repressed memory cases* or *non-repressed memory cases*. For a case to be classified as a repressed memory case, it had to satisfy the following criteria: The respondent had to have indicated that feature F20 in Table 10.1 (ritualistic abuse resulting in amnesic periods or preoccupation with dates) was a feature of the case (with the exceptions noted later). There also had to be clear language in response to any survey question to indicate that the memories of past experiences had allegedly been lost (e.g., "repressed memories," "amnesia," "lost memories," "blackout episodes," and "reliving forgotten experiences"). In three cases, although F20 was not checked, the respondent provided a clear indication of repressed memory (e.g., one respondent wrote, "therapy released repressed memory"). In some cases involving MPD, when the clinician told us that some "alter personalities" evidenced memory repression and some did not, the case was classified as a repressed memory case. Furthermore, we counted only repressed *explicit* memory in contrast to memories that took the form of physical reactions to stimuli without cognitive images or other explicit mental content. non-repressed memory cases were those in which respondents did not indicate that F20 was a feature and also gave no other indication of memory loss.

In most of the cases, the client's only role was that of abuse victim. These cases were referred to as *single-role cases*. In other cases, the client was a victim but also occupied other roles, such as perpetrator or relative of another victim. These cases were referred to as *multiple-role cases*. It seemed likely that the multiple-role cases would involve the most extreme allegations.

Using these two classifications (i.e., repressed vs. non-repressed memory case and single-role vs. multiple-role case), we identified 43 repressed memory cases (12 of which were multiple-role) and 447 non-repressed memory cases (38 of which were multiple-role). Because there were only three religion-related repressed memory cases, we grouped together ritual and religion-related cases for most purposes, although we distinguish between these two types of cases when it is informative to do so. Finally, the findings reported in this chapter were not generally affected by respondent profession (i.e., type of clinician), so we do not discuss differences among clinical psychologists, psychiatrists, and social workers (but see Goodman, Qin, Bottoms, & Shaver, 1993). Instead, our major goal was to compare the characteristics of repressed memory and non-repressed memory cases.[1]

Case Characteristics

Case Features

For each case in our sample, we were interested in examining the presence or absence of each case feature listed in Table 10.1. We did not concern ourselves with F20, however, because it was used in defining repressed and non-repressed memory cases. As Table 10.2 illustrates, respondents were generally more likely to indicate abuse features in repressed memory and multiple-role cases than in non-repressed memory and single-role cases. In addition, it was common for multiple-role repressed memory cases to involve extreme case features, such as "abuse associated with threats or activities involving grave-yards, crypts, bones, the dead, ghosts, etc." (F5) and "abuse involving actual or staged cannibalism" (F10). The pattern of results clearly indicates that repressed memory cases, especially those in which multiple roles of clients were claimed, were more likely to involve various bizarre and horrible abuse scenarios, such as sacrifice or killing of humans (F8), cannibalism (F10), and baby "breeding" for the purpose of ritual sacrifice (F19).

Abuse Types

Respondents indicated whether their cases included sexual abuse, physical abuse, psychological abuse, murder, or neglect. Repressed memory cases were more likely to involve murder than non-repressed memory cases, and multi-ple-role cases were more likely to involve neglect than single-role cases. When

TABLE 10.2. Proportion of Case Features

		Case type			Client role		
		RM	NRM	$F(1, 486)$	SR	MR	$F(1,486)$
F1	Cult member	.67	.33	14.84***	.33	.66	16.49***
F2	Repeated practices	.65	.30	16.82***	.30	.60	12.94***
F3	Devil symbols	.67	.22	37.44***	.23	.54	15.39***
F4	Supernatural	.44	.15	15.03***	.15	.48	28.37***
F5	Graveyards, etc.	.49	.12	35.03***	.13	.38	14.20***
F6	Excrement, blood	.74	.22	47.99***	.23	.64	29.93***
F7	Knives, candles	.79	.21	66.59***	.23	.56	15.73***
F8	Human sacrifice	.70	.20	45.15***	.20	.64	38.82***
F9	Human torture	.63	.22	27.37***	.21	.60	27.84***
F10	Cannibalism	.37	.07	29.45***	.06	.42	60.05***
F11	Animal sacrifice	.74	.19	62.50***	.21	.54	17.31***
F12	Forced sex	.84	.43	22.11***	.44	.70	7.34**
F13	Child pornography	.26	.10	5.62*	.09	.30	15.86***
F14	Drugs	.51	.14	35.43***	.15	.36	8.04**
F15	Medical neglect	.00	.03	—	.02	.08	5.41*
F16	Beating devil out	.07	.13	1.05	.13	.10	<1
F17	Abuse by clergy	.12	.30	4.94*	.30	.14	4.09*
F18	Religious setting	.07	.20	3.34	.20	.10	1.83
F19	Baby breeding	.35	.05	42.36***	.05	.28	23.09***
F20	Amnesia	.93	.00	—	.06	.24	—
F21	Dissociation, MPD	.86	.34	43.55***	.37	.54	1.36

Note. RM, repressed memory cases; NRM, non-repressed memory cases; SR, single-role cases; MR, multiple-role cases. Mean differences for F16, F17, and F18 were no longer significant when ritual versus religion-related abuse was statistically controlled through analysis of covariance.
* $p < .05$; ** $p < .01$; *** $p < .001$.

the total number of abuse types per case was considered, repressed memory and multiple-role cases involved more types of abuse than did nonrepressed and single-role cases. This is further indication that the alleged abuse was more severe in repressed and multiple-role cases than non-repressed memory and single-role cases.

Victim and Perpetrator Characteristics

Number of Victims and Perpetrators

Repressed and multiple-role cases involved more victims as well as more perpetrators than nonrepressed and single-role cases, respectively (see Table 10.3). The number of victims and number of perpetrators reported to be involved in the abuse cases were highest for multiple-role repressed memory cases: On average, a multiple-role repressed memory case allegedly involved 52 victims and 43 perpetrators. However, some cases were said to involve *hundreds* of victims and perpetrators! When these outlier cases were removed from the analyses, the alleged numbers of victims and perpetrators were still higher in repressed memory cases and multiple-role cases than in non-repressed memory cases and single-role cases, although statistically significant differences were eliminated. Thus, a few outlier cases exacerbated weak

TABLE 10.3. Victim and Perpetrator Characteristics: Means and *F* Values

	Case type			Client role		
	RM	NRM	F	SR	MR	F
Number of victims ($df = 1, 361$)						
All cases	17.5	3.6	14.53***	3.6	17.5	14.40***
Outliers excluded	3.4	3.6	< 1	3.6	3.4	< 1
Number of perpetrators ($df = 1, 316$)						
All cases	26.7	5.8	21.33***	6.7	17.4	2.49
Outliers excluded	6.9	4.2	5.29*	4.2	7.0	7.42**
Victims' ages						
Abuse began ($df = 1, 379$)	2.8	7.3	27.01***	7.1	5.3	2.71
Abuse ended ($df = 1, 344$)	14.6	14.0	< 1	14.0	15.5	1.97
Abuse discovered ($df = 1, 368$)	36.0	29.3	11.96***	30.0	31.3	< 1
Years elapsed from abuse to therapy ($df = 1, 412$)	19.0	16.6	2.39	17.1	14.9	2.24

Note. RM, repressed memory cases; NRM, non-repressed memory cases; SR, single-role cases; MR, multiple-role cases. Mean differences were no longer significant when outliers were excluded and ritual versus religion-related abuse was statistically controlled through analysis of covariance.
* $p < .05$; ** $p < .01$; *** $p < .001$.

general trends, making the findings particularly extreme for repressed memory and multiple-role cases.

Victims' Ages

Table 10.3 also presents the means of the victims' ages when the abuse began, ended, and was discovered and the years that elapsed between the abuse and therapy. The alleged abuse typically began earlier in repressed memory cases and tended to end later in multiple-role repressed memory cases ($M = 20.7$ years) than in any other types of cases. The abuse was also discovered later in repressed memory cases than in non-repressed memory cases. Interestingly, although one might suspect that repressed memory cases would involve longer delays before being disclosed in therapy, the years between abuse and therapy did not differ for different kinds of cases. Again, outliers' responses affected these results. When outliers were excluded, mean differences were no longer significant. In summary, the alleged abuse began earlier and lasted longer in repressed memory cases than in non-repressed memory cases. The alleged abuse in multiple-role repressed memory cases ended significantly later than in any other type of case. However, extreme claims by several respondents contributed to these findings.

Relationship between Perpetrators and Victims

Parents and persons in positions of trust were by far the most likely individuals to be accused of satanic and religion-related abuse. For instance, strangers were the alleged perpetrators in only 2% of the cases, whereas parents were the alleged perpetrators in 53% of the cases. The victim–perpetrator relationship was not significantly different for repressed and non-repressed memory cases. It is of interest that parents were so often reported as perpetrators of ritual abuse. There is little reason to suspect that should satanic child abusing cults exist, they would prefer to prey on their own children rather than those of others. However, in theory, it is possible that repeated parental abuse would lead to repressed memory. Thus it was surprising that the victim–perpetrator relationship did not significantly differ across case type.

Presenting Symptoms and Diagnoses

Bottoms and Davis (1997) proposed that certain vulnerable clients would be more likely than others to develop false memories of ritual abuse (see also Shaver et al., 1995; Spanos, 1996). It was therefore of interest to examine respondents' reports of the symptoms their clients exhibited when they first entered therapy. Regardless of case type (repressed vs. non-repressed memory), the majority of clients initially suffered from depression. A high proportion of clients in both kinds of cases also suffered from suicidal ideation.

Overall, however, no presenting symptom alone was associated with repressed memory cases.

Respondents were asked to provide diagnoses of their clients according to the revised third edition of the *Diagnostic and Statistical Manual of Mental Disorders* (DSM-III-R; American Psychiatric Association, 1987). Repressed memory cases included more diagnoses of MPD and eating disorders but fewer diagnoses of PTSD and other personality disorders than in non-repressed memory cases. The high proportion of MPD diagnoses in repressed memory cases was striking: 68% of the clients in repressed memory cases supposedly qualified for an MPD diagnosis. Also, multiple-role cases included more diagnoses of MPD than single-role cases.

A Critical Analysis of the Case Evidence

In the survey, respondents were asked to specify any evidence of which they were aware (but had not necessarily seen directly) for the abuse itself and, separately, for the ritual and religious aspects of the abuse. All relevant evidence was classified into four categories: corroboration from others, physical evidence, medical evidence, and perpetrator confession. We examined all statements of relevant evidence regardless of their likely quality. Thus, evidence that some would consider quite ambiguous or unconvincing (e.g., pentagrams on walls, satanic books, or artifacts) was nevertheless considered. Furthermore, it should be kept in mind that what we term "evidence" was based completely on clinicians' reports. We did not ask to see the evidence and do not know in most cases whether the clinician saw or verified the evidence described to us.

A perpetrator's confession would be strong evidence, though not indisputable proof, of the abuse itself and for the ritual and religious aspects of the abuse. However, respondents reported perpetrator confession in only a small proportion of single-role non-repressed memory cases, and no confessions were reported in any other type of case. When the evidence for abuse itself (not the ritual or religious aspects) was considered, a higher proportion of repressed memory than of non-repressed memory cases involved medical evidence. Repressed memory cases also had more total evidence than non-repressed memory cases. A higher proportion of multiple-role cases had corroboration from others and medical evidence than single-role cases. Multiple-role cases also had more total evidence than single-role cases. For evidence of ritual and religious aspects of abuse, there were no significant differences for repressed versus non-repressed memory cases or single- versus multiple-role cases.

We wanted to examine the exact nature of the evidence involved in repressed memory cases. There were 16 repressed memory cases involving evidence for the abuse itself; in 3 there was corroboration from others; in 1, physical evidence, and in the other 12, medical evidence. The reported physical evidence was, "Client talks of cemetery which we visited. She showed me babies' graves before she was close enough to read tombstones." The respondent implied that the client must have known about the babies' graves from satanic rituals, but surely the client could have become familiar with the cemetery in other ways. As for the 12 repressed memory cases with medical evidence, 7 were reported by one respondent who said there was "no supporting evidence other than scars, etc." (The respondent did not indicate whether the scars were actually visible to him or her.) Another three cases, also reported by one respondent, had "MPD, scars on body, ongoing attempts by cult to recontact patient." The other two cases had evidence such as "scars and marks on body areas patient unable to reach; carved symbols patient would be unable to self-inflict" and "patient memory, unable to have children; wagon wheel, electric prods up vagina, drugs, blood." In some of these cases, more than 100 victims and more than 100 perpetrators were said to be involved. Nearly all the ritual case features, such as rituals involving human or animal excrement or blood, torture and sacrifice or killing of humans, cannibalism, child pornography, forced participation in or observation of sexual practices, and so on, were supposedly involved in these cases. Yet despite the extreme brutality of the alleged abuse and the large number of people involved, the best evidence consisted of scars on the body, which by themselves do not unambiguously point to satanic ritual abuse. For example, even if these scars resulted from abuse, which is open to question, the abuse might not have included any satanic ritual component.

Regarding evidence of ritual and religion-related elements of abuse, only four repressed memory cases in our sample were bolstered by evidence—corroboration from others in one case and physical evidence in the other three cases. The case with corroboration from other people was a religion-related case: The client's friend remembered an abusing priest's name, the client's brother remembered specifics about the setting, but none of them corroborated the alleged abuse. The physical evidence for the other three cases included, respectively, (1) "patient gave detailed description of articles used in ritual"; (2) "voodoo dolls found, witchcraft"; (3) "satanic symbols carved on abdomen and limbs." None of the evidence indicated conclusively the existence of the bizarre and horrible satanic ritual abuse scenarios that allegedly occurred in many repressed memory cases. For instance, carvings of satanic symbols could be self-inflicted.

Overall, the results indicated that although repressed memory cases involved more evidence for abuse itself than non-repressed memory cases, they produced no more evidence for ritual and religion-related aspects of the abuse than non-repressed memory cases. More important, close examination of the evidence involved in repressed memory cases indicated that the evidence clinicians reported was weak and ambiguous.

Respondents' Case Validity Judgment

Clinician respondents were asked to make dichotomous judgments concerning the validity of allegations of ritual or religious aspects of the cases described in our survey. It is possible for a clinician to believe that the abuse itself had occurred but not believe the ritual or religion-related elements of the case. Thus, respondents were also asked to make judgments of the validity of allegations of harm (abuse, murder, etc.) separately. Because some respondents indicated "maybe," a third score was added (0 = false, 1 = maybe, and 2 = true). For the allegations of harm, the mean validity scores were 2.00 for repressed, 1.91 for nonrepressed, 1.92 for single-role, and 1.90 for multiple-role cases. For the ritual and religious features, the mean validity scores were 1.95 for repressed, 1.82 for nonrepressed, 1.82 for single-role, and 1.88 for multiple-role cases. In other words, therapists nearly always believed their clients. Interestingly, although the relations were not strong and accounted for only a small percentage of the variance in clinicians' responses, clinicians were particularly likely to believe the ritual and religion-related elements of a case when highly bizarre and extreme features were involved and the alleged abuse began early in a client's life. Disturbingly, we did not find a significant relation between validity judgments of allegations regarding ritual and religion-related elements and the amount of total evidence for ritual and religion-related elements of the abuse.

Thus, respondents overwhelmingly tended to believe their clients' claims both of harm and of the ritual or religious nature of the alleged abuse. Their judgments of allegations of ritual and religion-related elements were related to the number of bizarre features involved in the case and the victims' ages when the alleged abuse began but were unrelated to evidence of ritual and religious elements of abuse.

A SURVEY OF CLINICIANS

The findings from our initial survey sparked many questions, particularly about the respondents' convictions. What was the nature of the belief systems of clinicians who reported satanic ritual abuse and repressed memory? What was the level of these professionals' training? Was ritual abuse the most frequent type of repressed memory case or was ritual abuse simply a subset of a larger group of acts that allegedly resulted in repressed memory?

To address these questions, we distributed a second questionnaire, which we describe only briefly here (see Bottoms, Beety, Goodman, Tyda, & Shaver, 1995; Bottoms, Diviak, Goodman, & Shaver, 1996, for further details). Specifically, as a follow-up to our initial study, we surveyed 760 clinical members of the American Psychological Association, one-third of whom responded to our initial survey saying they had encountered a case of ritualistic or religion-related abuse, one-third of whom responded to our initial survey saying they had *not* encountered a case of ritualistic or religion-related abuse, and one-third of whom were randomly sampled from among 6,000 practicing clinicians who were not part of our original sample. The response rate was 47%. We asked a number of questions about the types of repressed memory cases the clinicians had encountered in their practice, the clinicians' own beliefs regarding satanic abuse and repressed memory, and the clinicians' training.

As part of the survey, we asked clinicians who had encountered repressed memory cases to describe the types of trauma allegedly repressed by their clients. Our findings were striking but not unexpected. Of the various repressed memory cases reported to us, those involving sexual abuse were by far the most likely to include repressed memory claims. In fact, 90% of the repressed memory cases involved alleged sexual abuse. Repressed memories of other acts such as satanic ritual abuse (16%), physical abuse (36%), and witnessed murder (10%) were also reported but less frequently. Thus, repressed memory cases were not specifically associated with allegations of satanic ritual abuse, but they were closely associated with allegations of sexual abuse.

In the survey, we measured clinicians' beliefs about a variety of issues related to satanic abuse and repressed memory. The beliefs fell into three categories: belief in ritual abuse, belief that ritual abuse is not a product of suggestion, and belief in repressed memory. Interestingly, these three kinds of beliefs were highly interrelated (correlations ranged from .52 to .62; $ps < .01$). There was thus a strong tendency for clinicians who believed in repressed memories also to believe in ritualistic abuse claims and to believe that such claims are not the product of suggestion, although there were many clinicians who did not adhere to this constellation of beliefs.

Some writers hypothesize that clinicians who do not hold PhD degrees or who obtained graduate degrees from less prestigious institutions are more likely to believe in ritual abuse and repressed memories (e.g., Dawes, 1994). In our sample (14% of which consisted of clinicians with PsyDs, EdDs, or MAs), however, there were no significant relations between, on the one hand, belief in repressed memory and ritual abuse and, on the other hand, respondents' highest academic degree or the prestige of the institution from which they obtained their highest degree.

In summary, allegations of repressed memory for ritual abuse are a subset of a larger group of repressed memory cases, the vast majority of which involve claims of sexual abuse. Clinicians who believe in the reality of satanic ritual abuse also tend to believe in repressed memory and believe that such memories are not the result of suggestion. These clinicians did not necessarily graduate from less prestigious institutions or obtain degrees other than the PhD.

IMPLICATIONS

A main goal of our initial study was to identify characteristics of repressed memory cases involving ritual or religion-related abuse allegations. Our results indicated that repressed memory cases, especially those in which clients allegedly occupied multiple roles, tended to be particularly extreme and often involved bizarre features. As compared to non-repressed memory cases, repressed memory cases were often associated with a diagnosis of MPD,

claims involving more types of abuse, and many more victims and perpetrators; abuse that allegedly began earlier and lasted longer; and more extreme
and severe case features. Consistent with the results of several previous studies
(e.g., Briere & Conte, 1993; Herman & Schatzow, 1987; Williams, 1994),
repressed memory cases in our sample were related to allegations of early
onset of abuse and severity of abuse. We also found that repressed memory
was related to allegations of a longer duration of abuse. However, we did not
replicate Williams's (1994) finding that repressed memory was related to a
close victim–perpetrator relationship. One important difference between
Williams's (1994) investigation and those of Briere and Conte (1993), Herman
and Schatzow (1987), and ours is that the abuse cases in Williams's research
were reported initially in childhood and did not rely exclusively on adults'
self-reports.

In our initial study, clinicians assigned high credibility to their clients'
claims. Regarding the ritual and religion-related case elements, there was a
trend for clinicians to believe the more extreme and severe allegations. In
repressed memory cases with multiple-role clients, clinicians unanimously
believed that allegations of harm were true, and they almost unanimously
agreed that the allegations of ritual and religion-related aspects of the abuse
were also true.

With the present results in hand, one has to wonder whether the clinicians'
beliefs were justified. One especially disturbing finding that emerged from our
study was that clinicians' acceptance of their clients' claims of ritual abuse was
not related to the evidence at hand but to the number of bizarre and extreme
features involved in the alleged abuse. However, even these latter relations were
not strong and accounted for a relatively small amount of the variability in
clinicians' responses concerning their acceptance of ritual abuse claims. Perhaps, as suggested by the findings of our second survey, individual-difference
factors among clinicians, such as belief in repressed memory, are better
predictors of clinicians' judgments than is case evidence.

Because our survey was based on reports regarding actual cases, we
cannot say with certainty which of the allegations were true and which were
false. However, it is instructive to examine the evidence that clinicians cited
(i.e., as reported to them by clients or that the clinicians actually had seen) for
repressed memory cases. Our close examination revealed no unequivocal
evidence for ritual or religious aspects of abuse, even when the abuse was
alleged to be quite severe. For example, in one case the abuse allegedly began
in 1955 when the patient was only 1 year old, and it "never ended" according
to the clinician respondent. The alleged abuse included actual or staged
sacrifice of humans and animals. According to the respondent, the "patient
was ritualistically abused by family of origin and also ritualistically abused by
psychiatrist and psychologist as an adult with MPD." Considering the severity
of these cases and the bizarre claims involved (e.g., ritualistic abuse by mental
health professionals), the evidence was astonishingly weak and ambiguous.
Almost all the physical evidence could be explained by factors other than

satanic ritual abuse. For example, the patient's detailed description of articles used and rituals enacted does not necessarily verify the allegations; the patient may have acquired the knowledge from other sources, such as popular writings and media stories about satanic ritual abuse (Coons, 1994).

Given the extreme claims associated with repressed memory cases (e.g., human sacrifice), one would expect that there would be more evidence of ritual or religious aspects of abuse in the repressed memory cases than in the non-repressed memory cases. Our findings indicate that based on clinicians' reports, repressed memory cases had more total evidence of abuse itself than non-repressed memory cases. This finding is in line with the view that although the ritual aspects of the abuse may not have been genuine, some kind of severe abuse may have occurred in at least a subset of the repressed memory cases (e.g., Ganaway, 1989; Lanning, 1991). However, when the total amount of evidence for ritual and religious aspects of abuse was considered, there was no significant difference between repressed memory cases and non-repressed memory cases despite the more extreme features of repressed memory cases. This means that the satanic ritual aspects of the alleged abuse were largely unsubstantiated.

What kind of evidence would one expect to exist? If hundreds of victims and perpetrators were involved, more corroboration (such as stories from other victims in the same cases) might be expected. (And in fact, in cases such as the one involving Father Porter, mentioned earlier, there was such multivictim corroboration.) If there were indeed torture and sacrifice of humans, murder, and cannibalism, more hard evidence, such as victims' remains, should have been found.

A high proportion of clients in the repressed memory cases were diagnosed with MPD. Despite the possibility of high suggestibility in MPD patients, clinicians who provided descriptions of these cases nevertheless believed their clients' claims and were willing to accept ambiguous evidence as verification of the abuse. For example, in response to the question "In your professional opinion, do you think the allegations of harm (abuse, murder, etc.) were true or false?," the respondent who provided seven cases with medical evidence, wrote: "Child has not made allegations. I suspect abuse based on parental memories." This same respondent also wrote: "For all patients, dissociated memories of abuse, previously unknown to patients, came to light during therapy. Specific details of abuse are difficult to list, because recollections by patients are partial and increase with duration of therapy. Much abuse is denied. Cult perpetrators are excellent at hiding/destroying evidence and doing 'unbelievable' acts." Such examples strengthen our suspicion that the belief systems of some clinicians foster allegations of ritual abuse and repressed memory.

Our second survey, which concentrated on clinicians' ideas and training, indeed revealed that some therapists possess belief systems that may contribute to allegations of repressed memories of ritualistic abuse. Clinicians who believed in repressed memory were also likely to embrace ritual abuse claims and believe that ritual abuse allegations are not the product of suggestion. However, certainly, there are also many clinicians who adhere to repressed memory theories but do not believe or encourage allegations of satanic abuse. It is notable that, consistent with Bottoms and Davis's (1997) model, a constellation of clinical assumptions exist which appear likely to foster the emergence of allegations of ritual abuse in the therapeutic context. When clinicians with such predispositions encourage ritual abuse memories in vulnerable (e.g., depressed, highly religious) clients, the co-creation of repressed memories of satanic abuse may result.

By way of caveats concerning our research, we want first to emphasize that the repressed memory cases in our first survey constitute a special subset of all repressed memory cases. We explicitly sought clinical cases that involved allegations of ritual or religion-related child maltreatment. As indicated by the findings of our second survey, ritual abuse cases generate only a small fraction of the total number of repressed memory claims, and they are among the most bizarre and extreme. Thus, our results cannot be generalized to all repressed memory cases. Second, the clinicians who reported cases to us constituted a select group. Not only did we oversample certain categories of clinicians, we then concentrated on ones who had encountered cases of ritual and religion-related abuse in their practices. Some of our results were colored by the few clinicians who reported a high number of dramatic cases, particularly a high number of ritual abuse cases involving large numbers of victims and perpetrators. Most clinicians had encountered few or no cases and thus were clearly not fostering false ritual abuse or repressed memory claims. However, our initial survey was constructed just before repressed memory cases gained widespread public and scientific attention and thus we did not mention "repressed memory" directly. Instead, we asked about amnesia, which had been mentioned in the ritual abuse literature. It is possible that if we had used the term "repressed memory," more cases would have been reported. In any case, a third caveat is that our results may not replicate today: Clinicians' belief in satanic cult abuse seems to have lessened since the time of our survey, partly because of the lack of evidence for widespread child abuse by satanic cults. Fourth, it is worth reemphasizing that our data do not permit us to say with certainty that the ritual or religion-related abuse cases included in our study were true or false. We also do not mean to imply that there are no valid cases of repressed memory or dissociation that make certain memories inaccessible. One of the great challenges for researchers today is to develop methods that allow us to determine scientifically whether there are various forms of inaccessible but recoverable memories and if so, to determine their precise nature. Current methods fall short of these important goals. Nevertheless, we hope our data are informative to professionals interested in the characteristics of repressed memory cases involving allegations of ritual and religion-related child abuse.

CONCLUSION

How can we best summarize our findings? First, the evidence that clinicians provided to us was weak given the extreme and bizarre nature of the ritualistic abuse allegations. Second, a large proportion of the "evidence" came only from a few clinicians. We are left wishing that we could observe the therapy sessions of these particular professionals. It is likely that a small subset of individuals played a disproportionate role in creating what some writers have called a "satanic panic" (Victor, 1994), and in damaging the public's and fellow professionals' (e.g., Dawes, 1994) impression of psychotherapists. Third, clinicians' acceptance of ritual and religious elements of cases was not related to the amount of evidence provided but to the bizarreness and extremity of the allegations. Fourth, there was no unequivocal evidence pointing to large-scale, well-organized satanic cults. Almost all the evidence could be explained by factors other than satanic ritual abuse. Fifth, a number of clinicians, regardless of highest level of their degrees or the prestige of the institution from which their degrees were obtained, hold a set of beliefs that may foster allegations of repressed memories of ritualistic abuse. We can thus hypothesize that there is a subset of clinicians who accept, and even help to create, "false memories" of satanic ritual abuse. These clinicians are willing to accept ambiguous evidence, some of which they unwittingly generate themselves, as proof of the existence of satanic cults.

Of course, one can always attribute the lack of good evidence to satanic cult members' extreme skillfulness in hiding and destroying it. This kind of paranoid and magical reasoning—common in discussions of ritual abuse—is difficult to counter decisively. We doubt that all the allegations involved in the repressed memory cases we studied were false. In fact, there may be considerable truth in some of the allegations. We are skeptical, however, that all the allegations in the repressed memory cases, especially those related to ritual and religion-related features, were literally true. One way to help resolve the ritual abuse debate, it seems to us, is to conduct further research on the particular kinds of clients and clinicians who account for the vast majority of allegations. If some special combination of sociocultural factors, client predisposition, and therapist beliefs and procedures accounts for most ritualistic and repressed memory cases, it is important to find out more about this special combination. It may continue to generate problems for clients and therapists under other than satanic guises long after the ritual abuse scare has passed. Claims of UFO abduction (Mack, 1994) provide a telling example.

ACKNOWLEDGMENTS

The research reported here was funded by the National Center on Child Abuse and Neglect (Department of Health and Human Services) and the University of Illinois at Chicago Campus Research Board. The studies were conducted in collaboration with Alexis Thompson and with the assistance of Kathleen Diviak, Jim Brandt, Jason H. Brown, Kathy Cavanaugh, Eugene Colucci, Maureen Coughlin, Leslie Dreblat, Brian Flaherty, Erica Howard, Charlotte Johnson, Noelle Kardos, Todd Karl, Wendy Landman, Ron Lelito, Tim Lundy, Lynn Nuzzo, Anne Orgren, Kimberly Packard, Steve Pawlowski, Chowdry Pinnamaneni, Isaura Pulido, Susan Reisch, Chris Rhoadhouse, Karleen Robinson, Julie Rothbard, Tracey Schneider, Lisa Thurbush, Chris Toonder, and Kimberly Tyda. Tina Brown and Michael Raulin kindly consulted on the use of DSM diagnostic categories. Phillips Stevens, Kenneth Lanning, Robin Mermelstein, and David McKirnan provided valuable consultation. We extend special thanks to the professionals who completed our surveys.

NOTE

1. When cell sizes rendered statistical analyses possible, results described in this chapter were based on a series of 2 (case type: repressed memory cases vs. nonrepressed memory cases) × 2 (client role: single vs. multiple) analyses of variance (ANOVAs). Also, because a larger percentage of religion-related abuse cases fell in the nonrepressed than the repressed memory category, we covaried the dichotomous ritual versus religion-related abuse variable from our analyses. When the analysis of covariance eliminated statistically significant mean differences, the lack of significance is indicated in table notes.

REFERENCES

Alpert, J. L., Brown, L. S., Ceci, S. J., Courtois, C. A., Loftus, E. F., & Ornstein, P. A. (1996). *Final conclusions of the APA working group on investigation of memories of childhood abuse* (pp. 1–14). Washington, DC: American Psychological Association.

American Psychiatric Association. (1987). *Diagnostic and statistical manual of mental disorders* (rev. 3rd ed.). Washington, DC: Author.

Bottoms, B. L., Beety, K., Goodman, G. S., Tyda, K., & Shaver, P. R. (1995, June). Repressed memory of childhood abuse: A survey of clinicians. In B. L. Bottoms (Chair), *Reactions to repressed memory cases*. Symposium conducted at the meetings of the American Psychological Society, New York.

Bottoms, B. L., & Davis, S. L. (1997). The creation of satanic ritual abuse. *Journal of Social and Clinical Psychology, 16,* 112–132.

Bottoms, B. L., Diviak, K. R., Goodman, G. S., & Shaver, P. R. (1996, March). *Individual differences in therapists' experiences with ritual abuse allegations.* Paper presented at the meetings of the American Psychology and Law Society, Hilton Head, SC.

Bottoms, B. L., Shaver, P. R., & Goodman, G. S. (1996). An analysis of allegations of ritualistic and religion-related child abuse. *Law and Human Behavior, 20,* 1–34.

Bottoms, B. L., Shaver, P. R., Goodman, G. S., & Qin, J. J. (1995). In the name of God: A profile of religion-related child abuse. *Journal of Social Issues, 51,* 85–111.

Briere, J. (1993). *The repressed memory debate.* Invited address to the American Psychological Association Convention, Toronto, Canada.

Briere, J., & Conte, J. (1993). Self-reported amnesia for abuse in adults molested as children. *Journal of Traumatic Stress, 6,* 21–31.

Cameron, C. (1996). Comparing amnesic and nonamnesic survivors of childhood sexual abuse: A longitudinal study. In K. Pezdek & W. Banks (Eds.), *The recovered memory/false memory debate* (pp. 41–68). San Diego, CA: Academic Press.

Coons, P. (1994). Reports of satanic ritual abuse. *Perceptual and Motor Skills, 78,* 1376–1378.

Courtois, C. A. (1992). The memory retrieval process in incest survivor therapy. *Journal of Child Sexual Abuse, 1,* 15–31.

Dawes. R. (1994). *House of cards: Psychology and psychotherapy build on myth.* New York: Free Press.

Elliot, D. M., & Briere, J. (1995). Post-traumatic stress associated with delayed recall of sexual abuse: A general population study. *Journal of Traumatic Stress, 8,* 649–673.

Freud, S. (1957). Repression. In J. Strachey (Ed.). *The standard edition of the complete psychological works of Sigmund Freud* (Vol. 14). London: Hogarth Press. (Original work published 1915)

Ganaway, G. K. (1989). Historical versus narrative truth: Clarifying the role of exogenous trauma in the etiological of MPD and its variants. *Dissociation: Progress in the Dissociative Disorders, 2,* 205–220.

Ganaway, G. K. (1995). Hypnosis, childhood trauma, and dissociative identity disorder: Toward an integrative theory. *International Journal of Clinical and Experimental Hypnosis, 43, 127–144.*

Goodman, G. S., Qin, J. J., Bottoms, B. L., & Shaver, P. R. (1993). *The repressed memory debate: Allegations of ritual and religion-related child abuse.* Paper presented at the Clark University Conference on Trauma and Memory, Worcester, MA.

Herman, J. L. (1992). *Trauma and recovery.* New York: Basic Books.

Herman, J. L., & Schatzow, E. (1987). Recovery and verification of memories of childhood sexual trauma. *Psychoanalytic Psychology, 4,* 1–14.

Holmes, D. S. (1990). The evidence for repression: An examination of sixty years of research. In J. Singer (Ed.). *Repression and dissociation: Implications for personality, theory, psychopathology, and health* (pp. 85–102). Chicago: University of Chicago Press.

Horn, M. (1993, November 29). Memories lost and found. *U.S. News and World Report,* pp. 52–63.

Hyman, I. E., Husband, T. H., & Billings, F. J. (1995). False memories of childhood experiences. *Applied Cognitive Psychology, 9, 181–197.*

Hyman, I. E., & Pentland, J. (1996). The role of mental imagery in the creation of false childhood memories. *Journal of Memory and Language, 35,* 101–117.

Jonker, F., & Jonker-Bakker, P. (1991). Experiences with ritualistic child sexual abuse: A case study from the Netherlands. *Child Abuse and Neglect, 15,* 191–196.

Kluft, R. (1985). *Childhood antecedents of multiple personality.* Washington, DC: American Psychiatric Press.

Lanning, K. V. (1991). Ritual abuse: A law enforcement view or perspective. *Child Abuse and Neglect, 15,* 171–173.

Lindsay, D. S., & Read, J.D. (1994). Psychotherapy and memories of childhood sexual abuse: A cognitive perspective. *Applied Cognitive Psychology, 8,* 277–280.

Lindsay, D. S., & Read, J.D. (1995). "Memory work" and recovered memories of child sexual abuse: Scientific evidence and public, professional, and personal issues. *Psychology, Public Policy, and Law, 4,* 846–908.

Loftus, E. F. (1993). The reality of repressed memories. *American Psychologist, 48,* 518–537.

Loftus, E. F., & Pickrell, J. E. (1995). The formation of false memories. *Psychiatric Annals, 25,* 720–725.

Loftus, E. F., Polonsky, S., & Fullilove, M. T. (1994). Memories of childhood sexual abuse: Remembering and repressing. *Psychology of Women Quarterly, 18,* 67–84.

Mack, J. (1994). *Abduction: Human encounters with aliens.* New York: Scribner's.

Mulhern, S. (1991). Satanism and psychotherapy: A rumor in search of an inquisition. In J. T. Richardson, J. Best, J., & D. G. Bromley (Eds.), *The satanism scare* (pp. 145–172). New York: Aldine de Gruyter.

Newman, L. S., & Baumeister, R. F. (1996). Toward an explanation of the UFO abduction phenomenon: Hypnotic elaboration, extraterrestrial sadomasochism, and spurious memories. *Psychological Inquiry, 7,* 99–126.

Ofshe, R. J. (1992). Inadvertent hypnosis during interrogation: False confession due to dissociative state, mis-identified multiple personality, and the satanic cult hypothesis. *International Journal of Clinical and Experimental Hypnosis, 40,* 125–156.

Ofshe, R. J. (1993). *The making of monsters.* Paper presented at the International Conference of Sex Researchers, Asilomar, CA.

Ofshe, R. J., & Watters, E. (1994). *Making of monsters: False memories, psychotherapy, and sexual hysteria.* New York: Charles Scribner's Sons.

Pendergrast, M. (1995). *Victims of memory: Incest accusations and shattered lives.* Hinesberg, VT: Upper Access Press.

Pezdek, K., Finger, K., & Hodge, D. (1997). Planting false childhood memories: The role of event plausibility. *Psychological Science, 8,* 437–441.

Poole, D. A., Lindsay, D. S., Memon, A., & Bull, R. (1995). Psychotherapy and the recovery of memories of childhood sexual abuse: U.S. and British practitioners' opinions, practices, and experiences. *Journal of Consulting and Clinical Psychology, 63,* 426–437.

Putnam, F. W. (1993). Dissociative disorders in children: Behavioral profiles and problems. *Child Abuse and Neglect, 17,* 39–45.

Richardson, J. T., Best, J., & Bromley, D. G. (1991). (Eds.). *The satanism scare.* New York: Aldine de Gruyter.

Rogers, M. L. (1992). A call for discernment—natural and spiritual: An introductory editorial to a special issue on SRA. *Journal of Psychology and Theology, 20,* 175–186.

Shaver, P. R., Bottoms, B. L., & Goodman, G. S. (1995). The co-creation of satanic ritual abuse. In R. Baumeister (Chair), *Bizarre phenomena: The social animal at the outer limits.* Symposium conducted at the American Psychological Association Convention, New York.

Sheler, J. (1993, November 9). Trials that test faith. *U.S. News and World Report,* p. 64.

Singer, J. L. (1990) Preface: A fresh look at repression, dissociation, and the defenses as mechanisms and as personality styles. In J. Singer (Ed.), *Repression and dissociation: Implications for personality, theory, psychopathology, and health* (pp. xi–xxi). Chicago: University of Chicago Press.

Smith, B., Elstein, S. G., Trost, T., & Bulkley, J. (1993). *The prosecution of child sexual and physical abuse cases* (Final report to the National Center on Child Abuse and Neglect, Washington, DC).

Smith, M., & Pazder, L. (1980). *Michelle remembers*. New York: Congdon & Lattes.

Spanos, N. P. (1994). Multiple identity enactments and multiple personality disorder. *Psychological Bulletin, 116*, 143–165.

Spanos, N. P. (1996). *Multiple identities and false memories*. Washington, DC: American Psychological Association.

Victor, J. S. (1993). *Sources of satanic ritual abuse memories in therapist–patient interaction*. Paper presented at the Clark University Conference on Trauma and Memory, Worcester, MA.

Victor, J. S. (1994). *Satanic panic*. Peru, IL: Open Court.

Waterman, J., Kelly, R.J., Oliveri, M. K., & McCord, J. (1993). *Behind the playground walls: Sexual abuse in preschools*. New York: Guilford Press.

Widom, C. S., & Morris, S. (1997). Accuracy of adult recollections of childhood victimization: Part 2. Childhood sexual abuse. *Psychological Assessment, 9*, 34–46.

Williams, L. M. (1994). Recall of childhood trauma: A prospective study of women's memories of child sexual abuse. *Journal of Consulting and Clinical Psychology, 62*, 1167–1185.

Williams, L. (1995). Recovered memories of abuse in women with documented child sexual victimization histories. *Journal of Traumatic Stress, 8*, 649–673.

Wright, L. (1994). *Remembering satan*. New York: Knopf.

Young, W. C., Sachs, R. G., Braun, B. G., & Watkins, R. T. (1991). Patients reporting ritual abuse in childhood: A clinical syndrome, report of 37 cases. *Child Abuse and Neglect, 15*, 181–189.

CHAPTER 11

ABDUCTED BY ALIENS
Spurious Memories of Interplanetary Masochism

Leonard S. Newman
Roy F. Baumeister

People have long speculated about the possible existence of life in the universe beyond our planet. A number of scientists have even argued that there are grounds for being optimistic that one day extraterrestrial life forms will be detected (see Sagan, 1979, 1996), but objective evidence for life on other planets is at this point nonexistent. Nonetheless, recent years have seen a rapid rise in the frequency with which people—especially American citizens—claim to have actually had contact with alien beings. These reported contacts are generally not pleasant ones: More often than not, meeting aliens means being abducted by them. By some estimates (Hopkins, Jacobs, & Westrum, 1992), hundreds or even thousands of Americans are captured every day by extraterrestrials, who take their helpless captives aboard their spacecrafts (or UFOs— unidentified flying objects) and subject them to intimate physical examinations and other indignities. These reports come from individuals who seem normal and well adjusted in other respects. That so many seemingly sane people would report experiences that stretch the bounds of common sense and credulity should be a matter of concern for social scientists, regardless of their beliefs about aliens.

In this chapter, we offer an account of how people come to remember being abducted by aliens. Our assumptions reject the extreme views that have dominated the often acrimonious debate about these reports. In particular, we assume that UFO abduction reports are neither based on actual experiences of abduction by aliens, nor are they outright, deliberate hoaxes. We also concur with the common observation that the people who report these experiences are not obviously mentally ill (Parnell & Sprinkle; 1990; Ring & Rosing, 1990; Spanos, Cross, Dickson, & DuBreuil, 1993). Our task, therefore, is to explain how otherwise sane and normal people could come to believe sincerely that they have been abducted by aliens even when they have not.

Explaining UFO abduction reports will require an understanding of how people can end up sincerely believing their own vivid memories for events that have not objectively occurred. To be more satisfying, however, any explanation of the UFO abduction phenomenon must shed light on why these memories take the particular form they do. Thus, we need to invoke both cognitive processes and motivational patterns to suggest both how and why people develop the false belief that they have been captured by aliens.

Our analysis is based on reports given by victims who claim to have survived such capture and subsequent release by the aliens, as documented in the growing literature on UFOs and UFO abductions. To anticipate our conclusions, we suggest that the cognitive processes that lie behind UFO abduction memories conform to what is already known about the genesis of spurious memories (i.e., that they can be constructed by a combination of suggestive cues, protracted retrieval efforts, and the elaboration of memories and knowledge with uncertain sources during free association or hypnosis) (Bowers & Farvolden, 1996; Clark & Loftus, 1996; Garry & Loftus, 1994; Lynn & Nash, 1994; Spanos, Burgess, & Burgess, 1994). The motivations involve the needs for an escape from self-awareness and loss of identity that have been shown in multiple spheres of motivated behavior and fantasy—particularly sexual masochism, which we argue, closely resembles in many respects the UFO abduction experience. In the typical case, then, a UFO abduction memory begins when someone with a prior interest in UFOs has an unusual and unexplained experience, feeling, or hallucinatory impression and then elaborates these impressions (often with the aid of a hypnotist) by drawing on his or her own latent masochistic fantasies.

Developing an understanding of the genesis of UFO abduction memories is of more than just theoretic interest. Those who identify themselves as abductees are generally people who initially sought out help because of persistent anxieties or other forms of psychological discomfort. If their problems are indeed the consequence of an extraterrestrial encounter, then perhaps uncovering memories of that experience could be a first step toward recovery. If, on the other hand, their discomfort stems from other causes, it is difficult to imagine how believing that one might at any moment be forcibly spirited away by alien life forms to be tormented and humiliated can be of much comfort. Uncritically accepting such disturbing memories may come at great personal cost (see Bottoms & Davis, 1997; Loftus, 1993; Powell & Boer, 1994).

ABDUCTION EXPERIENCES

Frequency

It is impossible to provide a firm estimate of the number of people who believe they have been abducted by aliens. Many abductees may be reluctant to disclose their memories for fear of being disbelieved (and possibly ridiculed or stigmatized). Nonetheless, when Bullard (1994b) surveyed 13 investigators of UFO-related phenomena, he found that even this small number of researchers had a total of 1,700 separate abduction reports in their files. And Whitley Strieber (1993) (author of a detailed first-person account of a series of abductions; Strieber, 1987) claimed that he alone had received 55,000 letters from people who believe that they are abductees, and as many as 200 a week were still arriving. Even more startling is Jacobs's (1992) suggestion that 15 million Americans may have had such experiences. His estimate, however, was based on a simple extrapolation from a survey of students at one university.

Other researchers assert that self-reports of abductions cannot form the basis of an accurate assessment of the extent of the phenomenon because most abductees have had their memories for the experience tampered with by their alien captors. Hopkins et al. (1992) thus included multiple indirect questions in a national survey conducted by the Roper organization designed to estimate the number of abductees in the United States (e.g., respondents were asked whether they recalled ever "waking up paralyzed with a sense of a strange person or presence or something else in the room"). Based on the survey data, Hopkins et al. concluded that 3.7 million Americans had been abducted as of 1992. Klass (1993) noted that if this conclusion is correct, then 340 Americans have been abducted every day since 1961, a number he regards as implausibly high.

Even if the numbers are much lower than some of these estimates, it is clear that there are many thousands of Americans who believe they have had such experiences. Conferences and support groups have even been organized by and for those who believe they are victims of alien abductions (see Bryan, 1995; Geist, 1987; Gordon, 1991; Klass, 1990; Pritchard, Pritchard, Mack, Kasey, & Yapp, 1994).

One difficulty in extrapolating beyond a carefully sampled population is that the reports of abductions do not seem to be uniformly distributed in either space or time. The first reported case was in 1961 (see Fuller, 1966), and the volume of reports has increased in each subsequent decade. Several books and movies have dealt with abductions by aliens, and each popular book or movie has been followed by increases in the frequency of reports (Klass, 1988). We interpret these increases as due to the influence of suggestion on the genesis of spurious memories, although believers would of course claim that the media attention makes people more willing to admit and explore such memories.

Believers might find it more difficult to explain the geographical distribution of abductions. Over half and perhaps as many as 80% of the abductions appear to have occurred in the United States, whereas Asia and Africa have produced almost no such reports (Bullard, 1987a, 1994a; Hynek, 1984; Randles, 1988; Rimmer, 1984). Although it may be flattering to Americans to think that the aliens have singled us out for special study, it is hard to believe that a scientifically advanced civilization would neglect to collect a more diverse and representative sample.

Typical Features

There are by now enough reports of UFO abductions that it is possible to form some generalizations about the experience. Our summary here is mainly based on the detailed accounts presented by Bullard (1987b), Fiore (1989), Hopkins (1987), Jacobs (1992), Lorenzon and Lorenzon (1977), Mack (1994), and Steiger (1988).

Many memories of UFO abductions begin with the sight of an alien spacecraft, sometimes seen merely as a bright light in the sky but at other times seen as a flying saucer or other actual craft. Other memories omit the UFO and begin with the appearance of the strange creatures who soon turn out to be alien beings. The victim, who is often at home or in his or her car, is rendered helpless and often paralyzed, following which he or she is transported aboard the alien craft. It is rare that people recall being transported onto the craft; many memories skip from the initial contact and immobilization by the aliens straight to the unpleasant events on the spaceship. The interior of the spacecraft is typically described as a strange, brightly lit room filled with complex machinery.

The victim is then subjected to what may be considered the "main event": a procedure usually described as a physical examination. He or she is undressed and placed on (or quite often, bound to) an examining table. The examination is usually described as painful, and it may include cutting the skin and probing the various apertures of the body. Apparently, medical procedures such as taking blood samples are often included. The examining aliens, who are described as grim and businesslike humanoids, pay special attention to the genitals of the victims. The genital part of the examination often goes beyond medical inspection and includes some form of sexual contact between the aliens and the victims. Indeed, in recent years more and more reports have emphasized sexual intercourse with the aliens, with some women claiming to have multiple offspring (kept by the aliens) that resulted from these acts (see Hopkins, 1987; Jacobs, 1992, 1994). Several aliens carry out the medical examination, but there are often others present who merely observe it. Subjects report that they feel utterly helpless and at the aliens' mercy during these procedures.

When the examination is finished, the aliens typically make some effort to ensure that the subject does not tell anyone what happened. Sometimes this is no more than a telepathic request not to talk about the event; other times the aliens seem to employ advanced technology to erase the victim's memory of the entire episode.

In some cases, subjects report being taken on a tour of the spacecraft or even being taken on a trip to the aliens' home planet, but these events are far from universal. Victims do not generally recall being returned to their home or car. Also, they do not usually remember the abduction experience itself until the memory is uncovered with the aid of therapy and hypnosis. The actual appearance of the memory may begin with a sense of having lost track of several hours of one's life, but "missing time" is far from a universal concomitant of abduction reports (Bullard, 1996). Other precursors include the discovery of unusual marks or scars on one's body and/or a more vague and uneasy feeling that something strange and inexplicable has occurred. Seeking insight into these unpleasant thoughts and feelings, people might end up consulting with a specialist who is familiar with UFO abductions and who helps them to recover (or reconstruct) the full memory.

COGNITIVE PROCESSES

We regard these reports of UFO abductions as one example of the broader phenomenon of spurious memories. Accordingly, our explanation for *how* people construct such memories is consistent with recent work in cognitive psychology on the genesis of false memories. Many of the same processes may lead people to construct a wide variety of confabulated memories, which may involve sexual abuse in early childhood (Loftus, 1993), victimization by Satanic cults (Bottoms & Davis, 1997; Ofshe, 1992), and even past lives (Spanos, 1987). As much of this work is covered elsewhere in this book, we confine ourselves here to a brief summary to emphasize the motivational aspect of our explanation, which is more unique to UFO abductions. Interested readers can find a fuller treatment of the cognitive genesis of UFO abduction memories in Newman and Baumeister (1996b).

The initial hint or "seed" of a UFO abduction memory may often be a hypnogogic or hypnopompic hallucination (Baker, 1992; Hufford, 1982). These hallucinations occur in the transitional or intermediate state between sleep and wakefulness. Such waking dreams (also known as "sleep paralysis") are fairly common and are in no way linked to psychopathology. They have many features (such as paralysis, the perceived presence of anomalous beings, and even musty smells and shuffling sounds) in common with UFO abduction memories (Baker, 1987; Ellis, 1987).

Why, though, should such experiences (or others) be transformed into memories of encounters with extraterrestrials? To begin with, it is necessary to appreciate that full-blown UFO abduction memories rarely emerge in a spontaneous, unaided fashion. Most of the currently available accounts have only emerged with the aid of hypnosis (Rimmer, 1984). Indeed, estimates of the proportion of UFO abduction accounts that have been obtained without hypnosis are rarely higher than about 30% (e.g., Bullard, 1994b; McLeod, Corbisier, & Mack, 1996). Unfortunately, the elaboration of spurious memories while hypnotized has long been widely recognized among researchers (Lynn & Nash, 1994; Pettinati, 1988). Hypnotic procedures may thus be *creating* rather than *uncovering* UFO abduction memories. Once the person has the beginnings of a memory of UFO abduction, hypnosis can facilitate the addition of many details to elaborate and fill out the episode.

Thus, the typical sequence is for a disturbing and inexplicable fragment of a memory (including hypnogogic or hypnopompic illusions, missing time, or marks on the body) to induce someone to consult a therapist or investigator who hypnotizes the confused and upset subject, whereupon a more thorough and detailed memory of a UFO abduction emerges. Clearly, not all therapists use hypnosis, nor do they all find themselves hearing UFO abduction stories, and so it is reasonable to assume that certain selection factors or predisposing attitudes may operate. It does appear that people who have a prior interest in UFOs are very likely to seek out a therapist who is an expert on such matters. For example, Fiore (1989) described a series of cases of UFO abduction reports, and predisposing factors were apparent in most of them. These antecedent factors included reading Strieber's (1987) book *Communion*, attending seminars on UFOs, and otherwise simply having a long-standing interest in UFOs. Thus, we suggest that people who are interested in UFOs and inclined to believe in them (who, according to Ring and Rosing's [1990] data, tend to be more generally open to paranormal phenomena) are consequently more likely to seek out therapists who specialize in UFOs to explain ambiguous feelings or memory fragments.

Hypnotically recovered memories are known to be susceptible to influence and suggestion by both the hypnotist's and the subject's beliefs (Orne, 1979; Spanos, 1986; Spanos, Menary, Gabora, DuBreuil, & Dewhirst, 1991). Hence, when both hypnotist and subject are inclined to believe in and suspect UFO experiences, the chances that a hypnotically elaborated memory will refer to such an experience is greatly increased. Hypnotherapy sessions relevant to UFO experiences often contain very blatant and obvious encouragement to recover UFO abduction memories (e.g., Fiore, 1989, p. 26; cf. Hall, 1996). And although hypnosis researchers generally support the influence of expectations with very subtle manipulations, subtle pressures may be enough; in fact, influences that are strong enough to have an effect but subtle enough so that they are not recognized as obvious influence attempts may have the strongest impact on people trying to reconstruct past events. People will be more likely to realize that their memories could be contaminated when they recognize obvious attempts to manipulate them (Bowers & Farvolden, 1996; Newman & Baumeister, 1996a).

One additional feature of hypnosis that is very relevant for understanding its role in the spread of the UFO abduction phenomenon is that it appears to increase confidence in the accuracy of one's memories while not increasing accuracy itself (Dywan, 1995; Nogrady, McConkey, & Campbell, 1985; Orne, 1979; Sheehan, 1988). Thus, not only will hypnosis help generate spurious memories of UFO abductions; it will also help people come to believe in the literal reality of the experiences they recall.

To be sure, some UFO abduction memories are not the result of hypnosis. Some critics dismiss these cases as coming from liars or attention seekers, but although there may be some of each, such a blanket condemnation is not necessary. Hypnosis merely facilitates the construction of false abduction memories; it is not a necessary precondition (see Garry & Loftus, 1994). As noted by Lynn and Kirsch (1996), the kind of "memory work" that promotes memory confabulation "encourages fantasy and imagination; is often conducted in a context of assumed accuracy of exhumed memories, which invites participants to adopt a lax standard for distinguishing fantasy and reality; and encourages participants to report more information independent of recall accuracy" (p. 152). Hypnotic inductions as carried out by many UFO abduction investigators arguably have all these important features. Other contexts and procedures do as well, and the most basic pathway to the construction of a false memory may simply be extended fantasizing, free association, and image generation with the guidance of authority figures predisposed to confirm the authenticity of pseudomemories (Loftus, 1993).

Other features of the circumstances in which abductees construct abduction accounts also encourage false memory construction. When people are encouraged to focus on the emotional aspects of real or imagined events, they are less able to distinguish between the two (Suengas & Johnson, 1988). The alleged recovery of abduction memories is often accompanied by intense affective reactions (e.g., see Bryan, 1995), something which may be encouraged by the therapeutic context in which abductees often attempt to recover memories (see Mack, 1994). In addition, Johnson, Foley, Suengas, and Raye (1988; also Johnson, 1995) found that when people are asked to report how they know that an imagined event did not really happen, they usually engage in logical reasoning and appeal to their real-world knowledge (e.g., "The event breaks physical laws about time and space"). Of course, a context that encourages people to seriously consider the possibility of frequent extraterrestrial visitation would undermine this reality monitoring strategy.

Finally, certain people might be more vulnerable than others to the circumstances that promote the construction of false memories in general and UFO abduction accounts in particular. Some researchers argue that abductees may be characterized by high levels of fantasy proneness (Baker, 1987; Bartholomew, Basterfield, & Howard, 1991; see discussions in Newman & Baumeister 1996a, 1996b), an individual difference associated with both high levels of involvement in vivid fantasies and difficulties distinguishing those fantasies from reality (Lynn & Rhue, 1988; Wilson & Barber, 1983). Nickell (1996), in fact, carefully analyzed the 13 alleged abduction cases in John Mack's (1994) heavily publicized book and concluded that all of them displayed many of the characteristics associated with fantasy proneness. Even without formal hypnotic procedures, such people may be willing to construct a full-scale report of an abduction out of puzzling memory fragments, prior knowledge of UFOs, and hallucinatory experiences (hypnogogic, hypnopompic, or otherwise). The ability of fantasy-prone people to mentally generate images without much effort could make them especially prone to confabulate memories; in general, the easier it is to mentally generate an image, the more likely a person is to assume that what they have imagined was once actually perceptually present (Durso & Johnson, 1980; Johnson, Raye, Foley, & Foley, 1981). Clearly, though, a fantasy-prone personality is not necessary for a person to develop the belief that he or she was abducted by aliens.[1]

MOTIVATIONAL PATTERNS

Certain people in certain contexts are thus especially prone to construct false memories, and we argue that when people claim to have been abducted by aliens they tend to be those kinds of people in those kinds of contexts. As for the content of a false memory, it is determined by a person's expectations, knowledge, and the cues to which he or she is exposed, and we also argue that abductees tend to be people with UFO-related knowledge and beliefs who develop their narratives with the help of others who share their biases. The material reviewed earlier, then, may be all that is needed for understanding why people claim to remember encounters with space aliens and why these memories take the particular form they do (see Arndt & Greenberg, 1996). In other words, maybe the prototypical abduction experience described previously is becoming increasingly common simply because it is a story that many people have now heard. If the abduction tales that people learned about in the tabloids and saw featured on television programs described people being welcomed on board spaceships and hailed as the saviors of extraterrestrial civilizations (to pick one hypothetical self-aggrandizing theme), then perhaps the typical abduction experience would instead take that form.

Indeed, many people now are so familiar with the standard abduction script that they can construct similar accounts with a little prodding. For example, Lynn and Pezzo (1994) asked students to role-play the behavior of a hypnotized subject. While doing so, participants were asked to "recall" the details of an incident that involved first seeing mysterious lights in the sky while driving in the country and then noticing 2 hours of missing time. With no more encouragement than that, close to 20% of the participants identified the lights in the sky as a UFO, and with a little more prodding, some reported boarding the craft and interacting with aliens. Other participants were more explicitly cued to imagine contact with extraterrestrials, and they not only did so willingly, but a few also embellished their stories with descriptions of "physical examinations" and even sexual activity. As Lynn and Kirsch (1996) concluded, these data "indicate that the elements of alien contact narratives are widely available to many college students" (p. 154).

Nonetheless, the fact that classic abduction accounts are dominated by pain, humiliation, and loss of control might mean more than just that the first heavily publicized abduction claims also featured these elements. The stories people tell about themselves—be they reconstructions of actual events, confabulations, or acknowledged fantasies—are heavily influenced by their needs and goals (Baumeister & Newman, 1994). In other words, when people recall past events and shape autobiographical accounts, more than just "cold cognitive" considerations are involved (Erdelyi, 1993). That is why we believe that a full explanation of UFO abductions as false memories requires both a cognitive and a motivational component. We turn now to the latter.

At first blush, an explanation of why people might *want* to believe that they experienced a painful and humiliating UFO abduction seems elusive, and several authors such as Jacobs (1992) and Randles (1988) have expressed open skepticism about the possibility that some internal wish, desire, or motive could contribute to the fabrication of such memories, mainly because the experiences seem unpleasant. In Randles's (1988) words, "Who would wish for the trauma these involve?" (p. 200). Yet the desire for seemingly unpleasant experiences is not unknown. The most obvious example of such a motivation is masochism, which is characterized by the quest for painful, helpless, and degrading experiences. We shall argue that masochistic fantasies and UFO abduction memories may spring from the same root. Indeed, the parallels between them seem sufficiently striking that it seems fair to regard many UFO abduction accounts as a form of extraterrestrial masochism. Moreover, the literature on masochism has included some examples of fantasies involving aliens (Schrim, 1982).

Noting parallels between UFO abductions and masochism is far from adequate as an explanation, in part because masochism itself has baffled psychological theorists for decades. Fortunately, recent empirical and theoretical work on masochism has allowed a clearer picture to emerge (see Baumeister, 1988b, 1989; Scott, 1983; Weinberg & Kamel, 1983). It is necessary to begin this explanation with an understanding of self-awareness and the urge to escape from it.

Self-Awareness, Escape, and Masochism

The notion that self-awareness is often an aversive state from which people may wish to escape has been central to self-awareness theory from its first formulations (Duval & Wicklund, 1972). Subsequent work acknowledged that in many cases people do like to be self-aware, but certainly many circumstances make it unpleasant (e.g., Greenberg & Musham, 1981).

Baumeister (1991) identified three main reasons for wanting to escape from awareness of oneself. The first is that failure, rejection, or other misfortunes reflect badly on the self, and so self-awareness becomes essentially an upsetting contemplation of one's inadequacies. The second is that the pressures and expectations associated with modern selfhood (i.e., demands to be liked, to be respected, and to be in control of one's life) make it difficult and even exhausting to maintain a highly attractive image of self, and so an occasional escape from self functions as a restful relief from stress. The third is that loss of self-awareness is apparently a prerequisite for various highly pleasant experiences, ranging from sexual pleasure to ecstatic religious experiences to mundane "flow" experiences in work or play (see Csikszentmihalyi, 1990). Thus, the desire to escape can appear in a broad variety of individuals and situations.

Many patterns of human behavior seem well designed to facilitate loss of self-awareness. Sexual masochism is an important one, and we emphasize it here, but several others deserve mention. Alcohol appears to have a direct effect of reducing awareness of self (as well as thinking about events in relation to the self; see Hull, 1981). Eating binges, ranging from an ordinary breach of diet to outright bulimia, appear to be marked by severe loss of self-awareness (Heatherton & Baumeister, 1991). Meditation and other spiritual exercises are often explicitly designed to reduce and remove self-awareness (Baumeister, 1991). Also, many of the activities leading up to a suicide attempt appear to be attempts at minimizing self-awareness, and often a suicide attempt is itself a search for selfless oblivion (Baumeister, 1990, 1991). In addition, many hobbies, pastimes, and exercise activities seem to promote loss of self.

These activities have a number of common features that are presumably the hallmarks of escaping the self. Meaningful thought is brought to a minimum, and time perspective shrinks to a narrow focus on the here and now. Thinking becomes rigid and concrete. Meaningful action and experience are replaced by simple, physical movement and sensation. Emotions and inhibitions are set aside.

Two general patterns subsume these diverse effects. The first can be called *cognitive deconstruction* or, more simply, mental narrowing. Constructs are generally understood to be the result of assembling multiple meaningful associations; deconstruction would therefore be dismantling them. A mental state that accomplishes such a dismantling of meaning would undermine the basis for many forms of thought, including self-awareness and evaluation. The second can be called *procedure orientation*, which means focusing attention on the details and methods of what one is doing rather than examining broader, more meaningful issues such as implications and justifications.

Sexual masochism appears to consist of a potent set of techniques for escaping from self-awareness (Baumeister, 1988b, 1989, 1991). The three main features of masochism are pain, bondage (and other loss of control), and humiliation. Because we argue later that UFO abduction accounts have many features in common with masochistic fantasies and activities, let us briefly examine each of these three masochistic patterns.

A desire for pain is inherently counterintuitive and seemingly irrational. Pain does, however, have several cognitive consequences that make it potentially useful for other ends. First, it captures attention and therefore prevents one from thinking about many other things. Second, it binds awareness to a very concrete, physical level, thereby impairing the capacity for highly abstract or meaningful thought (see Scarry, 1985). Together, these make pain a potent means of achieving cognitive deconstruction. The masochist's attention is kept very precisely and continually focused on the immediate present and is also kept at a very concrete level: He or she is acutely aware of being a body under the whip. As one eminent practitioner of sadomasochism commented, "A whip is a great way to get someone to be here now. They can't look away from it, and they can't think about anything else!" (Califia, 1983, p. 134).

Loss of control is central to many masochistic activities. Although bondage (i.e., physical restraint) is most vivid and well-known, masochists also submit to loss of control by accepting commands and rules imposed by their dominant partners. All these patterns deconstruct one of the most fundamental and essential functions of the self, which is to be the active agent that masters the environment, makes decisions, and initiates action. Relinquishing control relieves a person of the usual need to regulate his or her behavior in the service of maintaining esteem and dignity. In addition, it means that one does not have to accept responsibility for failing to live up to the standards typically used for self-evaluation. Being tied up can serve as an excellent excuse for not being at one's best and for not taking charge of a situation.

The third hallmark of masochism is humiliation: Masochists submit to many degrading, embarrassing, or humiliating experiences. These range from accepting verbal insults to enacting physical rituals such as kneeling, begging, and kissing feet. Male masochists often like to be symbolically transformed into a woman, a baby, or a dog. Female masochists are less inclined to report such status-loss transformations, but they do favor being displayed naked, such as tied up spreadeagled on a table or other piece of furniture, possibly being observed by several other (often fully clothed) people. Such experiences thwart another of the most fundamental and common operations of selfhood, namely the maintenance of self-esteem. Indeed, the temporary loss of dignity caused by some masochistic practices may help make it utterly impossible to maintain one's normal sense of identity.

In sum, the many puzzling aspects of sexual masochism actually serve the goal of escaping the self—that is, escaping both the aversive feelings that result from failing to meet the self's needs and standards and the relentless pressure to strive toward becoming a more adequate and competent person. In light of the existence of masochism, UFO abduction accounts are less unique and bizarre than they might at first seem. Many otherwise normal people desire, seek out, and apparently derive satisfaction from experiences and fantasies in which they receive pain, are rendered helpless and submissive to another's will, and/or are treated in a degrading or embarrassing way. The prototype UFO abduction experience has those same features. Thus, the same motives that might make some people fantasize about sexual masochism could make others construct fantasies about being abducted by UFOs.

Evidence: Parallels and Resemblances

We now turn to consider how UFO experiences resemble sexual masochism. If spurious memories of UFO abductions do spring from the same motivational root as sexual masochism, there should be multiple signs of similarity.

To begin with, it is clear that UFO abductions share many of the hallmarks of masochism. Pain is reported by many abductees, particularly in connection with the pseudomedical examination (Bullard, 1987b). Strieber, whose *Communion* (1987) is one of the best-known first person "accounts" of contact with aliens, has also written stories about ritualized masochistic activities in ways that suggest intimate familiarity with the escapist functions of pain.[2] Indeed, his comment that pain "lifts the burden of self from your shoulders" (1986, p. 276) aptly articulates the core idea of Baumeister's (1988b, 1989) analysis of masochism.

As already noted, loss of control is central to most UFO abduction experiences. In some cases the report seems to feature explicit bondage, such as shackles, collars, and other straps (see Lorenzon & Lorenzon, 1977, pp. 26, 59). In many others, the person is merely immobilized by unknown means, but the sense of passive helplessness is the same. In yet others, physical helplessness is downplayed in favor of a focus on being psychologically dominated by the aliens, such as in the case reported by Jacobs (1992), in which the abductee said, "I have no will. I have no will. I'm being absorbed and I'm not fighting it" while reliving her experience (p. 99). Hopkins (1987) observed that the feeling of being controlled by others was the single most common attribute of UFO abduction reports. As noted by Newman and Baumeister (1996a), loss of control does not only seem to be an "objective" aspect of the abduction experience (i.e., something that can be inferred from the details); it also plays a prominent role in how abductees talk about and frame their experiences. For example, 10 of the 13 abductees described in Mack's (1994) book explicitly focused on surrendering and losing control as a defining feature of their alleged alien encounters (see Newman & Baumeister, 1996b). Mack even concluded that "the helplessness and loss or surrender of control which are, at least initially, forced upon the abductees by the aliens—one of the most traumatic aspects of the experiences—seem to be in some way 'designed' to bring about a kind of ego death" (1994, p. 399).

Humiliation, especially with a sexual dimension, is the third main feature of masochism that is also found in UFO abduction reports. Being treated as a specimen for capture and observation is clearly degrading to many people, and so the entire episode has an aspect of humiliation. Many particular events intensify this sense. For example, male abductees often refer to devices being attached to their penises, often to vacuum sperm out of them (Hopkins, 1987; Jacobs, 1992). According to Conroy (1989), the editors of Strieber's *Communion* insisted on removing a brief discussion of how the aliens took hold of his penis to lead him around. Embarrassing probes of the anus were also reported in a number of cases (Fiore, 1989; Jacobs, 1992; Strieber, 1987). Some abductees make it quite clear that humiliation is an important feature of their stories:

> Recently I had a case of a woman who was forced to watch a "man" and "horse" engage in sexual contact. For various reasons, this was far more humiliating and shameful for her than for the average individual. She felt certain that they had used this image on purpose. Then the man came over to her and engaged in anal intercourse with her, much to her intense shame . . . she was given to believe during this event that the aliens were carefully monitoring her feelings of shame, guilt, and humiliation. (Jacobs, 1994, p. 65)

In general, being stripped naked and rudely examined by a group of aliens would very likely have a strong element of embarrassment for almost anyone.

Beyond these basic resemblances, several less obvious parallels provide further support for the hypothesized link between UFO abductions and sexual masochism. For one thing, both appeal to the same population segments. We already noted that most UFO abduction reports originate in the United States and are historically recent; sexual masochism has likewise been found to be mainly confined to the modern West (Baumeister, 1988b, 1989). While popular stereotypes arguably portray UFO abductees as being uneducated and unsophisticated people from isolated geographical regions, some samples indicate that abductees are instead very likely to be from the middle and upper classes, with white-collar jobs and above-average educational backgrounds (Bloecher, Clamar, & Hopkins, 1985; Parnell & Sprinkle, 1990; Rodeghier, Goodpaster, & Blatterbauer, 1991). Masochists have similarly been characterized as relatively well off and well-educated (Baumeister, 1989; Cowan, 1982; Janus, Bess, & Saltus, 1977; Scott, 1983; Spengler, 1977). American samples also suggest that masochism is disproportionately more common among whites than blacks (e.g., Baumeister, 1989), and the same seems to be true for UFO abductions (Randles, 1988; Rodeghier et al., 1991).

To provide a more subtle and falsifiable test of the hypothesis that UFO experiences resemble sexual masochism Newman and Baumeister (1996b) coded a large sample of abduction reports (from Bullard, 1987b) for several features that were already studied in masochism. Baumeister (1988a) showed significant sex differences in masochistic accounts on several dimensions. This work, of course, was completed and published prior to beginning our work on UFO abduction accounts, which makes at least the earlier work exempt from any suspicion of confirmation bias in the search for parallels with UFO accounts.

The UFO accounts showed several sex differences similar to the ones obtained in the earlier work on masochism. First, women's accounts were more likely than men's to include "display" humiliation, that is, being displayed in an embarrassing fashion (usually nude on the examination table, with an audience). Second, women's accounts were more likely than men's to refer to pain. Third, men's accounts were more likely than women's to feature some form of oral humiliation, although the count was too low for statistical significance. Taken together, these parallels provide further support for the view that the motivational roots are similar.

Various features of the process of escape from self (not necessarily specific to masochism) can also be seen in many UFO abduction accounts. In his synopsis of the typical abduction experience, Jacobs (1992) referred to forgetting most ongoing aspects of one's life and selfhood as one's "attention is continually fixed on the present" (p. 91). He also pointed out that the aliens seem only interested in physiological questions and show no curiosity at all about the more meaningful aspects of human life, such as careers and relationships. Likewise, Strieber (1987) said that while under the aliens' control he was reduced to "raw biological response" (p. 18). Also, the procedure orientation typical of escapist activities (see above) may account for the abundance of seemingly trivial details in many UFO accounts, such as detailed descriptions of spaceship interiors, the instruments and machinery on board, the devices used to torment abductees, and even the clothing worn by the aliens (see Jacobs, 1992, Chaps. 4 and 5).[3]

Taken together, these parallels and resemblances between UFO abductions and sexual masochism are too many to dismiss as coincidence. They seem best explained by suggesting that the two phenomena have a common motivational basis, namely, the desire of some people to achieve a release from selfhood by being thoroughly dominated by others. For some people, these desires are expressed in the form of sexual fantasies and occasionally sexual behavior. For others, they are expressed in the way the free associating or hypnotized mind fills in details to elaborate some confusing impressions into a spurious memory of mistreatment by alien beings.

CONCLUSION

In recent years more and more people have claimed that they have memories of a most unusual experience: They report that they were abducted by aliens into UFOs. Many of these individuals are quite convinced of the reality of these experiences. Moreover, an increasing number of researchers and therapists have been persuaded that these experiences are real (see Huyghe, 1993; Pritchard et al., 1994). Three features seem especially persuasive in this regard: the large number of such reports, the similarity in their features, and the seeming impossibility of offering any explanation of why people would fabricate such stories.

Our effort in this chapter is to offer an explanation that can potentially incorporate some of these troubling facts. Although most UFO abduction experiences seem unpleasant, some people (i.e., masochists) do invent and fantasize about being mistreated, so the possibility of motivated fabrication of UFO memories is not implausible. Moreover, the common features of many UFO accounts may be due to the common motivational roots as well as to the influence of well-publicized versions of what it is like to be taken prisoner aboard an alien spacecraft.

Hence, we argued that the widespread motivation to achieve a temporary escape from self-awareness may be a driving factor in the formation of spurious memories of UFO abductions. Sexual masochism is perhaps the phenomenon with the greatest number of similarities to UFO abductions, and both masochistic and abduction experiences may derive from the desire for a brief escape from the modern burden of selfhood. In support of this argument, we identified many parallels and resemblances between sexual masochism and UFO abductions. Both tend to involve moderately painful and embarrassing experiences of submitting to another's will, and both remove the person from his or her normal life and identity for a brief period.

Clearly, the fact that people might like to imagine such experiences does not sufficiently explain why they would actually come to believe that they have had them. We therefore propose that UFO abduction memories may be a product of processes that are known to lead to a breakdown in reality monitoring and to produce other spurious memories (such as those involving past lives, victimization at the hands of satanic cults, and even confabulated episodes of childhood sexual abuse). Typically, abductees begin with a vague sense of unease, a desire to understand why they feel the way they do, and ambiguous memory fragments. Some of the latter may originate in a sleep paralysis experience during the transition between sleep and wakefulness, when hallucinations and illusions may be relatively common. Prior belief in the physical reality of UFOs and UFO-related knowledge may predispose such people to interpret their hallucinations in terms of encounters with the occupants of those interplanetary vessels. UFO-related knowledge and beliefs may also lead one to seek out therapists or experts with similar beliefs. The use of hypnosis is a common step in the production of most full-fledged accounts of UFO abductions, and hypnosis helps to flesh out the details (and increases the confident belief in the veridicality) of these spurious memories, especially under the influence of subjects' and therapists' belief in UFOs and widely publicized models of similar experiences.

Any attempt to explain the baffling, counterintuitive phenomenon of widespread reports of UFO abductions must necessarily stretch the bounds of commonsense psychology. Our account has several advantages. It relies on firm parallels to documented patterns of cognition and motivation. In addition, it avoids the polarized positions that have dominated the debate over UFO abductions, namely, that the experiences are literally true and real, and (at the other extreme) that they are outright, deliberate hoaxes perpetrated by attention-seeking liars. Many individuals might sincerely believe that they were abducted and yet be mistaken. Our model explains how this might happen and also explains why people might *want* to believe that they have had such experiences. UFO abduction accounts can be understood as fantasies that, like masochistic ones, derive from the motivation to escape the self.

NOTES

1. We argue in this section that certain situations lead people to adopt looser standards for evaluating memories and that certain people are chronically less able to distinguish between reality and fantasy. A recent conversation between the first author and an alleged abductee, however, suggests that more subtle interactions between situational and dispositional factors may help foster abduction memories. The abductee in question revealed that he had recently become convinced that what he had long considered to be a bad dream was in fact a memory of an extraterrestrial encounter. He went on to note that he was in the process of reexamining other strange dreams that he could recall, including some that involved other members of his family. These too, he suggested, were probably fragmentary memories of abduction experiences. In sum, the experience of relabeling a dream or fantasy as a memory may lead to long-term changes in a person's reality monitoring criteria and processes.

2. Elsewhere, one of Strieber's (1990) characters talked about a ritualized beating as an experience that transported a person to "regions where suffering and pleasure were the same" (p. 288).

3. These "trivial" details may have consequences that are far from trivial. Johnson and Suengas (1989) found that the presence of concrete perceptual details plays an important role in people's judgments of the veridicality of others' memories. Hence, it is very likely that the minutiae of abduction accounts contribute to making many UFO abduction narratives seem like convincing accounts of real experiences. Interestingly, Johnson (1995) reported that when people are encouraged to be suspicious of others' stories, the number of perceptual details provided may correlate *negatively* with believability. These findings indicate that believers and skeptics are able to use the same aspects of abduction accounts to bolster their very different beliefs about the truthfulness of those accounts (see Ross & Newby, 1996, for a more detailed discussion of this possibility).

REFERENCES

Arndt, J., & Greenberg, J. (1996). Fantastic accounts can take many forms: False memory construction? Yes. Escape from self? We don't think so. *Psychological Inquiry, 7,* 127–132.

Baker, R. A. (1992). *Hidden memories: Voices and visions from within.* Buffalo, NY: Prometheus Books.

Baker, R. A. (1987). The aliens among us: Hypnotic regression revisited. *Skeptical Inquirer, 12,* 147–162.

Bartholomew, R. E., Basterfield, K., & Howard, G. S. (1991). UFO abductees and contactees: Psychopathology or fantasy-proneness? *Professional Psychology: Research and Practice, 22,* 215–222.

Baumeister, R. F. (1988a). Gender differences in masochistic scripts. *Journal of Sex Research, 25,* 478–499.

Baumeister, R. F. (1988b). Masochism as escape from self. *Journal of Sex Research, 25,* 28–59.

Baumeister, R. F. (1989). *Masochism and the self.* Hillsdale, NJ: Erlbaum.

Baumeister, R. F. (1990). Suicide as escape from self. *Psychological Review, 97,* 90–113.

Baumeister, R. F. (1991). *Escaping the self.* New York: Basic Books.

Baumeister, R. F., & Newman, L. S. (1994). How stories make sense of personal experiences: Motives that shape autobiographical narratives. *Personality and Social Psychology Bulletin, 20,* 676–690.

Bloecher, T., Clamar, A., & Hopkins, B. (1985). *Final report on the psychological testing of UFO abductees.* Mount Ranier, MD: Fund for UFO Research.

Bottoms, B. L, & Davis, S. L. (1997). The creation of satanic ritual abuse. *Journal of Social and Clinical Psychology, 16,* 112–113.

Bowers, K. S., & Farvolden, P. (1996). Revisiting a century-old Freudian slip—From suggestion disavowed to the truth repressed. *Psychological Bulletin, 119,* 355–380.

Bryan, C. D. B. (1995). *Close encounters of the fourth kind: Alien abduction, UFOs and the conference at M.I.T.* New York: Knopf.

Bullard, T. E. (1987a). *On stolen time: A summary of a comparative study of the UFO abduction mystery.* Mount Ranier, MD: Fund for UFO Research.

Bullard, T. E. (1987b). *UFO abductions: The measure of a mystery: Vol. 2. Catalogue of cases.* Mount Ranier, MD: Fund for UFO Research.

Bullard, T. E. (1994a). A comparative study of abduction reports update. In A. Pritchard, D. E. Pritchard, J. E. Mack, P. Kasey, & C. Yapp (Eds.), *Alien discussions: Proceedings of the abduction study conference* (pp. 45–48). Cambridge, MA: North Cambridge Press.

Bullard, T. E. (1994b). Addendum: The influence of investigators on UFO abduction reports: Results of a survey. In A. Pritchard, D. E. Pritchard, J. E. Mack, P. Kasey, & C. Yapp (Eds.), *Alien discussions: Proceedings of the abduction study conference* (pp. 571–619). Cambridge, MA: North Cambridge Press.

Bullard, T. E. (1996). Investigating the abduction investigators. *International UFO Reporter, 21*(2), pp. 6–10, 26–28.

Califia, P. (1983). A secret side of lesbian sexuality. In T. Weinberg & G. Kamel (Eds.), *S and M: Studies in sadomasochism* (pp. 129–136). Buffalo, NY: Prometheus.

Clark, S. E., & Loftus, E. F. (1996). The construction of space alien abduction memories. *Psychological Inquiry, 7,* 140–143.

Conroy, E. (1989). *Report on communion.* New York: Morrow.

Cowan, L. (1982). *Masochism: A Jungian view.* Dallas: Spring.

Csikszentmihalyi, M. (1990). *Flow: The psychology of optimal experience.* New York: Harper & Row.

Drew, H. (1992). The seduction of Earth and Rain. In Samois, *Coming to power* (pp. 125–131). Boston: Alyson.

Durso, F. T., & Johnson, M. K. (1980). The effects of orienting tasks on recognition, recall, and modality confusion of pictures and words. *Journal of Verbal Learning and Verbal Behavior, 19,* 416–429.

Duval, S., & Wicklund, R. A. (1972). *A theory of objective self-awareness.* New York: Academic Press.

Dywan, J. (1995). The illusion of familiarity: An alternative to the report-criterion account of hypnotic recall. *International Journal of Clinical and Experimental Hypnosis, 43,* 194–211.

Ellis, B. (1987). The varieties of alien experience. *Skeptical Inquirer, 12,* 263–269.

Erdelyi, M. H. (1993). Repression: The mechanism and the defense. In D. M. Wegner & J. W. Pennebaker (Eds.), *Handbook of mental control* (pp. 126–148). Englewood Cliffs, NJ: Prentice-Hall.

Fiore, E. (1989). *Encounters: A psychologist reveals case studies of abductions by extraterrestrials.* New York: Doubleday.

Fuller, J. G. (1966). *The interrupted journey.* New York: Putnam.

Garry, M., & Loftus, E. F. (1994). Pseudomemories without hypnosis. *International Journal of Clinical and Experimental Hypnosis, 42,* 363–378.

Geist, W. E. (1987, July 8). Group therapy for the victims of space aliens. *The New York Times,* p. B1.

Gordon, J. S. (1991, August). The UFO experience. *The Atlantic Monthly,* pp. 82–92.

Greenberg, J., & Musham, C. (1981). Avoiding and seeking self-focused attention. *Journal of Research in Personality, 15,* 191–200.

Hall, R. L. (1996). Escaping the self or escaping the anomaly? *Psychological Inquiry, 7,* 143–148.

Heatherton, T. F., & Baumeister, R. F. (1991). Binge eating as escape from self-awareness. *Psychological Bulletin, 110,* 86–108.

Hopkins, B. (1987). *Intruders: The incredible visitations at Copley Woods.* New York: Ballantine Books.

Hopkins, B., Jacobs, D. M., & Westrum, R. (1992). *Unusual personal experiences: An analysis of the data from three national surveys.* Las Vegas, NV: Bigelow Holding Corporation.

Hufford, D. (1982). *The terror that comes in the night.* Philadelphia: University of Pennsylvania Press.

Hull, J. G. (1981). A self-awareness model of the causes and effects of alcohol consumption. *Journal of Abnormal Psychology, 90,* 586–600.

Huyghe, P. (September, 1993). Dark side of the unknown. *Omni, 15,* pp. 35–45.

Hynek, J. A. (1984). Foreword. In P. Dong, *The four major mysteries of mainland China.* Englewood Cliffs, NJ: Prentice-Hall.

Jacobs, D. M. (1992). *Secret life: Firsthand accounts of UFO abductions.* New York: Simon & Schuster.

Jacobs, D. M. (1994). Subsequent procedures. In A. Pritchard, D. E. Pritchard, J. E. Mack, P. Kasey, & C. Yapp (Eds.), *Alien discussions: Proceedings of the abduction study conference* (pp. 64–68). Cambridge, MA: North Cambridge Press.

Janus, S., Bess, B., & Saltus, C. (1977) *A sexual profile of men in power.* Englewood Cliffs, NJ: Prentice-Hall.

Johnson, M. K. (1995, August). *The relation between memory and reality.* Paper presented at the meeting of the American Psychological Association, New York.

Johnson, M. K., Foley, M. A., Suengas, A. G., & Raye, C. L. (1988). Phenomenal characteristics of memories for perceived and imagined autobiographical events. *Journal of Experimental Psychology: General, 117,* 371–376.

Johnson, M. K., Raye, C. L., Foley, H. J., & Foley, M. A. (1981). Cognitive operations and decision bias in reality monitoring. *American Journal of Psychology, 94,* 37–64.

Johnson, M. K., & Suengas, A. G. (1989). Reality monitoring judgments of other people's memories. *Bulletin of the Psychonomic Society, 27,* 107–110.

Klass, P. J. (1988). *UFO abductions: A dangerous game.* Buffalo, NY: Prometheus Books.

Klass, P. J. (1990). Communion and intruders: UFO-abduction groups form. *Skeptical Inquirer, 14,* 122–123.

Klass, P. J. (1993). Additional comments about the "Unusual Personal Experiences" survey. *Skeptical Inquirer, 17*, 145–146.

Loftus, E. F. (1993). The reality of repressed memories. *American Psychologist, 48*, 518–537.

Lorenzon, C., & Lorenzon, J. (1977). *Abducted! Confrontations with beings from outer space.* New York: Berkley Medallion Books.

Lynn, S. J., & Kirsch, I. I. (1996). Alleged alien abductions: False memories, hypnosis, and fantasy proneness. *Psychological Inquiry, 7*, 151–155.

Lynn, S. J., & Nash, M. R. (1994). Truth in memory: Ramifications for psychotherapy and hypnotherapy. *American Journal of Clinical Hypnosis, 36*, 194–208.

Lynn, S. J., & Pezzo, M. (1994, August). *Close encounters of a third kind: Simulated hypnotic interviews of alien contacts.* Paper presented at the meeting of the American Psychological Association, Los Angeles.

Lynn, S. J., & Rhue, J. W. (1988). Fantasy Proneness: Hypnosis, developmental antecedents, and psychopathology. *American Psychologist, 43*, 35–44.

Mack, J. E. (1994). *Abduction: Human encounters with aliens.* New York: Macmillan.

McLeod, C. C., Corbisier, B., & Mack, J. E. (1996). A more parsimonious explanation for UFO abduction. *Psychological Inquiry, 7*, 156–168.

Newman, L. S., & Baumeister, R. F. (1996a). Not just another false memory: Further thoughts on UFO abduction narratives. *Psychological Inquiry, 7*, 185–197.

Newman, L. S., & Baumeister, R. F. (1996b). Toward an explanation of the UFO abduction phenomenon: Hypnotic elaboration, extraterrestrial sadomasochism, and spurious memories. *Psychological Inquiry, 7*, 99–126.

Nickell, J. (1996). A study of fantasy proneness in the thirteen cases of alleged encounters in John Mack's abduction. *Skeptical Inquirer, 20*, 18–20, 54.

Nogrady, H., McConkey, K. M., & Campbell, P. (1985). Enhancing visual memory: Trying hypnosis, trying imagination, and trying again. *Journal of Abnormal Psychology, 94*, 195–204.

Ofshe, R. J. (1992). Inadvertent hypnosis during interrogation: False confession due to dissociative state; mis-identified multiple personality and the satanic cult hypothesis. *International Journal of Clinical and Experimental Hypnosis, 40*, 125–156.

Orne, M. T. (1979). The use and misuse of hypnosis in court. *International Journal of Clinical and Experimental Hypnosis, 27*, 437–448.

Parnell, J. O., & Sprinkle, R. L. (1990). Personality characteristics of persons who claim UFO experiences. *Journal of UFO Studies, 2*, 45–58.

Pettinati, H. M. (Ed.). (1988). *Hypnosis and memory.* New York: Guilford Press.

Powell, R. A., & Boer, D. P. (1994). Did Freud mislead patients to confabulate memories of abuse? *Psychological Reports, 74*, 1283–1298.

Pritchard, A., Pritchard, D. E., Mack, J. E., Kasey, P., & Yapp, C. (Eds.). (1994). *Alien discussions: Proceedings of the abduction study conference.* Cambridge, MA: North Cambridge Press.

Randles, J. (1988). *Alien abductions: The mystery solved.* New Brunswick, NJ: Inner Light Publications.

Rimmer, J. (1984). *The evidence for alien abductions.* Wellingborough, Northamptonshire, UK: Aquarian Press.

Ring, K., & Rosing, C. J. (1990). The Omega project: a psychological survey of persons reporting abductions and other UFO encounters. *Journal of UFO Studies, 2*, 59–98.

Rodeghier, M., Goodpaster, J., & Blatterbauer, S. (1991). Psychosocial characteristics of abductees: Results from the CUFOS abduction project. *Journal of UFO Studies*, *3*, 59–90.

Ross, M., & Newby, I. R. (1996). Distinguishing memory from fantasy. *Psychological Inquiry*, *7*, 173–177.

Sagan, C. (1979). *Broca's brain*. New York: Random House.

Sagan, C. (1996). *The demon-haunted world: Science as a candle in the dark*. New York: Random House.

Scarry, E. (1985). *The body in pain: The making and unmaking of the world*. New York: Oxford University Press.

Schrim, J. (1982). Mirel. In Samois (Ed.), *Coming to power* (pp. 112–124). Boston: Alyson.

Scott, G. G. (1983). *Erotic power: An exploration of dominance and submission*. Secaucus, NJ: Citadel Press.

Sheehan, P. (1988). Confidence and memory in hypnosis. In H. M. Pettinati (Ed.), *Hypnosis and memory* (pp. 95–127). New York: Guilford Press.

Spanos, N. P. (1986). Hypnotic behavior: A social–psychological interpretation of amnesia, analgesia, and "trance logic." *Behavioral and Brain Sciences*, *9*, 449–502.

Spanos, N. P. (1987). Past-life hypnotic regression: A critical view. *Skeptical Inquirer*, *12*, 174–180.

Spanos, N. P., Burgess, C. A., & Burgess, M. F. (1994). Past-life identities, UFO abductions, and Satanic ritual abuse: The social construction of memories. *International Journal of Clinical and Experimental Hypnosis*, *42*, 433–446.

Spanos, N. P., Cross, P. A., Dickson, K., & DuBreuil, S. C. (1993). Close encounters: An examination of UFO experiences. *Journal of Abnormal Psychology*, *102*, 624–632.

Spanos, N. P., Menary, E., Gabora, N. J., DuBreuil, S. C., & Dewhirst, B. (1991). Secondary identity enactments during hypnotic past-life regression: A sociocognitive perspective. *Journal of Personality and Social Psychology*, *61*, 308–320.

Spengler, A. (1977). Manifest sadomasochism of males: Results of an empirical study. *Archives of Sexual Behavior*, *6*, 441–456.

Steiger, B. (1988). *The UFO abductors*. New York: Berkley Books.

Strieber, W. (1986). Pain. In D. Etchison (Ed.), *Cutting edge* (pp. 269–290). New York: Doubleday.

Strieber, W. (1990). *Billy*. New York: Berkley Books.

Strieber, W. (1987). *Communion: A true story*. New York: Avon Books.

Strieber, W. (1993, July 5). Appearance on *Larry King Live*, Cable News Network.

Suengas, A. G., & Johnson, M. K. (1988). Qualitative effects of rehearsal on memories for perceived and imagined complex events. *Journal of Experimental Psychology: General*, *117*, 377–389.

Weinberg, T., & Kamel, W. L. (Eds.). (1983). *S and M: Studies in sadomasochism*. Buffalo, NY: Prometheus Books.

Wilson, S. C., & Barber, T. X. (1983). The fantasy-prone personality: Implications for understanding imagery, hypnosis, and parapsychological phenomena. In A. A. Sheikh (Ed.), *Imagery: Current theory, research, and application* (pp. 340–390). New York: Wiley.

CHAPTER 12

REFLECTIONS ON
THE TRAUMATIC MEMORIES
OF DISSOCIATIVE IDENTITY
DISORDER PATIENTS

Richard P. Kluft

After briefly reviewing the literature on dissociative identity disorder (DID) and trauma, this chapter discusses findings corroborating memories of trauma recovered by DID patients in the course of treatment. It argues that the confirmation of memories recovered in treatments facilitated by hypnosis suggests that the circumspect use of hypnosis continues to deserve a role in the exploration of the experiences of DID patients. The complexity of memory work in the treatment of DID patients is discussed, and the influence of the inner realities experienced by the DID patient upon memory is addressed. The exploration of the autobiographical memories of DID patients remains a difficult area of inquiry that defies reduction to simplistic overgeneralizations. Clinical approaches to their memories must acknowledge this complexity and refrain from proposing premature and draconian restrictions on the use of techniques that have already demonstrated considerable clinical utility.

REVIEW OF THE LITERATURE

DID, formerly multiple personality disorder (MPD), is a chronic complex pleiomorphic and polysymptomatic dissociative psychopathology highly associated with traumatic antecedents (Braun, 1986; Kluft, 1984b, 1985a, 1996a; Loewenstein, 1991; Putnam, 1985, 1989; Putnam, Guroff, Silberman, Barban,

& Post, 1986; Ross, 1989; Ross, Norton, & Wozney, 1989; Schultz, Braun, & Kluft, 1989). However, the reality of DID patients' accounts of trauma, especially those of childhood trauma recovered in the course of psychotherapy, has been challenged, both generally (Brenneis, 1996; Frankel, 1993; Ganaway, 1989, 1994; Hacking, 1995; Piper, 1994, Simpson, 1995) and selectively (Kluft, 1984b, 1993, 1995a, 1995b, 1996b).

Because many articles on the relationship of trauma to DID rely on patient reports and are uncorroborated, those skeptical of the reality of DID and/or the traumatic memories of DID patients often feel entitled to dismiss the connection as unconfirmed, or as an instance of unwarranted assumptions leading to foregone conclusions with a disconcerting inevitability. That is, clinicians who endorse the trauma connection have been assumed to and/or accused of virtually creating confabulations consistent with their belief systems.

Without denying the possibility that interventions in the course of therapy, among many other forms of social influence, may lead to confabulated recollections, it is imperative to realize that there is no actual proof that this phenomenon is occurring with any degree of frequency (Brown, 1995a; Kluft, 1997a; Pope, 1996). Nor is there any proof that they account for a majority of the traumatic memories reported by DID patients, either always available memories shared during their assessments or previously unavailable memories encountered for the first time after treatment has begun. Even when it is patently clear that a patient's productions in psychotherapy are in the main confabulated or at least inaccurate, there is often no evidence, despite many accusations, that therapy is the origin of these phenomena rather than the locus of their being reported.

In fact, a number of studies indicate that DID patients are a genuinely traumatized group of patients. Several studies demonstrate documented abuse in the histories of DID cohorts. Bliss (1984) investigated the claims of nine DID patients and was able to document trauma for eight of the nine (89%). Fagan and McMahon (1984) present data from social service agencies on the abuse that affected their four young patients (100%). In the same year, I (Kluft, 1984a) found evidence of the abuse of five young patients (100%) but did not include all documentation in the published article.

In 1985, Bowman, Blix, and Coons provided exemplary documentation in a single case study. The following year Coons and Milstein (1986) documented abuse in 17 of 20 adults (85%) with DID. In 1992, Hornstein and Putnam showed that 61 of 66 children and adolescents with dissociative disorders (95%), had documentable trauma. Coons (1994) reported corroborating abuse histories in 21 of 22 children and adolescents (95%) with dissociative disorders. Working with adults, I (Kluft, 1995a) found that without taking special steps to document abuse allegations, I nonetheless could corroborate traumatic memories reported by 56% of my patients and demonstrate pseudomemories in 9%.

This study was unique in that it studied the confirmation of specific memories of abuse rather than the basic allegation that abuse had occurred. In it I studied 34 DID patients who had fulfilled criteria for DID according to the fourth edition of the *Diagnostic and Statistical Manual of Mental Disorders* (DSM-IV; American Psychiatric Association, 1994) for and who were in treatment with me during a specific 30-day period. The sample was 94% female and 94% Caucasian. The average patient was 44.4 years of age and had been in treatment for $5^1\!/_2$ years. Twenty, or 59%, were demonstrating classic DID behavior at the time of the study. The remainder were integrated, had greatly reduced the overtness of their DID phenomena, or had learned to restrict the emergence of alternate personalities only to therapy sessions, usually with the help of specialized hypnotic techniques (Kluft, 1989).

Charts were reviewed for instances of the confirmation and disconfirmation of abuse allegations. Confirmation or disconfirmation required a credible witness, a confession by a perpetrator, either verbal or in a legal document, or in other legal documentation. I accepted patients' accounts of witnesses' reports and confessions but received many in person as well. I did not consider an event documented if two witnesses (usually siblings) disagreed. I excluded memories that might have emerged after an event was mentioned to the patient.

For 19 of the 34 patients (56%) the recollection of abuse was confirmed. Ten of the 19 (53%) had always recalled the abuses the charts documented. However, 13 of the 19 were able to document events that they had not recalled prior to their work in therapy. Eleven of the 13 patients (85%) who recalled one or more later documented memories in treatment had recovered these memories with the assistance of hypnosis. One had retrieved the memory during eye movement desensitization and reprocessing (EMDR; Shapiro, 1995) treatment for a theme ostensibly unrelated to abuse; another did so during free association in the course of psychoanalytic psychotherapy.

The 34 memories definitively confirmed and the 3 disconfirmed, a total of 37, constituted a mere fraction of 1% of the recollections that were reported in the course of the therapies of these 34 patients. Furthermore, two of the three patients with disconfirmed accounts also had instances of confirmed mistreatment.

The sources of confirmation are reported in detail elsewhere (Kluft, 1995a). With regard to the confirmations of the 22 memories recovered in therapy, 8 (36%) came from siblings who witnessed the abuse. Three (14%) were from confessions by terminally ill incestuous fathers. Two (9%) were confirmed by abusive parents, two (9%) by one parent's confirming abuse by the other parent, and two (9%) by confession of abusive siblings. One confirmation (5%) came from each of the following sources: official records, confession by an exploitive therapist, observations by a childhood neighbor, the account of another relative who witnessed the abuse, and the revelations of a friend who witnessed the episode.

My initial article (Kluft, 1995a) focused on the fact that allegations of abuse by DID patients, both always recalled and those emerging in therapy, could be documented. No distinction was drawn between confirmations made directly to the investigator and confirmations made to the patient. However, in view of the intensity of the debate that surrounds such issues, some unpublished data from the study are of interest. It is useful to ask, How many confirmations would remain if all corroborations made from patients' reports were eliminated? This remainder would constitute a more stringent documentation, more respectful of the reservations of more skeptical colleagues (J. W. Schooler, personal communication, July 1996). Eleven of the 22 confirmed memories recovered in therapy, 50% of the total, were confirmed directly to the author. Table 12.1 summarizes these corroborations. Fifty percent direct confirmation is known to be an under-reporting because several events from these patients' lives confirmed *after* the study period are excluded. Also, one patient who found pornographic films of herself as a child begged me not to place this information on her chart. I declined to view these films in the interests of documentation, taking the stance that an implicit boundary violation outweighed any possible heuristic or scholarly imperative.

Several implications of the Kluft (1995a) study are summarized in Table 12.2. Taken as a whole, these findings suggest that it is premature to disambiguate the very complex dilemma posed by memories of childhood mistreatment encountered in the treatment of adult DID patients. Our knowledge is incomplete; there are data to corroborate that both the recovery of accurate, previously unavailable memories and the encountering of confabulated recollections of childhood mistreatment are genuine clinical phenomena. Polar-

TABLE 12.1. Confirmations Made Directly to or by the Investigator

Experience recovered	Corroboration
1. Childhood prostitution	Patient's sister described this shared experience to investigator
2. Usage in child pornography	Pictures of same in police custody
3. Rape by brother	Brother confessed to same in telephone conversation
4. Father–daughter incest known to mother	Mother apologizes for this and her complicity in letter given to investigator
5. Father–daughter incest	Deathbed confession to patient's husband reported to investigator by him
6. Disremembered war trauma	Military records confirm recovered incidents
7. Father–daughter incest	Taped discussion of this by mother left on patient's answering machine shared with investigator
8. Particular incidents of incest and beatings	Confirmed to investigator by six sibs and mother in family session
9. Father–daughter incest	Sister who witnessed same described incidents to investigator
10. Maternal physical abuse	Mother confessed to investigator
11. Attempted oral rape	Friend witness called investigator

TABLE 12.2. Summary of Significant Findings and Observations

1. DID patients' abuse experiences can be documented in many instances.
2. Once-unavailable memories of trauma retrieved in psychotherapy of DID patients can be documented in many instances.
3. Accurate recovered memories of abuse can be documented in clinical DID populations.
4. Confabulated memories of abuse can be documented in clinical DID populations.
5. Hypnotically retrieved memories of abuse from DID patients can be documented as accurate in many instances.
6. The proposition that recovered memories of childhood abuse are invariably inaccurate and can be discounted a priori is refuted.
7. The proposition that recovered memories of childhood abuse are invariably accurate and can be accorded credibility a priori is refuted.
8. Most memories of abuse reported by DID patients are neither confirmed nor disconfirmed in the course of their therapy.

ized stances are inappropriate and unscientific. Virtually all the strong claims made by advocates of the extreme false memory perspective are deeply flawed and unproven (Pope & Brown, 1996). Readers are referred to those authors who have tried to bring moderation and an acknowledgement of the complexity of the situation to the study of recovered memory (e.g., Alpert, 1995; Brown, 1995a, 1995b; Hammond et al., 1995; Kluft, 1984b; Nash, 1994; Schooler, 1994; Spiegel & Scheflin, 1994; van der Kolk, 1995; van der Kolk & Fisler, 1995).

Of special note is that 85% of the patients who had recovered memories confirmed had accessed those memories with the help of hypnosis. A considerable experimental literature, reviewed in Brown (1995a) and Hammond et al. (1995) demonstrates that hypnosis indeed can be associated with the distortion of recall and the creation of confabulations. However, the situation is far more complex than is generally appreciated by those who make global statements condemning the use of hypnosis in the treatment of the traumatized or in the exploration of patients' histories. The following discussion draws on observations from Kluft (1997a).

Heterohypnosis, that is, instances in which hypnosis follows (i.e, is invited or induced by) a deliberate ritual of induction administered by another individual (as opposed to spontaneous trance and autohypnosis), is a particular vehicle of interpersonal influence. Interpersonal influences and persuasions in general are often capable of having an effect on the mentation of those to whom they are applied.

Hypnosis as a form of influence is usually discussed as if it were a particular form of intervention with a predictable (and presumably distorting) effect on memory. In fact, scholars continue to debate the definition of hypnosis and to espouse a variety of theories to explain its phenomena. (For a discussion of prominent theories, see Lynn & Rhue, 1991.) Furthermore, hypnosis is a facilitator of interventions rather than a treatment intervention per se (Brown & Fromm, 1986; Frischholz & Spiegel, 1983). When hypnosis is employed to catalyze a directive intervention, its impact is different from when it is used in the service of a permissive intervention. Let us consider three instances in which hypnosis might be used to explore an amnestic period during which abuse, among other things, might have occurred. In the first case, after the induction of hypnosis, the patient is requested to return to the period in question and asked: "Were you being hurt?" "You see someone. Is it your father?" "Is he naked?" This line of inquiry, beyond question, is highly suggestive and leading. Its potential to mislead a patient toward confabulation is beyond question. In a second case, after the same preliminaries, the patient is asked, "What do you observe?" "Can you identify the person you noticed?" "Does anything more strike your attention?" This type of approach is rather open-ended and permissive in comparison. One cannot assume that it is likely to promote confabulation. In a third instance, the second type of intervention is undertaken, but the patient at some level expects to find abuse memories because of already known traumata, the hypotheses of friends or relatives, something noted on a talk show or in some media, a recent dream, the tenor of the therapy to date, and so on. Contaminating expectations need not have their source in the hypnosis or the therapy for them to contribute to the formation of a confabulated account that is reported in the context of the therapy.

In addition to the complexities noted previously, it is crucial to realize that hypnotic talent is not uniform, even among patients with a high level of hypnotizability. Furthermore, spontaneous trance and autohypnotic trance phenomena are not uncommon in high hypnotizables, and DID patients are a very hypnotizable group (Frischholz, Lipman, Braun, & Sachs, 1992).

Therefore, it is extremely important to appreciate that generalizations made about hypnosis are often dangerously misleading and must be interpreted with caution. Often what is attributed to hypnosis is due to other factors in a treatment situation (Frankel, 1976) or a scientific experiment (McConkey, 1992). McConkey found that given hypnotizability and the demand characteristics of a situation, the formal induction of hypnosis did not contribute to the likelihood that memory distortion would be increased. Recent arguments to the effect that even the memories of unhypnotizable individuals can be influenced by the hypnotic-context speak actually are powerful evidences that the nature of the influence about which concern is being raised is not hypnotic per se.

In legal situations it is often problematic to use hypnotic interventions because potential for the formation of pseudomemories and the creation of a sense of certainty about what has been recovered (concretization) may distort the pursuit of justice (Laurence & Perry, 1988; McConkey & Sheehan, 1995; Orne, 1979; Scheflin & Shapiro, 1989). However, it is questionable whether forensic concerns and practices should dictate rather than inform clinical practice. What is guarded against because it is a possible outcome of "hypnosis" (confabulation) is assumed without proof to be probable and then represented (without proof) by experts as having occurred in particular clinical circumstances. Such conclusions are several removes from any demonstrable data and become dubious guides to the clinician.

This may help the reader appreciate why, despite the widespread current tendency to disparage the use of hypnosis in uncovering material, it is not beyond the realm of possibility that the Kluft (1995a) study found hypnosis was associated with the recovery of the majority of the accurate recovered memories and was not associated with the confabulated instances. In this study the hypnosis to which the subjects were exposed was gentle and cautious with regard to issues of memory.

Overgeneralized and almost cartoon-like caricatures of hypnosis in the literature threaten to discredit the usefulness of this very important clinical tool. This is very dangerous because not only are DID patients highly hypnotizable (Frischholz et al., 1992), but many severe and chronic cases of posttraumatic stress disorder are also highly hypnotizable (Spiegel, Hunt, & Dondershine, 1988; Stutman & Bliss, 1985). It is often crucial to restructure the autohypnotic and spontaneous trance-related difficulties of these patient populations. Many dissociative and posttraumatic symptoms respond well to therapies facilitated by hypnosis (Kluft, 1982, 1984b; Maldonado & Spiegel, 1994; Spiegel, 1991). It would be unfortunate indeed to deprive such patients of the benefits of therapeutic hypnosis on the basis of legitimate but usually manageable concerns inflated to the level of unfounded overgeneralizations. We are offered three possible solutions to the dilemma of whether to use hypnosis under such circumstances: We can decline to use hypnosis and forfeit a valuable clinical tool. We can use hypnosis poorly. Or, we can use hypnosis carefully and in a manner that is informed by both clinical experience and scholarly findings (E. Frischholz, personal communication, April 1997). The latter course seems most circumspect.

THE CLINICAL SITUATION ILLUSTRATED

In clinical practice the mental health professional encounters all manner of perplexing material from DID patients. At one point I (Kluft, 1984b) observed that

> [The therapist] must remain aware . . . that material influenced by intrusive inquiry of iatrogenic dissociation may be subject to distortion. In a given patient, one may find episodes of photographic recall, confabulation, screen phenomena, confusion between dreams or fantasies and reality, irregular recollection, and willful misrepresentation. One awaits a goodness of fit among several forms of data, and often must be satisfied to remain uncertain. (pp. 13–14)

Although my mention of photographic recall may sound extreme and naive in the atmosphere of the current debate over false memory, it derived from my contact with some DID individuals who could indeed scan a book for the first time and report its contents accurately page by page thereafter.

Table 12.3 illustrates the complexity of actual clinical experience. The table offers some perspective on the allegations that may be presented to a therapist during the clinical encounter with a DID patient. The patient was a subject in a study (Kluft, 1995a), treated by me for approximately a decade, the latter 4 years in an integrated state. She is an intelligent woman, a mature and responsible health care professional with seniority in her field. Throughout most of her treatment she manifested a number of traits that distracted from her credibility. She was easily angered and affronted and overly sensitive and hyperreactive to environmental triggers. She often was paranoid and accusatory. Her transferences were venomously negative and often difficult to tolerate. Her accusations of her psychiatrist were so distorted as to be more absurd than psychotic. In short, she was the enemy of her own credibility until the last years of her treatment. At the time of the study, she had become temporarily disabled by the consequences of an accident, but prior to this event she had been gainfully employed in her profession for several years. Over a period of years, her father, whom she had described as her chief abuser, suffered a severe decline in health and gradually became incapacitated. He lost his ironclad grasp over his family. No longer fearful of displeasing him and risking severe retribution, the patient's mother and siblings began to talk openly of the abuse in the family and to validate one another's memories. This followed her brother's confession by several years. It is of note that the patient's recall of satanic ritual abuse occurred when, in the course of a hospital stay, she was exposed to a group therapy setting in which most participants claimed to have had such experiences and described them in vivid detail. The practice of dealing with the details of such allegations in detail in group settings is contraindicated (Kluft, 1993).

TABLE 12.3. Confirmations and Disconfirmations in an Illustrative Case of DID: A Professional Woman in Her 40s

Alleged abuse	Source of confirmation or disconfirmation
Father–daughter incest (general)	Three sisters, one brother, and mother were aware of incest; father confessed and apologized while terminally ill
Father–daughter incest (specific incidents)	Three sisters, one brother, and mother recall walking in on specific episodes; patient had recovered the memories in hypnosis and asked them for confirmation
Incest–rape by brother	Confession by brother dying of cancer confirmed hypnotically recovered memory
Abuse by physician mentor	No data
Satanic ritual abuse	School records demonstrate patient was not at the location of alleged abuses at times of alleged events

Four brief clinical vignettes establish the groundwork for some additional considerations:

Vignette 1. A mental health professional with DID discussed rather severe molestation by her father, with her alcoholic mother's passive acquiescence. In the course of therapy she recovered under hypnosis and reported that both she and her mother played a role in live sex shows and pornographic movies directed by her father. She also had many personalities with the names of characters from J. R. R. Tolkien's *Lord of the Rings*, who told stories of fantastic adventures and unspeakable hardships.

Vignette 2. A woman with DID on psychiatric disability was brought to the emergency ward complaining she had been raped and cut with wounds suggestive of satanic symbolism by a man whom she remembered from her days of participation in the cult, and who insisted that she return to the cult or be killed.

Vignette 3. A woman with DID was referred for assessment and treatment, in the context of her confessing her participation, with her homosexual lover, in the serial murder of several men. She described their tactics, motivations, and the characteristics of their victims. Currently disabled, she had had a successful career in social services.

Vignette 4. A woman with DID recovered under hypnosis her seduction by a previous psychotherapist. The previous therapist was a highly visible and highly regarded individual in the community.

In Vignette 1, a family doctor confirmed to the investigator that he had suspected abuse when he saw the patient as a child. He confirmed that the patient's grandmother had described her erotized childhood behavior to him. This material had been recovered with hypnotic age regression. The patient reported that her father, when confronted about the incest, admitted it and asked forgiveness. He denied the other allegations. Several years after therapy ended, the patient called me to inform me that her mother, as part of her recovery, felt obliged to tell her that her terrible stories about the sex shows and pornography were true, although she had denied this for years. Her many alters based on a work of literature were due to a creative transformation the patient had performed in her own mind. She succeeded in distancing the horror of her childhood by covering it over with an imaginary inner world based on Tolkien's "Middle Earth," about which she had read with delight in her early teens. By focusing on the imaginary hardships of this world, in which sexual concerns played no role, she successfully placed her own traumata even further out of mind. Thus, real trauma and its transformation into a mythic structure played a role in contributing to the history that her alters presented. Had she not created this transformation in the language and metaphors of a known work of literature, the appearance of such fantastic and clearly untrue material might have been attributed to iatrogenesis and/or fantasy proneness. There is no compelling reason to doubt her reports of her parents' confessions, but a skeptic might argue that they, too, were part of a confabulated fantasy world, or iatrogenic in origin.

In Vignette 2, a forensic pathologist was asked to examine the patient's wounds before they were treated. He concluded with a reasonable degree of medical certainty that they were self-inflicted. Further inquiry demonstrated that she had mistaken a flashback for external reality and that cult-identified alters inflicted wounds on the body. What was visualized, although it did not occur, was registered as historical reality, and the patient presented with a confabulated history of assault in which she firmly believed.

In Vignette 3, the patient's account was studied in detail and depth and understood to be unlikely. There were no homicides consistent with her alleged exploits reported in the city in which they were alleged to have occurred. A clinical inference was reached that the alleged homosexual partner was nonexistent or was an alter and that the patient reported events from her inner world as if they had occurred in the actual world. Under hypnosis, an alter consistent with the homosexual lover was reached and admitted it had created the illusion of being loved and of turning against men for this very lonely and seriously abused woman who felt helpless to resist the men who exploited her.

In Vignette 4, the patient was treated on the basis that her report was accurate. A decade later the therapist who she alleged had exploited her came to the same therapist who had treated her and confessed what he had done, confirming the patient's account in great detail.

These vignettes further illustrate the dilemma of truth and reality in work with DID, and they certainly do not demonstrate the full spectrum of situations that may be encountered. They should not be seen as representative of all clinical permutations one might encounter, but they do call into question the false dichotomy often implied in the literature and in presentations that are connected in some manner with the so-called recovered memory debate— that events reported by DID patients in psychotherapy are either historical truth or confabulation, the latter often as a result of iatrogenic influences. Often, it has been reasoned that whatever is shared after therapy has begun is unlikely to be true and must be a result of the therapy. This is a clear example of the *post hoc, ergo propter hoc* fallacy. It assumes, further, that all patients reveal all relevant information at their initial assessment, allowing the establishment of an accurate pristine baseline. It neglects resistance, reluctance, guilt, shame, shyness, and the fact that some people like to get to know their therapist for a while before putting their cards on the table. I recall a very shy and private teacher who saw me for 8 years before revealing that she was homosexual. I doubt that she finally succumbed to any suggestions on my part that she confabulate her lesbian experiences.

In fact, much discussion of the purported truth or falsity of memories reported by DID patients demonstrates an incredible lack of familiarity with clinical DID patients and their treatment, if not with clinical practice in general. Patients live in many realities, and those realities have the potential to become commingled. They live in the historical reality that they experienced, as best as they can recall it. They live in the narrative realities that they construct (Spence, 1982), either by themselves or in conjunction with their experiences and interactions, among which may be psychotherapy. They live in the fantasy-driven realities of the unconscious. They live in the reconstructed realities that emerge from interpersonal influences to which they are exposed, among which are psychotherapy and the media. It is often worth wondering whether an idea that is reported in therapy is iatrogenic, or Ophragenic (i.e., inspired by a television talk show). They also live in the realities that they create for themselves, for the purposes of compensation for hurts and difficulties, and for mastery, however illusory, of what threatens to overwhelm them.

That is, in terms of the realities to which DID patients respond, and in connection with which they guide their thoughts and behaviors, there is a reality that is relatively consistent with historical events, although these events may be altered even in the processes of perception and registration, let alone the processes of storage and recall. There is a constructed inner reality with both available and unavailable components that emanates from the needs and adaptational efforts of the patient. There is another form of reality, based on the influences that play on the patient. These three realities and their interplay, however crude a model they constitute, offer a more "realistic" perspective on the subjective reality and the autobiographical memory of the DID patient than the "truth or fiction" polarity that often permeates discussions of this issue. Because historical truth and confabulation are fairly familiar subjects to the student of memory and the clinician who tries to sort out what he or she is told in the consulting room, the following discussion explores some aspects of this third reality, which often is overlooked and may be relatively unfamiliar to those who do not do clinical work with DID patients.

THE THIRD REALITY: THE INNER
WORLD OF THE DID PATIENT

Although it is common to focus on the alters and amnesias in DID, because these are superficially the most dramatic and compelling phenomena traditionally associated with the condition, I (Kluft, 1991a, 1995c, 1996a) argue that they are simply the delivery system for a more basic underlying attempt to deal with the experience of being overwhelmed (i.e., MPD expresses a more crucial and more basic multiple reality disorder). Kluft (1995c) reasons that the alters are not so much aligned to the concept of the unconscious as they are to the phenomenon of parallel distributed processing, which he has described for the psychoanalytically oriented reader as the "elsewhere thought known." Alter creation allows the enactment of adaptational strategies that are at times incompatible and operate more efficiently without the burden of conflicting data and experiences imposed upon them. Table 12.4 represents an example of how a young girl of 5 might try to cope with the trauma, betrayal, and potential loss of an important good object. To understand this table, please consider the circumstances of "Lois," abruptly molested by a previously loved and positively valued "Uncle Ben."

Crucial to the topic at hand is a particular consequence of the adaptational purpose of the alters. For them to function efficiently and effectively in the midst of ongoing traumatization, there are certain implicit demands that result in their developing alternate realities and incorporating them into their autobiographical memories. The adaptations that facilitate their function under these circumstances are profoundly dysfunctional in their long-term impact, and result in significant "secondary loss." For example, if Uncle Ben is preserved as a positive object by the assumption of the blame for what occurred, and by the adaptation of provocative behaviors that further the illusion that the patient is bad but has a good and loving uncle, the patient has attached herself to an adaptation that is likely to be associated with repeated revictimization and a profoundly masochistic stance toward the world (Kluft, 1990a), described elsewhere as "the sitting-duck syndrome" (Kluft, 1990b). Much of the patient's autobiographical memory, in different alters, is distorted consistent with the alters' purposes.

Essential to the process of alter formation is a disidentification from a sense of self and a self-representation that is rendered intolerable, a repudiation of empathic connectedness with this intolerable sense of self and self-representation and the formation of a boundary between the newly formed sense of self and self-representation and the one that is rendered unacceptable. An

TABLE 12.4. Coping Strategies and Alter Formation

Coping strategy	Alter created
This did not happen	A Lois who knows, and a Lois who does not
I must deserve it	Bad Lois, whose behavior would explain trauma as punishment
I must have wanted it	A sexual alter, Sherrie
I can control it better if I take charge	An aggressively sexual alter, Vickie
I would be safe if I were a boy	Louis, Lois's male "twin"
I wish I were a big man who could prevent this	Big Jack, based on some person of power
I wish I were the one who could hurt someone, and not be hurt	Uncle Ben, or a more disguised identification with the aggressor
I wish I could feel nothing	Jessie, who endures all yet feels nothing
I wish someone could replace me	"The Girls," who encapsulate specific experiences of trauma unknown to Lois
I wish someone would comfort me	Angel, with whom Lois imagines herself to be while the body is being exploited and "The Girls" are experiencing the trauma

illusory but subjectively compelling embodiment of the fantasized personified adaptation is formed and autohypnotically envisioned. A cognitive restructuring that validates and accommodates to this embodiment takes place, secondary to changes in source and reality-monitoring capacities, and to their interpretation throughout the mind (Kluft, in press). This process makes it quite possible for modified versions of autobiographical memory to be endorsed as actual. For example, Bad Lois must somehow destroy or distort her connection to all historical information that would cause her to see herself as an innocent victim, and Louis must eschew femininity and all memory that would cause him to own it. Alters may either reconfigure their senses of their past, develop amnesia, or "observe" the occurrence of disowned experiences to other alters. Of course, additional alternatives and all manner of combinations are possible.

Furthermore, many DID patients reconfigure their alter systems and, *pari passu*, revise their autobiographical memory in certain alters as they undergo the adolescent passage (Kluft, 1985b). This was illustrated in an unusual form in Vignette 1 and may well occur when extreme and convoluted abuse scenarios involving allegations of uncertain historical reality are brought into play. The adolescent's attempts to resolve residual trauma, establish sexuality, and move through the second separation/individuation process (Blos, 1967, 1968) may instigate rearrangements and elaborations in the relatively uncomplicated alter systems often found in children (Kluft & Schultz, 1993). I (Kluft, 1997b) speculate that such reconfigurations may explain apparent memories of transgenerational satanic ritual abuse in which abusive parents are understood to themselves have weathered equivalent mistreatment and only passed on what they learned, a relative exculpation.

It is also important to appreciate that when alter systems are relatively small they may all interact with a shared external world and operate on many of the same shared assumptions about external reality. However, when alter systems become more complicated, which is generally thought to result from more severe and prolonged abuse, and/or from the employment of a variety of more complex adaptational strategies (Kluft, 1988), it is more common than not for an inner world to develop among the alters and to develop a secondary autonomy, or a life of its own.

> It is useful to bear in mind, however, that in most patients with more than a small number of personalities, the alters constitute a system of mind, and most of them subjectively have the experience of relating to one another as if they were actual people. It is not uncommon for significant constellations of individuals, such as family members and/or those involved in their traumatization, to be represented in a direct, derivative, or symbolic fashion within the system of personalities (Kluft, Braun, & Sachs, 1984). Consequently, they may have inner relationships, alliances, and enmities and experience themselves as constituting an inner family or society with its own rules and mores. (Kluft, 1991b, pp. 611–612)

As a result, not only does a series of interactions occur, but the capacity to see and perceive them as clearly as if they were external is developed and exploited in the service of this process. This is probably associated with a capacity for fantasy proneness (Wilson & Barber, 1983). A history of those interactions and their envisioned occurrences is developed, and although some DID patients can distinguish events in the inner world from those in the outer world, many if not most cannot, or can do so only in certain circumscribed areas.

Although such inner worlds certainly can become more elaborated in responses to treatment, and especially in response to errors and/or mistaken directions in therapy (Kluft, 1982, 1988), it would not be appropriate to assume that their origin resides in the matrix of therapy. I have collected more than two dozen unpublished examples of diaries and drawings depicting such inner worlds dating from years, and usually decades, before the patients in question ever experienced psychotherapy. This would suggest that inner-world formation occurs naturalistically and apart from the treatment setting.

In summary, the subjective autobiographical memory of the DID patient is a complex, multifaceted, and deeply layered phenomenon in which a sense of reality may be accorded to events and experiences that reflect and may take some degree of origin from genuine historical events as they become registered in memory, fantasy, dreams, the doings of an inner world, and external distorting influences. Furthermore, several versions of autobiographical events are commonly encountered and reflect the compelling subjective realities of the alters found in this disorder. Because DID patients have years of practice in constructing alternative scenarios as part of their manner of coping with their past and their circumstances, it is extremely illogical to maintain that initially unavailable alternative accounts that are shared in the course of therapy are most likely to be iatrogenic.

CONCLUSION

The fascinating and provocative title of a recent book is *The Truth about the Truth* (Anderson, 1995). Achieving the explicit goal of Anderson's fascinating title is beyond the grasp of this chapter, and perhaps beyond the grasp of the mental health sciences at this moment in time. However, this chapter tries to convey a straightforward description of some of the more controversial and hotly debated aspects of the memory and memories of DID patients.

Much of what has been written about the memory and the memories of DID patients is consistent with major paradigms and belief systems but is riddled with those errors so common in discussions and debates in the era of the "recovered memory debate": premature cognitive commitment (Langer, 1989), confirmatory bias, hindsight bias, false reliance on representativeness, defensive questioning, motivated skepticism, and paradigm-driven sophomorism (list derived from Pope & Brown, 1996, and Kluft, 1997a, with additions). Without a more sophisticated appreciation of the circumstances of the DID patient, especially an understanding of what here is designated "the third reality," it will be difficult to bring scholarly and clinical discussion of the false dichotomization of the caricatured quarrel, historical reality, or confabulation to a higher level. This progression is essential for the the mental health sciences to achieve if they wish to rise above an infantile polarized debate toward a more complex and sophisticated consideration of human memory and human reality monitoring and testing and their interaction. Viewed from this perspective, the bewildering dilemmas posed by the autobiographical memories of the DID patient may be understood as an unrivaled opportunity and laboratory with which to elevate the study of and the clinical approach to the memory of childhood trauma to a higher level.

REFERENCES

Alpert, J. L. (1995). Criteria: Signposts toward the sexual abuse hypothesis. In J. L. Alpert (Ed.), *Sexual abuse recalled: Treating trauma in the era of the recovered memory debate* (pp. 363–396). Northvale, NJ: Aronson.

American Psychiatric Association. (1994). *Diagnostic and statistical manual of mental disorders* (4th ed.). Washington, DC: Author.

Anderson, W. T. (Ed.). (1995). *The truth about the truth: Deconfusing and re-constructing the postmodern world.* New York: Tarcher/Putnam's.

Bliss, E. L. (1984). Spontaneous self-hypnosis in multiple personality disorder. *Psychiatric Clinics of North America, 7,* 135–148.

Blos, P. (1967). The second individuation process of adolescence. *Psychoanalytic Study of the Child, 22,* 162–186.

Blos, P. (1968). Character formation in adolescence. *Psychoanalytic Study of the Child, 23,* 245–263.

Bowman, E. S., Blix, S., & Coons, P. M. (1985). Multiple personality in adolescence: Relationship to incestual experience. *Journal of the American Academy of Child Psychiatry, 24,* 109–114.

Braun, B. G. (Ed.). (1986). *Treatment of multiple personality disorder.* Washington, DC: American Psychiatric Press.

Brenneis, C. B. (1996). Multiple personality: Fantasy proneness, demand characteristics, and indirect communication. *Psychoanalytic Psychology, 13,* 367–387.

Brown, D. (1995a). Pseudomemories, the standard of science, and the standard of care in trauma treatment. *American Journal of Clinical Hypnosis, 37,* 1–24.

Brown, D. (1995b). Sources of suggestion and their applicability to psychotherapy. In J. L. Alpert (Ed.), *Sexual abuse recalled: Treating trauma in the era of the recovered memory debate* (pp. 61–100). Northvale, NJ: Aronson.

Brown, D., & Fromm, E. (1986). *Hypnotherapy and hypnoanalysis.* Hillsdale, NJ: Erlbaum.

Coons, P. M. (1994). Confirmation of childhood abuse in childhood and adolescent cases of multiple personality disorder and dissociative disorder not otherwise specified. *Journal of Nervous and Mental Disease, 182,* 461–464.

Coons, P. M ., & Milstein, V. (1986). Psychosexual disturbances in multiple personality: Characteristics, etiology, and treatment. *Journal of Clinical Psychiatry, 47,* 106–110.

Fagan, J., & McMahon, P. P. (1984). Incipient multiple personality in children: Four cases. *Journal of Nervous and Mental Disease, 172,* 26–36.

Frankel, F. H. (1976). *Hypnosis: Trance as a coping mechanism.* New York: Plenum Medical Books.

Frankel, F. H. (1993). Adult reconstruction of childhood events in the multiple personality disorder literature. *American Journal of Psychiatry, 150,* 954–958.

Frischholz, E. J. Lipman, L. S., Braun, B. G., & Sachs, R. G. (1992). Psychopathology, hypnotizability, and dissociation. *American Journal of Psychiatry, 149,* 1521–1525.

Frischholz, E., & Spiegel, D. (1983). Hypnosis is not therapy. *Bulletin of the British Society of Clinical and Experimental Hypnosis, 6,* 3–8.

Ganaway, G. K. (1989). History versus narrative truth: Clarifying the role of exogenous trauma in the etiology of MPD and its variants. *Dissociation, 2,* 205–220.

Ganaway, G. K. (1994). Transference and countertransference shaping influences on dissociative syndromes. In S. J. Lynn & J. W. Rhue (Eds.), *Dissociation: Clinical and theoretical perspectives* (pp. 317–337). New York: Guilford Press.

Hacking, I. (1995). *Rewriting the soul: Multiple personality and the sciences of memory.* Princeton, NJ: Princeton University Press.

Hammond, D. C., Garver, R. B., Mutter, C. B., Crasilneck, H. B., Frischholz, E., Gravitz, M. A., Hibler, N. S., Olson, J., Scheflin, A., Spiegel, H., & Wester, W. (1995). *Clinical hypnosis and memory: Guidelines for clinicians and for forensic hypnosis.* Chicago: American Society of Clinical Hypnosis Press.

Hornstein, N. L., & Putnam, F. W. (1992). Clinical phenomenology of child and adolescent multiple personality disorder. *Journal of the American Academy of Child and Adolescent Psychiatry, 31,* 1055–1077.

Kluft, R. P. (1982). Varieties of hypnotic interventions in the treatment of multiple personality. *American Journal of Clinical Hypnosis, 24,* 230–240.

Kluft, R. P. (1984a). Multiple personality in childhood. *Psychiatric Clinics of North America, 7,* 121–134.

Kluft, R. P. (1984b). Treatment of multiple personality disorder. *Psychiatric Clinics of North America, 7,* 9–29.

Kluft, R. P. (Ed.). (1985a). *Childhood antecedents of multiple personality.* Washington, DC: American Psychiatric Press.

Kluft, R. P. (1985b). The natural history of multiple personality disorder. In R. P. Kluft (Ed.), *Childhood antecedents of multiple personality* (pp. 197–239). Washington, DC: American Psychiatric Press.

Kluft, R. P. (1988). The phenomenology and treatment of extremely complex multiple personality disorder. *Dissociation, 1*(4), 47–58.

Kluft, R. P. (1989). Playing for time: Temporizing techniques in the treatment of multiple personality disorder. *American Journal of Clinical Hypnosis, 32,* 90–98.

Kluft, R. P. (1990a). Dissociation and subsequent vulnerability: A preliminary study. *Dissociation, 3,* 167–173.

Kluft, R. P. (1990b). Incest and subsequent revictimization: The case of therapist–patient sexual exploitation, with a description of the sitting duck syndrome. In R. P. Kluft (Ed.), *Incest-related syndromes of adult psychopathology* (pp. 263–287). Washington, DC: American Psychiatric Press.

Kluft, R. P. (1991a). Multiple personality disorder. In A. Tasman & S. M. Goldfinger

(Eds.), *American Psychiatric Press review of psychiatry* (Vol. 10, pp. 161–188). Washington, DC: American Psychiatric Press.

Kluft, R. P. (1991b). Clinical presentations of multiple personality disorder. *Psychiatric Clinics of North America, 14,* 605–629.

Kluft, R. P. (1993). The treatment of dissociative disorder patients: An overview of discoveries, successes, and failures. *Dissociation, 6,* 87–101.

Kluft, R. P. (1995a). The confirmation and disconfirmation of memories of abuse in dissociative identity disorder patients: A naturalistic clinical study. *Dissociation, 8,* 253–258.

Kluft, R. P. (1995b). Current controversies surrounding multiple personality disorder. In L. Cohen, J. Berzoff, & M. Elin (Eds.), *Dissociative identity disorder* (pp. 347–377). Northvale, NJ: Aronson.

Kluft, R. P. (1995c). The psychodynamic psychotherapy of multiple personality disorder. In J. P. Barber & P. Crits-Cristoph (Eds.), *Dynamic therapies for psychiatric disorders (Axis I)* (pp. 332–385). New York: Basic Books.

Kluft, R. P. (1996a). Multiple personality disorder: A legacy of trauma. In C. R. Pfeffer (Ed.), *Severe stress and mental disturbance in children* (pp. 411–448). Washington, DC: American Psychiatric Press.

Kluft, R. P. (1996b, July). *True lies, false truths, and naturalistic raw data: Applying clinical research findings to the false memory debate.* Paper presented at Trauma and Memory: An International Research Conference, University of New Hampshire, Durham.

Kluft, R. P. (1997a). The argument for the delayed recall of trauma. In P. Appelbaum, L. Uyehara, & M. Elin (Eds.), *Trauma and memory: Clinical and legal controversies.* Northvale, NJ: Aronson.

Kluft, R. P. (1997b). Overview of the treatment of patients alleging that they have suffered ritualized or sadistic abuse. In G. A. Fraser (Ed.), *The dilemma of ritual abuse* (pp. 31–63). Washington, DC: American Psychiatric Press.

Kluft, R. P. (in press). Body ego integration in dissociative identity disorder. In J. Goodwin & R. Attias (Eds.), [*Title not yet determined*]. Washington, DC: American Psychiatric Press.

Kluft, R. P., Braun, B. G., & Sachs, R. (1984). Multiple personality, intrafamilial abuse, and family psychiatry. *International Journal of Family Psychiatry, 5,* 283–301.

Kluft, R. P., & Schultz, R. (1993). Multiple personality disorder in adolescence. *Adolescent Psychiatry, 19,* 259–279.

Langer, E. J. (1989). *Mindfulness.* Reading, MA: Addison-Wesley.

Laurence, J.-R., & Perry, C. W. (1988). *Hypnosis, will, and memory: A psycho-legal history.* New York: Guilford Press.

Loewenstein, R. J. (1991). An office mental status examination for complex chronic dissociative symptoms and multiple personality disorder. *Psychiatric Clinics of North America, 14,* 567–604.

Lynne, S. J., & Rhue, J. W. (Eds.). (1991). *Theories of hypnosis: Current models and perspectives.* New York: Guilford Press.

Maldonado, J., & Spiegel, D. (1994). The treatment of posttraumatic stress disorder. In S. J. Lynn & J. W. Rhue (Eds.), *Dissociation: Clinical and theoretical perspectives* (pp. 215–241). New York: Guilford Press.

McConkey, K. M. (1992). The effects of hypnotic procedures on remembering: The experimental findings and their implications for forensic hypnosis. In E. Fromm

& M. R. Nash (Eds.), *Contemporary hypnosis research* (pp. 405–426). New York: Guilford Press.

McConkey, K. M., & Sheehan, P. W. (1995). *Hypnosis, memory, and behavior in criminal investigation.* New York: Guilford Press.

Nash, M. R. (1994). Memory distortion and sexual trauma: The problem of false negatives and false positives. *International Journal of Clinical and Experimental Hypnosis, 42,* 346–362.

Orne, M. T. (1979). The use and misuse of hypnosis in court. *International Journal of Clinical and Experimental Hypnosis, 27,* 311–341.

Piper, A., Jr. (1994). Multiple personality disorder: A critical review. *British Journal of Psychiatry, 164,* 600–612.

Pope, K. S. (1996). Memory, abuse, and science: Questioning claims about the false memory syndrome epidemic. *American Psychologist, 51,* 957–974.

Pope, K. S., & Brown, L. S. (1996). *Recovered memories of abuse: Assessment, therapy, forensics.* Washington, DC: American Psychological Association.

Putnam, F. W. (1985). Dissociation as a response to extreme trauma. In R. P. Kluft (Ed.), *Childhood antecedents of multiple personality* (pp. 65–97). Washington, DC: American Psychiatric Press.

Putnam, F. W. (1989). *Diagnosis and treatment of multiple personality disorder.* New York: Guilford Press.

Putnam, F. W., Guroff, J. J., Silberman, E. K., Barban, L., & Post, R. (1986). The clinical phenomenology of multiple personality disorder: A review of 100 recent cases. *Journal of Clinical Psychiatry, 47,* 285–293.

Ross, C. A. (1989). *Multiple personality disorder: Diagnosis, clinical features, and treatment.* New York: Wiley.

Ross, C. A., Norton, G. R., & Wozney, K. (1989). Multiple personality disorder: An analysis of 236 cases. *Canadian Journal of Psychiatry, 34,* 413–418.

Scheflin, A. W., & Shapiro, J. L. (1989). *Trance on trial.* New York: Guilford Press.

Schooler, J. W. (1994). Seeking the core: The issues and evidence surrounding recovered accounts of sexual trauma. *Consciousness and Cognition, 3,* 452–469.

Schultz, R., Braun, B. G., & Kluft, R. P. (1989). Multiple personality disorder: Phenomenology of selected variables in comparison to major depression. *Dissociation, 2,* 45–51.

Shapiro, F. (1995). *Eye movement desensitization and reprocessing: Basic principles, protocols, and procedures.* New York: Guilford Press.

Simpson, M. A. (1995). Gullible's travels, or the importance of being multiple. In L. Cohen, J. Berzoff, & M. Elin (Eds.), *Dissociative identity disorder* (pp. 87–134). Northvale, NJ: Aronson.

Spence, D. P. (1982). *Narrative truth and historical truth: Meaning and interpretation in psychoanalysis.* New York: Norton.

Spiegel, D. (1991). Dissociation and trauma. In A. Tasman & S. M. Goldfinger (Eds.), *American Psychiatric Press review of psychiatry* (Vol. 10, pp. 261–275). Washington, DC: American Psychiatric Press.

Spiegel, D., Hunt, T., & Dondershine, H. F. (1988). Dissociation and hypnotizability in posttraumatic stress disorder. *American Journal of Psychiatry, 145,* 301–305.

Spiegel, D., & Scheflin, A. W. (1994). Dissociated or fabricated: Psychiatric aspects of repressed memory in criminal and civil cases. *International Journal of Clinical and Experimental Hypnosis, 42,* 411–432.

Stutman, R. K., & Bliss, E. L. (1985). Posttraumatic stress disorder, hypnotizability, and imagery. *American Journal of Psychiatry, 142*, 741–743.

van der Kolk, B. A. (1995). The body, memory, and the psychobiology of trauma. In J. L. Alpert (Ed.), *Sexual abuse recalled: Treating trauma in the era of the recovered memory debate* (pp. 29–60). Northvale, NJ: Aronson.

van der Kolk, B. A., & Fisler, R. (1995). Dissociation and the fragmentary nature of traumatic memories: Overview and exploratory study. *Journal of Traumatic Stress, 8*, 505–525.

Wilson, S., & Barber, T. (1983). The fantasy-prone personality: Implications for understanding imagery, hypnosis, and parapsychological phenomena. In A. Sheikh (Ed.), *Imagery: Current theory, research, and applications* (pp. 340–387). New York: Wiley.

CHAPTER 13

FROM MEMORIES OF ABUSE TO THE ABUSE OF MEMORIES

Jean-Roch Laurence
Duncan Day
Louise Gaston

When ideas go unexamined and unchallenged for a long time, certain things happen. They become mythological, and they become very, very powerful.

—E. L. DOCTOROW

The great tragedy of science — the slaying of a beautiful hypothesis by an ugly fact.

—T. H. HUXLEY

When Freud concocted and commercialized psychoanalysis, he was forced to come to terms with his failure to develop a scientific model of the mind (Esterson, 1993; Flax, 1981). He buried his dream in one of his desk drawers, a drawer that would be opened only after his death in an attempt to bolster the scientific depth of his work. Freud achieved what no other person has been able to achieve since: he influenced the minds of therapists, clients, and the lay public for generations to come. By creating what might be thought of as a new literary genre, pseudoscientific fiction (Laurence, 1995b), he distanced himself definitively from the scientific model. To do so, however, he had to resort to deception: he had to tell his listeners that he had achieved therapeutic success when in fact he had not (Laurence, 1995b; see also Crews, 1993, 1994; Kerr, 1993). Little did Freud know that he would be helped by an extremely powerful yet unexpected ally, the human memory system.

If anything, Freud understood one very basic fact of human life: We want to make sense of the world, especially when our own individual world is in chaos (Lakoff & Coyne, 1993; Powell & Boer, 1994). To achieve such a goal, we can count on our built-in cognitive and emotional processes to continuously reinterpret the past in light of the current situation. In search of causes, even the most tenuous link seems reasonable if it carries the promise of reestablishing order.

The same social factors that helped the psychoanalytical movement to become solidly implanted in Western thought are today at play in the controversy surrounding the existence of false memories of abuse: a powerful political lobby and a pseudoscientific intelligentsia capitalizing on the current *Zeitgeist*. All this, however, would amount to nothing without the same basic ingredient that led to Freud's success: the malleability of the human memory system.[1]

Although it has been well documented scientifically that the accuracy of our memories for past events is less than perfect (e.g., Bartlett, 1932), a number of important common misconceptions remain that continue to guide and shape our views of autobiographical memories. From the early memory research of Ebbinghaus (cited in Tulving, 1983), on how we remember, to the current studies in the area of declarative memory and suggestibility (e.g., Labelle, Lamarche, & Laurence, 1990; Loftus, Donders, Hoffman, & Schooler, 1989; Loftus & Loftus, 1980), we are becoming more certain that the ability to reminisce depends on more than just having witnessed or participated in a past event (Nelson, 1993). The current controversy surrounding the so-called false memory syndrome (Gardner, 1993) represents a clash between science (see, e.g., Kihlstrom, 1994) on the one side and clinical folklore (see, e.g., Fox, 1995) on the other. These positions represent two divergent ways of approaching the world, each founding their arguments ultimately on different conceptions of the memory system.

If memory is a reconstructive process,[2] variations in the content of autobiographical memory over time should be thought of as the rule rather than the exception (Laurence, 1988). Part of the difficulty in accepting the natural fluctuations of memory lies in the fact that it does not sit well with the notion that the current mental representation of ourselves is based on an accurate record of our past experiences. Our subjective feelings of unity and continuity are powerful determinants of uncritical acceptance of the historical veracity of our personal experiences. Pierre Janet (1889) had already described how the views we hold about ourselves are shaped and maintained by an intricate interaction between ongoing perception, memories, beliefs and expectations about oneself (our actual self-concept) and the current situation (Perry & Laurence, 1984).

The reconstructive nature of memory would thus be adaptive, yet there is a considerable reluctance to let go of the Aristotelian metaphor of memory as etchings in a waxen tablet: a permanent, complete, and accurate recording of our lives. This concept of permanent records was the dominant metaphor until only recently, and it is therefore understandable that it lingers in the face of current evidence. The form of the storage metaphor has changed to reflect the technology of the times. From the development of writing to telephone switchboards to audio and visual recordings, the message is the same. In von Feinaigle's paper on memory as a warehouse (cited in Tulving, 1983), the inventory (of memories for events) is all there, and whether it can be easily accessed or not depends on how well catalogued and how neatly stored the items in the warehouse are. It is a nice metaphor for those who like to think that they are in possession of a collection of their entire life's events, like a collection of fine art. Unfortunately, it is a collection of compelling forgeries and fakes mixed in with the masterpieces.

Most of us prefer to think of these inaccuracies as uncommon and usually happening to someone else. It is even claimed that the only errors that occur are small, concerning trivial details, whereas the essentials remain uncorrupted (Franklin & Wright, 1991). There is, however, no clear evidence to support this supposition, although considerable experimental evidence exists to support the notion that no one, and no type or quality of memory, is exempt from the rule. If the gist of an important event is usually correct (Loftus, 1979, 1993), the actual reconstruction of the event may be the subject of considerable variations.

Following the space shuttle *Challenger* disaster, Neisser and Harsch (1992) questioned subjects about their whereabouts and activities when they learned of the tragedy. Morning-after recollections were compared with the same individuals' accounts retold almost 3 years later. The results showed that although most subjects claimed that their recollections of the event were still vivid, they were almost always different from what they reported the morning after. Moreover, they found that approximately a third of their sample reported very different stories. Even when challenged with differences in the original and newer narratives, there was a considerable preference for the most recent accounts as being accurate.

Not only can we distort the details and sequence of memories for things that actually did happen, we are equally adept at creating memories for things that never happened. In a study by Laurence and Perry (1983), highly hypnotizable participants were asked during hypnosis to recount and relive the experience of preparing for and going to bed on a night from the previous week. During the night, the investigation suggested, a loud noise had been heard and had awakened them on that night. Nearly 40% of the participants incorporated that suggestion seamlessly into their own memories and stated *after* hypnosis that they had been awakened by a loud noise on that night. Even being told that the memory for a noise was suggested during hypnosis did not deter them. Hypnosis, however, is not a necessary condition to induce this kind of memory construction. Similar results can be obtained simply by asking individuals to imagine noises and then later recall separate events (Weekes, Lynn, Green, & Brentar, 1992).

To refer to these reconstructions in memory as false implies that these kinds of memories happen only under certain, relatively rare conditions. In a sense, we are making the way in which our memories normally function appear to be abnormal. By pathologizing the times when memory is imperfect, we are perpetuating the concept that when things are working normally, we are able to recall accurately the things that have happened to us. This is simply not so. Everything we can recall about our own past is the result of some accurate information about events gone by and a healthy dose of filling in the details. This filling in is where the reconstruction hazard arises. Based on what we have learned about the world and ourselves, we can come up with a good approximation of what should have happened. Most of the time, even when errors creep into the narratives of our own lives in the form of distortions of memories for things that happened, or pseudomemories for things that did not happen, they do not change the way we live our lives or the way we view ourselves.

Those errors go undetected simply because they are consistent with all the things we expect and believe about ourselves. Absolute accuracy simply is not all that important in how we tell ourselves (and others) our own stories. In fact, some of the changes happen precisely because they make for a better story or are more consistent with how we view ourselves in the present (see Laurence & Perry, 1988; Neisser, 1984, on John Dean's memories of his meetings with President Nixon). In a sense, these constructive editions reduce the strain of trying to match a current self-concept and belief structure with a past one that may differ.

The times that it matters whether or not our recollections are important, are when the claims are used to attribute causality. Most important, memory accuracy is required or at least expected when the information gleaned from one's recollections is used to remove freedoms of another individual, as in a courtroom testimony. As we move through our day-to-day lives, we rarely if ever question the veridical nature of our own recollections. In fact, most often we take for granted that our recollections are reasonably truthful to our past.

In 1980, over 80% of professional therapists believed that all our memories were recorded permanently in our brain (Loftus & Loftus, 1980). In a recent study (Legault & Laurence, 1996, 1997) the same high percentage was found among psychologists and social workers despite 15 years of research on autobiographical memories. How can we explain this remarkable stability in what is known scientifically to be a fallacy?

The path of the conceptual errors behind our current thinking in the role of memory leads us, in part, to Freud. His idea was that when one cannot recall an important event, the "recording" of that event is still there somewhere, just blocked or beyond access. This conceptual precursor to repression places the onus on the retrieval process, thus preserving and protecting the storage metaphor. To enhance the retrieval capabilities of the memory system, Freud used hypnosis and soon found himself having to explain some rather astounding "uncovered" narratives (see, e.g., Breuer & Freud, 1893–1895/1955; Kihlstrom, Chapter 1, this volume).

As a concept, repression is linked to Freud's early theory of neurosis whereby a traumatic event can come to be blocked from recall unconsciously, then return to haunt an individual later in life when the adaptive value of repressing the memory declines (Holmes, 1990; Loftus, 1993). An entire industry has emerged in the mental health sciences designed to assist people in regaining access to those memories (Hedges, 1994). These assumptions are flawed. Freud told his followers that when no memories exist, one should create them and convince the patient of their correctness. This constructive process could be used therapeutically and should lead to the same improvement as the one expected from the actual retrieval of a veridical memory. Freud's writings provide numerous examples of such constructions (see Bowers & Farvolden, 1996, for a detailed review of Freud's imaginative involvement in his patients' memories). We cite only a few:

> The work keeps on coming to a stop and they [the patients] keep on maintaining that this time nothing has occurred to them. We must not believe what they say, we must always assume, and tell them too, that they have kept something back. . . . We must insist on this, we must repeat the pressure and represent ourselves as infallible, till at last we are really told something. . . . There are cases, too, in which the patient tries to disown [the memory] even after its return. "Something has occurred to me now, but you obviously put it into my head." . . . In all such cases, I remain unshakably firm. I . . . explain to the patient that [these distinctions] are only forms of his resistance and pretexts raised by it against reproducing this particular memory, which we must recognize in spite of all this. (Freud. 1940/1964, pp. 279–280)

Freud's firmness is rooted in his own observations that very often the analysand cannot retrieve any appropriate memories (i.e., memories in line with Freud's expectations). The analyst's construction of the allegedly repressed memory does not frequently trigger the reemergence of the repressed. As Freud pointed out: "Quite often we do not succeed in bringing the patient to recollect what has been repressed. Instead of that, if the analysis is carried out correctly, we produce in him an assured conviction of the truth of the construction which achieves the same therapeutic result as a recaptured memory" (Freud, 1937/1964, pp. 265–266).

It is thus clear that these memories did not exist, as Freud recognized a few years later when he relabeled them "wishful fantasies." He also unfortunately misattributed them to the patients rather than to himself—an unfortunate habit that has been revived by current "memory therapists" uncovering alien kidnappings, multiple personalities, mass abuse in day-care centers, and satanic ritual abuses to name only a few of the currently fashionable topics (see Mulhern, 1991). It is also clear that the construct of repression was originally nothing else than a convenient inference to support the construction of memories that would validate Freud's theorizing. Repression later became the key that opened the doors to the interpretation of dreams, again seemingly corroborating Freudianism.[3] Dream imagery has also seen a recent revival as a source of validation for recovering memories (e.g., Bass & Davis, 1988; Mack, 1994; Terr, 1994). Once the basic techniques are in place, each new corroboration will reaffirm the correctness of the theory and the myth will become more established. This is what Grünbaum (1984) called the tally argument (see also Bowers & Farvolden, 1996). If all citizens wear emerald glasses, the city has to be emerald.

Freud recognized the facts that memories are not reliable records of our own past, that they are malleable and can sometimes be created. If his approach to life had been more positive he may have found that the malleability of the memory system could serve an adaptive function and could be used to further adaptation rather than minimize misery through the ventilation of, by the end, less than wishful fantasies. No wonder then that when he published *Interpretation of Dreams,* he borrowed from Virgil the following motto: "If Heaven I cannot bend, then Hell I will arouse!" (see Ellenberger, 1970, p. 452).

Today, three major areas of scientific research can help us understand how memories can be either distorted or created in unsuspecting individuals. First we look at the research on autobiographical memories emphasizing the importance of understanding the different factors at play in reminiscing. Then we examine the influence of the therapeutic relationship in furthering the construction and consolidation of suggested memories. Finally, we point to the broader impact of the sociopolitical *Zeitgeist* that allows the debate to perpetuate itself.

THE MALLEABILITY OF MEMORY

One of the arguments commonly leveled against the claims of false memories is that the victims of sexual abuse would never conjure up such horribly painful stories of abuse if they were not true. This is, on the face of it, a compelling and intuitively appealing argument: In fact, it does not make sense that someone would erroneously recall such traumatic events if they had a choice in the matter. But do they?

One of the most emphasized characteristics of a "repressed" memory is its involuntary quality. These memories or at least some details of a memory would emerge at first without consciously thinking about them. This intrusive quality is often believed by therapists to be a quasi-pathognomonic sign of the historical veracity of the memory (see, e.g., Fredrickson, 1992; Herman, 1992; Kristiansen, Gareau, Mittleholt, DeCourville, & Hovdestad, 1995). Many areas of research cast a strong doubt on this assumption, whether the research on flashback and flashbulb memories and memories recalled through hypnosis, or research on the ability of people to differentiate between externally generated events and internally generated events, what Johnson and Raye (1981) labeled reality monitoring.

A recent review on the experiences of flashbacks (Frankel, 1994) makes it clear that it is nearly impossible to differentiate between a flashback stemming from a lived event or one originating from an imaginary one. A flashback has as much chance of being historically correct as of being incorrect. In an attempt to capture the essence of flashbacks, researchers have developed the field of flashbulb memories, memories that are so subjectively vivid that they appear to be recalled without any forms of distortion. As Neisser and Harsh (1992) demonstrated, however, flashbulb memories are as subject to deterioration and reconstruction as are any other autobiographical memories. It is worth noting that the very concept of flasbulb memory emerged out of a practice that is customary in clinical interventions. In the seminal paper on flashbulbs examining the memories of people about President Kennedy's assassination (Brown & Kulik, 1977; see also Winograd & Killinger, 1983), the experimenters took at face value the narratives of their subjects. They never attempted to corroborate any of the details of the stories but rather relied on the subjective feelings of truthfulness reported by their subjects.

The subjective impression of accuracy when remembering is usually inferred from the automatic, effortless reemergence of memories. This feeling of involuntariness in the experience of recall is more the rule than the exception; we orient the search and depending on the context of recall, one cue triggers the next one until no more memories are recalled. Constructing memories or internally generating events is usually accompanied by the impression of having to use more cognitive efforts than remembering exter- nally generated events (Johnson & Raye, 1981). Cognitive effort, however, can be a misleading heuristic when determining the origins of a memory. "Spon- taneous" and effortless imagery can be generated in certain contexts that bypass the impression of cognitive effort. This may ultimately lead to a misidentification of source (Johnson, 1988; Johnson, Foley, Suengas, & Raye, 1988; see also Ceci, Loftus, Leichtman, & Bruck, 1994). This misattribution process has been particularly noted in aided recall whether it be by hypnosis or any other mnemonic techniques (e.g., sodium amytal interviews).

Research on hypnosis pays particular attention to the involuntary or effortlessness quality of hypnotic behaviors and experiences (see, e.g., Bowers, Laurence, & Hart, 1988). In fact, a behavior or an experience is rarely labeled as hypnotic when it is totally devoid of this involuntary quality. If an arm is hypnotically paralyzed, it is devoid of any interest if the subject recognizes that he or she is just not moving it voluntarily. What makes the experience of hypnosis fascinating for subjects is their reported inability to move the paralyzed arm in spite of their conscious efforts to do so. Does it mean that the arm is really paralyzed? Subjectively, yes; objectively, no.

Research on hypnotic hypermnesia over the last 20 years clearly demon- strates that the subjective reality of memories is quite at odds with their historical veracity (Nash, 1987). Not that hypnosis cannot be used from time to time to recover some aspects of an event that seemed forgotten. It does happen, but the price to pay is incredibly high when one considers the incorrect information produced (see, e.g., Laurence & Perry, 1988; Perry, Laurene, D'Eon, & Tallant, 1988). If anything, hypnosis increases productivity rather than accuracy of recall; more to the point, this productivity is not random but guided by the verbal and nonverbal cues of the recall setting (Kandyba & Laurence, 1996; see also Spanos, Burgess, & Burgess, 1994; Spanos & McLean, 1986). Knowing that hypnosis or other related techniques are used with increasing popularity by memory therapists is certainly not reassuring. In an ongoing study at our laboratory (Day & Laurence, 1996), individuals who claim to have been abducted by aliens are evaluated as well as hypnotized to assess how their story evolves with repeated hypnotizations. Preliminary data seem to indicate not only that the narratives complexify with each hypnotic recall but also that the story continues to evolve between sessions. This is particularly reminiscent of cases of satanic ritual abuse or complex multiple personalities publicized in the recent years (see, e.g., Mulhern, 1991, 1994).

Hypnosis is far from being a necessary ingredient in the production of incorrect material in recall (see, e.g., Loftus, 1993; Loftus et al., 1989; Loftus & Ketcham, 1994). Perhaps the most well-known area of research here is the "misinformation effect," where some postevent misinformation influences or changes subjects' recall of the original event. Although there are still contentions about the exact cognitive mechanisms at play in the misinformation effect, the available research indicates clearly that memories for observed events can be altered in many ways. Whether it be through leading questions aimed at selectively biasing the ways subjects report an event (Loftus, 1979) or leading questions aimed at creating an event that in fact did not happen (see also Ceci and Bruck, 1993; Hyman, Husband, & Billings, 1995; Maestri, Laurence, & Perry, 1996, for similar experiments with children), the traditional view of long-term memory as an exact repository of all that happened in one's life has been severely challenged in the last 20 years. Most important, not only does postevent misinformation change the content of what one remembers, but the same effects were found when preevent misinformation is presented (Kenney & Laurence, 1990; Laurence, Kenney, & Cassar, 1997). This is particularly relevant when clients and/or therapists convey their expectations and beliefs before engaging in the process of recovering memories (see also Jacoby & Whitehouse, 1989, for an experimental demonstration of nonconscious influences on memory; Harris, Lee, Hensley, & Schoen, 1988, on the nonconscious influence of cultural scripts on recall).

In fact, the reconstructive aspect of autobiographical memories is so well established that few researchers object to the process of reconstruction for any life events, traumatic or not (see, e.g., Kihlstrom, 1993, 1994). The more recent attempt to circumvent this challenging aspect of the memory system for proponents of the recovered memory movement is to affirm that emotional memories would be processed in a nonreconstructive but rather reproductive mode due to such mechanisms as repression and/or dissociation (Whitfield, 1995). These special mechanisms would preserve the pristine quality of the original memory to the day of its recovery. It is, of course, an interesting albeit self-serving hypothesis and it would be important to assess the literature that deals with emotionally traumatic memories.

Closer examination of the literature on the effects of trauma is sufficient to recognize that one of the least frequent sequelae of trauma is a global forgetting or a global amnesia for the event. It is rather the contrary: a spotty recollection of the main events with frequent intrusions in awareness. Not only can people not forget, but they appear to have no control on when and how parts of the event are replayed in their minds! Psychogenic amnesia has always been defined as a temporary inability to retrieve information pertaining to a traumatic event, an inability that usually vanishes in a few days. It is particularly distressing that this definition of psychogenic amnesia was modified in the fourth edition of the *Diagnostic and Statistical Manual of Mental Disorders* (DSM-IV; American Psychiatric Association, 1994), not based on scientific data but on publicized cases of "repressed" memories,[4] and the continued beliefs about repression and dissociation promulgated by the adherents of memory recovery therapy (see, e.g., Terr, 1994). The reluctance to relinquish this belief seems to be based on the emotional impact of the memories retrieved on the clinicians themselves. Memories of abuse are most of the time retrieved with an emotional intensity that is often overwhelming, leading both clinicians and clients to potentially misattribute the origin of the memory. Emotional concomitants of memories, however, are no guarantee of historical veracity (Loftus, 1993). In fact, memories from prior lives or from alien kidnappings or even from the womb are often accompanied by intense emotional abreactions; they are nonetheless imaginary constructions (Laurence, 1995b).

If trauma is linked to intrusive memories, maybe it is only a certain type of trauma, sexual in nature, that can trigger repression and/or dissociation. However, the literature on the consequences of rape in adults seems to convey the opposite conclusion. Victims of rape seem to be able to describe their abusers given that they had a chance to observe them (and register this information) and that they did not suffer brain concussions (Loftus & Ketcham, 1994).

That leaves us with the possibility that only sexually traumatic experiences during childhood are in one way or the other repressed and/or dissociated. This would be congruent with the abundance of reported recovered memories of childhood abuse in recent years. However, a recent review of the literature on child abuse, looking at the studies conducted with children and adolescents rather than with adults, seems to suggest otherwise (Kendall-Tackett, Williams, & Finkelhor, 1993). Once again, amnesia is a rare consequence of childhood abuse in children. In this recent review, the sole indication of a potential amnesic symptom is found under the label "posttraumatic stress disorder (PTSD) reaction" and is not as such mentioned. This PTSD reaction was seen in preschool children. However, as the authors mention, these data stemmed from one case of day-care abuse in California.

Since then, many of these cases have been dismissed by the courts due to the highly suggestive methods used to elicit the narratives of abuse from the children. Extreme care should be taken in evaluating these types of data before reaching any conclusion.

The belief in postabuse amnesia stems from the more pervasive belief in childhood amnesia, one of Freud's most clever constructs, designed to support his concept of repression and, as noted earlier, the belief that all that one has experienced in one's life is permanently recorded in the brain (see Legault & Laurence, 1996, 1997, for data supporting the popularity of these two beliefs among professional therapists). These two beliefs lead to a more than dangerous conclusion: that sexually traumatic events experienced during childhood have been recorded but cannot be retrieved.

Thus, no matter how one looks at it, there is at the moment no scientific evidence to support a mental process akin to repression and/or dissociation[5] at play in childhood abuse. Recent research on episodic memories in early childhood demonstrate that our conceptions of childhood memory are quite at odds with children's ability to remember their past (see, e.g., Bauer, 1994, 1995). Even young children demonstrate the ability to reconstruct personal events over long periods given appropriate repetitions and cuing. As in the adult, errors and forgetting occur but nothing akin to what would be expected from repression or dissociation or amnesia. The development of autobiographical memories parallels the sociocognitive development of the child. In fact, recent evidence from developmental research does not support the idea that young children's memories are especially threatening (Nelson, 1993).

In summary, recent research on autobiographical memories leads us to two general conclusions about an individual's quest for past events. The first is that the process of memory retrieval is reconstructive in nature. The second is that the reconstruction is guided by one's general metamemory assumptions (see, e.g., O'Sullivan & Howe, 1995) and influenced by beliefs, attitudes, expectations, and ongoing experiences. Reconstructing without being aware of the process leads an individual to equate "what was" to "what is," strengthening the current mental representation of the self. Reminiscing is a social behavior aimed at strengthening our current self-presentation and most of the time at convincing someone else of our current state of affairs (whether it be a job interview, a romantic encounter, or, for that matter, a political speech). In therapy, because of a continuously reinforced belief among the public that self-understanding is the key to good mental health, the search for causal events is of prime interest.[6] If a difficulty is important enough or if it has endured in spite of previous attempts at resolution, one can only conclude that the cause must also be important and enduring. If "what is" is very distressful, "what was" must also have been very distressful. Easily retrieved and emotionally ventilated memories are thus set aside if the difficulties persist and the search for more explanatory memories can begin.

THE THERAPEUTIC ACTIVATION OF PSEUDOMEMORIES

Up to this point we have argued that rewriting our memories is the norm, not the result of pathological processes. We would argue that this form of continual and subtle rewriting is adaptive and rarely harmful. However, there are situations in which these basic processes become extremely damaging when left unchecked. Any situation that demands that individuals' memories be accurate, truthful records of the past exerts pressure on their ability to recall. Courtroom testimony and psychotherapy are two examples of such artificial contexts in which memories are expected to be more accurate than they can be. This is where the normal filling in process that comprises the basic operation of memory can go awry. The legal arena seems to be aware of the limits of memory accuracy and the fallibility of eyewitness testimony. Forensic researchers have been present in courts explaining the limitations of human perception and memory more than ever in the last 20 years. Why is it that so many therapists who work daily with the complexities of their clients' perceptions and recollections seem to pay little attention to these issues?

The psychotherapeutic context does not necessarily demand historical veracity from the client. It often asserts that what the client believes to be true is more important than what the facts may be (see Legault & Laurence, 1996, 1997). But this contextual set may lead to an intricate dance of collusion between the client and the therapist where what should be adaptive will ultimately prove maladaptive (see Laurence & Cassar, 1997, for an application of associative learning models to the collaborative construction of narratives of abuse).

The client–therapist relationship has been the subject of considerable study from virtually all areas of clinical psychology (e.g., Beutler, 1991; Beutler, Crago, & Arizmendi, 1986; Frank & Frank, 1991). It is well understood that this relationship is an interactive one, affecting the desired changes in the client and, typically, few changes in the therapist. The balance of power in that relationship favors the therapist. Most theories would agree that the relationship that exists between the therapist and client is the fulcrum on which the lever of the therapeutic technique (regardless of the orientation) rests. What is perhaps not sufficiently stressed is the synergistic quality of that skewed relationship, a synergy that will ultimately reinforce the therapist's and the client's beliefs in their explanations of the presenting symptomatology.

It is not the purpose of this section to review what is known of the therapeutic context and all the variables that affect it. However, it is the intent to draw attention to the importance of the perceptions, beliefs, and expectations of both clients *and therapists* in that situation and the dangers inherent in such an imbalanced relationship, especially when the therapist is not fully cognizant of these factors while intervening (see Dawes, 1994, p. 131). Typically, a client seeks help from a therapist, hoping for relief from some form of distress. This places the therapist immediately in the role of the healer/expert. By simply entering into that relationship, the therapist accepts the role of expert and must somehow play the part, regardless of the existence of any actual expertise or not (Dawes, 1994; Faust, Hart, Guilmette, & Arkes, 1988). In a study reported by Smith and Dumont (1995), 14% of the participants (clinical psychologists and counseling psychologists) who had no formal training in the use of projective tests freely used data from a test to generate diagnostic and etiological inferences. Moreover, 87% of the participants who used the test for diagnostic purposes proffered inferences that had little justification in the scientific literature.

Recent research does point out the lack of understanding of the most basic scientific facts about memory among certain clinicians and the inability (or disinterest) in keeping track of recent developments in this area of research (see, e.g., Dawes, 1994; Legault & Laurence, 1996, 1997). This is a more than distressing state of affairs when one considers that autobiographical memories are the prime ingredients of a therapist's interventions.

Therapists are as vulnerable to moral dilemmas, biases, and prejudice as anyone. What information will be retained (availability heuristics), what links are drawn between narratives and symptoms (representativeness heuristics and illusory correlations), and how these links will be fed back to the client (confirmatory heuristics) are continuously at play in the interaction between therapist and client. If we add to this what Nisbett and Ross (1980) labeled the "fundamental attribution error," that is, "the assumption that behavior is caused primarily by the enduring and consistent dispositions of the actor, as opposed to the particular characteristics of the situation to which the actor responds" (p. 31) and the general overconfidence with which clinicians voice their diagnostics, clinicians quickly may be led to believe in their own expertise. Thus, they may let their personal views, beliefs, and biases enter into the therapeutic context unchecked. Moreover, they may even come to believe that those same biases and views are beneficial, even essential, to successful therapy (Dawes, 1994; Dumont, 1993; Smith & Dumont, 1995).

The more comfortable many therapists feel in their view of the world, the easier it is to cease questioning that view, to relax their vigilance over their own biases. Yet the therapy session continues to be an interaction of the client's system of beliefs and the therapist's system of beliefs. Two-way, reciprocal relationships are far more complex than one-way, top-down systems of causal effect, yet it is the former that more appropriately describe the therapeutic relationship, and the latter that seem to be what most people think therapy, an expertise-based approach, should be. This reciprocal determinism is described as "the continuous interaction between behavioral, cognitive and environmental influences" (Bandura, 1978, p. 344), meaning that situational and personal determinants are both important in explaining behavior. This same definition applies to the therapeutic situation.

Bidirectionality places emergent properties in a stronger role, in a sense returning to the perceptual theories of the Gestalt psychologists. Each member of the dyad attempts to meet the other's expectations while trying to shape those very expectations, arriving at an asymmetrical, emergent new whole, which exists entirely and exclusively within that context. In fact, it is the goal of most therapists to encourage the client to incorporate the therapist's viewpoint as a means of gaining insight into the nature of the processes underlying the current difficulties. The problem seems to lie in how far therapists go in "bending" the client to see things the way they do, to see things "more clearly" or to adopt a more adaptive approach to problems—invariably that of the therapist. Ideally, the synergistic effect of this unspoken collusion between therapist and client should lead to a satisfactory resolution of the current problem.

The synergistic effect of the therapeutic relationship is a crucial factor in understanding where pseudomemories come from. Pseudomemories, which would perhaps be more appropriately named collaborative reconstruction of inaccurate memory episodes, are actually a combined effort, requiring the active participation of both parties. It is a process that capitalizes on the normal reconstructive aspects of memory but within an artificial, goal-oriented context that seeks explanations for current symptoms in past events. As mentioned previously, the imbalance inherent in the therapeutic context places greater responsibility on the therapist when such reconstructions arise. A quick look at the scientific literature on social persuasion suffices to understand that a client can easily fall prey to the therapist expert position. The Barnum effect (the use of ambiguous personality interpretations that are applicable to most individuals), the acquiescence bias, the effects of demand characteristics, and even the demonstrated lack of introspective advantage from the part of a client (see, e.g., Lees-Haley, Williams, & Brown, 1993; Nisbett & Wilson, 1977; M. T. Orne, 1962) are well-documented examples of the subject's vulnerability to an expert's interpretation of their current distress.

When an individual arrives for therapy, it is almost a given that the therapist will hypothesize about the cause for that individual's woes. Ideally, the therapist will go through the process of successively entertaining then discarding a number of hypotheses until a clear working hypothesis can be established. Unfortunately, this process is too often cut short, leading the therapist to prematurely interpret or to divulge his or her initial hypothesis or suspicion for the cause of the client's symptoms in a very brief time—indeed, eliciting, albeit sometimes unconsciously, the appropriate responses from the client (Gauron & Dickinson, 1969). This initial labeling of the problem at hand has been shown to become quite resistant to change, triggering an anchoring effect that will then be vulnerable to the many heuristics already mentioned (Dumont, 1993). This collaborative process can lead to the two participants exploring irrelevant aspects of the client's past, indulging in making connections between events, real or imagined, that may be related to the problem by appearance only. The initiation and propagation of this collaborative process can be conceptualized as an experiment in associative learning, a conditioned emotional response (the client's distress) in search of a new conditioned stimulus (a narrative of abuse) (Laurence & Cassar, 1997). The whole process may be deceptively adaptive—for a while. As Janet had already observed (Perry & Laurence, 1984), a cathartic reaction may bring a temporary improvement of the client's mental state. The process leading to this temporary improvement is often misinterpreted as the solution to the problem at hand, the moment in therapy when most of the associative learning takes place. As the associative strength weakens, that is, when both therapist and client realize that the first "recovery" has no lasting positive effect, the problem reoccurs or worsens; more of the same solution is then sought, leading to the construction of a series of cathartic episodes, or, said otherwise, of learning episodes aimed at furthering the associative strength between the symptoms and the narratives of abuse.

To complicate this process, therapists are often reluctant to accept that there may be nothing of relevance to find along the lines of their prefered hypothesis. Even if the client states clearly that there is no connection between his or her symptoms and a past event, or any relevance to the therapist's hypothesis, there is a tendency to label it denial and continue pursuing that line of query (remember Freud). In time, the combined effect of the expertise and suggestion of the therapist and the collaborative search for a "smoking gun" result in enough self-doubt and confusion in the client that the therapist's hypothesis takes on its own reality. Through the therapeutic relationship and the special dynamic that exists within that context, memories for nonexistent events can be created and wrongly validated. In the long run, the effect is all too often damaging. However, it need not be. If therapists gain greater awareness of their role in this relationship, the power for benefit inherent in exactly the same processes can be activated. Reconstructing the past in light of what the present should be can be as rewarding and certainly more adaptive for both clients and therapists. Again, Janet at the beginning of this century warned that abreaction without restructuring of the past is worthless. This restructure could only succeed if the client's attention was brought back from the past to the present, a process he labeled "presentification." Therapists do not necessarily need to stop creating stories in the context of therapy, but they do need to stop believing their own stories while weaving them (Laurence, 1992).

THE SOCIAL VALIDATION OF VICTIMIZATION: ADAPTING TO THE *ZEITGEIST*

The question that arises from the awareness we are now gaining about the damage being done in therapy may very well resemble the questions asked by those individuals who witnessed or even participated in the famous witch trials of the 17th century: how did it get this far in the first place?

For change to happen, a global social climate must exist, along with its attendant beliefs, attitudes, and expectations. As the patient takes on the role of the consumer of health care services more and more, there is less sanctity in a physician's office (or a psychologist's or a therapist's); what was once a private ritual is now open to public scrutiny (Morfit, 1994).

Thus a number of factors are at play in bringing forth and exposing publicly psychotherapeutic rituals. We can certainly understand how the individual or at least his or her memory system is the basic ingredient. The individuals' sense of their own past is the object of the ritual, both fueling and perpetuating it. We can also understand that the ritual can only take place if there are ritualistic leaders. These are the acolytes of the inner sanctum who claim to possess the truth, who can conduct the rituals properly, and who believe profoundly in the righteousness of their cause (see, e.g., Mulhern, 1991). As Ellenberger (1970) discussed, however, the strength of the ritual can only reach its full potential if it is endorsed by the surrounding, greater social context.

When a social controversy arises, it often helps in bringing forth some apparently unrelated issues that previously escaped public attention. Perhaps one of the most apparent side-effects of this controversy is the public and professional realization that an important portion of what is actually practiced in psychotherapy and clinical psychology is largely without scientific foundation (Dawes, 1994; Laurence, 1995a). As Ellenberger (1970) so aptly observed, the psychotherapeutic rituals are much closer to the primitive healing rituals than to scientific models of healing. One of the consequences of building a profession on such a poor foundation is, on the one hand, the inability to eliminate old, inaccurate, and mostly epistemologically flawed theories and, on the other, the continuous acceptance of new rituals also devoid of any scientific underpinnings. Two recent examples of such uncritical acceptance—facilitated communication (Crossley, 1994) and EMDR (eye movement desensitization and reprocessing; Shapiro, 1994)—have already been linked to the elaboration of pseudomemories and the perpetuation of most memory myths (Bowers & Farvolden, 1996). These theories persist simply because they become ritualistically entrenched. This unfortunate state of affairs leads to "legitimized errors," that is, errors that are socially acceptable within the current *Zeitgeist* (see Victor, 1994).

The wide proliferation and acceptance of pseudomemories of abuse would not have happened without a larger communication and organizational network (Victor, 1993; Mulhern, 1991). The general perception of a social threat (e.g., child sexual abuse), the vocal influence of activist groups in general with specific emphasis on the victimization of women, and a socioculturally defined political correctness have given the controversy of recovered memories a national theater in which the personal dramas are played. These three factors have been widely publicized in the electronic medias, impregnating the minds of the viewers looking for some definite made-for-television explanations of their shattered dreams. A recent study showed for example, that the number of diagnosed dissociative disorders parallels closely the number of times the media publicized the issue. This observation is further supported by the results of surveys of public and professionals beliefs in the more occult functions of memory (see, e.g., Garry & Loftus, 1994; Labelle et al., 1990; Loftus & Loftus, 1980, for public beliefs about memory; Legault & Laurence, 1996, 1997; Yapko, 1994, for beliefs held by professionals).

The current tendency for many individuals to feel victimized, perhaps out of feelings of entitlement or other forms of disappointment, stems from discrepancies in what they were told they could expect through our cultural myths and what they actually get in life. The increasing expectations of individuals in all walks of life is a healthy stride away from oppression or victimization. However, to recover from victimization, one must first have identified, on some level, with the victim role. The unfortunate consequence of this empowerment is the associated increase in people, whether by group or as individuals, first having to become victims.

A number of possible gains can be made as the result of having been "wronged." The most obvious is simply that of gaining attention.[7] Once a victim is recognized as such, there is a changed perspective seen in the reactions of others. In addition, there is a gain in validation of the pain suffered by the alleged victim. With recognition of the victim comes a voice, group advocacy, and validation of the harm suffered. By receiving validation of harm, there is a tendency to more fully embrace that harm, possibly even to the point of overreaction or creating more pain than was actually there.

Perhaps the most potent gain in adopting the role of the victim is that of responsibility. If one has been victimized, the responsibility for consequences, problems, symptoms, and woes lie outside the individual's purview. Individuals given a ready-made explanation for why their lives are not as good as they should be, can find great relief in learning that they are not responsible for their difficulties. By abdicating responsibility, they then become even more entrenched in the role of victim and risk generalizing this attribution in other areas of life as well, perceiving themselves less as an active agent in their own lives and more as someone to whom tragic things happen. Once these secondary gains are recognized, victims may enter a cycle of seeking continued recognition and validation by further identifying with the victim role.

The debate over pseudomemories of abuse has become an overt political battle. Supporters of recovered memories have gone a long way in taking a public stance on the continued social victimization of women (see, e.g., Enns, McNeilly, Corkery, & Gilbert, 1995; Fox, 1995; Quirk & DePrince, 1995; Rockwell, 1994, 1995; Robbins, 1995). Fueled by political correctness, the problem of childhood abuse, of the imagined kind, has become a powerful weapon in the hands of those hoping to accelerate social changes. One may ask, however, if the individuals recovering memories of abuse are willing participants in this sociopolitical drama or if they are akin to the dispensable foot soldier in the name of a greater cause?

Unfortunately, these individuals do not have a choice in the matter. Given the original unresolved and apparently unresolvable distress, given the well-engrained beliefs about hidden memories, given the motivation to endorse a probable cause, given the conditional acceptance of therapists based on the proposed scenarios, there is little left for freedom of choice, little left for dignity. And when one's own memories turn against one's self, what is left but to be an unwilling foot soldier?

CONCLUSION

From individual distress to political stances and back to individual distress, one furthering the other, the entire process of memory recovery, usually conducted in a therapist's office, distorts what is and should serve an adaptive function. Memory was never meant to be all that accurate. Experimental research on memory was initially responsible for the notion that memory should be a faithful recording of one's history. The reproductive capacity of the memory system at one time was the simplest of its functions to study, at least at face value. Times have changed.

When one looks at the intrinsic malleability of the memory system, at the interactional processes that mold retrieved experiences, and the pervasive influence of the current *Zeitgeist,* it is difficult to come to any other conclusion than that autobiographical memories are adaptive. Even at the encoding stage, this adaptive interface is active and will continue to be, through storage and, ultimately, retrieval. It plays an integrative role in the lives of clients who seek relief from a distressful situation. At first, "recovered memories" play the same adaptive role as remembered memories in these same people when distress is absent. This new set of memories however, continuously reinforced and socially legitimized by therapists, takes a life of its own, furthering chaos in an already chaotic existence (see also Lockard & Paulhus, 1988). Members of the mental health profession should give careful consideration to this notion before embarking on the dangerous path of rebuilding their clients' pasts in light of their own perceptions and beliefs (Laurence, 1992).

There is always a price to pay to further a specific sociopolitical view, and to use what should be a therapeutic process to further victimize an already harmed portion of our society is not only antithetical to the goals pursued but conducive to more harm. To paraphrase Huxley, the role of science is often to replace a fantasy by an ugly fact. It may be time for psychotherapy and clinical psychology to face an ugly fact.

NOTES

1. Because of space limitation, only the literature on the malleability of the memory system is examined in some detail. The role played by sociocultural factors in maintaining both the therapists' beliefs in the righteousness of their goals and their clients' newly established delusional ideation are only briefly presented. The readers are referred, among others, to Dawes (1994), Grünbaum (1984, 1993), Mulhern

(1991, 1995), Ofshe and Watters (1994), Pendergrast (1995), and Victor (1994) for diverse yet incisive accounts of the social construction of memories.

2. The goal of memory retrieval is the reproduction of the information that one is looking for. Although memories can be reproduced correctly (e.g., retrieving the telephone number of a friend), the success of this memory function (exact copy of original information) depends largely on such factors as number of initial repetitions, importance of final results, and continuous rehearsal, which lead to perfect reproduction. This function, however, is also the end result of a reconstructive process.

3. Freud's interpretations of dreams were nothing other than a reversal of the usual ways of looking at dreams. Up to Freud, fortune tellers used dreams to predict the future. Freud used dreams to predict the past; he became a misfortune teller (Laurence & Perry, 1988).

4. A large proportion of this "evidence" comes from cases of mass abuse in day-care centers that proliferated in the 1980s. Unfortunately, most of these cases have by now been debunked and the evidence shown to be the end result of the misuse of suggestive techniques. In cases in which research has attempted to demonstrate the presence of repression, it failed lamentably (Briere & Conte, 1993; Herman & Schatzow, 1987; Williams, 1993, 1994).

5. Again, here the evidence supporting the notion of recovered memories comes mainly from cases of dissociative identity disorder (DID) and the well-accepted belief that sexual abuse lies at the core of this syndrome. However, when one reviews the research literature linking sexual abuse to DID, the evidence is at best tenuous. Again, the bulk of the evidence comes from clinical cases in which the therapists believe that abuse should be found to explain the pathology, a rather unfortunate state of affairs that has been vehemently denounced in many recent public documentaries.

6. Although we do recognize that many contemporary types of therapy emphasize current resolution of difficulties, a quick glance at the range of lay therapists as well as the percentage of official therapists who still cling to some variation of psychodynamism suffices to show why clients usually present themselves with the desire to identify the causes of their dysfunctions.

7. As many authors have noted, this highly publicized debate may become detrimental to all those who are or have been genuine victims of childhood abuse. It has been and still is imperative to bring physical, emotional, and sexual abuse of children to the attention of the public and take steps to eradicate it. However, publicized cases that are ultimately rejected on the ground of suggestive influence can bring more harm than good to this important social problem.

REFERENCES

American Psychiatric Association. (1994). *Diagnostic and statistical manual of mental disorders* (4th ed.). Washington, DC: Author.

Bandura, A. (1978). The self system in reciprocal determinism. *American Psychologist, 33*, 344–358.

Bartlett, F. C., (1932) . *Remembering: A study in experimental social psychology.* Cambridge: Cambridge University Press.

Bass, E., & Davis, L. (1988). *The courage to heal.* New York: Harper & Row.

Bauer, P. J. (1994). Episodic memory in 16- and 20-month-old children: Specifics are generalized. *Developmental Psychology, 30,* 403–413.

Bauer, P. J. (1995). Effects of experience and reminding on long term recall in infancy: Remembering not to forget. *Journal of Experimental Child Psychology, 59,* 260–298.

Beutler, L. E. (1991). Have all won and must all have prizes? Revisiting Luborsky et al.'s *Verdict. Journal of Counseling and Clinical Psychology, 59(2),* 226–232.

Beutler, L. E., Crago, M., & Arizmendi, T. G. (1986). Therapist variables in psychotherapy process and outcome. In S. L. Garfield, & A. E. Bergin (Eds.), *Handbook of psychotherapy and behavior change,* (pp. 257–310). New York: Wiley.

Bowers, K. S., & Farvolden, P. (1996). Revisiting a century-old Freudian slip: From suggestion disavowed to the truth repressed. *Psychological Bulletin, 119,* 355–380.

Bowers, P., Laurence, J.-R., & Hart, D. (1988). The experience of hypnotic suggestions. *International Journal of Clinical and Experimental Hypnosis. 36,* 336–349.

Briere, J., & Conte, J. (1993). Self-reported amnesia in adults molested as children. *Journal of Traumatic Stress, 6,* 21–31.

Breuer J., & Freud, S. (1955). Studies on hysteria. In J. Strachey (Ed. & Trans.), *The standard edition of the complete psychological works of Sigmund Freud* (Vol. 2). London: Hogarth Press. (Original work published 1893–1895)

Brown, R., & Kulik, J. (1977). Flashbulb memories. *Cognition, 5,* 73–99.

Ceci, S. J., & Bruck, M. (1993). Suggestibility of the child witness: A historical review and synthesis. *Psychological Bulletin, 3,* 403–439.

Ceci, S. J., Loftus, E. F., Leichtman, M., & Bruck, M. (1994). The possible role of source misattributions in the creation of false beliefs among preschoolers [Special Issue: Hypnosis and delayed recall: I]. *International Journal of Clinical and Experimental Hypnosis, 42,* 304–320.

Crews, F. (1993, November). The unknown Freud. *The New York Review,* pp. 53–66.

Crews, F. (1994, February). The unknown Freud: An exchange. *The New York Review,* pp. 34–43.

Crossley, R. (1994). *Facilitated communication training.* New York: Columbia Teachers College Press.

Dawes, R. M. (1994). *House of cards: Psychology and psychotherapy built on myth.* New York: Free Press.

Day, D., & Laurence, J.-R. (1996). *The UFO abduction phenomenon and the hypnotic context.* Unpublished manuscript, Concordia University, Montreal, Quebec, Canada.

Dumont, F. (1993). Inferential heuristics in clinical problem formulation: Selective review of their strengths and weaknesses. *Professional Psychology: Research and Practice, 24,* 196–205.

Ellenberger, H. F. (1970). *The discovery of the unconscious: The history and evolution of dynamic psychiatry.* New York: Basic Books.

Enns, C. Z., McNeilly, C. L., Corkery, J. M., & Gilbert, M. S. (1995). The debate about delayed memories of child sexual buse: A feminist perspective [Special section: Delayed memory debate]. *Counseling Psychologist, 23,* 181–279.

Esterson, A. (1993). *Seductive mirage: An exploration of the work of Sigmund Freud.* Chicago: Open Court Press.

Faust, D., Hart, K., Guilmette, T. J., & Arkes, H. R. (1988). Neuropsychologists' capacity to detect adolescent malingerers. *Professional Psychology: Research and Practice, 19,* 508–515.

Flax, J. (1981). Psychoanalysis and the philosophy of science: Critique or resistance? *Journal of Philosophy, 78,* 561–569.

Fox, R. E. (1995). The rape of psychotherapy. *Professional Psychology: Research and Practice, 26,* 147–155.

Frank, J. D., & Frank, J. B. (1991). *Persuasion and healing: A comparative study of psychotherapy.* Baltimore: Johns Hopkins University Press.

Frankel, F. H. (1994). The concept of flashbacks in historical perspective. [Special issue: Hypnosis and delayed recall: I]. *International Journal of Clinical and Experimental Hypnosis, 42,* 321–336

Franklin, E., & Wright, W. (1991). *Sins of the father.* New York: Crown Books.

Fredrickson, R. (1992). *Repressed memories: A journey through recovery from sexual abuse.* New York: Simon & Schuster.

Freud, S. (1964). An outline of psycho-analysis. In J. Strachey (Ed. and Trans.), *The standard edition of the complete psychological works of Sigmund Freud* (Vol. 23, pp. 139–207). London: Hogarth Press. (Original work published 1940)

Freud, S. (1964). Constructions in analysis. In J. Strachey (Ed. and Trans.), *The standard edition of the complete psychological works of Sigmund Freud* (Vol. 23, pp. 255–269). London: Hogarth Press. (Original work published 1937)

Garry, M., & Loftus, E. F. (1994). Pseudo-memories without hypnosis. [Special issue: Hypnosis and delayed recall. I.] *International Journal of Clinical and Experimental Hypnosis, 42,* 363–378.

Gardner, M. (1993). Notes of a fringe-watcher: The false memory syndrome. *Skeptical Inquirer, 17,* 370–375.

Gauron, E. F., & Dickinson, J. K. (1969). The influence of seeing the patient first on diagnostic decision-making in psychiatry. *American Journal of Psychiatry, 126,* 199–205.

Grünbaum, A. (1984). *The foundations of psychoanalysis: A philosophical critique.* Berkeley: University of California Press.

Grünbaum, A. (1993). *Validation of the clinical theory of psychoanalysis: A study in the philosophy of psychoanalysis.* New York: International Universities Press.

Harris, R. J., Lee, D. J., Hensley, D. L., & Schoen, L. M. (1988). The effect of cultural script knowledge on memory for story over time. *Discourse Processes, 11,* 413–431.

Hedges, L. E. (1994). Taking recovered memories seriously. *Issues in Child Abuse Accusations, 6,* 1–31.

Herman, J. L. (1992). *Trauma and recovery.* New York: Basic Books.

Herman, J. L., & Schatzow, E. (1987). Recovery and verification of memories of childhood sexual trauma. *Psychoanalytic Psychology, 4,* 1–14.

Holmes, D. S. (1990). The evidence for repression: An examination of sixty years of research. In J. L. Singer (Ed.), *Repression and dissociation* (pp. 85–102). Chicago: University of Chicago Press.

Hyman, I. E., Husband, T. H., & Billings, F. J. (1995). False memories of childhood experiences. *Applied Cognitive Psychology, 9,* 181–197.

Jacoby, L. L., & Whitehouse, K. (1989). An illusion of memory: False recognition influenced by unconscious perception. *Journal of Experimental Psychology: General, 118,* 126–135.

Janet, P., (1889). *L'automatisme psychologique.* Paris: Alcan.

Johnson, M. K. (1988). Discriminating the origin of information. In T. F. Oltmanns & B. A. Maher (Eds.). *Delusional beliefs* (pp. 34–65). New York: Wiley.

Johnson, M., Foley, M. A., Suengas, A. G., & Raye, C. L. (1988). Phenomenal characteristics for perceived and imagined autobiographical events. *Journal of Experimental Psychology: General, 117,* 371–376.

Johnson, M. K., & Raye, C. L. (1981). Reality monitoring. *Psychological Review, 88,* 67–85.

Kandyba, C., & Laurence, J.-R. (1996, August). *The modification and creation of memories in regression to early childhood and the uterus.* Poster presented at the 26th International Congress of Psychology, Montreal, Quebec, Canada.

Kendall-Tackett, K. A., Williams, L. M., & Finkelhor, D. (1993). Impact of sexual abuse on children: A review and synthesis of recent empirical studies. *Psychological Bulletin, 113,* 164–180.

Kenney, A., & Laurence, J.-R. (1990, October). *Finding memory creation between the lines of verbal report: The relation between individual differences and verbal style out of hypnosis.* Paper presented to the 41st annual scientific meeting of the Society for Clinical and Experimental Hypnosis, Tucson, AZ.

Kerr, J. (1993). *A most dangerous method: The story of Jung, Freud, and Sabina Spielrein.* New York: Knopf.

Kihlstrom, J. F. (1993, April). *The recovery of memory in laboratory and clinic.* Invited address at the joint annual meeting of the Rocky Mountain Psychological Association and Western Psychological Association, Phoenix, AZ.

Kihlstrom, J. F. (1994). Hypnosis, delayed recall, and the principles of memory. *International Journal of Clinical and Experimental Hypnosis, 42,* 337–345.

Kristiansen, C. M., Gareau, C., Mittleholt, J., DeCourville, N. H., & Hovdestad, W. E. (1995). *Social psychological factors sustaining the recovered memory debate.* Paper presented to the annual meeting of the American Psychological Association, New York.

Labelle, L., Lamarche, M. C., & Laurence, J.-R. (1990). Potential jurors' knowledge of the effects of hypnosis on eyewitness identification. *International Journal of Clinical and Experimental Hypnosis, 38,* 315–319.

Lakoff, R. T., & Coyne, J. C. (1993). *Father knows best: The use and abuse of power in Freud's case of Dora.* New York: Teachers College Press.

Laurence, J.-R. (1988, June). *Errors of memory: System failure or adaptive functioning?* Paper session presented at the 49th annual convention of the Canadian Psychological Association, Montreal, Quebec, Canada.

Laurence, J.-R. (1992, August 23–27). *Should we believe what we tell our patients? Toward a scientific psychotherapy.* Invited address at the Third National Assembly of the Federation of Canadian Societies of Clinical Hypnosis, Vancouver, British Columbia, Canada.

Laurence, J.-R. (1995a, November 7–12). *Let bygone be bygone: Cash only please.* Paper presented at the annual meeting of the Society for Clinical and Experimental Hypnosis, San Antonio, TX.

Laurence, J.-R. (1995b). *De la non-scientificité de la théorie psychanalytique.* Unpublished manuscript, Concordia University, Montreal, Quebec, Canada.

Laurence, J.-R., & Cassar, D. (1997). *Can associative learning models help us understand the phenomenon of recovered memories of abuse?* Unpublished laboratory document, Concordia University, Montreal, Quebec, Canada.

Laurence, J.-R., & Perry, C. (1983). Hypnotically created memory among highly hypnotizable subjects. *Science, 222,* 523–524.

Laurence, J.-R., & Perry, C. (1988). *Hypnosis, will, and memory: A psycho-legal history.* New York: Guilford Press.

Laurence, J.-R., Kenney, A., & Cassar, D. (1997). *The incorporation of pre-event misinformation in memory.* Unpublished laboratory document, Concordia University, Montreal, Quebec, Canada.

Lees-Haley, P. R., Williams, C. W., & Brown, R. S. (1993). The Barnum effect and personal injury litigation. *American Journal of Forensic Psychology, 11,* 21–28.

Legault, E., & Laurence, J.-R., (1996, August 16–21). *Therapists' beliefs and knowledge about memory processes.* Poster presented at the 26th International Congress of Psychology, Montreal, Quebec, Canada.

Legault, E., & Laurence, J.-R., (1997). *Elicited narratives of childhood sexual abuse: Social worker, psychologist, and psychiatrist reports of beliefs, practices and cases.* Unpublished laboratory document, Concordia University, Montreal, Quebec, Canada.

Lockard, J. S., & Paulhus, D. L. (Eds.). (1988). *Self-deception: An adaptive mechanism.* Englewood Cliffs, NJ; Prentice-Hall.

Loftus, E. F. (1979). The malleability of human memory. *American Scientist, 67,* 312–320.

Loftus, E. F. (1993). The reality of repressed memories. *American Psychologist, 48,* 518–537.

Loftus, E. F., Donders, K., Hoffman, H. G., & Schooler, J. W. (1989). Creating new memories that are quickly assessed and confidently held. *Memory and Cognition, 17,* 607–616.

Loftus, E. F., & Ketcham, K. (1994). *The myth of repressed memory: False memories and accusations of sexual abuse.* New York: St. Martin's Press.

Loftus, E. F., & Loftus, G. R. (1980). On the permanence of stored information in the human brain. *American Psychologist, 35,* 409–420.

Mack, J. E. (1994). *Abduction: Human encounters with aliens.* New York: Scribner's.

Maestri, D., Laurence, J.-R. & Perry, C. (1996). *Children's memory for a special event: Exploring the effects of repeated questioning on recall, suggestibility, and photo lineup identification.* Unpublished manuscript, Concordia University, Montreal, Quebec, Canada.

Morfit, S. H. (1994). Challenge to psychotherapy: An open letter to psychotherapists concerning clinical practice as seen through the lenses of the "recovered" or "false memory" debate. *Journal of Sex Education and Therapy, 20,* 234–245.

Mulhern, S. (1991). Satanism and psychotherapy: A rumor in search of an inquisition. In J. T. Richardson, J. Best, & G. Bromley (Eds.), *The satanism scare.* New York: Aldine de Gruyter.

Mulhern, S. (1994). Satanism, ritual abuse, and multiple personality disorder: A sociohistorical perspective. [Special Issue: Hypnosis and delayed recall: I.] *International Journal of Clinical and Experimental Hypnosis, 42,* 265–288.

Nash, M. (1987). What, if anything, is regressed about hypnotic age regression? A review of the empirical literature. *Psychological Bulletin, 102,* 42–52.

Neisser, U. (1984). John Dean's memory. *Social Action and the Law, 9,* 87–96.

Neisser, U., & Harsch, N. (1992). Phantom flashbulbs: False recollections of hearing the news about Challenger. In E. Winograd & U. Neisser (Eds.), *Affect and accuracy in recall: Studies of "flashbulb" memories* (pp. 9–31). New York: Cambridge University Press.

Nelson, K. (1993). The psychological and social origins of autobiographical memory. *Psychological Science, 4,* 7–14.

Nisbett, R. E., & Wilson, T. D. (1977). Telling more than we can know: Verbal reports on mental processes. *Psychological Review, 84*, 231–259.

Nisbett, R. E., & Ross, L. (1980). *Human inference: Strategies and shortcomings of social judgment.* New York: Prentice-Hall.

Ofshe, R., & Watters, E. (1994). *Making monsters: false memories, psychotherapy, and sexual hysteria.* New York: Scribner's.

Orne, M. T. (1962). On the social psychology of the psychological experiment: With particular references to demand characteristics and their implications. *American Psychologist, 17*, 776–783.

O'Sullivan, J. T., & Howe, M. L. (1995). Metamemory and memory construction. *Consciousness and Cognition: An International Journal, 4*, 104–110.

Perry, C., & Laurence, J.-R. (1984). Mental processing outside of awareness: The contributions of Freud and Janet. In K. S. Bowers and D. Meichenbaum (Eds.) *The unconscious reconsidered* (pp. 9–48). New York: Wiley.

Perry, C. W., Laurence, J.-R., D'Eon, J., & Tallant, B. (1988). Hypnotic age regression techniques in the elicitation of memories: Applied uses and abuses. In H. M. Pettinati (Ed.), *Hypnosis and memory* (pp. 128–154). New York: Guilford Press.

Powell, R. A., & Boer, D. B. (1994). Did Freud mislead patients to confabulate memories of abuse? *Psychological Reports, 74*, 1283–1298.

Quirk, S. A., & DePrince, A. P. (1995). Backlash legislation targeting psychotherapists. *Journal of Psychohistory, 22*, 258–264.

Robbins, A. D. (1995). False memories or hidden agendas? *Journal of Psychohistory, 22*, 305–311.

Rockwell, R. B. (1994). One psychiatrist's view of satanic ritual abuse. [Special Issue: Cult abuse of children: Witch hunt or reality?] *Journal of Psychohistory, 21*, 443–460.

Rockwell, R. B. (1995). Insidious deception. *Journal of Psychohistory, 22*, 312–328.

Shapiro, F. (1994). Eye movement desensitization and reprocessing: Treating trauma and substance abuse. *Journal of Psychoactive Drugs, 26*, 379–391.

Share, L. (1994). *If someone speaks, it gets lighter: Dreams and the reconstruction of infant trauma.* Analytic Press.

Smith, D., & Dumont, F. (1995). A cautionary study: Unwarranted interpretations of the Draw-a-Person test. *Professional Psychology: Research and Practice, 26*, 298–303.

Spanos, N. P., Burgess, C. A., & Burgess, M. F. (1994). Past-life identities, UFO abductions and satanic ritual abuse: The social construction of memories. *International Journal of Clinical and Experimental Hypnosis, 42*, 433–446.

Spanos, N. P., & McLean, J. (1986). Hypnotically created pseudo-memories: Memory distortions or reporting biases? *British Journal of Experimental and Clinical Hypnosis, 3*, 155–159.

Terr, L. (1994). *Unchained memories: True stories of traumatic memories, lost and found.* New York: Basic Books.

Tulving, E. (1983). *Elements of episodic memory* (Oxford Psychology Series No. 2). Oxford, UK: Clarendon Press.

Victor, J. S. (1994). Fundamentalist religion and the moral crusade against satanism: The social construction of deviant behavior. *Deviant Behavior, 15(3)*, 305–334.

Weekes, J. R., Lynn, S. J., Green, J. P., & Brentar, J. P. (1992). Pseudomemory in hypnotized and task-motivated subjects. *Journal of Abnormal Psychology, 101*, 356–360.

Whitfield, C. L. (1995). The forgotten difference: ordinary memory versus traumatic memory. *Consciousness and Cognition: An International Journal, 4,* 88–94.

Williams, L. M. (1993, October 27). *Recall of childhood trauma: A prospective study of women's memories of child sexual abuse.* Paper presented at the American Society of Criminology, Phoenix, AZ.

Williams, L. M. (1994). Recall of childhood trauma: A prospective study of women's memories of child sexual abuse. *Journal of Consulting and Clinical Psychology.*

Winograd, E., & Killinger, W. A., Jr. (1983). Relating age at encoding in early childhood to adult recall: Development of flashbulb memories. *Journal of Experimental Psychology: General, 112,* 413–422.

Yapko, M. D. (1994). Suggestibility and repressed memories of abuse: A survey of psychotherapists' beliefs. *American Journal of Clinical Hypnosis, 36,* 163–171.

FALSE MEMORIES IN THE DOMAINS OF THE LAW, TEXTBOOKS, AND THE MEDIA

CHAPTER 14

MEMORY, MEDIA,
AND THE CREATION
OF MASS CONFUSION

Jeanne Albronda Heaton
Nona Leigh Wilson

The debate about recovered memory has grown into one of the most prominent mental health controversies of the last decade (Enns, 1996; Fox, 1995). No longer confined to a limited professional audience, this debate has entered a commercial forum and as a result is markedly changed. Rather than being defined by researchers, clinicians, or experts in memory, the debate's parameters are now also set by journalists, television talk show hosts, self-help authors, and movie producers. These are the people who have called the public's attention to the issue of repressed memory, and it is they who help define the terms of the discussion.

Although mental health professionals express some concern about the media's influence in creating the current interest in, and misunderstanding about repressed memories, this role has not been adequately explored. Pope (1996) argues that professionals must attend not only to the central claims of the recovered memory debate but also to other factors that may "influence the degree to which people are inclined, willing, or free to question or reject certain claims" (p. 957). Despite such urging, professional reviews have largely ignored the media. We maintain, however, that it is just the kind of factor mentioned by Pope. The media use sophisticated techniques to secure top ratings. As a result, the media substantially affect the message.

Pope (1996) also advises professionals to examine the process by which claims about recovered memory "are evaluated and institutionalized, including tactics used to promote them" (p. 971). We argue that the media's tactics are highly confounding and significantly contribute to the current confusion about repression. Thus, rather than being relegated to a footnote, the media's role warrants the careful examination for which Pope has wisely called.

To further that examination, this chapter focuses on two components of the media: movies and television talk shows. We identify theatrical devices that are central to their commercial success and discuss the consequences of applying those devices to the study of repression. This chapter is not intended as an analysis of the credibility of recovered memories themselves; other chapters address such analysis. We do contend, however, that regardless of the credibility professionals accredit to recovered memories, professionals interested in the evolution of this debate should examine the media's role.

MOTION PICTURE MEMORIES

The topics of traumatic memory, amnesia, and multiple personality disorder were first introduced to the public in 1956 by the movie *The Three Faces of Eve*. The movie contributed to public confusion and misunderstanding by introducing a number of theatrical techniques that are still the hallmarks of popular culture depictions of repression and traumatic memory. *The Three Faces of Eve*:

- Offers dramatic portrayals as if they were fact, thus blurring the distinction between reality and fantasy;
- Represents memory storage and retrieval as analogous to videotaped recordings;
- Depicts questionable therapeutic techniques as standard practice;
- Oversimplifies a complicated and lengthy case;
- Prescribes memory retrieval as the key to improved functioning;
- Presents amnesia and repression as likely responses to childhood trauma;
- Links severe adult disturbance to repressed memories.

Other films followed, such as *Sybil, Ordinary People,* and *Prince of Tides*. But for the purposes of this chapter, we focus exclusively on *The Three Faces of Eve* and *Sybil*, with special attention to how cinematic maneuvers influence the movies' messages.

The Three Faces of Eve

The Three Faces of Eve, an entertainment project produced for profit, is presented to audiences as if it were an educational documentary. Viewers are informed at the beginning of the film that it is a "true story" which "needed no help from a fiction writer." The line between entertainment and education is further distorted by the involvement of Alistair Cooke, who is introduced as a "distinguished journalist and commentator." Throughout the film Cooke provides important details that could not be visually conveyed to the audience about the main character, her problem, and its treatment. His reputation as a reliable BBC-TV narrator of classical drama and his authoritative voice contribute to the sense that what viewers see is "real."

Joanne Woodward, a gifted actor, provides a highly compelling protrayal of Eve, a woman struggling with three personalities. Throughout the movie, viewers are permitted, via the camera, into her doctor's office as she recounts her "story." At times, while Eve is talking, the scene changes—cinematically becoming the stories that Eve tells. Although some events are outside of Eve's awareness, viewers are taken back in time to witness what she cannot remember.

What is significant about this cinematic maneuver is that what viewers see far exceeds in clarity and precision what is realistically possible (Loftus, 1993). Every detail, every image, movement, and emotion is crystalline, honed through professional acting, photography, and editing. The resulting scenes are vivid and compelling. This juxtaposing of compelling images with skeptical experts (Eve's doctors) creates a tension that is noteworthy on several counts.

First, a lay audience (exposed to a moving personal story) is in a better position to assess the veracity of Eve's story than are the trained experts, because the audience witnesses, via cinematic flashbacks, what Eve experienced—something that doctors have not been able to do. In fact, the audience sees the scenes with her, likely experiencing their own discomfort at the same time Eve reexperiences the anguish she felt as a child. Thus, there is an emotional linking between audience and protagonist from which the experts are excluded.

This highlights one of the central and ongoing conflicts in the recovered memory debate: whether recovered memories should be responded to on an emotional level or scrutinized by science. Mulhern (1991) has noted that emotionally compelling personal testimonies are the central piece of evidence used to verify repressed memories, despite the fact that a story's ability to provoke strong emotion is no indication of its truthfulness. By presenting graphic depictions of Eve's story as evidence, the movie clearly sides with emotional analysis. This is problematic in itself, but it is not the only problem here. The scenes that form the basis for the audience's more knowledgeable position are cinematically enhanced and do not represent "memory retrieval" but rather "movie production." Thus, the audience is positioned to believe they know more than the experts based solely on emotions aroused by cinematic technique.

Certainly, these cinematic maneuvers raise important questions about how viewers exposed to *The Three Faces of Eve* use the images to understand memory. Shifting in this way from Eve's words to vivid scenes reenacting her memories, then back again to her words, the movie strongly suggests that the two are the same. As a result, the cinematography promotes two dangerously erroneous assumptions that continue to plague the recovered-memory debate.

First, the filming technique creates the illusion that memory is literally recorded. In the movie, all the details of Eve's memories are accurately preserved, unaltered by other events in her life, and await retrieval. Second, the movie suggests that recovering repressed memories is a relatively easy, reliable task. Eve simply has to recall the memories and then tell them. In this way, it appears that the newly recovered memories are independent of Eve: she merely reports them rather than reconstitutes them. The significant point here is that the movie does not depict any influence on her remembrances of either her doctors' suggestions or Eve's emotional state at the time of the retrieval.

The conclusion to *The Three Faces of Eve* is similarly problematic. To send viewers home satisfied, some resolution must take place: it is accomplished through cinematic flashbacks to the original trauma. Viewers see Eve as a young girl being forced by her mother to lean over a coffin and kiss her dead grandmother good-bye. Once the young Eve stops yelling and resisting, the camera returns viewers to the adult Eve (now known as Jane) sitting in her doctor's office, much relieved and fully integrated. "Oh, I can remember," she cries, rapturous at her newfound release.

Then, just as cameras have taken viewers back in time, they also take them ahead to the second anniversary of "that day" when Jane recovered her memories. The audience sees Jane with her new husband and her daughter traveling down the highway eating ice cream as Alistair Cooke reveals that Jane has experienced a "total recovery."

Although Freud introduced the concept of repression into professional discussions more than 60 years earlier, *The Three Faces of Eve* brought the topic into public conversation. Reaching far more people than psychology texts or debates had reached in decades, this single entertainment event set the stage for the emergence of the current popularized version of traumatic memory. The movie suggests that adult difficulties stem from repressed memories and that such memories can suddenly and unpredictably intrude, making distant and evasive memories appear to be current events. Moreover, the film implies that the key to understanding adult problems may be an event from childhood, even if the actual event is not consciously remembered.

Further, hypnosis is presented as a remarkable "cure," allowing relief simply by retrieving memories of the original trauma. Although the movie was an Academy Award-winning financial and dramatic success, the underlying messages about trauma, repression, and treatment are highly inaccurate and misleading. Important details about the real case, such as information about the patient's lenghty therapy and her continuing difficulties after hypnosis, are omitted from the movie (Spanos, 1996).

For professionals who are skeptical of recovered memories, the problems generated by *The Three Faces of Eve* are self-evident: the movie portrays these memories as highly accurate and memory retrieval as an ideal treatment. Although perhaps not as evident, the movie's theatrical devices also present concerns for those who wish to validate the impact of repression and the benefits of recovery. The often long and arduous process of treatment is excluded. Further, the movie blurs distinctions between fact and fiction by encouraging emotionally based analyses and discouraging the kind of rigorous questioning needed to verify scientific claims.

Sybil

Following *The Three Faces of Eve*, the next movie to have widespread influence on public perceptions of repression was the made-for-television production of *Sybil* in 1976. Produced nearly 20 years after *The Three Faces of Eve*, *Sybil* was designed for an audience much more accustomed to public discussions of personal topics. The women's movement had worked actively to uncover childhood sexual abuse and had made significant contributions to changing attitudes about women and children. In addition, mental health services had become a more acceptable solution for personal problems. As a result, viewers were prepared for more graphic depictions of trauma and were more likely to accept therapy-based solutions. Despite such changes in the culture, many of the theatrical devices remained the same.

As with the *Three Faces of Eve*, *Sybil* is introduced as a documentary rather than an entertainment feature. It begins with the statement, "this is a strange story based on the experiences of a real woman known as *Sybil*." The movie also drew on the previously established credibility of its cast. Joanne Woodward, the star of *Three Faces of Eve*, returned in *Sybil*, but rather than appearing as the patient, she played the psychiatrist, Dr. Cornelia Wilbur. Sally Field appeared in the title role. She was known to many in the United States as the "Flying Nun," a character that epitomized sweetness and innocence. As such, her performance in *Sybil* was effective in underscoring the message that child sexual abuse damages the most vulnerable. But again, as with *The Three Faces of Eve*, *Sybil* is not the documentary it claims to be. The movie presents a stylized and emotionally provocative depiction of the story on which it is based. Further, the movie does not acknowledge that medical journals rejected Dr. Wilbur's case report on Sybil (Putnam, 1989).

In the opening scene, Sybil appears as a tortured art student, talking to herself and choking on vomit as she runs in tortured little steps into a Central Park fountain. Because nothing observable in the scene warrants such behavior, the immediate implication to viewers is that there must be something else, something hidden, causing her distress. Early in the movie, there are other similar scenes: Sybil passes out because of a smell, puts her hand through a window, and walks around on the furniture repeating, "I have to get out! I have to get out!"

The movie's message is that Sybil is a troubled woman with a story to tell, even though she is not aware of the reasons for her unusual behavior. Viewers are, however, once again in a more knowing position. Via cinematic flashbacks, the content of Sybil's hidden memories are reconstructed in vivid detail. The flashbacks, along with Sybil's behavior, make a persuasive case for the notion that there is no escape from the past even if it cannot be remembered. In fact, the on-screen doctors state directly that although Sybil's mind does not remember, "her body does."

Just as the film blurs the line between fact and fiction, it also obfuscates the distinction between personal and professional relationships. Joanne Woodward, in her role as psychiatrist, is intended to demonstrate the professional expertise needed to deal with Sybil's difficulties. Her portrayal, however, places little emphasis on professional skills. Instead, viewers are presented with a theatrical version of therapy more akin to idealized mothering than accepted clinical practice. During the movie, Dr. Wilbur takes her patient home and feeds her, is readily available any time day or night, and rocks Sybil in her arms to the soothing words of, "sweetie . . . oh sweetie." Furthermore, Dr. Wilbur makes a trip to Sybil's hometown to obtain highly confidential information from the family doctor about Sybil and her mother. This is done without Sybil's knowledge, much less her permission.

Dr. Wilbur's behavior ranges from questionable practice to serious breaches in professional ethics yet is presented as acceptable conduct. In fact, she is shown as a trustworthy character who truly cares about Sybil. And her character is influential, largely because of her personal—not professional—commitment to Sybil. Unfortunately, it is not clear from the movie which of these behaviors actually characterized the real Dr. Wilbur and which were simply added for entertainment value. In addition, the movie obscures the real criticism of Dr. Wilbur's ideas and treatment plans by depicting those contemporaries who objected to her work as less astute and as misguided in their assessments (Putnam, 1989). And again, the audience is in *the* most knowing position because they have seen the "evidence."

Taking cinematic license is undoubtedly successful for the entertainment industry, but it raises important questions about how such creative freedom influences the public understanding of mental health issues and therapeutic practice. The notion that professionals who feel strongly about their clients should be exempted from professional restrictions or that personal convictions can acceptably supplant professional training are dangerous propositions. In fact, such thinking has generated serious concerns within the recovered memory debate.

The movie's presentation of Dr. Wilbur's treatment is disconcerting and potentially confounding in other ways as well. Near the end of the movie, Dr. Wilbur tells Sybil, and therefore the audience, that the only escape from her internal torture is to reclaim the long-hidden memories. To overcome her pain, the "memories" have to be faced. Dr. Wilbur explains, "If we look at the scary stuff it will go away." Having already seen through flashbacks what awaits Sybil, audiences can anticipate how painful this task will be. Viewers have already seen the details: a sinister mother, button hooks, knives, and enema bags used to torture. Only Sybil does not yet know the secret. Dr. Wilbur offers hypnosis as the aid that will allow Sybil to remember but "without pain."

With the movie clock ticking, a quick resolution is in order. After several hypnotic sessions with Dr. Wilbur, Sybil is finally prepared to remember the worst of her abuse. It comes not in the doctor's office but in a personal setting. At a picnic in the park with Dr. Wilbur, Sybil again undergoes hypnosis and remembers the full horror of her childhood. Viewers see what Sybil remembers: Sybil as a small child laid out on a kitchen chopping block, legs strung up, her mother preparing to insert an enema. Then, with legs tied together, Sybil has to endure "holding her water" as her mother plays classical music on the piano. This gruesome scene undoubtedly makes audiences squirm and likely increases acceptance of the movie's version of recovered memory. Who would not want to forget such a scene?

Once she remembers the horror, Sybil is able to say, "I remember and I hate her. I hated her so much and I wanted her dead." Dr. Wilbur embraces Sybil and declares, "You can remember without pain." This cathartic scene in the park reinforces the notion that recall results in complete recovery. As the movie ends, Dr. Wilbur's voice tells viewers that "now 11 years later she tells me she is happy" and that Sybil became a professor of art.

Unquestionably, *Sybil* was more than merely a ratings winner. At the time of its release, this movie reinforced the public awareness campaign that was taking place about child abuse, particularly child sexual abuse, and in that way provided an important public service. It appealed to viewers on a personal level and showed them both the actual abuse and its potential consequences. As a result, it is likely that many who saw the movie were encouraged to seek help or to support efforts to stop childhood sexual abuse. But that is not all that *Sybil* did.

As an emotionally captivating movie, *Sybil* likely escaped viewers' more critical analysis of the psychological concepts presented. Such a critical examination quickly reveals that whereas this movie is presented as though it accurately presents psychological information, it is full of highly questionable ideas. Most notably, it reinforces the assumption that repression of childhood trauma will likely result in multiple personality disorder, with numerous competing personalities. Likewise, it suggests that current relationship problems, unusual behavior, or distress may signal the presence of repressed memories. Further, it clearly suggests that repressed memories are accurately preserved and can be accurately recalled. Finally, viewers are shown that the recovery of repressed memories will quickly "cure" the patient.

These controvertible notions were made all the more powerful by virtue of not being directly stated. Viewers witness "the truth." They are not told that multiple personality disorder exists; instead, they are convincingly given Sally Field in the role of Sybil. Viewers are not told that multiple personality disorder stems from repressed childhood trauma. They witness the connection over the course of the movie and then can believe that they have drawn their own conclusions from this "documentary."

In addition to presenting a rather heavy-handed picture of childhood trauma, the movie presents viewers unfamiliar with professional counseling a standard for treatment. That standard is one based more on bedside manner than on professional expertise. The point here is that it plays well with viewers and it likely shapes their expectations about mental health practice.

Such speculation about the film's impact on the general public seems reasonable given that professionals, whose expectations should be the least likely to be affected by such a depiction, also appear to have been significantly influenced. Putnam (1989) maintains that the book *Sybil*, written by journalist Flora Rheta Schreiber, became "a templete against which other patients could be compared and understood" (p. 35). Likewise, Ofshe (Ofshe & Watters, 1994) reports that "it was only after *Sybil* that therapists, often using hypnosis, began finding alter personalities and supposedly 'repressed' histories to match" (p. 221). In fact, it has only been since *Sybil* in 1976 that repressed memories have surfaced in large numbers. As late as 1979, only 200 recorded cases existed in all of medical history. Since 1980, however, thousands of recovered memory clients have been diagnosed with multiple personality disorder (Ofshe & Watters, 1994, p. 205). The difference in reported incidence is staggering and certainly gives rise to questions about what happened to produce such a change.

MEMORY IN SOCIAL CONTEXT

Some would argue that as a result of increased awareness, education, and sensitivity, both clinicians and the general public are better equiped to acknowledge and accept issues of sexual abuse and recovered memory. That certainly is true. A much-needed effort to remove the stigma associated with sexual abuse and to break the isolation experienced by survivors has wrought positive changes in the social climate. Many now find the help they need.

There is also evidence, however, that these needed efforts have resulted in other changes that are not as positive or helpful, including sensationalized media coverage (Heaton & Wilson, 1995) and growing alarm about unsubstantiated crimes (Ofshe & Watters, 1994). There is also growing suspicion, confusion, and skepticism about the very issues that the original effort strove to bring to light (Enns, 1996; Pope, 1996).

Sexual abuse is generally recognized as a hidden problem—a problem covered up by perpetrators, long denied by society, kept secret, and/or (some will argue) repressed by survivors. These layers of concealment easily and understandably contribute to a climate of suspicion in which silence—or even overt denial—no longer comfortably indicates the absence of abuse.

Further, as survivors of sexual abuse came forward in unprecedented numbers during the 1970s and 1980s, and as the media increasingly brought their stories to the general public, a growing sense of alarm developed that sexual abuse was everywhere and would have to be uncovered. The media have been instrumental in that uncovering.

The media have reported—in newspapers and magazines, through television news programs and after-school specials, and on radio programs—

much-needed information about sexual abuse. The same media sources, however, are motivated to sell products and to make money. As a result, they do not simply report issues; they use them to compete with other media for consumers in order to profit. For media reports to be successful, they must attract attention. Inevitably, this requirement results in attempts to find the most exciting stories and to tell them in the most shocking manner.

The consequences of applying attention-getting strategies to the issue of sexual abuse are alarming. A competition around the degree of trauma and victimization arises. Thus, when stories of sexual abuse were first surfacing, reports of a single rape or of a single incidence of father–daughter incest were shocking and therefore successful from a media perspective. After the public became accustomed to reports of rape and incest, however, such reports no longer provoked the degree of alarm necessary to ensure attention. Consequently, more dramatic accounts were needed, and partly because of the increasingly responsive climate created by the earlier reports, they were available. Gang rapes, sibling incest, mother–child incest, and abuses perpetrated by clergy, physicans, teachers, and others traditionally viewed as "helpers" were increasingly featured. Then came reports of repressed memories and cult abuse, followed by multigenerational, community-wide, and even international, conspiratorial rings of satanic ritual abuse.

We do not argue that media alone created such stories or that such claims are invalid merely because they are exploited by the media. We do assert, however, that the media's influence on the shape and timing of such stories requires closer examination. Many questions, such as the following, remain unanswered:

- What are the consequences for viewers of watching shocking accounts of sexual abuse?
- What effect does the media's competition for ratings have on the accuracy of their reports?
- Does the media's appetite for ever more dramatic accounts produce a similar desire within the general public?
- Does it do so within the mental health profession?
- Does the attention awarded shocking accounts suggest to survivors that their own victimization must be similarly dramatic to be noteworthy?

We pursue these questions with an examination of one of the principal sources of information about sexual abuse, repressed memory and satanic ritual abuse: competitively driven, daytime television talk shows.

MEMORY ON TALK TV

When talk TV first began, it gained a reputation for providing an eduational service that was otherwise unavailable to the general public. Beginning in

1967, Phil Donahue introduced daytime programming for women which centered around serious, though often controversial, discussions of important personal and political issues. Donahue provided information about such topics as abortion, sexual orientation, alcoholism, and sexual abuse. And unlike today's shows, his early programs featured only one or two guests and actually afforded a fairly sustained discussion by television standards.

Donahue's show set a standard. Each weekday, viewers were included in the discussions occurring among host, guests, experts, and audience. The format was immediately successful and maintained a credible level of conversation sufficient to establish talk TV as a legitimate source of information.

Unfortunately, Donahue's legacy provided talk TV with a great deal of latitude. Under the guise of education and "therapeutic" benefits, the talk TV shows that followed Donahue exploited mental health concerns. The exploitation was most evident when Oprah Winfrey led the move to a more therapeutic tone in 1985. Her show heralded a dramatic increase in personal disclosures and a simultaneous decrease in the critical evaluation of such disclosures. And because the producers misused the therapeutic function of both disclosure and evaluation, their ability to be "therapeutic" for guests or viewers was severely handicapped. But their popularity was not. Viewers rewarded indiscriminant public disclosures with higher-than-ever ratings, and thousands of potential guests clamored to make their way to the nation's most celebrated confessional.

During the period from 1986 to 1994, the number of nationally syndicated talk shows ranged from 15 to 30, with each seeking the attention of viewers. During their peak popularity in late 1980s and the early 1990s, viewers could choose from as many as 150 shows per week. And even with such a heavily saturated market, the top-rated shows still managed to attract an enormous audience. In 1992, for example, *The Oprah Winfrey Show* alone captured 8 to 10 million viewers *per show*. During this time, the combined audience for the most popular shows totaled on average 54 million viewing hours per day (Heaton & Wilson, 1995).

Sexual abuse and recovered memories were prominent themes, with such programs as "Satanists," "Male Incest Victims," "I Want My Abused Children Back," "Ramifications of Sexual Abuse," "MPD—Syndrome of the 90s," "Satanic Cults and Children," "Clergy Abuse," "Headlines That Shocked the Nation: Mexican Satanic Cult Murders," "Baby Breeders," "Too Scared to Remember," "Remembering Your Father Is a Murderer," and "Sexually Assaulted under Hypnosis." Talk TV also broadcast programs such as "Is Your Repressed Memory a Lie?," "False Memory Syndrome," and "Sex Abuse False Memory," which pitted those who "believed" against those who did not.

Although today the market is somewhat smaller, talk TV still attracts millions of viewers each weekday. No professional mental health organization or publication attracts such a large following. As a result, daytime television talk shows must seriously be considered a primary source of mental health information for the general public. Therefore, the process used to deliver that information warrants examination.

The shows take on many of the same devices used by movies:

- Blurring fact and fiction;
- Creating a sense of urgency;
- Rewarding disclosure;
- Alarming viewers with unsubstantiated checklists of symptoms;
- Utililizing "experts" to validate the production.

And just as with the movies, these strategies have been highly successful from an entertainment perspective but are potentially quite confounding. We turn now to an examination of the most common, and possibly the most problematic, techniques.

Blurring Fact and Fiction

Despite the lack of consensus among mental health professionals about repressed memories and satanic cult abuse, talk show hosts routinely speak authoritatively, suggesting that confounded information is established fact. For example, Sally Jessy Raphael told her viewers, " In fact, we've made a list of things that we think it's important to talk about, one of them is that something like 97% of all multiple personality disorder occurs because of sexual abuse in early childhood" (*Sally Jessy Raphael*, October 19, 1993). At the end of the same program Raphael summarized, "Points that we wanted to make here were: a lot of people who have this are not diagnosed and a lot of people mask this with drug and alcohol abuse. A lot of people know people like this, and they just have not sorted it out. And even a lot of therapists are completely confused. . . . We're attempting to educate and to share."

Similarly, Geraldo Rivera introduced his show titled "Married to a Multiple," on March 19, 1993, with the following verification, "Remember the movie *Sybil?* Well, some years ago it shocked the world with its dramatic portrayal of a woman cursed with multiple personalities." Just in case a viewer had not seen the original, he showed some footage from *Sybil* and then went on to explain, "Well, today after meeting these multiples and their husbands and their children, you'll come to realize the truly terrible scope of this awful dilemma."

Unfortunately, hosts typically do not provide information about how they obtained the statistics they report or how their guests were discovered or what, if any, efforts were made to verify their reports. Rather, the guests and their stories are presented as manifestly worthy of the attention of powerful hosts, the in-studio audience (of approximately 200 people per show), and millions of home viewers. When hosts do acknowledge the controversy surrounding these topics, they do so with virtually no detail and then proceed as usual with personal testimonies.

For example, in 1989 on the program titled "Baby Breeders," host Sally Jessy Raphael stated, "I do not think that we have ever had guests on this show with stories that were more shocking or stranger than the ones you're going to hear today." She went on to report that some officials were claiming that the stories being told on her program were fictitious and that one of her guests, an investigative journalist, believed that these stories might create a dangerous wave of mass hysteria. Despite these doubts and concerns, Raphael told her viewers that she thought the stories were worthy of consideration.

After issuing this cursory disclaimer, Sally Jessy Raphael devoted significant time to obtaining details about forced impregnations, aborted babies and satanic ceremonies. One guest reported that she had been forced to watch cult members drive a cross through her baby's chest, consume its flesh, and then bury the remains. Another guest reported that cult members "sacrificed my son over the spa with piranhas. They cut his arm off first and then started dismembering him." Throughout the program, Sally Jessy Raphael prompted the guests to provide further details. She expressed horror and sympathy but rarely skepticism (*Sally Jessy Raphael*, February 28, 1989).

Raphael's approach is characteristic of the hosts' interviewing technique. They ask questions that draw out details but do not help viewers evaluate the credibility of what is said. And it is here that the hosts contradict themselves. Sally, for example, said that she believed her viewers should think about the stories being told on her program, yet she did little during the program to encourage or assist their reflections. In fact, her apparently, unquestioning acceptance of the reports set the tone for the program and may have discouraged viewers from critically considering the material.

As the public receives more and more information about repressed memory and satanic ritual abuse it is critical that people (or consumers) be able to assess the quality of that information. But in the case of talk TV, how are they to do so? Most often the only evidence comes from the guests' assurances that their stories are true, confirmations from experts appearing on the show, and the hosts' purported belief.

This "evidence," however, is not very compelling when balanced against the knowledge that the shows' primary task is to provide successful entertainment in a highly competitive market. The shows report that they select guests who will tell their stories in interesting and entertaining ways that also fit the shows' fast-paced agenda. Further, guests are coached by the shows' staff to make their stories interesting and after the taping editors have the option to eliminate less compelling segments (Heaton & Wilson, 1995). Quite simply, the more assured and persuasive the guests, the more compelling their stories will be and, thus, the more successful the shows.

Again, the shows' practices do not discredit the reports of their guests. The shows' techniques, however, do render it exceedingly difficult to distinguish fact from fiction. And the consequences of repetitive presentations (on nationally syndicated shows watched by millions and hosted by powerful celebreties) of unverifiable but highly shocking and detailed personal testimonies need further study.

Creating Urgency

In addition to presenting dramatic, unsubstantiated accounts, the hosts use their authority to override viewer skepticism and then to create a sense of urgency about the reports. Again, the hosts often acknowledge that viewers may be incredulous, but then they dismiss viewer doubt and warn that what is discussed on the shows could also be happening to viewers or to people they know.

In this way hosts use their personal authority and influence, rather than verifiable data, to persuade viewers that the accounts presented are of urgent concern. This tactic is well illustrated by an Oprah Winfrey program entitled "Satanists," broadcast on September 30, 1986. Winfrey addressed her studio and home audience, stating, "What we are going to talk about today will sound unbelievable, unbelievable, to most of you. It will sound like the plot of an incredible horror story." Having acknowledged the potential for doubt, she then dismissed it, "But the fact is that it is very, very real. We are talking today about satanic cults, devil worship, and the terrifying ritual abuse of children."

According to Winfrey, not only were her *guests* vulnerable to cults, but virtually every TV *viewer* tuned into her program, which during 1986 typically amounted to approximately 8 million, was at risk as well. She stated, "Satanic cults are practicing underground, in your churches, in your neighborhoods, in your schools, abducting and brainwashing thousands of teenagers and adults into their evil and into their life threatening rituals." Acknowledging viewer reaction she continued, "You might be outraged to hear this type of conversation on television. . . . But the fact remains that it is happening to your children, and if you don't want to believe, I want you to meet my first guests." The guests were then introduced to tell their stories as if their statements alone constituted irrefutable evidence.

And again on her show "MPD–Syndrome of the 90s," Oprah Winfrey told viewers, "We used to think that it was rare, but it's not rare at all" (*The Oprah Winfrey Show*, April 20, 1992). Oprah Winfrey was not alone in issuing strong warnings based on unsubstantiated statistics. Geraldo Rivera, in 1988, told his viewers, "Satanic cults: every hour, every day their ranks are growing. . . . Estimates are that there are over one million Satanists in this country. . . . The odds are that this is happening in your town" (*Geraldo*, November 19, 1987). Other hosts issue similar statements with the same degree of certitude. On "Sons Raped by Their Mothers," Phil Donahue told viewers, "Well it doesn't get any worse than this. On our stage are four men who were sexually abused by their mothers. Do you believe this? A lot of people don't. It is perhaps the most underreported crime in all of criminology" (*Donahue*, May 4, 1992).

Our objection is that no information is provided about the basis for their urgent concern. If hosts have reputable sources for their data, they should reveal them. If they make their statements based on personal beliefs, they should say so. But they do neither. They simply make pronouncements without explanation and their authority to do so is rarely questioned.

Rewarding Disclosure

Talk shows depend on guests who are willing to reveal extremely personal, typically traumatic, information about themselves and others on national television. Without such guests there would be no programs. As a result, the shows' producers and hosts encourage potential guests to believe that appearing on the shows and disclosing their secrets will be beneficial—both for them and for the viewers (Heaton & Wilson, 1995). Once on the show, the guests are praised by hosts and audience members for their willingness to share their stories.

Although it may appear to viewers that the guests are naturally garrulous, demonstrative people, the guests have been specifically selected and then coached by assistant producers prior to the shows. In addition, guests are regularly placed on stage with many other guests with whom they have conflicts. They are frequently instructed not to hesitate to interrupt to demonstrate their points. This combination of selection and instruction contributes to the frenzied pace of self-disclosure that characterizes talk TV.

Once the host opens the show and announces the topic, the revelations begin. Guests are introduced primarily by the severity of their trauma and their willingness to talk about it. On her "Satanists" program mentioned previously, Oprah set the pace for disclosure when she introduced her first guest, Andy, who appeared with his mother. Oprah stated, "This young, red-haired, cute little boy, who looks like Opie Taylor, is a victim of ritual abuse. He has witnessed human sacrifice, he has witnessed animal killings, has been lowered into graves, he was given drugs, has been sexually molested. This all took place in their neighborhood by a group of seven people they all considered friends."

Her next guest, Julie, who also appeared with her mother, was similarily introduced. Julie was identified as a child who had been "in intense therapy for the past two and half years," but who was still telling her mother that "she is sorry for killing the animals." Oprah then asked the audience to "please welcome them all to the show, and thank them for their honesty and their courage to talk about such painful memories. Welcome them to the show."

It is virtually impossible to determine whether what is being disclosed actually occurred. Because of that, viewers are left to either believe guests or not based on impression. Impressionistic approaches to such complicated issues are problematic on several counts. Some viewers may feel that to question any of those appearing is "victim blaming" and thus unquestioningly accept all disclosure as true. This approach, in fact, is directly endorsed at times by the hosts.

In 1991, Oprah invited Eileen Franklin to discuss the memories she reports to have recovered about her father murdering her best friend in 1969. With the likely result of stifling any healthy criticism that Franklin's story might have provoked, Oprah emphatically stated, "I was really offended recently when I read in one of the newspapers that . . . people are coming forward so much with sexual abuse that it's now become chic. . . . I was so offended." She went on to address the Franklin case specifically, "I want to just say this, that their father, although he's in jail, denies that there was ever any sexual abuse. . . . I'm just sick of people denying it" (*The Oprah Winfrey Show*, October 28, 1991). Again, although the underlying message of support for survivors of sexual abuse is admirable, the outcome of a powerful host's vehement rejection of any questioning of any disclosure—and therefore an implicit message that all reports must be uncritically accepted and all those accused believed guilty—is potentially quite damaging.

Conversely, talk TV has been repeatedly criticized in the press as a modern-day "freak show" and several incidences of professional actors tricking the shows with completely fabricated, though elaborate, disclosures are well publicized. Other guests have been portrayed as willing to do or say anything for the chance to appear on television. The overly dramatic quality of the shows leads many to express doubt about the truthfulness of any of the disclosures. It is quite possible that these aspects of talk TV could reduce sympathetic responses to real disclosures of sexual abuse, thus reducing support for sexual assault survivors. The shows' unrestrained emphasis on personal disclosure may be problematic in at least one other way as well.

Many millions of viewers witness on a daily basis attention and praise being given almost always to the guests who have the most traumatic or dramatic stories to tell. Further, as viewers watch this pattern of interaction, they are encouraged by the shows to call in with their own stories to find out if they too could become guests. We question the influence of this combination of reward and solicitation. Viewers routinely listen to guests report that recovered memories of childhood sexual abuse suddenly explained what was wrong in their lives—and then witness those guests being praised by the audience and an influential host. Are viewers then more likely to believe that they would benefit from doing the same?

Alarming Viewers with Unsubstantiated Symptom Checklists

The hosts frequently introduce the topics for their programs with symptom checklists designed to encourage viewers to relate the problems of the guests to their own lives or to the lives of friends and family. On "Why Mothers Don't Tell," a program about sexual abuse, Oprah Winfrey explained that "people need to know those signs, it's the only way the abuse is going to be able to stop and everyone can get into the treatment process" (*The Oprah Winfrey Show*, May 8, 1992). Her basic idea was sound, but, unfortunately, the lists that follow such compelling lead-ins are typically generic.

For example, on another 1988 Winfrey show, "Ramifications of Sexual Abuse," viewers were warned that they too may have suffered from trauma they could not recall. In fact, Oprah encouraged viewers to look for their problems in a list of supposed symptoms. She instructed, "See if you recognize yourself in any of these characteristics of women who have been abused sexually as children." She went on with a listing of vague symptoms: "Do you have an aversion to sex? . . . Do you have an inability to have relationships? Are you leaning toward homosexuality or bisexuality? Have you been married many times, multiple marriages, Spider Woman-type—you snare the opposite sex only for sex? Are you overprotecting your children? Have drugs and alcohol played a major role in your life? Are you perfectionistic?" (*The Oprah Winfrey Show*, April 14, 1988).

Answering "yes" to any item on the list of questions could indicate all sorts of things or nothing at all, a dilemma characteristic of unvalidated assessments that provide no guidelines for scoring or interpretation. Although it may be true that survivors of sexual abuse experience, for example, a loss of interest in sexual contact, it is also true for those who are overworked, anxious about promotion, or angry with their partners. Thus, what the lists do best is present symptoms that apply to most people at least some of the time and thus persuade viewers to falsely identify with the problem.

The potential for difficulties does not end with the viewers themselves because they are also encouraged to analyze the behavior of their friends and family. Oprah's "Satanism" program included warning signs for identifying satanic ritual abuse of viewers' children. The list presented to viewers included fear of baby-sitters, fear of the house burning down, fear of being kidnapped, fascination with stars with circles around them, and interest in sex. The list undoubtedly proved fruitful. Most of the "symptoms" are descriptive of most children.

On the other hand, if viewers recognized none of these symptoms in their children, that was no assurance their children had not been victimized. One audience member reported that "what I thought was important for people to know is that most of the kids are asymptomatic. My son had no symptoms at all. He just—once they start disclosing. . . ." The fact that the show provided no verification of the information shared might be forgotten or go unnoticed by viewers. However, the emotionally disturbing message that even children who appear safe may not be was repeated throughout the show and is less easily forgotten.

Oprah Winfrey endorsed the presentation of these signs and symptoms, "If one parent out there recognizes a sign as a result of what happened to you, you save a child." This is an often repeated sentiment on talk TV. And in fact, it is true that it would be fortunate if the shows were actually able to assist their viewers in preventing sexual abuse. It would also be beneficial, however, to avoid encouraging viewers to interpret typical developmental struggles, ordinary parent–child conflicts, or mood disturbances of any kind as automatic indicators of sexual abuse.

Utilizing "Expert" Verification

Many talk TV shows call on mental health professionals to appear, usually near the end of their programs, to provide "expert" assessments of what was discussed and to offer advice to guests and viewers. In fact, 70% of these shows utilize an expert (Timney, 1991). Such appearances, perhaps more than any other aspect of the shows, distinguish talk TV from other entertainment shows.

The shows use "experts" to buttress their claims that they are providing a valuable services to guests and viewers. And the mental health professionals who appear do, in fact, lend an aura of credibility to whatever happens on the shows. They either explicitly confirm guests' and hosts' comments or they do not refute them and thereby tacitly condone what is said. Even on the rare occasions when mental health professionals dispute claims made on the shows, their appearances still suggest that talk TV is a legimate venue for debating professional ideas.

As discussed earlier, however, the shows are not primarily interested in evaluating the stories presented or in providing viewers with well-reasoned information. Because the shows are principally a for-profit endeavor, the majority of time is afforded to dramatic personal testimonies. Consequently, mental health professionals are rarely given more than a few minutes to express their ideas.

Professionals, in fact, are given so little time that they are reduced to speaking in sound bites, which seriously reduces their ability to provide any "expertise" at all. Typically, the problems presented on the shows are too complex to be dealt with during the time available. Therefore, analyses must be superficial. Professionals, then, are positioned to present generic information as if it were specialized advice. In addition, professionals are often at risk for overstepping the bounds of their expertise because they are frequently called on to comment on a wide range of problems in an extremely short period of time (Heaton & Wilson, 1995).

These problems are further compounded by the fact that many of the experts appearing are not credible professionals or even professionals at all. But, as with many other aspects of talk TV, it is virtually impossible to determine professional credentials from the information presented during the programs. The shows feature self-help authors, psychologists, relationship therapists, psychotherapists, researchers, counselors, motivational speakers, and psychiatrists. Little or no information about their licensing, academic training, or scope of practice is provided.

Most experts are introduced with nonregulated titles such as "relationship specialist," "communication expert," "therapist," or even "professional naysayer." These labels appear on the screen beneath their images. Such titles work well because they give the illusion of expertise without the obligation of allegiance to a code of professional ethics. Thus, the shows maintain some aura of credibility without the responsibility of accuracy.

On "Investigating Multiple Personalities: Did the Devil Make Them Do It?," Geraldo began the show by stating, "There are more than 1,200 guests on my panel today, all embodied in these three women, women with terrifying tales of multiple personality disorder, of human sacrifices and of other unspeakable acts. These ladies say the Devil made them this way, as you are about to hear" (*Geraldo*, September, 10, 1991).

Not surprisingly, the guests made some highly questionable claims. Kathleen reported that she had 800 personalities. Kayla stated that she had 400 personalities. And Jane claimed to have 49. Some guests went through transformations on stage and one described an incident when she was 3 years old in which she was ordered to curl up into a ball and was placed inside a woman's body so that she could be "rebirthed." The guest revealed that the woman was then sacrificed.

To create some semblance of credibility, Geraldo brought out the experts. First, the author of *Satan's Children: Case Studies in Multiple Personality* verified that that the women must be telling the truth because he witnesses these types of situations every day in his office. No information was provided about his credentials or how he obtained the information he reported in his book.

Geraldo then informed viewers, "We'll keep an open mind. The therapists and doctors of the three women are here, as is a professional naysayer." Geraldo asked the therapist directly, "Do you believe your patient?," perhaps looking for yet another confrontation for his show.

She answered with the following evasion: "Yes, but I think that—I come from a therapist's point of view. My patient showed fully documented signs of posttraumatic stress disorder, which multiplicity is really part of—she has flashbacks, all of that, and I treat her according to that." Her answer is largely unintelligible but draws on professional terminology to create the impression of expertise. She authoritatively reports to be providing treatment for a fully documented disorder, but no information is provided about either the disorder or the treatment.

In addition, this therapist is in the unenviable, and most likely unethical, position of being asked on national TV whether or not she believes her client. And she will likely be given little or no time to clarify her remarks. If she says "yes," which she did not, she misinforms the public; if she says "no" or "equivocates," which she did, she compromises her relationship to her client. Furthermore, the complexities of the ethics involved are never presented and so are most likely overlooked by viewers. Yet the impression remains that it is okay for therapists to appear on national TV with their clients to substantiate their clients' veracity, and that such opinions constitute "objective" and reasonable assurance of the truth.

At the end of the program, Geraldo called out his final expert for the day: the "professional naysayer," who was there to dispute the other two experts. Little in the way of a meaningful exchange of information occurred, but the program was certainly lively and provocative. Geraldo's closing comments perhaps best summarize the shows' approach to analysis and summary: "So, I don't know. Put that in your pipe and smoke it."

Although Geraldo's quick summary might work for the entertainment industry, such a carefree adjournment is neither responsible nor beneficial. His show and its conclusion, however, highlight tactics used by media, as well as illustrate the ways in which mental health professionals can either overtly or inadvertently endorse those strategies. We maintain that the media's methods, particularly when coupled with mental health professionals' endorsements, are contributing to the high level of confusion surrounding memory repression and recovery. We turn now to an examination of what concerned professionals can do to intervene.

RECOMMENDATIONS

We suggest three steps for those who wish to assist in reducing the confusion about recovered memories. First, profesionals must be knowledgeable about media tactics and question the influence those tactics have on both the general public's understanding of mental health issues and on professional opinions and training. Second, professionals must know and adhere to their professional codes of ethics about media involvement. Third, profesionals must actively inform the public about methods for evaluating professional theories and the parameters of responsible practice.

Examining Media Influence

Throughout this chapter we identified media strategies and raised questions about the outcomes of applying such strategies to the topics of memory repression and recovery. Although our primary focus is on the influence the media have on the general public, similar attention should be given to the influence the media have on professionals' understanding of these topics as well.

Experimental research is needed to answer questions about media influences, but until such studies are completed professionals should make themselves knowledgeable about media strategies. They should then use that knowledge to do the following:

- Question claims that are not well documented;
- Remain alert to stereotypes and overgeneralizations;
- Maintain skepticism about quick solutions to complicated problems;
- Challenge distorting portrayals;
- Respond to misleading media reports.

In addition, professionals should avoid using entertainment pieces for educational purposes. Movies and talk TV programs should not be used for demonstrating mental health concerns or practice, unless the instructors are prepared to examine in detail the distorting theatrical devices employed. Professionals should be especially cautious about using commercial media depictions when training novice professionals or the general public, who may have little or no exposure to the problems being represented.

Finally, when professionals encounter media depictions that misrepresent credible practice or promote unsubstantiated ideas, they should not hesitate to take action, either by addressing the media source directly or by contacting their ethics boards when appropriate.

Adhering to Professional Ethics

Although the likelihood of being reported for violating one's professional code of ethics is small, professionals could do much to reduce the confusion about recovered memories if they would adhere to the ethical mandates pertaining to media involvement (American Psychological Association, 1997). Ethical codes require professionals to base media presentations on accepted professional practice and literature (American Counseling Association, 1997; American Psychological Association, 1988, 1992). Mental health professionals are ethically bound to refuse to participate in any capacity in activities that are harmful. Further, mental health professionals must avoid establishing professional relationships that compromise client welfare. These mandates suggest that any ethical participation with talk TV would be extremely difficult to achieve. However, professionals who agree to participate in media presentations would do well to adhere to the following guidelines:

- Request detailed information about proposed role. Professionals should find out specifically what they are being asked to do, when they will do it, how long their involvement will last, and into what context their comments will be placed.
- Check the credibility of the proposed project. Professionals should question reporters and producers about their goals and request to see samples of previous relevant work.
- Refuse to solict previous or current clients as guests.
- Refuse to participate in questionable projects or in situations that involve risk or surprise to others.
- Refuse to oversimplify complicated issues.
- Differentiate between personal and professional opinions.
- Insist on knowing the manner in which professional credentials, training, and experience will be identified.
- Remain alert to the role of editors.

Although many media sources refuse to allow professionals to preview their work prior to publication or broadcast, they should ask to do so. Professionals should convey a sense of knowledge about media methods and a concern for accuracy.

Educating the Public

The media have been instrumental in conveying much-needed information about mental health concerns and services. And although such information clearly has had many positive effects, the image of the mental health profession and its professionals is often tarnished through media depictions (Raviv & Weiner, 1995). Further, clients may question their own experiences if they do not match media accounts (Enns, 1996).

The media are a powerful source of information and, unfortunately, when that information is distorted or misleading, professionals may have an extremely difficult time correcting the public perceptions it creates. Despite such difficulties, professionals have an obligation to combat inaccuracies (McCall & Stocking, 1982). The American Psychiatric Association has issued a series of *Mental Illness Awareness Guides* written for the media. The American Psychological Association has also released fact sheets to the media on sexual abuse and memory, such as *The Statement on Memories of Sexual Abuse* (American Psychiatric Association, 1993). Individual professionals can assist in increasing the availability of accurate information by keeping themselves informed, by critically questioning the material they encounter, and by sharing information they have with other professionals and their communities.

The combination of becoming knowledgeable about the media, adhering to professional codes of ethics, and helping to educate the public can do much to reduce the existing confusion about recovered memories. Although professionals may not always agree, professional codes of ethics provide an agreed-on method for establishing parameters for collective debate, professional practice, and public presentations.

CONCLUSION

Movies and talk TV depictions of recovered memories utilize a wide variety of strategies designed to enhance entertainment value to increase commercial success. Those strategies include presenting fictionalized accounts as though they were real, simplifying complicated mental health theories and practices, rewarding personal disclosures without verifying their truthfulness, presenting broad-based, unsubstantiated "symptom" lists, creating an aura of urgency, and then drawing on "expert" verification that is equally lacking in rigor. Not only are these strategies potentially quite dangerous, the movies and talk shows that utilize them are enormously popular. Unfortunately, the publications and presentations that counter such entertainment-driven sources are rather limited in reach—attracting relatively small, professional audiences.

The general public, then, is overexposed to distorted and misleading information. As a result, professionals interested in the current confusion about recovered memories would do well to give serious consideration to the influence that such information has on public perceptions. To date, little research has been conducted to examine the effects of media depictions, but such research is sorely needed. In addition, mental health professionals should examine their own contributions to confounding practices and take action to ensure ethical conduct within the profession.

The debate about recovered memory will not be an easy one to untangle, but no attempt to do so will be complete without a close examination of the media.

REFERENCES

American Counseling Association. (1997). *Code of ethics and standards of practice.* Alexandria, VA: Author.

American Psychiatric Association. (1993). *Statement on memories of sexual abuse.* Washington, DC: Author.

American Psychological Association. (1988). Trends in ethics cases, common pitfalls, and published resources. *American Psychologist, 43*(7), 564–572.

American Psychological Association. (1992). *Ethical principles of psychologists and code of conduct.* Washington, DC: Author.

American Psychological Association. (1997.) Report of the Ethics Committee, 1996. *American Psychologist, 52*(8), 897–905.

Borders, D. L. (1991). Report of the AACD Ethics Committee: 1989–1991. *Journal of Counseling and Development, 70*(2), 278–280.

Enns, C. Z. (1996). Counselors and the backlash: "Rape hype" and "false memory syndrome." *Journal of Counseling and Development, 74*(4), 358–367.

Fox, R. E. (1995). The rape of psychology. *American Psychologist, 26,* 147–155.

Heaton, J. A., & Wilson, N. L. (1995). *Tuning in trouble.* San Francisco: Jossey-Bass.

Loftus, E. F. (1993). The reality of repressed memories. *American Psychologist, 48,* 518–537.

McCall, R. B., & Stocking, H. S. (1982). Between scientist and public; communicating psychological research through the mass media. *American Psychologist, 37,* 985–995.

Mulhern, S. (1991). Satanism and psychotherapy: A rumor in search of an inquistion. In J. T. Richardson, J. Best, & D. G. Bromley (Eds.), *The satanism scare* (pp. 145–172). New York: Aldine de Gruyter.

Ofshe, R., & Waters, E. (1994). *Making monsters: False memories, psychotherapy, and sexual hysteria.* New York: Scribner's.

Pope, K. S. (1996). Memory, abuse, and science. *American Psychologist, 51,* 957–974.

Putnam, F. W. (1989). *Diagnosis and treatment of multiple personality disorder.* New York: Guilford Press.

Raviv, A., & Weiner, I. (1995). Why don't they like us? Psychologists' public image in

Israel during the Persian Gulf War. *Professional Psychology: Research and Practice, 26*, 88–94.

Spanos, N. P. (1996). *Multiple identities and false memories: A sociocognitive perspective on multiple personality disorder, hypnosis, and spirit.* Washington, DC: American Psychological Association.

Timney, M. C. (1991). *The discussion of social and moral issues on daytime talk shows: Who's really doing all the talking?* Unpublished master's thesis, Department of Communications, Ohio University.

CHAPTER 15

TEXTBOOK MODELS OF MULTIPLE PERSONALITY
Source, Bias, and Social Consequences

Jean Maria Arrigo
Kathy Pezdek

Multiple personality disorder[1] (MPD) provides a crucial example in the debate over the validity of recovered incest memories. At one extreme, dissociation of memory is postualted as an adaptive response to childhood incest. By this account, the strong dissociative condition of MPD typically results from severe and sustained sexual and physical abuse in childhood: "A diagnosis of multiple personality in a child ought to serve as *prima facie* evidence for child abuse, even if compelling physical evidence is lacking" (Elliott, 1982, p. 441). At another extreme of the debate, the recovery of memory of childhood incest is postulated as false, a creation of patients, therapists, or other players for covert gains. By this account, the more opportunistic role of a multiple personality represents a hoax of social influence or malingering: a "context-bounded, goal-directed, social behavior geared to the expectations of significant others ..." (Spanos, 1994, p. 143). Spanning the extremes, this chapter examines the portrayals of MPD in 84 recent introductory psychology textbooks and discusses the social implications of these portrayals.

Introductory psychology textbooks present psychological science to a broader cross-section of the population than any other single source. Over three-quarters of recent college graduates have taken one or more psychology courses (Stowe, 1993), and, as the prerequisite to many others, the introductory course is by far the most commonly enrolled psychology course. For lawyers and health care professionals, in particular, the introductory course often constitutes their only exposure to the academic discipline of psychology and their first exposure to the scientific depiction of MPD. We know from the memory literature that first depictions of phenomena outside our experience are especially salient and have a privileged status as organizers of memory. Also, we know that educators—teachers, therapists, health care professionals, judges, and journalists—tend to disseminate knowledge in the form they learned it, thus driving the institutional machinery that produces public knowledge. So, how do textbook writers, who usually have no direct knowledge of MPD, frame the problem? What references do they cite, and how true are they to these references? To borrow a maxim from risk assessment, the framing of the problem governs the range of solutions attempted.

The societal impact of textbooks has provoked many quantitative content analyses on topics of social concern, such as racism (Banks, 1969), ageism (Whitbourne & Hulicka, 1990), and sexism (Peterson & Kroner, 1992). These content analyses measured the divergence of textbook accounts of the selected topic from prevailing ideals (e.g., gender equality) or from consensus knowledge in an academic discipline (e.g., the impact of slavery on blacks). But there is no single ideal or standard in the academic community for evaluating textbook accounts of MPD. Our strategy was to invoke standards of scientific discourse, without reference to a social ideal or to particular knowledge claims about MPD. Textbook accounts of MPD were compared to their cited sources and reviewed against the background of available scientific literature and of nonscientific literature and films. Many previous content analysts complained of poor use of sources. For example, in their analysis of portrayals of mental illness in undergraduate psychology textbooks, Halter, Bond, and De Graaf-Kaser (1992) advocated "serious attempts by textbook authors to . . . reflect accurately current scholarship, both inside and outside psychological journals" (p. 40). By quantifying fidelity of textbooks to their cited sources, our study specifically articulates biases where they occur.

Beginning from a social policy perspective, four common models of MPD were discerned in textbooks. Content and citation analyses were conducted to characterize textbook writers' selection and use of sources that supported the models. These quantitative analyses converged on a differential pattern of reporting MPD models that could not be explained by textbook "demographics," such as edition and recency of references. Qualitative analysis of textbook presentations of three influential cases illustrated the social risks in the framing of cases according to different models.

Because of the methodological hazards of content analyses and because of the controversy surrounding multiple personality (MP), we retain technical details in this chapter.

TEXTBOOK MODELS OF MULTIPLE PERSONALITY DISORDER

The most prominent explanation for MPD was the internal defect model—*Trait MPD*. Nearly all textbook presentations of Trait MPD posited poor coping skills, a predisposition to self-hypnosis, and/or the good–evil split in the psyche. The following textbook passages are typical of Trait-MPD discussions.

> In a sense we are all multiple personalities in that we have conflicting tendencies, between the part of us that is socially conforming and the part that likes to cut loose. Most of us are able to find appropriate outlets for expressing different aspects of our personalities. However, not everyone is able to achieve a satisfactory synthesis. (Crooks & Stein, 1991, p. 570)

> In one [case] that became the subject of the film *The Three Faces of Eve*, a timid housewife named Eve White harbored two other personalities: Eve Black, a sexually aggressive, antisocial personality; and Jane, an emerging personality who was able to accept the existence of her primitive impulses yet show socially appropriate behavior. (Rathus, 1991, p. 434)

Trait MPD offers the least troublesome *social* explanation: multiple personalities, like epileptics and psychotics, simply have an internal defect.

As role playing becomes more voluntary and the gains more opportunistic, Trait MPD grades into self-deception and malingering—*Fake MPD*. With wider participation in the illusion, Fake MPD becomes the socially constructed reality theorized previously by Spanos (1994).

> Only 200 cases of multiple personality had been identified by 1979, but since 1979 more than 5000 have appeared. Some of these have been attempts by murderers to plead insanity: "*I* didn't kill her, my other personality did." (Wade & Tavris, 1990, pp. 593–594)

> Some researchers have suggested that doctors may be inadvertently creating [MPs] by the way they treat them (Spanos, Weekes, & Bertrand, 1985). A multiple-personality case is sensational and gets a lot of attention, so patients are encouraged to develop more than one personality. (D. L. Watson, 1992, p. 509)

A logical implication of the Fake-MPD model is a "get-tough" policy with malingerers, shrewd defense attorneys, and self-serving psychotherapists. A similar policy was proposed by "false memory syndrome" advocates for dealing with adults who claim to have delayed recovery of memories of childhood sexual abuse (e.g., Jaroff, 1993).

In the opposite direction, Trait MPD grades into the ecological model of *Trauma MPD* as stressors are seen to be more external, severe, chronic, and abusive and as commencing earlier in childhood. Here is Zimbardo (1992, p. 630) quoting Schultz et al.:

> "The dominant features of [these] 355 cases of multiple personality disorder (MPD) are an almost universal incidence among mostly female patients of being abused at a very early age, starting around 3 years old and continuing for

more than a decade . . . (Schultz et al. 1989)." . . . Psychologists believe that multiple personalities develop to serve a vital survival function.

The Trauma model calls for sympathetic treatment of MPs and for prevention of child abuse.

As a counterpoint to Fake MPD or to the uncertainties of Trait or Trauma MPD, some textbooks also presented a noncausal schema, *Measurable MPD*: there are psychometric or physiological differences between MPs and non-MPs.

"One major finding is that brain-wave activity of each of the personalities shown by an [MP] individual is distinct. . . . When control subjects, including skilled actors, are asked to pretend to be someone else, no such changes in brain wave patterns were evident . . ." (Putnam, 1982, quoted in Kagan & Segal, 1992, p. 503)

Other distinguishing measures reported were IQ, Minnesota Multiphasic Personality Inventory, semantic differential, and ophthalmological indices. Advocates of all three causal models, Fake, Trait, and Trauma MPD, claim corroboration in the measurability—or nonmeasurability—of MPD. (For ease of exposition, the schema of Measurable MPD is also referred to as a model.)

Textbook models are based on the biased sample of MPs who have come to the attention of mental health professionals. The 1988 *American Psychiatric Press Textbook of Psychiatry* (exhibiting the Trauma-MPD model; Talbott, Hales, & Yudofsky, 1988) warned that MPD is typically a secretive condition: Under 10% of MPs are flamboyant, and about 80% of MPs have only "windows of diagnosibility," according to Kluft (1988, p. 574). Proponents of Fake MPD would dispute these statistics as artifacts of observation. Self-reports in MPD-survivor newsletters are generally consistent with Kluft's view (e.g., Lynn, 1992). In any event, textbook MPs were confined to the flamboyant variety, and no child MPs were included.

OVERVIEW OF THE QUANTITATIVE ANALYSES

Three studies were conducted to characterize textbook presentations of MPD models. The first estimated the trends in scientific support for MPD models by examining the abstracts of MPD journal articles found in *Psychological Abstracts*. Here the aim was to portray the scientific background against which textbook authors wrote, in distinction to the popular lore of MPD. The second study established an MPD-model profile—Fake, Trait, Trauma, Measurable—for each textbook to represent strength of advocacy for the four positions. The third—and crucial—study assessed textbook writers' adherence to the MPD models of the references they themselves cited (biographies, films, scientific articles, etc.). As a check on the interpretation of findings, alternative explanations were sought in relationships between MPD-model support and textbook "demographics," such as edition and length of MPD section.

Ordinal scales (illustrated later) were developed to measure strength of support for the four MPD models in journal abstracts and in textbooks. Following Baker, Hardyck, and Petrinovich's (1966) Montecarlo study of the statistical properties of ordinal scales, the coding scales were treated as interval scales to the extent of computing sums, means, and standard deviations. However, Spearman correlations for ordinal scales were used throughout.

Examination of an estimated 80% of the entire set of 1987–1992 North American introductory psychology textbooks, all relevant MPD abstracts, and 93% of the textbooks' references to MPD permitted the use of robust descriptive statistics. The consistency of results with diverse measures across the three disparate databases established the validity of findings.

THE SCIENTIFIC BACKGROUND: MPD MODELS IN *PSYCHOLOGICAL ABSTRACTS*

Abstracts of MPD journal articles provide a rough indication of information available from scientific sources. The cumulative numbers of abstracts favorable to each MPD model are illustrated in Figure 15.1. At any point in time, the lines indicate the relative availability of different MPD models to textbook writers. The cumulative numbers of abstracts critical of Fake MPD are plotted below the baseline; only Fake MPD drew much criticism in abstracts. The biggest change over the 1974–1992 period was the increase in support for Trauma MPD, after early dominance by Trait MPD. Two surges in cumulative numbers of MPD-model abstracts occurred after the 1984 Bianchi murder case (described later) and after origination of the journal *Dissociation* in 1988.

Using a scale described later, Table 15.1 shows that relative support for different MPD models varied considerably by field of journal. Fake MPD was highest in hynposis journals. Trait MPD prevailed in psychoanalysis journals, which largely omitted the other models. Trauma MPD was highest in other psychiatry and in therapy and humanist journals. Most pertinent to introductory psychology textbooks, academic–scientific psychology journals gave strongest support to Measurable MPD and slightly less to Trauma MPD. The abstracts of articles referenced by textbook writers most resembled those of hypnosis journals and least resembled those of academic–scientific psychology journals.

Selection and Coding of *PsycLIT* Abstracts

For details of method, the electronic database *PsycLIT* supplied 455 abstracts of journal articles under the thesaurus subject heading "Multiple-Personality"[2] from 1974 to 1992, the last year of textbooks reviewed. These MPD abstracts were coded for strength of support for technical analogues of the four MPD

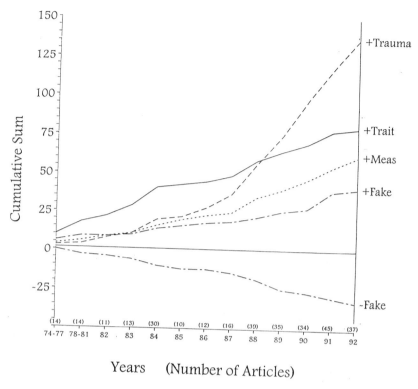

FIGURE 15.1. Cumulative number of *PsycLit* Abstracts that favor or oppose MPD models. Opposition to Fake MPD is plotted below the baseline. Opposition to other MPD models was negligible in *PsycLit* Abstracts.

models suggested by textbook usage. Here is a coding definition of the loosest category, Trait MPD.

> Trait MPD for *PsycLIT* Abstracts. The clear implication is that some traits, independent of environment, predispose to MPD. Key themes are: inadequate coping skills or defense mechanisms; alternative diagnoses, such as borderline personality, hysteria, narcissism, or Briquet's Syndrome; congenital hypnotizability or maladaptive self-hypnosis; and physiological defect, such as epilepsy or weak nervous system.

Abstracts were scored for each MPD-model position on a 6-point scale that ran from strong advocacy (3 points) to moderate (2 points) to weak (1 point), to omission (0 points), to criticism (–1 point), to contrary evidence (–2 points). Moderate support, for instance, meant that the model is clearly indicated, or it is used emphatically in a particular case without generalization. For the highly standardized and explicit abstracts of MPD journal articles, the

TABLE 15.1. Mean (Positive) MPD-Model Scores[a] for *PsycLit* Abstracts by Field of Journal, 1974–1989

	n^b	MPD model			
		Fake	Trait	Trauma	Measurable
Field of journal					
Hypnosis	25	**.60**	.48	.44	.28
Psychoanalysis	10	.00	**1.60**	.20	.00
Other psychiatry	112	.21	.53	**.82**	.56
Therapy/humanist	17	.12	.59	**1.35**	.06
Miscellaneous	9	.11	.67	**1.00**	.00
Academic–scientific psychology	21	.33	.57	.76	**.80**
All fields	194	.25	.60	**.79**	.46
MPD model journal articles cited by textbooks, 1974–1989					
Textbook reference pool	25	.44	.48	**.80**	.60
All textbook citations	90	**.83**	.57	.73	.24

Note. The largest model score for each class of journals is printed in **boldface**.
[a]Mean scores of positive support for MPD models on a 4-point scale from 0 to 3.
[b]The number of MPD articles published in journals in the field.

first author's intracoder reliability was deemed sufficient. On the first 124 abstracts, after a 3-month interval, the reliabilities were: Fake, .95; Trait, .92; Trauma, .93; and Measurable, .82.

Results

About two-thirds (68%) of the MPD abstracts addressed textbook models of MPD. Further analysis was restricted to these 309 *MPD-model abstracts*, of which 82% addressed only a single MPD model and another 16% addressed two models. The lines in Figure 15.1 represent the cumulative number of abstracts that gave at least weak support (score 1) to the MPD models, or, in the case of Fake MPD, at least weak criticism (score 1).

Positive (favorable) and negative (critical) scores for MPD models in journal abstracts were summed separately, not combined. As seen at the bottom of Table 15.1, in the 1974–1992 period, there was greatest mean positive support for Trauma MPD (.87 out of 3 points), declining in sequence for Trait (.47), Measurable (.45), and Fake (.25). In the shorter 1974–1989 period of textbook citations (see Table 15.1 under "All Fields"), the pattern of means was very similar. Mean strength of support for MPD models changed little over the entire 1974–1992 period: Trauma scores increased very slightly ($rs = .16$); Fake (−.01), and Measurable (−.03) showed no trend, and Trait (−.32) decreased. (The accelerations of lines in Figure 15.1 refer to numbers of favorable or critical articles, not to mean strength of support.) Standard deviations in scores, that is, variability in strength of advocacy for MPD models, were similar, ranging from a low of .69 for Fake MPD to a high of 1.17 for Trauma MPD.

Mean MPD-model scores differed characteristically according to field of journal for the 1974–1989 period of textbook citation, as shown in Table 15.1 and described earlier. (The pattern for the 1990–1992 period was similar.) For Fake MPD, both support, .60, and (not shown) criticism, –.36, were greatest in hypnosis journals.

The selection of MPD articles by textbooks authors showed a clear pattern. The authors gave a total of 90 citations to 25 different articles with MPD-model abstracts. The mean model scores over the 90 abstracts most resembled the profile for hypnosis journals ($rs = .80$) and least resembled the profile for academic-scientific psychology journals ($rs = -.80$).

MPD MODELS IN TEXTBOOK PRESENTATIONS

In the previous analysis, most *PsycLIT* MPD abstracts stated clear support for a single MPD model. In contrast, most textbooks presented two, three, or four unintegrated views with noncomparable forms of support, such as theoretical assertions and graphics. This section describes the textbook sample, develops scales for measuring textbook support for models, and identifies patterns of models in textbooks.

The Textbook Sample and Coding Scales

An attempt was made to obtain all introductory psychology textbooks published in the United States and Canada between 1987 and 1992 by searches of *Books in Print* (Anstaett, 1992) and publishers' lists. Of the 95 textbooks solicited through interlibrary loan, a total of 84 (88%) was obtained. This sample contained 20 textbooks with second editions (i.e., 40 books) and 4 textbooks with second and third editions (i.e., 12 books). (Textbooks were treated as later editions if they had the same first author.) Five textbooks omitted MPD, reducing the codable sample to 79. In each textbook the principal MPD section was coded along with MPD graphics, captions for graphics, and auxiliary MPD discussions.

To capture the great diversity of textbook support for each of the three causal MPD models (Fake, Trait, and Trauma), MPD-model scales were derived as the means of scores on four ordinal subscales, resulting in a (nearly) continuous scale from 0 to 4. These four (4-point) subscales measured (a) the strength of the general statement of MPD-model position, (b) the degree to which case histories exemplified the MPD model, (c) the ranked percentage of MPD-section text lines allocated to the MPD-model cases (ranked across all models), and (d) the degree of support from photographs, diagrams, and tables. The scales for the causal models were thus weighted in favor of case support, which exceeded all other types of support. For the Measurable MPD scale, the two case-support subscales of the causal models were replaced by (b′) strength of scientific evidence and (c′) completeness of scientific citation (e.g., "Putnam (1982)" versus "psychologists report . . ."). A second coder, whose field of psychology (behaviorism) and professional background (deputy district attorney) differed from the authors', provided the reliability check for the first author's coding of the irregular and ambivalent textbook accounts of MPD.[3]

Standard deviations for the four scales were all close to 1, as shown in Table 15.2, so raw scores were chosen over standardized scores. Each model scale performed similarly over the subset of textbooks that mentioned the model. This suggested that the wide range in scale means over the full set of textbooks was not an artifact of scale construction. The four model scales were essentially independent over the 79 textbooks, with pairwise correlations ranging from −.07 to .11, except for a negative Trait–Trauma correlation of −.32. That is, overall, textbook authors treated the models as unrelated to each other. None could be omitted from the content analysis without ignoring much content, and support of one model did not show up statistically as spurious support of another model.

Results for Textbook MPD-Model Scales

Ninety-four percent of textbooks addressed at least two MPD models, with a modal number of 3. As an informal impression, the models were more often juxtaposed than integrated. The mean score for Trait was highest, dropping about three-quarters of a standard deviation (*SD*) to Trauma, then one-quarter *SD* down to Fake, and another one-quarter *SD* down to Measurable, as shown in Table 15.2. In reviewing a stack of textbooks then, the reader would expect to find multiple models in most texts but with much more emphatic presentations of Trait MPD, often due to photographs or story from the film *The Three Faces of Eve.*

Textbook support for a model was considered *salient* for scores of .75 or higher. A moderately strong score of 3 on a single subscale could produce a scale mean of .75, for example, by a clear but not emphatic statement of general position ("many alleged MPs have been criminals seeking to evade

TABLE 15.2. Mean MPD-Model Scores[a] for Textbooks, and Salience[b] of Models

MPD models	*n*	Mean	SD	Salience (%)
Trait	79	1.74	.98	82
Trauma	79	1.03	1.02	49
Fake	79	.76	.92	44
Measurable	79	.53	.89	29
All models	316	1.02	1.05	96

[a]Mean scores of positive support for MPD models on a continuous scale from 0 to 4.
[b]Percentage of textbooks whose MPD-model score was .75 or higher.

responsibility"), by a case that implicitly demonstrated the mechanism of the model (e.g., a criminal faking MPD to escape the death penalty), or by a graphic with moderate impact (e.g., a photograph of an MP with ordinary appearance). As shown in the right column of Table 15.2, Trait MPD was found to be salient in four out five textbooks, Trauma and Fake MPD were both salient in almost a half of textbooks, and Measurable MPD was salient in less than a third.

MPD-model profiles of textbooks were so varied that the textbooks did not cluster naturally using any appropriate strategies of multivariate cluster analysis. The proportions of books that presented various combinations of causal models are displayed in Figure 15.2.

Several results are worth noting. In spite of the background scientific literature, for almost a quarter of the textbooks Trait MPD was the only salient model. For almost another quarter, Trait MPD and Fake MPD were the salient models. Trait MPD and Trauma MPD were the salient models in almost a fifth of textbooks. As a single causal explanation, Trauma MPD was uncommon. These proportions provide a general characterization of the textbook accounts of MPD. The distribution of emphasis resembles much more the MPD literature in psychoanalysis and hypnosis journals than in academic–scientific psychology journals (Table 15.1).

The crucial issue in this content analysis though is not the disciplinary affiliations of textbooks but their fidelity in reporting the MPD models in their references.

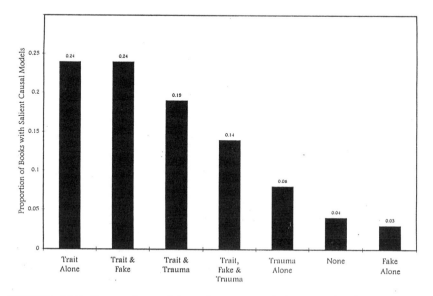

FIGURE 15.2. Proportions of introductory psychology textbooks (84 North American textbooks published between 1978 and 1992) with salient, causal MPD models.

TEXTBOOK FIDELITY TO MPD MODELS
IN THEIR REFERENCES

The Reference Pool

The MPD reference pool for the 79 textbooks consisted of 94 different sources cited in the textbooks, with an average of 4.7 citations per textbook. The scientific references (journals, monographs, science newsletters, *The New York Times* science section, etc.) constituted three-quarters of the reference pool items; the nonscientific references (films, biographies, magazines, etc.) constituted a quarter. But the scientific and unscientific each accounted for half of the textbook citations. The mean age of scientific references was 10.6 years, about half the mean age of nonscientific references (after omitting citations to 19th-century fiction). Ninety percent of textbooks cited a scientific source; 94% cited a nonscientific source. The Trauma model was most common in scientific citations, whereas the Trait model was most common in nonscientific citations.

Scientific and nonscientific references were examined separately to answer the questions: Did textbooks that cited an MPD-model reference actually report the model—*textbook fidelity?*[4]

Seventy percent of textbooks' scientific MPD references could be classified as strong supporters of a single MPD model, through either theory or MP case histories. For example, Spanos's experimental hypnotic induction in college students of a criminal personality modeled on "Hillside Strangler" Bianchi was classified with the Fake-MPD theory references, as a demonstration of role-playing MPD (Spanos, 1986; Spanos et al., 1985—12 citations). Lipton's (1943) case of Sara (three citations) was classified with the Trauma-case references because of Sara's childhood history of extreme physical and sexual abuse, even though the Trauma model did not appear until the 1970s. The Measurable model did not conflict with Trait or Trauma, so six references were permitted double classification. The 30% of unclassified references consisted of unknown or unobtained items—mostly conference presentations (unknown), items with two or more models (mixed model), and items with no MPD or no MPD models (no MPD). For each class of scientific references, 9% to 25% of textbooks cited one or more items in the class, except for the Trauma-theory class, which 60% of textbooks cited (see Table 15.3).

The *fidelity* of textbooks to a particular class of MPD-model references was defined as the percentage of citing textbooks in which the model was salient. To demonstrate the computation: There were 6 Trait-theory references (e.g., Janet, 1907); 13 of the 14 textbooks that cited 1 or more Trait-theory references had a Trait score of at least .75 (the salience criterion); so fidelity was calculated to be $^{13}/14$, or 93%.

Table 15.3 exhibits, in descending order, the fidelity of textbooks to MPD-model reference classes. Textbook fidelity to Fake case and Trait case was 100%, decreasing to 58% for Trauma case and 46% for Trauma theory.

By model, textbooks reported case references more faithfully than theory references.

The Trauma-Theory Anomaly

This analysis presents a puzzle: textbooks reported least faithfully the most-cited class of scientific references—Trauma theory. To explore this puzzle, textbook fidelities to the three most-cited Trauma-theory items were examined individually.

Multiple personality first appeared as a separate diagnosis in the 1980 third edition of the *Diagnostic and Statistical Manual of Mental Disorders* (DSM-III), with a weak, mixed Trait–Trauma position. The 1987 revised third edition DSM-III-R was updated to a moderate Trauma position: "*Predisposing*

TABLE 15.3. Fidelity[a] of Textbooks to MPD Models in Their References (*n* = 77[b])

	% of texts citing model	% fidelity
Scientific references		
MPD-model classes of scientific references		
Fake-case	10	100
Trait-case	13	100
Trait-theory	18	93
Measurable	22	71
Fake-theory	23	67
Trauma-case	25	58
Trauma-theory	60	46
Unclassifiable scientific references		
Mixed model	15	—
No MPD	9	—
Unknown	9	—
Nonscientific references		
MPD-model popular cases		
Fake—Bianchi	19	100
Trait—Eve	78	77
Trauma—Sybil	52	28
Trauma—Milligan	19	13
Mixed-model groups of cases		
Other human interest cases	26	—
Strictly clinical cases[c]	27	—

[a] Given the class of textbooks that cite references to a particular MPD-model, fidelity is the percentage of those textbooks that give salient account of the MPD model.
[b] Two textbooks with minimal MPD sections and no references were omitted from this analysis.
[c] Drawn from both scientific and nonscientific references.

factors. Several studies indicate that in nearly all cases, the disorder has been preceded by abuse (often sexual) or another form of severe emotional trauma in childhood" (American Psychiatric Association, 1980, p. 271). Four of the eight textbooks that cited the 1987 DSM-III-R gave a salient account of the Trauma model.

Boor (1982) provided one of the strongest, early Trauma-theory references. His abstract in the *Journal of Nervous and Mental Disease* stated: "These 29 case reports confirm that psychic and physical abuse, sexual trauma, and restrictive environments during childhood and consequent conflicts . . . are likely to have etiological significance for this disorder" (p. 302). However, only one of the seven textbooks that cited Boor reported faithfully its MPD etiology.

Putnam's (1982) one-page article in *Psychology Today* focused on Measurable MPD (brain-wave activity) but also included a strong Trauma paragraph. All seven texts that cited Putnam were faithful to the Measurable model, but only one was faithful to the Trauma model.

These findings highlight the fact that textbook authors are not consistent in their treatment of the background research they cite and may be presenting only the portions that support the models they choose to present.

Textbook Fidelity to Nonscientific References

Ambiguities, inconsistencies, and mixed models in the nonscientific references precluded classification by MPD model. However, four popular MPD cases captured the vast majority of citations, so fidelity to the MPD models for these cases was measured instead. Accepting court decisions and psychiatric biographies *at face value*, the four popular MPD-model cases were classified as follows: "Hillside Strangler" Kenneth Bianchi—Fake MP by defendent's court plea bargain (Allison, 1984); "Eve"—Trait MP by psychiatric biography (Thigpen & Cleckley, 1957); "Sybil"—Trauma MP by psychiatric biography (Schreiber, 1973); and "Campus Rapist" William Milligan—Trauma MP by court ruling on insanity defense (Keyes, 1981). Textbook fidelity was generously computed as the percentage of textbooks mentioning the case that gave a salient account of the corresponding model, whether or not associated with the case name.

The center portion of Table 15.3 shows textbook fidelity to these four popular MPD-model cases and percentages of texts that cited the cases. Fidelity to MPD-model cases exhibited the same pattern as fidelity to MPD-model scientific references: high fidelity for Fake and Trait and low for Trauma. But the pattern for frequency of citation differed: high (78% of textbooks) for Trait case Eve but lower for the Trauma cases Sybil and Milligan. For comparison, 26% of textbooks cited "other human interest" cases (mostly criminals) from nonscientific references, and only 27% cited "strictly clinical" cases, including those from scientific references.

TEXTBOOK "DEMOGRAPHICS" AS ALTERNATIVE EXPLANATIONS

To what extent can textbook demographics alone account for differential fidelity in the reporting of MPD models from references? Textbook data were collected for publication year, edition, number of authors, year of most recent MPD reference, number of references, and length of MPD section. Correlations of these demographic factors with mean MPD-model scores are reported in Table 15.4. Across the 1987–1992 period of textbooks, all mean MPD-model scores had *zero* correlation with publication year. Later textbook editions somewhat favored Trauma and Measurable and disfavored Fake and Trait MPD. Greater number of authors resulted in the same pattern. Recency of references showed a mild correlation (.28) with Measurable MPD scores but barely related to other models. More references and longer MPD-section line length uniformly corresponded to greater support for all models.

A simple explanation for the weak reporting of the Trauma model from references and for the infrequent reporting of the Measurable model would be the recency of emphasis on these models compared to the historically familiar Trait and Fake models. But the low correlations of MPD-model scores with age of most recent reference do not support this explanation. Moreover, almost all textbook authors relied on the *Diagnostic and Statistical Manual* in their general accounts of abnormal personality, and Trauma MPD first dominated in the 1987 edition (DSM-III-R). But there are no trends in MPD-model scores over the 1987–1992 period of textbook publication in response to the DSM-III-R.

The more vigorous reporting of Trait and Fake references might be attributed to the commercial appeal of sensationalist accounts. As an indicator of commercial success, later textbook editions favored Trauma and Measurable MPD though. Similarly, task specialization, as represented by greater number of authors, somewhat favored Trauma and Measurable MPD.

TABLE 15.4. Correlations of Textbook MPD-Model Scores with Textbook Demographic Factors

	MPD models			
Textbooks	Fake	Trait	Trauma	Measurable
Year (1987–1992)	.08	.00	.08	.00
Edition (1–13)	−.27	−.13	.19	.22
Number of authors (1–4)	−.29	−.13	.17	.26
Recency of references[a] (2–14 years)	−.14	.12	−.10	.28
Number of references (0–15)	.31	.25	.38	.37
MPD-section line length (31–755 cm)	.38	.31	.28	.34

[a]For a given MPD model, a positive correlation means that textbooks with high scores tend to have more recent references of any type.

Mere quantity of information, as represented by number of textbook references, and the perceived importance of the topic, as represented by length of MPD section, did not bear on choice of MPD models. Consequently, textbook author's attitude toward MPD, rather than impersonal factors, remains a reasonable explanation of differential support for MPD models.

QUALITATIVE SOCIAL ANALYSIS OF THREE PROTOTYPICAL MPD CASES

As a last analysis, textbook presentation of three influential MPD-model cases were scrutinized to reveal the social implications of the framing of cases and of the differential reporting of MPD models. These cases are Trait-MP Eve (in 76% of textbooks), Fake-MP Kenneth Bianchi (in 19%), and Trauma-MP Jonah (in 4%). The popular Trauma cases of Sybil and William Milligan ("the Campus Rapist") are not used in this section because they rest on trade book biographies. But the same perspective is found in the classic case history of Jonah, coauthored by Cornelia Wilbur, who treated Sybil and consulted in the Milligan case (Ludwig, Brandsma, Wilbur, Bendfeldt, & Jameson, 1972).

Eve

The good girl–bad girl version of Eve was promoted by her psychiatrists, Thigpen and Cleckley, who followed their 1954 case report with the bestseller *The Three Faces of Eve* (1957) and the sensational film starring Joanne Woodward. Thigpen and Cleckley (1957) created Eve in an era when American society defined women in terms of their sex roles for men: "Mrs. White was little more likely than a sweet Sister of Charity to draw boldly inquisitive glances from men on street corners. Everything about Eve Black seemed designed specifically to attract such attention" (p. 151). Eve's avoidance of sex, due to a "deep and specific frigidity" (p. 84), only highlighted her coquetry in their depiction. They confirmed their diagnosis of MPD, and their therapeutic integration of Eve's alters, with a blind analysis by Osgood and Luria of the semantic differentials of her personalities.

Later autobiographies (Lancaster & Poling, 1958; Sizemore & Pittillo, 1977) of the real Eve, Chris Sizemore, invalidated the image of the hedonistic "double." She had suffered debilitating shame and psychogenic blindness throughout her school years; had eloped, traumatically, at age 15 with a sexual sadist; and had struggled for decades with a severe eating disorder, sexual frigidity, and self-destructive personalities that had no defining relationship to men. Her husband thwarted her attempt to strangle her daughter with a cord—or she might have been cast as a child murderer instead of a seductress. Sizemore described how she had faked the cure of integration by having a single personality take the "postcure" semantic differential tests Thigpen mailed to her. The 1977 biography was chiefly written by Sizemore's childhood companion and cousin, Pittillo, who had just completed her doctoral dissertation at Duke University on gathering illusive data about decision making (Pittillo, 1976). Yet almost half of textbooks portrayed Eve as the hedonistic "double," and none, including the 19% of textbooks that cited Sizemore and Pittillo (1977), portrayed the wretchedness of her condition. Nor has the textbook Eve been allowed to mature into the dedicated lecturer, Sizemore, who earned a National Mental Health Association award for public service in 1982.

Bianchi

Between 1977 and his arrest in 1979, Kenneth Bianchi raped and strangled 7 to 12 young women. John Watkins, a professor of psychology and prison consultant, diagnosed Bianchi as an MP. Martin Orne, a professor of psychiatry, diagnosed Bianchi as a malingering sociopath (Allison, 1984). Orne had special expertise from previous investigations, for U.S. military intelligence, of how captured soldiers can pretend to be hypnotized to fool interrogators (Watson, 1978). Five other examiners of Bianchi supported variants of one diagnosis or the other (Allison, 1984). Testimony obtained from Bianchi under hypnosis, in the personality of the murderer, was essential to the conviction of his crime partner Buono (Allison, 1984). Watkins favored hypnotizing Bianchi to obtain verifiable details from the personality that had described the murders (Watkins, 1984; personal communication, January 27, 1995). Orne favored exposing Bianchi as a malingerer who had faked the hypnotic state so that Bianchi's prior testimony would be valid in court (Allison, 1984). Orne administered several "objective" tests of hypnotic state and concluded that Bianchi had never been hypnotized (Orne, Dunges, & Orne, 1984). Watkins challenged both the interpretation and the validity of the tests (Watkins, 1984). In a plea bargain to avoid the death penalty, Bianchi agreed to admit guilt and to testify against Buono (Allison, 1984).

Several of the citations above are to a special MPD issue of the *International Journal of Clinical and Experimental Hypnosis* in 1984 (under the general editorship of Orne), which laid out the Bianchi case controversy in four articles (Allison, 1984; Orne, Dunges, & Orne, 1984; Thigpen & Cleckley, 1984; Watkins, 1984—the issue received a total of 20 textbook citations). All textbook accounts of Bianchi emphasized the advantage to him of faking MPD. None reported the prosecution's advantage in construing Bianchi as a fake, to obtain valid testimony against his crime partner—at a time when the chief prosecutor, Attorney General Dukmejian, was campaigning for governor of California. From the perspective of self-interest, no conclusion could be drawn as to the correct diagnosis of Bianchi. Ironically, Bianchi himself firmly rejected the diagnosis of MPD; he still insists on his sanity and defends his innocence from prison (J. G. Watkins, personal communication, January 27, 1995).

The 35% of textbooks that presented Bianchi or other alleged MPD criminals did not distinguish the issue of accuracy of clinical diagnosis from the issues of moral culpability of MP criminals and of problematic procedures in the criminal justice system. Moreover, a search of case law for "multiple personality" (LEXIS/NEXIS, 1992) shows that MPD-related forensic cases do not center on criminals claiming MPD to evade punishment, as many textbooks implied.

Jonah

The Trauma-MPD model turns the risk around: Here the MP is the victim. Jonah's psychiatrists traced the origin of his personalities to such childhood traumas as being dressed by his mother in girls' clothes, seeing his mother stab his stepfather, and, as a young black boy, being attacked by a white gang (Ludwig et al., 1972). Four of Jonah's personalities produced widely discrepant, age-appropriate results on numerous personality tests, intelligence tests, learning and memory tasks, psychophysiological measures (e.g., galvanic skin response for emotionally laden words), and neurological measures (e.g., 2-point sensory discrimination). Textbook presentations of Jonah adhered to the Trauma- and Measurable-MPD models. But Jonah, too, might have been conceptualized as a hedonistic "double": "King Young," an alter personality, "views himself as pleasure-oriented and is quite a ladies' man" (Ludwig et al., 1972, p. 300). Trauma-MPD theory, however, considers the problems of the MP from the perspective of the MP. Jonah was frightened when he learned that he had attacked his wife with a butcher knife; he was surprised to wake up in jail, accused of beating up a man and a woman in a bar; when his unit came under fire in Vietnam he had a lapse and began firing his weapon crazily in all directions. Jonah might easily have become a murderer whose defense attorney then entered an insanity plea.

To disentangle the Fake, Trait, and Trauma models even in these prototypical cases would require a resolution of the problem of free will and determinism and a relinquishment of the archetypes of the *femme fatale* and the double—tasks beyond the reach of the positivist Measurable model.

SUMMARY

This study assessed textbook bias in reporting four models of MPD—Fake, Trait, Trauma, and Measurable. Extrapolating from *Psychological Abstracts* of MPD articles from 1974 to 1992, cumulative scientific support for Trait was greatest until surpassed by Trauma in 1988, cumulative support for Measurable was roughly third highest over the years, and it was lowest for Fake MPD. Journal articles cited by textbooks disproportionately reported Fake and slighted Measurable.

In textbook accounts of MPD, the Trait model strongly predominated. Textbooks averaged almost five MPD citations apiece. Textbook fidelity in reporting models from their scientific references varied considerably: 93%

for Trait (theory and case combined), 84% for Fake, 71% for Measurable, down to 50% for Trauma. Fidelity to primary sources in reporting popular MPD-model cases exhibited a similar decline, from Fake MP Bianchi, 100%, and Trait MP Eve, 77%, to Trauma MP Sybil, 28%, and Trauma MP Milligan, 13%. Examination of textbook demographics, such as recency of references and edition, suggested that this reporting pattern was not incidental to trends in the availability of references or to commercial pressures for sensational material.

Differential reporting of models manifested in textbook accounts in such ways as presenting Trait MP Eve, of 1958 movie fame, as the prototypical MP. *Eve captured 30% of all MPD citations, 55% of MPD graphics, and a mean of 17% of MPD-section text lines*—compared to 10% of text lines for all (unpopularized) clinical cases combined and 7% of text lines for Trauma MP Sybil of 1978 movie fame. Textbooks tended to extrapolate support for Fake MPD, as from a temperate article on conversion reactions which did not mention MPD (Ziegler, Imbroden, & Rodgers, 1963), and from criminal cases (e.g., Milligan), in which courts had accepted an MPD diagnosis. In contrast, textbooks tended to omit the Trauma model even when citing such clear-cut articles as Bowman's "Multiple Personality in Adolescence: Relationship to Incestual Experiences" (Bowman, Blix, & Coon, 1985). Sensationalist features of MP cases often eclipsed Measurable MPD indicators. *The common theme in these famous MPD-model cases was the importance of era and of professional context for the defining investigators, whether prosecutorial, psychotherapeutic, or medical* (Diesing, 1991). Close examination of the cases pointed to the inability of the Measurable model to resolve the social conflicts surrounding MPD.

CONCLUSION: SOCIAL CONSEQUENCES

Identified adult MPs—whatever the source of the diagnosis—have indeed presented social problems. A survey of 185 adults in treatment for MPD found a history of welfare for 55%, drug abuse by 57%, a criminal record for 15%, and an average of four psychiatric hospitalizations each (Rivera, 1991). Of 112 patients admitted with MPD to a dissociative disorders clinic between 1984 and 1991, 10% were discovered to be malingerers (Coons & Milstein, 1994). Some textbooks that emphasized the Trauma model overlooked larger issues of social order and justice, such as the possibility of remanding multiple-murderer Bianchi to a locked psychiatric ward until "cured" and freeing his crime partner.

On the other hand, identified child MPs have indeed been social victims. Over a 3-year period, the inpatient children's unit of a large neuropsychiatric hospital reported an incidence of 3% of cases of MPD, virtually all with documented histories of severe abuse (Hornstein & Tyson, 1991). All textbook accounts of Bianchi and most accounts of "Campus Rapist" Milligan (15 textbooks each) ignored their childhood torture. For instance, social services recorded that Bianchi's mother punished him by holding his hand over a stove burner (Watkins, 1984). Future health professionals who have not been exposed to the Trauma-MPD model may miss the opportunity to prevent revictimization, as did Bianchi's and Milligan's many documented professional helpers in childhood.

Given that all MPD-model advocates make claims that can be substantiated in the scientific literature, the question remains why textbook authors have not shown fidelity to the sources they cite. Although this question surpasses the scope of our study, the current debate regarding truth in memory directs us to consider the implications of the problem. Most college students take a psychology course, and introductory psychology is far and away the most popular course. Therefore, a very large segment of our population, including health care professionals, social service workers, educators, and legal professionals, bases its scientific understanding of MPD on these first impressions. Textbook writers collect and reformulate information about the hedonistic MP "double," the malingering MP criminal, and the severely abused child, and they broadcast these social risks to the public. That is, the introductory psychology textbook genre serves as a *social station of amplification* (Renn, Burns, Kasperson, Kasperson, & Slovic, 1992) of MPD-related risks. Multiple personality is an issue about which there are scientific data, if not firm conclusions, that are either ignored or misrepresented in textbook reports.

This chapter alerts memory researchers to the magnitude and the mechanisms of the institutional machinery producing opinion on multiple personality and related memory issues. This chapter also calls to action textbook writers and their editors to rely on scientific data when it is clearly available and to be true to their sources. Otherwise, the dissemination of faulty information from the scientific literature to the public domain infinitely perpetuates itself in the institutional machinery.

ACKNOWLEDGMENTS

We are grateful to librarian Ina Thomas for extraordinary assistance in obtaining textbooks and their references; to John C. Harris for the reliability check on textbook coding; and to Lucy Benjamin, Catherine Cameron, Charles Dicken, Robert Gable, Stuart Oskamp, and Allan Wicker for critiques of earlier versions of this work. This chapter is based on the master's thesis project of Jean Maria Arrigo.

NOTES

1. This chapter retains the older diagnostic category of multiple personality disorder to accord with usage in the 1987–1992 textbooks.

2. The 17 citations under related headings in *Psychological Abstracts* from 1927

to 1973 (e.g., Hall & Co., 1966) tended to lack standardized abstracts or not to address current MPD themes.

3. A second coder scored the 18 (then available) textbooks from 1987. Inter-coder reliabilities were Fake, .95; Trait, .70; Trauma, .95; and Measurable, .83. After further training, both coders scored a random sample of 23 of the remaining textbooks for Trait and raised the reliability to .90 on the Trait scale.

4. A second question was also addressed separately for scientific and nonscien-tific references: How big an effect did MPD-model references have on the textbooks' corresponding MPD-model scores? Findings from these two measures corroborated—and accentuated—the differential reporting pattern discovered for textbook fidelity.

REFERENCES

Allison, R. B. (1984). Difficulties in diagnosing the MP syndrome in a death penalty case. *International Journal of Clinical and Experimental Hypnosis, 32*, 107–117.

American Psychiatric Association. (1980). *Diagnostic and statistical manual of mental disorder* (3rd ed.). Washington, DC: Author.

American Psychiatric Association. (1987). *Diagnostic and statistical manual of mental disorders* (3rd ed., rev.). Washington, DC: Author.

Anstaett, H. B. (1992). *Books in print: Subject guide.* New York: Bowker.

Baker, G. O., Hardyck, C. F., & Petrinovich, L. F. (1966). Weak measurements vs. strong statistics: An empirical critique of S. S. Stevens' proscriptions on statistics. *Educational and Psychological Measurement, 26*(2), 291–310.

Banks, J. A. (1969). A content analysis of the black American in textbooks. In M. P. Golden (Ed.), *The research experience* (pp. 375–389). Itasca, IL: Peacock.

Boor, M. (1982). The multiple personality epidemic: Additional cases and inference regarding diagnosis, etiology, dynamics, and treatment. *Journal of Nervous and Mental Disease, 170*, 302–304.

Bowman, E. S., Blix, W., & Coons, P. M. (1985). Multiple personality in adolescence: Relationship to incestual experiences. *Journal of the American Academy of Child Psychiatry, 24*, 109–114.

Coons, P. M., & Milstein, V. (1994). Factitious or malingered multiple personality disorder: Eleven cases. *Dissociation, 7*(2), 81–85.

Crooks, R. L., & Stein, J. (1991). *Psychology: Science, behavior and life* (2nd ed.). New York: Holt, Rinehart & Winston.

Diesing, P. (1991). *How does social science work?: Reflections on practice.* Pittsburgh: University of Pittsburgh Press.

Elliott, D. (1982). State intervention and childhood multiple personality disorder. *Journal of Psychiatry and Law, 4*, 441– 456.

Hall, G. K., & Co. (Ed.). (1966). *Cumulated subject index to Psychological Abstracts, 1927–1960.* Boston: Author.

Halter, C. A., Bond, G. R., De Graaf-Kaser, R. (1992). How treatment of persons with serious mental illness is portrayed in undergraduate psychology textbooks. *Community Mental Health Journal, 28*, 29–42.

Hornstein, N. L, & Tyson, S. (1991). Inpatient treatment of children with multiple personality/dissociative disorders and their families. *Psychiatric Clinics of North America, 14*, 631– 638.

Janet, P. (1907). *The major symptoms of hysteria.* New York: Macmillan.

Jaroff, L. (1993, November 29). Lies of the mind. *Time*, pp. 52, 55, 56, 59.

Kagan, J., & Segal, J. (1992). *Psychology: An introduction* (7th ed.). San Diego, CA: Harcourt Brace Jovanovich.

Keyes, D. (1981). *The minds of Billy Milligan.* New York: Random House.

Kluft, R. P. (1988). The dissociative disorders: Multiple personality disorder. In J. A. Talbott, R. E. Hales, & S. C. Yudofsky (Eds.), *The American Psychiatric Press textbook of psychiatry* (pp. 569–583). Washington, DC: American Psychiatric Press.

Lancaster, E, & Poling, J. (1958). *The final face of Eve.* New York: McGraw-Hill.

LEXIS/NEXIS. (1992). [Online service.] Dayton, OH: Mead Data Central.

Lipton, S. (1943). Dissociated personality: A case report. *Psychiatric Quarterly, 17*, 35–46.

Ludwig, A. M., Brandsma, J. M., Wilbur, C. B., Bendfeldt, F., & Jameson, D. H. (1972). The objective study of a multiple personality. *Archives of General Psychiatry, 26*, 298–310.

Lynn. (1992, October). Portrait of a survivor. *SurvivorShip: A forum on survival of ritual abuse, torture and mind control*, p. 13.

Orne, M. T., Dunges, D., & Orne, E. C. (1984). On the differential diagnosis of multiple personality in the forensic context. *International Journal of Clinical and Experimental Hypnosis, 32*, 118–169.

Peterson, S. B., & Kroner, T. (1992). Gender biases in textbooks for introductory psychology and human development. *Psychology of Women Quarterly, 16*, 17–36.

Pittillo, E. S. (1976). *Decision flow analysis as perceived by different hierarchical levels within a selected educational organization.* (Doctoral dissertation, Duke University, 1975). *Dissertation Abstracts International, 36*, 4178–4179-A.

PsycLIT. (1974–1992). [CD-ROM]. Washington, DC: American Psychological Association. Available from SilverPlatter Information, Inc.

Putnam, F. W. (1982, October). Traces of Eve's faces. *Psychology Today*, p. 88.

Rathus, S. A. (1991). *Essentials of psychology* (3rd. ed.). Orlando, FL: Holt, Rinehart & Winston.

Renn, O., Burns, W. J., Kasperson, J. X., Kasperson, R. E., & Slovic, P. (1992). The social amplification of risk: Theoretical foundations and empirical applications. *Journal of Social Issues, 48*(4), 137–160.

Rivera, M. (1991). Multiple personality disorder and the social systems: 185 cases. *Dissociation, 4*(2), 79–82.

Schreiber, F. R. (1973). *Sybil.* Chicago: Regnery.

Sizemore, C. C., & Pittillo, E. S. (1977). *I'm Eve.* Garden City, NY: Doubleday.

Spanos, N. P. (1986). Hypnosis, nonvolitional responding, and multiple personality: A social psychological perspective. *Progress in Experimental Personality Research, 14*, 1–62.

Spanos, N. P. (1994). Multiple identity enactments and multiple personality disorder: A sociocognitive perspective. *Psychological Bulletin, 116*(1), 143–165.

Spanos, N. P., Weekes, J. R., & Bertrand, L. D. (1985). Multiple personality: A social psychological perspective. *Journal of Abnormal Psychology, 94*, 362–376.

Stowe, P. (1993). *Estimates of 1985–86 bachelor's degree recipients' course-taking behavior.* (NCES Report No. 93-078). Washington, DC: U.S. Department of Education,

Office of Education Research and Improvement, National Center for Education Statistics.

Talbott, J. A., Hales, R. E., & Yudofsky, S. C. (Eds.). (1988). *The American Psychiatric Press textbook of psychiatry*. Washington, DC: American Psychiatric Press.

Thigpen, C. H., & Cleckley, H. M. (1957). *The Three faces of Eve*. New York: McGraw-Hill.

Thigpen, C. H., & Cleckley, H. M. (1984). On the incidence of multiple personality disorder: A brief communication. *International Journal of Clinical and Experimental Hypnosis, 32*, 63–66.

Wade, C., & Tavris, C. (1990). *Psychology* (2nd ed.). New York: Harper & Row.

Watkins, J. G. (1984). The Bianchi (L.A. Hillside Strangler) case: Sociopath or multiple personality? *International Journal of Clinical and Experimental Hypnosis, 32*, 67–101.

Watson, D. L. (1992). *Psychology*. Pacific Grove, CA: Brooks/Cole.

Watson, P. (1978). *War on the mind: The military uses and abuses of psychology*. New York: Basic Books.

Whitbourne, S. K., & Hulicka, I. M. (1990). Ageism in undergraduate psychology texts. *American Psychologist, 45* (10), 1127–1136.

Ziegler, F. J., Imbroden, & J. B., Rodgers, D. A. (1963). Contemporary conversion reactions III: Diagnostic considerations. *Journal of the American Medical Association, 186*, 307–311.

Zimbardo, P. G. (1992). *Psychology and life* (13th ed.). Glenview, IL: Scott, Foresman.

CHAPTER 16

RECOVERED MEMORIES IN THE COURTROOM

Ralph Underwager
Hollida Wakefield

The rules of the courtroom have changed.

> Faced with the proffer of expert scientific testimony, the trial judge must determine at the outset, pursuant to Rule 104 (a), whether the expert is proposing to testify to (1) scientific knowledge that (2) will assist the trier of fact to understand or determine the fact at issue. This entails a preliminary assessment of whether the reasoning or methodology underlying the testimony is scientifically valid and of whether that reasoning or methodology properly can be applied to the facts in issue. We are confident that federal judges possess the capacity to undertake that review. (*Daubert v. Merrell Dow Pharmaceuticals, Inc.*, 1993)

The ruling has two concepts. The first supersedes the *Frye* (*Frye v. United States*, 1923) standard by Federal Rules of Evidence. Rule 702 states that testimony is admissible if the scientific knowledge of the expert will assist the trier of fact. However, the second concept of the *Daubert* ruling is that the substance of the testimony must qualify as "scientific knowledge." The ruling then goes on to give requirements for determining what is scientific knowledge. This is most crucial to understanding the way claims of recovered memory are likely to be treated in the courtroom. Now, under Rule 702, the judge's task is to screen out testimony that cannot be described as scientific knowledge. Then a methodological definition of scientific knowledge is given, rather than any particular body of propositions (Imwinkelried, 1996). The trial judge has this responsibility. "This entails a preliminary assessment of whether the reasoning or methodology underlying the testimony is scientifically valid and of whether that reasoning or methodology properly can be applied to the facts in issue" (*Daubert*, 1993, p. 12).

This Supreme Court decision constitutes a paradigm shift in what the justice system accepts as scientific evidence (Underwager & Wakefield, 1993). The decision adopts the position of Sir Karl Popper's philosophy of science and, thus, repudiates logical positivism and the naive view that science proves what is true. Instead, as the first consideration, it adopts the statement of Popper that the criterion for science is falsifiability, refutability, or testability: "Ordinarily, a key question to be answered in determining whether a theory or technique is scientific knowledge that will assist the trier of fact will be whether it can be (and has been) tested . . . ('The criterion of the scientific status of a theory is its falsifiability, or refutability, or testability')" (*Daubert*, 1993, pp. 12–13).

The second consideration is whether there has been peer review and publication. The third is the known or potential rate of error and the standards of controlling the technique's operation. Finally, there may be some significance in the level of acceptance in the scientific community. The Supreme Court clearly wants fact finders to have available credible scientific knowledge to make the most accurate decisions. Therefore, it requires trial judges to think like scientists in order to select admissible evidence (Thomas, 1994).

Although general acceptance in the scientific community (the *Frye* test; *Frye v. United States*, 1923[1]) is retained as one consideration, the lack of such by itself does not preclude the proposed testimony. This will make admissible new scientific evidence that was excluded under *Frye*. At the same time, if properly understood and followed, *Daubert* should render inadmissible "junk science" in the courtroom (Underwager & Wakefield, 1993). Scientific theories must always be able to make predictions in such a way that they can be falsified, that is, shown to be wrong. Unscientific theories are those, such as Marxism and Freudianism, that explain everything. Nothing can occur that cannot be accommodated by these theories; therefore they are not falsifiable. Science advances by the process of producing hypotheses about how things work, finding a way to test them, and discarding those that do not work out. The number of times a theory has been supported is not the crucial element. Although there may be a large number of supportive studies, a single credible and well-done study that falsifies the theory means the theory must be discarded (Meehl, 1967). The goal now must be to demonstrate that the proposition rests on sound scientific procedure. This involves the factors of falsifiability and level of error as direct evidence while the publication and general acceptance are circumstantial evidence only (Imwinkelried, 1993).

After the *Daubert* decision on June 28, 1993, there were 40 cases through May 18, 1994, that reached the reporting level in which the new rules establishing what is admissible as scientific evidence were applied (Bernstein, 1994). In most of the 40 cases the courts used *Daubert* to reject scientifically unsound evidence. Although most of these have involved toxic tort and traditional tort cases, there were four cases in which *Daubert* was applied to the social sciences, that is, testimony by mental health professionals, psychiatrists, psychologists, and social workers. Testimony based on weakly supported psychological theories has been excluded (e.g., the use of posttraumatic stress disorder and the child abuse accommodation syndrome to buttress, by inference, claims of prior abuse). Because of the recognition of suggestibility, hypnotically refreshed testimony has been excluded.

CLAIMS OF RECOVERED MEMORIES OF CHILDHOOD ABUSE

Beginning in the late 1980s, claims were made that childhood sexual abuse was banished from consciousness through some type of active filtering process termed "repression" or "dissociation." This alleged abuse was often highly traumatic and intrusive, but the victim had no memories until adulthood. The memories generally returned with the aid of a therapist or after reading a sexual abuse survivors' book (e.g., Bass & Davis, 1988; Blume, 1990; Dolan, 1991; Fredrickson, 1992).

These recovered memories claims have created fierce controversy and massive polarization in the professional community. Although some professionals attempt to take a "middle" position, this is difficult to do and those involved are generally on one side or another. A task force established by the American Psychological Association with three researchers and three therapists (Alpert et al., 1996) was unable to reach a consensus on the question of repressed memories and recovered memory therapy.

In 1992, a small group of parents whose adult children accused them of abuse based on recently recovered memories and several sympathetic professionals formed the False Memory Syndrome Foundation (FMSF) in Philadelphia.[2] It now has a large professional advisory board, has put on scientific conferences, and disseminates information concerning claims of repressed or dissociated memories and the techniques often used to recover memories. Recovered memory advocates have reacted to the FMSF with anger and defensiveness and have attacked the organization and its director and advisory board in books, newsletters, and conference presentations. The claims of recovered memories as well as the skeptical responses have received significant media attention.

As with all disputes about facticity that cannot be resolved elsewhere in our society, many of these allegations end up in the courtroom. One party claims to have recovered memories of childhood abuse and the other party denies ever committing any abuse. The new rules for scientific evidence are directly applicable to these claims and counterclaims. Therefore, the question becomes which party has the sustainable claim to scientific knowledge, methodology, and techniques under *Daubert.*

Approximately 200 cases involving claims of recovered memories of childhood abuse have now reached the appellate level. Some have been ruled on while others are still at the appeal level. Four legal postures have emerged from the appellate rulings on recovered memory claims. First, the discovery rules (i.e., the date a person discovers an injury) may not apply to recovered memory claims. Then, recovered memory claims do not extend the statute of limitations as a statutory disability. Next, independent corroboration is required to apply the discovery rule. Finally, and most recently, the reliability of the repressed memory theory must be determined before any extension of the statute of limitations. A pretrial hearing on admissibility is where the *Daubert* standards of scientific knowledge are most likely to be applied to recovered memory claims. The history of appellate rulings gives some indication of which direction is likely to emerge from such hearings.

In the first repressed memory case to reach the appellate level, the Washington Supreme Court (*Tyson v. Tyson*, 1986) did not extend the discovery rule to repressed memories because of the lack of "empirical verifiable evidence of the original wrongful act and the resulting injury." The court reasoned that when an alleged recollection of events repressed from consciousness had no way to be independently verified, "the potential for spurious claims would be great and the probability of the court's determination of truth would be unreasonably low" (p. 230). The Michigan Supreme Court (*Lemmerman v. Fealk*, 1995) also refused to extend the discovery rule because it would be very difficult to resolve the issue "given the state of the art regarding repressed memory and the absence of objective verification." The weakness of scientific support for claims of repressed memories has also been noted by the supreme courts of New Hampshire, Wisconsin, Alabama, Michigan, Texas, and Maryland (*Pritzlaff v. Archdiocese of Milwaukee*, 1996; *Travis v. Ziter*, 1996; *Lemmerman v. Fealk*, 1995; *S.V. v. R.V.*, 1996; *Doe v. Maskell*, 1996; *New Hampshire v. Hungerford/Morahan*, 1997; *New Hampshire v. Walters*, 1997), and appellate courts in Illinois, Tennessee, California, and North Carolina (*M.E.H. v. L.H.*, 1996; *Hunter v. Brown*, 1996; *Engstrom v. Engstrom*, 1997; *Barrett v. Hyldburg*, 1997).

Trial courts in Pennsylvania, North Carolina, and New Hampshire (*Pennsylvania v. Crawford*, 1996; *New Hampshire v. Hungerford*, 1995; *Barrett v. Hyldburg*, 1996), as well as others, have held that claims of recovered memories cannot proceed because of the lack of scientific support for the concepts advanced. The *Daubert* standards were cited by some trial judges as in North Carolina (*Barrett v. Hyldburg*, 1996), where the court stated, "This court is of the opinion, considering all of the evidence that has been presented . . . that the evidence sought to be introduced is not reliable and should not be received into evidence in this trial." The Rhode Island Supreme Court (*Kelly v. Marcanonio*, 1996) ruled that the scientific reliability and validity of repressed memory theories must first be determined before a trial or extension of discovery. Requiring a judgment about the scientific status of recovered memory claims is the most likely direction for the courts to go. Given the indications of decisions made thus far, when a *Daubert* analysis is used to determine the scientific status of repressed memory claims, such claims are likely to be found wanting and not allowed in the courtroom. Several trial courts and appellate courts ruled that the statute of limitations applies when a plaintiff has always known of the abuse but asserts lack of knowledge of the damage done (see *Marshall v. First Baptist Church of Houston*, 1997; *John BBB v. Archdiocese of Milwaukee*, 1997).

But the final implications of *Daubert* are not clear because judges will have great latitude in determining whether evidence meets the criterion for admissibility. Some judges may be mistaken, uninformed, or biased. Dershowitz (1982) comments, "Most judges have little interest in justice. . . . They want to make sure criminals are convicted and sent away . . . many judges will do everything within their lawful power—and some things beyond it—to convict defendants who they believe should be in jail. . . . Beneath the robes of many judges, I have seen corruption, incompetence, bias, laziness, meanness of spirit, and plain, ordinary stupidity (pp. xvii–xviii). Huff, Rattner, and Sagarin (1996) report finding a systemic error in the justice system. Higher courts do not reverse lower courts but systematically incorporate their errors into the case law system. "The further a case progresses in the system, the less chance there is that an error will be discovered and corrected, unless it involves a basic issue of constitutional rights and due process" (p. 144).

The ruling of the U.S. Court of Appeals for the Second Circuit (*Borawick v. Shay*, 1995) establishes a legal precedent for interpreting the *Daubert* decision guidelines by considering the totality of the circumstances in determining admissibility of evidence. This was a recovered memory of childhood abuse claim. While the ruling affirms the district court's summary judgment in the specific case, it leaves open an exercise of judicial discretion that permits evasion of the *Daubert* ruling's guidelines for admissibility of scientific evidence. Errors by a biased or incompetent judge claiming to consider the totality of the circumstances and admitting evidence with no scientific validity or credibility would be very difficult to reverse. This may effectively prevent the application of the *Daubert* ruling to prevent junk science from dominating the courtroom. Given the high level of emotional involvement of all participants when there is an allegation of sexual abuse, this may be the type of case in which the potential risk of error is greatest.

THE IMPACT ON PSYCHOLOGY

The shift represented in the *Daubert* ruling exposes the science of psychology to what may turn out to be startling influence by the judicial system. With judges passing on the nature of scientific knowledge, scientific methodology, and what is or is not scientific, it is almost assured that what is affirmed by judicial decisions will gain prestige and status whereas what is rejected will lose out. Theories, procedures, and concepts judged to be unscientific may well be vulnerable to malpractice actions, ethical complaints, and loss of insurance coverage.

The period when scientists alone determined what was science and what ideas could be pursued is over. Now if there is any hint of a judicial rejection of scientific recognition, the future of an idea is likely pretty bleak. As science entered the courtroom, it became reasonable for the justice system to hold putative scientists and their testimony to standards of accountability and responsibility. Nobody really wants pseudoscience to be on an equal footing in the courtroom with responsible and empirically supported science.

At the same time, ethical positions taken by the American Psychological Association strongly urge psychologists to maintain the autonomy of the science and the profession. The Committee on Professional Standards (1981) states, "As a member of an autonomous profession, a psychologist rejects limitations upon his [or her] freedom of thought and action other than those imposed by his [or her] moral, legal, and social responsibilities" (p. 650 17. 19).

When judges make decisions regarding the admissibility of expert testimony, they cannot avoid becoming participants in a particular construction of scientific facts. Judges can, and most likely, will shape an image of science that is affected by their own preferences and biases as to how the world should work. A recent ruling by the Court of Appeals for the Eighth Circuit (*United States v. Rouse et al.*, 1996) overturned a verdict because the trial judge had inappropriately and mistakenly applied the *Daubert* standards to the admissibility of expert testimony.[3] The process of bringing *Daubert* to bear on the science of psychology is one that psychologists need to observe carefully and thoughtfully and interact with the judiciary in any way possible. The controversy around claims of recovered memory offers the first opportunity to do so.

RECOVERED MEMORY ASSUMPTIONS

Proponents of recovered memories often maintain that from one-third to one-half of all women were sexually abused in childhood. Although the various studies of prevalence yield widely divergent estimates (Miller, Johnson, & Johnson, 1991; Salter, 1992), the higher figures of Russell (1983) and Wyatt (1985) are often cited as support for this claim. (These high prevalence estimates have been sharply disputed by Gilbert, 1991, 1994, and Okami, 1990.) Discussions of prevalence statistics also often include assertions that many instances of child abuse are unreported and many victims never tell anyone. Some professionals believe that up to half of adults who were abused as children have amnesia for their abuse (e.g., Blume, 1990; Demause, 1991; Gleaves, 1994; Maltz, 1990; Summit, 1990).

Advocates for recovered memories claim that "survivors" have a variety of symptoms that indicate abuse even when the person has no memories (e.g.,

Blume, 1990; Dolan, 1991; Fredrickson, 1992). (See Kihlstrom Chapter 1, this volume, for a discussion of checklists of symptoms.) They believe that sexual abuse survivors must retrieve their memories so they can process the trauma and eliminate their symptoms (Bass & Davis, 1988; Blume, 1990; Courtois, 1992; Dolan, 1991; Everstine & Everstine, 1989; Fredrickson, 1992). Memory recovery work is described as the basic healing force: "The bulk of your repressed memories need to be identified, retrieved, and debriefed for healing to occur" (Fredrickson, 1992, p. 223). Without retrieving memories, the person cannot heal and recover (Courtois, 1992).

The recovered memory assumptions are supported by referring to one or more of several concepts. The person is said to have "repressed" the memory because it was too painful, or to have "dissociated" during the abuse as protective mechanism. The victim may have developed "traumatic amnesia" for the abuse and, if the abuse was severe and repeated, may have formed "alter personalities" and will develop "multiple personality disorder." It is believed that, although not available to conscious memory, childhood abuse can be observed through a variety of later problems and "body memories," "flashbacks, or "nightmares" (see Wakefield & Underwager, 1994b, for a detailed discussion of these concepts).

Vague feelings about abuse are interpreted to mean that the person has been abused but cannot remember it. Demands for details or corroboration are seen as unreasonable and, once the person begins "recovering" memories, the veracity of these memories is seldom questioned. In *The Courage to Heal*, sometimes referred to as the "Bible" of the recovered memory movement, Bass and Davis (1988) state:

> "If you think you were abused and your life shows the symptoms, then you were" (p. 2).
>
> "If you don't remember your abuse you are not alone. Many women don't have memories, and some never get memories, This doesn't mean they weren't abused" (p. 81).
>
> "You are not responsible for proving that you were abused" (p. 137).

Information about the basic assumptions and therapy that elicits recovered memories comes from several sources. Descriptions of the type of treatment offered are found in the reports of people who have undergone such treatment (Goldstein & Farmer, 1993; Nelson & Simpson, 1994; Wakefield & Underwager, 1994b). Several therapists describe their techniques in books, articles, and workshop presentations (e.g., Bass & Davis, 1988; Blume, 1990; Courtois, 1992; Dolan, 1991; Fredrickson, 1992; Grand, Alpert, Safer, & Milden, 1991; Lundberg-Love, 1989, n.d.). There have been instances in which a journalist joins a survivors" group or goes to a therapist and records what happens (e.g. Nathan, 1992) or a parent sends a private investigator to their adult child's therapist to act as a pseudopatient (Wakefield & Underwager, 1994b). In a questionnaire project conducted by the FMSF, lengthy questionnaires were sent to people whose adult children accused them of recovered memories of repressed childhood sexual abuse (Freyd, Roth, Wakefield, & Underwager, 1993; Wakefield & Underwager, 1992, 1994b). Many of the respondents were able to provide information about the type of therapy their adult child received.

Many different techniques may be used to help patients recover memories of sexual abuse. These include direct questioning, hypnosis, age regression, reading survivors' books, attending survivors' groups, free association, massage therapy, dream interpretation, ideomotor signaling with the unconscious, and expanding on imagistic memories. In the FMSF questionnaire, respondents also were aware of a variety of other unconventional techniques, including prayer, meditation, neurolinguistic programming, reflexology, channeling, psychodrama, casting out demons, yoga, trance writing, and primal scream therapy.

After memories are retrieved, the "survivor" may be encouraged to express her rage at the perpetrator in a variety of ways, such as throwing darts at his photograph, writing him angry letters, or confronting him during a family gathering. The patient is often referred to a survivors' group, where further abuse memories may develop in response to group norms and influence. The goal of the therapist is to be accepting, reassuring, encouraging, and validating of the disclosures.

The number of therapists accepting these assumptions and techniques appears to constitute a significant minority. Poole, Lindsay, Memon, and Bull (1995) found that 71% of three random samples of doctoral-level therapists taken from the National Register of Health Services Providers in Psychology (NRHSPP) in the United States and the Register of Chartered Clinical Psychologists (RCP) in Britain used techniques to help clients recover suspected repressed memories of sexual abuse. Out of their total sample of 202 therapists, 25% reported a constellation of beliefs and practices suggestive of a focus on memory recovery, and this latter group reported relatively high rates of memory recovery in their clients. If the Poole et al. (1995) sample is typical of doctoral-level clinical psychologists, there are thousands of clinical psychologists performing recovered memory therapy. Poole et al. (1995) estimate that the number of clients working with recovered memory-focused therapists from the NRHSPP and the RCP during the time covered by the survey would exceed 100,000. This number does not include other psychologists, social workers, psychiatrists, and assorted "counselors." Poole et al. (1995) observe that their findings argue against the claim that these therapists are a small group of uncredentialed and untrained therapists. Dawes (1995) notes that using the Poole et al. estimates, a conservative estimate is that in a 2-year period, 1,475,833 women have seen therapists who use two or more recovered memory techniques.

More recently, some clinicians have shifted toward a less dogmatic position and are more open to discussion and modification of previous positions. For example, in 1992, Courtois recommended hypnosis, guided imagery, drawing, guided movement, body work, and psychodrama for retrieving memories. But in 1996, she acknowledges that some of the techniques previously used in recovering memories may not be well supported and states that such techniques are used mostly by untrained and unlicensed therapists. She now describes a consensus on treatment that is phase oriented and aimed at healing rather than full remembering or reexperiencing the trauma and abreaction, and she declares that therapists must pay careful attention to social influence and risk factors that may generate erroneous beliefs. There is no mention of the techniques she advocated in 1992.

In 1991, Alpert was a presenter in an APA symposium (Grand et al., 1991) in which the role of the therapist was declared to be to help the patient become convinced of the historical reality of the recovered memory of abuse even when there was no external corroboration and even when the patient doubted the memory was real. Techniques of body work, dream analysis, imaging, and the like were touted. But in 1996, Alpert states that the "search for buried memories is not promoted by professional programs in psychology or by the mainstream professional literature on treatment of adult survivors. . . . There is no training program or mainstream literature that presents memory retrieval to the exclusion of other therapeutic tasks as the treatment goal, or that promulgates the utilization of techniques that are suggestive" (Alpert, 1996, p. 328).

Alpert and Courtois were members of the American Psychological Association's working group on investigations of memories of childhood sexual abuse (Alpert et al., 1996). In the three clinicians' report, Alpert, Courtois, and Brown[4] conclude that the majority of sexually traumatized individuals remembered their abuse, that there are no symptoms pathognomic of childhood sexual abuse, and that clinicians must use care to avoid errors of commission or omission.

There now appears to be general agreement among both researchers and clinicians that most sexual abuse victims remember their abuse, that sometimes abuse many be forgotten and later remembered, but that it is possible to construct convincing pseudomemories of abuse that never happened.

MEMORY AND FORGETTING

The nature of memory itself is central to evaluating a recovered memory claim. The popular view of memory is that it operates like a videotape in which everything that happens to us is recorded and stored in our brain, waiting for the correct playback button to be found so that the memory can be retrieved. This view of memory is basic to the belief in recovered memories and is widely accepted by both laypersons and professionals (Loftus & Ketcham, 1991).

But this view of memory is completely mistaken. In reality what we remember is a combination of the original encoding of the event, intervening events that happen to us since the original event occurred, and our current beliefs and feelings (Dawes, 1988; Goodman & Hahn 1987; Loftus & Ketcham, 1991; Loftus, Korf, & Schooler, 1989). Reconstructed memories can sometimes include detailed and subjectively real pseudomemories of events that never happened (Loftus & Ketcham, 1991; Wakefield & Underwager, 1994b).

Many things that happen are forgotten. People regularly forget significant life events even a year after they occurred. Studies indicate that even events such as job loss, injuries, robbery, assaults, hospitalizations, or accidents are sometimes forgotten (e.g. Loftus, 1993; Raphael, Cloitre, & Dohrenwend, 1991; Rettig, 1993). However, although forgotten, such events are generally readily recalled when there are cues.

But even with cues, people are seldom able to remember incidents from before the age of 3 or 4 because of the phenomenon of infantile amnesia. Infantile amnesia is part of the normal process of growth and development and has nothing to do with dissociation, repression, or traumatic amnesia. Although some researchers report slightly younger estimates of how far back adults can remember, these bits of memory may well represent educated guesses about what was likely to have happened (Loftus, Garry, Brown, & Rader, 1994). No researchers report reliable memories in adults for events that occurred before the age of 2 (see Malinoski, Lynn, & Sivec, Chapter 5, this volume).

Sexual abuse may be forgotten—not "repressed," not "dissociated," not remembered only by an "alter personality," but simply forgotten. No one disputes this. Not all sexual abuse is traumatic. Almost every study on the effects of sexual abuse reports a substantial group of subjects with little or no symptomology (Finkelhor, 1990). Some adults do not view their childhood abuse as traumatic and may not even define themselves as sexual abuse victims. They may have been too young at the time of the abuse to fully understand what was happening, especially if the abuse consisted only of fondling. For many children, the abuse may have been an unpleasant but relatively unimportant event in the same category as countless other unpleasant childhood events (Spence, 1993).

In addition, as Schacter (1996) observes, people may attempt to avoid or suppress painful experiences. Because sexual abuse is unlikely to be discussed if not disclosed, victims may be deprived of opportunities to talk about their abuse, which could in turn weaken their memories for those experiences. Schacter notes that this kind of explanation could apply to cases in which the initial experience was not highly traumatic but was disturbing or confusing enough to make the victim avoid thinking about it. The forgotten memories then may return years later through prompted recall. We have described an example of corroborated abuse that was forgotten until the victim's recall was triggered by reading a letter she had written years before at the time of the abuse (Wakefield & Underwager, 1994b).

It is therefore not surprising that some sexual abuse victims forget about it until they are reminded in some way. It is not necessary to hypothesize a mechanism of repression, dissociation, or traumatic amnesia for such cases.

MEMORY FOR DOCUMENTED TRAUMA

It is also unlikely that persons for whom the abuse was highly traumatic will forget it. There is information on the reactions of people to documented trauma, such as fires, airplane crashes, terrorist attacks, automobile accidents, hurricanes, and being held hostage. Such trauma victims may report feelings of unreality, detachment, numbing, disorientation, depersonalization, and flashbacks, but a response of total amnesia for the entire event is not reported in the literature (e.g., Eth & Pynoos, 1985; Schacter, 1996; Spiegel, 1991; Wilson & Raphael, 1993). Although memories may be fragmented and impaired, complete amnesia for traumatic episodes is extremely rare.

Terr (1985, 1988, 1990, 1991, 1994) studied many children who underwent verified trauma. Terr differentiates repression from simple forgetting and believes that sexual abuse can be repressed or dissociated and later recovered. But, despite her beliefs about recovered memories, there are no reported cases in her research in which children over the age of infantile amnesia have no memories for the trauma.

Terr's findings that children subjected to documented trauma remember the trauma are consistent with other studies of traumatized children. In discussing the effects on children who witnessed acts of personal violence, including homicide, rape, or suicide, Pynoos and Eth (1985) state that such children "do not display traumatic amnesia" (p. 24). Children who witnessed a parent being murdered have not been found to develop amnesia; instead, they are likely to be troubled by intrusive thoughts (Black, Kaplan, & Hendriks, 1993; Malmquist, 1986). Gordon and Wraith (1993) studied more than 100 families affected by disasters and traumas, including physical and sexual abuse, and there are no accounts of anyone developing amnesia. The types of trauma occurring in wartime will include some cases of repeated trauma, such as when the child is subjected to repeated bombardment and shelling. Macksoud, Dyregrov, and Raundalen (1993) discuss the effects of such wartime experiences on children and amnesia for the trauma is never mentioned.

THE SCIENTIFIC STATUS OF CONCEPTS USED BY RECOVERED MEMORY PROPONENTS

Repression

Repression is the original concept used to explain how people can have no memories of sexual abuse but can later retrieve these memories in accurate detail (e.g. Blume, 1990; Briere & Conte, 1989, 1993; Fredrickson, 1992; Maltz, 1990; Terr, 1991, 1994, 1996; Williams, 1992). Although repression is usually differentiated from dissociation and traumatic amnesia, these concepts are often used interchangeably.

Repression is seen as a psychological defense that results in the person losing all memory for events that were too traumatic to be borne by the conscious mind. This protective mechanism is thought to be powerful enough to completely block out repeated instances of sexual abuse, rape, torture, and murder. It is assumed that the repressed abuse still affects us in powerful ways. The long list of "symptoms" of childhood sexual abuse described earlier are said to result from such repressed abuse.

Repression comes from Freudian psychodynamic theory and is seen as an active, filtering process that is different from ordinary forgetting. The concept of repression that involves the banishment from consciousness of a series of traumatic and intrusive events that take place in different circumstances over a number of years has been termed "robust repression" (Ofshe & Watters, 1993).

Repression is used in different ways by different researchers and theorists (Singer & Sincoff, 1990). If it is defined narrowly as intentional suppression of thoughts about an event, there is no dispute that it exists. But, if repression is defined as an unconscious defense mechanism used to block out all memories of overwhelming events, it is highly controversial and most experimental psychologists do not believe it exists. There are no empirical quantified data to support the theory of repression; the only evidence comes from impressionistic clinical case studies and anecdotal reports. Although hundreds of studies have tested the concept of repression (Hoch, 1982; Holmes, 1974, 1990, 1994; Hornstein, 1992; Mackinnon & Dukes, 1963), none has produced unequivocal support for the concept. In 1974, Holmes published a review in which he concluded that there was no reliable evidence for repression. In 1990, he stated that he has not seen anything new in the literature to change this conclusion. In 1994, he observed that "the many elegant theoretical explanations of repression may seem convincing, but they are meaningless because its existence has never been demonstrated" (p. 5).

In addition, traditional psychodynamic theorists object to the way repression has been used by recovered memory proponents. Traditional analytical therapists are concerned with the patient's perceptions of reality rather than the historical accuracy of the material uncovered in therapy. They do not assume that childhood memories retrieved in therapy are historically truthful (Hedges, 1994; Nash, 1992; Wakefield, 1992).

There is nothing in the literature on repression supporting the belief that repeated episodes of sexual abuse can be "repressed" and inaccessible to memory and to be only remembered years later in bits and pieces. There is no support for a concept of "robust repression" that underlies the use of recovered memory techniques.

Dissociation, Psychogenic Amnesia, and Posttraumatic Stress Disorder

As the concept of repression was attacked, many people began abandoning it as the operative mechanism and dissociation is now often used to describe the process by which traumatic memories are banished from consciousness. Dissociation refers to the failure of the person to integrate all relevant aspects of an experience so that it becomes difficult or impossible to recall the experience.

There is no disagreement about the concept of dissociation comparable to that surrounding repression. All of us are familiar with minor forms of dissociation, such as daydreaming, becoming lost in a book, or "spacing out" while driving. Dissociation can be seen as lying on a continuum from such ordinary forms to pathological forms such as amnesia, depersonalization, and fugue states (Bernstein & Putnam, 1986). Trauma victims often report having had dissociative experiences while in the midst of a rape, accident, terrorist attack, and so on. They may feel unreal or detached during the trauma and the experience may feel like a dream or like it happened to somebody else. Later they may show some memory impairment or perceptual distortions (Spiegel, 1991; Terr, 1991).

Persons undergoing repeated trauma are believed to learn to use dissociation as a defense against the trauma (e.g., Courtois 1992, 1996; Dolan, 1991; Fredrickson, 1992; Putnam, 1991a; Putnam & Trickett, 1993; Terr, 1991, 1994, 1996). Because psychiatric patients report disproportionately high abuse histories (Bernstein & Putnam, 1986), this is seen as supporting the trauma–dissociation hypothesis. The repeatedly abused child is thought to learn to dissociate as a way of defending against the trauma so that the trauma is lost from conscious awareness. Sometimes, after undergoing repeated severe trauma, the child is said to develop alter personalities and multiple personality disorder. It is assumed that adults cannot recall their childhood sexual abuse because they dissociated the abuse and were in an altered state of consciousness. Therefore, hypnosis and age regression are used to retrieve these memories by attempting to replicate the state in which the abuse occurred.

There are difficulties with this use of dissociation as a way of supporting recovered memories assumptions. If up to one-quarter of the women in the United States have been abused but do not remember it because they dissociated it, we would expect the symptoms of childhood dissociation to be frequently seen and for dissociation to be a common diagnosis in the literature on psychopathology in children. But review articles (Lahey & Kazdin, 1988, 1989, 1990) on childhood disorders do not even mention dissociative disorders. In addition, the connection between childhood trauma and dissociation has been questioned (Tillman, Nash, & Lerner, 1994). People who have dissociative symptoms have more psychopathology in general and the research claiming a link between trauma and dissociation is plagued by conceptual and design problems.

There are changes between the revised third edition and the fourth edition of the *Diagnostic and Statical Manual of Mental Disorders* (DSM-III-R and DSM-IV; American Psychiatric Association, 1987, 1994) in the dissociative amnesia disorder that reflect the attention given to recovered memory claims. A new type, *systematized* amnesia, is added. Whereas DSM-III-R states that psychogenic amnesia (now called dissociative amnesia in DSM-IV) "is rarely diagnosed under normal circumstances; it is more common in wartime and during natural disasters" (p. 274), according to DSM-IV the acute form that occurs during wartime and in natural disasters is *less* common. The main manifestation is now said to be a gap or series of gaps for aspects of the person's life history. The phrase "series of gaps" is added in DSM-IV. DSM-IV notes that there has been an increase in the reports of dissociative amnesia that involve previously forgotten early childhood traumas, but it acknowledges that this increase is subject to very different interpretations, with some professionals maintaining that the increase is due to improved identification but others due to overdiagnosis in suggestible individuals.

Although Loewenstein (1991) broadens the concept of psychogenic amnesia to include a *group* of events, which allows psychogenic amnesia to account for repeated instances of sexual abuse, no research supports this assumption. No empirical data support a concept of psychogenic amnesia for a category of events stretching across several years. Literature reviews on the consequences of sexual abuse (Beitchman, Zucker, Hood, daCosta, & Akman, 1991; Beitchman, Zucker, Hood, daCosta, Akman, & Cassavia, 1992; Cole & Putman, 1992) do not include psychogenic amnesia as a sequelae of sexual abuse.

In addition, neither Loewenstein nor anyone else has explained just how traumatic amnesia (or "repression" or "dissociation") is supposed to work in eradicating sexual abuse memories. Does the person completely dissociate the abuse and therefore develop traumatic amnesia immediately following each event? If this is the case, each new instance of abuse would be like the very first time as the child would have no memories of any of the previous incidents. Or, at some point after the abuse stops, does the person suddenly develop total amnesia for all memories of all the abuse incidents that were previously remembered? Proponents of memory-recovery techniques have not addressed these questions.

In clinical case studies of psychogenic amnesia, the person suffers a trauma that can be verified. But corroboration is seldom found in recovered memory claims. In contrast, people who have experienced documented trauma rarely develop amnesia unless they are physically injured. Although dissociation may occur and memories may be fragmented and incomplete, this is quite different from having no memory whatsoever of the incident. With the exception of dissociative identity disorder (discussed later), nothing in the literature on dissociation describes selective amnesia for a series of traumatic events that occur at different ages and at different times and places.

The diagnosis of posttraumatic stress disorder (PTSD) is often found in recovered memory claims where it may be used to explain the lack of memories. Survivors of severe sexual abuse are often reported to have PTSD symptoms, including disturbances of memory (Briere, 1996; Harvey & Herman, 1996). According to DSM-IV (American Psychiatric Association, 1994), the PTSD diagnosis is given when a person develops characteristic symptoms following exposure to an extremely traumatic event that involves actual or threatened death or serious injury, or a threat to the physical integrity of self or others and the person's response involves intense fear, helplessness, or horror. The symptoms involve reexperiencing the traumatic event, avoidance of stimuli associated with the event or numbing of general responsiveness, and increased arousal. But although the criteria for PTSD include numbing and efforts to avoid thoughts or feelings along with psychogenic amnesia for an important *aspect* of the event, there is no mention of total amnesia for the *entire* event.

Also, to diagnose PTSD, there must be a *known* stressful event (Fisher & Whiting, 1996). The diagnosis cannot be given on the basis of the symptoms alone without verification of the event. A task force of the American Psychiatric Association (Halleck, Hoge, Miller, Sadoff, & Halleck, 1992) makes it clear that it is inappropriate to use the presence of symptoms related to PTSD as evidence that prior abusive events such as rape and child sexual abuse took place. Nevertheless, Fisher and Whiting (1996) note that PTSD symptoms are frequently misused as diagnostic criteria for the validation of sexual abuse.

Dissociative Identity Disorder

Dissociative identity disorder (DID; formerly multiple personality disorder, or MPD) often appears in recovered memory cases when the alleged abuse is violent and sadistic. DSM-IV (American Psychiatric Association, 1994) defines DID as the presence of two or more distinct identities or personality states. The disorder is believed to begin early in life and mainly to affect women.

It is assumed that most people with DID were abused as children (e.g., Dunn, 1992; Kluft, 1987, 1991; Putnam, Guroff, Silberman, Barban, & Post, 1986; Ross et al. 1990). A "protector" personality is believed to develop and take over for the child, who therefore escapes psychologically from the abuse (Spiegel, 1991). The theory is that the traumatized child learns to dissociate from the repeated abuse so that DID is found in people with a history of severe physical or sexual abuse.

But the main support for this belief comes from clinical case reports. In a review of the empirical literature on the long-term effects of child sexual abuse, Beitchman et al. (1991) conclude that there is insufficient evidence to confirm a relationship between childhood sexual abuse and multiple personality disorder.

In addition, even though it is found in DSM-III-R and DSM-IV, DID itself is controversial (Dunn, 1992; North, Ryall, Ricci, & Wetzel, 1993). This controversy has increased as this diagnosis was given to people claiming recovered memories of child sexual abuse. Many researchers and clinicians believe there is little empirical evidence supporting DID as a distinct mental disorder and that it is heavily dependent on cultural influences for both its emergence and its diagnosis (Aldridge-Morris, 1989; Fahy, 1988; Frankel, 1993; McHugh, 1995; Merskey, 1992, 1995; Underwager & Wakefield, 1996; Weissberg, 1993). Spanos (1994, 1996) notes that few patients show clear signs of MPD at the beginning of therapy but learn to act out the role of the multiple personality patient during therapy. He and his colleagues have performed a series of role-playing and hypnosis experiments that support the interpretation of DID as a learned role.

The interpretation of DID as an artifact of psychotherapy is criticized by researchers and clinicians who see DID as a distinct mental disorder and who maintain that although some of the symptoms of DID can be created by therapists, there is no evidence that the disorder itself can be created. Spiegel and Cardeña (1991) state, "Although it is possible that the inappropriate handling by a therapist of a highly suggestible person may give rise to inaccurate reports of early abuse and MPD-like symptomatology, this mechanism does not seem sufficient to explain all or even most of the cases of MPD" (pp. 371–372). Gleaves (1996) maintains that Spanos (1994) makes "numerous false assumptions about the psychopathology, assessment, and treatment of DID" (Gleaves, 1996, p. 42). He believes that treatment recommendations arising from such assumptions may be harmful to patients, since posttraumatic symptoms will not be addressed.

But, although the existence of DID as a distinct mental disorder is debated, there is agreement that suggestible patients, with unwitting encouragement from their therapists, can learn to show symptoms of DID (e.g., North et al., 1993).

Body Memories

The "body memory" concept assumes that although there are no conscious memories, the body remembers and the client has physical symptoms that correspond to the childhood abuse. For example, Fredrickson (1992) describes a man whose anus hurt when he talked about his father because his body remembered the father's anal rapes. Grand et al. (1991) state that the analyst can observe the body memories and therefore be certain that abuse happened, even though the patient is confused.

Body memories are believed to occur when memories are repressed because the body has no intellectual defenses and therefore cannot screen out memory imprints. Later, a "survivor," who may have no abuse memories, will retrieve colors, hear sounds, or experience smells, odors, and taste sensations and her body may react in pain reflecting the purported abuse as the memory is retrieved. The body memory can even be an actual physical representation of an event, such as hand prints appearing around the neck of a person who was allegedly choked during the abuse. There is no empirical support for the body memory concept. (See Smith, 1993, for a critical analysis of the body memory concept.)

Trauma Memory

An assumption underlying recovered memory theories is that trauma memory is different from other memories. Herman (1992) says that whereas normal memory is "the action of telling a story," traumatic memory is "wordless and static" (p. 175), and Harvey (1993) maintains that traumatic memories are acquired in an altered state and are not stored in the same way as ordinary memories. Freyd (1993) postulates a "betrayal–trauma theory" in which childhood incest produces conflict between external reality and a necessary system of social dependence. When the abuser (betrayer) is someone we depend on, such as a parent, we need to ignore the betrayal so we block out information about sexual abuse in order to preserve our attachments. There is no convincing empirical support for these trauma-memory theories.

van der Kolk (1988a, 1988b; van der Kolk & van der Hart, 1989) developed a model of the biological changes associated with trauma along with the effect of this on later memory. He postulates a complicated biological theory to explain how traumatic events are handled differently from nontraumatic events. But van der Kolk's biological trauma memory concepts do not explain how repeated, intrusive abuse, occurring in different circumstances and places and over a number of years, can completely disappear from memory and then be recovered many years later. His explanations of how biological changes can explain PTSD symptomatology and contribute to later psychopathology do not need the assumption of some type of repression process during the trauma.

CIVIL LITIGATION

Lawsuits against Parents

Survivor's groups and books may suggest suing the alleged perpetrator (Bass & Davis, 1988; Crnich & Crnich, 1992; Nohlgren, 1991). Some therapists and attorneys believe such lawsuits are an essential part of the healing process. One attorney, quoted in *The Courage to Heal*, says, "In my experience, nearly every client who has undertaken this kind of suit has experienced growth, therapeutic strengthening, and an increased sense of personal power and self-esteem as a result of the litigation" (Bass & Davis, 1988, p. 310). Mallia (1993) believes civil litigation can bring closure to the victim and claims that winning the lawsuit "can cleanse the victim's tortured psyche" (p. 129). Lamm (1991) lists several benefits, including exoneration of the victim through publicly blaming and punishing her abuser, deterring future abuse, financial rewards and healing for the victim, and increasing public awareness of the problem of abuse. Clute (1993) describes the effect on a survivor she represented who won $3 million: "It was clearly a victory of the human soul, a liberation from a bondage that had changed him for a long time. . . . I knew I had participated in a significant healing experience" (p. 122). Walker (1992) describes such lawsuits as a "new and exciting tool in the war against child sex offenders" (p. 125).

But others (e.g., Ewing, 1992; Thompson, 1993) are pessimistic about the psychological benefits of civil litigation and observe that, especially if the abuse never happened, such a lawsuit can be harmful not only to the falsely accused but to the person initiating the lawsuit. Nevertheless, there is evidence that such lawsuits are not uncommon. The FMSF reports that 1 out of 16 of the accused parents who have contacted them have had lawsuits filed against them.

Statutes of Limitations

The statute of limitations restricts the period during which lawsuits may be filed after the date of injury. This protects defendants from having to defend themselves in court years later when witnesses have died, evidence is lost, documents have disappeared, and memories have faded. When the plaintiff is a minor, the statute of limitations does not begin to run until the age of majority.

The law, however, recognizes circumstances in which the person could not reasonably have discovered the injury within the statutory time period. Common examples are in medical malpractice (i.e., a former surgery patient experiences pain and discovers that a sponge was left in his abdomen years before) and asbestos damage. To account for such circumstances, courts have developed a "delayed discovery rule." This rule delays tolling the statute of limitations until the plaintiff discovers or reasonably should have discovered the injury. Many courts have applied the delayed discovery rule to lawsuits brought by plaintiffs claiming childhood sexual abuse. Some courts have limited the delayed discovery rule to cases in which the plaintiff claims to have completely repressed her memory of the abuse, only to recall it as an adult. In others, the plaintiff only has to claim that she did not discover within the statutory period that her current psychological problems were caused by the abuse (Lamm, 1991).

Several states have passed legislation extending the statutory period in civil cases so that the statute of limitations does not begin until 2 or 3 years after the alleged abuse is remembered and/or after the claimant understands that the abuse caused injury (Bulkley & Horwitz, 1994; Colaneri & Johnson, 1992; Loftus, 1993; Loftus & Rosenwald, 1993; Slovenko, 1993). Courts and legislatures in many states have created legal mechanisms for both criminal and civil actions based on recovered memories (Loftus & Rosenwald, 1993; Sargeant, 1994).

Recovered Memory Claims and *Daubert*

The concepts and theories used by proponents of recovered memories are vulnerable under *Daubert*. For example, the concept of repression is not falsifiable because all the behaviors of the client can be accommodated by this concept. Innumerable symptoms are said to be caused by repressed sexual abuse, even when there are no memories. Parents who are outwardly normal as well as those who are clearly dysfunctional are seen as capable of abusing their children in a way that produces repression. When there is no corroboration from the accused, the accused is said to be either denying or repressing the act.[5] If the "survivor" later retracts her recovered memories, she is said to be "rerepressing" the abuse or retracting it under pressure from her family. If the alleged abuse is implausible (i.e., bizarre satanic ritual abuse), it is claimed that these things really happen and that the satanists are clever conspirators with positions in high places who therefore can cover it up. If the alleged abuse is completely impossible (i.e., a woman who is found to have never been pregnant alleges multiple forced births as a breeder in a cult), the memories are said to be distorted but based on actual abuse or to be symbolic of emotional abuse. If everything can be explained by the theory and it is not capable of being tested or falsified, the theory should not be allowed under *Daubert*.

As mentioned previously, the concept of repression is controversial and not supported by empirical research. There are a few studies examining amnesia for childhood abuse (Briere & Conte, 1993; Feldman-Summers & Pope, 1994; Herman & Schatzow, 1987; Loftus, Polonsky, & Fullilove, 1994; Williams, 1994), but none assess repression or provide credible scientific evidence to support the assumptions underlying recovered memory therapy. They all have methodological problems concerning the manner in which trauma and amnesia are documented. None support the view that large numbers of people are so amnesiac for actual abuse that intrusive therapy techniques must be used to help them remember and heal. (For a critique of these studies see Kihlstrom, 1996; Lindsay & Read, 1994; Pope & Hudson, 1995; Wakefield & Underwager, 1994b.)

Faced with both the lack of support and the lack of testability for repression, the court should rule that testimony based on the concept is not scientific and cannot be relevant or helpful to the finder of fact. Therefore, it is not admissible. This could make it impossible for civil litigation based on a claim of recovered repressed memories to be pursued. The other concepts should be treated similarly.

Lawsuits against Therapists

An increasing number of people who recovered "memories" of abuse in therapy are now retracting these memories (Freyd, 1994). Some of them are suing their former therapists for malpractice. A suit by a Texas woman, Laura Pasley, against the therapists who persuaded her that she had been sexually abused by her mother, brother, grandmother, and a neighbor ended in a significant out-of-court settlement and a Minnesota psychiatrist, Diane Humenansky, is currently being sued by five women who claim that she implanted false memories of satanic ritual abuse (Gross, 1994). Two of the cases went to trial and the juries awarded multi-million-dollar settlements. Dr. Humenansky's license has also been suspended (Gustafson, 1994).

Many therapists are becoming worried about ethical complaints and malpractice suits. At a conference entitled "Memories of Abuse" in Minneapolis in June 1993, several therapists expressed anxiety over this. But the worried therapists do not appear to be seriously considering the possibility that their techniques may be creating false memories and harming their clients. Peterson (1994) describes her "inescapable" pain and "shattered soul" after her patient "sadistically turned on [her]" by filing a malpractice suit, but she still believes her client was abused. "Kill the messenger. Lie. This client relived the trauma by victimizing me" (pp. 26–27).

Accused parents often want to sue the therapist they hold responsible for their adult children's false memories of abuse. However, they lack legal standing to sue for malpractice because, as they were not patients, the therapist owes them no duty. For a cause of action for negligence against a therapist to succeed, the plaintiff must establish (1) the duty of the professional to use such skill, prudence and diligence as other members of his profession commonly possess and exercise; (2) a breach of that duty; (3) a proximate causal connection between the negligent conduct and the resulting injury; and (4) actual loss or damage resulting from the professional's negligence. The difficulty in third-party professional negligence cases is in establishing the duty of the therapist to the parent. If the law fails to recognize a duty between the therapist and the parent, the parent lacks standing to sue, no matter how egregious the behavior of the therapist (Simons, 1994).

But in *Ramona v. Isabella* (1994), the judge ruled that as a parent and as someone who had been substantially affected by the therapist's alleged malpractice, the accused father, Gary Ramona, did have standing to sue his daughter's therapists. In May 1994 the jury awarded Ramona $500,000 in damages.

In *Ramona*, the daughter, who sought therapy for bulimia nervosa, originally had no memories of sexual abuse. However, the therapist told the girl's mother that 70% to 80% of bulimics had been sexually abused and the daughter was placed in group therapy where abuse was discussed. Eventually she began having vague flashbacks of abuse by her father. The therapist then referred her to a psychiatrist for a sodium amytal interview. During this interview, she accused her father of repeated rape from the time she was age 5 to age 7. Afterwards, the therapist and the psychiatrist assured her that it was impossible to lie under the influence of sodium amytal and that her memories were real. They arranged a confrontation session with the father (Ewing, 1994; Loftus & Rosenwald, 1993).

As a result of the accusations, Ramona was fired from his $500,000-a-year job and his wife divorced him. In granting Gary Ramona standing to sue his daughter's therapists, the trial judge referred to a California Supreme Court ruling (*Molien v. Kaiser Foundation Hospitals*, 1980). In this case, the court ruled that the husband of a woman misdiagnosed as having syphilis had standing to sue his wife's physicians because, as he had to be treated for syphilis also, they had a duty to care for him as well as the wife (Gross, 1994). In similar cases of lawsuits by parents or relatives, settlements have been reached in several, including one against an attorney for wrongful use of civil proceedings (*Bean v. Peterson, Peterson*, 1995; *Downing v. McDonough*, 1997).

Ramona is seen as a landmark case, both because a third party was granted standing to sue and because it was the first courtroom challenge to the recovered memory assumptions and techniques. It has been interpreted by skeptics as a judgment against recovered memory therapy and a warning to psychotherapists who engage in it. It is expected to result in more malpractice suits. It is also expected to change the behavior of many therapists.

EVALUATING CLAIMS OF RECOVERED MEMORIES

The only way to test the accuracy of a memory is through independent corroboration (Schacter, 1996; Spiegel & Scheflin, 1994). Mental health experts have no special abilities to tell whether a memory is true or is the product of imagination, social influence, or fabrication. Without external corroboration, there is no truly satisfactory way to reliably determine the truth of a given "memory." At the same time, we believe psychologists can provide helpful information to the finder of fact. This information includes facts about the nature of memory, the scientific credibility and status of the assumptions underlying memory-recovery techniques, the reliability and validity of these techniques, the nature of social influence and suggestibility, and the probabilities of the behaviors alleged. This information is not generally known by either laypeople or many professionals.

When a mental health professional becomes involved in a civil lawsuit involving recovered memories, it is necessary to get as much information as possible about the circumstances surrounding the disclosure and accusations. Here is a paraphrasing of the information Daly and Pacifico (1991) suggest should be gathered:

1. All medical, psychiatric, and school records of the person claiming abuse from childhood to the present.
2. Any information concerning relationships with peers, siblings and parents, or any childhood behavior problems of the person claiming abuse.
3. Any information concerning the sexual history of the person claiming abuse, including rapes, other childhood sexual abuse, abortions, and so on.
4. The nature and origin of the disclosure, in as much detail and specificity as possible.

5. Information about any current problems or stresses in the life of the person claiming abuse.
6. The nature of any current therapy, e.g. whether techniques such as hypnosis and survivors' groups were used, the training and background of the therapist, and whether he or she specializes in treating MPD or "recovered" abuse.
7. Any books, television shows, or workshops about sexual abuse or rape to which the person claiming abuse may have been exposed.
8. Any exposure to recovered memory cases though a highly publicized case in the media or through friends who may have reported that this happened to them.
9. The work history of the person claiming abuse, including any problems with supervisors or coworkers, especially any allegations of sexual harassment.
10. The psychological characteristics and social and family history of the accused adult(s), including any drug or alcohol use, sexual history, family relationships, and job history.
11. Any criminal record or prior behaviors in the accused adult which would support or undermine the credibility of the allegations.
12. A detailed description of the behaviors alleged to have occurred.
13. Possible ways by which the person making the accusation might benefit from or receive reinforcement from making the accusation (e.g., a civil lawsuit, an explanation for why life has not gone well, the expression of anger for perceived childhood injustices, power over a dominant parent, attention, acceptance, new friends [in survivor group], etc.).

After obtaining the available documents and information, it is helpful to create a chronology of events. In the chronology, it is particularly important to note information about how the memory returned and how it was disclosed; the impact of therapy, books, or survivors' groups, and so on; any changes in the nature of the allegations over time; and any possible secondary reinforcement.

Some professionals have proposed ways of evaluating claims of alleged sexual abuse based on recently recovered memories (Gardner, 1992a, 1992b; Rogers, 1992, 1994; Wakefield & Underwager, 1992). There is little empirical research on this, so all such suggestions are based primarily on existing knowledge about memory, social influence, suggestibility, conformity, the psychotherapy process, hypnosis, and the characteristics and behavior of actual sexual abusers.

The Nature of the Alleged Behaviors

When the allegations are of extremely deviant, low-probability behaviors rather than of behaviors more typical of actual abusers, the memory is less likely to be for a real event. This appears to be self-evident, but cases of alleged sexual abuse often involve highly implausible allegations. For example, preliminary data from a survey by the the American Bar Association indicated that approximately one-fourth of local prosecutors have handled cases involving "ritualistic or satanic abuse" (Victor, 1993).

Recovered memory claims may include allegations of highly deviant abuse, such as anal or vaginal rape of toddlers, violence, sadism, sex with animals, feces and urine, abuse by several adults, and satanic ritual abuse. The accused are not just fathers; mothers and other relatives are also accused, often of acting together. These allegations can be assessed in terms of what is known about the behavior of actual child sexual abusers (Wakefield & Underwager, 1994a, 1994b).

Information is available about the behavior of actual sexual abusers, although the studies vary somewhat as to the behaviors reported. This is not surprising because the studies differ in terms of the sample studied (community, college, clinical, prison, hospital, etc.), whether victims or offenders are sampled, the method of obtaining the data (interviews, questionnaires, hospital records, etc.), the sex of the victim, the definition of terms, the specificity of the description of the behavior, whether the abuse is intrafamilial or extrafamilial, and the adequacy of the verification of the abusive acts. Despite these considerations, the research literature provides helpful information about what actual child molesters do when they sexually abuse a child (Erickson, Walbek, & Seely, 1988; Gebhard, Gagnon, Pomeroy, & Christenson, 1965; Kendall-Tackett & Simon, 1987; Kinsey, Pomeroy, Martin, & Gebhard, 1953; Tollison & Adams, 1979).

Most sexual abuse victims are girls (Erickson et al., 1988; Tollison & Adams, 1979). Although some preschoolers are abused, most are older. Tollison and Adams (1979) report that average age of female victims is ages 6 to 12 and male victims appear to be somewhat older. Erickson et al. found that one-fourth of the victims of both sexes were under age 6, one-fourth were between 6 and 10, and half were between the ages of 11 and 13.

Most sexual behavior consists of fondling, exhibitionism, masturbation, and oral or genital contact. Anal and vaginal penetration of very young children is rare but penetration becomes more likely with an older child. Males are more likely to be victims of attempted or actual anal penetration than are females (Erickson et al., 1988; Gebhard et al., 1965; Kinsey et al., 1953; Tollison & Adams, 1979). Vaginal penetration is more common in clinical samples compared to community samples (Kendall-Tackett & Simon, 1987). Most victims know the offender; abuse by strangers is much less common. It is rare for the offender to have a partner who participates in the abuse or to molest children in groups.

Many professionals believe that a grooming process is generally involved in incest (e.g., Christiansen & Blake, 1990; Erickson et al., 1988; Gebhard et al., 1965; Kendall-Tackett & Simon, 1987, 1992). Aggression and violence are not usually part of the behavior, although Lang and Langevin (1991) indicate that at least one in five child victims appear to be subjected to force or "gratuitous physical violence" as part of the abusive act.

Although sadistic, bizarre, or homicidal forms of child sexual abuse do occur (e.g., Dietz, Hazelwood, & Warren, 1990), they are extremely rare. Dietz et al. (1990) observe that such cases occur so infrequently in any one jurisdiction that it is difficult for researchers to gather information about them. Kinsey et al. (1953) state that in only one case was appreciable physical injury done to the child. Gebhard et al. (1965) report that only 6.6% of their sample used force. Erickson et al. (1988) note that there were no reports in their sample of sadistic or bizarre abuse. There is no evidence supporting allegations of organized satanic ritual abuse conspiracies (Hicks, 1991; Lanning, 1992; Putnam, 1991b; Richardson, Best, & Bromley, 1991; Victor, 1993).

Contrasted with this are the results from 398 surveys from the questionnaire project from the FMSF (Freyd et al., 1993; Wakefield & Underwager, 1994a, 1994b). The respondents were people who contacted the FMSF after their adult child recovered a memory of sexual abuse that the caller denied. No effort was made to make an independent determination of the veracity of the denial or of the information obtained. Many of the purported behaviors reported by the respondents are impossible and others have such low base rates that the probability of their actually occurring is extremely small. Examples of such allegations include the following:

- Abused by parents and grandparents in satanic rituals while wearing hooded black robes. Forced to drink urine and blood. Raped by grandfather while grandmother and mother watched. Hung by her heels. Abused with a hot poker, freezer, and washer wringer.
- Abused by mother, father, strangers, blind uncle, and nursery school teacher. Raped with scissors, killed babies, worshiped Satan, and ate ears and other organs. Was sold into child prostitution.
- Forced to have sex with a neighbor's dog and subsequently had a baby that was half dog.

In the FMSF survey, although fathers were usually the ones accused, mothers were often accused along with the fathers and in one-third of the cases, a variety of other persons were accused, most often along with the parents. Over half of the respondents appeared to have little idea concerning just what it was they were supposed to have done, but when this information was known, the allegations included a very high proportion of extremely deviant and intrusive behaviors. In the 203 cases in which the respondents knew the nature of the allegations, violence was alleged in 41%, rape in 44%, witnesses to the abuse in 42%, and satanic ritual abuse in 34%.

Therefore, in evaluating a case of alleged childhood abuse, when the allegations are of extremely deviant, implausible, and low-probability behaviors, the memory is unlikely to be for a real event. Allegations of ritual abuse by intergenerational satanic cults are especially unlikely to be true.

Because there is no scientific evidence to support a mechanism of "robust repression," if there are allegations of a series of violent and abusive incidents across time in different places and situations, the recovered memory is less likely to be true than if it is for a single traumatic incident. When the disclosures progress across time to ever more intrusive, abusive, and highly improbable behaviors, the growth and embellishment of the story may represent the suggestions and reinforcement in therapy. Anecdotal evidence (Wakefield & Underwager, 1994b) suggests this can happen in survivors' groups where group members spend the sessions talking about their newly recovered memories and flashbacks.

The Age the Abuse Is Said to Have Occurred

If the memory is for abuse that occurred at a very young age, such as abuse during infancy or under age 3 or 4, the memory is less likely to reflect a real event. This is younger than documented sexual abuse victims whose average age is between 6 and 12. In addition, the phenomenon of childhood or infantile amnesia makes it less likely that the memory is of a real event because adults and older children seldom remember incidents from their lives that happen prior to age 3 or 4.

But in the FMSF survey, the abuse typically was said to have begun at a very young age. For 29% of the cases, the alleged events began at under age 2. For 55%, the alleged events began from ages 2 to 6. Only in 16% did the alleged events first happen at age 6 or older. The median age for the age the accusing child claims the abuse began is between ages 3 and 4 (Freyd et al., 1993; Wakefield & Underwager, 1994a, 1994b).

Gardner (1992a, 1992b) believes that an important factor in evaluating the truthfulness of recently remembered abuse is the length of time the alleged abuse took place. The longer the period of abuse, the less the likelihood of its being forgotten. He sees it as more credible that a person would forget abuse that occurred over a 2- or 3-year period at age 6 or 7 compared to abuse that took place from ages 2 to 18. The age at which the abuse is said to have stopped is another factor. Although events taking place at age 5 or 6 may be forgotten, it is much less likely that events taking place during the teen years would not be remembered.

Characteristics of the Accused

Especially when the behaviors alleged are highly deviant, the allegations are less likely to be true when they include the mother and when a psychological evaluation of the defendant indicates no discernible pathology. There is no single child sex offender personality type. But despite the fact that sex offenders are heterogeneous in personality characteristics, they tend to have psychological problems (Ballard et al., 1990; Kalichman, Shealy, & Craig, 1990; Langevin, 1983; Overholser & Beck, 1986; Wakefield & Underwager, 1988; Weinrott, & Saylor, 1991).

Psychological evaluations are less helpful when the behaviors alleged are of nonviolent fondling and other less deviant behaviors. It is not unusual in such cases for the perpetrator to show a "normal" personality based on psychological testing. Therefore, the Minnesota Multiphasic Personality Inventory (MMPI) or other assessment techniques do not rule out the possibility that the person is a sexual abuser because some sex offenders produce normal MMPIs.

Although no psychological test or evaluation procedure can determine whether or not a given individual has, in fact, sexually abused a child or committed any other specific behavior (Erickson, Luxenberg, Walbek, & Seely, 1987; Myers, 1992; Nagayama Hall & Crowther, 1991), a psychological evaluation of the person accused can provide information concerning the *likelihood* that an individual would engage in the behaviors alleged. Normal, functional persons do not ordinarily act in bizarre, unusual, and totally idiosyncratic ways. Therefore, it may be helpful to evaluate the accused, especially when the allegations are of more intrusive, deviant, or sadistic behaviors. The person must be evaluated in light of the specific behaviors he is accused of committing. When it cannot be demonstrated that an accused person has the level of pathology expected given the behaviors alleged, the likelihood of a false accusation increases.

Accusations that a woman has sexually abused a child must be treated very cautiously. Although awareness about women perpetrators of sexual abuse has increased in recent years, sexual contact between children and women represent a minority of child–adult sexual contacts. Many studies depict women who sexually abuse children as being loners, socially isolated, alienated, likely to have had abusive childhoods, and apt to have emotional problems, although most are not psychotic (see Wakefield & Underwager, 1991, for a review). It is unlikely that a psychologically healthy and well-adjusted woman would sexually abuse a child.

Research claiming large numbers of outwardly normal female perpetrators must be examined very cautiously because false allegations may have contaminated the samples. For example, a large study using a sample of day-care facilities where there were abuse allegations (Finkelhor, Williams, & Burns, 1988; Finkelhor, Williams, Burns, & Kalinowski, 1988) reported that 40% of the perpetrators were intelligent, educated, highly regarded women who had no histories of known deviant behavior. But their sample includes many cases that ended in dismissals, acquittals, or convictions or that were overturned on appeal (e.g., Kelly Michaels and McMartin preschool). In fact, the authors admit that charges were filed and arrests were only made in half of their cases and less than a tenth resulted in guilty pleas or convictions. In another example, Waterman, Kelly, Oliveri, and McCord (1993) describe research on the effects of ritualistic sexual abuse, but their sample was mostly the McMartin preschool children.

The Type of Therapy and Therapist Characteristics

When memories first emerge following reading *The Courage to Heal* or therapy with a practitioner who uses memory-recovery techniques, the possibility of influence must be considered. Techniques such as hypnosis, survivors' group participation, dream analysis, ideomotor questioning, and guided imagery may increase the risk of creating memories for events that never happened, especially when the therapist believes abuse occurred. Therefore, the medical notes and records should be carefully examined. Rogers (1992, 1994) notes that valid claims may arise in therapy, but in these cases the therapist did not use intrusive techniques and the individual was not placed in group treatment until the abuse had already been fully detailed and documented.

Although some professionals believe that a lack of credentials and inadequate scientific training are major factors in false recovered memories (Dawes, 1992; Gardner, 1992a, 1992b; Gravitz, 1994; Rogers, 1992, 1994), therapists who have erroneous ideas of concepts such as the nature of memory, suggestibility and social influence, and the veracity of memories uncovered through techniques such hypnosis include those with advanced degrees. In the FMSF survey (Freyd et al., 1993), the therapists reported by the parents included all disciplines, including psychiatrists and social workers as well as less credentialed therapists. Bottoms, Shaver, and Goodman (1991) surveyed doctoral-level clinical psychologists and report that of those who encountered cases of ritual or religious abuse, the great majority, 93%, accepted the clients' claims as true. Many of these cases involved adult survivors who reported amnesiac periods. Yapko (1994a, 1994b) found that 22% of therapists who believed in age regression and past lives held PhDs and 28.1% held MDs. All of the Poole et al. (1995) sample mentioned earlier were doctoral-level therapists with good credentials; one-quarter of these reported beliefs and practices consistent with recovered memory therapy.

Therefore, the fact that the therapist has a PhD or MD from a major university does not mean that the therapist has avoided using misguided and suggestive therapy techniques. However, the lack of training and understanding in relevant scientific issues may make some therapists more vulnerable to engaging in poor clinical practices.

Psychiatric History and Characteristics of the Plaintiff

Although psychopathology in some individuals may well make them more susceptible to developing pseudomemories, the data from the FMSF survey (Freyd et al., 1993) suggest that many people who recover memories of childhood abuse are not psychologically disturbed. In fact, the questionnaire responses suggest that most of the accusing adult children are well educated and occupationally successful and come from functional, intact, and successful families. Most of the accusers had no history of significant psychiatric problems prior to the recovered memories. These data are consistent with the work of Spanos, Cross, Dickson, and DuBreuil (1993), who found that subjects reporting UFO experiences were not psychologically disturbed.

Claims that the individual must have been abused because of problems in her life must be viewed cautiously. The existence of eating disorders, sexual dysfunction, anxiety, depression, or low self-esteem cannot be used to support abuse claims because these can be caused by a variety of factors. Beitchman et al. (1992) concluded there is insufficient evidence to confirm a relationship between childhood sexual abuse and borderline or multiple personality disorder. Pope and Hudson (1992) reviewed studies on bulimia and sexual abuse and report that these studies did not find that bulimic patients show a higher prevalence of childhood sexual abuse than do control groups.

Rogers (1992, 1994) notes that in evaluating a case for civil litigation, an important consideration is whether the claimant is a bona fide patient or is in treatment for reasons other than pain or dysfunction.

Corroborating Evidence

Corroborating evidence, such as a childhood diary with unambiguous entries, pornographic photographs, or an uncoerced admission by the perpetrator, clearly makes the allegations much more likely to be true. Some cases may have this type of corroboration.

Ambiguous evidence, however, such as a childhood story or drawings now reinterpreted in light of the believed-in abuse, cannot be used as proof that the abuse actually occurred. The nature and quality of the corroboration must be looked at carefully. For example, Herman and Schatzow (1987) claim that 3 out of 4 of 53 women in their group were able to "validate their memories by obtaining corroborating evidence from other sources" (p. 1), but most of the women in their group had either full or partial recall of the abuse prior to therapy; only a minority of their sample addresses the issue of repressed memories. In discussing the claimed corroboration, no distinction is made between women who always remembered the abuse and those who did not recall it until entering therapy. In addition, the details of the corroboration are vague and depended on the reports of the women in group therapy. Herman and Schatzow (1987) presented two case examples to describe the validation process in women who had no memories prior to therapy. In one, there was no corroboration. For the other, the corroboration consisted of the woman's report in group therapy of discovering her brother's pornography collection and diary after he was killed in Vietnam. But there is no indication that anyone else saw the diary or verified what the woman said she found. Herman (Joseph DeRivera, personal communication, 1993) acknowledges that the diary was not seen by the group leaders.

Daubert Analysis

An examination of the scientific status of the competing claims of recovered memories and the assertion that therapists can teach vulnerable patients to have false memories suggest that the claim that abuse can be repressed and later recovered is not supported. In addition, the concept of repression as it is generally used is so broad that nothing can occur that cannot be accommodated by the concept and therefore it is not falsifiable.

The level of error in recovered memory claims is dealt with by Lindsay and Read (1994), who offer a Bayesian analysis of the error involved in such claims. Although they view the implantation of false memories by therapists as the best explanation for the claims, to assess the level of error, they accept the hypothetical possibility that the phenomenon may occur as the proponents describe it. Using the most liberal figures offered by the proponents of recovered memories for base rates of occurrence and assuming an unrealistic accuracy for the test of 90%, the level of error is five false positives for every false negative. One-third of the diagnoses of repressed memory will be wrong. If the accuracy of test is dropped to 80%, still unrealistically high, half of the diagnoses of repressed memories will be wrong.

There is no general acceptance of the claims of recovered repressed memory in the science of psychology. There may be publications in peer-reviewed journals, but they are subject to criticism as primarily anecdotal and case study material and demonstrating severe weaknesses and flaws in design and procedures. Using the criteria of the *Daubert* decision, expert testimony advancing the concept of recovered memories as accurate accounts of prior historic events should not be allowed in the courtroom.

The position that people can develop subjectively real memories for events that did not happen is supported by laboratory research (Ceci & Bruck, 1995; Hyman, Husband, & Billings, 1995; Loftus, 1993; Loftus & Ketcham, 1994) as well as anecdotal and case study evidence (Gavigan, 1992; Goldstein & Farmer, 1993; Gondolf, 1992; Nelson & Simpson, 1994; Wright, 1993). It must be noted, however, that the extent to which the laboratory research can be generalized to psychotherapy is debated (e.g., Alpert et al., 1996; Olio, 1994; Pezdek & Banks, 1996).

When there is no corroboration, denial by the alleged perpetrator with support of the denial by others, and claims of improbable, bizarre, or even impossible acts, the level of error is likely to be very low. This points to a much lower level of error than the proponents of uncorroborated recovered memory can suggest. The *Daubert* circumstantial evidence of general acceptance and publication are also met. Therefore, scientific testimony refuting claims that the human mind can produce accurate memories with the help of memory-recovery techniques should be permitted in the courtroom.

CONCLUSION

Some survivors of childhood sexual abuse forget about their childhood sexual abuse, particularly if the abuse was not highly traumatic. This lack of memory is most likely due to some combination of the normal forgetting process, conscious suppression, and lack of rehearsal if the abuse was never talked about. But there is no credible evidence that people subjected to repeated incidents of violent and traumatic abuse after early childhood will lose all memories for the abuse. The research on the nature of memory and forgetting does not support the assumption that some abuse is so traumatic that all memories for it will be removed from consciousness by an active filtering process of repression or dissociation.

Sexual abuse may not be talked about until the victim is an adult and real abuse may be forgotten until the person is reminded in some way. In such cases, there is no need for concepts of repression, dissociation, or traumatic amnesia. Intrusive and traumatic abuse that occurs after early childhood is likely to be remembered. The research on victims of documented trauma supports this assumption.

Schacter (1996) notes that because of ethical considerations, there can be no conclusive scientific evidence from controlled laboratory studies demonstrating that false sexual abuse memories can be created. However, there is good scientific evidence that pseudomemories for other events can be created in some people. The difficulty, as Spiegel and Scheflin (1994) note, is that it is just as possible to dissociate and retrieve a real memory as it is to convince oneself of a false belief. But there is no easy way to know the difference. Without independent corroboration, memory cannot be trusted. Although there is dispute over the prevalence, there is also no doubt that some therapists have helped create false memories of sexual abuse. The techniques used for memory recovery risk creating memories for events that never happened.

Many recovered memory cases are appearing in court. In such cases, although there is no substitute for external corroboration, mental health professionals can provide information to help the finder of fact sort out the truth and falsity of an allegation. Although each case must be evaluated on its own merits, we are skeptical of the truthfulness of allegations involving satanic ritual abuse, abuse said to be remembered from infancy, claims that repeated, traumatic abuse has been completely repressed only to be remembered years later, and abuse that is not recalled until after intrusive therapy techniques.

NOTES

1. Under the *Frye* test a scientific technique is not admissible unless the technique is "generally accepted" in the scientific community. Giannelli (1980) notes that the *Frye* rule envisions a process by which a novel technique must pass through an "experimental" stage where it is scrutinized by the scientific community. Only after

it has passed successfully through this process and has entered into the "demonstrable" stage can it be admissible. Under the *Frye* rule it is not enough that a qualified expert or experts believe the technique is valid and reliable; it must have been generally accepted by the relevant scientific community.

    2. The False Memory Syndrome Foundation, a tax-exempt research and education institute, is located at 3401 Market Street, Suite 130, Philadelphia, PA 19104.

    3. This ruling was later reconsidered and overturned by the full Eighth Circuit. Nevertheless, it remains a good example of a *Daubert* analysis.

    4. The three clinicians were Judith L. Apert, Laura S. Brown, and Christine A. Courtois. The three researchers who prepared a separate statement were Peter A. Ornstein, Stephen J. Ceci, and Elizabeth F. Loftus.

    5. In some cases, the accused may be hypnotized or helped in other ways to "remember" his abusive behaviors. Ofshe (1992) provides an account of the Paul Ingram case where such efforts resulted in Ingram falsely confessing to abusing his daughters in a satanic cult.

REFERENCES

Aldridge-Morris, R. (1989). *Multiple personality: An exercise in deception*. East Sussex, UK: Erlbaum.

Alpert, J. L. (1996). Professional practice, psychological science, and the recovered memory debate. In K. Pezdek & W. P. Banks (Eds.), *The recovered memory/false memory debate* (pp. 325–340). San Diego: Academic Press.

Alpert, J. L., Brown, L. S., Ceci, S. J., Courtois, C. A., Loftus, E. F., & Ornstein, P. A. (1996). *Working group on investigation of memories of childhood abuse: Final report*. Washington, DC: American Psychological Association.

American Psychiatric Association. (1987). *Diagnostic and statistical manual of mental disorders* (3rd ed., rev.). Washington, DC: Author.

American Psychiatric Association. (1994). *Diagnostic and statistical manual of mental disorders* (4th ed.). Washington, DC: Author.

Ballard, D. T., Blair, G. D., Devereaux, S., Valentine, L. K., Horton, A. L., & Johnson, B. L. (1990). A comparative profile of the incest perpetrator: Background characteristics, abuse history, and use of social skills. In A. L. Horton, B. L. Johnson, L. M. Roundy, & D. Williams (Eds.), *The incest perpetrator: The family member no one wants to treat* (pp. 43–64). Newbury Park, CA: Sage.

Barrett v. Hyldburg, Case No. 94-CVS-0793 (N.C. Buncombe County, Jan. 23, 1996).

Barrett v. Hyldburg, 1997 WL 434876 (N.C. App.).

Bass, E., & Davis, L. (1988). *The courage to heal*. New York: Harper & Row.

Bean v. Peterson, Peterson, Case No. 95-E-0038 (N.H. Super. Cheshire County 1995).

Beitchman, J. H., Zucker, K. J., Hood, J. E., daCosta, G. A., & Akman, D. (1991). A review of the short-term effects of child sexual abuse. *Child Abuse and Neglect, 15*, 537–556.

Beitchman, J. H., Zucker, K. J., Hood, J. E., daCosta, G. A., Akman, D., & Cassavia, E. (1992). A review of the long-term effects of child sexual abuse. *Child Abuse and Neglect, 16*, 101–118.

Bernstein, D. E. (1994). *Daubert one year later*. Unpublished manuscript.

Bernstein, E. M., & Putnam, F. W. (1986). Development, reliability, and validity of a dissociation scale. *Journal of Nervous and Mental Disease, 174,* 727–735.

Black, D., Kaplan, T., & Hendriks, J. H. (1993). Father kills mother: Effects on the children in the United Kingdom. In J. P. Wilson & B. Raphael (Ed.), *International handbook of traumatic stress syndromes* (pp. 551–559). New York: Plenum.

Blume, E. S. (1990). *Secret survivors: Uncovering incest and its aftereffects in women.* New York: Wiley.

Bottoms, B. L., Shaver, P. R., & Goodman, G. S. (1991, August). *Profile of ritualistic and religion-based allegations reported to clinical psychologists in the United States.* Paper presented at the 99th annual meeting of the American Psychological Association, San Francisco.

Borawick v. Shay, 1995, LEXIS 29707 (2nd Cir. Oct. 17, 1995).

Briere, J. (1996). *Therapy for adults molested as children: Beyond survival* (rev. & expanded ed.). New York: Springer.

Briere, J., & Conte, J. (1989, August). *Amnesia in adults molested as children: Testing theories of repression.* Paper presented at the 97th annual convention of the American Psychological Association, New Orleans.

Briere, J., & Conte, J. (1993). Self-reported amnesia for abuse in adults molested as children. *Journal of Traumatic Stress, 6*(1), 21–31.

Bulkley, J. A., & Horwitz, M. J. (1994). Adults sexually abused as children: Legal actions and issues. Behavioral Sciences and the Law, *12,* 65–87.

Ceci, S. J., & Bruck, M. (1995). *Jeopardy in the courtroom: A scientific analysis of children's testimony.* Washington, DC: American Psychological Association.

Christiansen, J. R., & Blake, R. H. (1990). The grooming process in father–daughter incest. In A. L. Horton, B. L. Johnson, L. M. Roundy, & D. Williams (Eds.), *The incest perpetrator: The family member no one wants to treat* (pp. 88–98). Newbury Park, CA: Sage.

Clute, S. (1993). Adult survivor litigation as an integral part of the therapeutic process. *Journal of Child Sexual Abuse, 2*(1), 121–127.

Colaneri, J. K., & Johnson, D. R. (1992, March). Coverage for parents' sexual abuse. *For the Defense,* pp. 2–5.

Cole, P. M., & Putnam, F. W. (1992). Effect of incest on self and social functioning: A developmental psychopathology perspective. *Journal of Consulting and Clinical Psychology, 61,* 174–184.

Committee on Professional Standards. (1981). Specialty guidelines for the delivery of services by clinical psychologists. *American Psychologist, 36*(6), 640–651.

Courtois, C. A. (1992). The memory retrieval process in incest survivor therapy. *Journal of Child Sexual Abuse, 1*(1), 15–31.

Courtois, C. A. (1996). Informed clinical practice and the delayed memory controversy. In K. Pezdek & W. P. Banks (Eds.), *The recovered memory/false memory debate* (pp. 355–370). San Diego: Academic Press.

Crnich, J. E., & Crnich, K. A. (1992). *Shifting the burden of truth. Suing child sexual abusers: A legal guide for survivors and their supporters.* Lake Oswego, OR: Recollex.

Daly, L. W., & Pacifico, J. F. (1991, December). Opening the doors to the past: Decade delayed disclosure of memories of years gone by. *The Champion,* pp. 42–47.

Daubert v. Merrell Dow Pharmaceuticals, 113 S. Ct. 2786 (1993).

Dawes, R. M. (1988). *Rational choice in an uncertain world.* San Diego, CA: Harcourt Brace Jovanovich.

Dawes, R. M. (1992). Why believe that for which there is no good evidence? *Issues in Child Abuse Accusations, 4,* 214–218.

Dawes, R. M. (1995, January). Review of "Return of the furies: An investigation into recovered memory therapy" by Hollida Wakefield and Ralph Underwager. *FMS Foundation Newsletter,* pp. 11–13.

Demause, L. (1991). The universality of incest. *Journal of Psychohistory, 19*(2), 123–164.

Dershowitz, A. M. (1982). *The best defense.* New York: Random House.

Dietz, P. E., Hazelwood, R. R., & Warren, J. (1990). The sexually sadistic criminal and his offenses. *Bulletin of the American Psychiatry and the Law, 18,* 163–178.

Doe v. Maskell, 1996 Md. LEXIS 68.

Dolan, Y. M. (1991). *Resolving sexual abuse.* New York: Norton.

Downing v. McDonough, *FMSF Newsletter,* Sept. 1997, *6*(8).

Dunn, G. E. (1992). Multiple personality disorder: A new challenge for psychology. *Professional Psychology: Research and Practice, 23,* 18–23.

Engstrom v. Engstrom, B098146 (Cal. App. 2nd Dist. Div. 2 June 18, 1997).

Erickson, W. D., Luxenberg, M. G., Walbek, N. H. & Seely, R. K. (1987). Frequency of MMPI two-point code types among sex offenders. *Journal of Consulting and Clinical Psychology, 55,* 566–570.

Erickson, W. D., Walbek, N. H., & Seely, R. K. (1988). Behavior patterns of child molesters. *Archives of Sexual Behavior, 17*(1), 77–86.

Eth, S., & Pynoos, R. S. (Eds.). (1985). *Post-traumatic stress disorder in children.* Washington, DC: American Psychiatric Press.

Everstine, D. S., & Everstine, L. (1989). The problem of molestation. In *Sexual trauma in children and adolescents: Dynamics and treatment* (pp. 1–11). New York: Brunner/Mazel.

Ewing, C. P. (1992). Suing your perpetrator: Response to a survivor's story. *Journal of Child Sexual Abuse, 1*(2), 129–132.

Ewing, C. P. (1994, July). Plaintiff awarded $500,000 in landmark "recovered memories" lawsuit. *APA Monitor,* p. 22.

Fahy, T. A. (1988). The diagnosis of multiple personality disorder: A critical review. *British Journal of Psychiatry, 153,* 597–606.

Feldman-Summers, S., & Pope, K. S. (1994). The experience of forgetting childhood abuse: A national survey of psychologists. *American Psychologist, 38,* 636–639.

Finkelhor, D. (1990). Early and long-term effects of child sexual abuse: An update. *Professional Psychology: Research and Practice, 21,* 325–330.

Finkelhor, D., Williams, L. M., & Burns, N. (1988). *Nursery crimes.* Newbury Park, CA: Sage.

Finkelhor, D., Williams, L. M., Burns, N, & Kalinowski, M. (1988, March). *Sexual abuse in day care: A national study.* Family Research Laboratory, Durham, NH: University of New Hampshire.

Fisher, C. B., & Whiting, K. A. (1996). The [mis]use of posttraumatic stress disorder to validate child sexual abuse. *Register Report, 22*(1), 8–10.

Frankel, F. H. (1993). Adult reconstruction of childhood events in the multiple personality literature. *American Journal of Psychiatry, 150,* 954–958.

Fredrickson, R. (1992). *Repressed memories: A journal to recovery from sexual abuse.* New York: Simon & Schuster.

Freyd, J. J. (1993, August 7). *Theoretical and personal perspectives on the delayed memory debate.* Center for Mental Health at Foote Hospital's conference on controversies around recovered memories of incest and ritualistic abuse, Ann Arbor, MI.

Freyd, P. (1994, July 6). Editor's column. *FMS Foundation Newsletter*.

Freyd, P., Roth, Z., Wakefield, H., & Underwager, R. (1993, April 16–18). Results of the FMSF family survey. Paper presented at the conference on "Memory and Reality," False Memory Syndrome Foundation, Valley Forge, PA.

Frye v. United States, 293 F. 1013, 1014 (D.C. Cir. 1923).

Gardner, R. A. (1992a). Belated realization of child sex abuse by an adult. *Issues in Child Abuse Accusations, 4*, 177–195.

Gardner, R. A. (1992b). *True and false accusations of child sex abuse*. Cresskill, NJ: Creative Therapeutics.

Gavigan, M. (1992). False memories of child sexual abuse: A personal account. *Issues in Child Abuse Accusations, 4*(4), 246–247.

Gebhard, P. H., Gagnon, J. H., Pomeroy, W. B., Christenson, C. V. (1965). *Sex offenders*. New York: Harper & Row.

Giannelli, P. C. (1980). The admissibility of novel scientific evidence: Frye v. United States, a half-century later. *Columbia Law Review, 80*, 1197–1250.

Gilbert, N. (1991). The phantom epidemic of sexual assault. *The Public Interest, 103*, 54–65.

Gilbert, N. (1994, March/April). Miscounting social ills. *Society*, 18–26.

Gleaves, D. H. (1994). On "the reality of repressed memories. *American Psychologist, 49*(5), 440–441.

Gleaves, D. H. (1996). The sociocognitive model of dissociative identity disorder: A reexamination of the evidence. *Psychological Bulletin, 120, 42–59.*

Goldstein, E., & Farmer, K. (1993). *True stories of false memories*. Boca Raton, FL: SIRS Books.

Goodman, G. S., & Hahn, A. (1987). Evaluating eyewitness testimony. In I. B. Weiner & A. K. Hess (Eds.), *Handbook of forensic psychology* (pp. 258–292). New York: Wiley.

Gondolf, L. P. (1992). Traumatic therapy. *Issues in Child Abuse Accusations, 4*, 239–245.

Gordon, R., & Wraith, R. (1993). Responses of children and adolescents to disaster. In J. P. Wilson, J. P., & B. Raphael (Eds.), *International handbook of traumatic stress syndromes* (pp. 561–575). New York: Plenum.

Grand, S., Alpert, J. L., Safer, J. M., & Milden, R. (1991, August 17). *Incest and amnesia:How do we know what really happened?* Symposium presented at the 99th annual convention of the American Psychological Association, San Francisco.

Gravitz, M. A. (1994). Are the right people being trained to use hypnosis? *American Journal of Clinical Hypnosis, 36*, 179–182.

Gross, J. (1994, April 8). Suit asks, does "memory therapy" heal or harm? *New York Times*, pp. A1, B9.

Gustafson, P. (1994, March 18). Psychiatrist sues after order to have exams. *Star Tribune* (Minneapolis), pp. 1B, 4B.

Halleck, S. L., Hoge, S. K., Miller, R. D., Sadoff, R. L., & Halleck, N. H. (1992). The use of psychiatric diagnoses in the legal process: Task force report of the American Psychiatric Association. *Bulletin of the American Academy of Psychiatry and Law, 20*(4), 481–499.

Harvey, M. (1993, June). *Traumatic memory: Research and practice*. Paper presented at the "Memories of Abuse" conference, Minneapolis, MN.

Harvey, M. R., & Herman, J. L. (1996). Amnesia, partial amnesia, and delayed recall among adult survivors of childhood trauma. In K. Pezdek, & W. P. Banks (Eds.), *The recovered memory/false memory debate* (pp. 29–40). San Diego, CA: Academic Press.

Hedges, L. E. (1994). Taking recovered memories seriously. *Issues in Child Abuse Accusations, 6*, 1–32.

Herman, J. L. (1992). *Trauma and recovery.* New York: HarperCollins.

Herman, J. L., & Schatzow, E. (1987). Recovery and verification of memories of childhood sexual trauma. *Psychoanalytic Psychology, 4*(1), 1–14.

Hicks, R. D. (1991). *In pursuit of Satan.* Buffalo, NY: Prometheus Books.

Hoch, E. L. (1982). Perspective on experimental contributions to clinical research. In P. C. Kendall & J. N. Butcher (Eds.), *Handbook of research methods in clinical psychology* (pp. 13–57). New York: Wiley.

Holmes, D. S. (1974). Investigations of repression: Differential recall of material experimentally or naturally associated with ego threat. *Psychological Bulletin, 81*, 632–53.

Holmes, D. S. (1990). The evidence for repression: An examination of sixty Years of research. In J. L. Singer (Ed.), *Repression and dissociation* (pp. 85–102). Chicago: University of Chicago Press.

Holmes, D. S. (1994). Is there evidence for repression? Doubtful. *Harvard Mental Health Newsletter, 10*(3), 4–6.

Hornstein, G. A. (1992). The return of the repressed: Psychology's problematic relations with psychoanalysis, 1909–1960. *American Psychologist, 47*, 254–263.

Huff, C. R., Rattner, A., & Sagarin, E. (1996). *Convicted but innocent: Wrongful conviction and public policy.* Thousand Oaks, CA: Sage.

Hunter v. Brown, 1996 Tenn. App. LEXIS 95.

Hyman, I. E., Husband, T. H., & Billings, F. J. (1995). False memories of childhood experiences. *Applied Cognitive Psychology, 9*(3), 181–197.

Imwinkelried, E. J. (1993). The *Daubert* decision. *Trial, 29*(9), 60–65.

Imwinkelried, E. J. (1996, July). Evidence law: Uncertainty of scientific enterprise. *The Champion*, pp. 12–15.

John BBB v. Archdiocese of Milwaukee, 365 N.W.2d 94 (Wis. June 27, 1997).

Kalichman, S. C., Shealy, L., & Craig, M. E. (1990). The use of the MMPI in predicting treatment participation among incarcerated adult rapists. *Journal of Psychology and Human Sexuality, 3*(2), 105–119.

Kelly v. Marcanonio, 678 A.2d 873 (R.I. 1996).

Kendall-Tackett, K. A., & Simon, A. F. (1987). Perpetrators and their acts: Data from 365 adults molested as children. *Child Abuse and Neglect, 11*, 237–245.

Kendall-Tackett, K. A., & Simon, A. F. (1992). A comparison of the abuse experiences of male and female adults molested as children. *Journal of Family Violence, 7*, 57–62.

Kihlstrom, J. F. (1996). The trauma–memory argument and recovered memory therapy. In K. Pezdek & W. P. Banks (Eds.), *The recovered memory/false memory debate* (pp. 297–311). San Diego, CA: Academic Press.

Kinsey, A. C., Pomeroy, W. B., Martin, C. E., & Gebhard, P. H. (1953). *Sexual behavior in the human female.* Philadelphia: Saunders.

Kluft, R. P. (1987). The parental fitness of mothers with multiple personality disorder: A preliminary study. *Child Abuse and Neglect, 11*, 273–280.

Kluft, R. P. (1991). Multiple personality disorder. In A. Tasman & S. M. Goldfinger (Ed.), *Review of psychiatry* (pp. 161–188). Washington, DC: American Psychiatric Press.

Lahey, B. B., & Kazdin, A. E. (Eds.). (1988). *Advances in clinical child psychology* (Vol. 11). New York: Plenum.

Lahey, B. B., & Kazdin, A. E. (Eds.). (1989). *Advances in clinical child psychology* (Vol. 12). New York: Plenum.

Lahey, B. B., & Kazdin, A. E. (Eds.). (1990). *Advances in clinical child psychology* (Vol. 13). New York: Plenum.

Lamm, J. B. (1991). Easing access to the courts for incest victims: Toward an equitable application of the delayed discovery rule. *Yale Law Journal, 100*, 2189–2208.

Lang, R. A., & Langevin, R. (1991). Parent–child relations in offenders who commit violent sexual crimes against children. *Behavioral Sciences and the Law, 9*, 61–71.

Langevin, R. (1983). *Sexual strands: Understanding and treating sexual anomalies in men.* Hillsdale, NJ: Erlbaum.

Lanning, K. V. (1992). *Investigator's guide to allegations of "ritual" child abuse.* Quantico, VA: National Center for the Analysis of Violent Crime.

Lemmerman v. Fealk, 534 N.W.2d 695 (Mich. 1995).

Lindsay, D. S., & Read, J. D. (1994). Psychotherapy and memories of childhood sexual abuse: A cognitive perspective. *Applied Cognitive Psychology, 8*, 281–338.

Loewenstein, R. J. (1991). Psychogenic amnesia and psychogenic fugue: A comprehensive review. In A. Tasman & S. M. Goldfinger (Ed.), *Review of psychiatry* (pp. 189–221). Washington, DC: American Psychiatric Press.

Loftus, E. F. (1993). The reality of repressed memories. *American Psychologist, 48*, 518–535.

Loftus, E. F., Garry, M., Brown, S. W., & Rader, M. (1994). Near-natal memories, past-life memories, and other memory myths. *American Journal of Clinical Hypnosis, 36*, 176–179.

Loftus, E. F., & Ketcham, K. (1991). *Witness for the defense.* New York: St. Martin's Press.

Loftus, E., & Ketcham, K. (1994). *The myth of repressed memory: False memories and allegations of sexual abuse.* New York: St. Martin's Press.

Loftus, E. F., Korf, N. L., & Schooler, J. W. (1989). Misguided memories: Sincere distortions of reality. In J. C. Yuille (Ed.), *Credibility assessment* (pp. 155–174). Dordrecht, The Netherlands: Kluwer Academic.

Loftus, E. F., Polonsky, S. & Fullilove, M. T. (1994). Memories of childhood sexual abuse: Remembering and repressing. *Psychology of Women Quarterly, 18*, 67–84.

Loftus, E. F., & Rosenwald, L. A. (1993, November). Buried memories shattered lives. *ABA Journal*, pp. 70–73.

Lundberg-Love, P. (1989, August). *Research and treatment issues concerning adult incest survivors.* Paper presented as part of a symposium titled "Treating Incest Victims and Offenders: Applying Recent Research" at the 97th annual meeting of the American Psychological Association, New Orleans.

Lundberg-Love, P. J. (n.d.). *Treatment of adult survivors of incest.* Unpublished manuscript, University of Texas, Tyler, TX.

M.E.H. v. L.H., 1996 WL 49272 (Ill. App. 2nd Dist.).

Macksoud, M. S., Dyregrov, A., & Raundalen, M. (1993). Traumatic war experiences and their effects on children. In J. P. Wilson, & B. Raphael (Eds.), *International handbook of traumatic stress syndromes* (pp. 625–633). New York: Plenum.

Mackinnon, D. W., & Dukes, W. F. (1963). Repression. In L. Postman (Ed.), *Psychology in the making: Histories of selected research problems* (pp. 662–744). New York: Knopf.

Mallia, M. (1993). Adult survivor litigation as an integral part of the therapeutic process: A reply. *Journal of Child Sexual Abuse, 2*(1), 129–130.

Malmquist, C. P. (1986). Children who witness parental murder: Posttraumatic aspects. *Journal of the American Academy of Child Psychiatry, 25*, 320–325.

Maltz, W. (1990, December). Adults survivors of incest: How to help them overcome the trauma. *Medical Aspects of Human Sexuality*, pp. 42–47.

Marshall v. First Baptist Church of Houston, 1997, WL 398859 (Tex. App. Hous. 14th Dist.).

McHugh, P. (1995). Resolved: Multiple personality disorder is an individually and socially created artifact. *Journal of American Child and Adolescent Psychiatry, 34*, 957–959.

Meehl, P. E. (1967). Theory-testing in psychology and physics: A methodological paradox. *Philosophy of Science, 34*, 103–115.

Merskey, H. (1992). The manufacture of personalities: The production of multiple personality disorder. *British Journal of Psychiatry, 160*, 327–340.

Merskey, H. (1995). Multiple personality disorder and false memory syndrome. *British Journal of Psychiatry, 166*, 281–283.

Miller, R. S., Johnson, J. A., & Johnson, J. K. (1991). Assessing the prevalence of unwanted childhood sexual experiences. *Journal of Psychology and Human Sexuality, 4*(3), 43–54.

Molien v. Kaiser Foundation, 27 Cal. 3d 916, 616 P.2d 813, 167 Cal. Rptr. 831 (1980).

Myers, J. (1992). *Evidence in child abuse and neglect cases* (2nd ed., Vol. 1). New York: Wiley.

Nagayama Hall, G. .C, & Crowther, J. H. (1991). Psychologists' involvement in cases of child maltreatment: Additional limits of assessment methods. *American Psychologist, 46*, 79–80.

Nash, M. R. (1992, August). *Retrieval of childhood memories in psychotherapy: Clinical utility and historical veridicality are not the same thing*. Paper presented at the centennial meeting of the American Psychological Association, Washington, DC.

Nathan, D. (1992, October). Cry incest. *Playboy*, pp. 84–86, 162, 164.

Nelson, E. L., & Simpson, P. (1994). First glimpse: An initial examination of subjects who have rejected their recovered visualizations as false memories. *Issues in Child Abuse Accusations, 6*(3), 123–133.

New Hampshire v. Hungerford, 1995 WL 37571.

New Hampshire v. Hungerford/Morahan, 1997 WL 358620 (N.H. July 1, 1997)

New Hampshire v. Walters, 1997 WL 9370224 (N.H. Aug. 6, 1997).

Nohlgren, S. (1991, April 28). Making a case to punish incest. *St. Petersburg Times*, pp. 1B, 5B.

North, C. S., Ryall, J. M., Ricci, D. A., & Wetzel, R. D. (1993). *Multiple personalities, multiple disorders: Psychiatric classification and media influence*. New York: Oxford University Press.

Ofshe, R. J. (1992). Inadvertent hypnosis during interrogation: False confession due to dissociative state: Mis-identified multiple personality and the satanic cult hypothesis. *The International Journal of Clinical and Experimental Hypnosis, 40*(3), 125–156.

Ofshe, R., & Watters, E. (1993, March/April). Making monsters—Psychotherapy's new error: Repressed memory, multiple personality and satanic abuse. *Society, 30*(3), 4–16.

Okami, P. (1990). Sociopolitical biases in the contemporary scientific literature on adult human sexual behavior with children and adolescents. In J. Feierman (Ed.), *Pedophilia: Biosocial dimensions* (pp. 91–121). New York: Springer-Verlag.

Olio, K. A. (1994). Truth in memory. *American Psychologist, 49*(5), 442–443.

Overholser, J. C. & Beck, S. (1986). Multimethod assessment of rapists, child molesters, and three control groups on behavioral and psychological measures. *Journal of Consulting and Clinical Psychology, 54*, 682–687.

Pennsylvania v. Crawford, 1996 Pa. Super. LEXIS 2507.

Peterson, J. A. (1994). When the therapists who have sat with shattered souls are themselves shattered. *Treating Abuse Today, 4*(2), 26–27.

Pezdek, K., & Banks, W. P. (Eds.). (1996). *The recovered memory/false memory debate*. San Diego, CA: Academic Press.

Poole, D. A., Lindsay, D. S., Memon, A., & Bull, R. (1995). Psychotherapy and the recovery of memories of childhood sexual abuse: U.S. and British practitioners' opinions, practices, and experiences. *Journal of Consulting and Clinical Psychology, 63*(3), 426–437.

Pope, H. G., & Hudson, J. I. (1992). Is childhood sexual abuse a risk factor for bulimia nervosa? *American Journal of Psychiatry, 149*, 45–463.

Pope, H. G., & Hudson, J. I. (1995). Can individuals "repress" memories of childhood sexual abuse? An examination of the evidence. *Psychiatric Annals, 25*, 426–437.

Pritzlaff v. Archdiocese of Milwaukee, 533 N.W.2d 780 (Wis. 1996).

Putnam, F. W. (1991a). Dissociative phenomena. In A. Tasman & S. M. Goldfinger (Eds.), *Review of psychiatry* (pp. 145–160). Washington, DC: American Psychiatric Press.

Putnam, F. W. (1991b). The satanic ritual abuse controversy. *Child Abuse and Neglect, 15*, 175–179.

Putnam, F. W., Guroff, J. J., Silberman, E. K., Barban, L., & Post, R. M. (1986). The clinical phenomenology of multiple personality disorder: Review of 100 recent cases. *Journal of Clinical Psychiatry, 47*(6), 285–293.

Putnam, F. W., & Trickett, P. K. (1993). Child sexual abuse: A model of chronic trauma. *Psychiatry, 56*, 82–95.

Pynoos, R. S., & Eth, S. (1985). Children traumatized by witnessing acts of personal violence: Homicide, rape, or suicide behavior. In S. Eth & R. S. Pynoos (Eds.), *Post-traumatic stress disorder in children* (pp. 17–43). Washington, DC: American Psychiatric Press.

Ramona v. Isabella, Case No. 61898 (Cal. Super. 1994).

Raphael, K. G., Cloitre, M., & Dohrenwend, B. P. (1991). Problems of recall and misclassification with checklist methods of measuring stressful life events. *Health Psychology, 10*, 62–74.

Rettig, S. (1993). Can relating the past disclose the future. *Journal of Mind and Behavior, 14*(2), 133–144.

Richardson, J. T., Best, J., & Bromley, D. G. (Eds.). (1991). *The satanism scare*. New York: Aldine de Gruyter.

Rogers, M. L. (1992). Evaluating adult litigants who allege injuries from child sexual abuse: Clinical assessment methods for traumatic memories. *Issues in Child Abuse Accusations, 4*, 221–238.

Rogers, M. L. (1994). Factors to consider in assessing adult litigants' complaints of childhood sexual abuse. *Behavioral Sciences and the Law, 12*, 279–298.

Ross, C. A., Miller, S. D., Reagor, P., Bjornson, L., Fraser, G. A., & Anderson, G. (1990).

Structured interview data on 102 cases of multiple personality disorder from four centers. *American Journal of Psychiatry, 147,* 596–601.

Russell, D. (1983). The incidence and prevalence of intrafamilial and extrafamilial sexual abuse of female children. *Child Abuse and Neglect, 7,* 133–146.

S.V. v. R.V., 39 Tex. Sup. J. 386 (Tex. 1996).

Salter, A. C. (1992). Epidemiology of child sexual abuse. In W. O'Donohue, & J. H. Geer (Eds.), *The sexual abuse of children: Theory and research* (Vol. 1, pp. 108–138). Hillsdale, NJ: Erlbaum.

Sargeant, G. (1994, May). Victims, courts, academics debate truth of recovered memories in abuse cases. *Trial,* pp. 12–14, 91.

Schacter, D. L. (1996). *Searching for memory.* New York: Basic Books.

Simons, J. (1994, June). Analysis of the Ramona decision. *FMS Foundation Newsletter,* pp. 10–12.

Singer, J. L., & Sincoff, J. B. (1990). Summary chapter: Beyond repression and the defenses. In J. L. Singer (Ed.), *Repression and dissociation: Implications for personality theory, psychopathology and health* (pp. 471–496). Chicago: University of Chicago Press.

Slovenko, R. (1993, Spring). The "revival of memory" of childhood sexual abuse: Is the tolling of the statute of limitations justified? *Journal of Psychiatry and Law,* 7–34.

Smith, S. E. (1993). Body memories: And other pseudo-scientific notions of "survivor psychology." *Issues in Child Abuse Accusations, 5,* 220–234.

Spanos, N. P. (1994). Multiple identity enactments and multiple personality disorder: A sociocognitive perspective. *Psychological Bulletin, 116,* 143–165.

Spanos, N. P. (1996). *Multiple identities and false memories: A sociocognitive perspective.* Washington, DC: American Psychological Association.

Spanos, N. P., Cross, P. A., Dickson, K., & DuBreuil, S. C. (1993). Close encounters: An examination of UFO experiences. *Journal of Abnormal Psychology, 102,* 624–632.

Spence, D. P. (1993, August). *Narrative truth and putative child abuse.* Address given at the 101st annual convention of the American Psychological Association, Toronto, Ontario, Canada.

Spiegel, D. (1991). Dissociation and trauma (1991). In A. Tasman & S. M. Goldfinger (Ed.), *Review of psychiatry* (pp. 261–275). Washington, DC: American Psychiatric Press.

Spiegel, D., & Cardeña, E. (1991). Disintegrated experience: The dissociative disorders revisited. *Journal of Abnormal Psychology, 100,* 366–378.

Spiegel, D., & Scheflin, A. W. (1994). Dissociated or fabricated? Psychiatric aspects of repressed memory in criminal and civil cases. *International Journal of Clinical Hypnosis, 42*(4), 411–432.

Summit, R. (1990, October 29–November 1). *Reaching the unreachable.* Presentation at the Midwest conference on child abuse and neglect, Madison, WI.

Terr, L. C. (1985). Children traumatized in small groups. In S. Eth & R. S. Pynoos (Eds.), *Post-traumatic stress disorder in children* (pp. 45–70). Washington, DC: American Psychiatric Press.

Terr, L. C. (1988). What happens to early memories of trauma? A study of twenty children under age five at the time of documented traumatic events. *Journal of the American Academy of Child and Adolescent Psychiatry, 27*(1), 96–104.

Terr, L. C. (1990). *Too scared to cry.* New York: Harper & Row.

Terr, L. C. (1991). Childhood traumas: An outline and overview. *American Journal of Psychiatry, 148*, 10–20.

Terr, L. C. (1994). *Unchained memories: True stories of traumatic memories, lost and found.* New York: HarperCollins.

Terr, L. C. (1996). True memories of childhood trauma: Flaws, absences, and returns. In K. Pezdek & W. P. Banks (Eds.), *The recovered memory/false memory debate* (pp. 69–80). San Deigo, CA: Academic Press.

Thomas, J. (1994). Supreme court rejects "anything goes" approach to expert scientific testimony. *Skeptical Inquirer, 18*(2), 118–120.

Thompson, J. E. (1993). Healing is an unenforceable order. *Journal of Child Sexual Abuse, 2*(1), 131–133.

Tillman, J. G., Nash, M. R., & Lerner, P. M. (1994). Does trauma cause dissociative pathology? In S. J. Lynn & J. W. Rhue (Eds.), *Dissociation: Clinical and theoretical perspectives* (pp. 395–414). New York: Guilford Press.

Tollison, C. D., & Adams, H. E. (1979). *Sexual disorders: Treatment, theory, and research.* New York: Gardner.

Travis v. Ziter, 1996 WL 390629, 1996 Ala. LEXIS 180.

Tyson v. Tyson, 107 Wash. 2d 72, 727 P.2d 226 (1986).

Underwager, R., & Wakefield, H. (1993). A paradigm shift for expert witnesses. *Issues in Child Abuse Accusations, 5*, 156–167.

Underwager, R., & Wakefield, H. (1996). Therapeutic influuence in DID and recovered memories of sexual abuse. *Issues in Child Abuse Accusations, 8*(3/4), 160–169.

United States v. Rouse et al., No. 95–1554 (8th Cir. Nov. 12, 1996).

van der Kolk, B. A. (1988a). The biological response to psychic trauma. In F. M. Ochberg (Ed.), *Post-traumatic therapy and victims of violence* (pp. 25–38). New York: Brunner/Mazel.

van der Kolk, B. A. (1988b). The trauma spectrum: The interaction of biological and social events in the genesis of the trauma response. *Journal of Traumatic Stress, 1*, 273–289.

van der Kolk, B. A., & van der Hart, O. (1989). Pierre Janet and the breakdown of adaptation in psychological trauma. *American Journal of Psychiatry, 146*, 1530–1540.

Victor, J. S. (1993). *Satanic panic: The creation of a contemporary legend.* Chicago: Open Court.

Wakefield, H., & Underwager, R. (1988). *Accusations of child sexual abuse.* Springfield, IL: C. C. Thomas.

Wakefield, H., & Underwager, R. (1991). Female child sexual abusers: A critical review of the literature. *American Journal of Forensic Psychology, 9*(4), 43–69.

Wakefield, H., & Underwager, R. (1992). Recovered memories of alleged sexual abuse: Lawsuits against parents. *Behavioral Sciences and the Law, 10*, 483–507.

Wakefield, H., & Underwager, R. (1994a). Abusive behaviors alleged in two samples of likely false allegations. *Issues in Child Abuse Accusations, 6*, 72–86.

Wakefield, H., & Underwager, R. (1994b). *Return of the furies: An investigation in recovered memory therapy.* Peru, IL: Open Court Press.

Wakefield, J. (1992, June 20). Recovered memories of alleged sexual abuse: Memory as production and as reproduction. *Issues in Child Abuse Accusations, 4*, 219–220.

Walker, L. E. (1992). When an incest survivor sues her father: A commentary. *Journal of Child Sexual Abuse, 1*(2), 125–127.

Waterman, J., Kelly, R. J., Oliveri, K., & McCord, J. (1993). *Behind the playground walls*. New York: Guilford Press.

Weinrott, M. R., & Saylor, M. (1991). Self-report of crimes committed by sex offenders. *Journal of Interpersonal Violence, 6*, 286–300.

Weissberg, M. (1993). Multiple personality disorder and iatrogenesis: The cautionary tale of Anna O. The *International Journal of Clinical and Experimental Hypnosis, 41*(1), 15–32.

Williams, L. M. (1992, Summer). Adult memories of childhood abuse: Preliminary findings from a longitudinal study. *APCAC Advisor*, pp. 19–21.

Williams, L. M. (1994). Recall of childhood trauma: A prospective study of women's memories of child sexual abuse. *Journal of Consulting and Clinical Psychology, 62*, 1167–1176.

Wilson, J. P., & Raphael, B. (1993). *International handbook of traumatic stress syndromes*. New York: Plenum.

Wright, L. (1993, May 17 & 24). Remembering Satan: Part I, & Part II. *New Yorker*, pp. 60–83, & pp. 54–76.

Wyatt, G. E. (1985). The sexual abuse of Afro-American and White-American Women in childhood. *Child Abuse and Neglect, 9*, 507–519.

Yapko, M. D. (1994a). Suggestibility and repressed memories of abuse: A survey of psychotherapists' beliefs. *American Journal of Clinical Hypnosis, 36*, 163–171.

Yapko, M. D. (1994b). Response to comments. *American Journal of Clinical Hypnosis, 36*, 185–187.

A WAY FORWARD

CHAPTER 17

PSYCHOTHERAPY WITHOUT REPRESSED MEMORY

A Parsimonious Alternative Based
on Contemporary Memory Research

George A. Bonanno
David J. Keuler

The dominant psychotherapeutic model of memory functioning has histori-cally included and in many cases centered on the concept of repressed memory. Although repression serves as a convenient explanation for the way memories appear to emerge during psychotherapy, it has become increasingly clear that it is no longer tenable as a scientific construct. The construct of repressed memory evidences a number of conceptual weaknesses, does not appear to be verifiable empirically, and produces a decidedly unparsimonious contrast with the general findings to emerge over the past several decades in experimental cognitive psychology. Moreover, the continued espousal of the construct by psychotherapists has resulted in myriad intractable professional and ethical dilemmas. In its stead, we propose an alternative model of memory and psychotherapy based on contemporary concepts derived from experimental cognitive psychology. It is important to note that we do not propose this model in answer to or as an explanation of public claims of repressed memories. Rather, we advance these ideas as part of a broader effort (Bonanno, 1990a, 1990b, 1995) to integrate the literatures of experimental and clinical psychology and to advance clinical theory toward more parsimo-nious models for practical application in the psychotherapeutic treatment of emotional and behavioral problems.

THE PROBLEM WITH REPRESSED MEMORIES

The fundamental assumption inherent in the construct of repressed memory is that distressing or traumatic experiences are stored fully intact in memory but, because of the intolerable emotion with which they are associated, are prohibited from reentering conscious awareness (Freud, 1915/1957, 1917/1966). The mechanism of repression is assumed to block what are otherwise normal retrieval processes and to produce an amnestic inability to recall the details and, in extreme cases, even the occurrence of the events (Kaszniak, Nussbaum, Berren, & Santiago, 1988). Repressed memories find their expression, instead, in the form of conversion disorders and somatic symptoms (Freud, 1894/1924, 1926/1966).

Psychotherapy, in the context of the repression model, dictates that patients find their way back to the hidden memories of the antecedent traumatic event and that they reexperience these memories fully in consciousness. This procedure was originally enacted in psychotherapy through hypnotic induction (Breuer & Freud, 1895/1955), free association, transference interpretation, and other techniques of the classic psychoanalytic approach (Freud, 1917/1966). Once the repressed memories are made conscious, their unconscious force is expected to diminish and the patient's symptoms are presumed to abate.

The repression model is alive and well in the contemporary psychoanalytic literature (cf. Lindy, 1986; van der Kolk & Kadish, 1987). Importantly, current treatment approaches that are *not* explicitly aligned with the psychoanalytic school also appear to utilize techniques based on the repression model. For example, the literature on traumatic experience continues to espouse the importance of reexperiencing the traumatic past (Peterson, Prout, & Schwarz, 1991; T. Williams, 1988). Yet, although it may be effective in many instances to have patients attempt to remember antecedent events as fully as possible, such a practice often proves unnecessary (Bonanno, 1995) and, in many cases, even inadvisable (Ehrlich, 1988; Kinzie, 1988).

One of the more likely explanations for the endurance of the construct of repressed memories is its phenomenologic appeal—even cursory introspection suggests that we can manage to block from awareness ideas and images that we experience as unpleasant. Certainly, the phenomenologic appeal of the construct was crucial to the inductive observations of Breuer, Freud, and others who followed them in attempting to explain the surprising effectiveness of the "talking cure." Unfortunately, introspection alone is clearly not a sufficient evidentiary basis to sustain a psychological construct. It is equally likely that when we are considering something as subtle as repression, or for that matter any mechanism that might have to do with regulating conscious awareness, our capacity to introspect is seriously limited (Schneider, 1993). Further, individuals vary in their ability to report accurately on complex emotional responses (Katkin, 1985; Keuler & Safer, 1997; Leventhal, 1991). Thus, there are probably as many, if not more, people who might claim to have never experienced repressed memory as those who would swear to its existence.

Perhaps more seriously, when we move beyond the phenomenologic to a consideration of underlying theoretical assumptions, the construct of repressed memory appears conceptually indigent. One of the primary difficulties with the repression model is that it hinges on the troublesome concept of an unconscious and autonomous regulator or "censor"—the gatekeeper of the boundary to conscious awareness. Consider this passage:

> The crudest idea of these systems is the most convenient for us—a spatial one. Let us therefore compare the system of the unconscious to a large entrance hall, in which the mental impulses jostle one another like separate individuals. Adjoining this entrance hall there is a second, narrower room—a kind of drawing room—in which consciousness, too resides. But on the threshold between the two rooms a watchman performs his function: he examines the different mental impulses, acts as a censor, and will not admit them into the drawing-room if they displease him. (Freud, 1917/1966, pp. 365–366)

The spatial metaphor—the concept of a place called "the" unconscious—and its compatible assumption of a censor or gatekeeper—raises a number of intractable conceptual problems (J. M. G. Williams, Watts, MacLeod, & Matthews, 1988). If our conscious mind cannot bear to process certain memories, then the decision to keep these memories repressed elsewhere, in "the" unconscious, could only originate in the unconscious. Consequently, "the" unconscious must have an autonomous quality—an inner "homunculus" which must somehow possess the omnipotence or wisdom to "know" what is best for the conscious self. The problem is, however, that a century of research in psychology and the neurosciences has yet to reveal anything remotely similar to such a mechanism. Indeed, the now abundant contemporary research on unconscious processes suggests not a wise, autonomous system but a dramatically limited capacity for processing independent of conscious awareness (Greenwald, 1992; Greenwald, Klinger, & Liu, 1989). Thus, the ideas of a place or region of the mind called "the" unconscious which is separated from consciousness by a wise and autonomous censor are decidedly lacking in theoretical parsimony.

Given the serious nature of these limitations, why the concept continues to appear in the psychotherapeutic arena is interesting in its own right. This question becomes particularly intriguing when we consider that after years of seemingly endless controversy, there is as yet no unassailable experimental evidence for the existence of repressed memories (Holmes, 1974, 1990). In contrast, there is abundant empirical evidence on perceptual and memory processes which allows us to explain "repression-like" processes using far more flexible and parsimonious concepts (Bonanno, 1990a, 1990b, 1995). Many professionals within the psychotherapeutic community have simply been unwilling or unable to keep abreast of the developments in experimental psychology and to weigh such developments against the formidable inertia of previously accepted ideas about the workings of human memory (Bonanno, 1990a). Thus, modern-day practitioners may espouse the repression model not so much from the inspiration they may have found in the original works as from complacent loyalty to a Zeitgeist that has yet to succumb to scholarly revolution. What is more, many of the researchers and theorists in scholarly psychology who developed and propagated the ideas that might lead to alternatives to the repression construct are themselves uninterested in this application of their work. Indeed, for many in experimental psychology, repression is an old and outmoded idea unworthy of further consideration (Holmes, 1990).

THE HISTORICAL ORIGINS OF THE REPRESSION CONSTRUCT

The idea of repressed memories originated in the late 19th century, when physicians were confronted with myriad psychosomatic maladies—strange physical symptoms and unusual pains or paralyses that could not be explained by organic causes (Ellenberger, 1970). An important avenue toward understanding these seemingly intractable problems appeared in the 1880s with Charcot's startling demonstrations of hysteria-like somatic symptoms induced in healthy individuals by hypnotic suggestion (Ellenberger, 1970). Several years later, and still prior to Freud's initial psychoanalytic works, Pierre Janet (1889) published what is generally acknowledged as the first detailed evidence of the unconscious representation of traumatic experience and its symbolic manifestation as physical symptoms (Ellenberger, 1970; Veith, 1965). Janet described patients whose traumatic experiences resulted in idée fixe, or unconscious fixed ideas that were organized into automated patterns of thought, emotion, and movement associated with the patient's response to the trauma. Because Janet believed that fixed ideas existed "below consciousness," his descriptions were "undoubtedly what modern psychology has come to consider Freudian" (Veith, 1965, p. 252). However, Janet (1889, 1893/1901) never evoked repression as an explanatory mechanism. Rather, he conceived of fixed ideas as dissociated aspects of the personality that resulted from a general narrowing or "retraction of the field of consciousness" (Janet, 1907, p. 303). Further, although Janet believed that the conscious identification of unconscious or dissociated fixed ideas would promote the disappearance of symptoms, he repeatedly emphasized that this procedure alone would not be enough to cure a patient (Ellenberger, 1970).

The primary difference between Janet's nascent system and Freud's writings that were soon to follow was that Freud included the etiological significance of early sexual experience. Whereas Janet (1893/1901) felt that the problems presented by hysterical patients were not necessarily of a sexual nature, Freud (1898/1924) was soon to conclude that "factors arising in the sexual life represent the nearest and practically the most momentous causes of *every single case* of nervous illness" (p. 221, italics added). Eventually, of course, as his theory developed, Freud came to locate the origins of sexual disturbances in the earliest stages of childhood, a thesis that could not exist without the mechanism of repressed memory. Freud spent the remainder of his career elaborating on this model.

At the heart of Freud's repression construct was the censor that insured that painful unconscious contents would only appear consciously in symbolic or "disguised" form as a symptom, commonly a somatic symptom. Freud (1917/1966) felt that such manifestations contained "the sense of the symptom," their repressed unconscious meaning, and that, "as soon as the unconscious processes concerned have become conscious, the symptom must disappear" (p. 346). Thus, Freud (1917/1966) argued that such symptoms "offer the plainest indication of their being a special region of the mind, shut off from the rest . . . to a conviction of the existence of the unconscious in the mind" (p. 345).

This was the hinge on which Freud hung his therapeutic model—the recovery of antecedent repressed memories during psychotherapy. The "fact" that such memories could be produced, Freud believed, perfectly illustrated the workings of repression. Similar assumptions of "proof," of course, fuel the continued espousal of the repression model in the popular psychological literature as well as the seemingly ubiquitous legal and ethical battles that inevitably accompany many such reports. Close examination of this early case material, however, reveals that the conceptual role of repressed memory in therapeutic intervention was by no means simple and straightforward. Consider the famous case of Anna O., reported by Breuer and Freud (1895/1955). The patient was a seemingly bright young woman who developed a host of debilitating symptoms while caring for her physically ill father. She was so hydrophobic, for example, that she "found it impossible to drink" and suffered a constant "tormenting thirst" (p. 34). She also experienced unusual paralyses and numbing of her limbs, blurred vision, and hearing difficulties. Each of these symptoms appeared to be psychological in origin and were reported to have abated as the putative antecedent events were remembered, fully intact, during the therapy. Based on this unequivocal conclusion, the "therapeutic technical procedure" (p. 35) used to discover these antecedent memories would at first consideration appear to be deceptively simple. These procedures were in fact quite protracted and required considerable searching and effort on the patient's part. As Breuer and Freud (1895/1955) note:

> It turned out to be quite impracticable to shorten the work by trying to elicit in her memory straight away the first provoking cause of her symptoms. She was unable to find it, grew confused, and things proceeded even more slowly than if she was allowed quietly and steadily to follow back the thread of memories on which she had embarked. Since the latter method, clearly differentiated, that if she happened to make a mistake in their sequence she

> would be obliged to correct herself and put them in the right order; if this was
> not done her report came to a standstill. (pp. 36–37)

What remains suspect here is not the pursuit of associations, the "thread of
memories," but the insistence that a culpable, repressed memory lay couched
in the corner of the unconscious resisting discovery.

The emphasis on recovering a veridical past is particularly susceptible to
myriad problems of memory augmentation and distortion. Breuer and Freud
(1895/1955) make only brief mention of these possibilities and then dismiss
them without further ado. They note that many of the remembered "incidents" were internal experiences and could not be verified. Still other aspects
of the patient's recollections, they point out, could be verified by others in her
experience. As additional proof, they unconvincingly note that the events
described by Anna were "so lacking in interest and significance and were told
in such detail that there could be no suspicion of their having been invented"
(p. 37). In a later writing, Freud (1917/1966) appears to have anticipated that
some readers might question the legitimacy of the memories his patients
produced in therapy or in the way he used these memories to demonstrate
his views of the mind. Lest his conclusions be dismissed as "wild thoughts,"
Freud defended his approach by stating, "You must not forget, I did not make
these things but only interpreted them."

With the benefit of subsequent research in normal memory biases and
distortions, however, it seems obvious that Freud probably did do more to
mold his patient's memories than he was aware of or at least willing to
acknowledge. It is well-known, for instance, that patients in these early days
of psychoanalysis were apprised explicitly of Freud's methods and expectations and well knew that their "cure" depended on the uncovering of
antecedent memories (Freud, 1913/1963, 1913/1976b, 1914/1976c; Wolf-
Man, 1971). Indeed, Breuer and Freud (1895/1955) note that "On one
occasion our whole progress was obstructed for some time because a recollection *refused to emerge*" (p. 37, italics added).

An abundant corpus of research data are now available which demonstrate just how readily memories for specific events can be distorted or even
fabricated to fit the demands of the recall situation (Loftus, 1979; Loftus &
Banaji, 1989; Loftus & Palmer, 1974; Ross, 1989; Ross & Conway, 1986; Smith
& Ellsworth, 1987). Thus it is quite probable that patients in psychotherapy
could twist or bend even slightly whatever accessible fragments of memory
they could recollect until these fragments fit the emerging therapeutic story.
Of particular relevance to the psychotherapy process, memory distortion
during eyewitness accounts appears to occur even more readily when the
interrogator is perceived as a knowledgeable expert (Smith & Ellsworth, 1987).
Psychotherapists, of course, are usually perceived by their patients with just
such an expert status. In a similar vein, there is abundant evidence that actual
and imagined events are relatively easily confused, and that imagined events
are more readily taken for "real" memories when one's focus is on thoughts

and feelings rather than the concrete perceptual aspects of the events (Suengas & Johnson, 1988). Again, this evidence holds important implications for psychotherapy process, which focuses primarily on the emotional aspects of memory and suggests that during psychotherapy, the normal human susceptibility to confuse actual and imagined events would be even more pronounced.

It was also sometimes true, as it is today, that hypnosis was used to aid the process of remembering the past. Research demonstrates, however, that remembering under the condition of hypnosis tends to result in even greater willingness to accept misleading information and to produce even greater distortion or "pseudomemories" than does remembering in a normal or nonhypnotized state (McCann & Sheehan, 1988; Murray, Cross, & Whipple, 1992; Sheehan, Grigg, & McCann, 1984). One study, of particular relevance to the use of hypnosis in psychotherapy (Sheehan & Statham, 1989) showed that the greatest memory distortion occurred when hypnotized participants attempted "free recall," a form of recollection not dissimilar to the analytic technique of recall by "free association."

MEMORY AVAILABILITY, ACCESSIBILITY, AND RECONSTRUCTION

In the remainder of this chapter, we expand on previous attempts (Bonanno, 1990a, 1990b, 1995) to move beyond the concept of repressed memory and, in its stead, to provide a scientifically tenable, parsimonious model of memory in psychotherapy based on the integration of clinical theory with the contemporary experimental literature. To this end, In the next sections we describe experimentally derived concepts relevant to the availability and accessibility of information in memory and then consider these concepts in light the processes of dissociation and the reconstructive nature of autobiographical recollection.

Encoding, Availability, and Traumatic Experience

To begin with, it now seems clear that virtually all human perception and memory processes are selective and thus incomplete. What and how much might be perceived varies greatly across individuals and situations (Johnson & Dark, 1986). Consequently, only a portion of the possible information from any experience is encoded. In terms of subsequent retrieval, only some of the possible information from any given situation is ever *available* for remembering.

The limitations of human encoding process are particularly pronounced for traumatic memories, the very type of memories historically associated with repression. For example, T. Williams (1988) summarized his work with over 2,000 trauma victims by noting two primary types of emotional shock reactions, both of which would limit the amount of information encoded and, thus, the amount of information that might be available. One type of shock reaction, according to Williams, is characterized by confusion, disorganization, and a feeling of being frozen or immobilized so that even simple tasks became impossible. For example, during a robbery, the victims sometimes become so paralyzed by fear that they cannot even open the cash register drawer. In the second type of shock reaction, in contrast, the trauma seems surreal, as if it is occurring in slow motion or not really happening. Sometimes the opposite occurs and events are experienced as if they are speeded up or as if they occurred out of sequence (Peterson et al., 1991) or have an "out-of-body" quality (T. Williams, 1988). Most important to our concerns here, sometimes these perceptual aberrations result in a kind of tunnel vision in which selected aspects of the traumatic events are perceived in vivid, almost exaggerated detail while other crucial aspects are not encoded. This phenomenon is illustrated in the classic example of a robbery victim who becomes transfixed by the assaulter's weapon to the exclusion of other crucial details such as the assailant's face. Experimental studies of this phenomenon, knowns as "weapon focus" (cf. Kramer, Buckhout, & Eugenio, 1990), similarly demonstrate the narrowing of attention, and encoding, that can accompany traumatic events.

Accessibility and Motivated Forgetting

The extent to which the partial representation of any event is remembered later further depends on additional cognitive activity, such as the degree that the features of an event are remembered and rehearsed on subsequent occasions, associated with the same event in time, or connected with other events, ideas, and categories (Craik & Lockhart, 1972). Factors that influence the encoding and representation of an event over time also influence the degree that the details of the event are *accessible* to retrieval (Crowder, 1985). The accessibility of a memory representation, in turn, is influenced by, among other things, the compatibility of the encoding and retrieval context (Tulving & Thomson, 1973).

A useful metaphor for understanding the role of accessibility in memory is learning one's way around in an unfamiliar city in an unfamiliar country. We may know parts of the city from a previous visit. In this case, if we had an appointment somewhere in one of the familiar areas, we could probably find it with little or no problem. Thus, the familiar part of the city is relatively accessible. Now imagine that we are taken to a wonderful restaurant in another part of the city, an area with which we are completely unfamiliar. We have a great time and, because the restaurant was so wonderful, we would want to visit it again. The problem is that we are not sure we could find our way. In this case, the restaurant is like a memory that is available but relatively inaccessible. We might stumble on the restaurant accidentally—just as we might suddenly remember something we had not thought of in years—but we would accept that this was not likely to happen. Now imagine that we are taken to the restaurant for a second visit and that this time we pay attention to the route. The restaurant should become more accessible. Once we have a better idea of its location, in fact, we decide on a third occasion to attempt to find it on our own. When we do so, however, we discover that it is only one block away from a street we visited many times in the past. Suddenly, the accessibility of the restaurant is dramatically increased. Because it was such a good restaurant, we dine there every at every opportunity. Eventually it becomes almost impossible to not think of the restaurant whenever we think of the city or of the neighborhood in which the restaurant is located.

This same process can also explain how memory contents become less accessible over time. Imagine that shortly after our second visit to the restaurant, we discover a number of interesting neighborhoods, each full of wonderful places to eat. Indeed, we learn that the city provides a veritable cornucopia of fine dining. In this case, over time we would have visited so many good restaurants that our memory of the original restaurant is interfered with. In other words, it becomes less accessible. To take this a step further, memory contents may also become less accessible because we wish to avoid reexperiencing them. Imagine that our second visit to the restaurant did not go so well; in fact, it was a complete disaster. The food was terrible, the waiter surprisingly unpleasant, and our complaints to the manager casually dismissed. In this case, we probably would not return and thus we would not likely discover the close proximity of the restaurant to other more familiar parts of the city. We would probably stop thinking about the restaurant. In fact, we might find ourselves within only a few blocks of it without even knowing it. In this way, not returning to the restaurant is similar to not thinking about a particular piece of information in memory—it remains available (i.e., not repressed) but relatively unrehearsed and thus relatively inaccessible.

In much the same way, when an event is experienced as highly stressful or traumatic, undesirable thoughts and images associated with the event may remain relatively inaccessible. Note here that again there is no need to evoke the concept of repressed memory, because the memory fragments associated with the event would be fully available for retrieval. Indeed, traumatic ideation is often characterized by an intrusive "unbidden" quality (Horowitz, 1986). Even when distressing contents enter awareness, however, they can be avoided by changes in the focus of conscious attention. In this case, the fragmentary information—a fleeting image or frightening thought—would not form strong associative connections with other information in memory and would thus remain relatively inaccessible. When this is achieved, such information becomes over time less and less likely to reenter conscious awareness.

Even more important, if it were possible to fully avoid thoughts and images related to a traumatic event, such memories would not look much like the elaborate, and almost mythically complete, repressed memories typically reported in the media. As we have noted, traumatic memories tend to be fragmentary and markedly incomplete. If they are not further elaborated and rehearsed in the days or even hours subsequent to the trauma, they would likely hold little concrete information. Under such conditions, reconstructions of such events are likely to include a considerable portion of retrospective insertion and distortion. In other words, memories for disturbing events that are relatively immediately avoided would likely bear little resemblance to the original perceptual experience.

A more likely scenario is that highly emotional or traumatic events will remain active in the sufferer's consciousness for a considerable length of time, for days, weeks, even years after the event took place. The seemingly autonomous nature of most intrusive thoughts and images makes them highly disturbing and, thus, demanding of further consideration. Such continued processing would increase the accessibility of the memory so that it would not be easily kept from consciousness. More important, the processes of distortion and augmentation that characterize normal remembering would undoubtedly be at work almost immediately after a traumatic event is experienced. As this happens, the continual reconstruction and replaying of the event would result in the addition, removal, or revision of its various details and qualities. As such a process is extended over time, the original aspects of the event would likely become less crucial to the memory. Thus, even relatively accessible memories of traumatic experiences are necessarily incomplete and unreliable.

Trauma Victims, White Bears, and Repressors

One result of the attempt to "not think" about something is that this very goal may actually make us think about it even more. This seeming paradox was cleverly demonstrated in a series of experiments by Daniel Wegner and his colleagues. For example, in a now classic study, Wegner, Schneider, Carter, and White (1987) found that when participants were instructed to do all that they could to "try not to think of a white bear," this instruction actually increased the prevalence of thoughts about white bears, what Wegner et al. have labeled a "rebound" effect. They speculated that when people tried not to think of a white bear, they did so by switching their attention to other thoughts or to other features of the environment. Eventually, in such a situation, attention drifts and we remind ourselves that we had a task to accomplish, which in this case was to not think of a white bear. This realization, of course, immediately brings to mind a white bear. Further, the image of the white bear is then associated with whatever the person was thinking about as a means of distraction. Thus, trying not to think of white bears by distraction links the concept "white bear" to a range of ideas and images and makes it even more accessible in memory.

The artificial nature of the white bear experiment suggests obvious limitations. It is noteworthy, however, that the rebound effect demonstrated after attempted suppression in the laboratory is not unlike the observation of intrusive and unbidden thoughts (Horowitz, 1986) and nightmares (Wood, Bootzin, Rosenhan, Nolen-Hoeksma, & Jourdan, 1992) reported by actual trauma sufferers. The intrusive nature of traumatic memories also appears to go hand in hand with deliberate attempts at avoidance (Creamer, Burgess, & Pattison, 1990).

By the same token, some individuals do manage to successfully restrict unpleasant thoughts and emotions from consciousness awareness (Bonanno & Singer, 1993). Consider, for example, individuals who typically respond to threatening information with a "repressive" style (Weinberger, Schwartz, & Davidson, 1979)—the term comes from a propensity to use avoidant processes at the level of perception and encoding rather than from any evidence linking them to repressed memories (Bonanno & Singer, 1990; Gur & Sackeim, 1979). Repressors show a unique ability to restrict or narrow the focus of their attention (Bonanno, Davis, Singer, & Schwartz, 1991) such that they manage to experience genuinely reduced levels of subjective distress in presumably stressful situations (Newton & Contrada, 1992; Weinberger et al., 1979) and to encode only discrete aspects of emotional events (C. Hansen, Hansen, & Shantz, 1992). As a result, repressors appear to form simple (R. Hansen & Hansen, 1988) and relatively inaccessible (Davis, 1987, 1990; Davis & Schwartz, 1987) memories for emotional events.

How repressors respond to the memories of traumatic experience is not yet known. Interestingly, however, in a recent study of conjugal bereavement it was found that although all participants had increased psychological and physical symptoms soon after the loss, repressors showed the earliest reductions in grief symptoms as rated by clinical interviewers (i.e., they got over their grief more quickly) (Bonanno, Siddique, Keltner, & Horowitz, 1995). Thus, there appears to be an adaptive side to such avoidant habits.

Becoming Famous Overnight and Other Distorted Reconstructions

Given the limitations of human encoding retrieval processes reviewed thus far, we must next ask why our subjective experience of the past seems to provide us with such marked continuity, such a coherent and fluid narrative? An important and often grossly underestimated aspect of human memory is that autobiographical remembering is a reconstructive process (Barclay, 1986; Bonanno, 1990a; Erdelyi, 1990; Ross, 1989; Ross & Conway, 1986). This reconstructive illusion is nicely described by Rosenfield (1988).

> There are not specific recollections in our brains, there are only the means for reorganizing past impressions, for giving the incoherent, dreamlike world of memory a concrete reality. Memories are not fixed but are constantly evolving generalizations—recreations—of the past, which give us a sense of continuity, a sense of being, with a past, a present, and a future. They are not discrete units that are linked up over time but a dynamically evolving system. (p. 76)

The capacity limits of the human cognition (Fehling, Baars, & Fisher, 1990) necessitate that we effectively organize what we experience at each stage of information processing. When we remember something, in essence we are reconstructing an event into a narrative logic based on whatever information is available and accessible at the time.

The human propensity to reconstruct the past points up just how difficult it would be to support the veridicality of even the simplest of memories. Consider this wonderful experimental demonstration of everyday memory distortion provided by Jacoby, Kelley, Brown, and Jasechko (1989). They had participants read aloud a list of names described explicitly as people who were not well-known or famous. Some of the participants were then immediately shown a series of test names, which included the nonfamous names they had just read aloud as well as some new nonfamous names and also some names of actual moderately famous people. The task was to judge whether each name was the name of a famous person or not. As we might expect, these participants could remember with relative ease the nonfamous names they had previously read aloud and thus rarely made the mistake of categorizing these names as famous. Interestingly, however, when the remaining participants were asked to make the famous–nonfamous judgments a day later, they often mistakenly attributed fame to nonfamous names they had previously read out loud. It seems that these participants did not possess an *explicit* memory for the names they had read aloud the day before; that is, they did not remember reading these particular names but reacted to *implicit* information (i.e., the global familiarity of the name), which they then reconstructed as fame. In other words, the implicitly remembered nonfamous names became "famous overnight."

The distorting effects of memory reconstruction are even more pronounced when we consider individuals who have suffered traumatic experiences. Trauma victims are commonly subject to an imperative social pressure of describing their experience in great detail. Generally well intended, this pressure from therapists, law enforcement authorities, family, and friends creates an additional push to remember the missing details and to make sense of partial information. There is perhaps also a personal need to fill in the blanks based on the logic of the narrative. Indeed, humans are more than capable of altering memories when the situation calls for it (Johnson, 1985). Therapists working with trauma victims have also noted the tendency to distort or fill in the missing details based on stories pieced together from putative "facts" supplied by others (Silver, 1986).

DISSOCIATION AND NARRATIVE RECONSTRUCTION IN PSYCHOTHERAPY

Considering the era of its formulation, Freud's hydraulic model of repressed memory stands as scholarship of remarkably erudition; integrated inductive psychological observations, etiological theories about sexuality, and the dominant models in physics at the time, such as the first law of thermodynamics—the conservation of energy (Erdelyi, 1985). We must keep in mind that Freud's speculations about the "talking cure" were nascent. We now take the seemingly ubiquitous influence of the psychotherapist for granted, but in Freud's time there was only a small number of physicians specializing in psychological disorders. By the same token, it is of the utmost importance to move beyond Freud's charismatic but now outdated stance. Contemporary scholars writing from within the psychoanalytic tradition have attempted to honor Freud's brilliant psychological insights while simultaneously advancing his ideas to better accommodate the conceptual gains in other areas of psychology.

As a case in point, consider the landmark contributions of Spence (1982, 1987). The importance of Freud's insight is evident in Spence's conclusion that "Freud, the first *psychoanalyst*, was also one of the first great synthesizers. He was a master at taking pieces of the patient's associations, dreams, and memories and weaving them into a coherent pattern that is compelling, persuasive, and seemingly complete, a pattern that allows us to make important discoveries about the patient's life and to make sense out of previously random happenings" (p. 21). Spence's homage is tempered, however, by the observation that Freud based his integrative portraits on the false assumption of a *historical truth* or veridical past that can be traced through the analytical process. In expounding on the weakness of this view, Spence (1982) cites the fallacy of the accompanying assumptions that the patient can serve as an "unbiased reporter" (p. 25) and that the therapist can listen with unbiased attention, the latter which he termed "the myth of the innocent analyst" (p. 25).

Consider, for instance, Freud's (1912/1976) description of the recommended form of psychoanalytic listening as "not directing one's notice to anything in particular and in maintaining the same 'evenly suspended attention' in the face of all that one hears" (pp. 111–112). The sheer impossibility of such "evenly suspended attention" is pointed up by the ubiquitous and unavoidable influence of selective processes in human cognition. This same conclusion is also evident from a clinical standpoint in Chessick's (1989) review of the literature on "listening" in intensive psychotherapy.

> The question of whether the therapist really can give such equal notice to everything communicated by the patient has often been raised, but only recently has it been answered increasingly in the negative. Many experienced therapists have learned that everyone approaches the data provided by the patient's free associations and behavior during sessions with a certain mental set—one that is based on either conscious or preconscious theoretical and philosophical conceptions. This mental set determines what is perceived and what is selected, *regardless* of the therapist's effort to listen with evenly suspended attention. (p. 4, italics in original)

How then can therapists listen? Spence (1987) proposed that therapists must in general aspire to accept their natural human limitations and unavoidable listening biases and work toward developing "truly respectful listening." In contrast to the assumption of unbiased understanding, truly respectful listing "endeavors to uncover the potentialities of meaning implied by what the patient is saying, latent contents of which he is unaware" (p. 66) and "acknowledges from the outset that our context of understanding is significantly different from the patient's" (p. 66). The majority of the therapist's perceptions and assumptions, from Spence's point of view, "are probably little more than pathetic fallacies which say more about the [therapist's] subjective state than about the patient's" (p. 68).

We propose a more generous stance toward the psychotherapist (Bonanno 1990a, 1990b, 1995). As trained listeners, we believe therapists may indeed generate useful intuitions about the patient's experience. Expressing these intuitive hunches or tentative interpretations might be confused with historical information only if they are labeled inappropriately as fact or as informed conclusions. On the other hand, interpretative comments may play an essential role when they are *explicitly labeled as tentative or intuitive*, for example, "I'm getting a sense that . . . ," or "What do you think about . . ." and, thus, provide patients with a safer, less invasive environment in which they might reconsider the meanings of their own experiences.

A particularly useful method for understanding and expressing tentative interpretations is the metaphor (Bonanno, 1990b). Metaphors can "represent symbolically what are often no more than vague 'felt meanings and experiences' (Gendlin, 1962), images, or other forms of nonconceptual representations, within the broader conceptual context of the therapeutic dialogue" (Bonanno, 1990b, p. 466). The metaphor offers both a context for intuitive listening and a form of creative expression and communication which maintains the emphasis on tentative and emergent interpretation. The therapist's use of creative, metaphoric language also appears to increase the expressiveness in patients (Wexler & Butler, 1976) and encourages an evolving rather than a fixed perspective on meaning. Metaphors tend to change of the course of a therapy and sometimes even within a single session (Angus & Rennie, 1988). Thus, metaphoric listening moves naturally toward closer approximations of private experience (Bonanno, 1990b). Even in the flexible expression of metaphor, however, it is necessary to repeatedly and explicitly note its tentative nature. As Spence (1987) again wisely notes, "When metaphor masquerades as explanation, we have lost the sense that the concepts are provisional and tentative, that they can, if necessary be replaced and discarded" (p. 168). Thus, in contrast to traditional analytical interpretations aimed at demarcating previously repressed motives and memories, the metaphor provides only the most transient and necessarily global structures from which to integrate the emergent therapeutic dialogue.

NARRATIVE TRUTH AND NARRATIVE REVISION

Despite the limits of the therapist's listening and the unreliability of historical information, Spence (1982) argues that the effectiveness of Freud's interpretations demonstrates his awareness of the "persuasive power of a coherent narrative" (p. 21).

> There can be no doubt that a well-constructed story possesses a kind of *narrative truth* that is real and immediate and carries an important significance for the process of therapeutic change. Although Freud would later argue that every effective interpretation must also contain a piece of historical truth, it is by no means certain whether this is always the case; narrative truth by itself seems to have a significant impact on the clinical process. (pp. 21–22, italics added)

Thus, psychotherapy is effective not as Freud believed, and uncritical exponents of the repression model continue to claim, because a repressed memory previously masquerading as a symptom was made conscious but, on the contrary, because patients were able to substitute a faulty construction of reality with a more suitable or effective construction, one created by the patient with the therapist and one containing elements of narrative truth. The development of the narrative truth occurs gradually, evolving naturally from the many communications and mutual exchanges between the patient and therapist across the course of psychotherapy. The process of *narrative revision* (Bonanno, 1990a, 1995), when carefully monitored and explicitly identified as tentative, can lead to the gradual emergence of a more healthy and more effective construal of the world—one that integrates memory fragments and constructions of the past with a more efficacious and functional "story."

Dissociated Fragments and the Organizing
Nature of Narrative Meaning

One means by which narrative revisions influence psychotherapeutic change is that they help organize the patient's experience around the meaning of events rather than the veridicality of events. The telling and retelling of traumatic or difficult experiences helps patients to consciously structure and organize their often fragmented recollections and various associated emotional responses into somewhat of a coherent narrative picture, one that integrates the past, present, and anticipated future and is intimately bound up with our personal sense of identity and purpose (McAdams, 1988, 1991).

An important consideration in this endeavor is that many patients, particularly those suffering from the *disorganizing* effects of traumatic experience, find it initially quite difficult to present a coherent narrative account of the past. This difficulty points up the crucial distinction between repressed memory and dissociative mechanisms which operate by prohibiting the

simultaneous experience in consciousness of various fragmented representations of the same event (Bonanno, 1990b). Each piece of information
related to the disturbing event may capture some feature or form of the
traumatic experience but, in isolation, lacks a cohesive, narrative element. In
other words, what may seem like repressed memory is more accurately
conceptualized as relatively inaccessible and isolated memory fragments—a
fleeting image, a vague but powerful sense of helplessness, a bodily memory
of a frantic movement or gesture—that, by virtue of the reluctance to reexperience the event, remain isolated from each other.

The work of therapy in this case may sometimes center on the "translation" of these various fragments into a unified and integrated reconstruction
of a single moment in time. Clinicians working with trauma victims often
believe it is necessary to assist patients in reconstructing antecedent events by
providing provocative cues, such as historical facts or actual fragments of a
patient's history garnered from the treatment records. Sometimes, particularly in the case of known traumatic events, actual materials from the
antecedent events are brought into the treatment. In the safety of the proper
treatment atmosphere, with an adequate emphasis on the tentative nature of
memory reconstruction, techniques of this sort stimulate retrieval and associative processing. We propose, however, that the more important therapeutic
consideration must always involve the eventual integration of such memory
fragments into the broader evolving narrative. Clearly, the treatment situation
must provide the patient with a sense of safety and trust (Silver, 1986; van der
Kolk & Kadish, 1987) to ensure the readiness to make such connections. Too
great an emphasis on the details of the past often blurs the quality of the
therapeutic relationship and may foster unnecessary suspicion about powerful repressed memories or hidden meanings.

Dissociation and the Pathogenic Meaning

An obvious conclusion at this point is that, in addition to its function of
bringing fragmentary representations into the therapeutic dialogue, the
gradual emergence of a narrative account of the past may inform the treating
clinician, not so much about *what* had occurred in the past but *how* the patient
construes the past. To some extent, this meaning is intimately bound up with
the patient's general expectations, hopes, beliefs, and fears, what Frank and
Frank (1991) referred to as the patient's "assumptive world." The unfolding
stories told by patients suffering from traumatic experience are often their
first fully realized narrative versions of the events that brought them into
therapy and their first glimpses of their full meaning and significance (Lifton,
1988). For those who have suffered from traumatic events of a particularly
random or cruel nature, the development of a coherent meaning may be next
to impossible. In many cases, such traumatic experiences challenge an individual's fundamental sense of safety and well-being in the world (Harber &
Pennebaker, 1992; Horowitz, 1986).

Regardless of the actual nature of the antecedent event, however, virtually any traumatic experience that produces a dissociated or fragmented representation will with great likelihood be linked to primitive or irrational, unconscious interpretations of the event—a simple, global *pathogenic meaning* (Bonanno, 1995) not unlike Janet's (1889) *idée fixe*.

When this happens, the pathogenic meaning or unconscious fixed ideas are likely to reveal the patient's preexisting, personal dysfunctional meaning structures, for example, core-conflicted themes (Luborsky, 1984), nuclear scripts (Tomkins, 1979), or negative schema of the self, world, and future (Greenberg & Beck, 1990).

Such core understandings are, of course, not easily changed or for that matter challenged without strong resistance. Organized meaning structures are part of the fabric of human cognitive functioning: They are economic, become increasingly automated over time (Hayes-Roth, 1977; Langer, 1978), and allow us to condense or "crystallize" a lifetime of experience (Horn & Cattell, 1966). As part of this economic function, we typically remain unaware of the organized or "schematic" nature of our beliefs (Greenwald, 1980; Singer & Salovey, 1988) and of the narrative or reconstructed quality of memory (Johnson, 1985; Ross, 1989). Even in the absence of traumatic experience, we tend to cling to our organized ways of knowing the world, not because the actual underlying events were repressed but, rather, out of the human need to maintain a sense of safety and predictability in a complex world (Kelly, 1955). This is an essential difference.

The difficulty confronted by the clinician in helping patients confront the complex tangle of fragmented bits of memory, pathogenic meanings, and core beliefs is no doubt one of the reasons that the concept of repressed memory has endured. It is simply easier to assume that a hidden memory is behind a patient's dysfunction than to confront the formidable task of untangling the complex web of memories and meanings. It is also easier to assume the role of expert authority when the burden of remembering rests squarely on the patient's shoulders. In contrast, the process of helping patients express and understand the complicated and often confusing narratives that they might bring to the therapy is likely to challenge a therapist's own sense of efficacy. Further, the therapist must contain his or her own desire to hasten the narrative revision process and to provide the patient with a neatly packaged explanation for his or her difficulties.

In this light, it is important for clinicians to keep in mind that neat narrative explanations are not always forthcoming. In other words, the patient's avoidant responses may serve a useful adaptive function of allowing a gradual assimilation of meaning. Recent research into conjugal bereavement shows, for example, that the individuals who minimized the experience and expression of negative emotion while describing their relationships with the deceased had a less severe grief course than those who did not (Bonanno & Keltner, 1997; Bonanno, Keltner, Holen, & Horowitz, 1995). Thus, it may be important to allow some patients to describe the memories and emotions related to a stressful event at a more moderated pace (Bonanno & Castonguay, 1994). Indeed, for those who have endured extreme trauma and deprivation, exploratory work may even be impossible (Ehrlich, 1988; Kinzie, 1988). In such cases, clinicians may need to monitor their own desire to hasten the patient's narrative understanding and to focus instead on establishing and maintaining a useful and safe bond, or on addressing general social supports and adaptive issues with which the patient is struggling (Van Boemel & Rozee, 1992). We would propose that such interventions, although not directly addressing avoided experiences, nonetheless do effectively influence the patient's more encompassing narrative understanding of life and to some extent help to ameliorate the pathogenic meaning of the traumatic events.

CONTEMPORARY PSYCHOSOMATIC MANIFESTATIONS OF TRAUMA

To illustrate the inappropriateness, as well as the temptation, of treatment models based on repressed memory, we conclude this chapter with an example of a repression-like phenomenon that can be more effectively explained and treated by normal, everyday memory concepts such as accessibility and reconstruction. In this last case, we look at a type of psychosomatic problem that bears a striking resemblance to the classic "hysterical" symptoms that inspired Freud's original theory of repression, that of psychosomatic blindness—the inability to "see" when no apparent organic visual deficits.

Psychosomatic blindness has been relatively rare at this point in the late 20th century, limited to just a few reported cases each year. A startlingly abundant number of cases have appeared recently, however, in southern California, with all the cases turning out to be women who had recently emigrated to the United States as refugees from the Cambodian holocaust(Rozee & Van Boemel, 1989; Van Boemel & Rozee, 1992). In the late 1970s, Cambodia suffered an almost unimaginable "autogenocide"—approximately 3 million of the country's 7 million people were killed at the hands of its own Khmer Rouge government. Many Westerners glimpsed the horror as it was dramatized in the film *The Killing Fields*— a mass torture and slaughter on a scale unparalleled since the Nazi holocaust of the World War II (Kinzie, 1988; Rozee & Van Boemel, 1989). The refugee survivors who somehow made their way to Long Beach were primarily women—nearly 80% of Cambodia's male population were killed (Cook, 1991). Their suffering was almost unimaginable. They were separated from their children, forced to work years in labor camps often without adequate food, and forced to witness the apparently random and graphic torture and execution of family and friends. They lived in constant fear for their own lives. The women who managed to slip away often spent many months in the jungle before reaching the Thai border. There they found a different set of traumatic conditions—overcrowded refugee camps, starvation, disease, and often rape or sexual assault at the hands of Thai guards.

Somehow, some of these women made their way to the Los Angeles area in the United States where a large Cambodian community already existed. It was at this time, when many of the refugees received medical attention for the first time, that it became apparent that an inordinate number had lost their sight. When ophthalmological examinations revealed the startling fact that most of these women showed no detectable physical impairments, it became apparent that they suffered from "psychosomatic blindness," as well as a number of other somatic complaints, such as leg pain or dizziness, in the absence of verifiable organic pathology. The visual acuity in these women was worse the longer they had been held in the labor camps. Those with the poorest visual acuity also tended to have trauma-related nightmares (Rozee & Van Boemel, 1989).

This leaves us with the difficult task of explaining how such psychosomatic manifestations come about. Because all the patients suffered from remarkably similar experiences, there can be little question that the symptoms were a response to those traumatic experiences. What is more, malingering can all but be ruled out if for no other reason than simply because not only did these women have little knowledge of the possible gains they might obtain from their illnesses but most were as a result of their experiences profoundly suspicious or even deathly afraid of the medical establishment.

What of the repressed memory explanation? Almost all the elements evident in the lives of these unfortunate victims are compatible with the classic picture of repressed memory. A defining consistency in their stories is the traumatic past coupled with a pressing need to put the events out of consciousness and to somehow push forward toward survival. Further, these women exhibited a profound reluctance to think back to the horrible events they had endured. It is tempting to conclude then that they had repressed significant portions of their frighteningly distressing past. For this reason, as Freud proposed, their unconscious opted for a partial or symbolic expression of their traumatic memories in the form of the somatic symptom of functional blindness.

As much as we might wish to apply the repression explanation in this case, several facts render it untenable. Most important, none of the women appeared to have repressed their memories of the traumatic events. As much as they might have wished to forget what they saw, published interviews attest to the fact that, when requested to do so, they could recall the horrors of their recent pasts in all-too-vivid detail (Cook, 1991). Further, *primary repression* (of events in childhood), which is a cornerstone of the repression explanation, is clearly not an issue here because the blindness-producing traumatic events took place in the adulthood, or adolescence, of the women. Finally, even though psychotherapy was a completely foreign and nearly incomprehensible idea to these women, several who participated showed considerable improvement regardless of whether the treatment was a standard "talk" therapy or a more instructive type of living skills training aimed at fostering adaptation to cultural practices in the United States and at least a partial return to normalcy (Van Boemel & Rozee, 1992). Thus, improvement seemed to have little to do with directly remembering the past but was more generally a function of having engaged in some form of "treatment" with a concerned clinician.

How then might we explain functional blindness using the concepts of dissociation and reconstruction? Recall that the crux of this approach is the *organizing* function of narrative meaning. Perhaps the most important factor to consider, then, is the shear incomprehensibility of the events through which these women have suffered. In general, when people endure severe traumatic experiences, the overwhelming sense of horror and disbelief, coupled with the perceptual omissions and distortions that often accompany psychological trauma, typically leave survivors more or less unable to comprehend what has happened to them. They may remember the events in terms of basic "facts" or sequences of events, vivid images and sensory details, or *enactive* representations of visceral and motor responses (Bruner, 1964; Horowitz, 1983; Loewald, 1976). Gestures and other motor actions, in particular, can represent "separate manifestations of meaning" than those contained in speech and conceptual representations (McNeill, 1989) and, thus, may capture more of the traumatic experience than victims can really understand. The possibility that psychological trauma might be "represented" as a disruption of an otherwise automatic function, such as vision, is suggested by the fact that visual development necessarily requires a certain degree of neural plasticity (Held, 1965). Human infants "learn" to coordinate visual and motor reflexes and to decode the visual array into meaningful perceptual experiences (Aslin & Banks, 1978; Banks & Salapatek, 1983). Congenitally blind individuals who only later gain the use of their sight experience extreme difficulties attempting to make sense of the visual world and typically suffer serious emotional consequences as a result (Gregory, 1974; Sacks, 1995). In a similar manner, then, individuals who experience "unbearable" psychological trauma might manage to "unlearn" or at least disrupt this same visual function.

In the case of Cambodian refugees, we propose that psychosomatic blindness is linked to a dissociated cluster of primitive meanings, horrific images, and behavioral responses or muscular representations loosely organized around the incomprehensibility of the events and the desire or "need not to see" (Rozee & Van Boemel, 1989). We further propose that these representational components may each be accessible to conscious experience but fragmented and nearly impossible for the survivors to comprehend as a meaningful whole. One survivor's understanding of the experience, for example was summed up simply as, "My family was killed in 1975 and I cried for 4 years. When I stopped crying, I was blind" (Rozee & Van Boemel, 1989). Although a full understanding of such "lexically inexpressible" (Geller, 1987) trauma might be an impossible goal, a gradually developing sense of order may eventually return to the patient's life and, thus, enable a "translation" of meaning (Bonanno, 1990b) from the immediacy of enactive and imagistic memories and the urge to block perception of them to a more fully realized comprehension that the traumatic events happened in the past and that the present environment holds at least some protection from such events ever being repeated. Stated another way, the gradual acceptance of the traumatic past is essentially a *realization* that the world might once again be perceived as a relatively safe and predictable place. This change, or translation of meaning, will in turn produce a richer set of associative connections between the trauma and other related but less distressing events, including those in which patients may see themselves as safer or more efficacious human beings (Harber & Pennebaker, 1992) and ideally the safety and efficacy of the treatment context (Kingsbury, 1992; Silver, 1986).

In contrast, we can imagine the type of treatment dynamics that would occur if, instead of general, broad-based supportive treatment, the therapist emphasized the search for the putative repressed memories. Such an approach would require a concerted focus on the traumatic past and would presuppose a level of tolerance probably far out of reach of patients as fragile and as reluctant as these. Judging from what these women had already been through, the search for repressed memories would probably be quite difficult to understand and would likely be experienced as authoritarian and punitive. In terms of the associative structure of memory, then, such an approach would probably result in the encoding of the treatment experience, not as a benign or helpful process to balance the horror of the past but as invasive and for that matter quite consistent with their previous experiences. In short, the emphasis on recovering repressed memories *that may not even exist* may only replicate rather than revise the patient's narrative understanding.

CONCLUSION

We reviewed the evidential, conceptual, and scientific limitations of the construct of repressed memory. We devoted significant portions of this review to early historical material, including Janet's nascent writings on subconscious processing and Breuer and Freud's extension of these concepts to include the mechanism of repression, and to the writings of contemporary clinical theorists, most notably Spence, who have acknowledged the limitations of human memory and perceptual processes. As an alternative to the construct of repressed memory, we reviewed contemporary memory concepts derived from experimental research which may serve as the basis of a more parsimonious model of memory functioning during psychotherapy. In particular, we emphasized the distinction between memory availability and accessibility and the important role played by the processes of dissociation and of narrative reconstruction and revision. The application of these concepts to common problems in psychotherapy, such as memory for traumatic events, deemphasizes the importance of recounting the details of the past and places crucial emphasis, instead, on the subjective meaning of a gradually emerging narrative understanding. To illustrate these distinctions and to highlight the advantages of integrating clinical theory with concepts derived from experimental research, we reviewed the compelling examples of psychosomatic blindness found among the survivors of the recent Cambodian holocaust.

Clearly, the issues we raised in this chapter are of sufficient import to warrant far more detailed consideration than is possible in this space. We believe, however, that the examples we provided should illustrate adequately how the seemingly intractable problems associated with an outdated clinical construct, such as repressed memory, can be remedied by a broader understanding and integration of related experimental research. In the end, the alternative memory model we propose should not be viewed as a plea for radical shifts in therapeutic orientation. Rather, we outlined these subtle but important conceptual distinctions about the role of memory in psychotherapy in the spirit of providing practicing clinicians with a more efficacious framework from which to conceptualize their patients' experience during therapy.

REFERENCES

Angus, L. E. , & Rennie, D. L. (1988). Therapist participation in metaphor generation: Collaborative and noncollaborative styles. *Psychotherapy*, *25*, 552–560.

Aslin, R. N., & Banks, M. S. (1978). Early visual experience in humans: Evidence for a critical period in the development of binocular vision. In S. Schneider, H. Liebowitz, H. Pick, & H. Stevenson (Eds.), *Psychology, from basic research to practice*. New York: Plenum.

Banks, M. S., & Salapatek, P. (1983). Infant visual perception. In P. H. Mussen (Ed.), *Handbook of child psychology* (4th ed., Vol. 2). New York: Wiley.

Barclay, C. B. (1986). Schematization of autobiographical memory. In D. S. Rubin (Ed.), *Autobiographical memory* (pp. 82–99). Cambridge, UK: Cambridge University Press.

Bonanno, G. A. (1990a). Remembering and psychotherapy. *Psychotherapy*, *27*, 175–186.

Bonanno, G. A. (1990b). Repression, accessibility, and the translation of private experience. *Psychoanalytic Psychology*, *7*, 453– 473.

Bonanno, G. A. (1995). Accessibility, reconstruction, and the treatment of functional memory problems. In A. Baddeley, B. A. Wilson, & F. Watts (Eds.), *Handbook of memory disorders* (pp. 616–637). Sussex, UK: Wiley.

Bonanno, G. A., & Castonguay, L. G. (1994). On balancing approaches to psychotherapy: Prescriptive patterns of attention, motivation, and personality. *Psychotherapy*, *31*, 571–587.

Bonanno, G. A., Davis, P. J., Singer, J. L., & Schwartz, G. E. (1991). The repressor personality and avoidant information processing: A dichotic listening study. *Journal of Research in Personality*, *25*, 386–401.

Bonanno, G. A., & Keltner, D. (1997). Facial expressions of emotion and the course of conjugal bereavement. *Journal of Abnormal Psychology*, *106*(4) 126–137.

Bonanno, G. A., Keltner, D., Holen, A., & Horowitz, M. J. (1995). When avoiding unpleasant emotion might not be such a bad thing: Verbal-autonomic response dissociation and midlife conjugal bereavement. *Journal of Personality and Social Psychology, 69*, 975–989.

Bonanno, G. A., Siddique, H. I. L., Keltner, D., & Horowitz, M. J. (1996). *Correlates and consequences of dispositional repression and self-deception following the loss of a spouse.* Unpublished manuscript, Catholic University of America, Washington, DC.

Bonanno, G. A., & Singer, J. L. (1990). Repressive personality style: Theoretical and methodological implications for health and pathology. In J. L. Singer (Ed.), *Repression and dissociation* (pp. 435–470). Chicago: University of Chicago Press.

Bonanno, G. A., & Singer, J. L. (1993). Controlling the stream of thought through perceptual and reflective processing. In D. Wegner & J. Pennebaker (Eds.), *Handbook of mental control* (pp. 149–170). New York: Prentice-Hall.

Breuer, J., & Freud, S. (1955). Studies on hysteria. In J. Strachey (Ed. & Trans.), *The standard edition of the complete psychological works of Sigmund Freud* (Vols. 4 & 5). London: Hogarth Press. (Original work published 1895)

Bruner, J. S. (1964). The course of cognitive growth. *American Psychologist, 19*, 1–15.

Chessick, R. D. (1989). *The technique and practice of listening in intensive psychotherapy.* Northvale, NJ: Aronson.

Cook, P. (1991, June 23). They cried until they could not see. *New York Times Magazine*, pp. 24–25, 45–48.

Craik, F. I. M., & Lockhart, R. S. (1972). Levels of processing: A framework for memory research. *Journal of Verbal Learning and Verbal Behavior, 11*, 671–684.

Creamer, M., Burgess, P., & Pattison, P. (1990). Cognitive processing in posttrauma reactions: Some preliminary findings. *Psychological Medicine, 20*, 1–17.

Crowder, R. G. (1985). On access and the forms of memory. In N. M. Weinberger, J. L. McGaugh, & G. Lynch (Eds.), *Memory systems of the brain* (pp. 433–441). New York: Guilford Press.

Davis, P. J. (1987). Repression and the inaccessibility of affective memories. *Journal of Personality and Social Psychology, 53*, 585–93.

Davis, P. J. (1990). Repression and the inaccessibility of emotional memories. In J. L. Singer (Ed.), *Repression and dissociation.* Chicago: University of Chicago Press.

Davis, P. J., & Schwartz, G. E. (1987). Repression and the inaccessibility of affective memories. *Journal of Personality and Social Psychology, 52*, 155–163.

Ehrlich, P. (1988). Treatment issues in the psychotherapy of Holocaust survivors. In J. P. Wilson, Z. Harel, & B. Kahana (Eds.), *Human adaptation to extreme stress: From the Holocaust to Vietnam* (pp. 285–303). New York: Plenum.

Ellenberger, H. F. (1970). *The discovery of the unconscious.* New York: Basic Books.

Erdelyi, M. H. (1985). *Psychoanalysis: Freud's cognitive psychology.* New York: Freeman.

Erdelyi, M. H. (1990). Repression, reconstruction, and defense: History and integration of the psychoanalytic and experimental frameworks. In J. L. Singer (Ed.), *Repression and dissociation* (pp. 1–32). Chicago: University of Chicago Press.

Fehling, M., Baars, B., & Fisher, C. (1990). A functional role for repression in an autonomous, resource-constrained agent. In *Program of the XII annual conference of the Cognitive Science Society.* Hillsdale, NJ: Erlbaum.

Frank, J. D., & Frank, J. B. (1991). *Persuasion and healing: A comparative study of psychotherapy.* Baltimore, MD: Johns Hopkins University Press.

Freud, S. (1924a). The defense neuro-psychoses. In E. Jones (Ed. & Trans.), *The collected papers of Sigmund Freud* (Vol. 1, pp. 59–75). London: Hogarth Press. (Original work published 1894)

Freud, S. (1924b). Sexuality and the etiology of the neuroses. In E. Jones (Ed. & Trans.), *The collected papers of Sigmund Freud* (Vol. 1, pp. 220–248). London: Hogarth Press. (Original work published 1898)

Freud, S. (1957). Repression. In J. Strachey (Ed. & Trans.), *The standard edition of the complete psychological works of Sigmund Freud* (Vol. 14, pp. 146–158). London: Hogarth Press. (Original work published 1915)

Freud, S. (1963). Further recommendations in the technique of psychoanalysis. In P. Rieiff (Ed.), *Freud: Therapy and technique* (pp. 135–156). New York: Collier Books. (Original work published 1913)

Freud, S. (1966a). Introductory lectures on psychoanalysis. In J. Strachey (Ed. & Trans.), *The standard edition of the complete psychological works of Sigmund Freud* (Vols. 15, 16, pp. 146–158). London: Hogarth Press. (Original work published 1917)

Freud, S. (1966b). Inhibition, symptoms and anxiety. In J. Strachey (Ed. & Trans.), *The standard edition of the complete psychological works of Sigmund Freud* (Vol. 20, pp. 87–172). London: Hogarth Press. (Original work published 1926)

Freud, S. (1976a). The dynamics of transference. In J. Strachey (Ed. & Trans.), *The standard edition of the complete psychological works of Sigmund Freud* (Vol. 12). London: Hogarth Press. (Original work published 1912)

Freud, S. (1976). On beginning the treatment. In J. Strachey (Ed. & Trans.), *The standard edition of the complete psychological works of Sigmund Freud* (Vol.12, pp. 146–158). London: Hogarth Press. (Original work published 1913)

Freud, S. (1976). From the history of an infantile neurosis. In J. Strachey (Ed. & Trans.), *The standard edition of the complete psychological works of Sigmund Freud* (Vol. 12, pp. 7–122). London: Hogarth Press. (Original work published 1914)

Geller, J. D. (1987). The process of psychotherapy: Separation and the complex interplay among empathy, insight and internalization. In J. Bloom-Feshbach & S. Bloom-Feshbach (Eds.), *The psychology of separation and loss.* San Francisco: Jossey-Bass.

Gendlin, E. T. (1962). *Experience and the creation of meaning: A philosophical and psychological approach to the subjective.* Toronto: Free Press of Glencoe.

Greenberg, M. S., & Beck, A. T. (1990). Cognitive approaches to psychotherapy: Theory and therapy. In R. Plutchik & H. Kellerman (Eds), *Emotion: Theory, research and experience* (Vol. 5, pp. 177–194). New York: Academic Press.

Greenwald, A. G. (1980). The totalitarian ego: Fabrication and revision of personal history. *American Psychologist, 35,* 603–618.

Greenwald, A. G. (1992). New look 3: Unconscious cognition reclaimed. *American Psychologist, 47,* 766–779.

Greenwald, A. G., Klinger, M. R., & Liu, T. J. (1989). Unconscious processing of dichoptically masked words. *Memory and Cognition, 17,* 35–47.

Gregory, R. L. (1974). *Concepts and mechanism of perception.* London: Duckworth.

Gur, R. C., & Sackeim, H. A. (1979). Self-deception: A concept in search of a phenomenon. *Journal of Personality and Social Psychology, 37,* 147–169.

Hansen, C. H., Hansen, R. D., & Shantz, D. W. (1992). Repression at encoding: Discrete appraisals of emotional stimuli. *Journal of Personality and Social Psychology, 63,* 1026–1035.

Hansen, R. D., & Hansen, C. H. (1988). Repression of emotionally tagged memories: The architecture of less complex emotions. *Journal of Personality and Social Psychology, 55,* 811–818.

Harber, K. D., & Pennebaker, J. W. (1992). Overcoming traumatic memories. In S.-A. Christianson (Ed.), *The handbook of emotion and memory: Research and theory* (pp. 359–387). Hillsdale, NJ: Erlbaum.

Hayes-Roth, B. (1977). Evolution of cognitive structures and processes. *Psychological Review, 84,* 260–278.

Held, R. (1965). Plasticity in sensory motor systems. *Scientific American, 21,* 84–94.

Holmes, D. S. (1974). Investigations of repression: Differential recall of material experimentally or naturally associated with ego threat. *Psychological Bulletin, 81,* 632–653.

Holmes, D. S. (1990). The evidence for repression: An examination of sixty years of research. In J. L. Singer (Ed.), *Repression and dissociation* (pp. 85–102). Chicago: University of Chicago Press.

Horn, J. L., & Cattell, R. B. (1966). Refinement and test of the theory of fluid and crystallized intelligence. *Journal of Educational Psychology, 57,* 253–270.

Horowitz, M. M. (1983). *Image formation and psychotherapy.* New York: Aronson.

Horowitz, M. J. (1986). *Stress response syndromes* (2nd ed.). Northvale, NJ: Aronson.

Jacoby, L. L., Kelley, C., Brown, J., & Jasechko, J. (1989). Becoming famous overnight: Limits on the ability to avoid unconscious influences of the past. *Journal of Personality and Social Psychology, 56,* 326–338.

Janet, P. (1889). *L' automatisme psychologique.* Paris: Librairie Félix Alcan.

Janet, P. (1901). *The mental state of hystericals: A study of mental stigmata and mental accidents* (C. R. Carson, Trans.). New York: Putnam. (Original work published 1893)

Janet, P. (1907). *The major symptoms of hysteria.* New York: Macmillan.

Johnson, M. K. (1985). The origin of memories. In P. C. Kendall (Ed.), *Advances in cognitive-behavioral research and therapy* (Vol. 4, pp. 1–27). New York: Academic Press.

Johnson, W. A., & Dark, V. J. (1986). Selective attention. *Annual Review of Psychology, 37,* 43–75.

Kaszniak, A. W., Nussbaum, P. D., Berren, M. R., & Santiago, J. (1988). Amnesia as a consequence of male rape: A case report. *Journal of Abnormal Psychology, 97,* 100–104.

Katkin, E. S. (1985). Blood, sweat, and tears: Individual differences in autonomic self-perception. *Psychophysiology, 22,* 125–135.

Kelly, G. A. (1955). *The psychology of personal constructs: Vol 1. A theory of personality.* New York: Norton.

Keuler, D. J., & Safer, M. A. (1997). *Recall bias in the assessment and recall of pre-therapy distress.* Manuscript submitted for publication.

Kingsbury, S. J. (1992). Strategic psychotherapy for trauma: Hypnosis and trauma in context. *Journal of Traumatic Stress, 5,* 85–95.

Kinzie, J. D. (1988). The psychiatric effects of massive trauma on Cambodian refugees. In J. P. Wilson, Z. Harel, & B. Kahana (Eds.), *Human adaptation to extreme stress* (pp. 305–318). New York: Plenum.

Kramer, T. H., Buckhout, R., & Eugenio, P. (1990). Weapon focus, arousal, and eyewitness memory: Attention must be paid. *Law and Human Behavior, 14,* 167–184.

Langer, E. J. (1978). Rethinking the role of thought in social interactions. In J. Harvey, W. Ickes, & R. Kidd (Eds.), *New directions in attribution research* (Vol. 2). Hillsdale, NJ: Erlbaum.

Leowald, H. (1976). Perspectives on memory. *Psychological Issues, 9,* 298–325.

Leventhal, H. (1991). Emotion: Prospects for conceptual and empirical development. In R. G. Lister & H. J. Weingartner (Eds.), *Perspective on cognitive neuroscience* (pp. 325–348). Oxford, UK: Oxford University Press.

Lifton, R. J. (1988). Understanding the traumatized self. In J. P. Wilson, Z. Harel, & B. Kahana (Eds.), *Human adaptation to extreme stress* (pp. 7–31). New York: Plenum.

Lindy, J. D. (1986). An outline for the psychoanalytic psychotherapy of posttraumatic stress disorder. In C. R. Figley (Ed.), *Trauma and its wake: Volume II. Traumatic stress theory, research, and intervention* (pp. 195–212). New York: Brunner/Mazel.

Loftus, E. F. (1979). *Eyewitness testimony.* Cambridge, MA: Harvard University Press.

Loftus, E. F., & Banaji, M. R. (1989). Memory modification and the role of the media. In V. A. Gheorghiu, P. Netter, H. J. Eysenck, & R. Rosenthal (Eds.), *Suggestion and suggestibility* (pp. 279–193). Berlin: Springer-Verlag.

Loftus, E. F., & Palmer, J. C. (1974). Reconstruction of automobile destruction: An example of the interaction between language and memory. *Journal of Verbal Learning and Verbal Behavior, 13,* 585–589.

Luborsky, L. (1984). *Principles of psychoanalytic psychotherapy: A manual for supportive-expressive (se) treatment.* New York: Basic Books.

McAdams, D. P. (1988). *Power, intimacy, and the life story: Personological inquiries into identity.* New York: Guilford Press.

McAdams, D. P. (1991). The development of a narrative identity. In D. M. Buss & N. Cantor (Eds.), *Personality psychology: Recent trends and emerging directions* (pp. 160–176). New York: Springer-Verlag.

McCann, T., & Sheehan, P. (1988). Hypnotically induced pseudomemories—sampling conditions among hypnotizable subjects. *Journal of Personality and Social Psychology, 54,* 339–346.

McNeill, D. (1989). A straight path—to where? A reply to Butterworth and Hadar. *Psychological Review, 94,* 175–179.

Murray, G. J., Cross, H. J., & Whipple, J. (1992). Hypnotically created pseudomemories: Further investigation into the "memory distortion or response bias" question. *Journal of Abnormal Psychology, 101,* 75–77.

Newton, T. L., & Contrada, R. J. (1992). Repressive coping and verbal-autonomic response dissociation: The influence of social context. *Journal of Personality and Social Psychology, 62,* 159–167.

Peterson, K. C., Prout, M. P., & Schwarz, R. A. (1991). *Posttraumatic stress disorder: A clinician's guide.* New York: Plenum.

Rosenfield, I. (1988). *The invention of memory.* New York: Basic Books.

Ross, M. (1989). Relation of implicit theories to the construction of personal histories. *Psychological Review, 96,* 341–357.

Ross, M., & Conway, M. (1986). Remembering one's own past: The construction of personal histories. In R. M. Sorrentino & E. T. Higgins (Eds.), *Handbook of motivation and cognition: Vol. 1. Foundation of human behavior* (pp. 122–144). New York: Guilford Press.

Rozee, P., & Van Boemel, G. (1989). The psychological effects of war trauma and abuse on older Cambodian refugee women. *Women and Therapy, 8,* 23–50.

Sacks, O. (1995). *An anthropologist on Mars.* New York: Knopf.

Schneider, D. J. (1993). Mental control: Lessons from our past. In D. M. Wegner & J. W. Pennebaker (Eds.), *Handbook of mental control* (pp. 13–35). Englewood Cliffs, NJ: Simon & Schuster.

Sheehan, P. W., Grigg, L., & McCann, T. (1984). Memory distortion following exposure to false information in hypnosis. *Journal of Abnormal Psychology*, *93*, 259–265.

Sheehan, P. W., & Statham, D. (1989). Hypnosis, the timing of its introduction, and acceptance of misleading information. *Journal of Abnormal Psychology*, *98*, 170–176.

Silver, S. M. (1986). An inpatient program for posttraumatic stress disorder. In C. R. Figley (Ed.), *Trauma and its wake: Vol. II. Traumatic stress theory, research, and intervention* (pp. 213–231). New York: Brunner/Mazel.

Singer, J. A., & Salovey, P. (1988). Mood and memory: Evaluating the network theory of affect. *Clinical Psychology Review*, *2*, 211–251.

Smith, V. L., & Ellsworth, P. C. (1987). The social psychology of eyewitness accuracy: Misleading questions and communicator expertise. *Journal of Applied Psychology*, *72*, 294–300.

Spence, D. P. (1982). *Narrative truth and historical truth*. New York. Norton.

Spence, D. P. (1987). *The Freudian metaphor*. New York: Norton.

Suengas, A. G., & Johnson, M. K. (1988). Qualitative effects of rehearsal on memories for perceived and imagined complex events. *Journal of Experimental Psychology: General*, *117*, 377–389.

Tomkins, S. S. (1979). Script theory: Differential magnification of affects. In H. E. Howe (Ed.), *Nebraska Symposium on Motivation* (Vol. 26). Lincoln: University of Nebraska Press.

Tulving, E., & Thomson, D. M. (1973). Encoding specificity and retrieval processes in episodic memory. *Psychological Review*, *80*, 352–373.

Van Boemel, G. B., & Rozee, P. D. (1992). Treatment for psychosomatic blindness among Cambodian refugee women. *Women and Therapy*, *13*, 239–266.

van der Kolk, B. A., & Kadish, W. (1987). Amnesia, dissociation, and the return of the repressed. In B. A. van der Kolk (Ed.), *Psychological trauma*. Washington, DC: American Psychiatric Press.

Veith, I. (1965). *Hysteria: The history of a disease*. Chicago: University of Chicago Press.

Wegner, D. M., Schneider, D. J., Carter, S. R., III, & White, T. L. (1987). Paradoxical effects of thought suppression. *Journal of Personality and Social Psychology*, *53*, 5–13.

Weinberger, D. A., Schwartz, G. E., & Davidson, J. R. (1979). Low- anxious and repressive coping styles: Psychometric patterns of behavioral and physiological responses to stress. *Journal of Abnormal Psychology*, *88*, 369–380.

Wexler, D., & Butler, J. (1976). Therapist modification of client expressiveness in client-centered therapy. *Journal of Consulting and Clinical Psychology*, *44*, 261–265.

Wolf-Man, The. (1971). My recollections of Sigmund Freud. In M. Gardiner (Ed.), *The Wolf-Man by the Wolf-Man* (pp. 135–152). New York: Basic Books.

Williams, J. M. G., Watts, F. N., MacLeod, C., & Matthews, A. (1988). *Cognitive psychology and emotional disorders*. New York: Wiley.

Williams, T. (1988). Diagnosis and treatment of survivor guilt: The bad penny syndrome. In J. P. Wilson, Z. Harel, & B. Kahana (Eds.), *Human adaptation to extreme stress* (pp. 319–336). New York: Plenum.

Wood, J. M., Bootzin, R. R., Rosenhan, D., Nolen-Hoeksema, S., & Jourdan, F. (1992). Effects of the 1989 San Francisco earthquake on frequency and content of nightmares. *Journal of Abnormal Psychology*, *101*, 219–224.

CHAPTER 18

PRACTICAL TRUTHS IN MEMORY

Michael M. Gruneberg
Douglas J. Herrmann

The last 100 years have witnessed a considerable intellectual effort to understand human memory. Starting with Ebbinghaus (1885), many memory studies have investigated memory in the context of controlled laboratory settings. Ever since Ebbinghaus used controlled procedures to rule out the meaningfulness of stimuli to understand "pure" forgetting, the major tradition in seeking to understand the nature of memory has been to use materials and tasks not normally encountered in real life (e.g., recognizing and recalling lists of unrelated words and recalling lists of letter strings or digits).

Many "truths" of a general nature appear to have emerged from the Ebbinghaus tradition. For example, after studying meaningless syllables, forgetting occurs rapidly. When a word list is learned and then recalled at a later date, similar material learned in the interval between the original learning of the word list and later recall causes increased forgetting of the original material. This finding led to the view that the cause of at least some forgetting is due to the interference of similar kinds of material with each other.

Many other truths in memory were established in the laboratory, and models and theories of memory are based largely on rigorous experimentation. Unfortunately, many of these "truths" are subject to dispute. It is not clear, for example, that forgetting is solely due to interference. Moreover, memory models (e.g., Baddeley, 1990; Craik & Lockhart, 1972) based on artificial conditions in the laboratory are not entirely satisfactory models of our current knowledge of memory, especially in real life.

Nevertheless, few would argue that at an empirical level many truths have

464

been established in the laboratory. In learning a sequence of unrelated words, for example, it is well established that the first items are best recalled at a later retrieval attempt, with the last items well retained, at least temporarily. It is the words in the middle that are the most vulnerable to forgetting. In addition, research indicates that concrete nouns are better recalled than abstract nouns, and that word lists that can be organized into semantic categories are better recalled than when semantic organization is impossible. Many other memory phenomena were established on the basis of laboratory investigations and have contributed in meaningful ways to our understanding of memory (see Morris & Gruneberg, 1994, for a review).

THE BEGINNINGS OF THE EVERYDAY MEMORY MOVEMENT

These developments notwithstanding, by the 1970s there was an emerging sense, among certain workers in the field, that the ability to translate laboratory-based knowledge into applications of value outside the relatively narrow domain of psychology was limited. This perception was the impetus for the First International Conference on Practical Aspects of Memory. In their introduction to the conference, Gruneberg, Morris, and Sykes (1978) wrote that one of the objectives of the conference was "to examine ways in which the considerable advances recently made in our theoretical understanding of memory could be applied to real life memory problems."

Other participants were much less satisfied that the progress made in the laboratory was of practical signficance and argued that the truths revealed in the laboratory were trivial and perhaps even irrelevant to the way memory operates in real life. Neisser (1978) went so far as to state that "If 'X' is an interesting or socially significant aspect of memory, then psychologists have hardly ever studied 'X' " (p. 4).

The conference provided a forum for scientists who formerly believed they were "working largely in isolation against what was perceived as the dominant experimental paradigm" (Baddeley & Wilkins, 1984). In fact, at the end of the meeting, Neisser acknowledged that he was mistaken about the lack of interest in practical aspects of memory. Indeed, seminal papers that were presented focused and accelerated interest in areas of inquiry that continue to receive attention today. For instance, Brandimonte, Einstein, and McDaniel (1996) recently published a book on prospective memory (i.e., remembering to do things in the future such as a doctor's appointment) that recounts significant advances in our understanding of this phenomenon since Harris (1978) and Wilkins and Baddeley (1978) presented their seminal work in this area at the conference. Relatedly, Rubin (1996) recently provided an extensive account of the current state of knowledge of autobiographical memory that illustrates how much the field has advanced since Linton's (1975, 1978) influential papers were presented at the meeting. Finally, the study of the maintenance of knowledge stimulated initially by Bjork and Landauer (1978) was promoted by Bahrick's (1984) research documenting very long-term retention of material learned in college.

Gruneberg and Morris (1992a) identified three strands of interest pursued by those involved in the contemporary "everyday memory movement": (1) explicating memory processes and principles, (2) identifying and understanding interesting phenomena in the laboratory with potential relevance to "real world" memory, and (3) searching for practical solutions to real-life problems. In this chapter, we review methodological issues raised by the applied/everyday memory movement, as well as the general and specific contributions of applied memory research and technologies in improving memory in children, the elderly, and cognitively impaired populations.

THE NEW METHODOLOGY:
PROBLEMS WITH EXPERIMENTAL CONTROL

It could be argued that Neisser's real impact was not so much his call for psychologists to study "interesting or socially significant" phenomena, because many psychologists were doing so already. More important, perhaps was Neisser's challenge to researchers to devise ecologically valid methodologies (i.e., methodologies that studied memory where it occurred in the real world, outside the confines of the laboratory).

Yet this approach was not without critics. Banaji and Crowder (1989) disputed the idea that any truths about memory could be discovered apart from the rigorous control afforded in the laboratory that ultimately made it possible to generalize beyond the scope of the individual experiment. In short, their argument was that without scientific control, the science of psychology is not possible. Kihlstrom (1996), while in favor of applying memory research, maintained that Banaji and Crowder's stance on experimental control was "incontrovertible." Banaji and Crowder's position certainly is one to which many basic researchers would subscribe. But is it incontrovertible?

THE PROBLEM OF GENERALIZING FROM LABORATORY
EXPERIMENTS TO MEMORY MECHANISMS

We believe that the experimental approach is limited, if not unsatisfactory, for investigating certain memory phenomena. When a phenomenon is new to investigation, several factors must be taken into consideration. First, it is typically assumed that uncontrolled variables are randomized between control and experimental situations. However, this is not alway the case; sometimes they are not randomly distributed across situations.

Second, ethical considerations can preclude investigating memory phenomena in an experimental situation. A case in point would be that emotional factors have been shown to materially affect eyewitness testimony (Johnson, 1993), yet it is difficult, if not impossible, to replicate the level of emotionality experienced in real-life situations in the laboratory. Because emotionality cannot be fully captured in the laboratory, it is not possible to generalize from the laboratory to real life.

Third, traditional laboratory studies of serial learning, paired associate learning, and free recall do not yield consistent findings across recall paradigms (Underwood, Borsch, & Malmi, 1978). Because memory is a composite of different skills, the ability to generalize from controlled laboratory settings to the real world is constrained unless it can be shown that specific experiments access memory processes or identify memory principles that can be generalized beyond the particular paradigm employed.

THE PROBLEM OF GENERALIZING FROM THE LABORATORY TO REAL LIFE

Generalizing from the laboratory to the real world is fraught with difficulties. A number of examples illustrate this point. The first example is derived from the arena of research on eyewitness confidence and accuracy. Deffenbacher's (1996) recent review of the literature concluded (as have many others) that the underlying relationship between confidence and accuracy is relatively small, ranging from an average correlation of .3 under ordinary conditions, to about .5 when memory conditions are optimal. Even under optimal conditions, the correlation between confidence and accuracy is so low that it is not reliable in forensic or courtroom situations that require that certainty judgments parallel the accuracy of eyewitness identification.

However, as Gruneberg and Sykes (1993) point out, the evidence that supports these correlations is based on studies that are limited in their generalizability to the real world. All experiments involve situations in which subjects vary in the accuracy and the confidence in their memories. Otherwise, statistical analysis would not be possible. Often, in fact, the experiment involves the attempt to identify the perpetrator of a "crime" by selection of possible individuals from an array of possible "criminals." In such an experimental situation the correlation between eyewitness confidence and accuracy is almost always low.

Yet in many real-life situations, individuals are both extremely confident and extremely accurate (e.g., "What did you have for breakfast this morning?") in their judgments or memories. Statistical evaluation of research questions is difficult in situations in which there is little or no variability in the data. However, in real life, many confidence–accuracy judgments can be corroborated or supported by other information. For instance, it may be possible to state with reasonable accuracy and certitude that an accident happened at a particular time because it coincided with the start of a regularly attended football match and it takes 5 minutes to walk to the scene of the accident. At present, we have no means of knowing how many statements of the confidence–accuracy relationship are of the kind "I had coffee for breakfast, I'm certain" and how many statements are buttressed by other evidence.

Additionally, as Robinson and Johnson (1996) argue, most previous studies have involved recognition memory, and when recall is examined, the confidence–accuracy relationship is higher than for recognition. This phenomenon may occur because the ease of retrieval in recall is a good cue for accuracy, as Robinson and Johnson argue. Robinson and Johnson also show that within-subject analysis of the confidence–accuracy relationship yielded higher correlations than between-subject analysis. However, it is doubtful that within-subject analysis in any one study can be used to indicate the magnitude of a general relationship between confidence and accuracy, since the magnitude of a relationship depends on the number of easy questions where subjects will be both confident and accurate.

Of course, laboratory experiments on the confidence–accuracy relationship do tell us something important: When viewing conditions are less than optimal, even highly confident individuals' recognition is often inaccurate. One experiment involved a realistic incident staged in a classroom in front of 109 students. Nineteen students were certain that their answer to a particular question about the event was correct. However, only two of these students answered the question correctly. Interestingly, we found that the more the group as a whole answered a particular item correctly, the greater was the likelihood that each accurate response would be endorsed with greater confidence (Gruneberg & Sykes, 1981).

Clearly, there are limits to the degree to which experiments generalize to real-life circumstances. Certain relationships may apply under certain conditions and not under others. Indeed, juries may be wrongly informed that there is a weak relationship between confidence and accuracy if the basis of such information is experiments that do not consider the range of possible factors moderating the confidence–accuracy relationship in the real world. In short, experimental truth and real-life truth can be at variance with one another.

A second example of the danger of generalizing from experimentally controlled materials to the real world comes from two studies on the retention of football (soccer) scores. Morris, Gruneberg, Sykes, and Merrick (1981) established subjects' knowledge of soccer by administering a questionnaire on football facts, such as who was the goalkeeper for Liverpool, who played at Highbury, and so forth. Later, subjects listened to soccer results presented on a Saturday afternoon on a BBC sports program. The correlation between subjects' ability to recall the correct scores and their knowledge and, presumably, interest regarding football was .81, a highly significant relationship.

A second experiment (Morris, Tweedy, & Gruneberg, 1985) on the retention of soccer results presented soccer results under two different conditions. In the first condition, actual results were presented to subjects. In the second condition, subjects received plausible yet fictional results, which subjects knew were generated by the experimenter. In this study, there was a highly significant difference beween the correlations of knowledge with recall of soccer scores across conditions. For the "real results" group, the corrlation was virtually identical to the results obtained in the initial study: $r = .82$. In contrast, for the "made-up scores" group, the correlation was only .36. In short, the real-life versus artificial nature of the materials moderated the results secured.

The experiment clearly demonstrates that the use of laboratory materials may not generalize to the use of real-life materials. In this particular case the difference between real and artificial material probably was due to differential participant motivation, such that individuals who received the fictional results were less motivated to process the material (i.e., even material that is "automatically" processed is affected by motivation to process the material). Whatever the reason for the pattern of findings, it is clear that what happens in the laboratory may not be consistent with what happens outside the laboratory (Yuille & Cutshall, 1986).

A third experiment shows that not only the magnitude of an effect but its nature may be changed by bringing the investigation into the laboratory. Ceci and Bronfenbrenner (1991) had children monitor when cupcakes they were baking should be taken out of the oven. In one condition, children carried out the task at home; in a second condition they carried out the task in the laboratory. The investigators found that the children performed the monitoring task considerably more competently in their home surroundings. But just as important, the children's actual pattern of behavior, in terms of monitoring the clock, was different in the laboratory compared to the home situation.

ESTABLISHING PRACTICAL TRUTHS

The previous discussion supports two conclusions about the experimental method. First, the experimental method does guarantee a certain kind of truth—namely, that in the context of a particular paradigm there is a given probability that the findings will be replicated. However, the experimental paradigm does not guarantee that it is possible to make generalizations about the "true" nature of memory beyond the confines of the actual experiment.

A second conclusion is that to apply findings to the real world, it is not sufficient to conduct laboratory experiments. They cannot be expected to generalize to real-life phenomena in every case. For example, Johnson (1993) reports that real-life research on eyewitnesses to crimes yields higher accuracy levels than most laboratory studies do. Of course, this does not mean that the experimental method should be abandoned. However, at the very least, it implies that laboratory findings have to be tested against what happens in the real world.

Unfortunately, real-life research sometimes precludes adequate control and statistical analysis due to small sample sizes. What memory researchers need to do, in our view, is what is commonly done in other research areas such as organizational psychology. Organizational psychologists' solution to these sorts of difficulties has been to conduct a form of meta-analysis wherein as many studies (e.g., job enrichment) as possible are assembled and common features are assessed. When, in spite of wide variations in features manipulated and in statistical adequacy, virtually all studies point to the conclusion that a manipulation is successful in producing a particular effect, the greater mistake might be to reject evidence that is in support of the manipulation than to accept the value of the manipulation with reservations.

In applied memory research we need to conduct repeated studies in real-life situations until we have enough studies to carry out some form of meta-analysis. Then we have to live with less than scientific certainty and accept sensible judgment. Of course, we no longer have truth and certainty. What such tactics yield are approximations to the truth and the possibility of taking applied work further.

THE ACHIEVEMENTS OF THE EVERYDAY/APPLIED MEMORY MOVEMENT

Earlier we alluded to a variety of theoretical advances in our understanding of human memory stimulated by the everyday/applied memory movement (e.g, prospective memory, autobiographical memory, and maintenance of knowledge). In addition, the study of meta-memory (i.e., the knowledge that an individual has about the workings and content of his or her memory system) arguably started by examining a practical problem—how to overcome the tip-of-the-tongue phenomenon. Such phenomena have been studied extensively in the laboratory, but our understanding of them has benefited from diary studies of real-life experiences (Reason & Lucas, 1984). Each of these areas of study has been enriched by nonstandard modes of investigation.

In addition to theoretical advances, substantial progress has been made in the arena of actual application. At this point, a distinction advocated by Herrmann and Gruneberg (1993) and Gruneberg, Morris, Sykes, and Herrmann (1996) must be made between applicable research and actual application. Applicable research involves research of an applied nature that is usually conducted in a laboratory but, if exported to the outside world in a sustained and systematic way, would affect real-life application. Real-life application involves just that, applying the findings of the laboratory and/or trying to solve real-life problems *in situ*. This latter application often involves the development of cognitive technology in its widest sense (i.e., procedures or products that can be widely applied in the real world).

Both laboratory and nonlaboratory studies have contributed to finding empirical truths at the level of applicable research. In solving practical problems, the issue is not whether laboratory or nonlaboratory studies are better, in general, but what type of investigatory strategy is appropriate in a given set of circumstances. In this chapter we can do no more than "cherry-pick" what we feel are some of the major findings of practical significance (for many more findings of practical import, interested readers are referred to Baddeley, Wilson, & Watts, 1995; Brandimonte et al., 1996; Cohen, 1996; Gruneberg & Morris, 1992b; Gruneberg, Morris, & Sykes, 1978, 1988; Herrmann, McEvoy, Hertzog, Hertel, & Johnson, 1996; Payne & Conrad, 1997).

Eyewitness Research

Perhaps the most successful area in applied memory research in terms of generating a body of useful findings is eyewitness research. The early work of Loftus and Palmer (1974) showed how eyewitness accuracy was affected by slight differences in how questions are asked. A study by Loftus, Miller, and Burns (1978) demonstrated the postevent information effect: When misleading information was presented after an event was witnessed, recall for the event was compromised. The postevent information effect is one of the best established truths in eyewitness research. However, another important finding with practical significance is that in lineups of potential perpetrators of criminal activity, false-positive identifications are considerably reduced if witnesses make a yes–no judgment of each suspect in turn rather than choosing from an array of suspects all present and lined up at the same time (Sporer, Malpass, & Koehnken, 1996).

The Repressed Memory Controversy

One controversial area that has captured the attention of eyewitness memory researchers, as well as cognitive and clinical psychologists more generally, is the "repressed" or "false memory" debate discussed elsewhere in this volume. The clearest findings to date in this contentious area are that it is possible to implant false memories that subjects insist are true (Loftus & Ketcham, 1994). The great concern is that some therapists might initiate treatment with a hypothesis that their client's problem is related to childhood sexual abuse and subtly "plant" that possibility in the client's mind, after which the client may come to mistakenly believe it is a real memory. This does not, of course, mean that all memories are false. Indeed, Pope (1996) questions whether current research on the false memory syndrome is relevant to highly emotional memories such as child sexual abuse memories.

Just as problematic as the instantiation of false memories in clients by way of suggestive therapeutic procedures might be what Payne and Blackwell (Chapter 2, this volume) term "reperception." For example, almost all parents take part in bathing their children, in cleaning, and in hugging and caressing behavior after children have hurt themselves. In bathing children, genital areas are often touched as part of the cleaning process. Such activities are entirely healthy, natural, and universal. Yet under certain circumstances, someone who remembers incidents in an innocent light might be induced to construe such contact in a sinister light, and, for example, "reperceive" the events as "abusive."

The problem is that the consequences of a "mistake"—either of accepting a false memory as valid or, conversely, of mislabeling a memory of a real historical event as a false memory—are considerable. To deny the genuine suffering caused by sexual abuse can have disastrous consequences, as can implicating innocent parents as abusers, a charge that can demolish the family unit.

There is no doubt that child abuse occurs and is, in fact, a widespread problem. The recent horrifying case of the Rosemary West murder trial in the United Kingdom is just one example. In this instance, West persuaded her 8-year-old daughter that sexual abuse perpetrated by her husband was normal. Moreover, a survey by Polusny and Follette (1996) found that the majority of clinical psychologists who dealt with child abuse cases in the previous 12 months noted that clients who reported sexual abuse almost always did so *before* therapy commenced, which would seem to counter the charge of therapist influence. It is certainly possible to acknowledge the terrible reality of child abuse while also acknowledging that it is possible to implant false memories that are held with great conviction. Although ethical considerations preclude testing whether it is possible to implant memories of child sexual abuse, it is reasonable to infer that this could be done.

It is worth noting that despite the important input of memory researchers in calling for caution about arriving at premature conclusions regarding the false memory controversy, the debate has had two unfortunate side effects. The first is that the focus on the possibilty of false memories of childhood sexual abuse detracts from the fact that the majority of individuals receiving therapy for this problem had memories of the abuse before therapy started (Polusny & Follette, 1996). It is imperative that the discussion of the false memory syndrome not detract from the real distress experienced by many sexual abuse survivors, or from the value of clinical work with this population. The danger is that the profession of clinical psychology is being "overcriticized" for a problem whose true dimensions are difficult, if not impossible, to establish (Pope, 1996).

Pope (1996) also draws attention to a second unfortunate side effect of the false memory debate. He observes that scientific evaluation appears to be giving way to unscientific intolerance in the academic community, where, in certain instances, those who hold opposing views are being demonized to the point that it has been suggested that their books be banned. As Pope (1996) points out, at a scientific level, at least, the case for either side—that repressed memories can be exhumed in therapy or that experiments showing that false memories generated in the laboratory can be generalized to actual cases of child sexual abuse—has yet to be conclusively made. Our position, as noted earlier, is that both possibilites are potentially viable and that caution, patience, and tolerance are required to achieve resolution of the questions that are at the heart of current controversies.

Memory Improvement

Memory improvement is an area in which applied research has made significant progress. Apart from confirming that imagery strategies are effective in a number of everyday tasks such as face–name association, foreign vocabulary acquisition, and the recall of ideas, recent research also shows that strategies can facilitate the learning of number sequences and can be applied to examination preparation, learning in the elderly, and learning in the neurologically impaired. Sheikh, Hill, and Yesavage (1987), for example, found that learning of name–face associations could be facilitated in the elderly for up to 6 months after initial learning, and Wilson (1987) used imagery strategies to help elderly brain-damaged patients to acquire the names of those around them (see Gruneberg, 1992; Herrmann, Weingartner, Searleman, & McAvoy, 1992; Higbee, 1988, for reviews of memory improvement).

Many other strategies facilitate memory ranging from the spaced retrieval strategy (Landauer & Bjork, 1978) to strategies for enhancing retrieval such as context reinstatement (Wilkinson, 1988), repeated recall attempts (Payne & Wenger, 1992), and the retrieval strategies that comprise the cognitive interview (Geiselman & Fisher, 1987). Furthermore, there is a growing realization that memory improvement depends on a considerable range of "nonmemory" factors such as physical health, mental well-being, and self-efficacy (Herrmann & Searleman, 1990).

Work on memory in the elderly has also achieved a great deal of attention (see West & Sinnott, 1992). One welcome development is an improvement in the ability to differentiate behaviors associated with normal aging memory loss versus behaviors associated with Alzheimer's and other memory-damaging diseases. Advances in the management of Alzheimer's patients have been spurred by evidence that both implicit and motor memory may be relatively preserved, making it possible to improve adapation in the home by way of cuing patients' recall. Camp and McKitrick (1992), for example, found that spaced practice in Alzheimer's patients promoted implicit learning of name–face associations.

Additional work has focused on helping the elderly with memory problems concerning future actions (i.e., prospective memory), with related technological developments including pillboxes designed to signal to patients when it is time to take their next medication, and to remind people where they have parked their cars. Camp and Foss (1997) reported that they "solved" a major social problem experienced by an elderly person who could not remember she had been fed supper and became angry when she was refused further food. The simple expedient involved leaving cues to previous meals that were prominently displayed—unwashed dishes! It is worth emphasizing that small advances in application can reap major social benefits.

Cognitive Rehabilitation

Recent developments in the field of applied memory have contributed to the cognitive rehabilitation of neurologically damaged persons (Parente & Herrmann, 1996). Because neurological damage following car accidents, for example, is a major problem affecting young and old alike, advances in this area are likely to have long-term benefits for many patients. Of course, one cannot retrieve what is not retrievable, but several studies demonstrate that it is possible to adapt the environment to ensure that appropriate cuing leads to a continuation or implementation of acquired behavior. Glisky and Schacter (1987), for example, show how a computer program that trained individuals with a method known as vanishing cues (where learners are taught to rely on fewer and fewer cues over time) led to one amnesiac patient gaining employment as a computer programmer.

Relatively simple yet important environmental modifications reported by Wilson (1995) involved painting the men's and women's toilet doors a different color and getting care providers to wear name badges to facilitate appropriate social behaviors. An interesting approach devised by Parente, Elliot, and Twum (1996) involves using large financial inducements to improve the atttention and cognitive functioning of brain-damaged individuals. It is notable that the examples reported represent highlights from a much larger body of findings that, in their totality, evidence the breadth and depth of progress that has been made in applied memory research.

ACTUAL APPLICATION AND COGNITIVE TECHNOLOGY: PROBLEMS OF ATTITUDE

Yet relative to what is known about memory and the potential application of memory strategies and techniques to improve the human condition, progress has been slower at the level of actual application (Gruneberg et al. 1996; Herrmann & Gruneberg, 1993; Herrmann & Raybeck, 1996). This is not because real-life problems are insoluble; rather, it is because the social climate in academia does not encourage and may, in fact, discourage academic careers that focus on applied memory research.

Banaji and Crowder (1991) capture what we believe may be an all too prevalent attitude among certain academics: "We would be delighted to see a Steve Jobs of human memory technology emerge some day but we are of the belief that our goal is to advance science and not come up with an occasional memory aid" (p. 48). We believe this position is ill advised for at least two reasons. First, technological advance often feeds into theoretical understanding and can provide guideposts and methods for addressing and assessing theoretical questions. Second, without a significant and increasing output of pragmatic and useful findings and applications, basic research is perceived as irrelevant and self-indulgent to those who ultimately pay for the research—the public.

In addition to the current academic climate that does little if anything to foster the develoment of new technologies, other factors that impede the application process include the difficulty of publishing applied research in high-level journals, the fact that applied research is often more time-consuming than basic research, the perception that financial gains made by application somehow corrupt scientific standards or the researchers themselves, and the fact that communicating with the public is not a high priority of academic research (see Gruneberg et al., 1996, for a full discussion of these issues). There are, however, a number of hopeful develoments that may diminish some of these problems in the future.

First, a learned society devoted to the application of research in memory and cognition (SARMAC) was recently established and has already attracted a considerable membership and established a successful series of conferences. Second, a journal, *Cognitive Technology*, has been established to publish articles of an applied rather than an applicable nature. And third, as the saying goes, "Nothing succeeds like success": A growing body of useful applied knowledge and technological advances are likely to attract researchers to the area of aplied memory research.

A Case Study of Successful Application

One major success story, which is a paradigm case of real-life aplication, is the development of the cognitive interview by Geiselman and his colleagues (see Geiselman & Fisher, 1997, for a review). Starting with Tulving's work on cue-dependent forgetting, Geiselman and his colleagues assembled a set of retrieval strategies which they found produced greater recall than uninstructed recall. The improvement in recall with such retrieval strategies has been found to be substantial, with some studies showing gains on the order of 40% with respect to accurate retrieval, with little increase in inaccurate material. There are, of course, some failures to replicate these findings, but studies by a number of independent investigators imply that it is reasonably safe to conclude that memory gains associated with the cognitive interview are a robust phenomenon (see Sporer et al., 1996).

After Geiselman and his colleagues were convinced of the usefulness of their procedure, they conducted real-life fieldwork trials with police officers. These efforts revealed problems in variability of effectiveness of different interviewers and how training and modifying the techniques could surmount many of the problems encountered. Geiselman and his colleagues not only advanced their work from applicable to applied research but also were successful in convincing an initially skeptical "market"—police officers—that the cognitive interview was a useful and valuable technique. In the long run, human well-being will be enhanced if the cognitive interview does, indeed, increase the likelihood of more accurate eyewitness information, an achievement that would also increase the perceived relevance of psychology to society.

There are, of course, other areas of eyewitness research in which cognitive technology has enjoyed conserable success, including, among many examples, lineup research and videorecording of child witnesses. Outside the domain of eyewitness research, cognitive technology has been applied successfully in the develoment of external memory aids (see Herrmann & Petro, 1991), in facilitating human–computer interactions (Payne & Conrad, 1997), and in the area of cognitive rehabilitation, where psychologists such as Wilson, Cockburn, and Baddeley (1985) developed diagnostic tests of brain injury.

DISCUSSION

Overall, the achievements of applied memory research are considerable, despite the fact that compared to applicable research, real-life application is underdeveloped. Of course, all in the garden is not rosy. As we noted earlier, a climate still exists in which the pursuit of practical solutions to practical problems is regarded as a secondary, indeed second-rate activity. We are certainly not the first authors to point out that the argument about whether basic or applied research is "better" is futile. Indeed, few, if any, applied researchers would argue that basic research is devoid of value. To understand how to solve practical problems, it is often necessary to first understand underlying memory mechanisms (see Gruneberg, 1992). Time and again in the history of science, what seemed unimportant or merely curious becomes the starting point of a significant development. Nor need basic research justify its value in terms of the real-world applicability of any particular piece of work. It is justification enough that basic research advances our fundamental understanding of a particular or general phenomenon. That said, it is also true that the natural and biological sciences have gained enormously from the major applications that flow, in large measure, from fundamental scientific work. Without this flow of applications, it is anything but clear that funding for fundamental research in these areas would be forthcoming in amounts sufficient to support the global research agenda.

Our belief is that we have to do more than establish practical truths. We have to use them in a way that serves society. Yet the argument that it is necessary to "convince those outside" of the value of applied memory research is not the main impetus for applying memory research in the real world. Applied research for the benefit of society is for many of those involved in the applied memory movement the primary justification for the practice of psychology in the first place. The truths of psychology, if not used to benefit society, are arguably inconsequential truths. If the benefit of society is not one focus of our research, then the truths we seek are likely to end up, as Neisser noted in his 1978 address, as intellectually arid.

This is not to argue against the value of basic research. An understanding of the basic architecture of memory is of value in its own right as an intellectual achievement, and it is impossible to predict when the pursuit of "essential" truths in memory will reap practical rewards. However, the effort to understand basic memory mechanisms cannot be the only goal of memory researchers if the whole exercise of understanding memory is not to be jeopardized by a failure to meet the needs of society which pays for our intellectual curiosity in the first place.

REFERENCES

Baddeley, A. D. (1990). *Human memory: Theory and practice*. Hove, UK: L.E.A.

Baddeley, A. D., & Wilkins, A. J. (1984). Taking memory out of the laboratory. In J. Harris & P. E. Morris (Eds.), *Everyday memory, actions and absentmindedness* (pp. 1–17). London: Academic Press.

Baddeley, A. D., Wilson, B. A., & Watts, F. N. (Eds.). (1995). *Handbook of memory disorders*. Chichester, UK: Wiley.

Bahrick, H. P. (1984). Semantic memory in permastore: 50 years of memory for Spanish learned in school. *Journal of Experimental Psychology, 113*, 1–29.

Banaji, M. R., & Crowder, R. J. (1989). The bankruptcy of everyday memory. *American Psychologist, 44*, 1185–1193.

Banaji, M. R., & Crowder, R. J. (1991). Some everyday thoughts on ecologically valid methods. *American Psychologist, 46*, 78–79.

Bjork, R. A., & Landauer, T. K. (1978). On keeping track of the present status of people and things. In M. M. Gruneberg, P. E. Morris, & R. N. Sykes (Eds.), *Practical aspects of memory* (pp. 52–60). London: Academic Press.

Brandimonte, M. A., Einstein, G. O., & McDaniel, M. A. (1996). *Prospective memory: Theory and applications*. Mahwah, NJ: Erlbaum.

Camp, C. J., & Foss, J. N. (1997). Designing ecologically valid memory interventions for persons with dementia. In D. G. Payne & F. G. Conrad (Eds.), *Intersections of basic and applied memory research*. Mahwah, NJ: Erlbaum.

Camp, C. J., & McKitrick, L. A. (1992). Memory interventions in Alzheimer's-type dementia populations: Methodological and theoretical issues. In R. L. West & J. D. Sinnot (Eds.), *Everyday memory and ageing* (pp. 155–172). New York: Springer-Verlag.

Ceci, S., & Bronfenbrenner, U. (1991). On the demise of everyday memory: The rumors of my death are much exaggerated (Mark Twain). *American Psychologist, 46*, 27–31.

Cohen, G. (1996). *Memory in the real world* (2nd ed.). Hove, UK: Psychology Press.

Craik, F. I. M., & Lockart, R. S. (1972). Levels of processing: A framework for memory research. *Journal of Verbal Learning and Verbal Behavior, 11*, 671–687.

Deffenbacher, K. A. (1996). Updating the scientific validity of three key estimator variables in eyewitness testimony. In D. J. Herrmann, C. McAvoy, C. Hertzog, P. Hertel, & M. K. Johnson (Eds.), *Basic and applied memory research* (Vol. 1, pp. 421–438). Mahwah, NJ: Erlbaum.

Ebbinghaus, H. E. (1886). *Memory: A contribution to experimental psychology*. New York: Dover.

Geiselman, R. E., & Fisher, R. P. (1997). Ten years of cognitive interviewing. In D. G. Payne & F. G. Conrad (Eds.), *Intersections in basic and applied memory research* (pp. 291–310). Mahwah, NJ: Erlbaum.

Glisky, E. L., & Schachter, D. L. (1987). Long-term retention of computer learning by patients with memory disorders. *Neuropsychologia*, 173–178.

Gruneberg, M. M. (1992). The new approach to memory improvement: Problems and prospects. In D. J. Herrmann, H. Weingartner, A. Searleman, & C. McAvoy (Eds.), *Memory improvement: Implications for memory theory*. New York: Springer.

Gruneberg, M. M., & Morris, P. E. (1992a). Applying memory research. In M. M. Gruneberg & P. E. Morris (Eds.), *Aspects of memory: The practical aspects* (Vol. 1, 2nd ed., pp. 1–17). London: Routledge.

Gruneberg, M. M., & Morris, P. E. (Eds.). (1992b). *Aspects of memory: The practical aspects* (Vol. 1, 2nd ed.). London: Routledge.

Gruneberg, M. M., Morris, P. E., & Sykes, R. N. (Eds.). (1978). *Practical aspects of memory*. London: Academic Press.

Gruneberg, M. M., Morris, P. E., & Sykes, R. N. (Eds.). (1988). *Practical aspects of memory: Current research and issues* (2 vols.). Chichester: Wiley.

Gruneberg, M. M., Morris, P. E., Sykes, R. N., & Herrmann, D. J. (1996). The practical application of memory research: Practical problems in the relationship between theory and practice. In D. J. Herrmann, C. McAvoy, C. Herzog, P. Hertel, & M. K. Johnson (Eds.), *Basic and applied memory research: Vol. 2. Practical applications* (pp. 63–82). Mahwah, NJ: Erlbaum.

Gruneberg, M. M., & Sykes, R. N. (1981). Eyewitness accuracy and feelings of certainty. *IRCS Medical Science*, *9*, 935–936.

Gruneberg, M. M., & Sykes, R. N. (1993). The generalizability of confidence-accuracy studies in eyewitnessing. *Memory*, *1*, 185–189.

Harris, J. (1978). External memory aids. In M. M. Gruneberg, P. E. Morris, & R. N. Sykes (Eds), *Practical aspects of memory*. London: Academic Press.

Herrmann, D. J., & Gruneberg, M. M. (1993). The need to expand the horizons of the practical aspects of memory. *Applied Cognitive Psychology*, *7*, 553–566.

Herrmann, D. J., McAvoy, C., Hertzog, C., Hertel, P., & Johnson, M. K. (Eds.). (1996). *Basic and applied memory research* (2 vols.). Mahwah, NJ: Erlbaum.

Herrmann, D. J., & Petro, S. (1991). Commercial memory aids. *Applied Cognitive Psychology*, *4*, 439–450.

Herrmann, D. J., & Raybeck, D. (1996). A clash of cultures and basic and applied cognitive researchy. In D. Payne & F. Conrad (Eds.), *Intersections in basic and applied memory research* (pp. 24–44). Mahwah, NJ: Erlbaum.

Herrmann, D. J., & Searleman, A. L. (1990). The new multimodal approach to memory improvement. In G.H. Bower (Ed.), *Advances in learning and motivation* (pp. 26, 175, 205). New York: Academic Press.

Herrmann, D. J., Weingartner, H., Searleman, A., & McAvoy, C. (1992). *Memory improvements: Implications for memory theory*. New York: Springer-Verlag.

Higbee, K. (1988). *Your memory*. Englewood Cliffs, NJ: Prentice-Hall.

Johnson, M. T. (1993). Memory phenomena in the law. *Applied Cognitive Psychology*, *7*, 603–618.

Kihlstrom, J. F. (1996). Memory research: The convergence of theory and practice. In D. Herrmann, C. McAvoy, C. Hertzog, P. Hertel, & M. K. Johnson (Eds.), *Basic and applied memory research: Vol. 1. Theory and context.* (pp. 5–25). Mahwah, NJ: Erlbaum.

Landauer, T. K., & Bjork, R. A. (1978). Optimal rehearsal patterns and name learning. In M. M. Gruneberg, P. E. Morris, & R. N. Sykes (Eds.), *Practical aspects of memory* (pp. 625–632). London: Academic Press.

Linton, M. (1975). Memory for real-world events. In D. A. Norman & E. D. Rumelhart (Eds.), *Explorations in cognition.* San Francisco: Freeman.

Linton, M. (1978). Real-world memory after six years: An in vivo study of very long-term memory. In M. M. Gruneberg, P. E. Morris, & R. N. Sykes (Eds.), *Practical aspects of memory* (pp. 69–76). London: Academic Press.

Loftus, E.F., & Ketcham, K. (1994). *The myth of repressed memory: False memories and allegations of sexual abuse.* New York: St. Martin's Press.

Loftus, E. F., & Palmer, J. C. (1974). reconstruction of an automobile deconstruction: An example of the interaction between language and memory. *Journal of Verbal Learning and Verbal Behavior, 13,* 585–589.

Loftus, E. F., Miller, D. G., & Burns, H. J. (1978). Semantic integration of verbal information into a visual memory. *Journal of Experimental Psychology: Human Learning and Memory, 4,* 19–31.

Morris, P.E., & Gruneberg, M. M. (1994). The major aspects of memory. In P. E. Morris & M. M. Gruneberg (Eds.), *Aspects of memory: Vol. 2. The theoretical aspects* (pp. 29–49). London: Routledge.

Morris, P. E., Gruneberg, M. M., Sykes, R. N., & Merrick, A. (1981). Football knowledge and the acquisition of new results. *British Journal of Psychology, 72,* 479–483.

Morris, P. E., Tweedy, M., & Gruneberg, M. M. (1985). Interest, knowledge, and the memory of soccer scores. *British Journal of Psychology, 76,* 417–425.

Neisser, U. (1978). Memory: What are the important questions? In M. M. Gruneberg, P. E. Morris, & R. N. Sykes (Eds.), *Practical aspects of memory* (pp. 3–24). London: Academic Press.

Parente, R., Elliott, A., & Twum, M. (1996). Curious memory phenomena: Implications for treatment after traumatic brain injury. In D. J. Herrmann, C. McAvoy, C. Hertzog, P. Hertel, & M. K. Johnson (Eds.), *Basic and applied memory research: Vol. 2. Theory and context* (pp. 455–468). Mahwah, NJ: Erlbaum.

Parente, R., & Herrmann, D. J. (1996). *Retraining cognition.* Gaithersburg, MD: Aspen.

Payne, D. G., & Conrad, F. G. (Eds.). (1997). *Intersections in basic and applied research.* Mahwah, NJ: Erlbaum.

Payne, D. G., & Wenger, M. J. (1992). Improving memory through practice In D. J. Herrmann, C. McAvoy, C. Hertzog, P. Hertel, & M. K. Johnson (Eds.), *Basic and applied memory research: Vol. 2. Theory and context* (pp. 184–209). Mahwah, NJ: Erlbaum.

Polusny, M. A., & Follette, V. M. (1996). Remembering childhood sexual abuse: A national survey of psychologists, clinical practice, beliefs, and personal experiences. *Journal of Professional Psychology, 27,* 41–52.

Pope, K. S. (1996). Memory abuse and science: Questioning claims about the false memory syndrome. *American Psychologist, 51,* 957–974.

Reason, J. T., & Lucas, D. (1984). Using cognitive diaries to investigate naturally occurring memory blocks. In J. E. Harris & P. E. Morris (Eds.), *Everyday memory, actions, and absentmindedness* (pp. 53–70). London: Academic Press.

Robinson, M. D., & Johnson, J. T. (1996). Recall memory, recognition memory, and the eyewitness cofidence-accuracy correlation. *Journal of Applied Psychology, 81*, 587–594.

Rubin, D. (Ed.). (1996). *Remembering the past*. Cambridge, UK: Cambridge University Press.

Sheikh, J. I., Hill, R. D., & Yesavage, J. A. (1987). Long-term efficacy of cognitive training for age associated memory impairment: A six month follow-up study. *Developmental Neuropsychology, 2*, 413–421.

Sporer, S. L., Malpass, R. S., & Koehnken, G. (Eds.). (1996). *Psychological issues in eyewitness research*. Mahwah, NJ: Erlbaum.

Underwood, B. J., Borsch, R. F., & Malmi, R. A. (1978). Composition of episodic memory. *Journal of Experimental Psychology: General, 107*, 393–419.

West, R. L., & Sinnot, J. D. (Eds.). (1992). *Everyday memory and aging*. New York: Springer-Verlag.

Wilkins, A. J., & Baddeley, A. D. (1978). Remembering to recall in everyday life: An approach to absentmindedness. In M. M. Gruneberg, P. E. Morris, & R. N. Sykes (Eds.), *Practical aspects of memory* (pp. 27–34). London: Academic Press.

Wilkinson, J. (1988). Context effects in childen's event memory. In M. M. Gruneberg, P. E. Morris, & R. N. Sykes (Eds.), *Practical aspects of memory: Current research and issues* (Vol. 1, pp. 107–111). Chichester: Wiley.

Wilson, B. A. (1987). *Rehabilitation of memory*. New York: Guilford Press.

Wilson, B. A. (1995). Management and remediation of memory problems in brain injured adults. In A. D. Baddeley, B. A. Wilson, & F. N. Watts (Eds.), *Handbook of memory disorders* (pp. 451–480). Chichester, UK: Wiley.

Wilson, B. A., Cockburn, J., & Baddeley, A. D. (1985). *The Rivermead Behavioral Memory Test manual*. Reading, UK: Thames Valley Test Co.

Yuille, J. C., & Cutshall, J. L. (1986). A case study of everyday eyewitness memory of a crime. *Journal of Applied Psychology, 71*, 291–301.

CHAPTER 19

DEPOLARIZING VIEWS ON RECOVERED MEMORY EXPERIENCES

D. Stephen Lindsay

When I first began writing and speaking about the recovered memories controversy in 1993, my primary objective was to persuade trauma-oriented practitioners of the potential risks of therapeutic approaches intended to help clients "explore the possibility" that they have nonremembered histories of childhood sexual abuse (CSA). I use the term "memory-recovery work" to refer to such approaches. I am not going to belabor the point here, but I believe that there is solid ground to believe that over the last decade a small percentage of therapists have used approaches to memory-recovery work that inadvertently led substantial numbers of clients to develop illusory memories and/or false beliefs in nonexperienced CSA (see, e.g., Lindsay & Read, 1994, 1995; Loftus, 1993; Pendergrast, 1996; Poole, Lindsay, Memon, & Bull, 1995). I have always sought to make this argument in ways that do not undermine support for victims of CSA, but nonetheless in the last year or two I have become increasingly concerned about the extent to which criticisms of potentially suggestive therapies may contribute to an antivictim and antitherapist "backlash." Furthermore, I am concerned that polarization around this topic may sustain extremist views on both sides. Thus I find my own agenda shifting slightly, from a focus on criticizing suggestive approaches to a focus on reducing polarization and enhancing communication with the aim of cultivating an approach that equally emphasizes the importance of supporting genuine victims of CSA and the importance of minimizing the risk of iatrogenic illusory memories and false beliefs.

In this chapter, I focus on a consideration of certain aspects of the recovered memories controversy that contribute to its difficulty and contentiousness and summarize my views of what existing scientific evidence does and does not yet allow us to say about recovered memory experiences.

PSYCHOSOCIAL DYNAMICS

Lindsay and Briere (1997) offer an analysis of some of the many psychosocial factors that exacerbate the contentiousness of the recovered memories controversy. Some of the factors considered are specific to the topic of recovered memories. For example, (1) CSA is an intrinsically upsetting topic, and one that is related to more general sociopolitical issues having to do with Western society's long history of political–physical–sexual–economic oppression of women, (2) there is a long-standing tension between experimentalist research psychologists and clinical psychologists, and (3) many participants in the debate have some degree of personal involvement in it (trauma-oriented therapists who do difficult work and now find themselves threatened and attacked, psychologists who have worked with people they believe have been falsely accused on the basis of recovered memories, etc.). Also discussed in Lindsay and Briere (1997) is the role of more general characteristics of life in the 1990s, such as the polarizing influence of sensationalized popular media presentations on either side of the controversy[1]; the ease with which people can disseminate their views, unreviewed, via electronic communication systems and, relatedly, the extent to which some professionals involved in the debate appear to have relied on secondhand accounts; and our culture's passion for litigation, which threatens the reputations and financial security of accused parents and accused therapists.

Also considered in Lindsay and Briere (1997) are some even more general factors that may contribute to polarization of discussion of virtually any socially divisive issue. For example, evidence (recently reviewed in an excellent article by Keltner & Robinson, 1996) is cited regarding individuals' perceptions of the opposing positions on socially divisive issues. A consistent finding in this research is that people dramatically overestimate the extremity and the uniformity of the views held by individuals on the opposing sides. What is most striking is that people often tend to exaggerate the extremity and uniformity of beliefs among members of their own side as well as among the opposition. One interesting consequence is that many individuals describe themselves as "lonely moderates" on socially divisive issues. I found this observation and Keltner and Robinson's discussions of the psychological processes that contribute to it particularly fascinating because I have often fancied myself a "lonely moderate" on the recovered memories controversy. This social psychological research encourages me to believe that many readers, too, will view themselves as holding moderate views on the issues at hand; perhaps with better efforts toward communication moderates can begin to feel a bit less lonely.

Another general-level contributor to the contentiousness of the recovered memories controversy discussed in Lindsay and Briere (1997) is the human tendency to simplify and dichotomize complex phenomena, using language (if not ideas) that describes subtle and multifaceted phenomena in stark, black-and-white terms. I do not mean to suggest that psychologists have explicitly made dichotomized arguments, but rather, that dichotomizing often creeps into our language in ways that may be unhelpful. For example, participants in this debate often use language that implies that people can be neatly divided into those who experienced CSA and those who did not. Of course, this would be true if we had a widely agreed-on operational definition of CSA with good reliability, but in fact ideas about what does and does not constitute CSA are often not only vague but unstated. Moreover, even if we did have an operational definition that reliably divided the world into two groups (abused and not abused), both categories would consist of people with a wide variety of histories, and attention to such differences may be important if we are to make progress on understanding memory for and forgetting and rerememebering of CSA.

Similarly, participants in the debate sometimes use language that implies that therapists either do or do not use potentially suggestive forms of memory-recovery work (i.e., practices intended to help clients remember suspected hidden histories of CSA). Yet it is likely that approaches to memory-recovery work range across a wide continuum, from practices that likely pose little if any risk of iatrogenic illusory memories or false beliefs regarding CSA to those that likely pose substantial risk. It is true that existing science is insufficient to enable precise specification of which approaches do and do not pose substantial risk, but although this ignorance may contribute to the tendency to use dichotomizing language, it does not justify it.

Dichotomizing language also creeps into descriptions of adult survivors' memories of CSA: Discussions sometimes imply that adult CSA victims neatly divide into those who have always remembered the abuse in full detail versus those who have always been completely amnestic about the abuse. Critics of memory-recovery work (including me) have tended to focus their discussions almost exclusively on cases in which an adult who initially denies any history of CSA, and appears to have had a more or less normal childhood, later reports new memories of repeated and extreme CSA. There is no doubt about the existence of such cases, but I see little reason to believe that they are the norm. For example, in some other cases, people may know that abuse occurred but not be able to recollect any specific episodic details.[2] In some cases, people who previously (during adulthood) reported histories of CSA later falsely believe they had no awareness of an abuse history until they had a dramatic memory-recovery experience (see Schooler, Ambadar, & Bendiksen, 1997). In yet other cases, people who experienced an isolated instance of CSA may recollect some details but not others, and people who experienced multiple instances of CSA may recollect some instances but not others. In the latter sort of case, some such people may later report recovered memory experiences that are consistent with the sorts of abuse they have always remembered, and others may later report memories of qualitatively more extreme kinds of abuse. And, of course, many abuse victims remember their abuse all too well. The point is that dichotomizing adults with CSA histories into those who have always versus never remembered the abuse may not be helpful.

Perhaps the most pernicious of dichotomizations in this controversy are the ones between those who take the view that all (or virtually all) recovered memory experiences are essentially accurate versus those who take the view that all (or virtually all) are essentially false. As discussed in the next section, I believe that this dichotomization is in error, that it partly arises from inconsistent use of poorly defined terms, and that it results in misunderstandings that have played a major role in inflaming the controversy about recovered memories of CSA.

Before leaving this section, I want to emphasize that the extent to which proponents of different sides of the recovered memories controversy take dichotomized, extremist views has sometimes been exaggerated. That is, polarization on the various issues may be more illusory than real, or at least may be an exception rather than the rule. For example, my impression is that the False Memory Syndrome Foundation (FMSF) and prominent critics of memory-recovery work, such as Elizabeth F. Loftus (1993), are often perceived by trauma-oriented clinicians as asserting that all recovered memory reports reflect iatrogenic illusions. Certainly the FMSF and many psychologists critical of memory-recovery work have vehemently attacked the notion of "massive repression" (see next section) and have strongly emphasized their belief that iatrogenic false memories occur and are a serious problem, but very few have asserted that recovered memory reports are always false. When I recently put the question to several prominent critics of memory-recovery work, they strenuously denied saying, believing, or meaning to imply that all recovered memory reports are false (Pamela Freyd, personal communication, April 21, 1997; Elizabeth F. Loftus, personal communication, April 21, 1997; Mark Pendergrast, personal communication, April 22, 1997). (For published statements to this effect, see, e.g., Freyd, 1997, p. 1; Lindsay & Read, 1994, pp. 281–282; Loftus, 1993, pp. 524, 533; Pendergrast, 1996, pp. 71, 91, 536; Underwager & Wakefield, Chapter 16, this volume.)

The exaggerated perception of extremity may partly have to do with the one-sided focus of materials on either side of the debate. For example, critics of recovered memory work quite understandably focus on the potential risk of false recovered memory experiences, and countercritics equally understandably focus on evidence for accurate recovered memory experiences. Misperceptions of the extremity of claims made on either side of the controversy may also partly have to do with biases on the part of readers producing distorted perceptions. Consistent with the latter possibility, I have had the honor of being mischaracterized by some people as arguing that "recovered memories are false" and mischaracterized by other people as arguing that "recovered memories are true." As per Keltner and Robinson's (1996) article, it may be helpful if participants in this debate strive to resist the tendency to assume that those on the opposing side of the issue all hold common and extreme views. Finally, as discussed in the next section, different under-standings of the term "recovered memories" may also have contributed to exaggerated perceptions of the extremity of the views held by opposing sides of the recovered memories controversy.

RECOVERED MEMORY EXPERIENCES

The term "recovered memories" is a vexing one, for two reasons. First, for many readers the term means "repressed and then recovered memories," and hence any statement allowing for accurate recovered memories is taken by such readers as affirming the existence of a special repression mechanism. Indeed, for some readers the term "recovered memories" means "instantly-completely-repressed-and-then-recovered-in-pristine-form-via-suggestive-memory-recovery-work-memories-of-years-of-extreme-CSA." It may seem ridiculous that a term could carry this much baggage (indeed, I think it *is* ridiculous), but nonetheless it appears that this is the case for a substantial percentage of critics of memory-recovery work. Thus, for example, a statement such as "it is likely that most recovered memories are essentially accurate" is understood by some to mean that most cases in which people who appear to have had normal childhoods and who initially disclaimed an abuse history but who later reported new memories of years of brutal victimization are essentially accurate. Of course, some therapists do believe that most such cases are accurate (and, as reported by Qin, Goodman, Bottoms, & Shaver, Chapter 10, this volume, a very small percentage of clinicians report large numbers of clients with recovered memories of this form). Nonetheless, it is my belief that the fact that the term "recovered memories" carries this kind of baggage for some participants in the debate but not for others has greatly hampered mutual understanding.

A second drawback of the term "recovered memories" is that the words themselves imply that the phenomenon is necessarily one of recovering accurate memories. Clearly, the term was used initially because those who coined it believed that this was what happened whenever a person reported remembering previously nonremembered CSA. Just as cleary, this is precisely the main bone of contention, and it is not helpful that the term used to label the phenomenon to be explained (reports of remembering CSA that the person believes was previously not remembered) implies a particular expla-nation (retrieval of memories of CSA).

Schooler et al. (1997) proposed the term "discovered memories," because it (1) focuses attention on the central phenomenon to be explained (the subjective experience of "discovering" new material about one's past) and (2) does not imply a particular mechanism, such as recovery from repression, for this phenomenon. I agree that "discovered memories" is an improvement over "recovered memories," but both terms imply that the phenomenon involves memory retrieval. My current preference is to use the term "recovered memory experiences" (RMEs). Though somewhat ungainly, this term makes contact with existing terminology yet emphasizes that it is the subjective experience that constitutes the phenomenon to be explained.

MECHANISMS OF FORGETTING CSA

Most proponents of approaches to psychotherapy that include attempts to foster RMEs use the term "repression" to account for cases in which a person is thought to have a history of nonremembered CSA. These writers differ widely—one might almost say wildly—in what they appear to have in mind when they use the term "repression." At one extreme, the term refers to a hypothesized special mechanism, qualitatively different from and perhaps even based in different brain regions than the processes that govern ordinary forgetting. With the special mechanism, the mind more or less instantly encapsulates more or less perfect records of traumatic experiences and maintains them in pristine form outside consciousness unless and until they are recovered. Various less extreme (and, in my view, less ridiculous) variations of the special-mechanism hypothesis include those in which repression is not assumed to be instant but rather to occur gradually over extended periods and those in which the encapsulated memories are not held to be complete and perfect. I refer to such hypotheses, collectively, as "special-mechanism repression." At another extreme, the term "repression" is used relatively loosely to refer to processes (perhaps simply those of ordinary forgetting) that lead to nonremembering of childhood events that one would, intuitively, have expected people to remember. For example, an abuse victim may avoid thinking about the to-be-forgotten event and avoid environmental cues likely to stimulate retrieval of such memories and hence eventually develop a "habit of forgetting" (Larry L. Jacoby, personal communication, 1990) the event. At this extreme, "repression" does not appear to differ from the motivated use of ordinary mechanisms of forgetting, and hence I refer to these hypothesized mechanisms of forgetting CSA as "ordinary forgetting."

I am skeptical of the existence of special-mechanism repression. My skepticism is strongest for the most extreme claims (as described earlier) but extends to all claims of a special mechanism, unique to CSA or trauma, by which memories are formed and maintained but excluded from consciousness in such a way that they could later be retrieved (see Pope & Hudson, 1995). As noted by Payne and Blackwell (Chapter 2, this volume), ideas about the special quality of traumatic memories are similar to ideas about the uniqueness of so-called flashbulb memories (e.g., vivid and detailed recollections of the experience of learning of a momentous event, such as Kennedy's assassination or the Challenger disaster). In the original article on this hypothesized phenomenon, Brown and Kulik (1977) proposed that we may be biologically equipped with a special "now print!" mechanism that engages on such occasions and takes a snapshot of all brain activity, subsequently giving rise to vivid multimodal memories. People can and do experience extraordinarily detailed recollections, but such recollections (1) are not necessarily accurate, (2) appear to be affected by the same variables that are known to affect other recollections, and (3) are not restricted to momentous events (see, e.g., Winograd & Neisser, 1992, for reviews). In the words of Christianson (1989), flashbulb memories are "special, but not so special." Although the science base is too limited at present to justify definitive claims, my suspicion is that trauma memories, too, will turn out to be special, but not so special. Specifically, it is likely that variables such as arousal, salience, perceptual intensity, attention, distinctiveness, and rehearsal play major roles in producing differences between memories of CSA versus memories of mundane events, but at present I see little reason to conclude that CSA or trauma engages a special and separate memory system that differs in qualitative ways from ordinary memory.

Does the existence of accurate RMEs hinge on the existence of special-mechanism repression? That is, if research somehow definitively determined that there is no special mechanism that handles forgetting of CSA, would that mean that all RMEs are false? The answer to that question depends on whether or not mechanisms of ordinary memory could account for cases in which abuse victims forget about the abuse for extended periods, in the sense of not remembering the abuse even when prompted to search for such memories, and then later recover such memories.

From my perspective, it seems extremely likely that people can forget and then later remember at least some kinds of CSA histories via ordinary mechanisms of memory. Existing evidence indicates that, all else being equal, people are less likely to forget highly salient and/or repeated experiences than mundane or one-time experiences, which suggests that most people who experienced extreme and/or repeated CSA after the age of 3 or 4 years are aware of having such a history (e.g., Koss, Tromp, & Tharan, 1995). But that does not mean that there are no adults who experienced CSA who are unaware of their abuse histories. It is well established that people sometimes forget quite dramatic life events. In addition to the recent surveys demonstrating that substantial percentages of people who report CSA also report prior periods of not remembering CSA (e.g., Briere & Conte, 1993; Feldman-Summers & Pope, 1994; cf. Read, 1997) and several compelling case studies of RMEs (e.g., Corwin & Olafson, 1997; Dalenberg, 1997; Schooler et al., 1997), there are a variety of prospective studies in which people apparently failed to remember quite well-documented and quite dramatic events, including CSA (e.g., Loftus, 1993, p. 522; Widom, 1997; Williams, 1995). It is also well established that memories that are inaccessible under some conditions can be retrieved under other conditions, as anyone who has revisited childhood haunts can attest. Overall, it would be difficult to argue that ordinary mechanisms of memory cannot lead people to forget and then reremember CSA.

Although scientific data on the issue are lacking, and would be difficult to obtain, it seems likely that there are limits on the sorts of histories that can be forgotten via ordinary forgetting. For example, it seems unlikely that ordinary forgetting could lead a person to be unaware of years of violent abuse such that they would think they had a normal relationship with a parent who repeatedly raped and tortured them. Because it seems unlikely that ordinary forgetting could lead to forgetting of repeated and extreme abuse, and because I think that the evidence for special-mechanism repression is weak, I am skeptical of cases in which a person initially appeared to remember no abuse and then subsequently experienced recovered memories of years of extreme abuse. My skepticism is further fueled if there is evidence that the "memories" were recovered via prolonged, multifaceted, socially influenced recovered memory work. On the other hand, I see no reason to doubt that ordinary forgetting mechanisms can sometimes lead people to forget isolated instances of CSA, especially if the abuse was not physically violent or intensely salient when it occurred. Retrospective self-report studies suggest that the most common forms of CSA involve one or a few isolated instances of nonviolent abuse (e.g., Finkelhor, 1994). Given what we know about memory and remembering, it seems likely that some adults who experienced such abuse will fail to remember it in adulthood, and that some such adults could recover essentially accurate memories of the abuse if appropriately cued.

I have argued so far in this chapter and elsewhere (e.g., Lindsay & Read, 1994) that ordinary forgetting mechanisms cannot easily account for cases in which adults who initially appeared to believe that their childhoods were more or less normal later experience recovered memories of years of brutal CSA. Many other critics of recovered memory work have made this argument as well, which may have contributed to the misperception that critics are claiming that all RMEs are false. As noted earlier, even if this argument is correct it does not suggest that all or even most RMEs are false because many RMEs may be of less extreme experiences that could well be forgotten via ordinary mechanisms. Moreover, we really do not know what kinds of events can versus cannot be forgotten via ordinary forgetting mechanisms. Most memory researchers seem to have the intuition that people could not forget violent and/or repeated CSA via ordinary forgetting. Combined with skepticism regarding special-mechanism repression, this amounts to a hypothesis that people cannot forget such experiences, but we lack sufficient long-term prospective studies to assess the accuracy of this intuition. Generally, even if the intuition is accurate, it is not clear just how memorable an event must be before it becomes essentially impossible for people to forget it via ordinary mechanisms.

MECHANISMS OF ILLUSORY MEMORIES/FALSE BELIEFS

Ample evidence supports the claim that people can develop illusory memories or false beliefs of CSA that they did not really experience (see, e.g., Coons,

1994; Goldstein & Farmer, 1992, 1993; Lindsay & Read, 1995; Loftus & Ketcham, 1994; Pendergrast, 1996; Spanos, 1994; Underwager & Wakefield, Chapter 16, this volume). It seems likely that false RMEs usually arise through a constellation of fairly powerful suggestive influences, perhaps sometimes augmented by a high level of vulnerability on the part of the recipient of those influences. That is, there is little reason to think that people are likely to develop false RMEs spontaneously or in response to a few suggestive questions. As Pendergrast (1996) argued, a few suggestive comments may sometimes be sufficient to set in motion a sequence of events that will bring substantial suggestive pressures to bear (e.g., a suggestion that current psychological problems might arise from hidden memories of CSA could lead a person to buy self-help books on memory recovery which could in turn lead the person to seek out questionable forms of therapy, join a support group for survivors, etc.), but the point remains that existing evidence suggests that most people are unlikely to develop illusory memories or false beliefs of CSA in response to a few suggestive questions per se.

My argument that illusory RMEs require substantial suggestive influences is based on an extrapolation of across- and within-experiment comparisons that indicate a strong and consistent relationship between (1) the perceived "plausibility" of suggestions, (2) the strength of suggestive influences, and (3) the likelihood of false memory reports. "Plausibility" may be codetermined by (1) how well the suggestions fit with the person's beliefs about his or her past and (2) the person's beliefs concerning the memorability of the suggested event. For example, if I suggest to you that you were mugged at gunpoint yesterday I am unlikely to succeed in inducing an illusory memory, even if I resort to hypnosis or related techniques. This is partly because you feel that being mugged at gunpoint would be a spectacularly unusual event and that you would remember it vividly if it had really occurred. If you are from a major urban area in the United States, I might be more successful, especially if I suggested that the mugging happened years ago, because these factors would increase the perceived plausibility both of the event having occurred and of your not remembering it clearly. If I convinced you that muggings are vastly more common than most people realize, that you would be unlikely to have easy access to memories of the mugging because people often repress such memories, that your current behaviors suggest that you may indeed have experienced nonremembered muggings, and that your psychological well-being would be enhanced if you remembered them, I would have laid a fertile ground for false memories.

Interacting with the perceived plausibility of suggestions to determine the likelihood of false memories is the overall strength of suggestive influences. Scientific research has not yet progressed sufficiently to allow us to specify how the various factors that co-determine the strength of suggestive influences should be weighted, but we can say that such factors include the perceived authority and trustworthiness of the source(s) of suggestions, repetition of suggestions, imagability of the suggestions, and memory-monitoring criteria (i.e., the amount and kind of evidence people require before they experience thoughts and images as memories of the suggested event). The kinds of approaches to memory-recovery work that most alarm critics are those that simultaneously increase the perceived plausibility of nonremembered CSA and bring to bear all the factors that have been shown to increase the overall strength of suggestive influences.

It appears likely that individual differences play important roles in susceptibility to suggestion, both in terms of mediating the perceived plausibility of suggestions and in terms of mediating the overall strength of suggestions. Some people are highly hypnotizable, some are highly responsive to authority, some have vivid imagery skills, and so on, and such individual differences could heighten susceptibility to suggestions. Of particular note, Hyman and Billings (in press) found that people with high scores on the Dissociative Experiences Scale (Bernstein & Putnam, 1986) were particularly likely to "remember" a suggested childhood event (e.g., knocking over a punchbowl at a wedding reception).

It must be acknowledged that we do not know exactly what conditions are sufficient to constitute substantial risk of false memories of CSA. No one has reported an experiment comparing memory reports of people known not to have a CSA history who were exposed to varying levels of suggestion regarding such histories. Several recent studies have, however, demonstrated manipulations that lead some subjects to report pseudomemories of nontrivial life experiences (e.g., being lost in a shopping mall, in Loftus & Pickrell, 1995; Pezdek, Finger, & Hodge, 1997; knocking over a punchbowl at a wedding [and similar events], Hyman & Billings, in press; Hyman, Husband, & Billings, 1995; Hyman & Pentland, 1996; being discouraged from using one's left hand, Kelley, Lindsay, & Amodio, described in Lindsay, 1997). I think only a reckless person would claim that because the studies were not conducted with psychotherapy clients and did not induce illusory memories of CSA per se, they do not provide a basis for concern about suggestive therapies. It is also worth noting that none of these studies comes near to approximating the power of the suggestive influences that are brought to bear in some forms of memory-recovery work, in which individuals may be exposed to suggestions several hours per week for months or even years before reporting RMEs.

CONCLUSION

It seems extremely likely that some RMEs are essentially accurate and that some are essentially illusory. In my view, RMEs range along a continuum of plausibility. Even in cases in which individuals initially disclaimed an abuse history, some RMEs are relatively plausible (i.e., the kind of abuse reported is relatively common and is said to have happened a small number of times and after the first few years of life, no extensive memory work was involved in recovering the memories, and there is at least some evidence in support of the report). Others are relatively implausible (i.e., the reported abuse is bizarre and extreme and is said to have happened on numerous occasions over a period of many years, the reports emerged via extensive memory-recovery work, and there is little or no evidence supporting the report). Note that I do not mean to imply that all "plausible" cases are accurate or that all "implausible" cases are illusory.

We may be able crudely to estimate likelihood of accuracy of RMEs by weighing a constellation of kinds of evidence including (1) how the RME came about (the less evidence of suggestive memory-recovery work the greater the confidence), (2) the nature and clarity of the RMEs (with more credence given to detailed, integrated recollections than to vague feelings), (3) the likelihood of the suggested events being forgotten, (4) the plausibility of having memories to recover (e.g., less credence given to reports of events said to have occurred before 2 years of age), and (5) the base rate of the alleged type of abuse. At this point, it is not known exactly how these factors should be weighted, nor how well this approach would work: It is likely that even an optimal solution would sometimes erroneously reject essentially accurate RMEs as false and erroneously accept essentially illusory RMEs as accurate.

In my view, more important than postdicting the accuracy of RMEs is taking steps to reduce the incidence of essentially false RMEs. In this regard, it seems likely to me that suggestive forms of memory-recovery work are contraindicated with psychotherapy clients. Although existing knowledge is insufficient to enable specification of precisely which approaches pose substantial risk, absent any convincing evidence of benefits of such approaches it seems best to take a conservative, cautious approach. Happily, it appears that many trauma-oriented clinicians increasingly appreciate the importance of minimizing suggestive influences when working with clients who may or may not have a nonremembered CSA history (e.g., see Briere, 1997; Courtois, 1997).

In closing, I want to emphasize that I believe that most people involved in the recovered memories controversy wish to promote good and minimize harm. Some people may have focused overexclusively on promoting one kind of good (detecting and supporting victims of CSA, or minimizing false beliefs), and this may sometimes have had the unfortunate consequence of creating other kinds of harm (unintentionally promoting false RMEs or undermining support for genuine victims). I do not, however, believe there is any necessary trade-off between the two goods—that is, I believe that psychologists can simultaneously maximize support for victims of CSA and minimize risk of iatrogenic illusory memories. Progress toward these dual goals requires a depolarized, collaborative approach to the many unanswered questions raised by the recovered memories controversy. This book offers valuable steps in that direction.

NOTES

1. Heaton and Wilson (Chapter 14, this volume) provide a very informative discussion of popular-media popularization of ideas regarding recovered memories of satanic ritual abuse. An analogous analysis of popular-media promulgation of exaggerated ideas about false memories would also be interesting.

2. Note that I do not mean here to refer to cases in which people who have recovered memories of CSA retrospectively form the belief that they "always knew"; there are many reasons to view such claims of having always known with substantial skepticism. Rather, I refer to cases in which people report, prior to any memory-recovery experience, that they have knowledge about an abuse history although they cannot recollect the experiences themselves (e.g., Corwin & Olafson, 1997).

REFERENCES

Bernstein, E. M., & Putnam, F. W. (1986). Development, reliability, and validity of a dissociation scale. *Journal of Nervous and Mental Disease*, *174*, 40–54.

Briere, J. (1997). An integrated approach to treating adults abused as children, with specific reference to self-reported recovered memories. In J. D. Read & D. S. Lindsay (Eds.), *Recollections of trauma: Scientific research and clinical practice* (pp. 25–41). New York: Plenum.

Briere, J., & Conte, J. (1993). Self-reported amnesia for abuse in adults molested as children. *Journal of Traumatic Stress*, *6*, 21–31.

Brown, R., & Kulik, J. (1977). Flashbulb memory. *Cognition*, *5*, 73–99.

Christianson, S.-A. (1989). Flashbulb memories: Special but not so special. *Memory and Cognition*, *17*, 435–443.

Coons, P. M. (1994). Reports of satanic ritual abuse: Further implications about pseudomemories. *Perceptual and Motor Skills*, *78*, 1376–1378.

Corwin, D., & Olafson, E. (1997). Videotaped discovery of a reportedly unrecallable memory of child sexual abuse: comparison with a childhood interview videotaped 11 years before. *Child Maltreatment*, *2*, 91–112.

Courtois, C. A. (1997). Informed clinical practice and the standard of care: Proposed guidelines for the treatment of adults who report delayed memories of childhood trauma. In J. D. Read & D. S. Lindsay (Eds.), *Recollections of trauma: Scientific research and clinical practice* (pp. 337–361). New York: Plenum.

Dalenberg, C. J. (1997). The prediction of accurate recollections of trauma. In J. D. Read & D. S. Lindsay (Eds.), *Recollections of trauma: Scientific research and clinical practice* (pp. 449–454). New York: Plenum.

Feldman-Summers, S., & Pope, K. S. (1994). The experience of "forgetting" childhood abuse: A national survey of psychologists. *Journal of Consulting and Clinical Psychology*, *62*, 636–639.

Finkelhor, D. (1994). Current information on the scope and nature of child sexual abuse. *The Future of Children*, *4*, 31–53.

Freyd, P. (1997). Dear friends. *FMSF Newsletter*, *6*(1), 1.

Goldstein, E., & Farmer, K. (1992). *Confabulations*. Boca Raton, FL: Upton Books.

Goldstein, E., & Farmer, K. (1993). *True stories of false memories.* Boca Raton, FL: SIRS Books.

Hyman, I. E., Jr., & Billings, F. J. (in press). Individual differences and the creation of false childhood memories. *Memory.*

Hyman, I. E., Jr., Husband, T. H., & Billings, F. J. (1995). False memories of childhood experiences. *Applied Cognitive Psychology, 9,* 181–197.

Hyman, I. E., Jr., & Pentland, J. (1996). The role of mental imagery in the creation of false childhood memories. *Journal of Memory and Language, 35,* 101–117.

Keltner, D., & Robinson, R. J. (1996). Extremism, power, and the imagined basis of social conflict. *Current Directions in Psychological Science, 5,* 101–105.

Koss, M. P., Tromp, S., & Tharan, M. (1995). Traumatic memories: Empirical foundations, forensic and clinical implications. *Clinical Psychology: Science and Practice, 2,* 111–132.

Lindsay, D. S. (1997). Increasing sensitivity. In J. D. Read & D. S. Lindsay (Eds.), *Recollections of trauma: Scientific evidence and clinical practice* (pp. 1–16). New York: Plenum.

Lindsay, D. S., & Briere, J. (1997). The contoversy regarding recovered memories of childhood sexual abuse: Pitfalls, bridges, and future directions. *Journal of Interpersonal Violence, 12,* 631–647.

Lindsay, D. S., & Read, J. D. (1994). Psychotherapy and memories of childhood sexual abuse: A cognitive perspective. *Applied Cognitive Psychology, 8,* 281–338.

Lindsay, D. S., & Read, J. D. (1995). "Memory work" and recovered memories of childhood sexual abuse: Scientific evidence and public, professional, and personal issues. *Psychology, Public Policy, and the Law, 1,* 846–908.

Loftus, E. F. (1993). The reality of repressed memories. *American Psychologist, 48,* 518–537.

Loftus, E. F., & Ketcham, K. (1994). *The myth of repressed memory: False memories and allegations of sexual abuse.* New York: St. Martin's Press.

Loftus, E. F., & Pickrell, J. (1995). The formation of false memories. *Psychiatric Annals, 25,* 720–724.

Pendergrast, M. (1996). Victims of memory: Incest accusations and shattered lives (2nd ed.). Hinesburg, VT: Upper Access Press.

Pezdek, K., Finger, K., & Hodge, D. (1997). Planting false childhood memories: The role of event plausibility. *Psychological Science, 8,* 437–441.

Poole, D. A., Lindsay, D. S., Memon, A., & Bull, R. (1995). Psychotherapy and the recovery of memories of childhood sexual abuse: U.S. and British practitioners' beliefs, practices, and experiences. *Journal of Consulting and Clinical Psychology, 63,* 426–437.

Pope, H. G. Jr., & Hudson, J. I. (1995). Can memories of sexual abuse be repressed? *Psychological Medicine, 25,* 121–126.

Read, J. D. (1997). Memory issues in the diagnosis of unreported trauma. In J. D. Read & D. S. Lindsay (Eds.), *Recollections of trauma: Scientific evidence and clinical practice* (pp. 79–108). New York: Plenum.

Schooler, J. W., Ambadar, Z., & Bendiksen, M. (1997). A cognitive corroborative case study approach for investigating discovered memories of sexual abuse. In J. D. Read & D. S. Lindsay (Eds.), *Recollections of trauma: Scientific research and clinical practice* (pp. 379–388). New York: Plenum.

Spanos, N. P. (1994). Multiple identity enactments and multiple personality disorder: A sociocognitive perspective. *Psychological Bulletin, 116*, 143–165.

Widom, C. S. (1997). Accuracy of adult recollections of early childhood abuse. In J. D. Read & D. S. Lindsay (Eds.), *Recollections of trauma: Scientific research and clinical practice* (pp. 49–78). New York: Plenum.

Williams, L. M. (1995a). Recall of childhood trauma: A prospective study of women's memories of child sexual abuse. *Journal of Consulting and Clinical Psychology, 62*, 1167–1176.

Winograd, E., & Neisser, U. (Eds.). (1992). *Affect and accuracy in recall: Studies of "flashbulb" memories* (Emory Symposium on Cognition). New York: Cambridge University Press.

INDEX